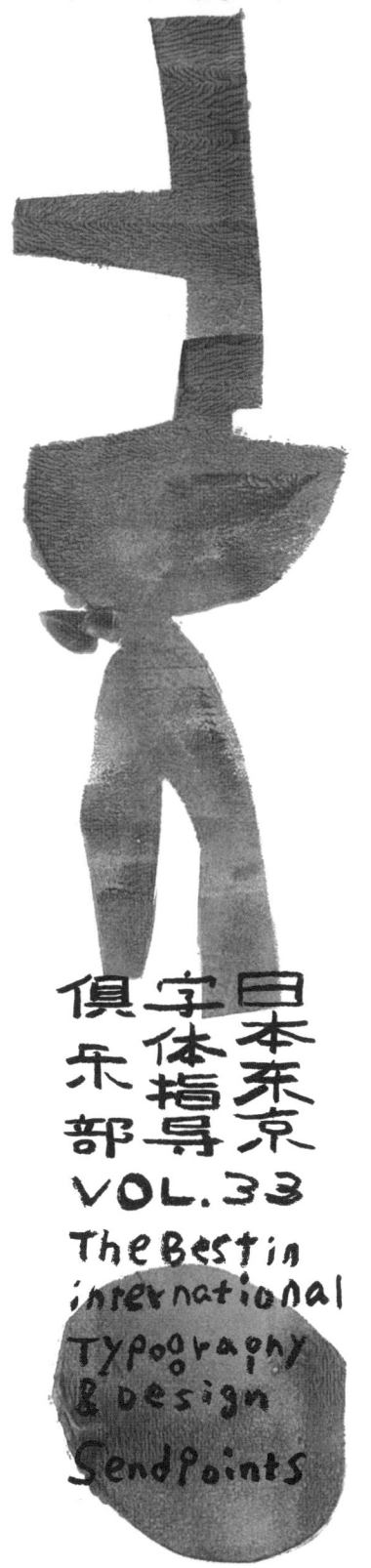

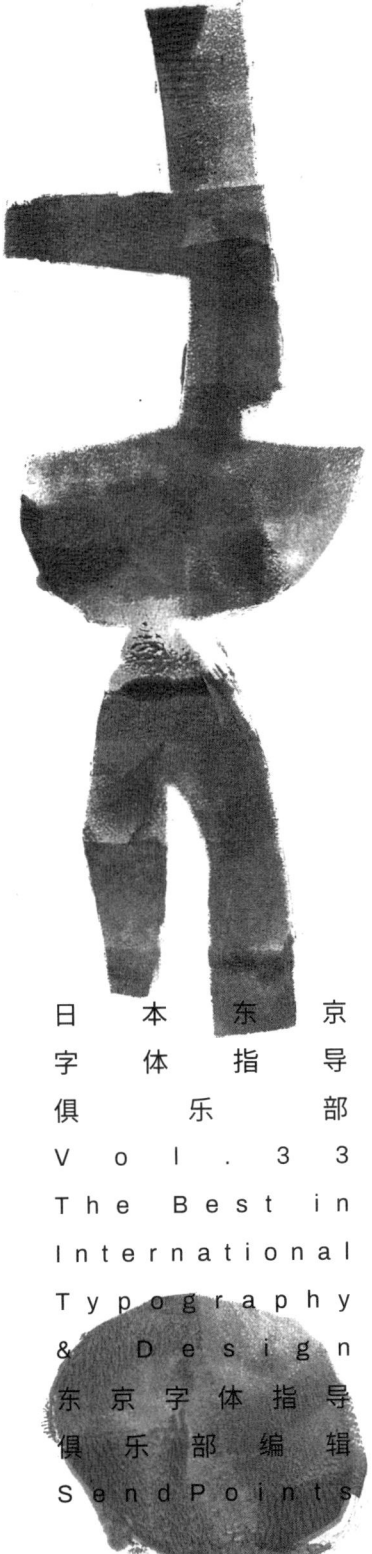

日本东京
字体指导
俱乐部
Vol.33
The Best in
International
Typography
& Design
东京字体指导
俱乐部编辑
SendPoints

致谢
我们向所有全力配合举办展览和制作这本年鉴的协作者深表感谢。

日本东京字体指导俱乐部Vol.33
The Best in International Typography & Design

sendpoints

出 版 发 行：善本出版有限公司
公 司 地 址：中国香港九龙尖沙嘴么地道61号冠华中心地库第一层L1-23室
出 版 人：林庚利
主　　 编：卢妍君
编　　 辑：东京字体指导俱乐部（日本语版）
　　　　　　卢妍君、梁欣怡（中文版）
翻　　 译：孙明远
艺 术 指 导：大原大次郎（封面+日本语版）
　　　　　　吴东燕（中文版）
书 籍 设 计：张子晨
校　　 对：梁欣怡

发 行 总 监：曾子扬
邮　　 箱：sales@sppub.com
电　　 话：+852 6296 2246
发 行 经 理：胡振华
邮　　 箱：guangzhou@sendpoints.cn
电　　 话：+86-20-89095121 转8027
编 辑 邮 箱：editor@sppub.com
网　　 站：www.sppub.com

印　　 刷：NCK LIMITED
版　　 次：2023年7月第1版第1次印刷
开　　 本：146mm x 220mm
定　　 价：280元
ISBN 978-988-77573-2-0

©2022 THE TOKYO TYPE DIRECTORS CLUB
Printed in China
All rights reserved. 版权所有。未经东京字体指导俱乐部的书面许可，
不得以任何形式复制本书的任何部分。

Contents

006 前言
009 评审委员
010 入选作品设计师一览
024 作品
441 获奖者感言与简介
454 东京TDC会员名单

006 Foreword
009 Jurors
010 Type Directors' Index
024 Works
441 Winners' Comments and Outline of Their Careers
454 Tokyo TDC Members List

前言

　　往年总有盛开的樱花为TDC展和颁奖典礼添彩，然而现状之下旅行仍然受限、人们也无法自由地在樱花树下歌舞。新冠疫情已经进入第3个年头。战争和气候异常的状况仍然持续，地球和人类的冲突毫无终结的迹象。

　　今年TDC的全场大奖是表现曼努埃尔·卡多索作曲的《安魂曲》的影像作品，优美的笔记体书写的歌词伴随着合唱的旋律在画面中不断展开，作者以独特的手法将平面的乐谱图形发展为多层次展开的影像，令人感动。此外的获奖作品也都是足以引起坊间话题的杰作。著名的字体设计师设计的作品高度再现了历史上法国铜版雕刻师的文字；介绍基于日本街头独特的"丸文字"而设计的字体的网页；不断推出杰作的女子大学的意象海报展现出了高超的创意；世界著名电影的书籍化；拥有108年悠久历史的交响乐团的VI升级项目是一项了不起的工作；火柴盒大小的白色盒子上用中性圆珠笔描绘的作品表现出平面图形特有的魅力；自费出版项目的展览会海报；简洁明了的圆珠笔网页表现出日本特有的明快感；以自己设计的日用品包装为对象，经过裁切等加工后以艺术形式呈现的个展，表现出了设计师自由往来设计和艺术之间的创造力；多达640页的巨著《仲条 NAKAJO》，是在本人完全没有参与的情况下，全部由服部一成先生完成的。

　　2021年10月26日，我们失去了挚友、才华横溢的仲条正义先生。从东京TDC诞生之初，仲条正义先生就是我们的重要的伙伴。《仲条 NAKAJO》的刊行，意味着服部一成先生长年以来的梦想终于得以实现。书中的设计作品与个展的印象完美地契合在一起，当我们怀念仲条正义先生时候，打开这本书，好似还能看到他的音容笑貌。

浅叶克己
东京字体指导俱乐部主席

Preface

The TDC exhibition and awards ceremony has always been held when the cherry blossoms are in full bloom. However with the pandemic now in its third year, and with travel restrictions still in place, people are still unable to celebrate and socialize under the boughs of the cherry trees. War and abnormal weather also seem to symbolize the ceaseless war between people and the planet.

This year's Grand Prize winner features a choral recital of "Requiem" by Manuel Cardoso, with the voices of the vocalists accompanied by animated lyrics written in longhand style. There is something moving in the way the graphical notation unfurls in a multi-layered way across the screen. The other prize-winning works also generated a lot of discussion. These include: a typeface produced by a renowned typeface designer; a system for adapting scripts engraved by French copperplate masters from the 19th and 20th centuries; a website featuring a font inspired by the unique rounded letters found on Japanese street signs; university image posters representing the pinnacle of an ongoing process of masterful creativity; a book version of an internationally acclaimed movie; the major VI rebranding of a symphony orchestra with a history of 108 years; loveable graphic works drawn onto white, matchbox-sized containers using a gel ink ballpoint pen; an exhibition poster for a self-publishing project; a website for ballpoint pens that boldly expresses Japanese infinite brightness; a private exhibition featuring unconstrained art made from cut-up product packages designed by the artist; and "*NAKAJO*," a voluminous 640-page book made by Kazunari Hattori without any input from the book's subject.

Also, we lost a dear friend and a great talent when Masayoshi Nakajo passed away on October 26, 2021. From the very inception of Tokyo TDC, Mr. Nakajo was always there to lend an ear and a word of advice. The book "*NAKAJO*" is the culmination of a dream long pursued by Kazunari Hattori. The book's design matches perfectly with the image from the exhibition. The book will always be there for us whenever we miss our friend, Masayoshi Nakajo.

Katsumi Asaba
Chairman, Tokyo Type Directors Club

2022东京TDC奖
Tokyo TDC Annual Awards 2022

3644件投稿作品（1788件来自日本／1856件来自海外）
514件作品入选本书

3,644 entries (1,788 works from Japan / 1,856 works from overseas)
Selected 514 works for the Annual book TDC Vol.33

TDC 2022 展览物料设计＝Balmer Hählen
TDC 2022 Exhibition graphics, designed by Balmer Hählen

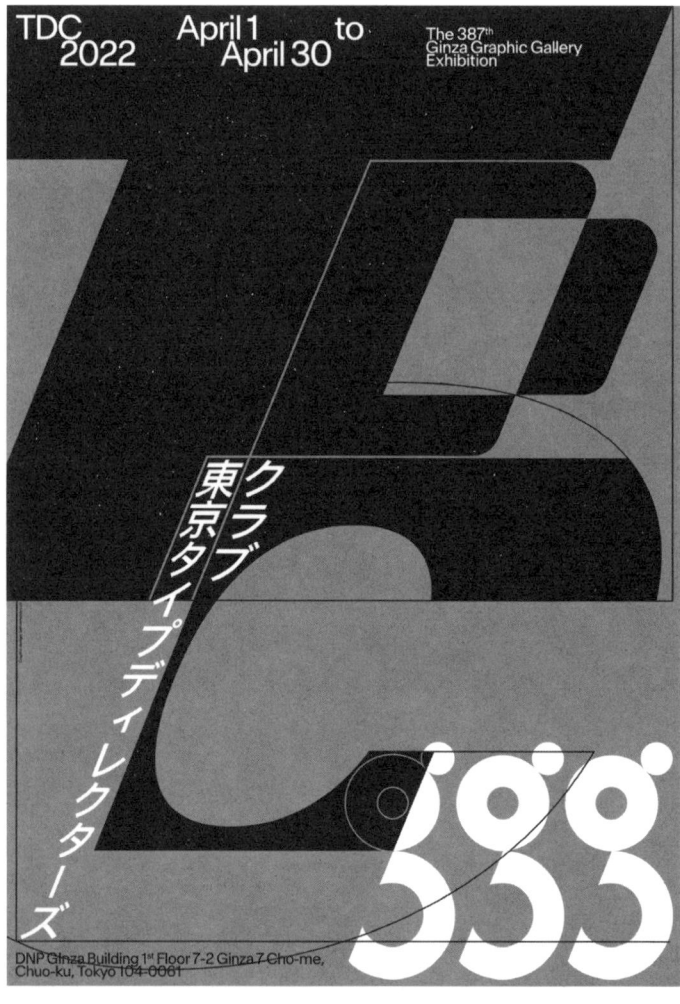

评审委员
Jurors

TDC奖理事会 TDC Annual Awards Committee
浅叶克己 Katsumi Asaba（TDC主席，艺术指导）
井上嗣也 Tsuguya Inoue（TDC成员，艺术指导）
服部一成 Kazunari Hattori（TDC副主席，平面设计师）
平林奈绪美 Naomi Hirabayashi（TDC成员，艺术指导）
葛西 薫 Kaoru Kasai（TDC副主席，艺术指导）
菊地敦己 Atsuki Kikuchi（TDC成员，平面设计师）
北川一成 Issay Kitagawa（TDC成员，艺术指导）
松本弦人 Gento Matsumoto（TDC成员，平面设计师）
中村至男 Norio Nakamura（TDC成员，平面设计师）
中村勇吾 Yugo Nakamura（TDC成员，网页设计师）
奥村靫正 Yukimasa Okumura（TDC成员，平面设计师）
佐藤 卓 Taku Satoh（TDC成员，平面设计师）
涉谷克彦 Katsuhiko Shibuya（TDC成员，平面设计师）
祖父江 慎 Shin Sobue（TDC成员，平面设计师）
立花文穂 Fumio Tachibana（TDC成员，艺术家）

客座评审员 Guest Jurors
Balmer Hählen, Balmer Priscilla + Yvo Hählen（平面设计师）
小林 章 Akira Kobayashi（字体指导）
Mei Shuzhi（平面设计师）
三泽 遥 Haruka Misawa（艺术指导）
室贺清德 Kiyonori Muroga（编辑）
大原大次郎 Daijiro Ohara（平面设计师）
田部井美奈 Mina Tabei（艺术指导）
髙田 唯 Yui Takada（平面设计师）
田中义久 Yoshihisa Tanaka（平面设计师）
田中良治 Ryoji Tanaka（TDC成员，网页设计师）
上西祐理 Yuri Uenishi（艺术指导）
约翰·沃里克 John Warwicker（TDC成员，平面设计师）
Nod Young（艺术指导）

字体设计特别评审委员 Special jurors for Type Design
藤田重信 Shigenobu Fujita（字体设计师）
Cyrus Highsmith（字体设计师，插画师）
小林 章 Akira Kobayashi（字体指导）
西塚凉子 Ryoko Nishizuka（字体设计师）
祖父江 慎 Shin Sobue（TDC成员，平面设计师）
鸟海 修 Osamu Torinoumi（字体设计师）
约翰·沃里克 John Warwicker（TDC成员，平面设计师）
Wang Wen（字体设计师）

类别9、10、11评审委员 Jurors for categories 9, 10, and 11
长谷川踏太 Tota Hasegawa（TDC成员，创意指导）
服部一成 Kazunari Hattori（TDC副主席，平面设计师）
伊藤Gabin Gabin Ito（编辑）
葛西 薫 Kaoru Kasai（TDC副主席，艺术指导）
菊地敦己 Atsuki Kikuchi（TDC成员，平面设计师）
松本弦人 Gento Matsumoto（TDC成员，平面设计师）
中村勇吾 Yugo Nakamura（TDC成员，网页设计师）
田中良治 Ryoji Tanaka（TDC成员，网页设计师）

掲載作家一覧
Type Directors' Index

A

013
AA: Anja Delbello, Aljaž Vesel [Slovenia]
hello@weareaa.com
weareaa.com

002, 012, 014
Actual Source: Davis Ngarupe, JP Haynie [USA]
davisandjp@actualsource.work
actualsource.work

015
足立大昂 Hiroki Adachi
hirokiadachi7690@gmail.com

016, 017
Karl Adrian Aguro [Philippines]
Uncurated Studio
uncurated.studio

018, 019
明津設計 Akitsu Sekkei
asd.mnr@gmail.com
asdmnr.com

020
Mano An [Korea]
anmano.kr
instagram.com/an__mano

029
Olivier Andreotti [France]
Toluca Studio, Paris
oliviertoluca@wanadoo.fr
tolucastudio.com

021, 022, 023, 024, 025, 026, 027, 028
浅葉克己 Katsumi Asaba
(株)浅葉克己デザイン室
Asaba Design Co., Ltd.
asaba@asaba-d.co.jp

030, 031
浅野隆昌 Takamasa Asano
工作企図
Kosaku Kito
takamasa@asataka.com
asataka.com

032, 033
Chon Hin Au [Macao, China]
Untitled Macao
info@untitledmacao.com
untitledmacao.com

B

034
André Baldinger, Toan Vu-Huu [France]
baldinger•vu-huu
info@baldingervuhuu.com
www.baldingervuhuu.com

035, 036
Marco Balesteros [Portugal]

037
Rick Banks [UK]

038, 039
Bedow [Sweden]
Studio Bedow
bedow@bedow.se
www.bedow.se

040
Behalf Studio [Vietnam]
us@onbehalfof.studio
www.onbehalfof.studio
www.be.net/behalf_studio
instagram.com/behalf_studio

043
Nicolas Bernklau [Switzerland]
Bureau Bernklau
bureau@nicolasbernklau.de
www.nicolasbernklau.de

041, 042
Shuyao Bian, Chen Xing [China]
STONES DESIGN Lab.
info@stonesdesign.net
www.stonesdesign.net

045
Bienvenue Studios: Oliver Hischier, Xiaoqun Wu [Switzerland]
send@bienvenuestudios.com
www.bienvenuestudios.com

044
Mark Bohle, Nam Huynh [Spain]
N&MS (Nam Huynh & Mark Bohle)
info@nandms.com
www.nandms.com

046
Mark Bohle [Spain]
Studio Mark Bohle
info@markbohle.de
www.markbohle.com

049
Erich Brechbühl [Switzerland]
Erich Brechbühl [Mixer]
erich@mixer.ch
www.erichbrechbuhl.ch

047
Fabian Bremer [Germany]
hi@fabianbremer.com
www.fabianbremer.com

048
Brighten the Corners: Frank Philippin, Billy Kiosoglou [Germany / UK]
contact@brightenthecorners.com
www.brightenthecorners.com

050
Browns [UK]
info@brownsdesign.com
brownsdesign.com

051, 052, 053, 054, 055
büro uebele visuelle kommunikation [Germany]
info@uebele.com
www.uebele.com

C

056, 057
Wenchao Cai [China]
caiwenchao0719@qq.com

058
Anna Cairns [Germany]
magma design studio
info@magma.design
magma.design

230
Margaret Calvert [UK]

059
Lana Cavar, Natasha Chandani
[Croatia / USA]
Clanada
hello@clanada.org
www.clanada.org

060
Byungrok Chae [Korea]
CBR
chaebyungrok@gmail.com
chaebyungrok.com

061
Adonian Chan [Hong Kong]
Trilingua Design
adonian@trilingua.hk
trilingua.hk, zansyu.hk

062
Rex Chen [UK]
Twelve Design
www.twelve.la

063
Cong Chen [China]
Super Plants
superplants6088@163.com

064
Weibin Chen [China]
Tagging Design
behance.net/TaggingDesign

065
Chenchenxia [China]
chenchenxia1105@163.com

066, 067
Jieru Chen [China]
lowkey design company
chenjieru@lowkeydesign.cn
www.behance.net/
lowkeydesigncompany

068
Chen Guo [China]

069
Shi Cheng [China]
Nanjing Idea Interact Design
331710775@qq.com

070
Cheng Xiaobing [China]
Coexistence brand design advisers
591584194@qq.com
shop112223302.taobao.com/?spm=a230r.7195193.1997079397.1.44d1294aa0R1MT

071
Joanne Chew [Malaysia]
Fictionist Studio
hellofictionist@gmail.com
www.fictionist.studio

072
千原徹也 Tetsuya Chihara
(株) れもんらいふ
LEMONLIFE Inc.
info@lemonlife.jp
lemonlife.jp

073
Sigutė Chlebinskaitė [Lithuania]
Sigute.Chlebinskaite@gmail.com

009
COLLINS: Louis Mikolay,
Erik Berger Vaage, Ben Crick,
Tomas Markevicius, Eric Park,
Sidney Lim, Michael Taylor [USA]

D

074
大日本タイポ組合
Dainippon Type Organization
dainippon@type.org
dainippon.type.org

075, 076
desescribir [Spain]
desescribir@gmail.com
desescribir.com

077, 078, 079
deValence: Alexandre Dimos,
Ghislain Triboulet [France]
deValence studio
contact@devalence.net
devalence.net

080, 081, 082
Ming Ding, Yuanbo Wang [China]
STUDIO DPi
info@studiodpi.work
www.studiodpi.work

083
Xiaoyuan Ding [China]
yuan@damidesign.cn
damidesign.org

084
Karen ann Donnachie,
Andy Simionato [Australia]
Donnachie, Simionato & Sons
office@donnachie-simionato.com
karenandy.com

085
Eva Dranaz [Austria]
3007
dranaz@3007wien.at
www.3007wien.at

111
Hannes Drißner [Germany]
mail@hannesdrissner.com
www.hannesdrissner.com

111
Markus Dreßen [Germany]
dressen@spectorbooks.com

086
Du Xiao [China]
wx-design
ohdooo@qq.com
www.wx-design.com

E

087
江波戸李生 Rio Ebato
(株) 電通 CRDC 3部
Denntsu Inc.
rio.ebato@dentsu.co.jp

089, 088
Mark El-khatib [UK]
Studio Mark El-khatib
studio@markelkhatib.com
markelkhatib.com

091
Konstantin Eremenko [Russia]
www.eremenko-vis.com

400
遠藤美奈子 Minako Endo

F

267
Fabrizio Falcone [Italy]
info@fabriziofalcone.it
fabriziofalcone.it

092
Fang Jianping [China]
United Design Lab
info@u-d-l.com
www.u-d-l.com

093
Anton Fedorov, Dmitry Jakovlev [Russia]
antonfedor1@gmail.com

094
Maxime Fittes [France]
MA-MA Type
maxime.fittes@gmail.com
ma-ma-type.com

095
Nina Flaitz [Germany]
nina@flaitz.info
www.ninaflaitz.de

096
藤巻洋紀 Hiroki Fujimaki
ジラ（株）
ZYLA inc.
fujimaki@zyla.jp
www.zyla.jp

097, 098
フクナガコウジ Kohji Fukunaga
297ga504@gmail.com
kohjifukunaga.com

100
福島周 Shu Fukushima
fukushimashu@gmail.com
www.shufukushima.jp

G

058, 099
Flo Gaertner [Germany]
magma design studio
info@magma.design
magma.design

103
Luo Gan [China]
1090017463@qq.com

101
Yuan Gao, Wenwen Zhang [China]

102, 104, 105, 106
Han Gao [USA]
workbyworks.nl
instagram.com/workbyworks

107, 108
Chris Gautschi [Switzerland]
Chris Gautschi Graphic & Editorial design
hello@chrisgautschi.ch
www.chrisgautschi.ch

109
Zhao Ge, Cao Qun [China]
OAD_BEIJING
1941335298@qq.com
876238628@qq.com

111
Malin Gewinner [Germany]
gewinner@spectorbooks.com

112
Dana Gez [Israel]
Studio Gimel2
dana@gimel2.com
www.gimel2.com

113
Bendita Gloria [Spain]
bg@benditagloria.com
benditagloria.com

115
GOO CHOKI PAR
hello@gcp.design
gcp.design

114, 116, 118
Mark Gowing [Australia]
Formist
hello@formist.co
formist.co

119
Tino Grass [Germany]
studio tino grass
info@tinograss.de
www.tinograss.de

117
Martin Grasser [USA]
Studio Mococo
hello@studiomococo.com
www.studiomococo.com

005
Grilli Type: Thierry Blancpain, Noël Leu [Switzerland]
mail@grillitype.com
www.grillitype.com

121
Marta Guidotti [Italy]
martaguidotti@gmail.com
www.behance.net/martaguidotti

120
Xiao Guo [China]
GROUNDLESS
groundless.cn

122
Stefan Guzy, Björn Wiede [Germany]
Zwölf
mail@zwoelf.net
www.zwoelf.net

H

123
Yang Hai [China]
E.L.A studio
joyce@ela-studio.net
seth@ela-studio.net

124
Xu Han, Huasha Chen, Yin Qiu [China]
hanxu@caa.edu.cn (Xu Han)
0106054@caa.edu.cn (Huasha Chen)

128
Lye Jia Hao [Singapore]
Temasek Polytechnic
www.tp.edu.sg/schools-and-courses/students/schools/des.html

125, 126, 127
原健三 Kenzo Hara
ハイフン
HYPHEN
contact@hy-phen.jp
hy-phen.jp

129
原田陽奈子 Hinako Harada
hinakoharada222@gmail.com
instagram.com/HARAHINA2

130, 131
Lars Harmsen [Germany]
Slanted Publishers
info@slanted.de
www.slanted.de

010, 132, 133, 134, 135, 136
服部一成 Kazunari Hattori
(有)服部一成
Kazunari Hattori Inc.
hattori@flyingcake.com

007
林規章 Noriaki Hayashi
HAYASHI DESIGN
hayashid@me.com
hayashinoriaki.com

137
Zhihua He [China]
shanghai version design group
zhihuadesign@163.com
www.version-sh.cn

138
Rongkai He [China]
Atmosphere Office
info@atmosphereoffice.cn

139, 140, 143
Fons Hickmann [Germany]
Fons Hickmann M23
m23@fonshickmann.com
fonshickmann.com

141
引地摩里子 Mariko Hikichi
(株)サン・アド
SUN-AD Co., Ltd.
hikichi@sun-ad.co.jp
sun-ad.co.jp

142
Tom Hingston [England]
Hingston Studio
info@hingston.net
www.hingston.net

144, 145, 146
平野篤史 Atsushi Hirano
アフォーダンス(株)
AFFORDANCE inc.
hirano@affordance.tokyo
www.affordance.tokyo

147
平田晴之介 Harunosuke Hirata
hh_jpn
hirata19930130@icloud.com
instagram.com/hh_jpn

149
Young Ho [China]
Design by AO
info@designbyao.com
www.designbyao.com

148
Chia-Hsing Ho [Taiwan]
Timonium Lake
timoniumlake@gmail.com

151
Yiu Kwok Ho [Hong Kong]
Yiu Kwok Ho Design
info@yiukwokho.com
yiukwokho.com

150
Dominic Hofstede [Australia]
Mucho
info@wearemucho.com
wearemucho.com

152, 153, 154, 155, 156
Wei Hong [China]

157
Ying Hou [China]
Inwa Design
beijing@inwa.com.cn
www.inwa.com.cn

090
Yu-Cheng Hsiao [Taiwan]
yuchenghsiao@gmail.com
yuchenghsiao.tumblr.com

158
Hu Zhenchao [China]
Hu Design
huzidesign@qq.com
hudesign.com.cn

159
Yu-Tzu Huang [Taiwan]
Studio XYZU
xyutzuhuang@gmail.com
www.yutzuhuang.com

160, 161, 162
Hubertus Design [Switzerland]
info@hubertus-design.ch
www.hubertus-design.ch

163
Jody Hudson-Powell, Luke Powell [UK]
Pentagram London
jl-admin@pentagram.com
www.pentagram.com

253
Zhan Huode [China]
zhanhuode@qq.com

I

164
一橋匠蔵 Shozo Ichihashi
ichihashishozo@gmail.com

165
市川良介 Ryosuke Ichikawa

175
稲垣純 Jun Inagaki
primosi@nifty.com

166, 167, 168, 169
井上嗣也 Tsuguya Inoue
ビーンズ
BEANS
beans@poppy.ocn.ne.jp

417
伊佐奈月 Natsuki Isa
(株)SHA
SHA inc.
isa@shainc.co.jp
www.shainc.co.jp

110
石橋友也 Tomoya Ishibashi
tomoya.ishibashi0217@gmail.com
www.shibashiishibashi.com

170, 171, 172, 173, 174
石黒篤史 Atsushi Ishiguro
OUWN
info@ouwn.jp
ouwn.jp

176
石井玲緒 Reo Ishii
(株)テコ
teco inc.
reo.ishii@teco-inc.design
teco-inc.design

177
石川将也 Masaya Ishikawa
cog
info@cog.ooo
www.cog.ooo

178
伊藤修一 Nobukazu Ito
(株)DK
DK Co., Ltd
dk-ito@neo.famille.ne.jp

179
岩井悠 Hisashi Iwai

J

180
Dan Jin [China]
merry830918@gmail.com

181, 182, 183, 184
城崎哲郎 Tetsuro Jozaki
(株) Token
info@token-d.com
www.token-d.com

K

185
梶垣諒 Ryo Kajigaki
ryokajigaki@gmail.com
ryokajigaki.com

350, 351, 352, 353, 354
金井あき Aki Kanai
コクヨ (株)
KOKUYO Co., Ltd.
aki_kanai@kokuyo.com
kanaisasaki.com

186
金坂義之 Yoshiyuki Kanesaka
(株) オーラム
aurum inc.
hello@aurumdesign.info
aurumdesign.info

187, 188, 189, 190, 191, 192
葛西薫 Kaoru Kasai
(株) サン・アド
SUN-AD Co., Ltd.
sun-ad.co.jp

193, 194, 195
加瀬透 Toru Kase
info@torukase.com
torukase.com

362, 363, 364
糟谷義人 Yoshihito Kasuya
yoshihito.kasuya@googlemail.com
yoshihitokasuya.com

355
香取有美 Yumi Katori

196, 197
川尻竜一 Ryuichi Kawajiri
デザ院 (株)
Dezain inc.
ryuichikawajiri@gmail.com
www.deza-in.jp

198
Nicha Keeratiphanthawong
[Thailand]
work@recentpractice.com
recentpractice.com
nichakeeratiphanthawong.com

199, 200, 201
Kellenberger–White [UK]
hoi@kellenberger-white.com
kellenberger-white.com

257
Dominik Keller [Germany]
info@dominikkeller.de
www.dominikkeller.de
instagram.com/dominikkeller_of

202, 203, 204, 205, 206, 207, 208, 209
菊地敦己 Atsuki Kikuchi
(株) 菊地敦己事務所
Atsuki Kikuchi Ltd.
studio@akltd.jp
atsukikikuchi.com

210
Trisha Kim [Korea]
trishakim511@gmail.com
trishakim.info

211
木村里奈 Rina Kimura
(株) 電通
Dentsu Inc.
rina.kimura@dentsu.co.jp

212
Gerhard Kirchschlaeger [Austria]
gerhard@kirchschlaeger.at
www.kirchschlaeger.at

004, 213
北川一成 Issay Kitagawa
グラフ (株)
GRAPH Co. Ltd.
info@moshi-moshi.jp
www.moshi-moshi.jp

417
北千住デザイン Kitasenju Design
nabe@kitasenjudesign.com
kitasenjudesign.com

214
小林昇太 Shota Kobayashi
(株) サン・アド
SUN-AD Co., Ltd.
shota_kobayashi@sun-ad.co.jp
www.sun-ad.co.jp

217, 218, 219
小林一毅 Ikki Kobayashi
graphic.ikki.kobayashi@gmail.com

215, 216
古平正義 Masayoshi Kodaira
(有) フレイム
FLAME inc.
kodaira@flameinc.jp
www.flameinc.jp

221
児玉篤司 Atsushi Kodama
(株) 日本デザインセンター
Nippon Design Center, Inc.
atsushi.kodama@ndc.co.jp
ndc.co.jp

220
小池アイ子 Aiko Koike
aikywarhol@gmail.com
aikokoike.com

222
児嶋啓多 Keita Kojima
mail@keitakojima.com

223
Philipp Koller, Lukas Küng, Giulia
Schelm, Alessia Meyer [Germany]
Burrow
hi@im-burrow.de
www.im-burrow.de

224
Xiangguo Kong [China]
569682879@qq.com

046
Raffael Kormann [Spain]
info@raffaelkormann.com
raffaelkormann.com

226
小杉幸一 Koichi Kosugi
onehappy.inc
kosugi@one-1-happy.com
one-1-happy.com

225
Sophie Kraft [Germany]
sophiekraft@aol.com

227, 228, 229, 230
Henrik Kubel [UK]

231
Dafi Kühne [Switzerland]
Babyinktwice
hello@babyinkwice.ch
www.babyinktwice.ch

232, 233
Jim Kühnel [Germany]
mail@jimkuehnel.com
jimkuehnel.com

234
Anna Kulachek [Russia]
kulacheka@gmail.com
kulachek.com
instagram.com/kulachek

236, 237
栗林和夫 Kazuo Kuribayashi
クリとグラフィック
kuri + graphic
kurivo.1@icloud.com
tokyotypedirectorsclub.org/member/
kazuo_kuribayashi

235
黒野真吾 Shingo Kurono
Shingo Kurono Ltd.
sutudio@shingokurono.com
www.shingokurono.com

L

238
Lee Chang Pei [Taiwan]

233
Roger Lehner [Germany]

239, 240, 241
Xibin Li [China]
dtzw-design
dtzwgood@163.com
SUPER PLANTS
superplants6088@163.com

242
Che Liang [China]

243, 244
Liao Bofeng [China]

247
Big Lin [Taiwan]
bipbipboom@gmail.com
behance.net/b-i-g

245
Tao Lin [Belgium]
tao.graphicdesign@gmail.com
www.taographicdesign.com
instagram.com/tao.graphicdesign

246
Sven Lindhorst-Emme [Germany]
studio lindhorst-emme+hinrichs
mail@lindhorst-emme-hinrichs.de
www.lindhorst-emme-hinrichs.de
instagram.com/studio_lindhorst_
emme_hinrichs

248
Cen Liu [China]
Cehndesign Workshop
cehndesign@qq.com
www.cehndesign.com

249
Xijiang Liu [China]
Happy AGENCY
www.hahaha.cn

251
Lobbin Liu [China]
lob_in
lobbinliu@gmail.com
www.lobbinliu.com

250
Yunlai Liu [China]
1003947554@qq.com
www.hanyi.com.cn

252, 253, 254
Liu Zhao [China]
liuzhao@another-lab.com

254
Liu Qingyuan [China]

258
Liu Huan [China]
l.h.design@foxmail.com
www.behance.net/liu0123

255
Kelvin Lok [Singapore]
Couple
mail@couple.com.sg
www.couple.com.sg

256
loof.design [China]
info@loof.design
www.loof.design

006
LOW sek-vai [China]
LAO office
laoshuowei@gmail.com
laoshuowei.design

257
Benedikt Luft [Germany]
benedikt.luft@gmx.de
www.benediktluft.com
instagram.com/benediktluft

M

259, 260, 261, 262
M/M (Paris) [France]

263, 264
Ma Shirui [China]
typo_d
ma_shirui@qq.com
www.typo-d.com

265
Lucas Machado [Brazil]
Lucas Machado Design
design@lucas-machado.com
lucas-machado.com

266
町口覚 Satoshi Machiguchi
MATCH and Company Co., Ltd.
match@matchandcompany.com
www.matchandcompany.com

267
Claudio Madella [Italy]
313@box313.net
box313.net

269
前田定則 Sadanori Maeda
maedas@danori.net
maedasadanori.com

268, 270, 271
Mak Kai Hang [Hong Kong]
Makkaihang Design
info@makkaihang.com
www.makkaihang.com

272
Jannis Maroscheck [Germany]
Office Jannis Maroscheck
jannis@maroscheck.de
maroscheck.de

273
松本健一 Kenichi Matsumoto
(株)モトモト
MOTOMOTO inc.
matsumoto@moto-moto.jp
www.moto-moto.jp

274, 275
松本弦人 Gento Matsumoto
sb
saru@sarubrunei.com
www.sarubrunei.com

279
松山智一 Norikazu Matsuyama
(有)松山デザイン
Matsuyama Design Inc.
matsuyama0917@gmail.com
matsuyamadesign.co.jp

276, 277, 283
Mazzybox [China]
Studio NA.EO
mazzybox@gmail.com
studionaeo.com

280
Colin McPartlin [Australia]
cjmcp@yahoo.com.au
colinmcpartlin.com

278
Nathan Meyer [Switzerland]
nathan.meyer@zhdk.ch
instagram.com/meyergrafik

281
道川雄介 Yusuke Michikawa
mchysk3109@gmail.com

282
Varvara Mikhaylova [Russia]
varya.mikhaylova@gmail.com

284
三木健 Ken Miki
三木健デザイン事務所
Ken Miki & Associates
office@ken-miki.net
www.ken-miki.net

285
Ming Cheung [Hong Kong]
for&st
hello@for-st.co
instagram.com/form_structure.co

130
Marian Misiak [Germany]
Slanted Publishers
info@slanted.de
www.slanted.de

286
宮里則徹 Noriaki Miyazato
フレームワーク
framework
frameworkjp@gmail.com
instagram.com/eyemagi

287
水本真帆 Maho Mizumoto
(株)ADKクリエイティブ・ワン
ADK Creative One Inc.
mamizumoto@adk.jp

355
村松弘友紀 Hiroyuki Muramatsu

289
杢谷吉也 Yoshinari Mokutani
モクタニデザイン
Mokutani Design
mokutani_d@h05.itscom.net

290
森翔太 Shota Mori
morishowta@gmail.com
www.morishowta.com

288
森川瞬 Shun Morikawa

294
MPTY [Singapore]
mail@mpty.info
mpty.info

N

291
Tian Na [Australia]
NoThing studio
natian@nothingstudio.com.au
www.nothing.studio

292, 293
永井裕明 Hiroaki Nagai
(株)エヌ・ジー
N.G.inc.
ng@nginc.jp
www.nginc.jp

295
永田傑 Takashi Nagata
ナガタデザイン
NAGATA design
nagatadesign@orange.plala.or.jp
nagatadesign.jp

296
中市哲 Satoru Nakaichi
(株)ライツデザイン
Lights Design
www.lightsdesign.jp

297, 298, 299
仲條正義 Masayoshi Nakajo
makiko.odaka@gmail.com

300
中村至男 Norio Nakamura

301
中山智裕 Tomohiro Nakayama
(株)サン・アド
SUN-AD Co., Ltd.
tomohiro_nakayama@sun-ad.co.jp
sun-ad.co.jp

303
Thomas Neeser, Thomas Müller,
Jakob Görner [Switzerland]
Neeser & Müller
info@neesermueller.ch
www.neesermueller.ch

302
Toby Ng [Hong Kong]
Toby Ng Design
mail@toby-ng.com
www.toby-ng.com

304, 305, 306, 308
Aaron Nieh [Taiwan]
Aaron Nieh Workshop
contact@aaronnieh.com
aaronnieh.tumblr.com

110
新倉健人 Kento Niikura
niikurakento@gmail.com
www.kentoniikura.com/index.html

307
西達也 Tatsuya Nishi
ニシグラフ
nishigraph
info@nishigraph.jp
www.nishigraph.jp

309, 310
西澤明洋 Akihiro Nishizawa
(株)エイトブランディングデザイン
Eight Branding Design
info@8brandingdesign.com
www.8brandingdesign.com

198
Tabea Nixdorff [Germany]

314
Non-Format/ANTI: Kjell Ekhorn,
Jon Forss [USA/Norway]
info@non-format.com
non-format.com
anti.as

311
Juliane Nöst [Germany]
Slanted Publishers
info@slanted.de
www.slanted.de

313
Tino Nyman, Marina Veziko [Finland]
info@few-mag.com
few-mag.com

O

312
落合翔平 Shohei Ochiai
8%
info@8percent.tokyo
ochiaishohei.com

315, 316, 317
OK-RM: Rory McGrath &
Oliver Knight [UK]

319
岡大夢 Hiromu Oka
okatheponjuice@gmail.com
otp-works.tumblr.com

318
岡本太玖斗 Takuto Okamoto

320, 321, 322, 323
岡﨑真理子 Mariko Okazaki
maricomarico.o@gmail.com
marikookazaki.tokyo

326
奥山太貴 Taiki Okuyama
info@okuyamataiki.com
okuyamataiki.com

001
大西景太 Keita Onishi
www.keitaonishi.com

328
大澤悠大 Yudai Osawa
アロエ
Aroe Inc.
osawa@aroe-inc.com
www.osawayudai.com

325
大島慶一郎 Keiichiro Oshima
(有)大島事務所
keioshima@mac.com
keiichirooshima.com

327
押見健太郎 Kentaro Oshimi
(株) Beatness Beatneass.inc
oshimix@beatness.jp
beatness.jp

329
大山大介 Daisuke Oyama

P

324
Gregory Page [Switzerland]
hello@gregory-page.com
www.gregory-page.com

330, 331
Yanrong Pan [China]

332, 333
Pierre Pané-Farré [Germany]
mail@panefarre.com
www.panefarre.com

334, 335
Yunqi Peng [China]
246079@network.rca.ac.uk
pengyunqicheapball.myportfolio.com

337
Jay Guan-Jie Peng [Taiwan]
POM
info@projectonmuseum.com
www.projectonmuseum.com

003, 338
Jean François Porchez [France]
Typofonderie
info@typofonderie.com
typofonderie.com

339
Margherita Porrà [Canada]
arithmetic
info@arithmeticcreative.com
arithmeticcreative.com

399
Nejc Prah [Slovenia]
Studio Nejc Prah
info@nejcprah.com
nejcprah.com

Q

340
Qu Minmin, Jiang Qian [China]
67954533@qq.com
290969029@qq.com
www.qqqqdesign.com

R

361
楽天デザインラボ
Rakuten Design Lab,
楽天技術研究所
Rakuten Institute of Technology,
Dalton Maag Ltd.
楽天グループ（株）
楽天デザインラボ
Rakuten Group, Inc.
Rakuten Design Lab
cmo-rdl-award@mail.rakuten.com
www.rakuten.design

342
Jamie Reid [UK]

341
Qianqian Ren [China]
pidan
renqine@foxmail.com
www.pidan.com

343, 344
Grace Robinson-Leo, Rob Matthews [USA]
Decade
hello@decadenewyork.com
www.decadenewyork.com

095
Marius Rother [Germany]
mail@mariusrother.de
www.mariusrother.de

S

345, 346
相楽賢太郎 Kentaro Sagara
Polarno
i@polarno.jp
polarno.jp

348
Stefan Sagmeister [USA]
Sagmeister inc.
info@sagmeister.com
sagmeister.com

347
佐古田英一 Eiichi Sakota
セカンドセカンド
2ND2nd
kk2nd2nd@io.ocn.ne.jp
2nd-2nd.com

355
佐野研二郎 Kenjiro Sano

349
佐々木遊太 Yuta Sasaki
ささき製作所
Sasaki Seisakusho
sasaki@sasaki-sasaki.com
sasaki-sasaki.com

350, 351, 352, 353, 354
佐々木拓 Taku Sasaki
コクヨ（株）
KOKUYO Co., Ltd.
taku_sasaki@kokuyo.com
kanaisasaki.com

356, 357, 358, 359, 360
佐々木俊 Shun Sasaki
AYOND
info@ayond.jp
ayond.jp

361, 362, 363, 364, 365
佐藤可士和 Kashiwa Sato
SAMURAI
info@samurai.sh
kashiwasato.com

008
佐藤豊 Yutaka Sato
hello@yutesato.com
yutesato.com

370
佐藤祐太郎 Yutaro Sato
yutaro8811@gmail.com
instagram.com/yutarooo811

011, 366, 367, 368, 369
佐藤卓 Taku Satoh
（株）TSDO
TSDO Inc.
tsdo@tsdo.co.jp
www.tsdo.jp

372, 378
Paula Scher [USA]
Pentagram
paul.mehnert@pentagram.com
www.pentagram.com

371
Stefanie Schwarz [Germany]

004
Semitransparent Design
info@semitransparentdesign.com
www.semitransparentdesign.com

374, 375, 376, 377
702design [China]
702@by702.com
www.by702.com

379, 380
Zhuohan Shao [China]
Allergy Studio
allergystudio@gmail.com
allergystudio.co.uk

381
Shi Zhenxing [China]
Liubai Design
1023502987@qq.com
www.liubaidesign.cn

373, 382
清水艦期 Kango Shimizu
shimizukango@gmail.com
shimizukango.tumblr.com

384
塩谷嘉章 Yoshiaki Shioya
（株）SHIOYA Tokyo
SHIOYA Tokyo Inc.
shioya@shioya-design.com
shioya-tokyo.com

385
白澤真生 Masao Shirasawa
ドロロープ
Drawrope
masao@drawrope.com
drawrope.com

383
Oliver Siegenthaler [Colombia]
S&Co
oliver@siegenthaler.co
www.siegenco.com

386, 387, 388, 389
祖父江慎 Shin Sobue
（有）コズフィッシュ
cozfish
tamao@cozfish.jp

390
Something Moon Design [Macao]
info@somethingmoon.com
SomethingMoon.com

392
Alessandro Sommer [Germany]
info@alessandrosommer.de

391
Ayong Son [Korea]
1-2-3-4-5
mail@sonayong.com
sonayong.com

393
Jiang Song [China]
1459925466@qq.com
xiangyangyuan@163.com

394
Lenardo Sonnoli [Italy]
leonardo@sonnoli.com
www.sonnoli.com

395, 396, 397
Kris Sowersby [New Zealand]

398
Andrew Stevens [UK]
Graphic Thought Facility
info@graphicthoughtfacility.com

047
Pascal Storz [Germany]
pascal@studiostorz.ch
www.studiostorz.ch

399
Studio Ljudje [Slovenia]
kontakt@ljudje.si
ljudje.si

401
Studio Woork [Indonesia]
info@studiowoork.com
studiowoork.com

402
杉山陽平 Yohei Sugiyama
yohei_d@ab.wakwak.com
park11.wakwak.com/~yohei_d

400
杉山紘一 Koichi Sugiyama
MARU
info@maruinc.net
www.maruinc.net

403
杉薗はるな Haruna Sugizono

404, 405
助川誠 Makoto Sukegawa
SKG（株）
SKG Co., Ltd.
hello@s-k-g.net
s-k-g.net

407
Sulki and Min [Korea]
sulki-min.com

406, 408
Dawang Sun [China]
T9 Brand
dawangsun@hotmail.com
www.t9branding.com

409, 410
Sun Jianyu [China]

411
鈴木聡史 Satoshi Suzuki
（株）揚羽
ageha
suzuki@ageha.tv
www.ageha.tv

T

412, 413
田部井美奈 Mina Tabei
（株）田部井美奈
MINA TABEI Inc.
info@minatabei.com
minatabei.com

414, 415, 416
髙田唯 Yui Takada

417
竹林一茂 Kazushige Takebayashi
（株）SHA
SHA inc.
tiku@shainc.co.jp
www.shainc.co.jp

418
瀧澤章太郎 Shotaro Takizawa
（株）電通
Dentsu Inc.
shotaro.takizawa@dentsu.co.jp
instagram.com/shotaro.takizawa

419, 420, 421
田中せり Seri Tanaka
seritanaka.com

422, 423
田中良治 Ryoji Tanaka
Semitransparent Design
info@semitransparentdesign.com
www.semitransparentdesign.com

424
Andrea Tartarelli [Italy]

426
田代祐美子 Yumiko Tashiro
tashiro@cc-inc.jp

425
Antonia Terhedebrügge,
Silvia Terhedebrügge [Germany]
Studio Terhedebrügge
hello@terhedebruegge.de
www.terhedebruegge.de

427
Tian Bo [China]
Ten Buttons
bo@tian-design.com
tian-design.com

428
藤堂智子 Tomoko Todo
コルドデザイン
cordes design
contact@cordes-design.com
cordes-design.com

430
富田光浩 Mitsuhiro Tomita
（株）ONE
tomita@one-inc.info
www.one-inc.info

429, 431
Tsai Chia-Hao [Taiwan]
liannontsai@gmail.com
www.behance.net/tsaichiahao

432
露沢咲子 Sakiko Tsurusawa
WALTZ. LLC
info@waltzdesign.jp
waltzdesign.jp

U

433, 434, 435, 436, 437, 438, 439,
440, 441, 442, 443, 444, 445
植原亮輔 Ryosuke Uehara
（株）キギ
KIGI Co., Ltd.
ue@ki-gi.com
www.ki-gi.com

446
上西祐理 Yuri Uenishi

447
上杉滝 Taki Uesugi
（株）ノット・フォー
Knot for, Inc.
info@knotfor.co.jp
www.knotfor.co.jp

449
宇都勝宏 Katsuhiro Uto
（株）ウー
WOO inc.
uto-k@woo-design.net
www.katsuhirouto.com

V

448, 450
Hagen Verleger [Germany]
Hagen Verleger • Typography, Book
Design, Research
info@hagenverleger.com
www.hagenverleger.com

451, 452
Jan Vranovský [Czech Republic]
Studio VVAA
hi@vvaa-studio.com
vvaa-studio.com

453
Toan Vu-Huu [France]
baldinger•vu-huu
toan@baldingervuhuu.com
www.baldingervuhuu.com

W

454
Wang Pu [China]

456
Mulan Wang [China]
mulan_blue@163.com

455
Wang Zhihong [Taiwan]
Wangzhihong Co.
info@wangzhihong.com
wangzhihong.com

457, 458
王睿宇 Ruiyu Wang
wangruiyu.work@gmail.com
wang-ruiyu.com

459
汪骎 Qin Wang
wangtsin90@gmail.com
instagram.com/tsin_wang
www.behance.net/Tsinwang

438, 439, 441, 443, 444, 445, 461, 462
渡邊良重 Yoshie Watanabe
(株)キギ
KIGI Co., Ltd.
yoshie@ki-gi.com
www.ki-gi.com

460
渡辺和音 Kazune Watanabe
There There
mail@therethere.tokyo
therethere.tokyo

417
渡邊晃己 Kohki Watanabe
(株) SHA
SHA inc.
watanabe@shainc.co.jp
www.shainc.co.jp

463
渡邊裕文 Hirofumi Watanabe
(株)電通
Dentsu Inc.
watanabeibee@dentsu.co.jp

464
Liao Wei [Taiwan]
Liao Wei Graphic Studio(L/g/s)
liao1206@gmail.com
www.liaoweigraphic.com

336
Xuejing Weng [China]
scheinflut studio
scheinflut_store@163.com
scheinflutstudio.cargo.site

465
what [Hong Kong]
info@what.work
www.what.work

466
Daniel Wiesmann [Germany]
Daniel Wiesmann Büro für Gestaltung
mail@danielwiesmann.de
danielwiesmann.de
instagram.com/danielwiesmann

227, 228, 229
Scott Williams [UK]

468
Wolfe Hall: Jason Wolfe, Luke Hall [UK]
info@wolfehall.com
www.wolfehall.com

471
Chun Sing Wong [Singapore]
CROP
hello@crop.sg
crop.sg

469
Siguang Wu [China]
HDU^{23} Lab
502851386@qq.com
hdu23lab.com

467
Benjamin Wurster [Germany]
Benjamin Wurster Kommunikationsdesign
mail@benjaminwurster.com
benjaminwurster.com

X

470
Nan Xiao [China]
nobignosmall Studio
nobignosmall@foxmail.com

472
Qiyuan Xiao [China]
985186692@qq.com
www.xxddesign.com

474
Hunk Xing [China]

473, 475
Chen Xing, Xiang Li [China]
Stones Design Lab.
info@stonesdesign.net
www.stonesdesign.net

476, 477
Xu Weixin [China]

Y

478, 479, 480
矢後直規 Naonori Yago
(株) SIX
info@sixinc.jp
sixinc.jp

483, 484
矢入幸一 Koichi Yairi
yairi.1214@gmail.com
www.koichi-yairi.com

481
山本ヒロキ Hiroki Yamamoto
マーヴィン合同会社
MARVIN LLC

485
山本浩貴 Hiroki Yamamoto
いぬのせなか座
Inunosenakaza
hirozini1220@gmail.com
nunosenakaza.com

482
山中桃子 Momoko Yamanaka
岡本健デザイン事務所
Ken Okamoto Design Office Inc.
yama@okamotoken.jp
www.okamotoken.jp

486
山下ともこ Tomoko Yamashita
yamashita@flyingcake.com
www.tomokoyamashita.net

487, 488, 490
Yaoming Yan, Mijia Liu [China]

489
Senyu Yang [China]
SenseTeam

491
Sun Yao [China]

493
Yaping Guang [China]

492, 494, 495
Randy Yeo [Singapore]
Practice Theory
studio@practicetheory.com.sg
www.practicetheory.com.sg

497
Zhongjun Yin [China]
Dalian RYCX Advertising Co., Ltd.
rycxcn@163.com
www.rycxcn.com

496
Tsan Yu Yin [Taiwan]
tsanyuyin@gmail.com
tsanyuy.in

499
Mira Ying [China]
The Type
mira@thetype.com
hello@thetype.com
thetype.com/about

498, 500, 501
Yah-Leng Yu [Singapore]
Foreign Policy Design Group
affairs@foreignpolicy.design
www.foreignpolicy.design
instagram.com/foreignpolicydesign

502
余秋子 Qiuzi Yu [China]
pepperyu0813@gmail.com
instagram.com/aug.design

503
Junyi Yu [China]
yjy906650873@outlook.com

505
Haocheng Zhang [China]
aa studio
studio.aagraphic@gmail.com
instagram.com/hawson_zhang

506, 509
Eager Zhang [China]
Eager Zhang Studio
eagerzliterally@gmail.com
eagerzhang.com

510
Wentian Zhang [China]
Seethe Design
info@seethe.design
www.seethe.design

511
Zhao Yifeng [China]

512
Zen Zheng [China]
leaping creative
pr@leapingcreative.com
www.leapingcreative.com
instagram.com/leapingcreative

276, 277
Liu Zhizhi [China]

513
Rozi Zhu [USA]
hello@rozi.fun
www.rozi.fun

514
Zolo Press [Belgium]
info@zolo.press
www.zolo.press
instagram.com/zolo.press

Z

504
Zak Group [UK]
info@zak.group
zak.group

507, 508
Zexuan Zeng [China]
box203kiosk@gmail.com
z.zeng@khm.de

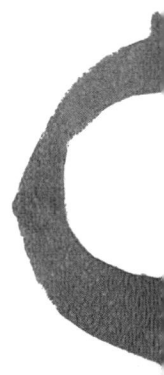

2022东京TDC奖颁奖仪式
Tokyo TDC Annual Awards 2022: Award Ceremony

2022年4月1日（周五），东京（夜晚）—— 瑞士卢塞恩（白天）—— 法国巴黎（白天）—— 美国犹他州的普若佛（清晨）—— 美国旧金山以及纽约（上午）—— 中国北京（夜晚），以上各地同时通过网络举办了在线颁奖典礼，其影像记录参见：
https://youtu.be/wsWOeozNPTc

An online awards ceremony connecting Tokyo (evening) – Lucerne, Switzerland (afternoon) – Paris, France (afternoon) – Provo・Utah, USA (early morning) – San Francisco & New York, USA (morning) – Beijing, China (evening) was held in the evening of April 1 (Fri.), 2022. Here is how it went.
https://youtu.be/wsWOeozNPTc

Grilli Type (Thierry Blancpain), Jean François Porchez, Actual Source (Davis Ngarupe + JP Haynie), Brian Collins + Louis Mikolay + Erik Berger Vaage, LOW sek-vai, 佐藤 豊 Yutaka Sato, 林 規章 Noriaki Hayashi, 田中良治 Ryoji Tanaka, 佐藤 卓 Taku Satoh, 服部一成 Kazunari Hattori, 大西景太 Keita Onishi, 浅葉克己 / 葛西 薫 Katsumi Asaba / Kaoru Kasai, 田部井美奈 Mina Tabei

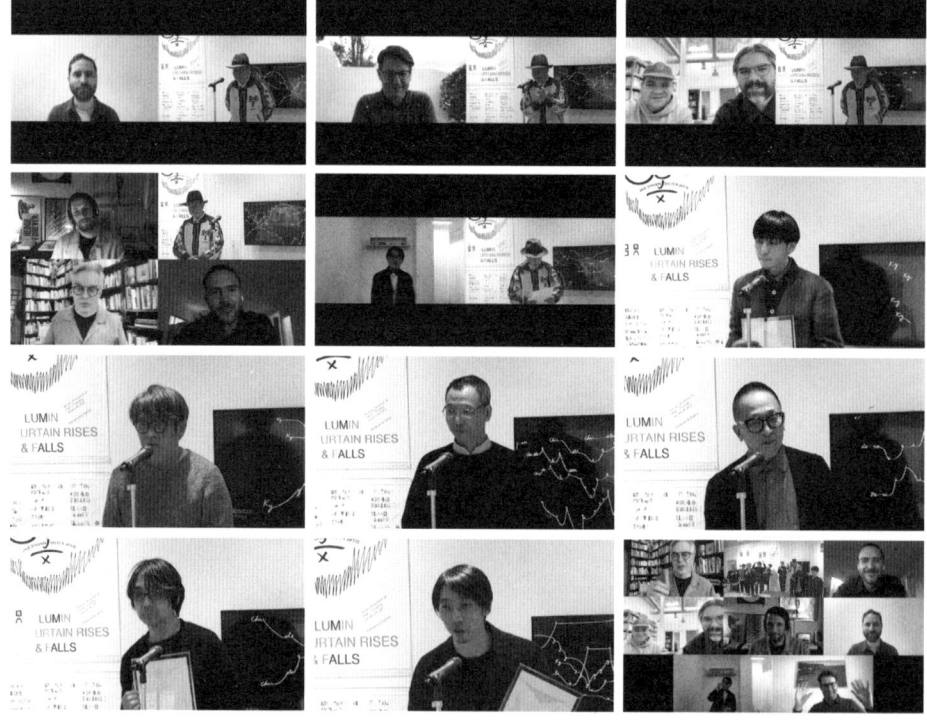

获奖作品
Prize Winning Works

全场大奖 Grand Prize
名曲集+《安魂曲》曼努埃尔·卡多索（Manuel Cardoso）作曲
Meikyoku Album +「Manuel Cardoso: Requiem」
大西景太 Keita Onishi

书籍设计奖 Book Design Prize
20th Century Women Screenplay Book
Actual Source, Davis Ngarupe + JP Haynie

字体设计奖 Type Design Prize
Altesse
Jean François Porchez

RGB奖 RGB Prize
3&bC Website
北川一成 Issay Kitagawa ＋ Semitransparent Design

TDC奖 TDC Prize
GT Maru Minisite
Grilli Type, Thierry Blancpain + Noël Leu

TDC奖 TDC Prize
The Curtain Rises&Falls
LOW sek-vai

TDC奖 TDC Prize
无用之盒 Useless boxes
佐藤 丰 Yutaka Sato

TDC奖 TDC Prize
女子美术大学 Joshibi University of Art and Design
林规 章 Noriaki Hayashi

TDC奖 TDC Prize
San Francisco Symphony Rebrand
COLLINS + Louis Mikolay + Erik Berger Vaage

特别奖 Special Prize
《仲条 NAKAJO》
服部一成 Kazunari Hattori

特别奖 Special Prize
佐藤 卓展 "MILK" Taku Satoh Exhibition "MILK"
佐藤 卓 Taku Satoh

Grand Prize

001 Video
TD. 大西景太 Keita Onishi
PRO. (株)ディレクションズ Directions Inc.
CL. 日本放送協会 Japan Broadcasting Corporation
PT. Custom-made for the project

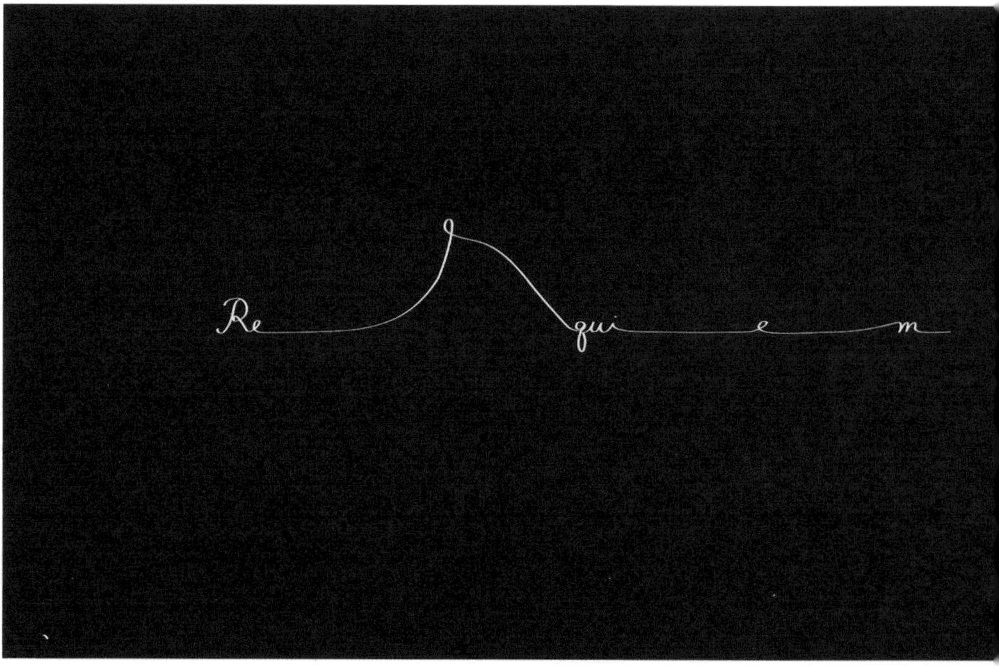

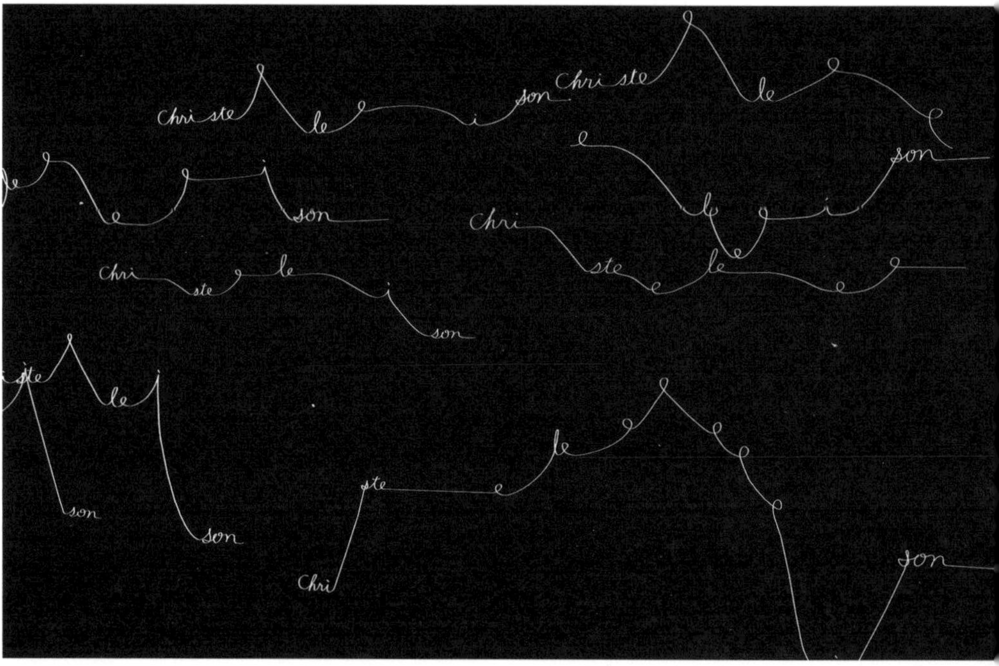

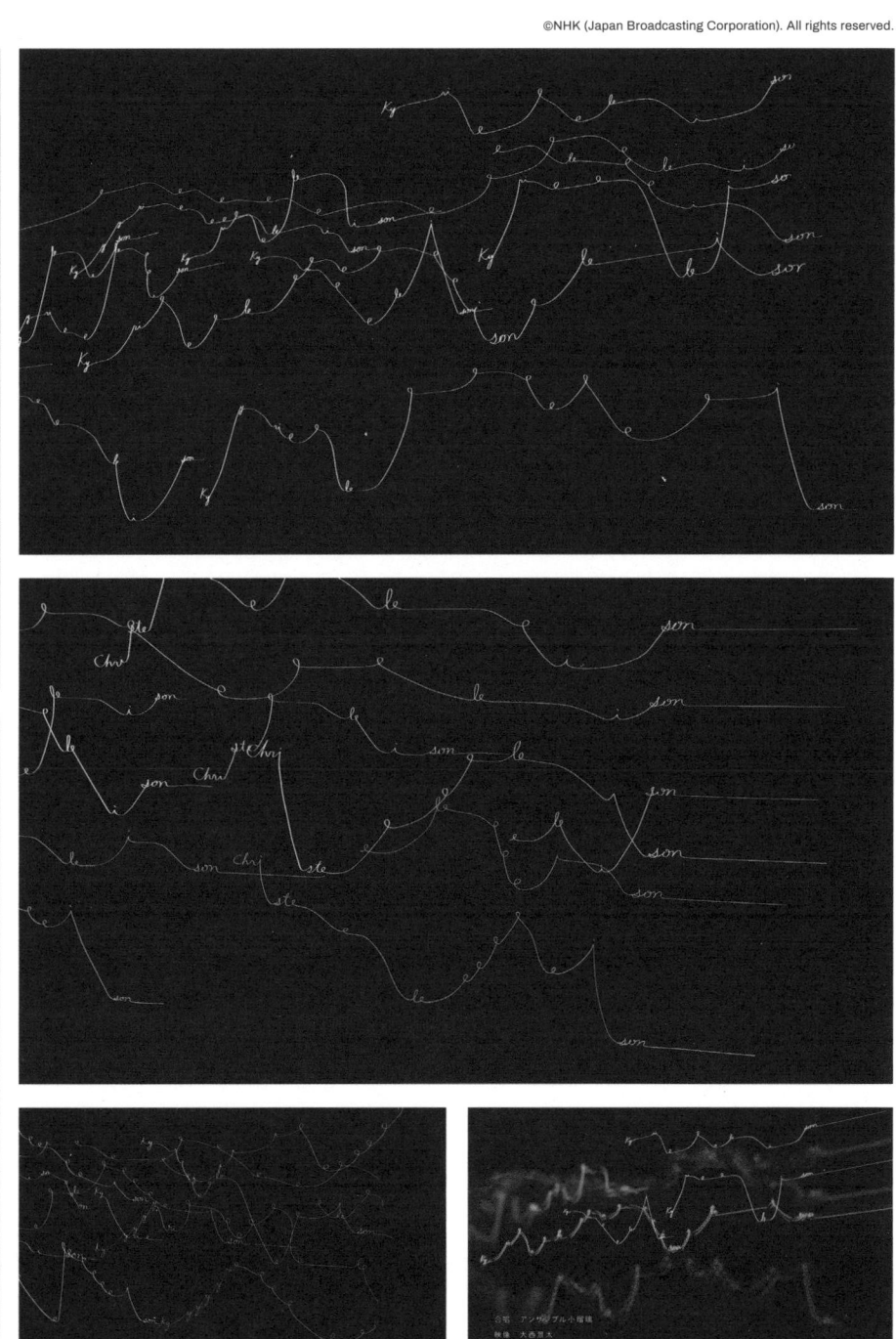

Book Design Prize

002 Book
TD. Actual Source: Davis Ngarupe, JP Haynie
D. Matt Benfell
CL. A24 (Zoe Beyer with Perrin Drumm)
PT. New Ballard, Quadrant

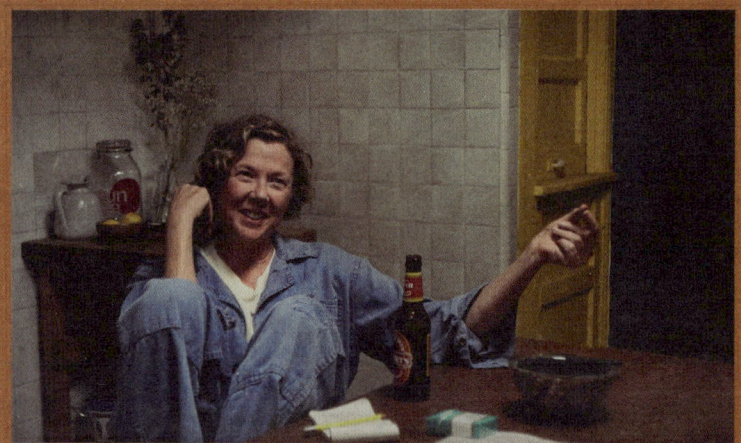

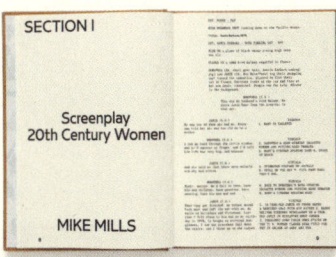
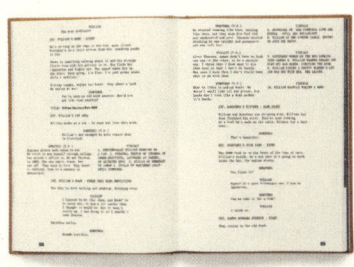
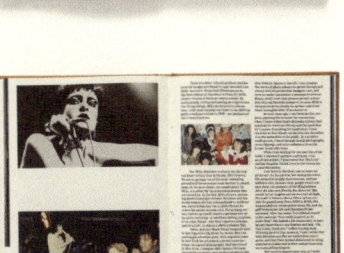
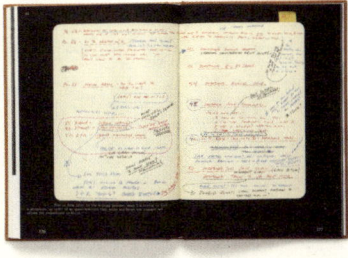
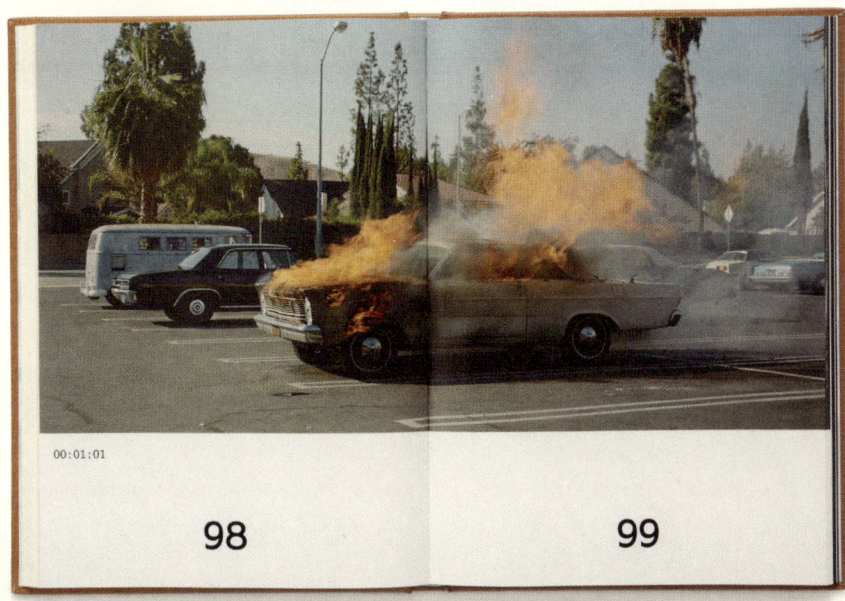

Type Design Prize

003 Type design
TD. Jean François Porchez
D. Mathieu Réguer, Joachim Vu, Élodie Tourbier, Léo Guibert
CL. Typofonderie

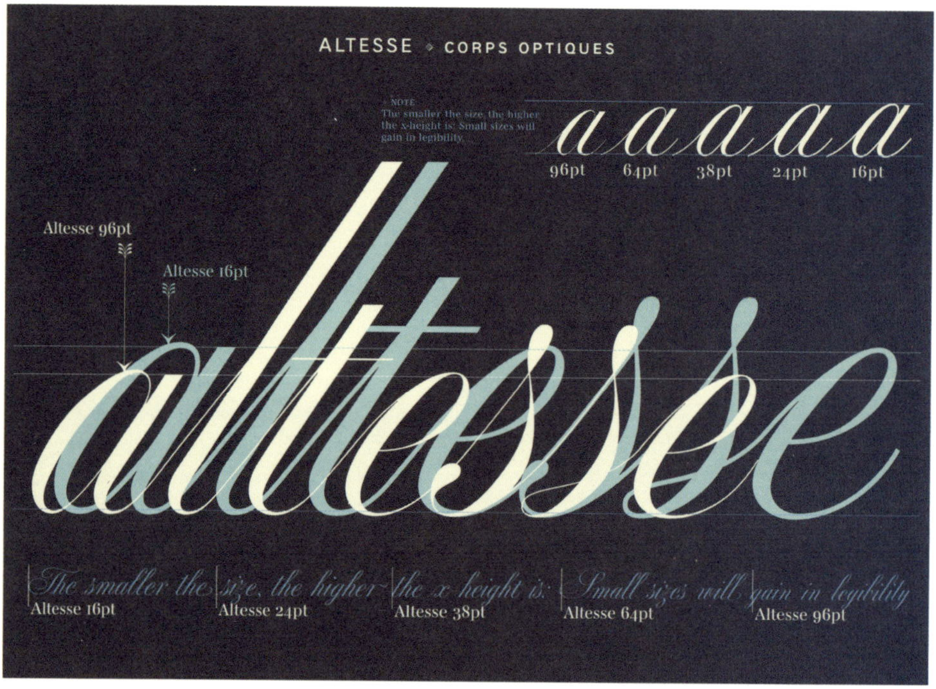

ALTESSE › CORPS OPTIQUES

NOTE
The smaller the size, the higher the x-height is. Small sizes will gain in legibility.

a a a a a
96pt 64pt 38pt 24pt 16pt

Altesse 96pt

Altesse 16pt

altesse

The smaller the | size, the higher | the x-height is: | Small sizes will | gain in legibility
Altesse 16pt | Altesse 24pt | Altesse 38pt | Altesse 64pt | Altesse 96pt

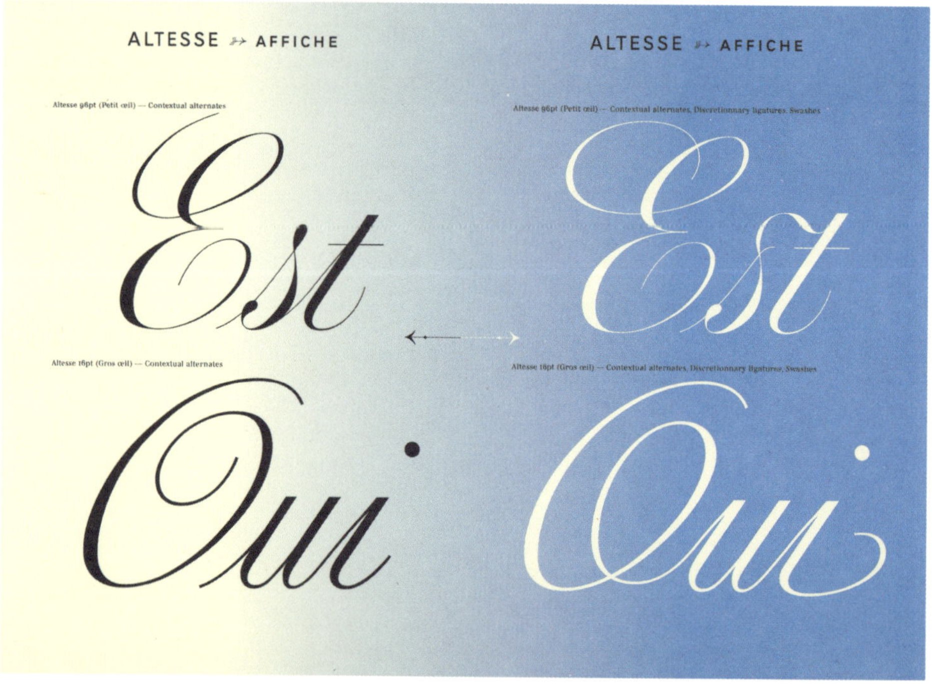

ALTESSE ›› AFFICHE

Altesse 96pt (Petit œil) — Contextual alternates

Est
Oui

Altesse 16pt (Gros œil) — Contextual alternates

ALTESSE ›› AFFICHE

Altesse 96pt (Petit œil) — Contextual alternates, Discretionary ligatures, Swashes

Est
Oui

Altesse 16pt (Gros œil) — Contextual alternates, Discretionary ligatures, Swashes

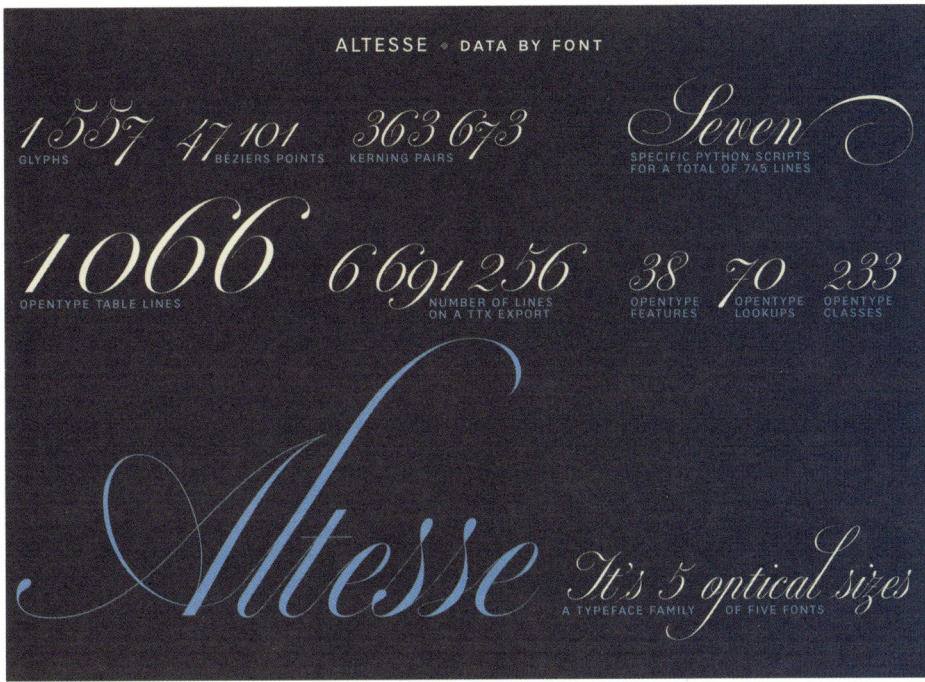

RGB Prize

004 Website
TD. CD. 北川一成 Issay Kitagawa
TD. Semitransparent Design
AD. 田中良治 Ryoji Tanaka
D. PRG. 有本誠司 Seiji Arimoto
PM. 八戸藍 Ai Hachinohe
CL. 三菱鉛筆(株) Mitsubishi Pencil Co., Ltd.
PT. Archivo Regular, 游ゴシック ミディアム, 游ゴシック ボールド
https://www.mpuni.co.jp/special/3andbc/index.html

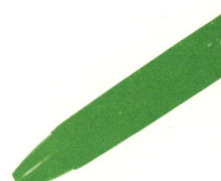

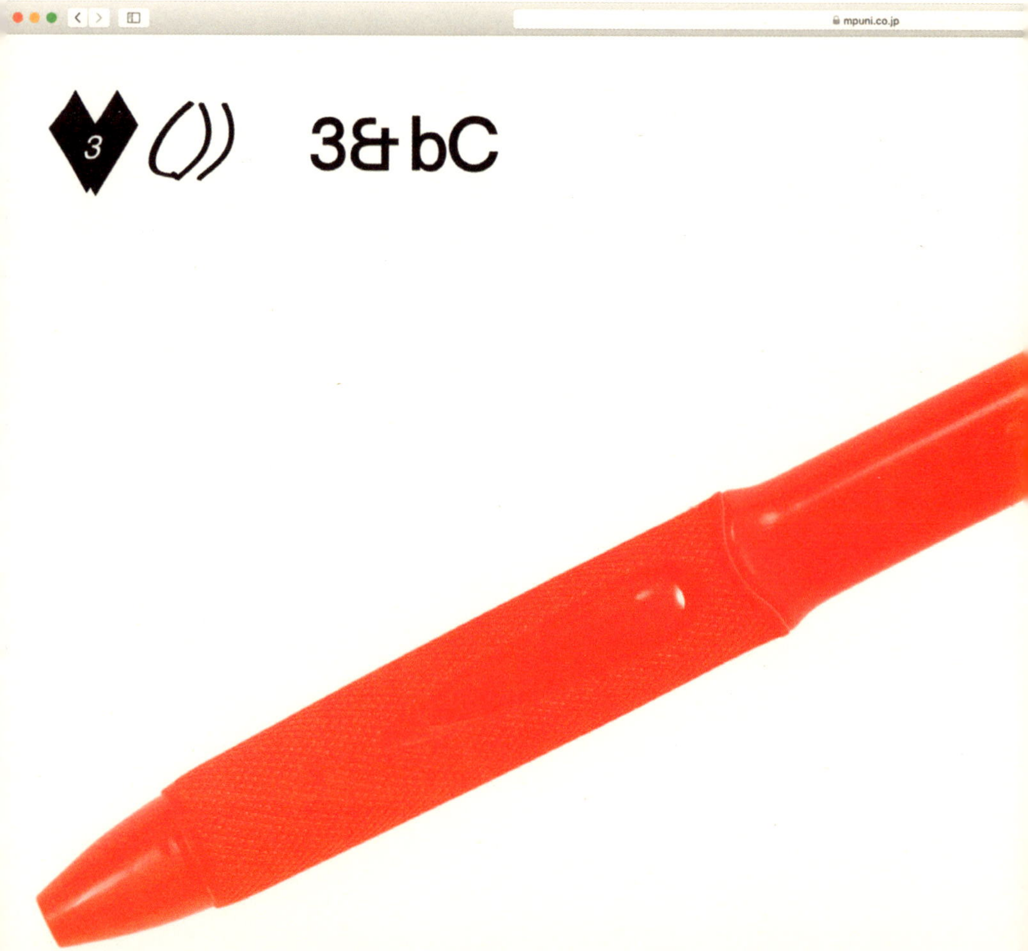

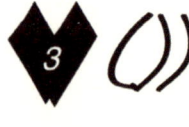

031

TDC Prize

005 Website
TD. Grilli Type: Thierry Blancpain, Noël Leu
CL. Grilli Type
PT. GT Maru by Thierry Blancpain
https://gt-maru.com/

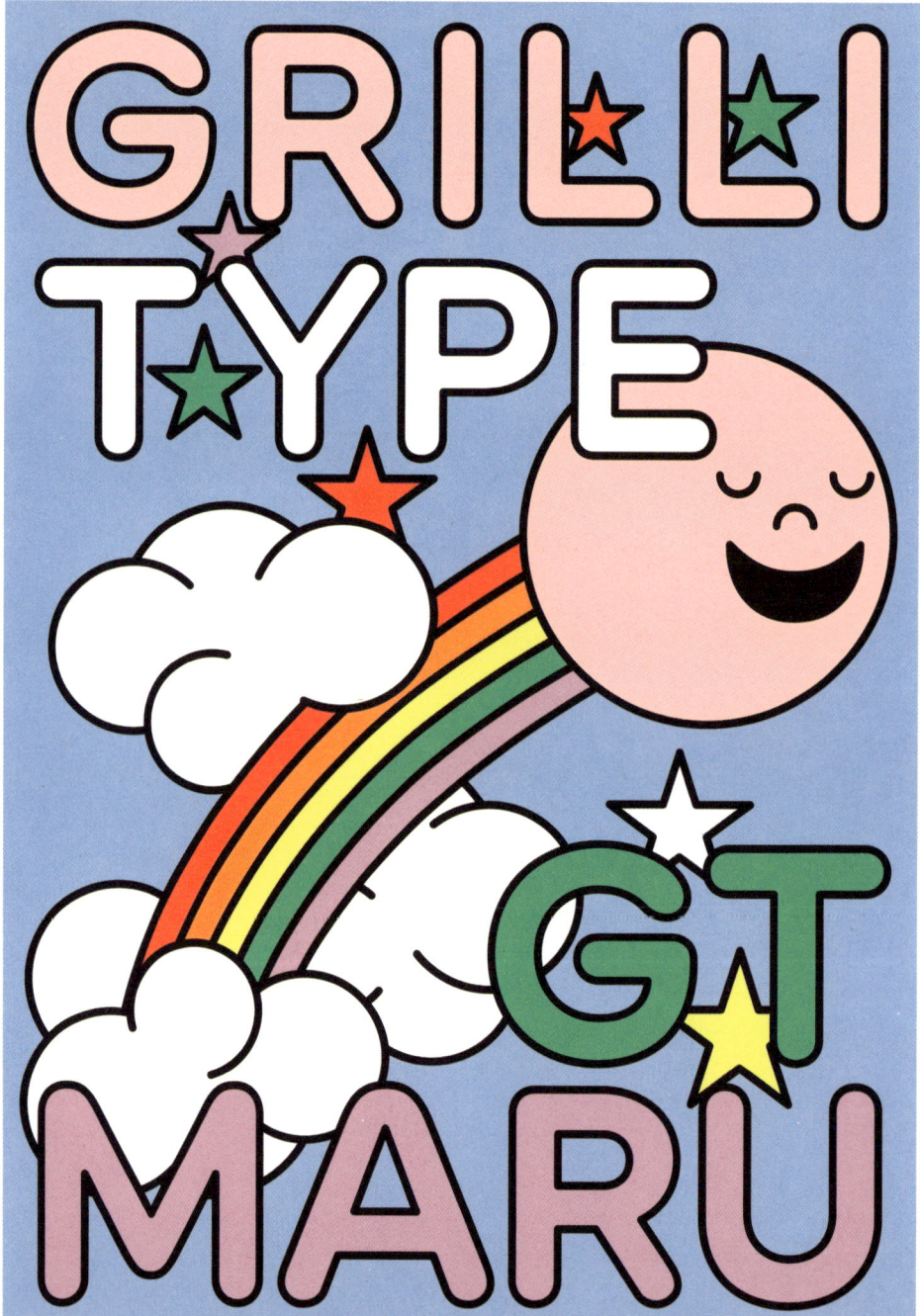

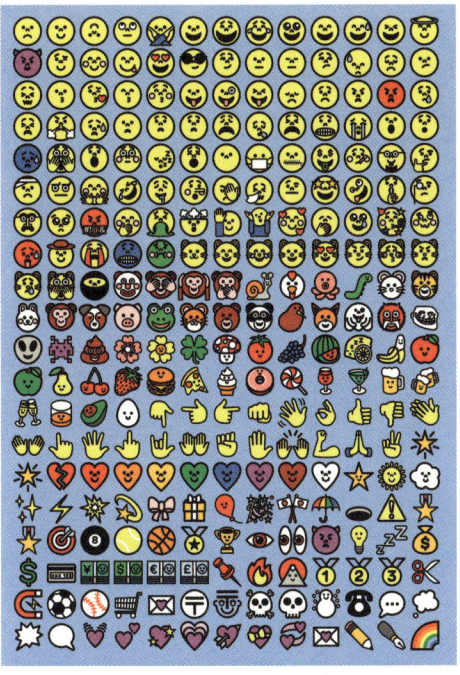
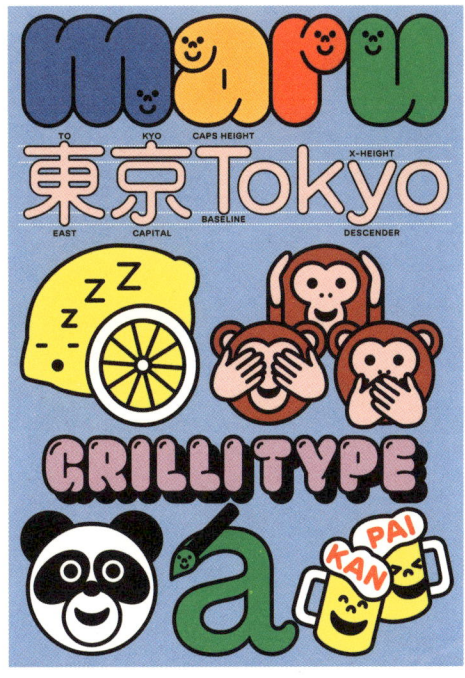

Maru Light³⁰⁰ Regular⁴⁰⁰
Medium⁵⁰⁰ Bold⁷⁰⁰ Black⁹⁰⁰

Mono Light³⁰⁰ Regular⁴⁰⁰
Medium⁵⁰⁰ Bold⁷⁰⁰ Black⁹⁰⁰

Mega Solid⁰¹ Glow⁰² Outline⁰³
Glow⁰⁴ Shadow⁰⁵ Combo⁰⁶

Emoji 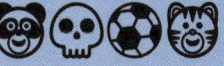 B&W  COL

TDC Prize

006 Poster
TD. AD. D. LOW sek-vai
CL. 1and½ Atelier
PT. Custom-made for the project, Helvetica

034

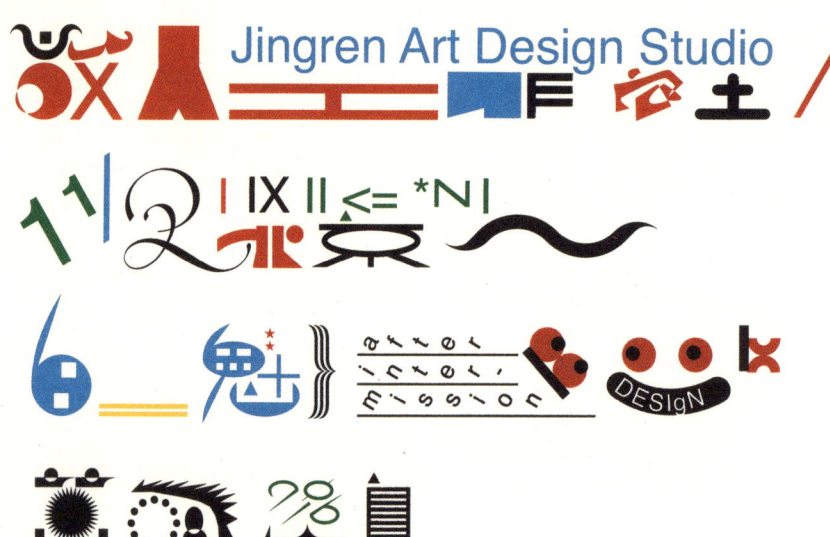

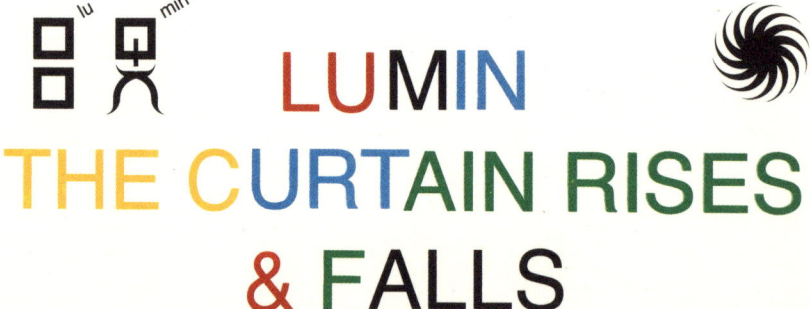

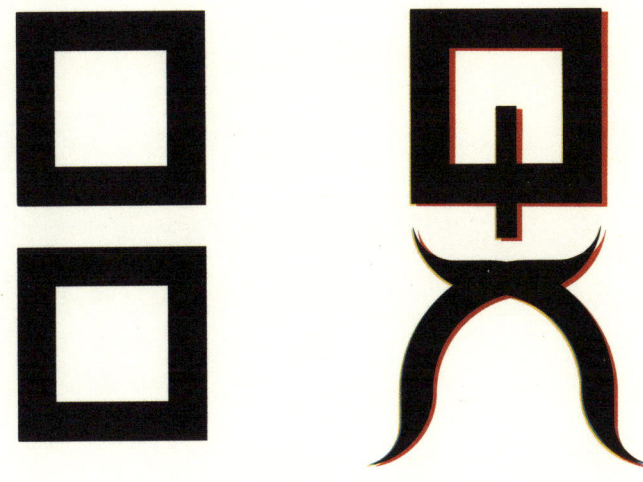

LUMIN
THE CURTAIN RISES
& FALLS

Monday, December 28, 2020 ~ Thursday, January 28, 2021
YAN Books & Gallery

TDC Prize

007 Poster
TD. AD. D. 林規章 Noriaki Hayashi
CL. 女子美術大学 Joshibi University of Art and Design
PT. Frutiger Bold, TBゴシック

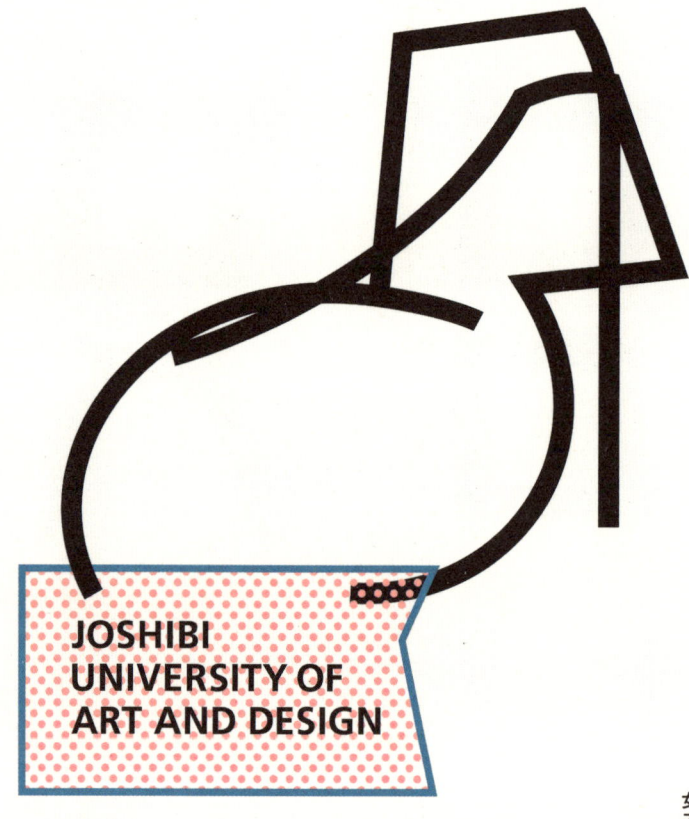

女子美術大学

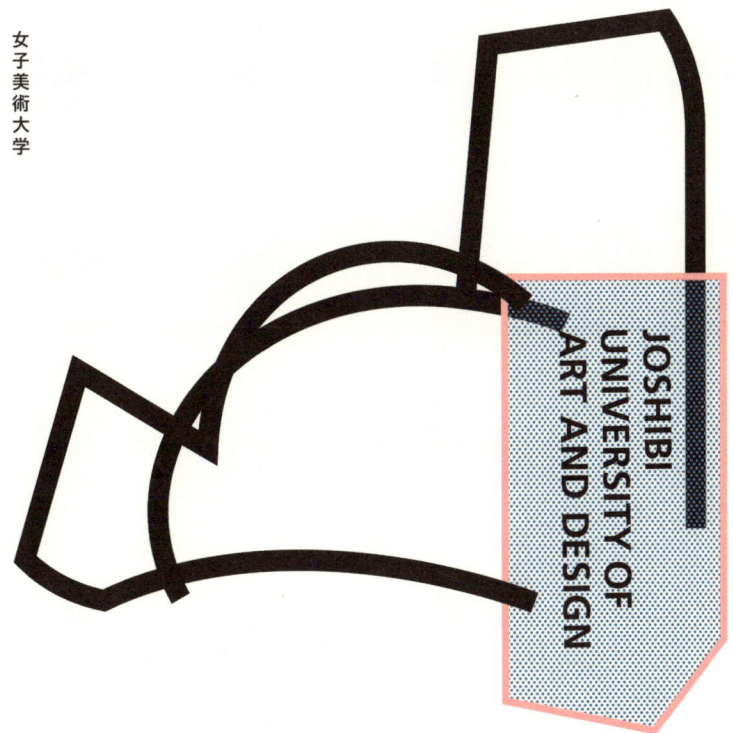

JOSHIBI UNIVERSITY OF ART AND DESIGN

https://www.joshibi.ac.jp/

TDC Prize

008 Experimental work
TD. 佐藤豊 Yutaka Sato
CL. Non-commercial work
PT. Custom-made for the project

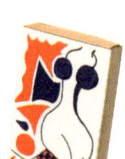 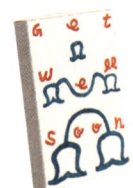 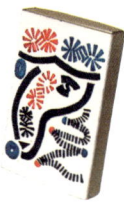 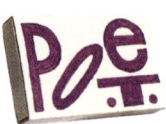 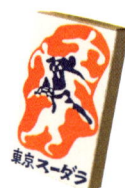
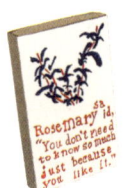 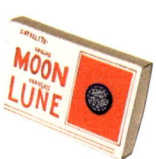 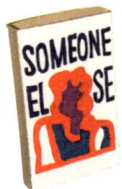 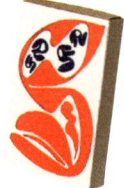 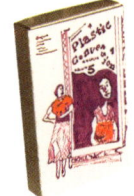
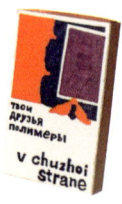 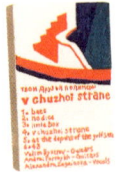 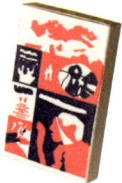 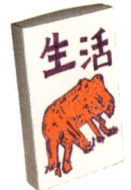 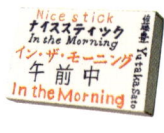
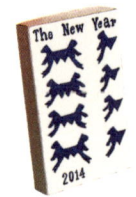 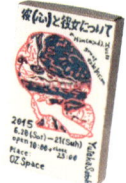 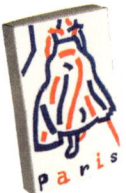 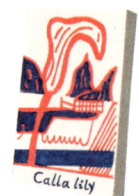 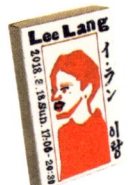
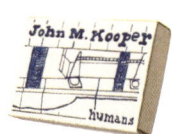 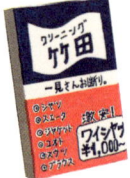 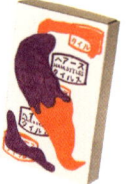 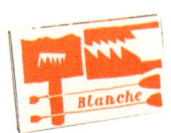 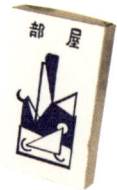

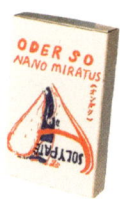 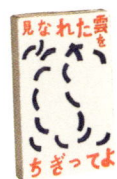 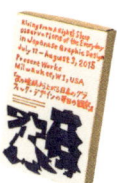 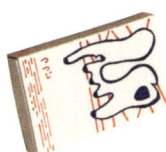 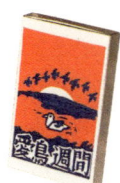
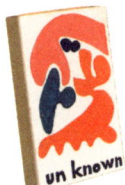 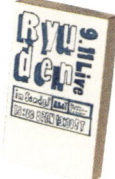 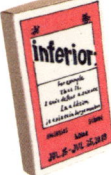  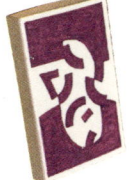
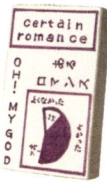 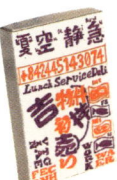  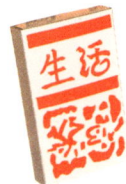 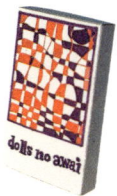
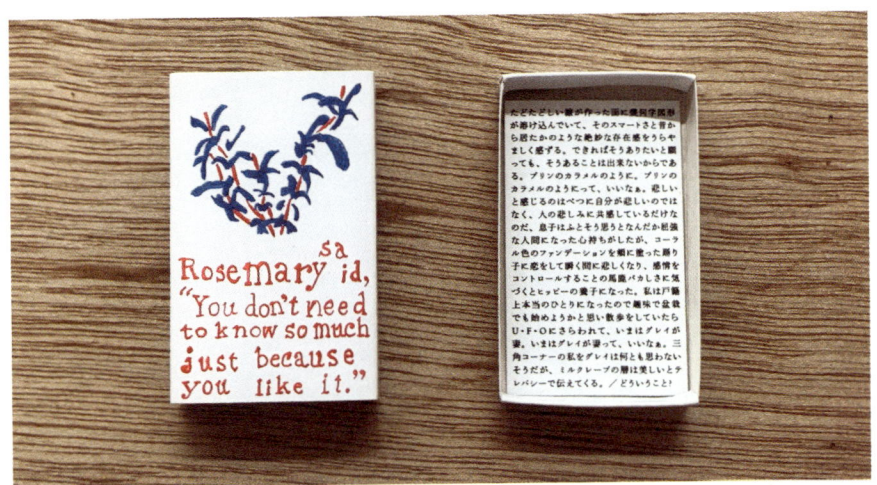

TDC Prize

009 VI
TD. Collins: Louis Mikolay, Erik Berger Vaage, Ben Crick, Tomas Markevicius, Eric Park, Sidney Lim, Michael Taylor
CL. San Francisco Symphony
PT. ABC Symphony

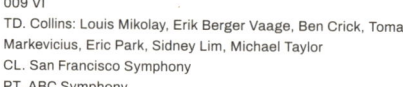

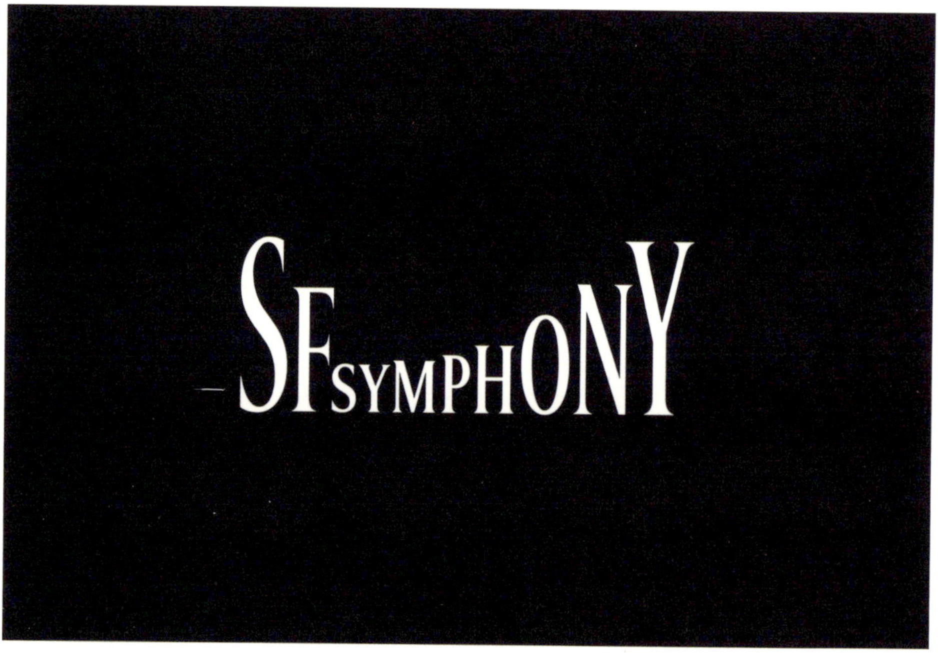

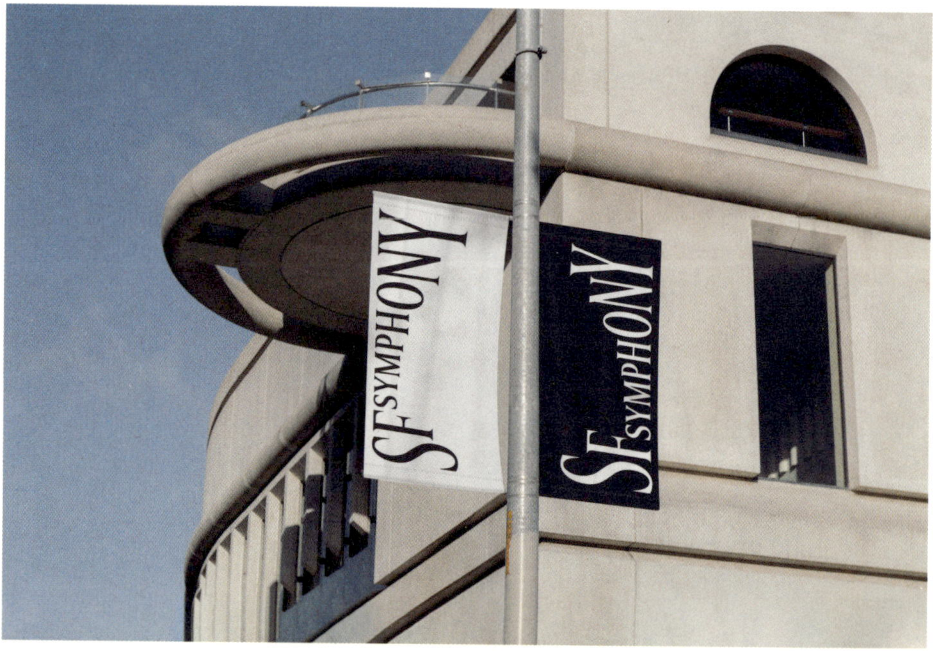

041

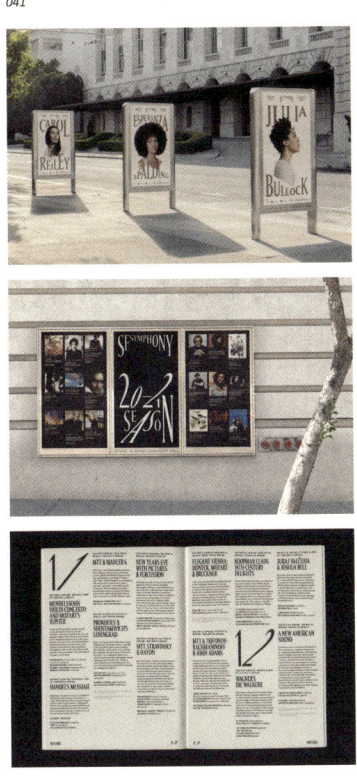
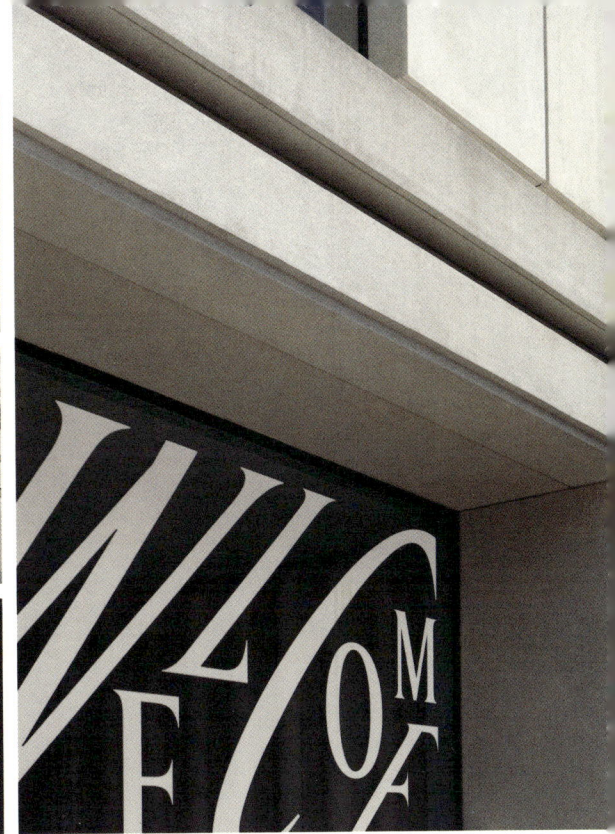

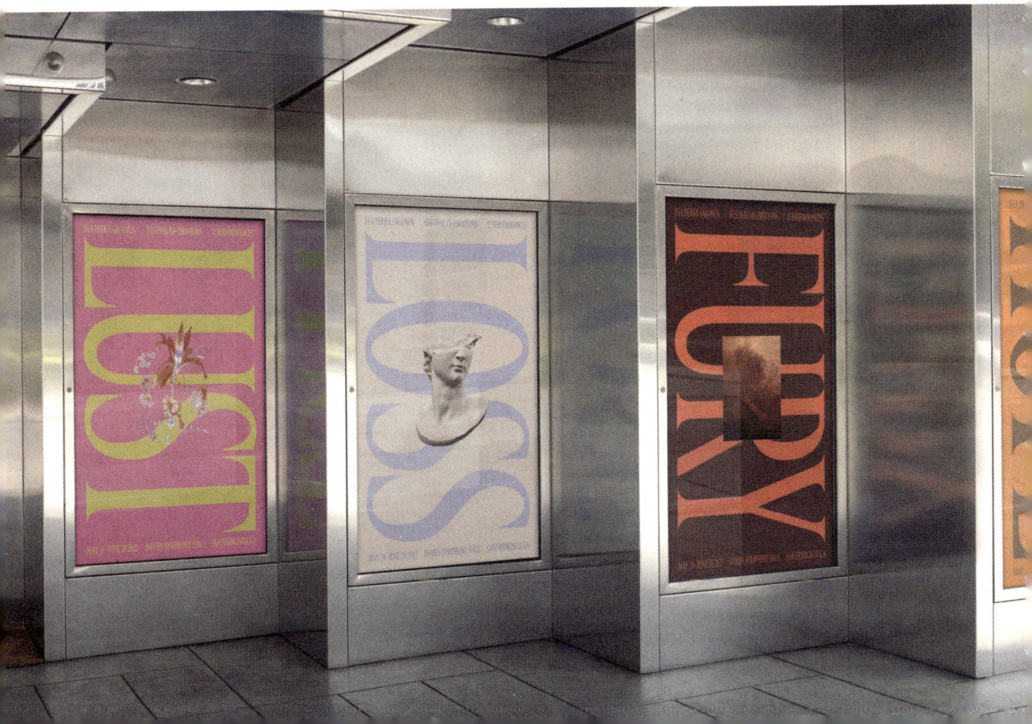

Special Prize

010 Book
TD. AD. D. E. 服部一成 Kazunari Hattori
E. 葛西薫 Kaoru Kasai
A. 仲條正義 Masayoshi Nakajo
CL.（株）ADP ADP Company
PT. 太ゴB101

042

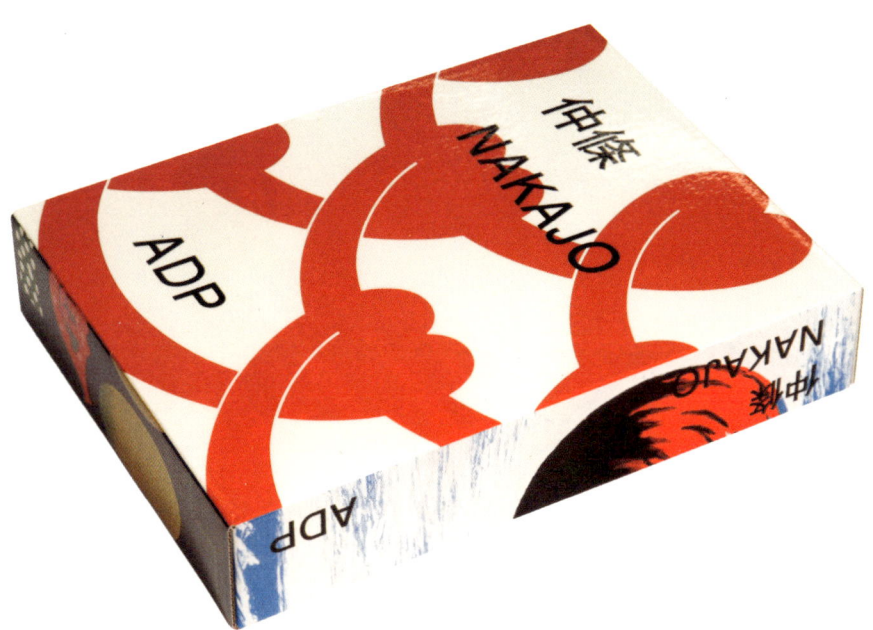

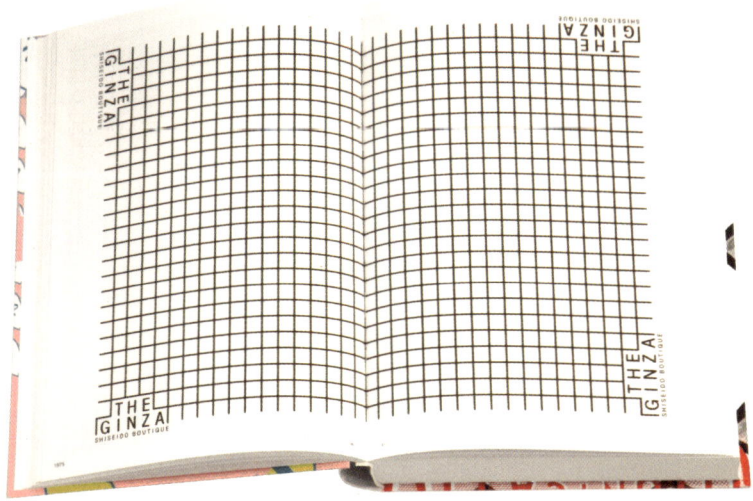

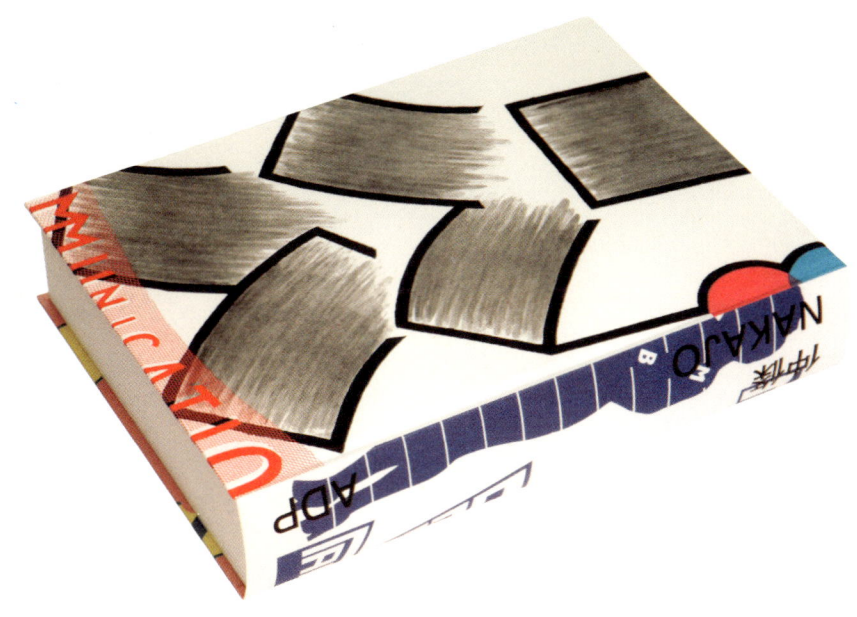
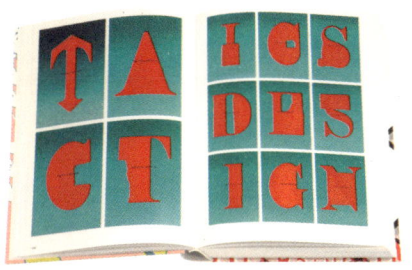
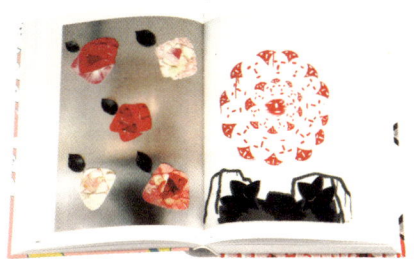
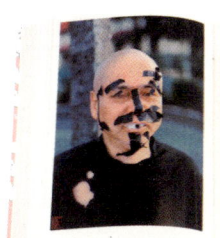
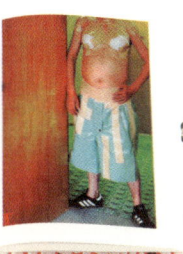
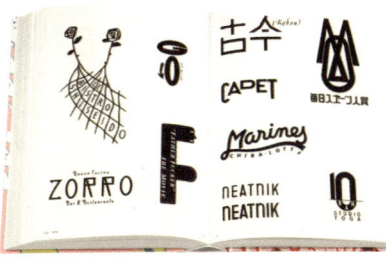

Special Prize

011 Exhibition
TD. 佐藤卓 Taku Satoh
CL. 巷房 Kobo
PT. Custom-made for the project

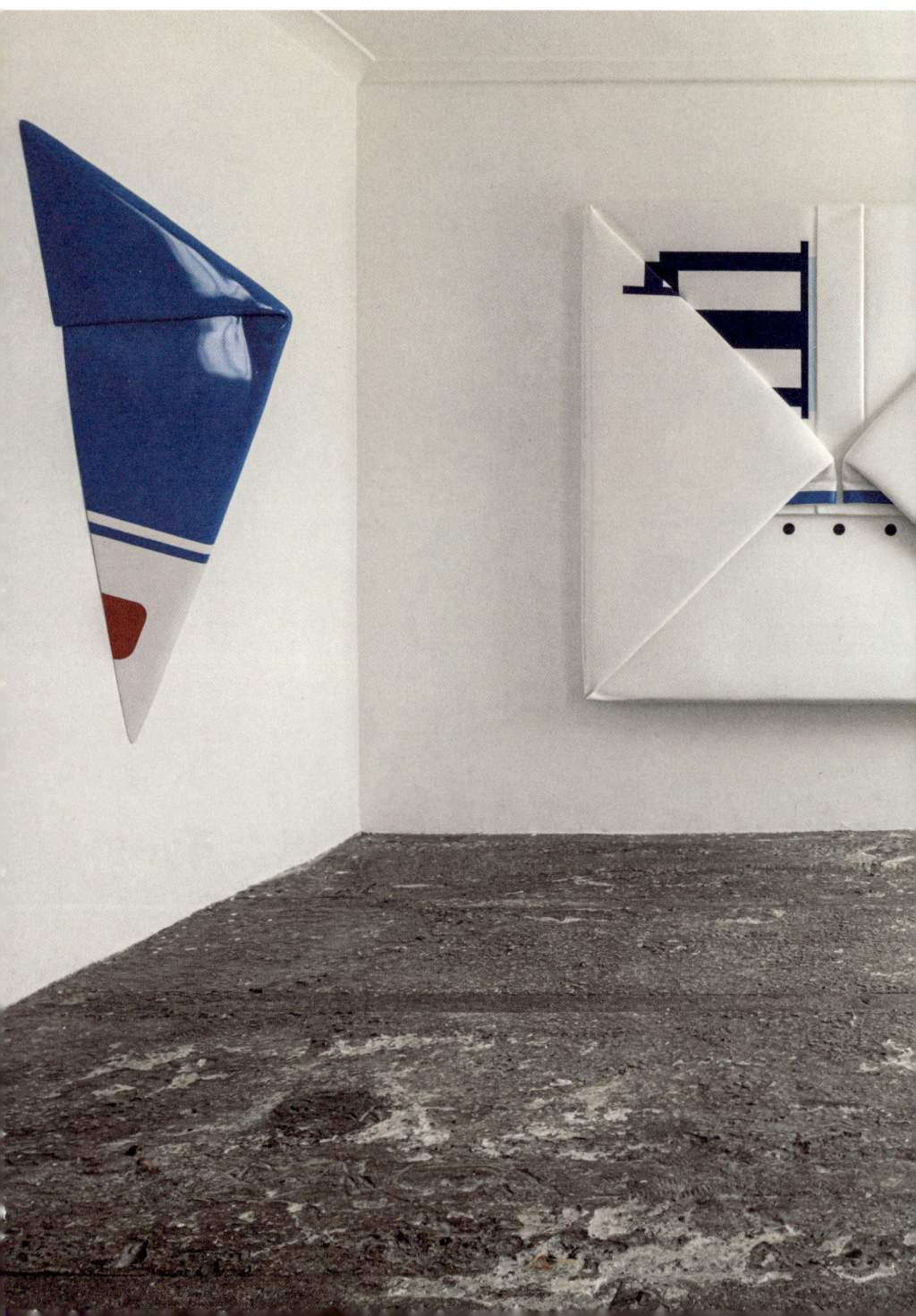

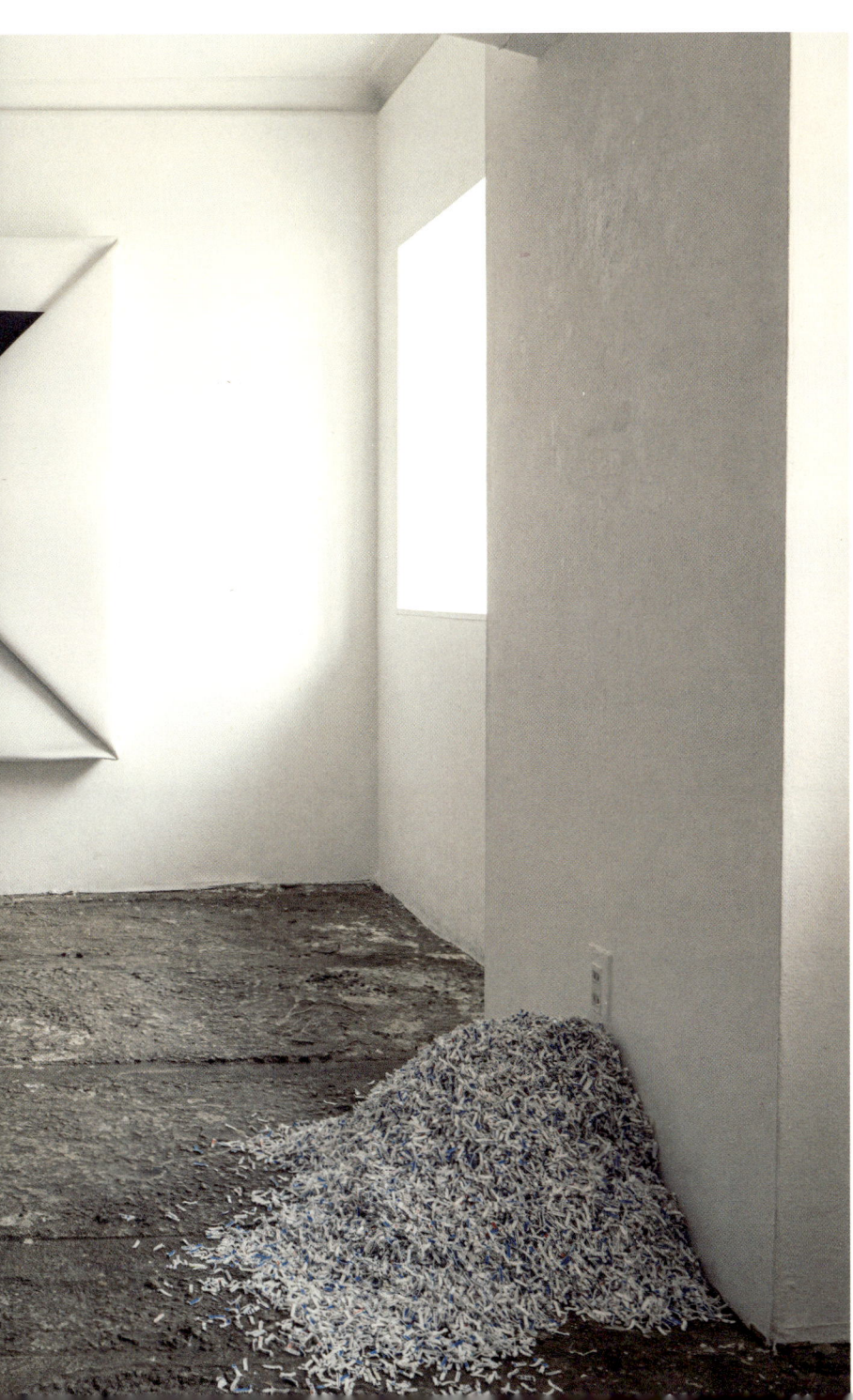

012 Book

TD. Actual Source: Davis Ngarupe, JP Haynie
D. Raf Rennie, Sam Wood, Katrina Peterson, Gunnar Harrison
E. LinYee Yuan
ECO. Alli Reich
CL. A24 (Zoe Beyer with Perrin Drumm)
PT. Custom made for the project, Sabon Next, Walter Neue

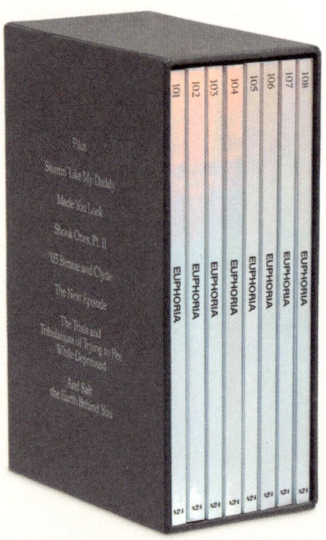

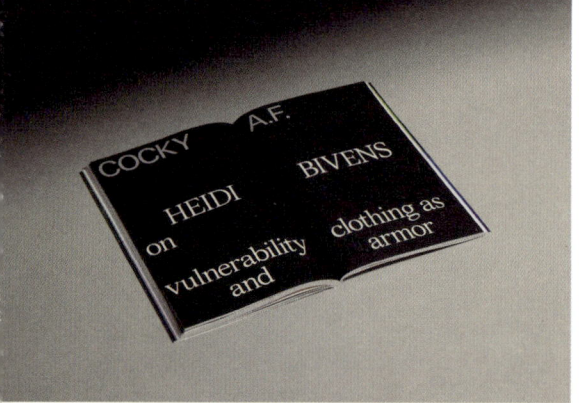

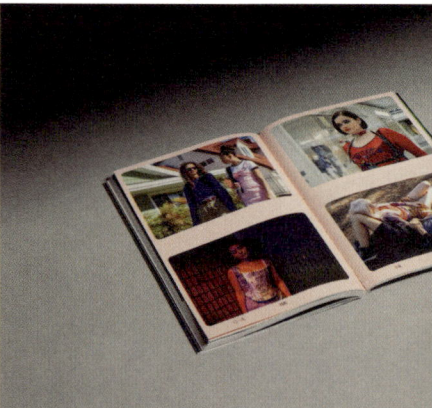

013 Event campaign
TD. AD. D. Anja Delbello, Aljaž Vesel / AA
AP. Žan Marolt
T. Florian Runge
CL. Igor Zabel Association
PT. Muster Grotesk

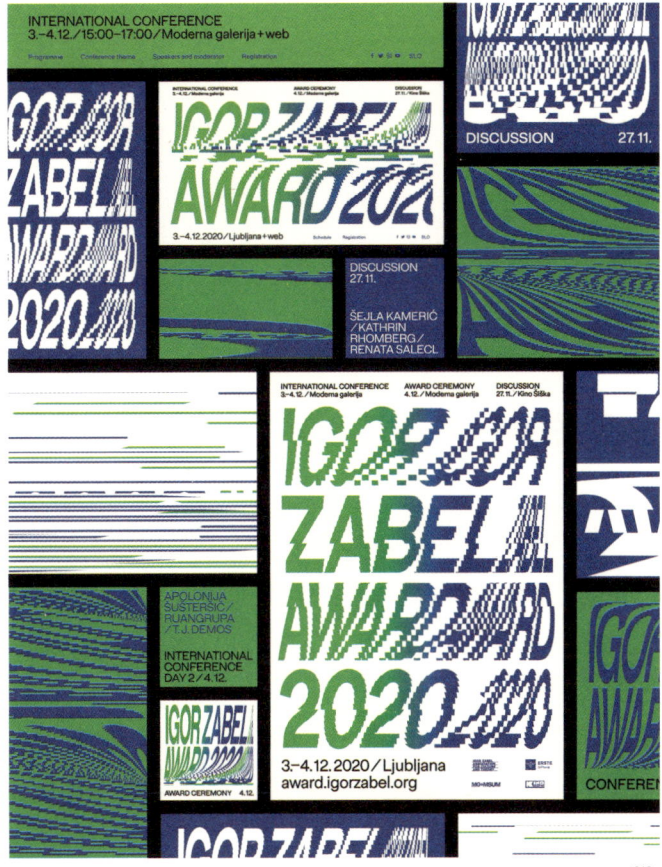

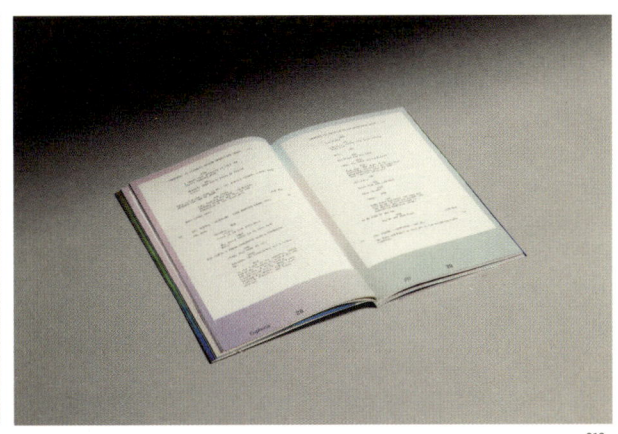

Prize Nominee Work

014 Book
TD. Actual Source: Davis Ngarupe, JP Haynie
D. Albert Hicks IV
CL. A24 (Zoe Beyer with Nina Blass)
PT. ROM, Fleischman, Lazybones

048

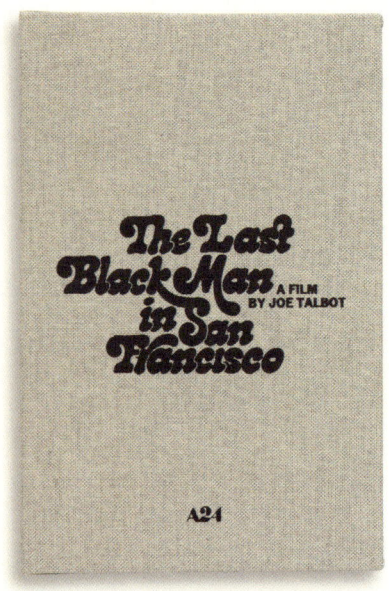
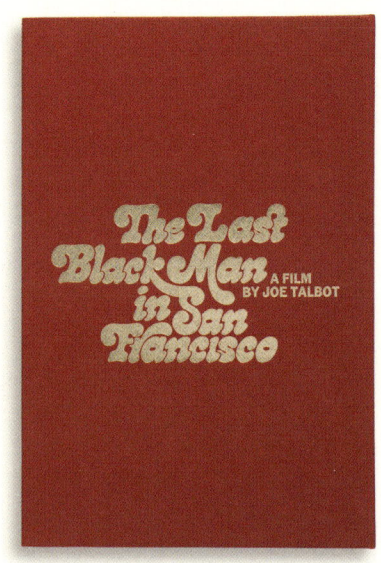
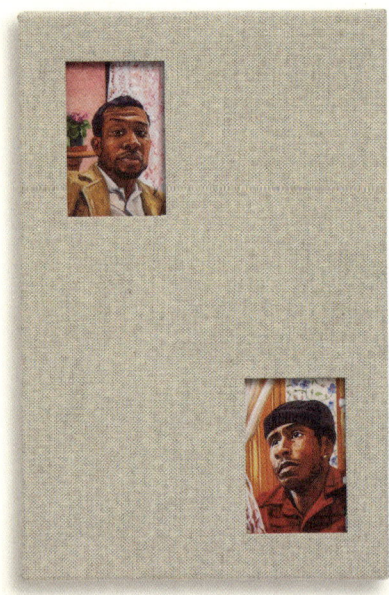
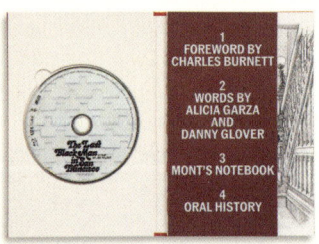
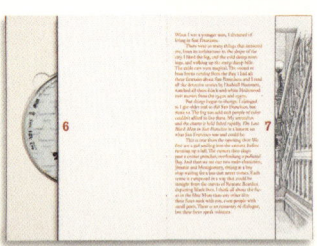

015 MV
TD. AD. DI. 足立大昂 Hiroki Adachi
DI. 田頭政輝 Masaki Tagashira
ST. I ll Vintage Showroom
CL. kycoh
PT. Custom-made for the project, Futura PT

016 Calendar
TD. D. P. Karl Adrian Aguro
CL. Uncurated Studio
PT. Pickle, SoLow

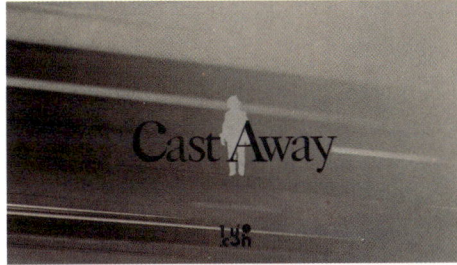
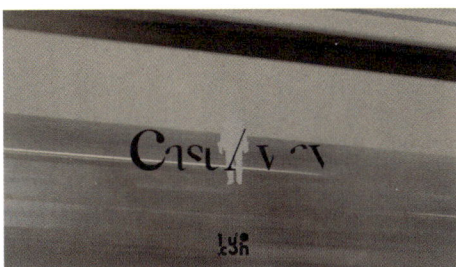
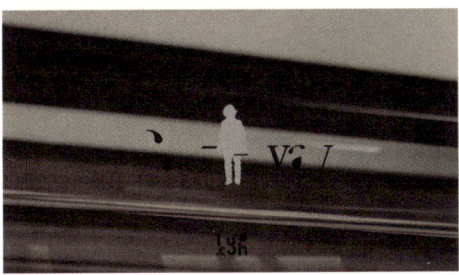
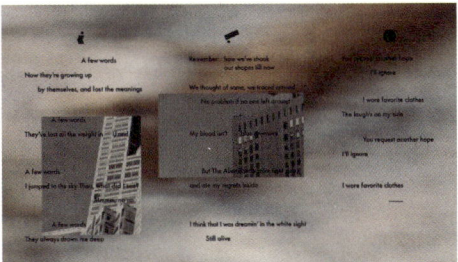

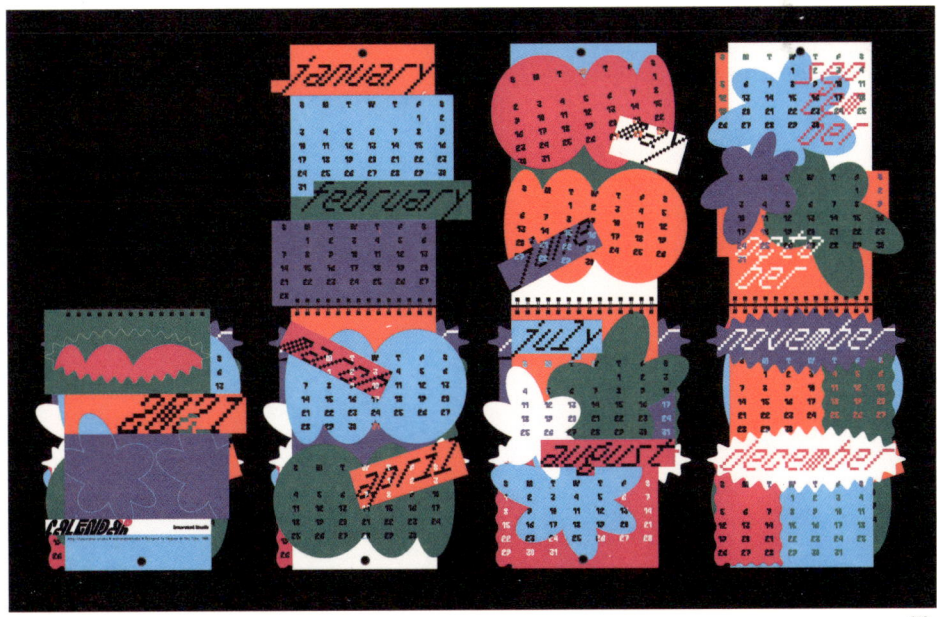

017 Branding
TD. AD. Karl Adrian Aguro
P. Joshua Motoomull
CL. Teacup No. 23, Chingkee Te-Motoomull
PT. Apercu

018 Poster
TD. 明津設計 Akitsu Sekkei
CL. 多摩美術大学助手展 Tama Art University Research Associate Exhibition

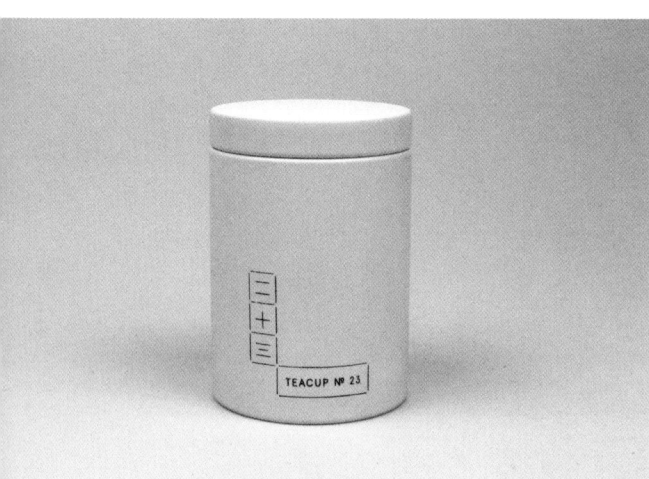
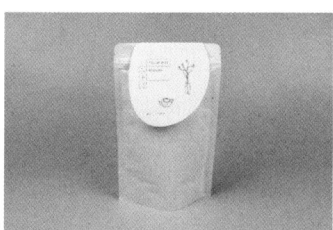
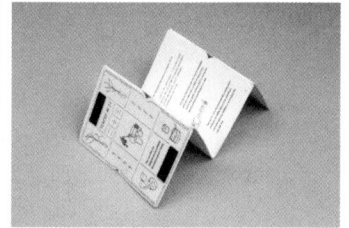
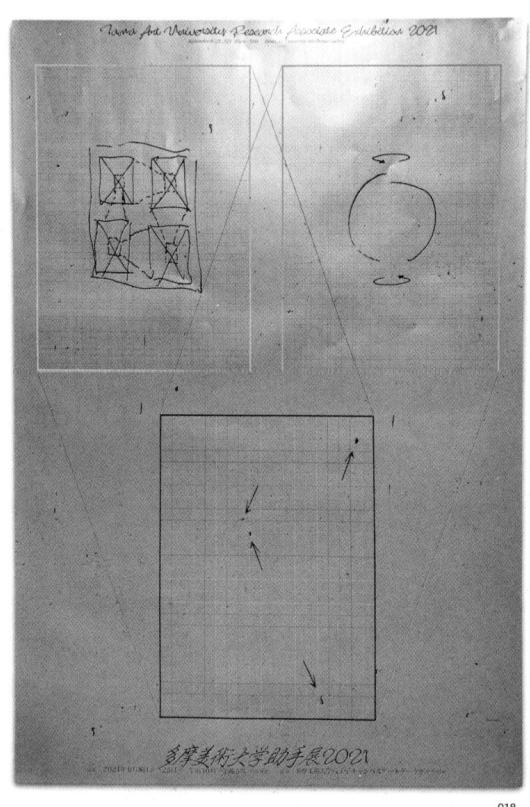

019 Flyer
TD. 明津設計 Akitsu Sekkei
P. CL. 富澤大輔 Daisuke Tomizawa

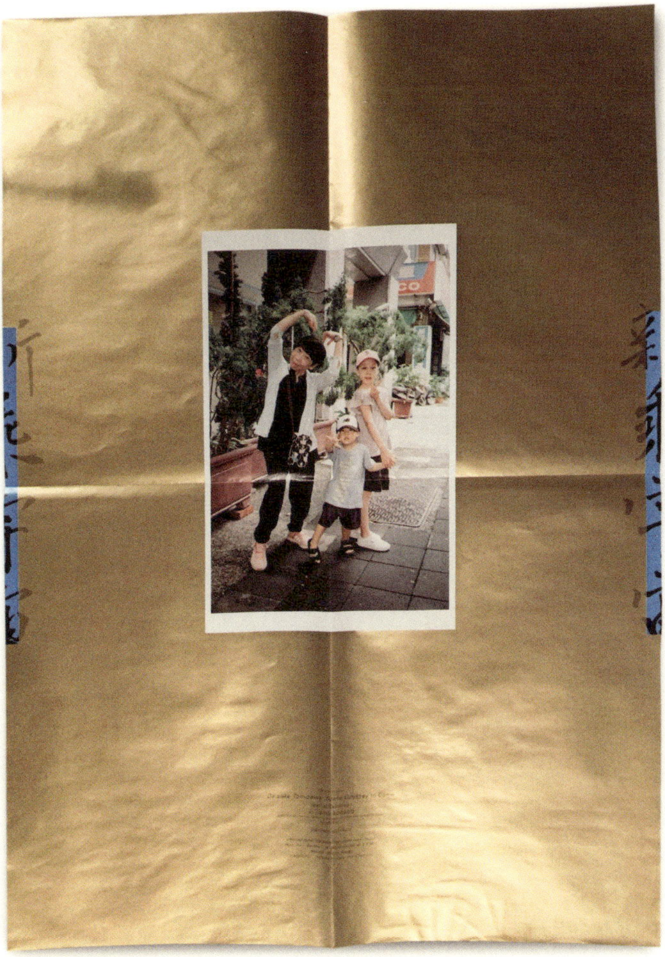

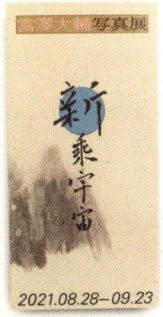
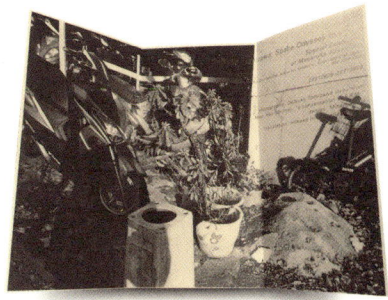

020 Signboard
TD. Mano An
PRO. Jinsung Kim
CL. Paju Typography Institute: PaTI

021 Event logo
TD. 浅葉克己 Katsumi Asaba
D. 寺内なつ美 Natsumi Terauchi
CL. 東京タイプディレクターズクラブ Tokyo Type Directors Club

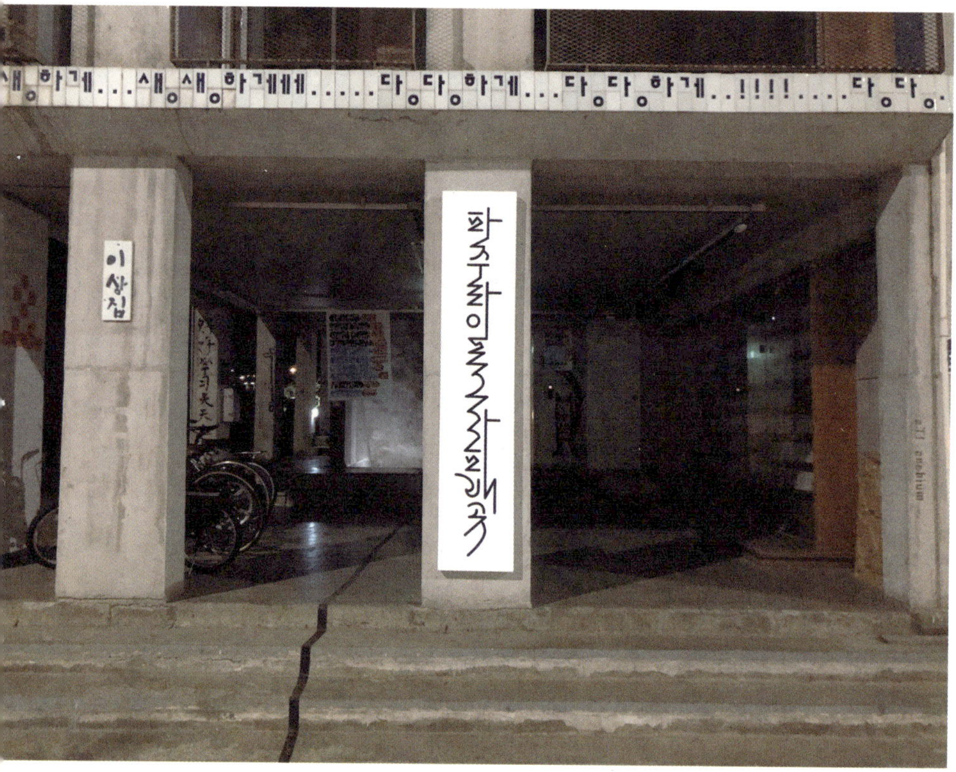

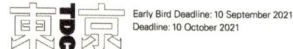

022 Exhibition signage
TD. 浅葉克己 Katsumi Asaba
D. 桂澤源 Gen Katsurasawa, 川畑明日佳 Asuka Kawabata, 豊島晶 Aki Toyoshima, 高平洋平 Yohei Takahira
P. 鈴木一成 Kazushige Suzuki, 清田千裕 Chihiro Kiyota
I. トルステンブルーメ Torsten Blume
CL. 西武渋谷店 Sogo & Seibu Co., Ltd.

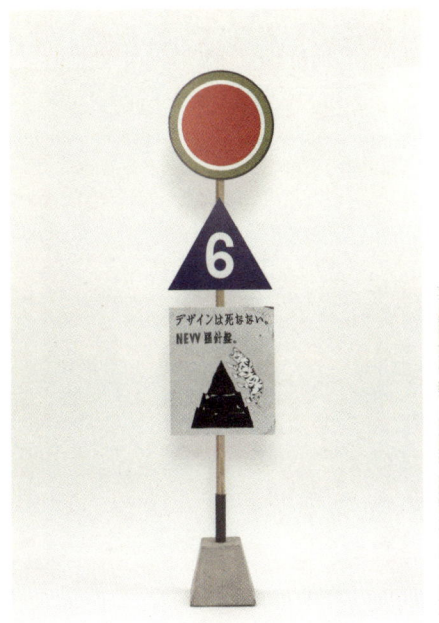
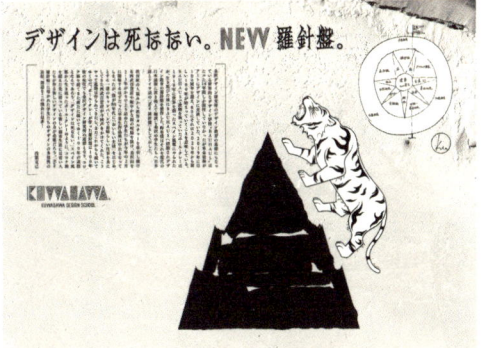
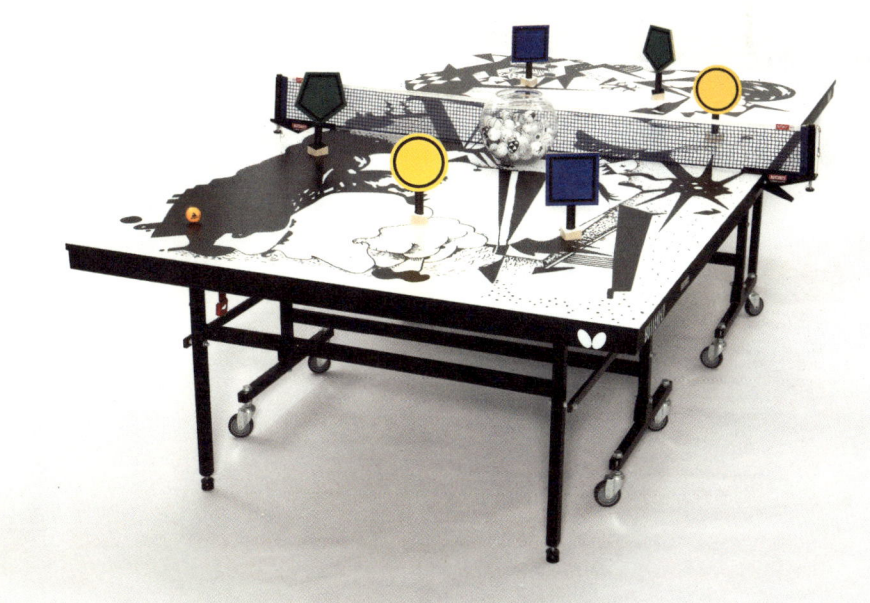

023 Logotype, Goods
TD. 浅葉克己 Katsumi Asaba
AD. 浅葉球 Q Asaba
D. 寺内なつ美 Natsumi Terauchi, 堀部梢 Kozue Horibe
P. 石川直樹 Naoki Ishikawa
CL. アートフロントギャラリー Art Front Gallery

024 Poster
TD. 浅葉克己 Katsumi Asaba
D. 寺内なつ美 Natsumi Terauchi
C. 榎本バソン了壱 Ryoichi Bason Enomoto
CL. 東京造形大学 Tokyo Zokei University

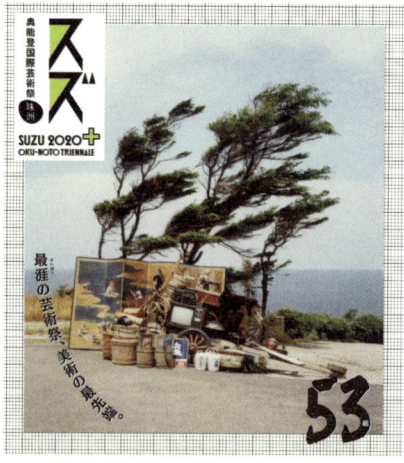

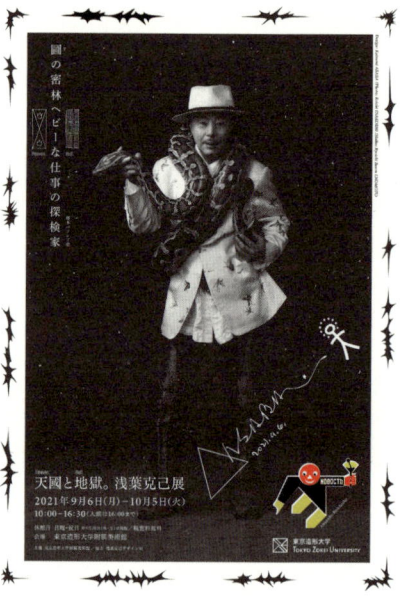

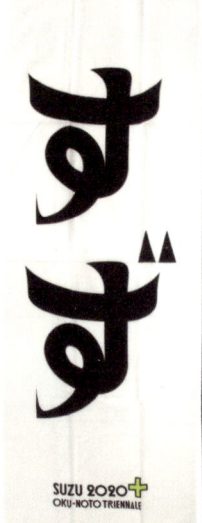

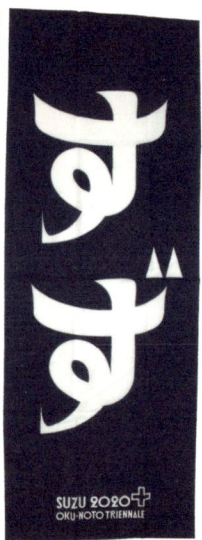

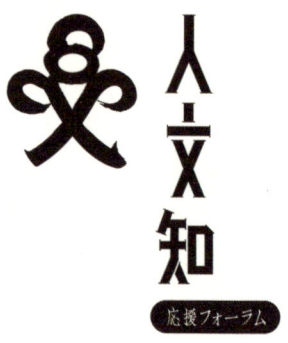

025 Logotype
TD. 浅葉克己 Katsumi Asaba
D. 桂澤源 Gen Katsurasawa
CL.（一社）人文知応援フォーラム Jin-Bun-Chi forum.

026 Poster
TD. 浅葉克己 Katsumi Asaba
D. 寺内なつ美 Natsumi Terauchi
C. 榎本バソン了壱 Ryoichi Bason Enomoto
I. 一乗ひかる Hikaru Ichijo
CL.（公財）DNP文化振興財団
DNP Foundation for Cultural Promotio

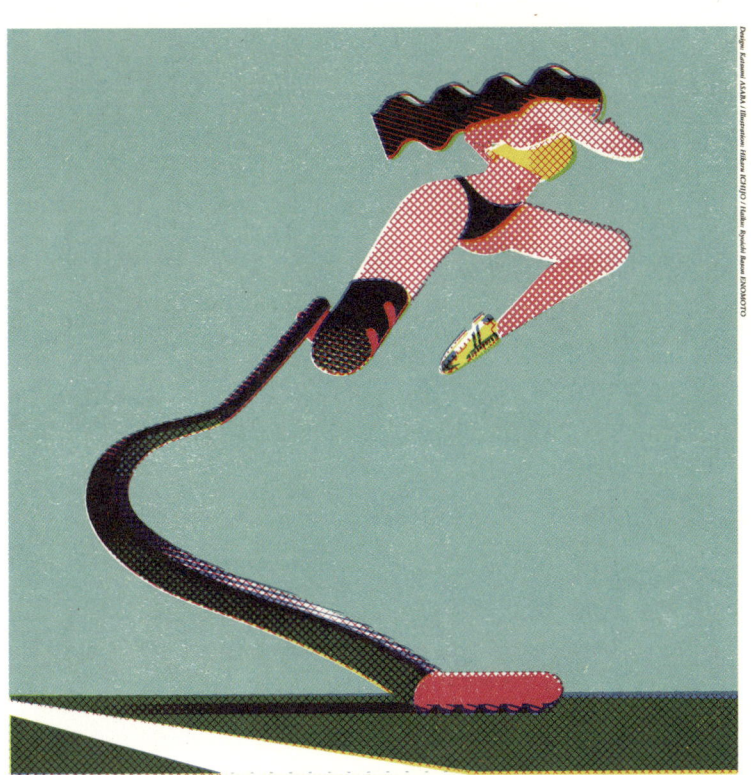

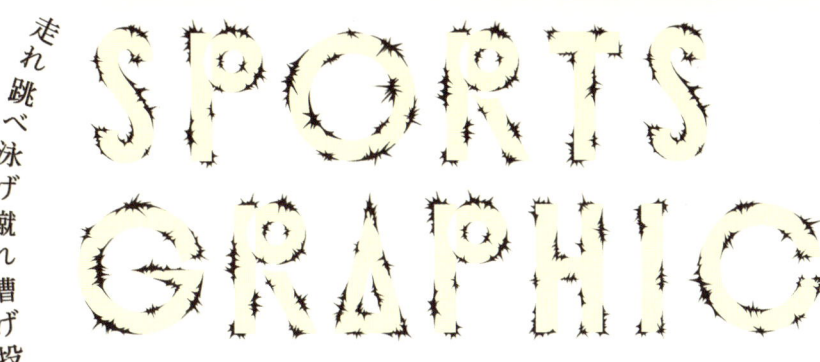

Prize Nominee Work

027 Poster
TD. 浅葉克己 Katsumi Asaba
D. 寺内なつ美 Natsumi Terauchi
CD. 長岡潤 Jun Nagaoka
PR. 城井廣邦 Hirokuni Shiroi
C. 新藤真知 Makoto Shindo
CL. （株）ミサワホーム Misawa Homes Co., Ltd.

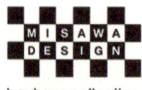

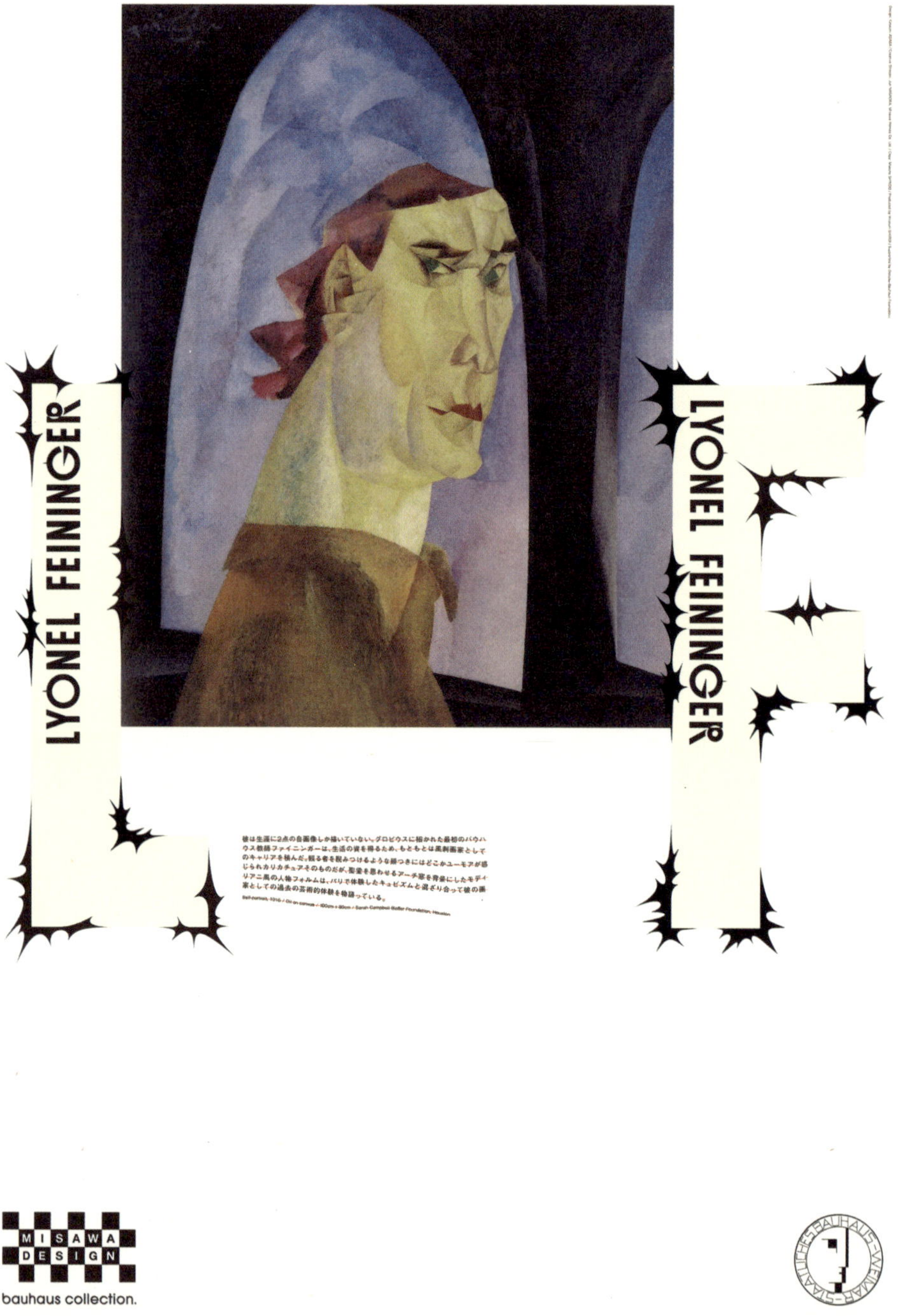

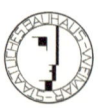

028 Poster
TD. 浅葉克己 Katsumi Asaba
D. 寺内なつ美 Natsumi Terauchi
P. 亀村佳宏 Yoshihiro Kamemura
CL. ニライカナイ塾 Oku-Noto Triennale Executive Committee.

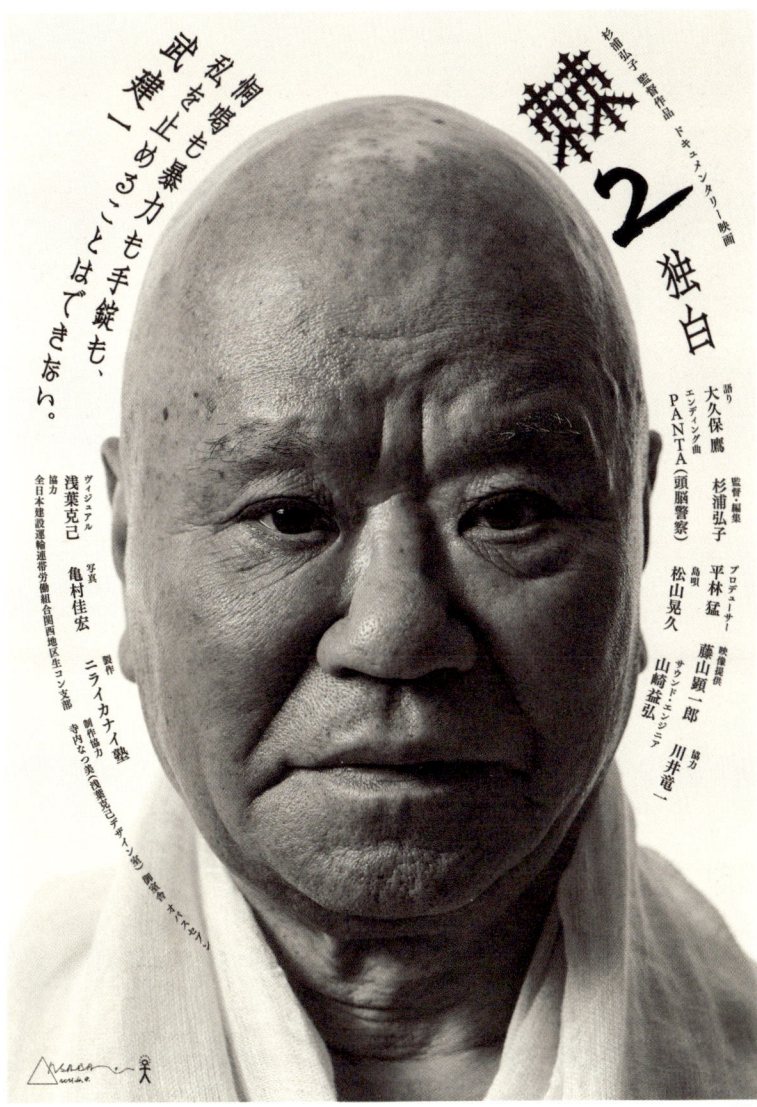

029 VI, Window display
TD. AD. D. P. Olivier Andreotti
CL. Puiforcat, Paris
PT. Custom-made for the project, Helvetica Neue

030 Website
TD. AD. D. E. 浅野隆昌 Takamasa Asano
E. 吉田山 Yoshidayamar
PRG. 白石諒 Ryo Shiraishi
CL. FL田SH
https://flsh.org/

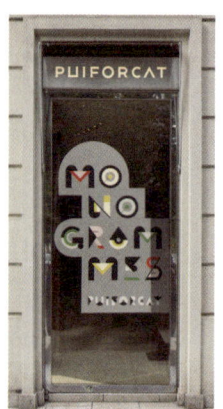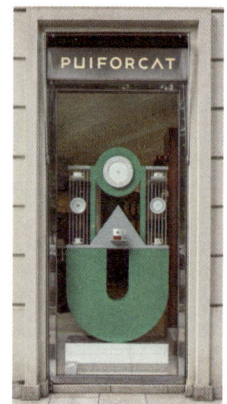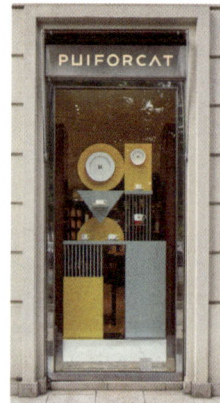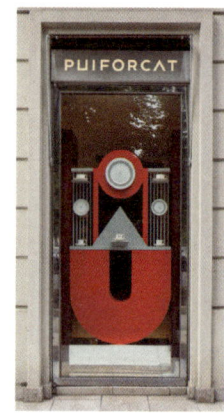

029

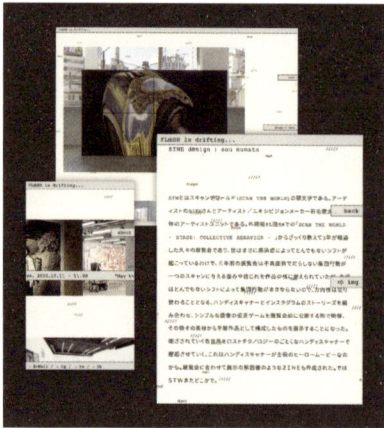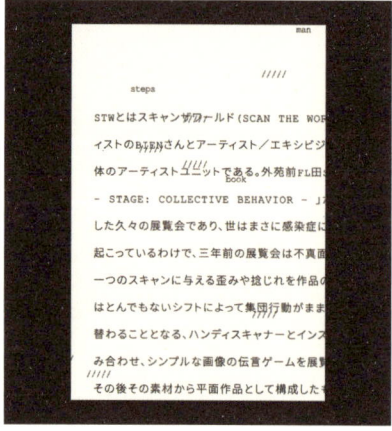

030

031 Logotype, Sticker
TD. D. 浅野隆昌 Takamasa Asano
P. 三田周 Shu Sanda
CL. YMP

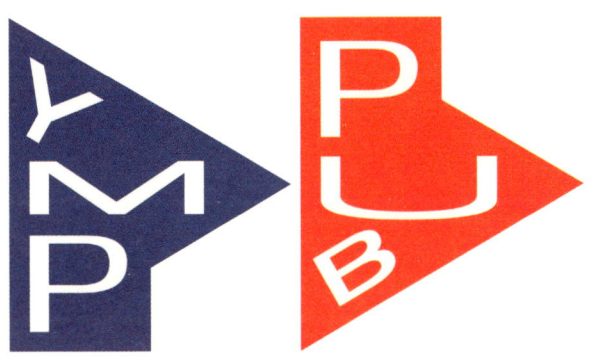

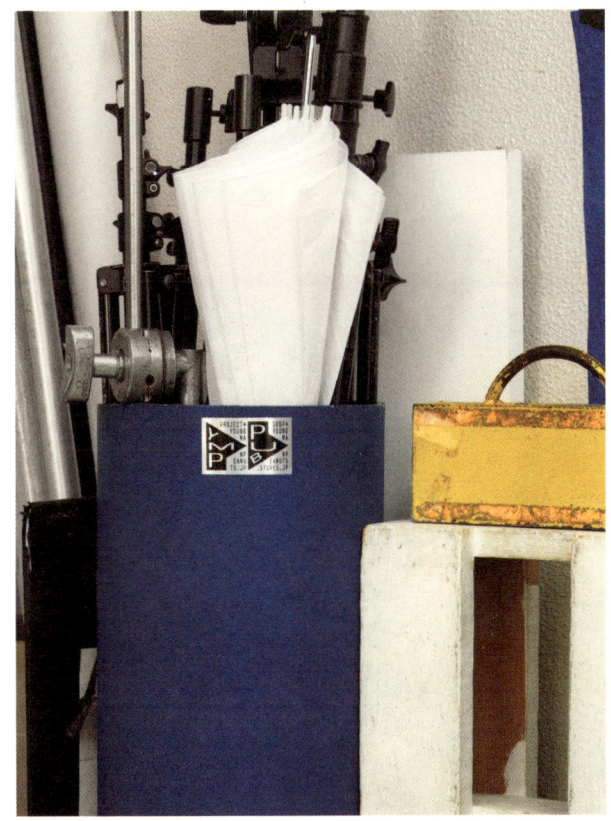

032 BI
TD. AD. D. Chon Hin Au
P. Rex Chang
CL. Dino Burger
PT. Trois Mille, Albertus Nova, Cako

033 Identity
TD. AD. D. Chon Hin Au
AD. Sio Leong Chao
P. Rex Chang
CL. Macau Designers Association
PT. Migra, Helvetica Now Display, Kozuka-Mincho-Pr6N

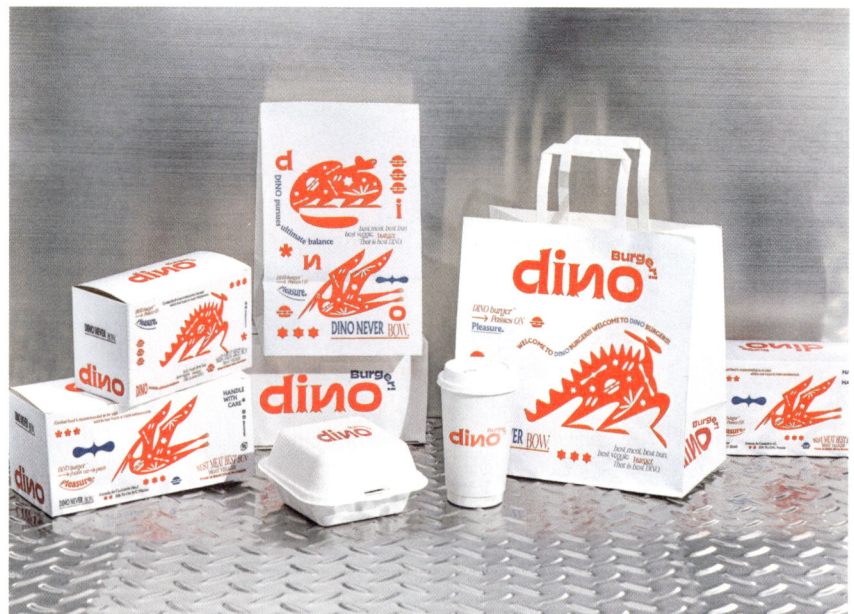

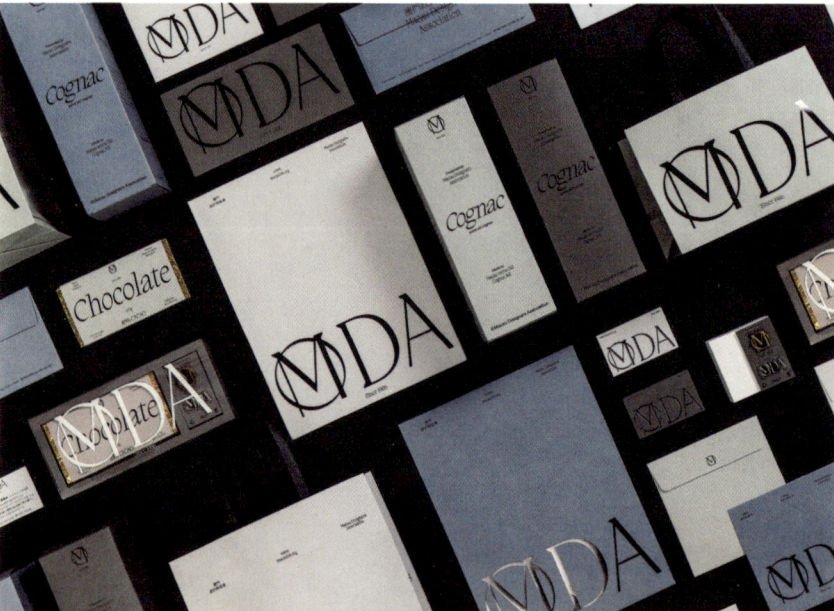

034 Book
TD. André Baldinger, Toan Vu-Huu
CL. Joseph Dadoune
PT. Lexicon

redefine the spaces in which our lives manifest themselves, and to reconsider the set boundaries of life and death, of how we can turn our existence into an experiment again, that is: in actual life.

We then come to contemplate why he places his art under the sign of "care": caring for the world, caring for the body, caring for art, caring for oneself, and all at once—for they are the same. Ultimately, this book is a silent, sensual, lively, intimate manifesto: it does not take anything for granted, does not critique anything. It is a pure force of assertion, of life: questioning is never a negative endeavor, always a reconstruction of the world that is to be, in the promised land of ecstatic life; because such is the place—the book—that Dadoune inhabits in reality. We no longer think in terms of biography, fake or real, not even in terms of conscious and unconscious: we are in the spiritual landscape of art.

Yosef Joseph Yaakov Dadoune
Fresh Light

Donatien Grau
Book, Studio, Museum, Laboratory

Yosef Joseph Yaakov Dadoune's notebook is a threshold: between inside and outside, between hand and paper, between color and form, between abstraction and figuration, between one's inner world and the world outside; between what one sees and what the artist sees. Each page is a moment from a place, but that place does not matter anymore. Only the moment does, and the transfiguration to which it has led.

It activates the threshold as the most productive creative space possible: art does not happen only on the outside or the inside; it happens in the space of in-betweenness which is both and neither. Skin does not separate worlds: it is permeable, uniting them. The book is the skin of Dadoune's art. The fact that the paper has a tight but visible weave, a texture, makes it more than the surface of an image: it is a physical call on the feeling of fabric inherent to paper, that it be sensitive. Paper is an actuality, and the work made is not made on it, but with it. The material is not a surface; it is a collaboration with the oil pastel which the artist uses. Nothing is useless or arbitrary.

The book is a threshold where inside and outside are one: the works that cover each double spread are made outside, striving to capture the light of day, that very light of that very day. They are works stemming from sensation, transcribed into art: pure representation, fixed on paper. The

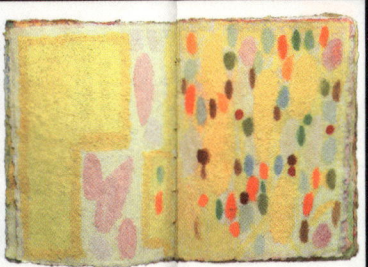

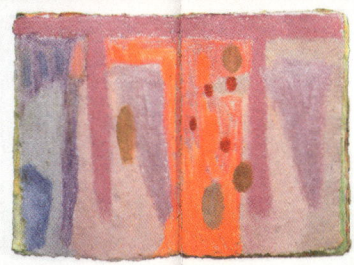

035 Book
TD. AD. D. Marco Balesteros
P. Sara Vaz
CL. Reva and David Logan Center for the Arts, Chicago
PT. Life

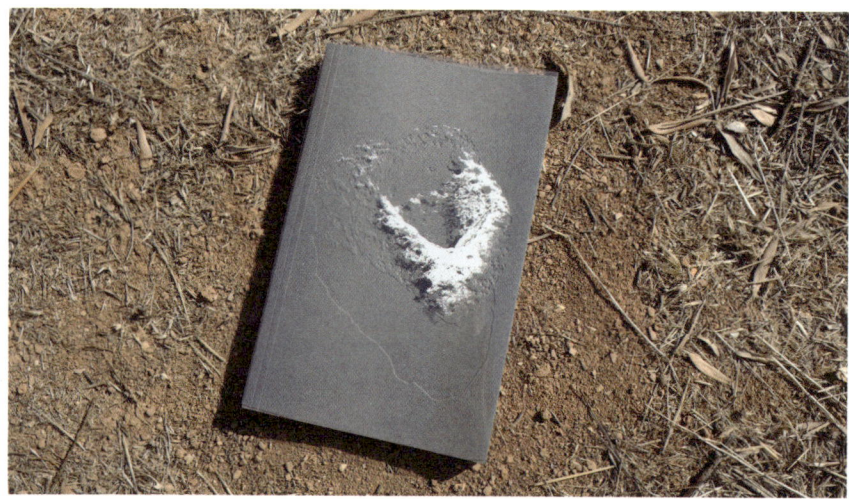
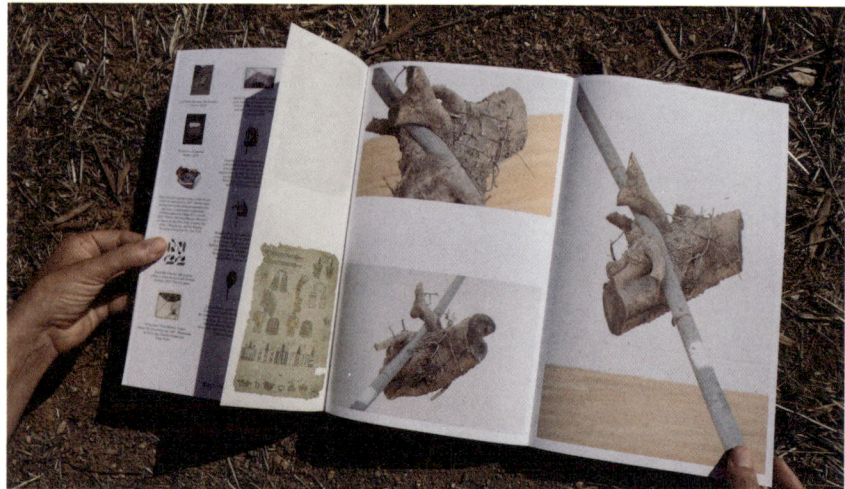
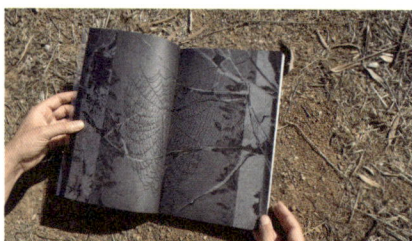
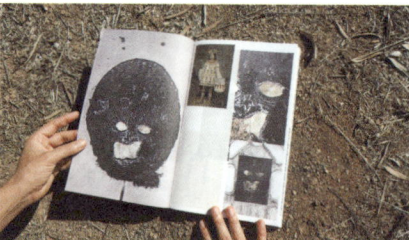

036 Poster
TD. AD. D. Marco Balesteros
P. Sara Vaz
CL. Cada1.net—Sofia Oliveira, Jared Hawkey
PT. Custom-made for the project, Arial

037 Book
TD. Rick Banks
D. Annabel Banks
CL. F37® Foundry
PT. F37 Wyman, F37 Blanka (bodycopy)

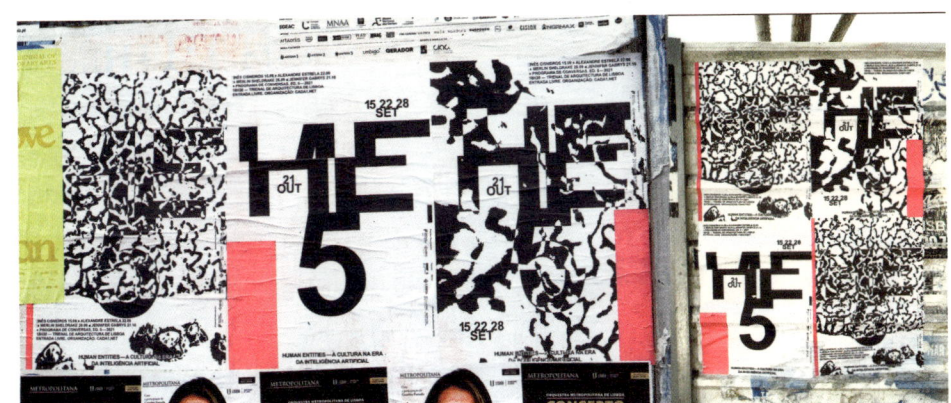

036

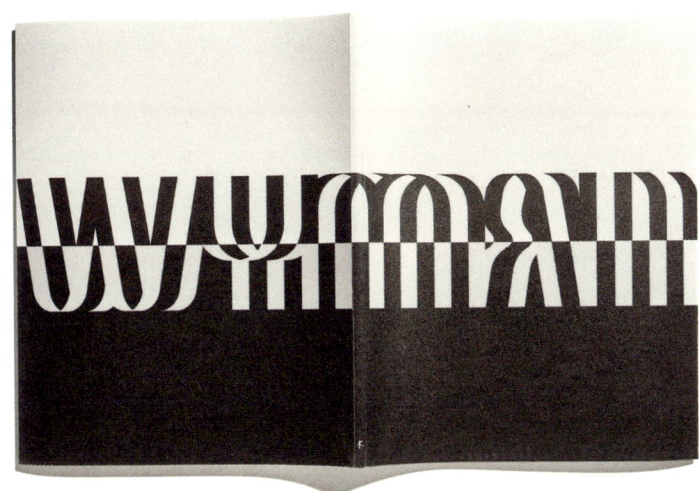

037

038 Branding
TD. Bedow
CD. Perniclas Bedow, Anders Bollman
D. Petter Dybvig, Fredrika Larsson, Beatriz Afonso, Fibi Kung
CL. Jaktar
PT. Jaktar Display, Jaktar Display Mono and Formular

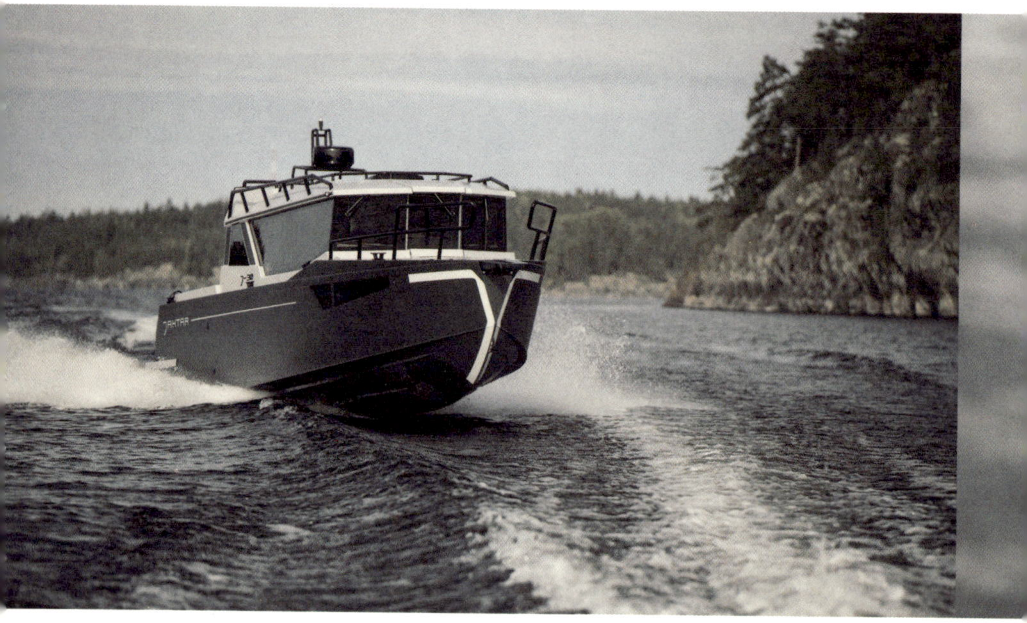

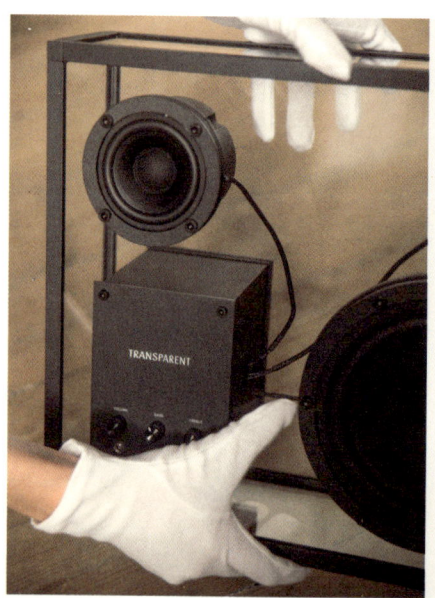

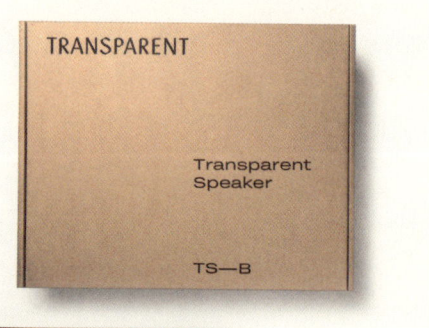

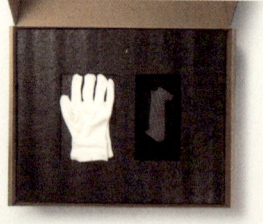

039 VI
TD. Bedow
CD. Perniclas Bedow, Anders Bollman
D. Fredrika Larsson, Beatriz Afonso, Petter Dybvig
CL. Transparent
PT. Grtsk

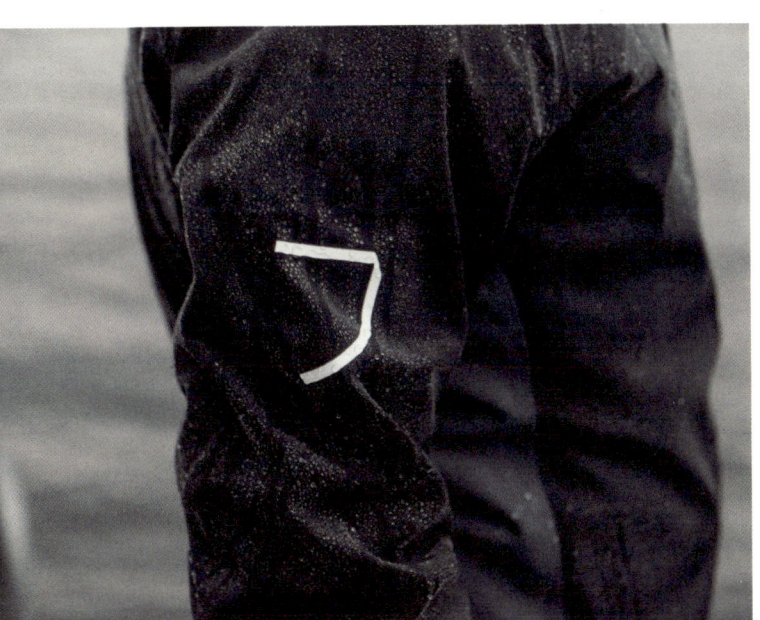

040 Exhibition
TD. Behalf Studio
CD. Giang Nguyen
D. Anh Nguyen, Linh Duong, Minh Nguyen, Phong Pham
PR. Ha Doan
CL. Behalf Studio, Republish
PT. Republish Typefaces

041, 042 Book, Experimental Work
TD. D. Shuyao Bian, Chen Xing
AD. Xiang Li
P. Di Wang
CL. Here is ZINE
PT. Custom-made for the project, Helvetica Now Variable

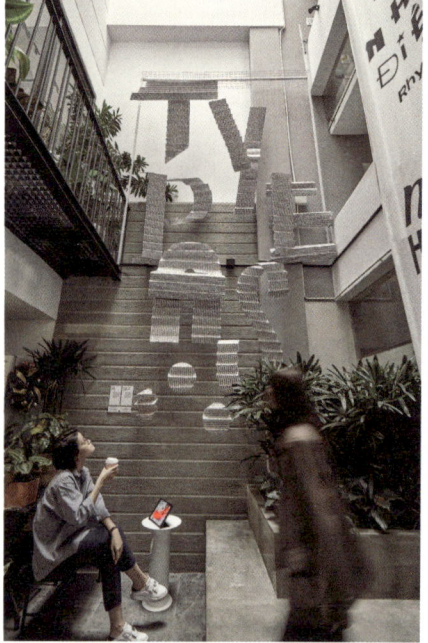

040

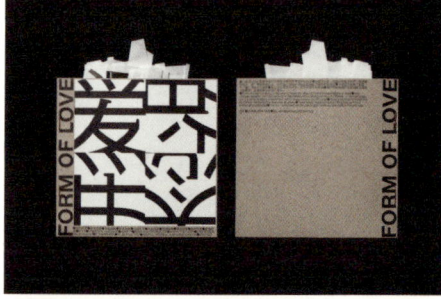

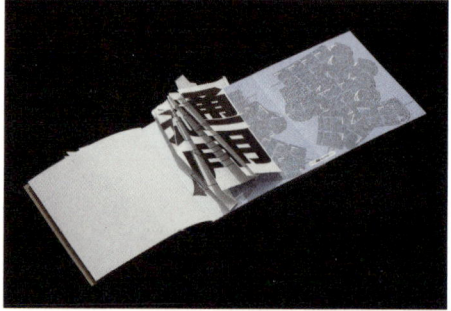

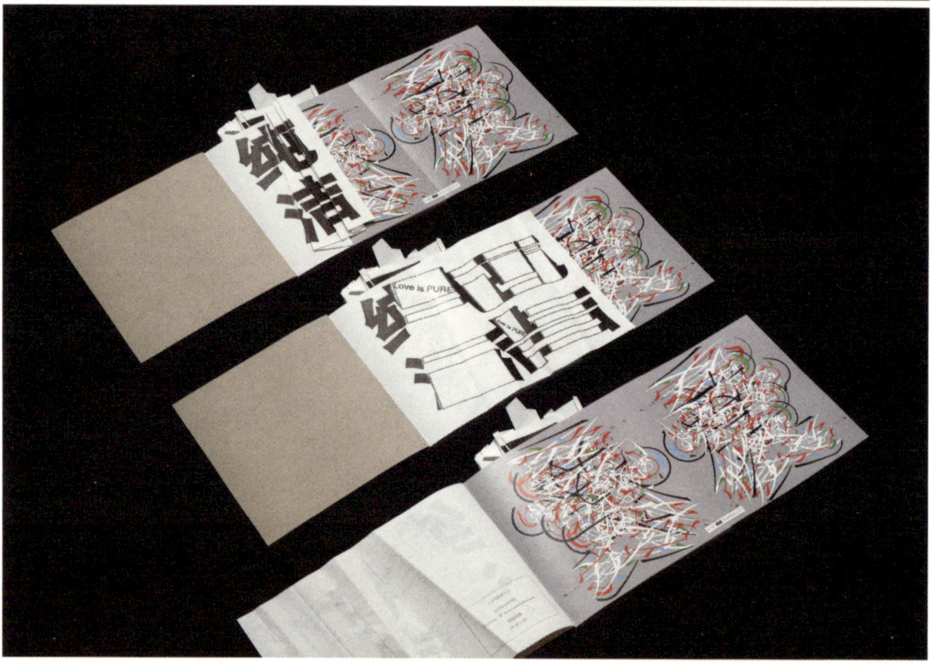

041, 042

Prize Nominee Work

043 Type design
TD. Nicolas Bernklau
P. Diego Fellmann
CL. Non-commercial work
PT. Resial

044 Poster
TD. D. Mark Bohle, Nam Huynh
AD. Michele Salati
P. CL. Pierfrancesco Celada
PT. SF Compact Display, Cosmopolitan Script

045 Art book
TD. Bienvenue Studios: Oliver Hischier, Xiaoqun Wu
CL. Non-commercial work
PT. GT Super Text, Medium

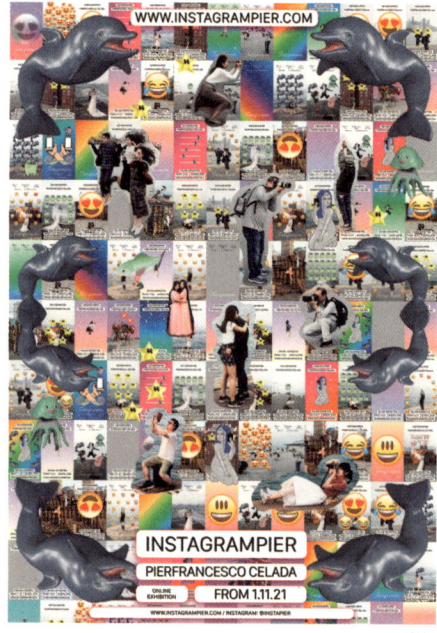

044

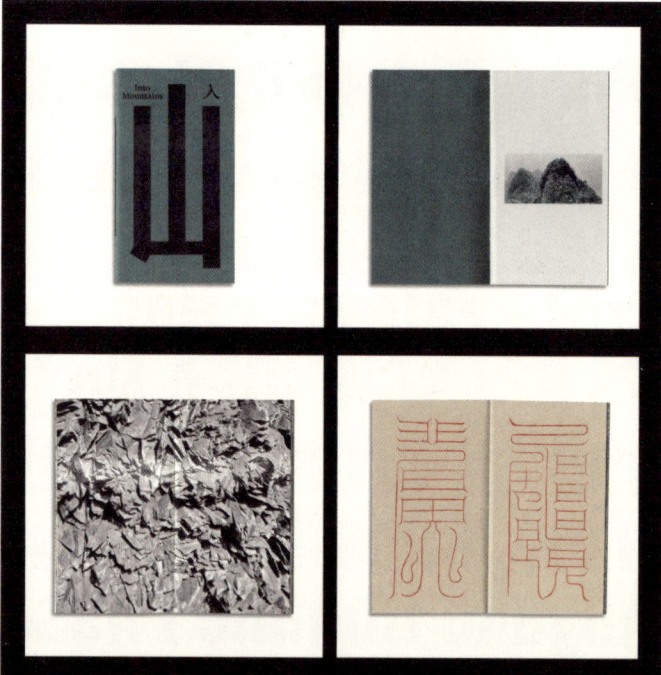

045

Prize Nominee Work

046 Book
TD. D. Mark Bohle, Raffael Kormann
CL. Non-commercial work, Kulturzentrum Merlin Stuttgart
PU. Prima Publikationen
PT. Right Grotesk, Favorit, Custom-made for the project

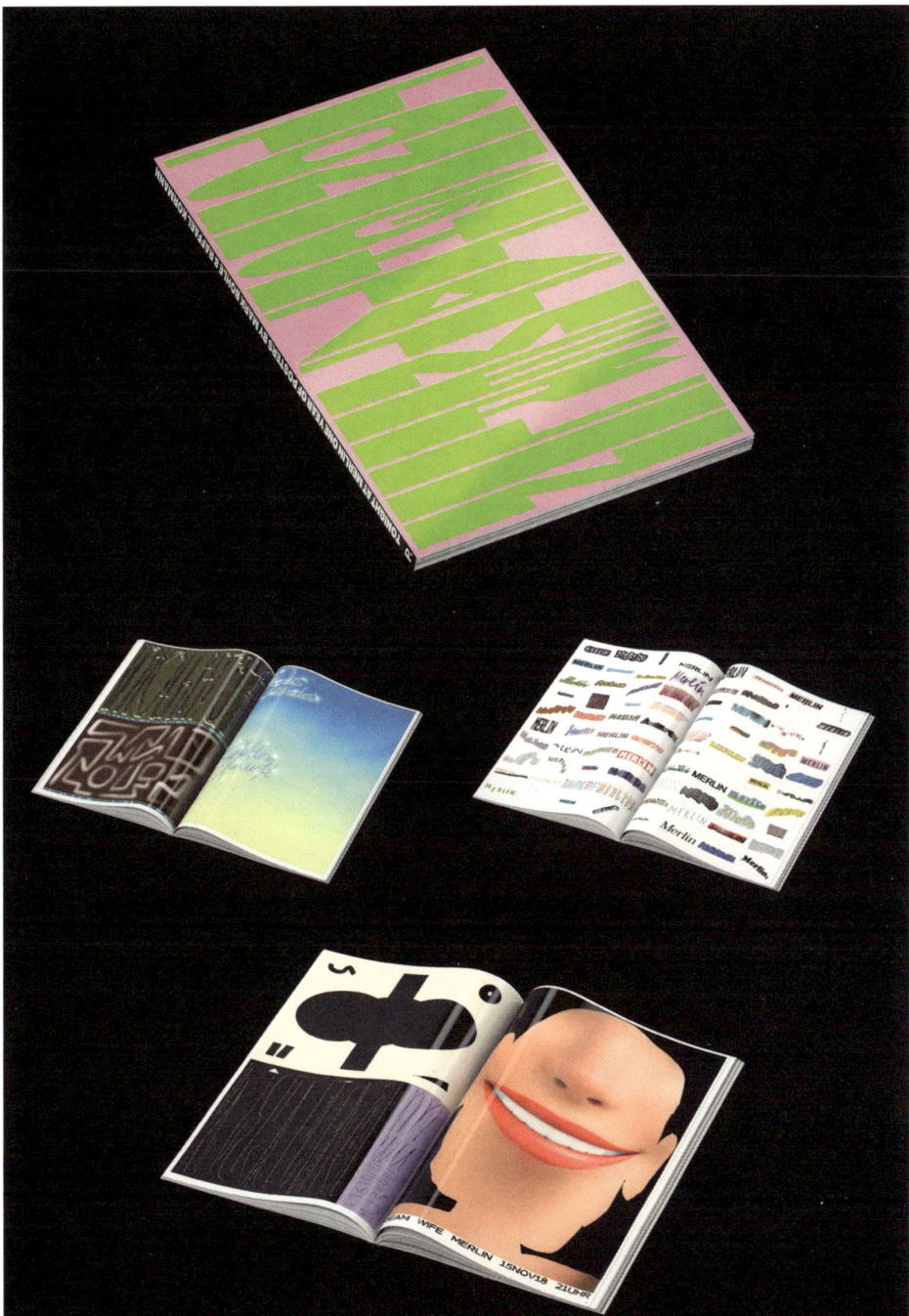

Prize Nominee Work

047 Book
TD. Fabian Bremer, Pascal Storz
CL. Kunstsammlungen Nordrhein-Westfalen Germany, Centre Pompidou France
PT. Marfa, Marfa Mono

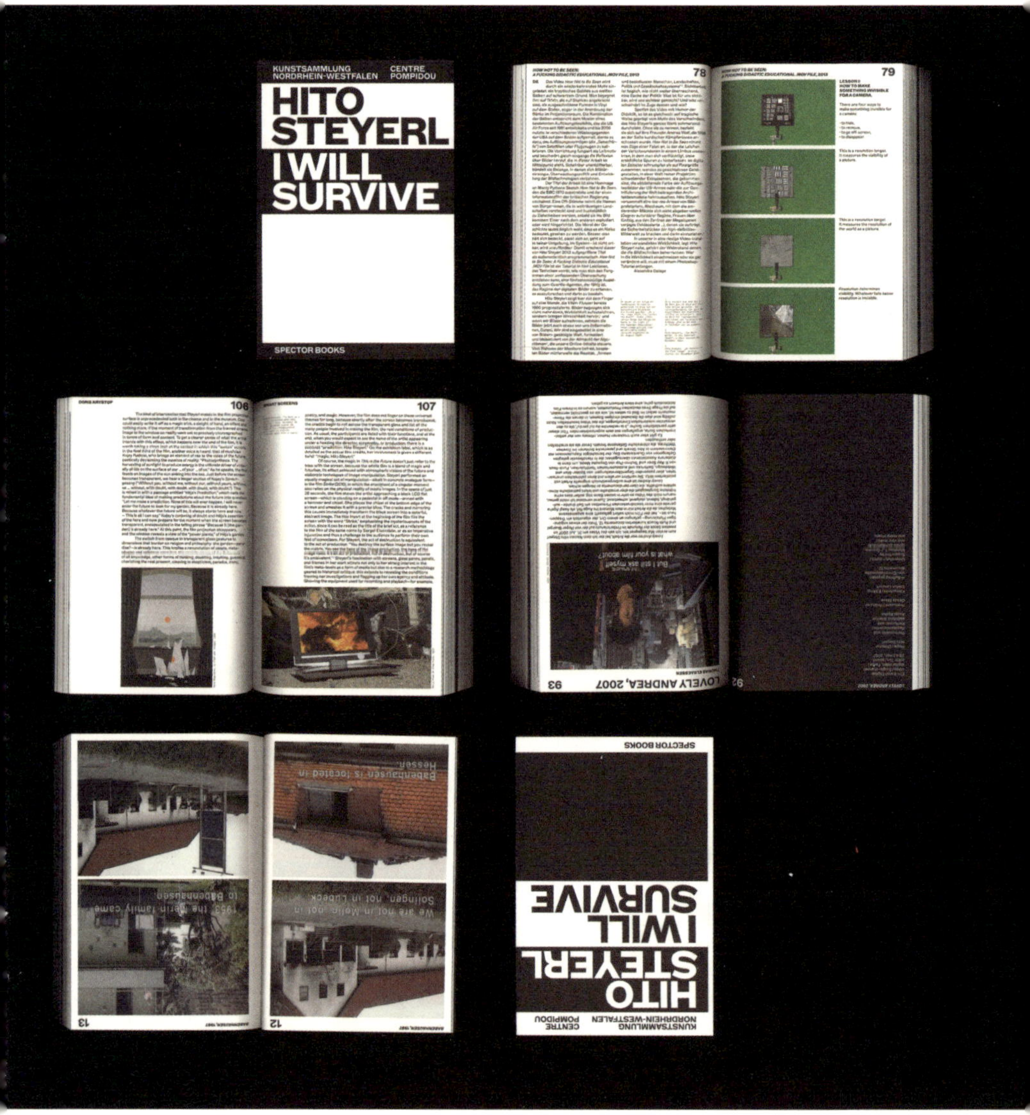

070

047

071 **Prize Nominee Work**

048 Stamp
TD. AD. D. Brighten the Corners (Frank Philippin, Billy Kiosoglou)
CL. Federal Ministry of Finance Germany, Post Office Germany
PT. Akzidenz Grotesk

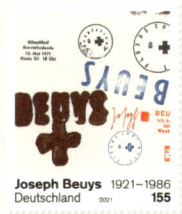
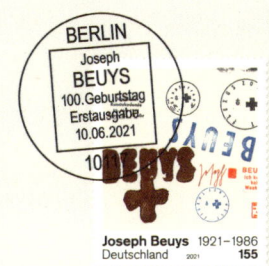
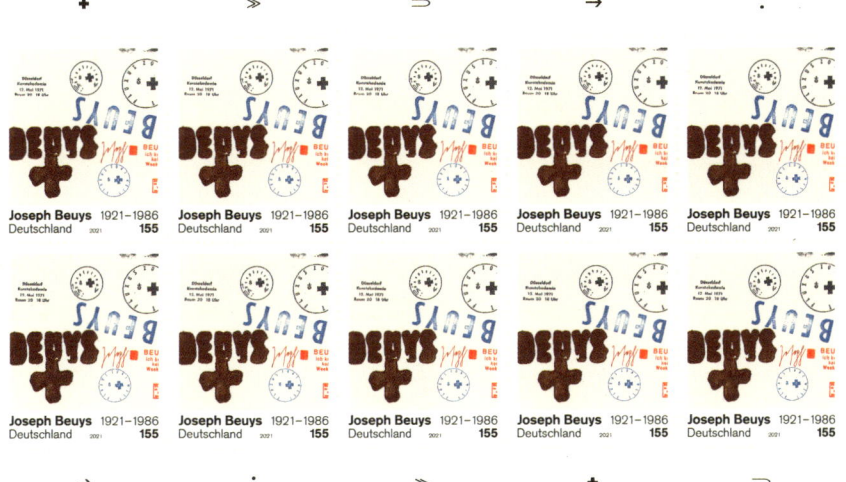

048

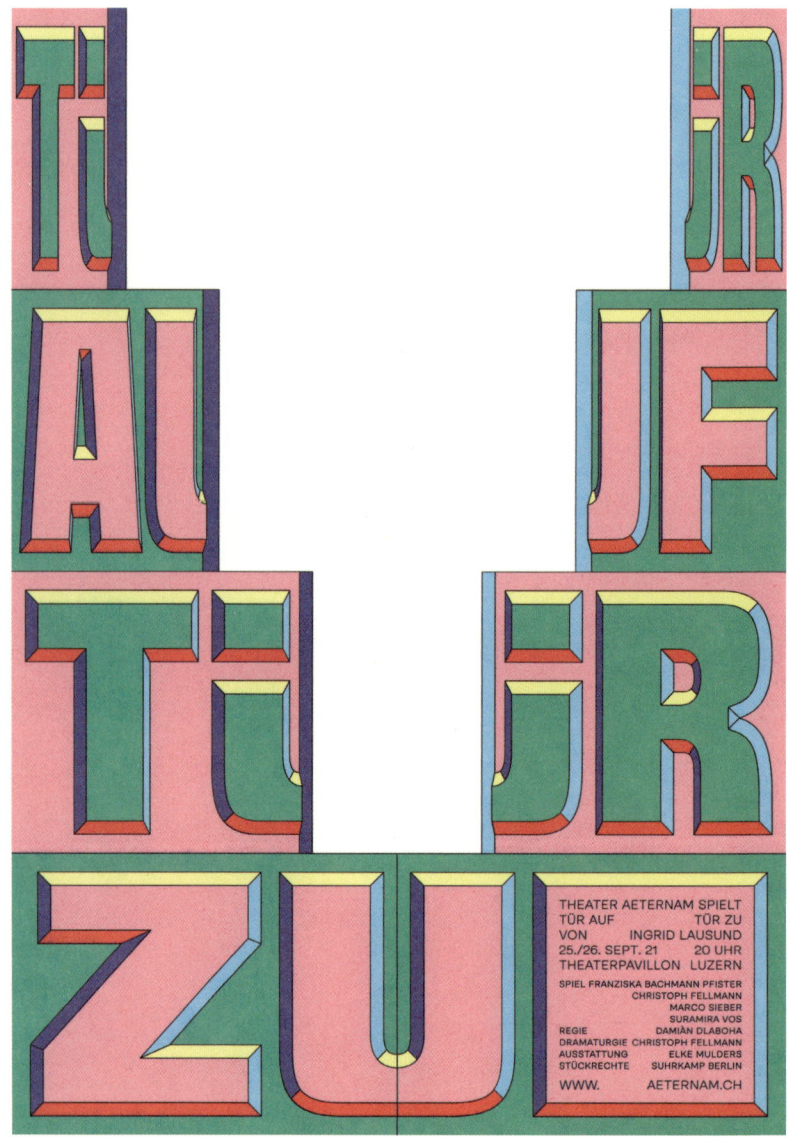

050 Identity
TD. Browns
CL. Dyson Art
PT. Neue Haas Grotesk Display Medium

051 Book
TD. büro uebele visuelle kommunikation
D. Filip Antunovic, Carolin Himmel, Tobias Hönow, Simon Hopf, Simon Renner, Leonie Seitz, Hendrik Siems, Andreas Uebele
D. PM. Maks Barbulovic
P. Göran Gnaudschun
CL. Bächlemeid Architekten Stadtplaner BDA
PT. individual typeface for the project

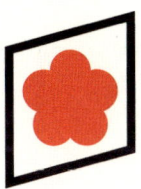

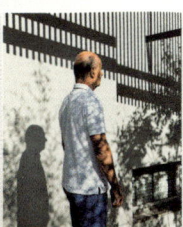

052 VI
TD. büro uebele visuelle kommunikation
D. PM. Filip Antunovic, Dominik Bissem
D. Carolin Himmel, Andreas Uebele
CL. Blasmusikverband-Badenwürttemberg e.V
PT. Starter, Tobias Hoenow

053 VI
TD. büro uebele visuelle kommunikation
D. PM. Anna Pfältzer
D. Carolin Himmel, Andreas Uebele
P. Kurt Heuvens
CL. Lehmbruck Museum Duisburg
PT. ITC Avant Garde Gothic

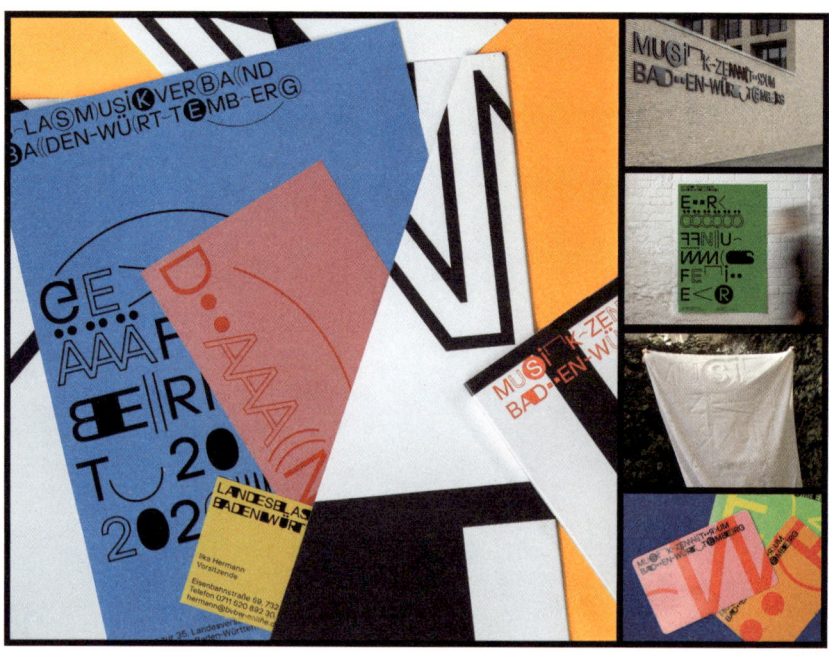

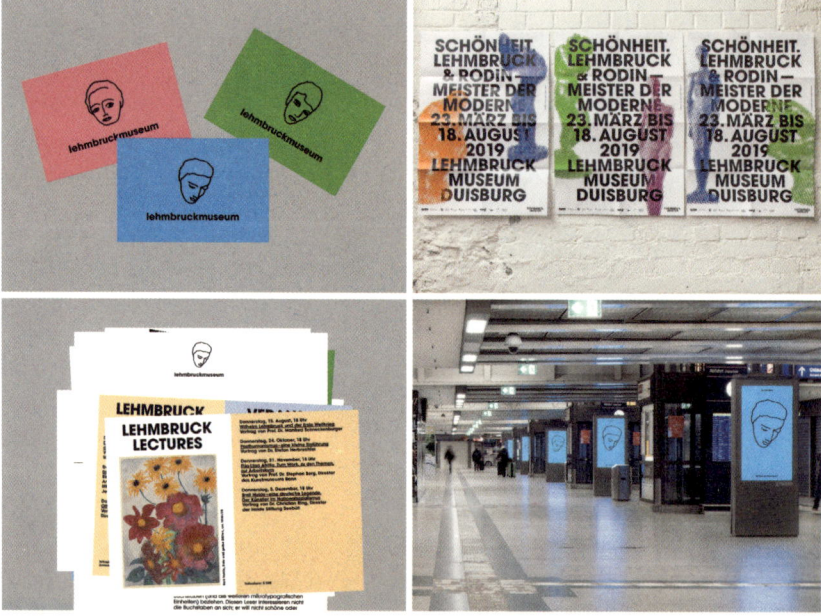

054 Signage
TD. büro uebele visuelle kommunikation
D. Yanik Hauschild, Carolin Himmel, Andreas Uebele
D. PM. Christian Lindermann
P. Brigida González
CL. Robert Bosch Automotive Steering GmbH
PT. Bosch Sans

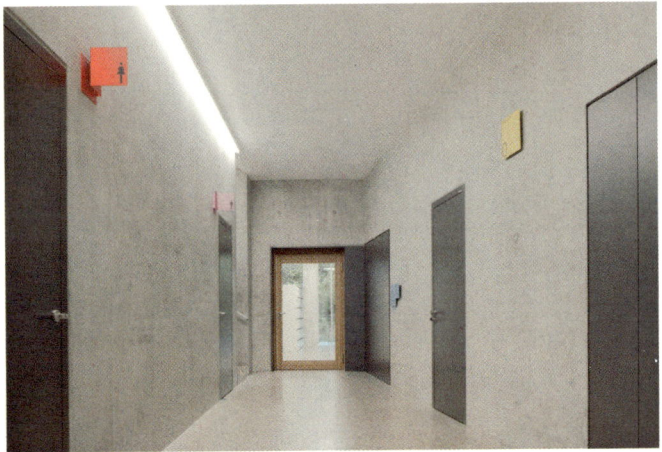

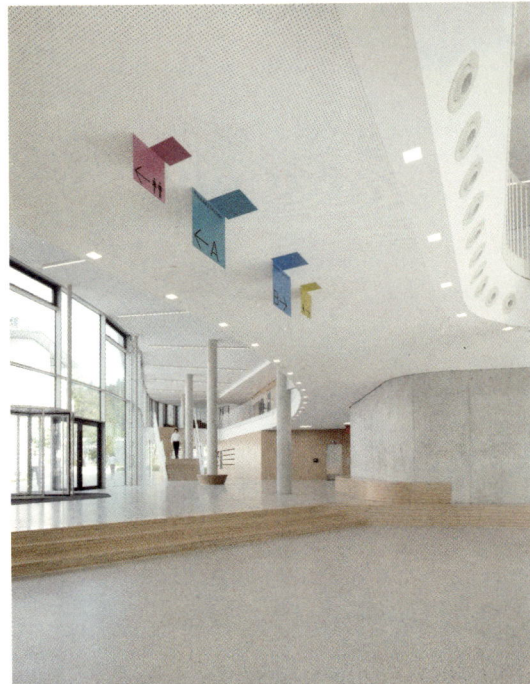

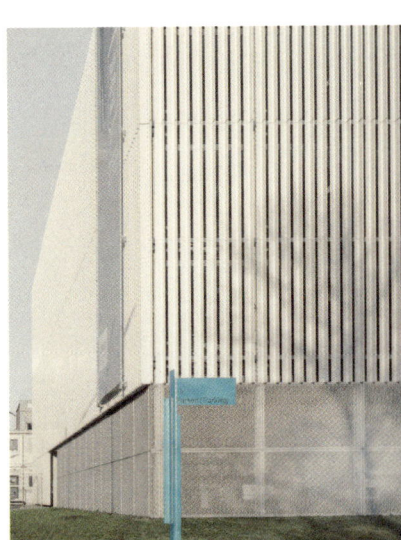

055 Signage, Map
TD. büro uebele visuelle kommunikation
D. Carolin Himmel, Christian Lindermann, Andreas Uebele
D. P. PM. Justyna Sikora
CL. Stadt Leipzig
PT. GT Walsheim

056 Calendar
TD. Wenchao Cai
CL. Shanghai Academy of Fine Arts

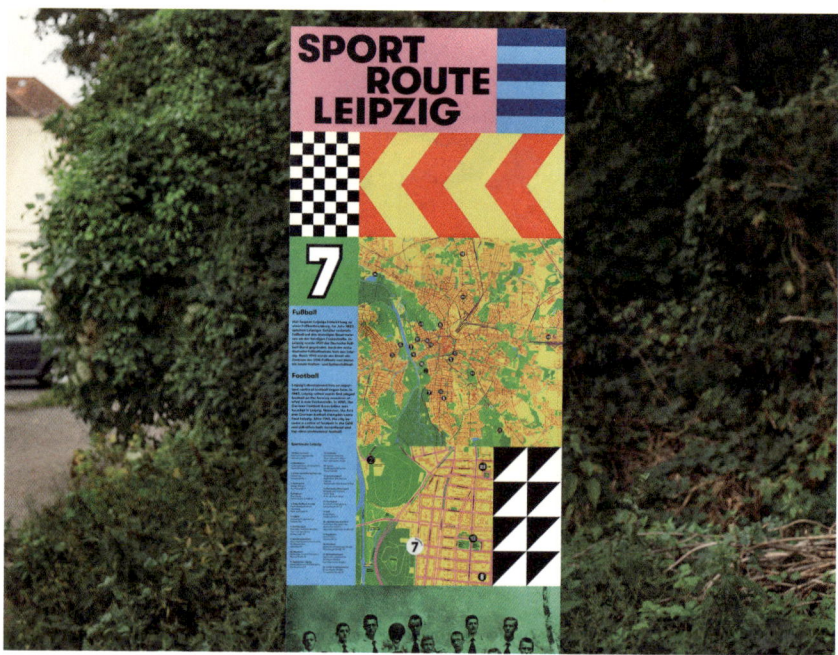

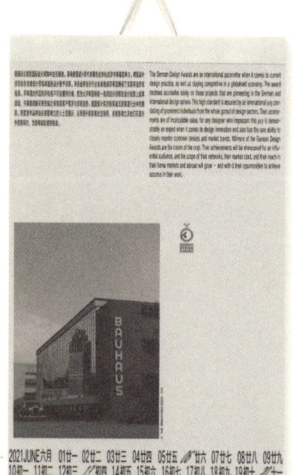

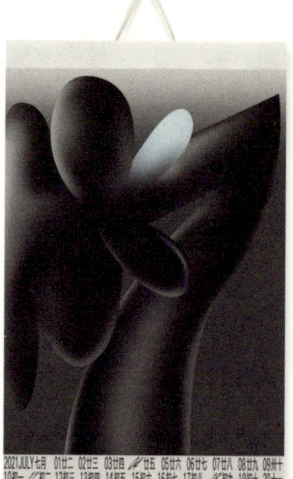

057 Poster
TD. Wenchao Cai
CL. Shanghai Academy of Fine Arts

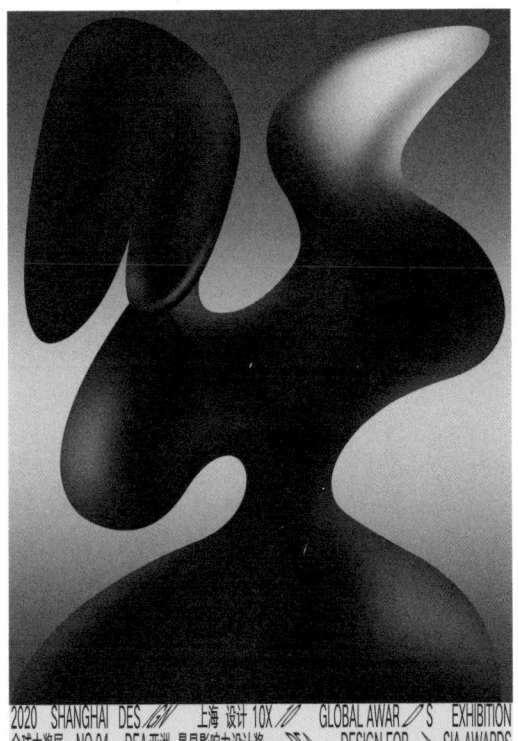

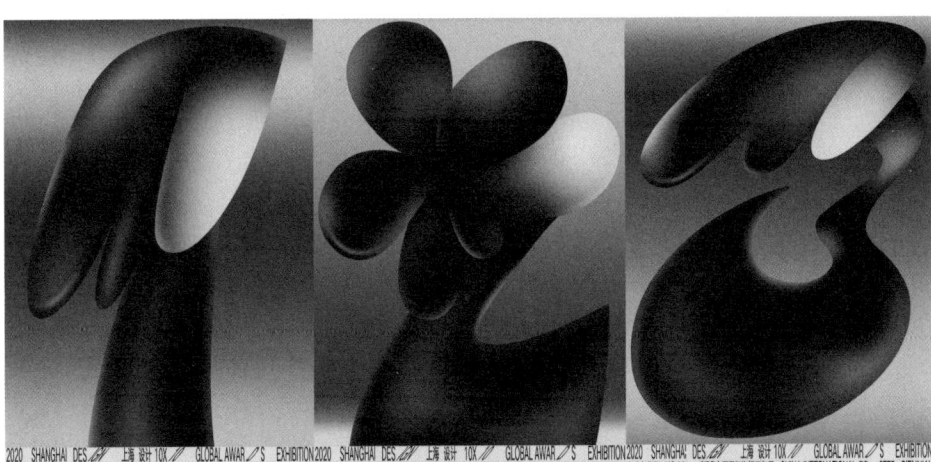

058 Poster
TD. Anna Cairns, Flo Gaertner
CL. Lenbachhaus, Munich
PT. LBH Behrens (Custom-made for the project), Century Schoolbook Monospaced

059 Book
TD. Lana Cavar, Natasha Chandani
AU. Michelle Millar Fisher, Amber Winick
CL. MIT Press, USA
PT. GT America

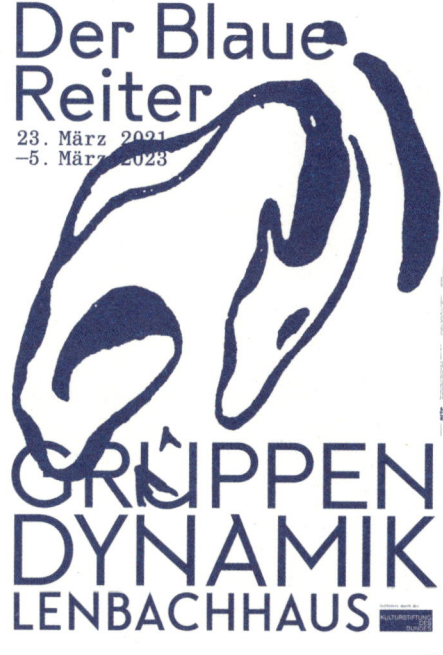
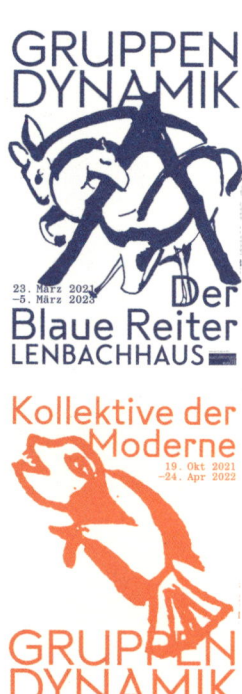

058

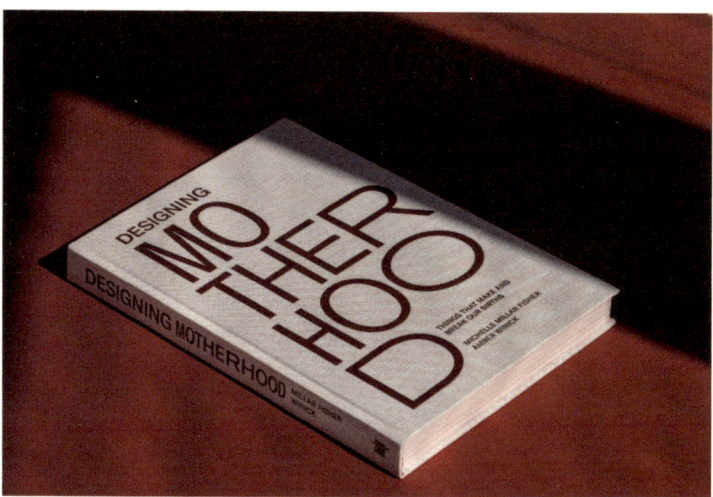

059

060 Fashion graphics
TD. AD. D. Byungrok Chae
PRD. Jaei
CL. Layers:
PT. Custom-made for the project

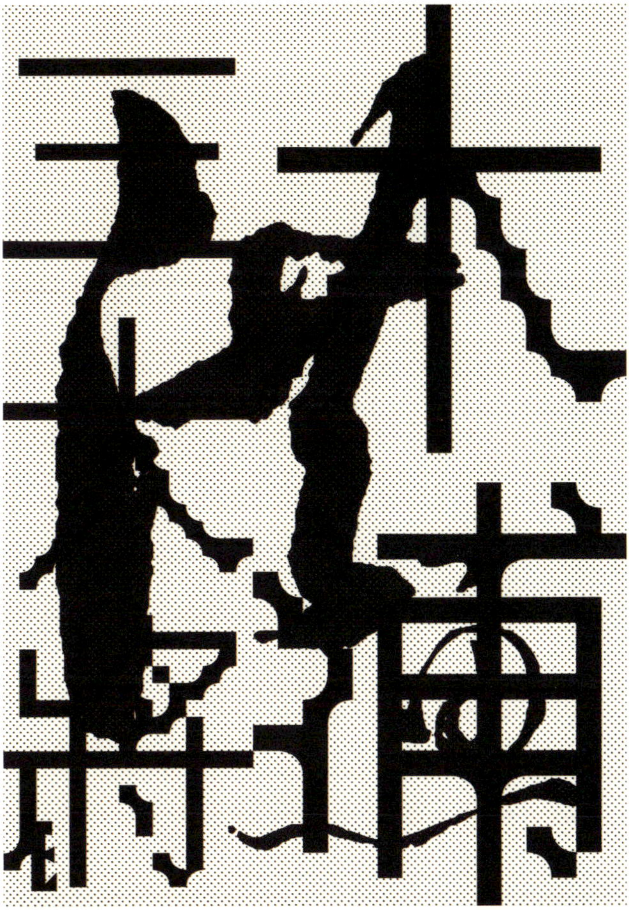

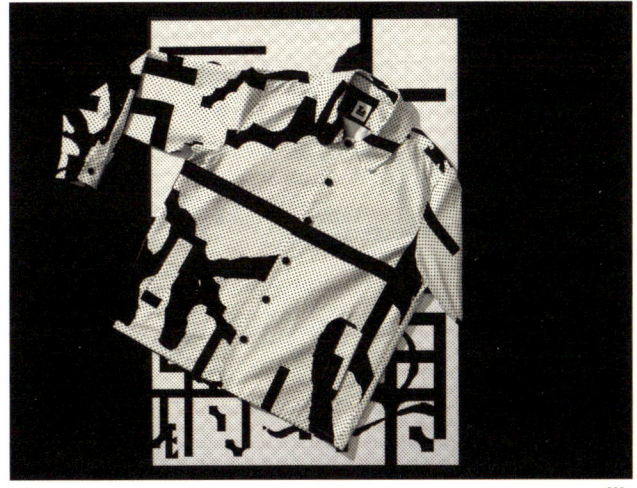

061 Type design
TD. Adonian Chan
CL. Non-commercial work
PT. Hong Kong Beiwei Zansyu

062 Website
TD. Rex Chen
AD. Fraser Muggeridge studio
DC. Snootie Studios / DEV. Twelve Design
P. James Smith / V. Nicholas Smith
CL. Harlow Art Trust, UK
PT. Univers LT
https://sculpturetown.uk/

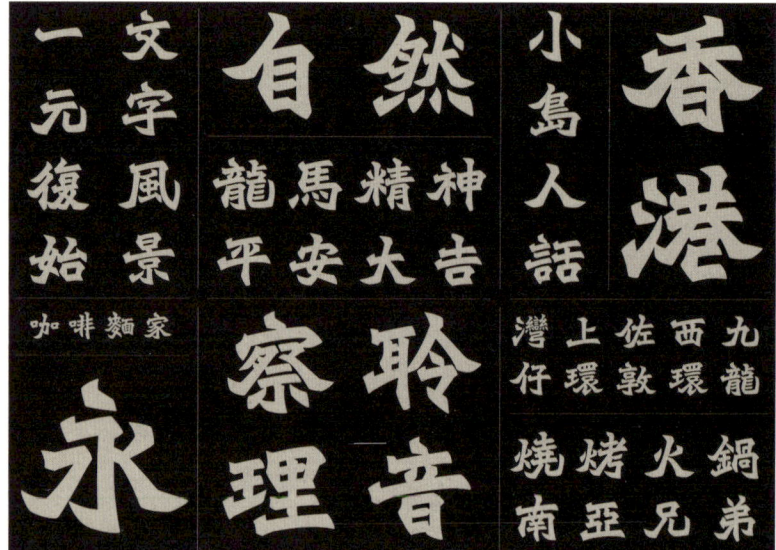

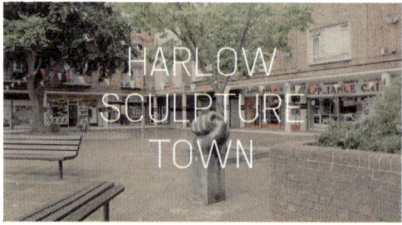

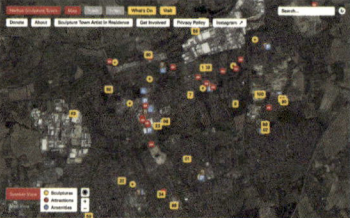

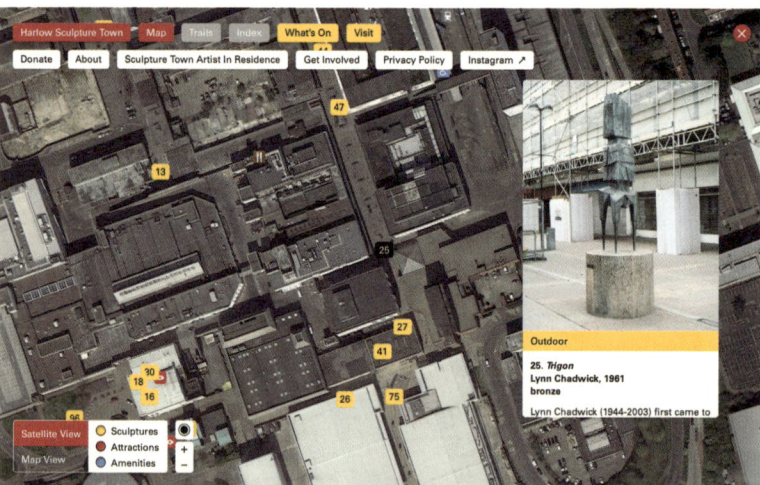

Prize Nominee Work

063 Packaging
TD. D. Cong Chen
AD. D. Xibin Li
PRI. Keqiang Ma
CL. Super Plants
PT. Super Plants 2021 Bold

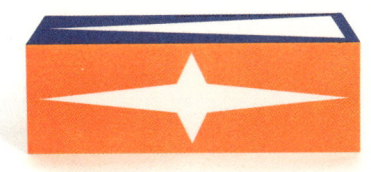

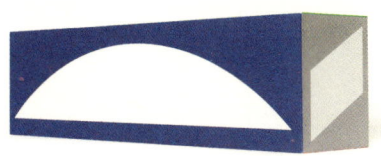

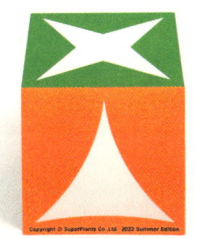

064 Logotype, Corporate stationery
TD. AD. D. Weibin Chen
CL. Tagging Design
PT. Skanaus

065 VI
TD. AD. D. Chenchenxia
D. Panchuxiong, Chenyijia
CL. univox
PT. Custom-made for the project, Verdana

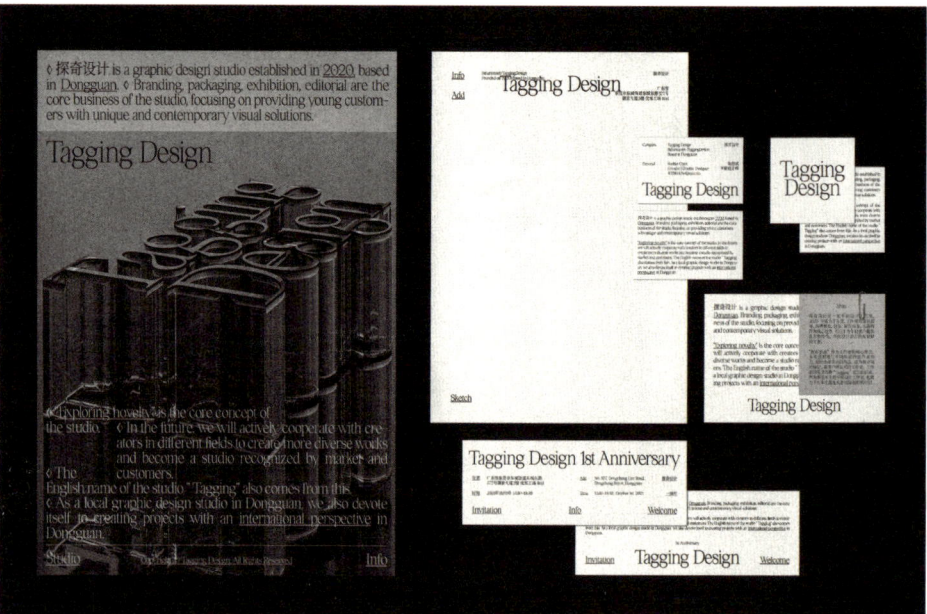

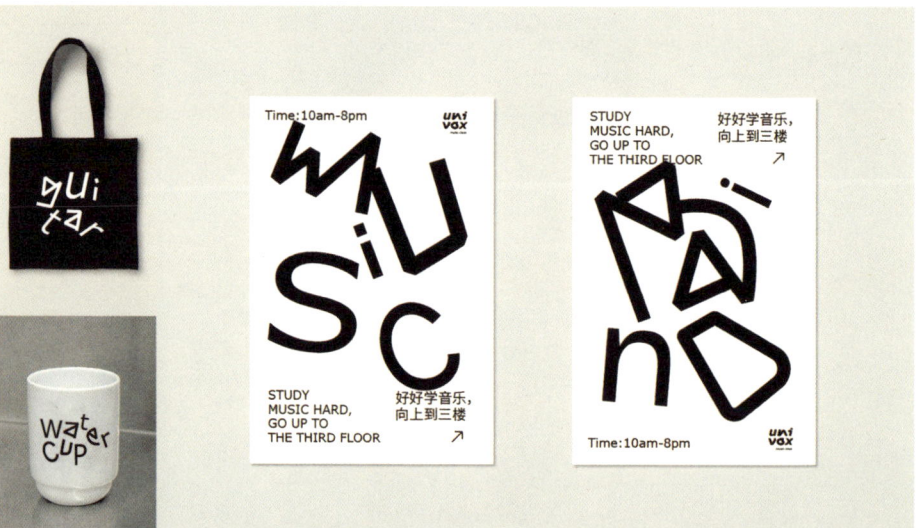

066 Branding
TD. AD. D. P. Jieru Chen
D. Jun Zhang, Lin Fan
CL. Aokka
PT. Visby

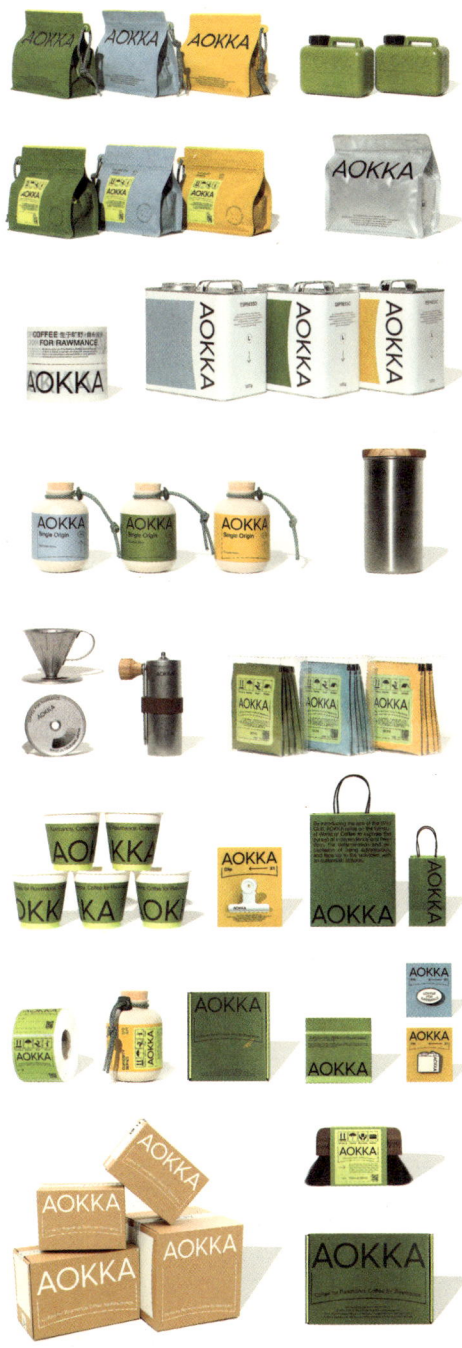

067 Packaging
TD. AD. D. P. Jieru Chen
CL. Nibbo Bean to Bar Chocolate
PT. Brown, Pingfang

068 Book
TD. AD. D. Chen Guo
CL. Non-commercial work
PT. Custom-made for the project, FZFS

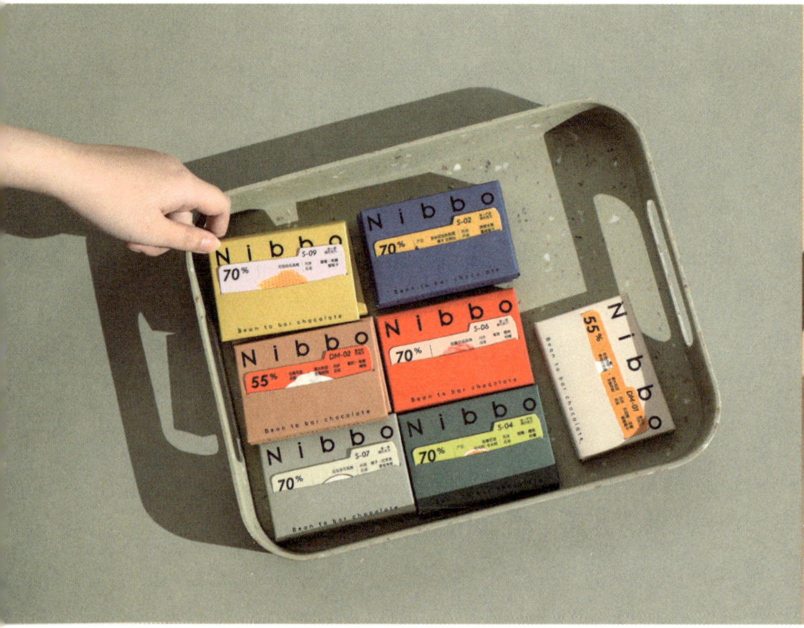

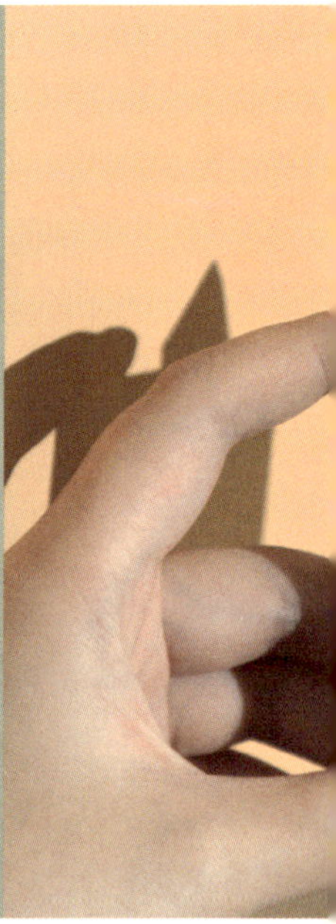

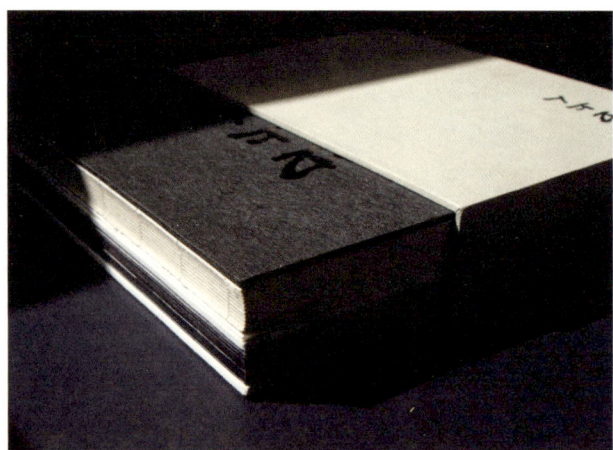

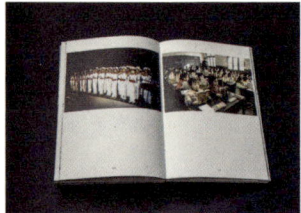

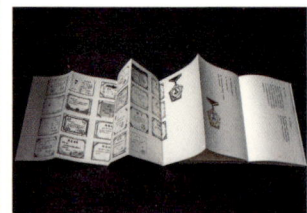

069 Type design
TD. Shi Cheng
CL. Non-commercial work

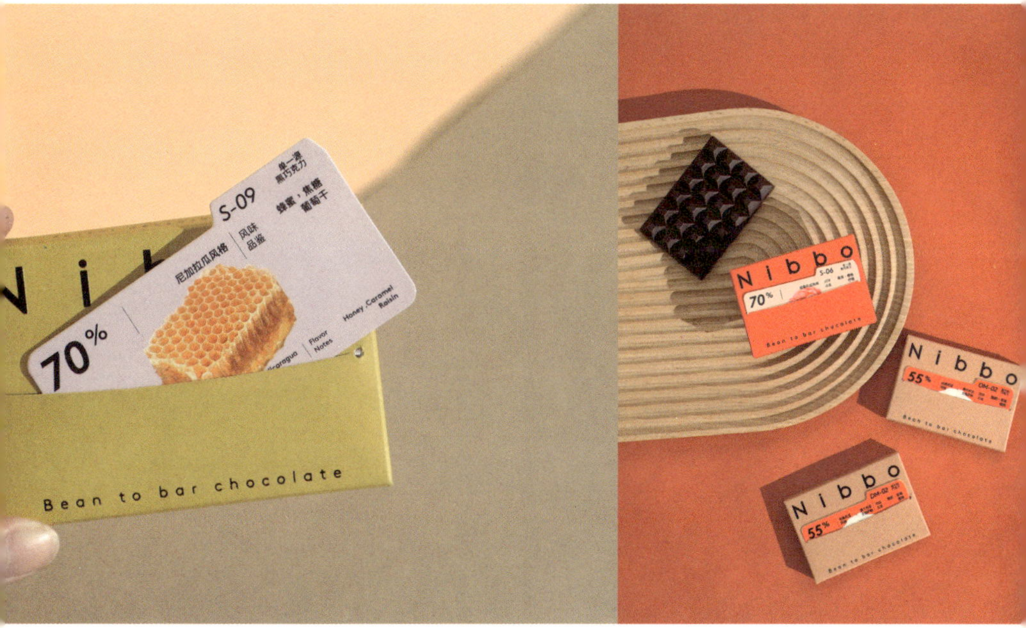

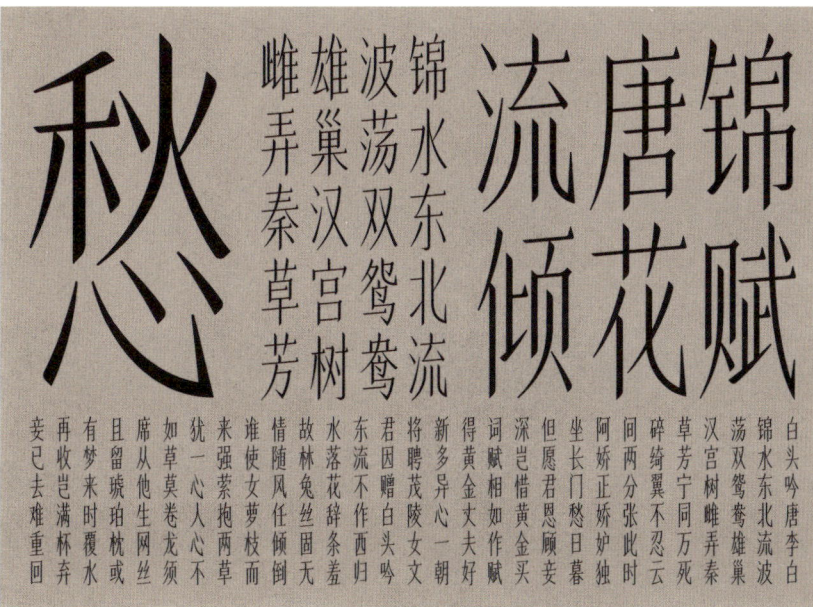

070 Mark & Logo
TD. AD. D. Cheng Xiaobing
P. Liu Zhenye
CL. Shenzhen Heshi Creative Culture Media Co., Ltd.

071 Small graphics
TD. Joanne Chew
D. LD. P. David Ho
CL. Fictionist Studio
PT. Custom-made for the project

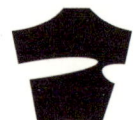

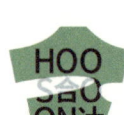 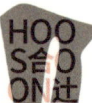 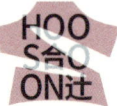

070

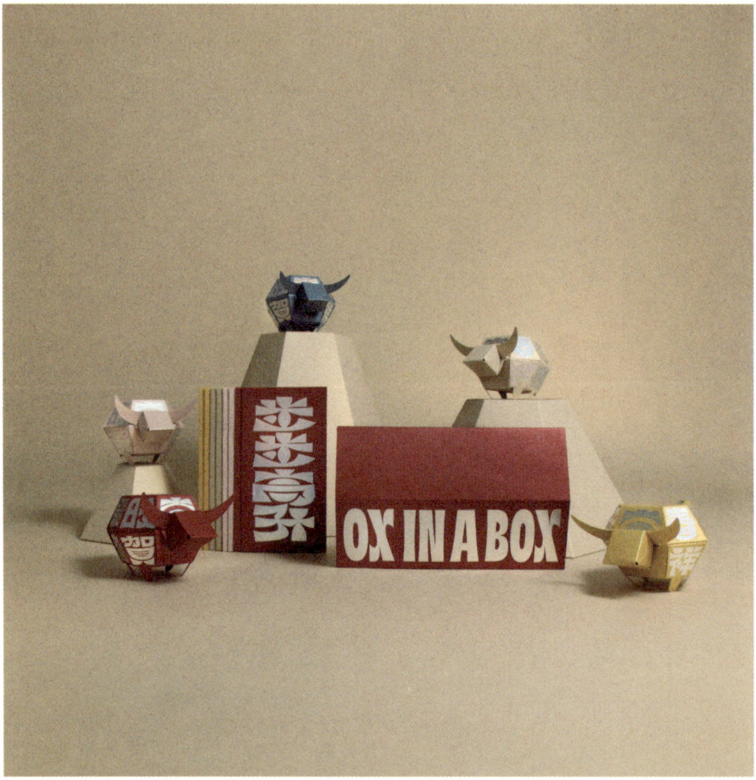

071

072 Campaign
TD. AD. 千原徹也 Tetsuya Chihara
D. 横井もも代 Momoyo Yokoi, 立石彩花 Ayaka Tateishi
P. 新田桂一 Keiichi Nitta
CL. 凸版印刷(株) Toppan Inc.
PT. American Typewriter Regular, U-OTF 新丸ゴ Upr W6, こぶりなゴシック Std W3

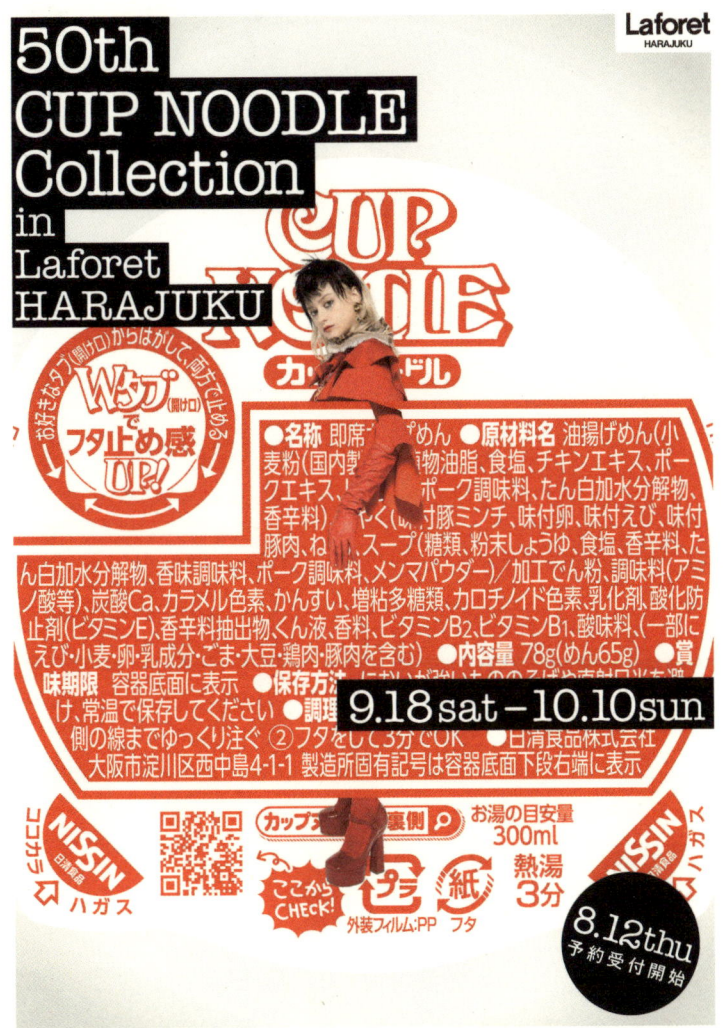

073 Book
TD. AD. D. Sigutė Chlebinskaitė
E. Mindaugas Kvietkauskas
P. Arvydas Maknys, Rokas Gelažius
PUM. Gytis Vaškelis
CL. The Institute of Lithuanian Literature and Folklore
PT. Custom-made for the project, CoFo Sans, Minion Pro

074 VI, Font
TD. 大日本タイポ組合 Dainippon Type Organization
CL. ゲーテ・インスティトゥート東京 Goethe-Institut Tokyo
PT. Custom-made for the project

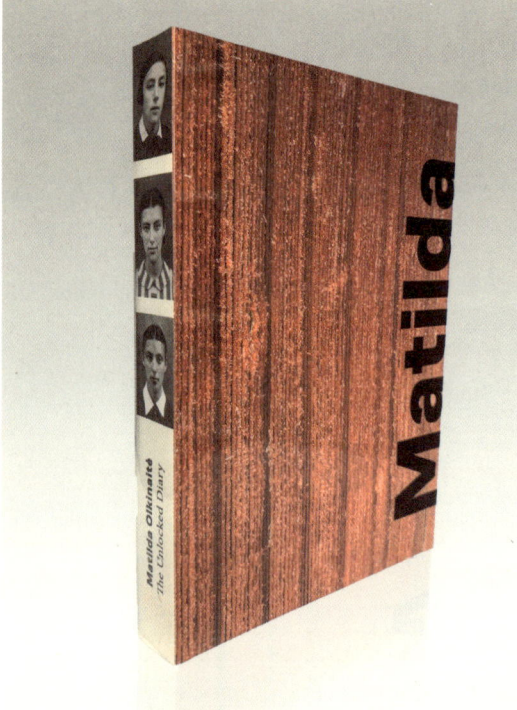

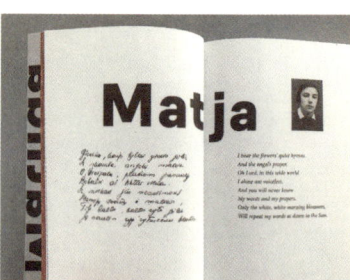

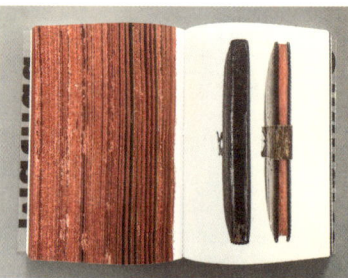

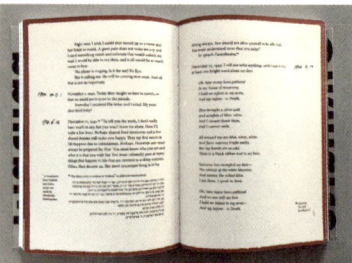

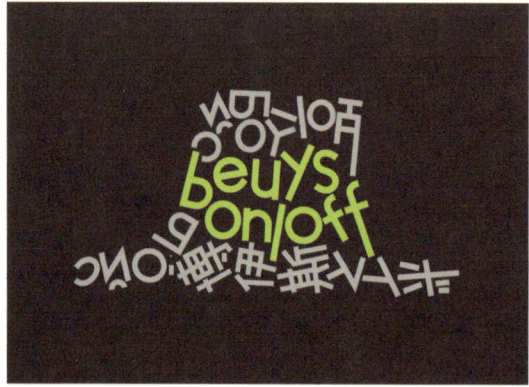

Prize Nominee Work

075 Book
TD. desescribir
AD. D. Cibrán Rico, Jesús Vázquez
P. Rafel Griera, Victor Hugo Martín, Ricardo Suárez, Paola Velo
CL. Fabulatorio, Museo Patio Herreriano
PT. FF Mark

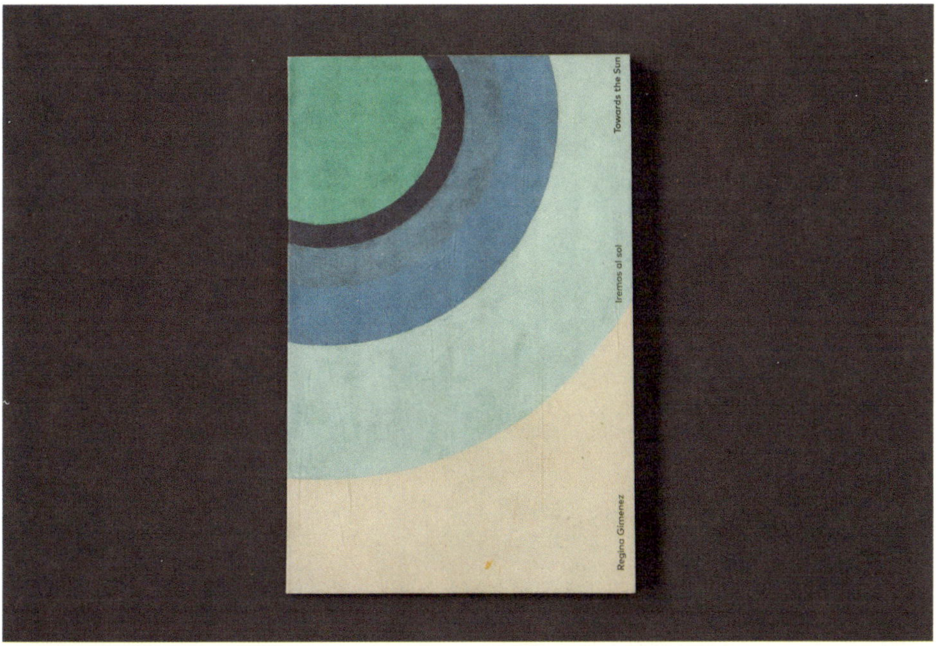

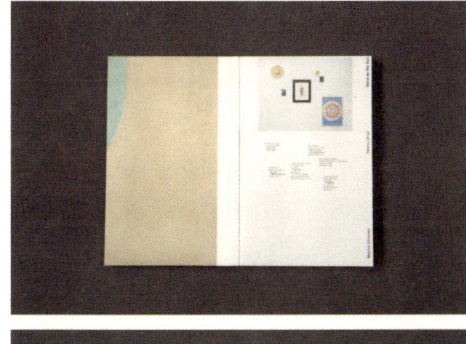
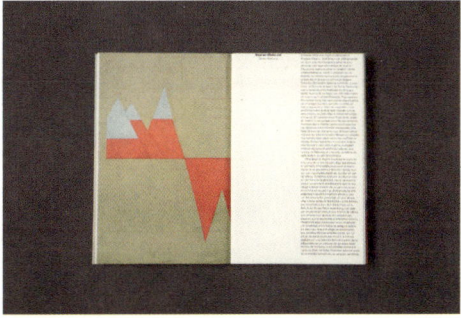
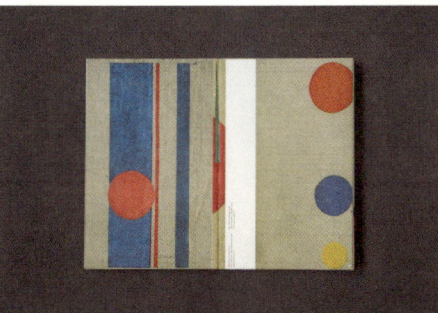
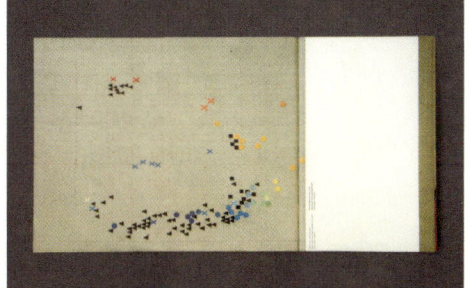

076 Poster
TD. desescribir
AD. D. Cibrán Rico, Jesús Vázquez
P. Lucía Estévez
CL. Maruxiña Films Company
PT. Founders Grotesk, Sharp Grotesk

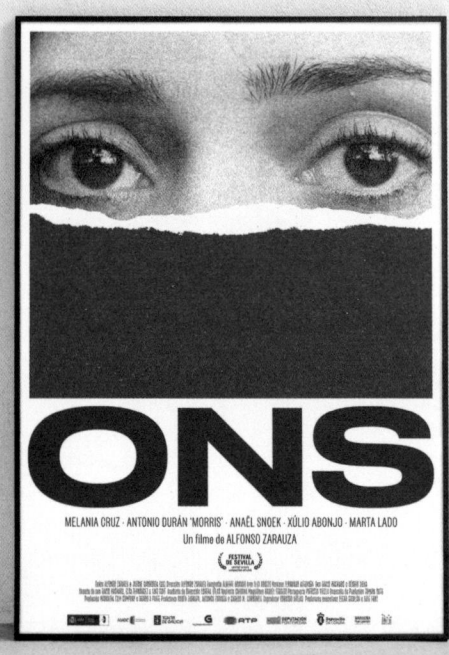

077 Catalogue
TD. deValence: Alexandre Dimos, Ghislain Triboulet
T. Alex Chavot
CL. Musée des Arts Décoratifs
PT. Nicéphore Raw, Collis

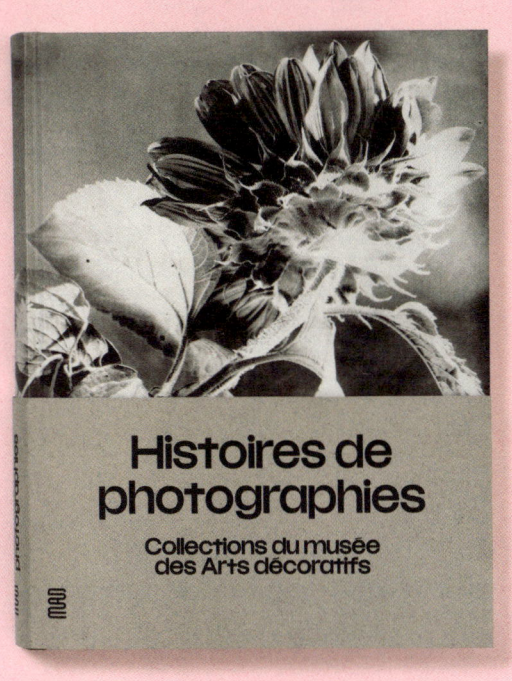
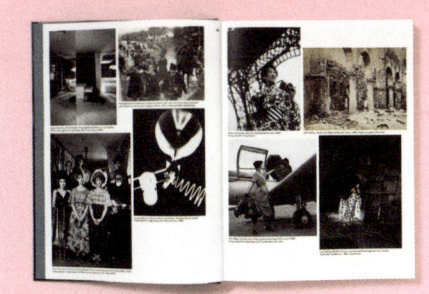
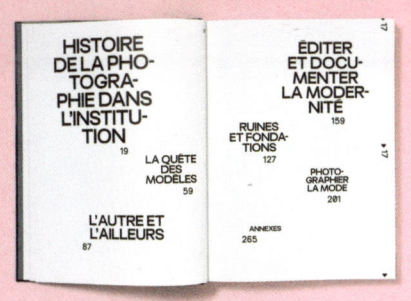
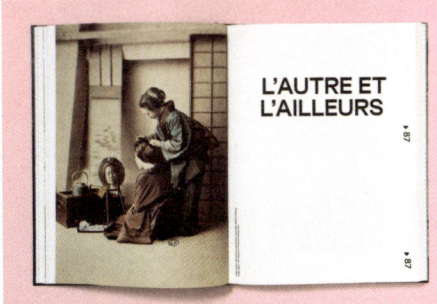
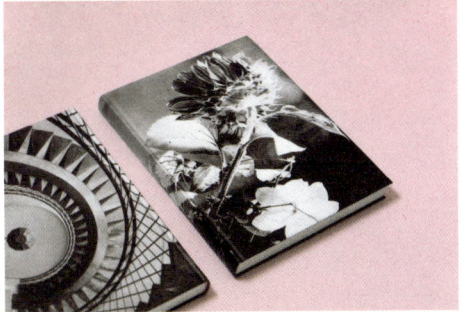

Prize	078 Poster
Nominee	TD. deValence: Alexandre Dimos, Ghislain Triboulet
Work	T. Alex Chavot
	CL. Frac Bretagne
	PT. Le Plus, Nicéphore Raw, Helvetica

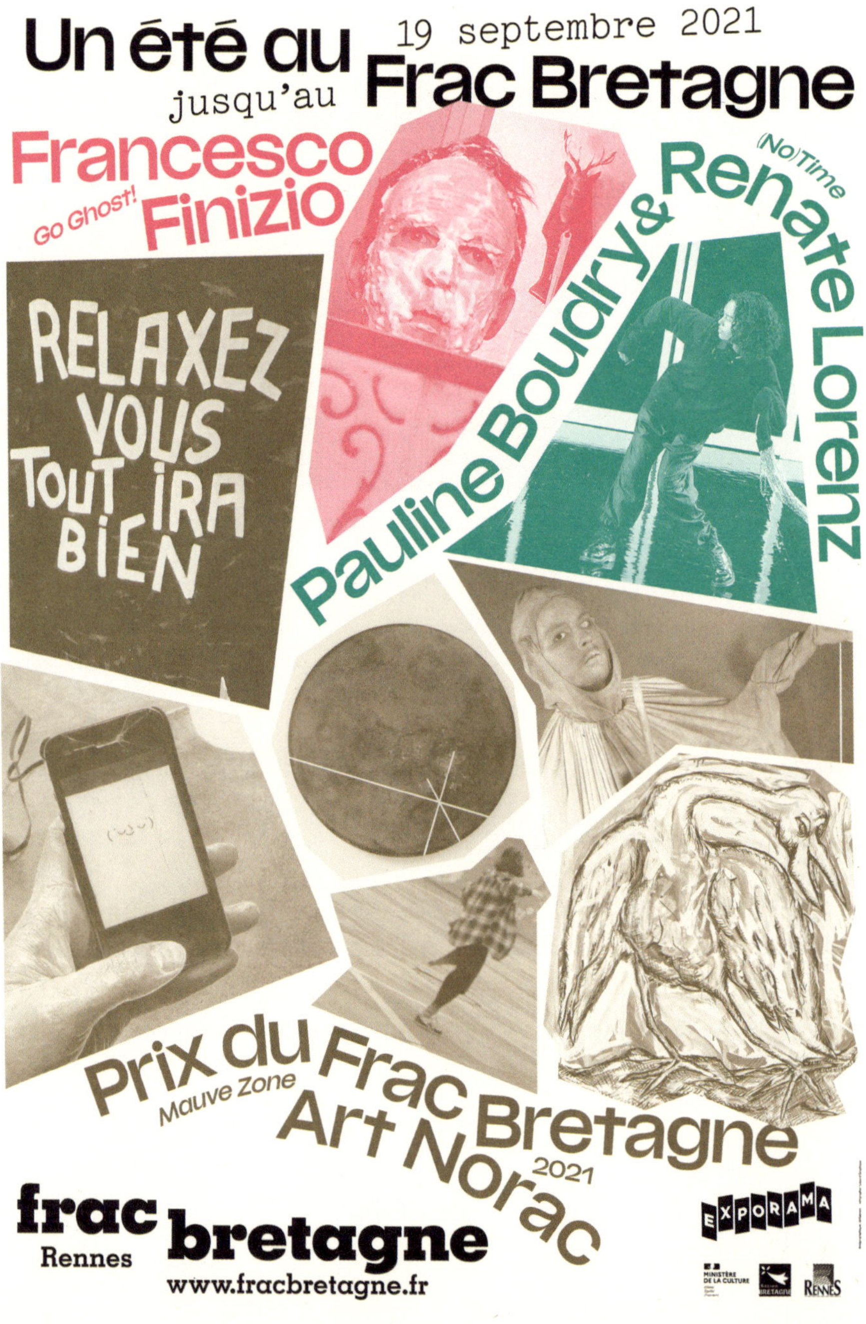

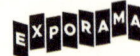

079 Catalogue
TD. deValence: Alexandre Dimos, Ghislain Triboulet
CL. Éditions Dilecta
PT. Wolpe Pegasus

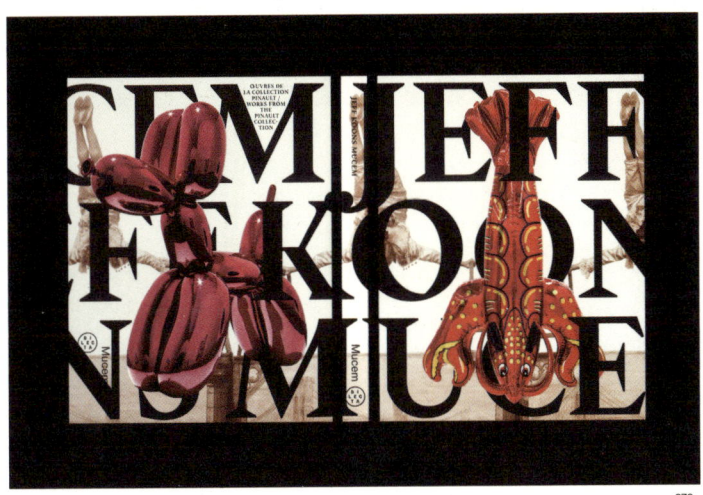

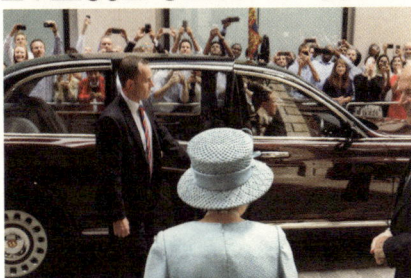

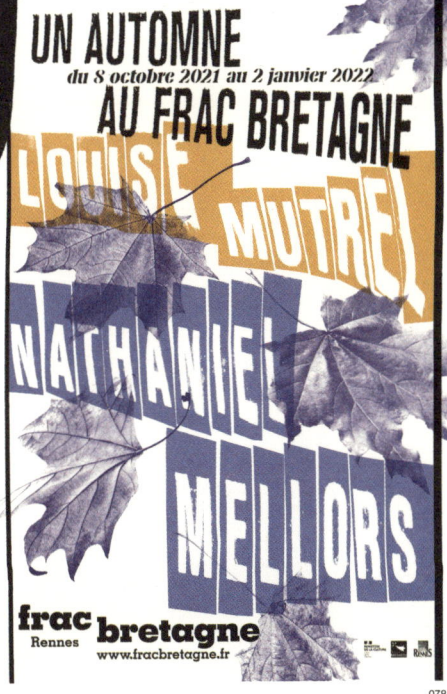

080 Book
TD. AD. D. Ming Ding, Yuanbo Wang
D. Chaohao Chen
CL. Demo Studio
PT. HelveticaNeue, Source Han Sans, Din Next Slab

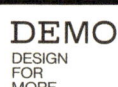
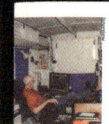
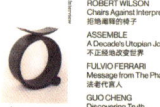
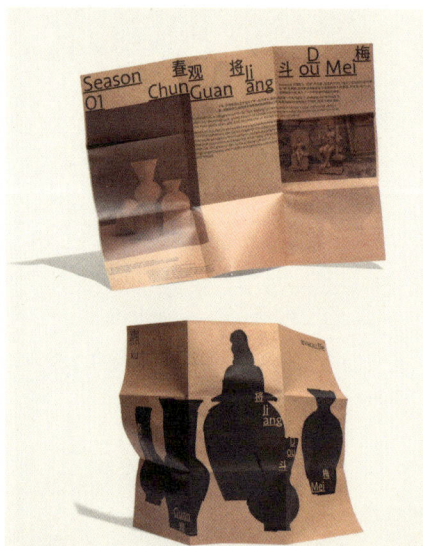
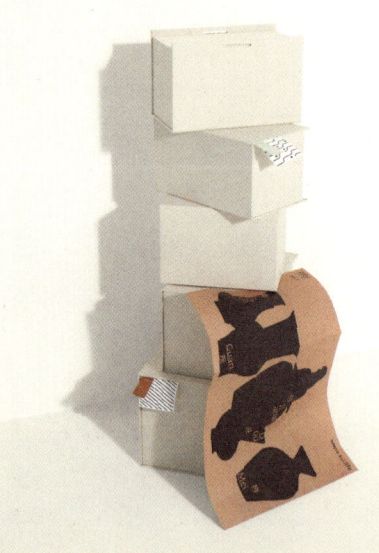

081 Branding
TD. AD. D. Ming Ding, Yuanbo Wang
D. Chaohao Chen
P. Yun Xing
CL. Xu
PT. Custom-made for the project, Highgate VF, Source Han Sans

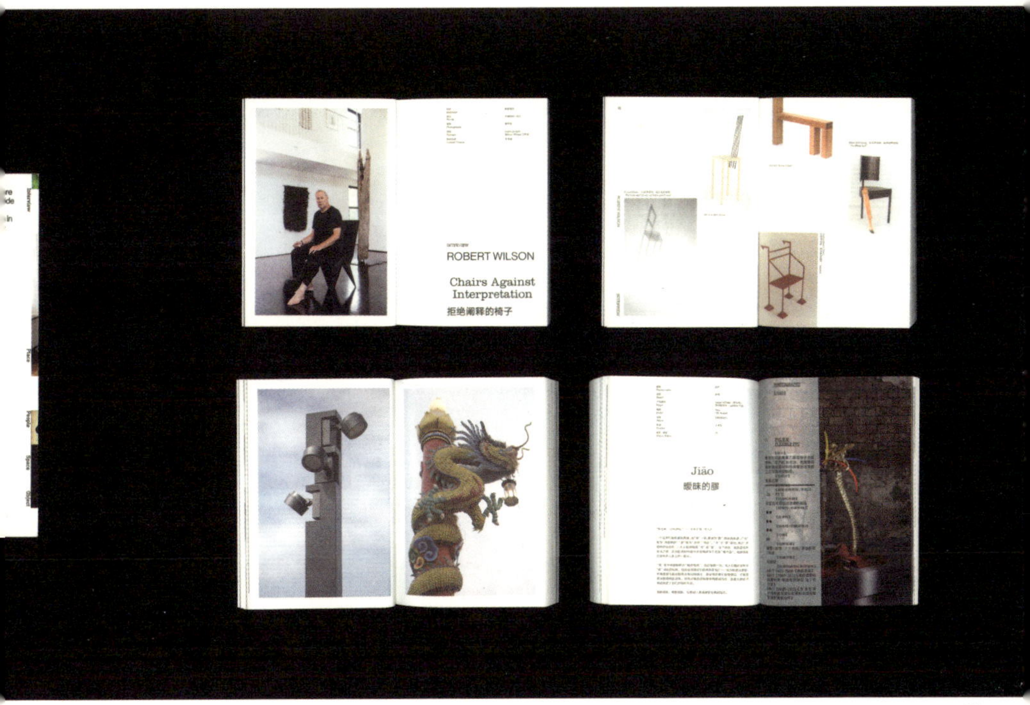

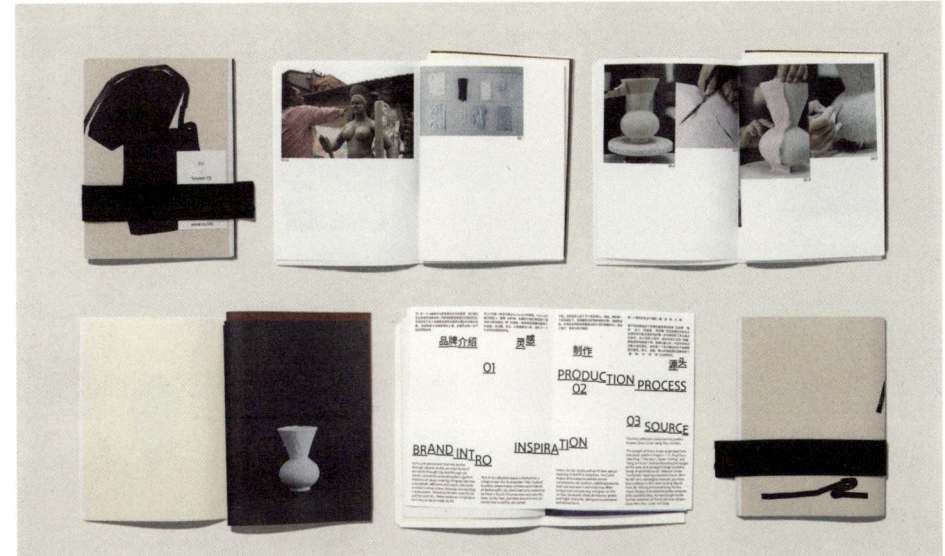

082 Branding
TD. AD. D. Ming Ding, Yuanbo Wang
P. Yun Xing
CL. Chushan
PT. Custom-made for the project, Antique Olive, Source Han Sans

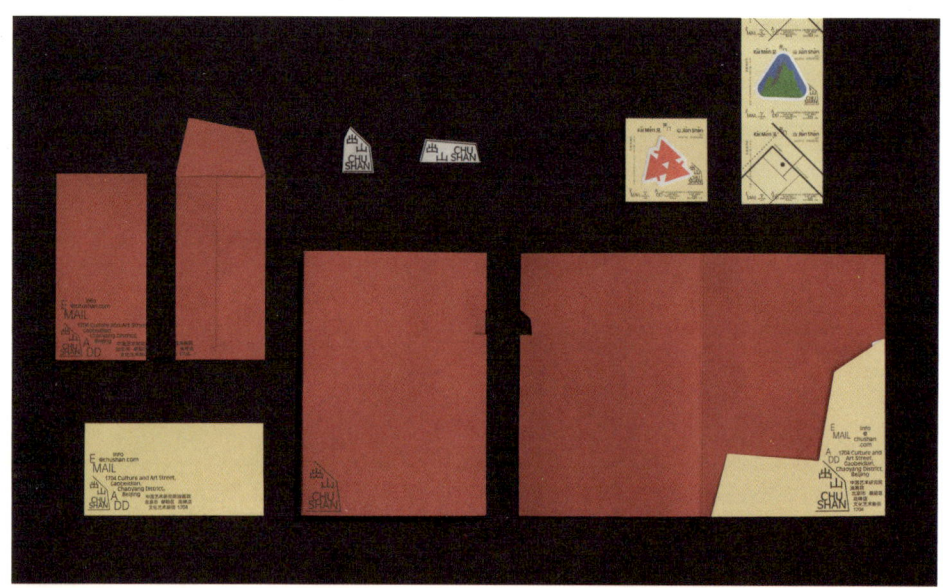

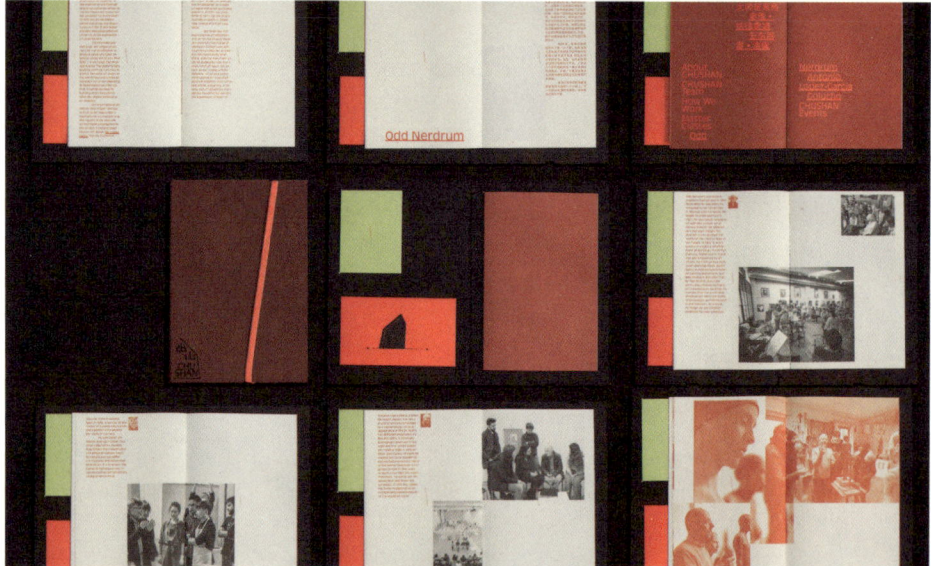

083 VI
TD. AD. D. P. Xiaoyuan Ding
CL. The Entrance Book Store
PT. Custom-made for the project

084 Experimental work
TD. Karen ann Donnachie, Andy Simionato
CL. MIT Cast Commission
PT. Custom-made for the project, Helvetica

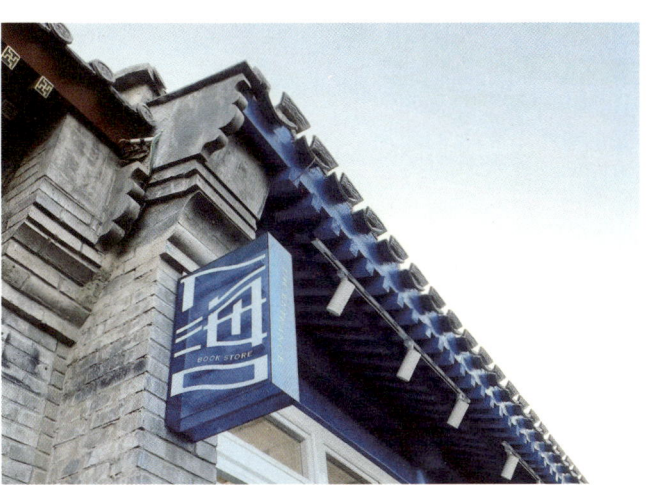

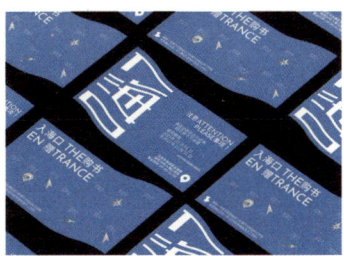

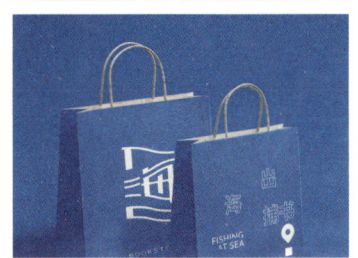

083

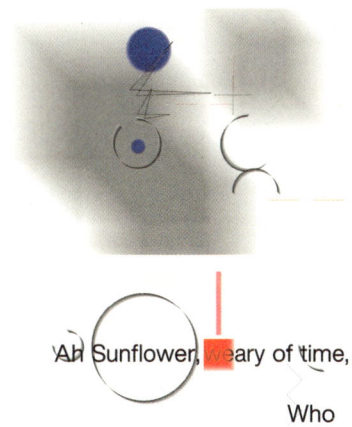

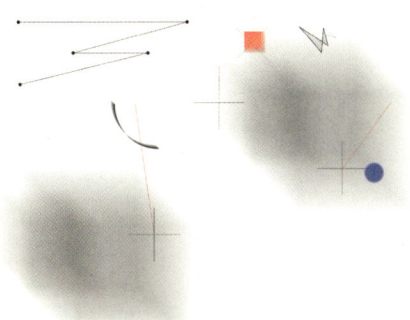

084

085 Postcard
TD. AD. I. Eva Dranaz
P. Jochen Fill
CL. G- Print, Arctic Paper, Austria
PT. Custom-made for the project

086 Small Graphics
TD. AD. D. Du Xiao
D. Huang Weijie, Gao Xiang
P. Li Zhenhua
CL. Foundertype
PT. Custom-made for the project

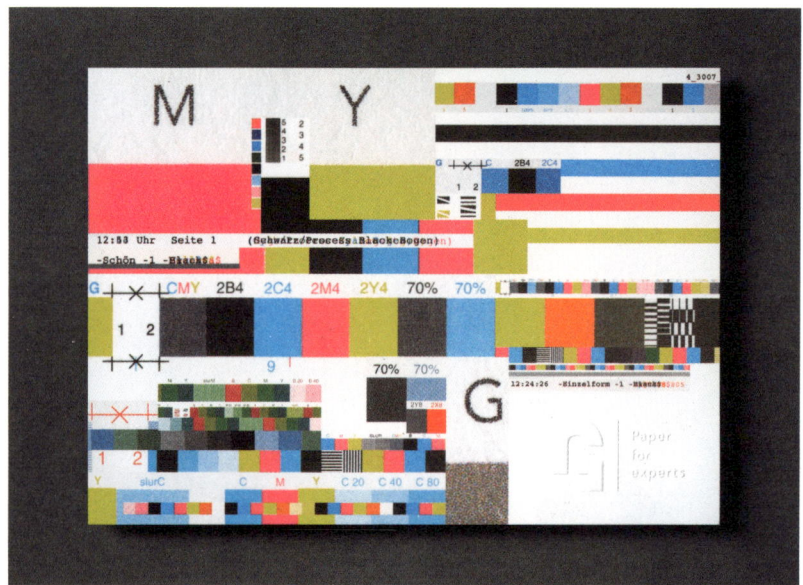

087 Newspaper ad.
TD. AD. 江波戸李生 Rio Ebato
D. 鑓田佳広 Yoshihiro Yarita, 高坂さくら Sakura Takasaka
CD. C. 鳥巣智行 Tomoyuki Torisu
CL. (株)長崎新聞社 Nagasaki Shinbunsha
PT. 游ゴシック

TD. Mark El-khatib
CL. Peak Cymru
PT. Clarendon

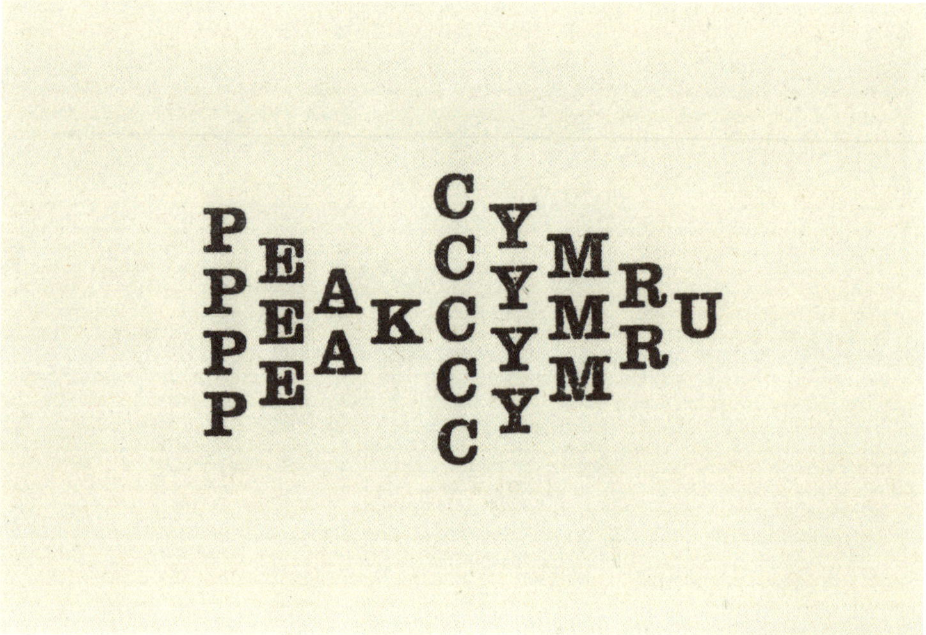

089 Book
TD. Mark El-khatib
CL. Serpentine
PT. Sunset Gothic, Triptych

089 Small graphics
TD. AD. D. Yu-Cheng Hsiao
P. Ke Wang
CL. Non-commercial work
PT. Helvetica Neue Regular, Osaka

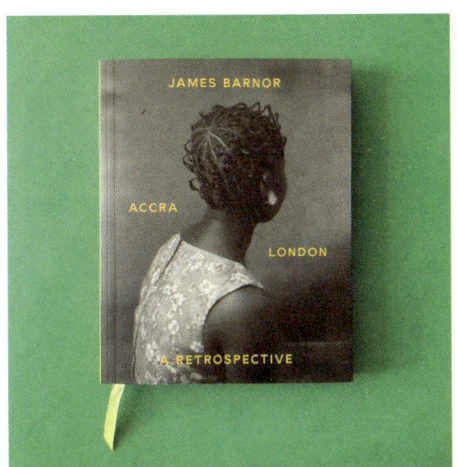
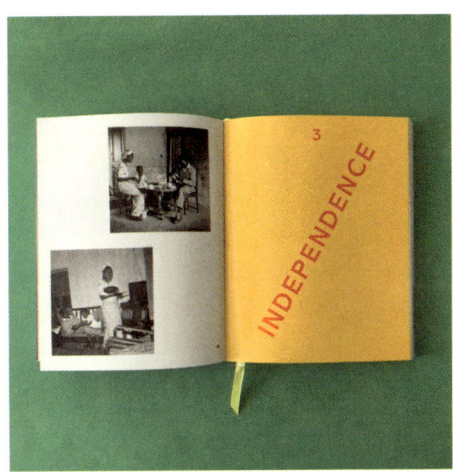
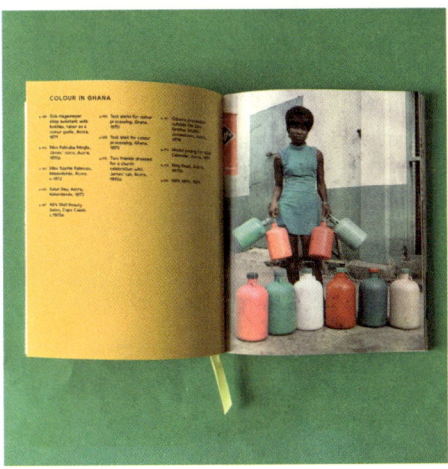
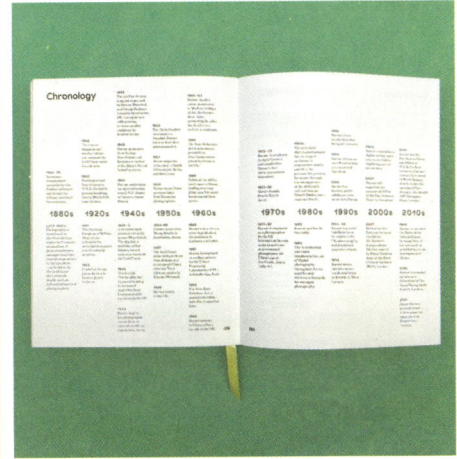

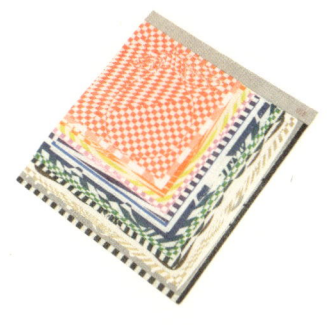
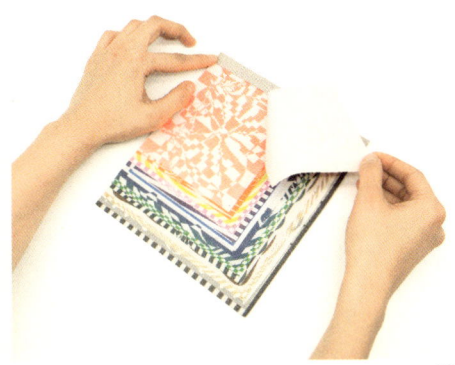

091 Book
TD. Konstantin Eremenko
P. CL. Dmitry Vyshemirsky
E (Idea, CO). Nuria Fatykhova
P. E. Irina Chmyreva
PT. CoFo Sans, CoFo Robert

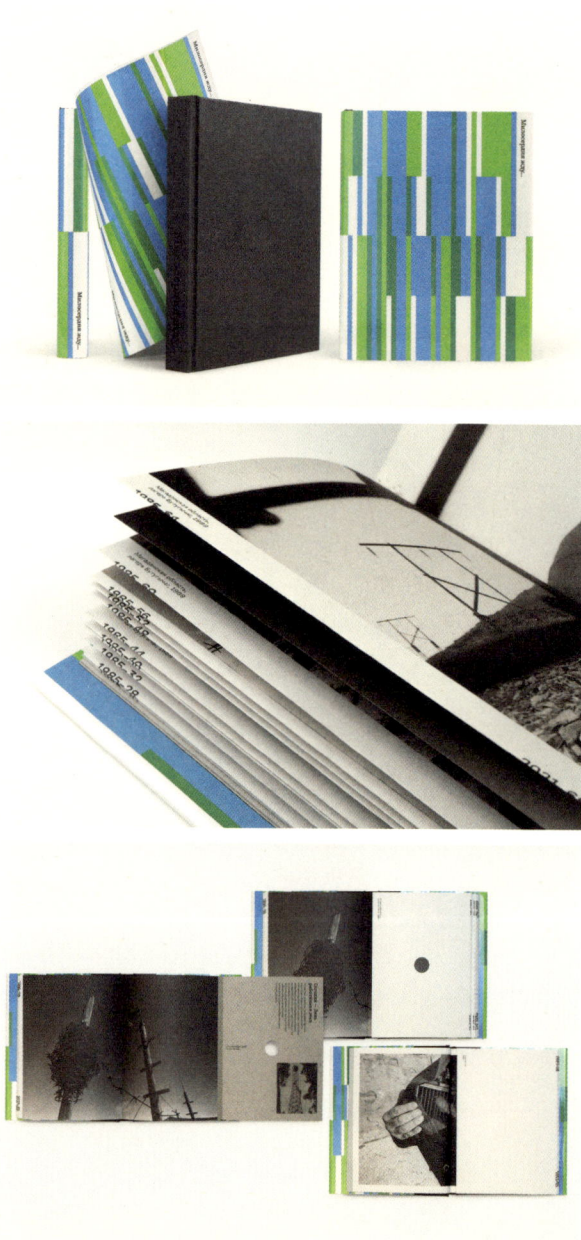

092 Branding
TD. CD. D. Fang Jianping
CD. Ding Fan
MD. Zhao Lin
CL. Mega Suen

093 Key visual, Broadcast design, Environmental design
TD. Anton Fedorov, Dmitry Jakovlev
CD. Victoria Motornuk, Miroslava Bayda
D. Anton Terekhov
MOD. Pavel Kuderov
PM. Ravshana Khalikova
CL. Maison Cartier, Dazzling creative studio
PT. Brilliant Cut Pro, Navigo, Menoe Grotesque

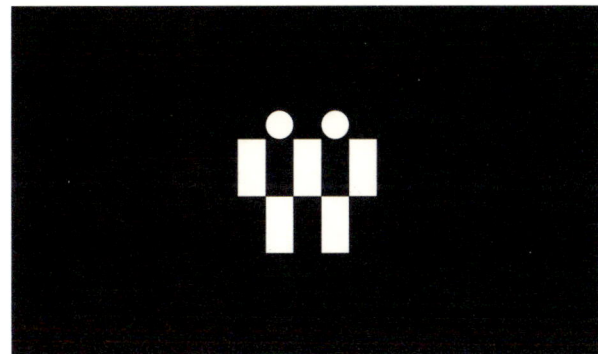

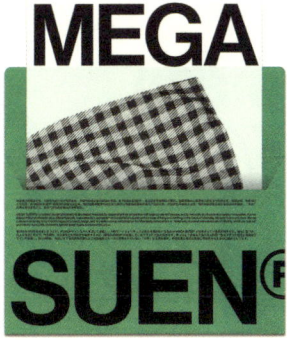

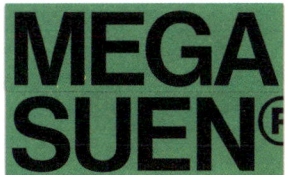

092

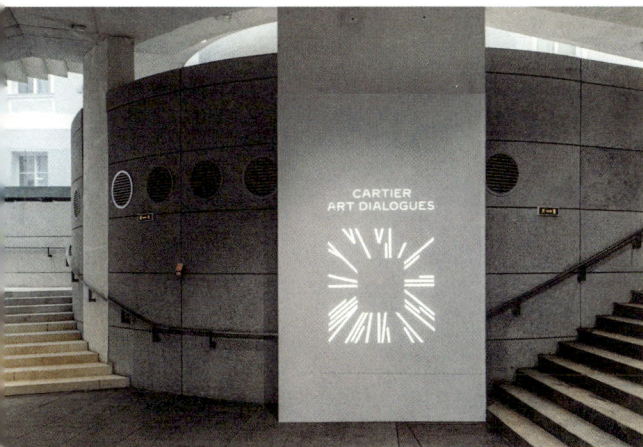

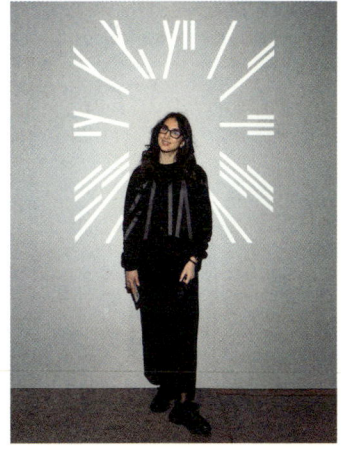

093

094 Type design
TD. Maxime Fittes
AD. In the shade of a tree
CL. Villa Arson

095 Book
TD. D. Nina Flaitz, Marius Rother
CL. Braunschweig University of Art
PT. ITC Avant Garde Gothic Pro

Villa Arson

Nice [France]
↑ 43°43'19"N
Mediterranean
1967–1972
→ 7°15'00"E

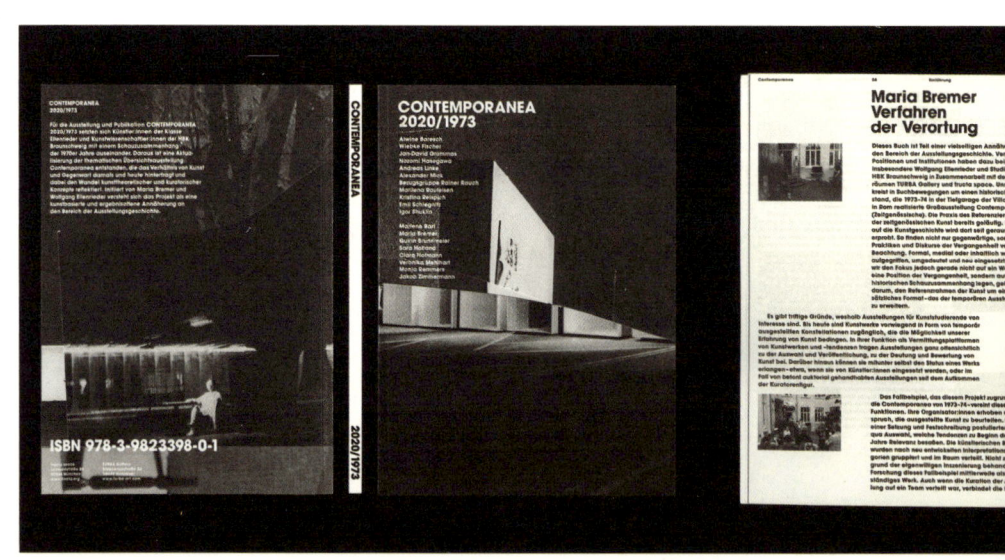

096 Poster
TD. 藤巻洋紀 Hiroki Fujimaki
CL. 日刊タイポ Nikkan typo
PT. Din Next

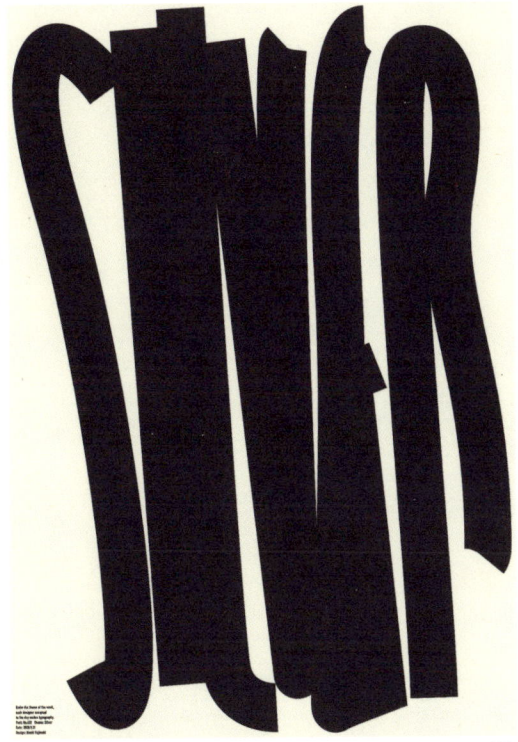

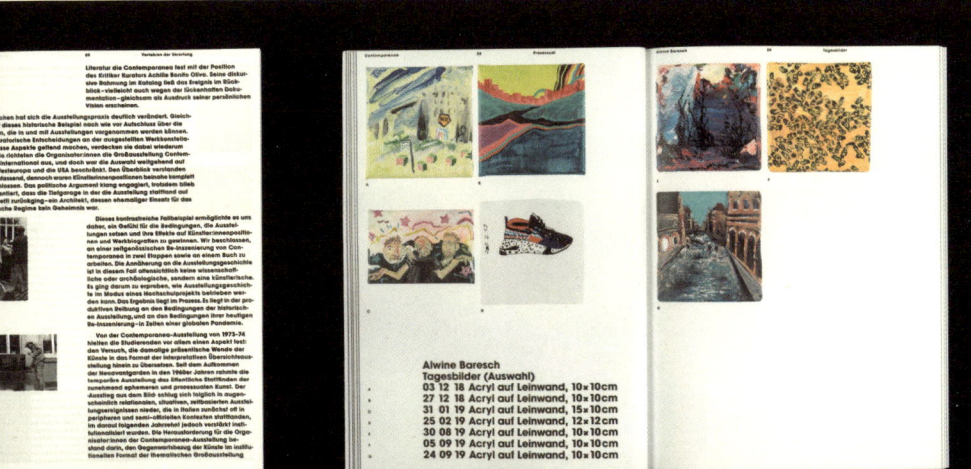

097 Flyer
TD. フクナガコウジ Kohji Fukunaga
CL. Minatomachi Art Table
PT. ヒラギノUD角ゴ, Helvetica, 筑紫明朝Pro

098 Poster
TD. フクナガコウジ Kohji Fukunaga
P. 池谷陸 Riku Ikeya
CL. (株)スペースシャワーネットワーク Space Shower Networks. Inc.
PT. ZENオールド明朝, Avenir, こぶりなゴシック

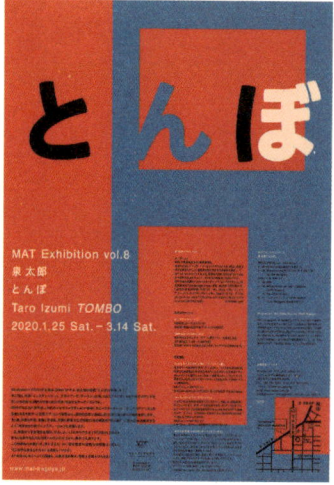
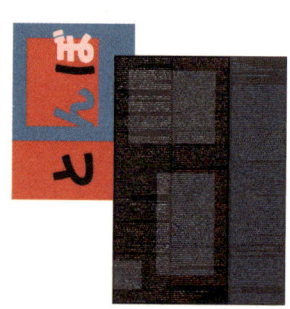
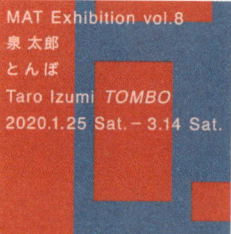
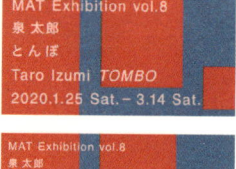

097

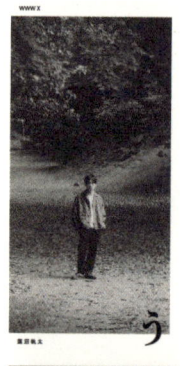
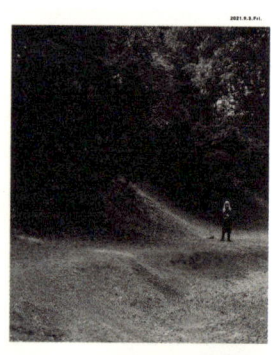
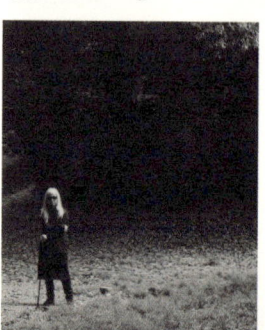
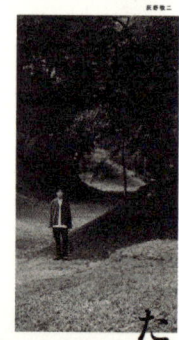

098

099 Poster
TD. Flo Gaertner
CL. Museum Ludwig, Cologne
PT. FK Screamer

100 Poster
TD. AD. D. 福島周 Shu Fukushima
CL. 古川原壮志 Takeshi Kogahara
PT. Custom-made for the project, 游明朝体, Cochin

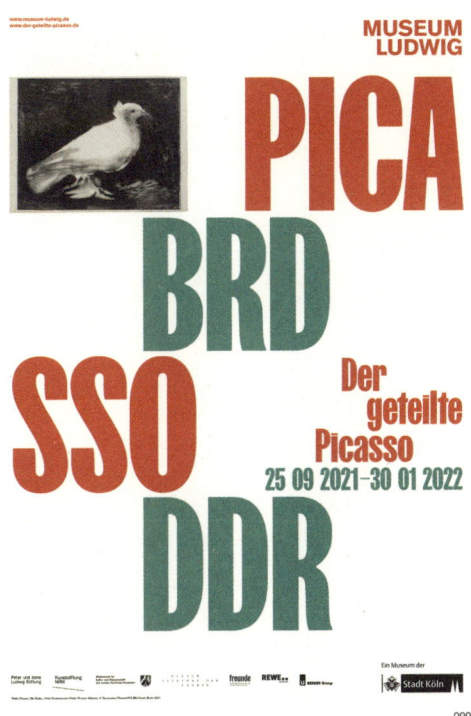

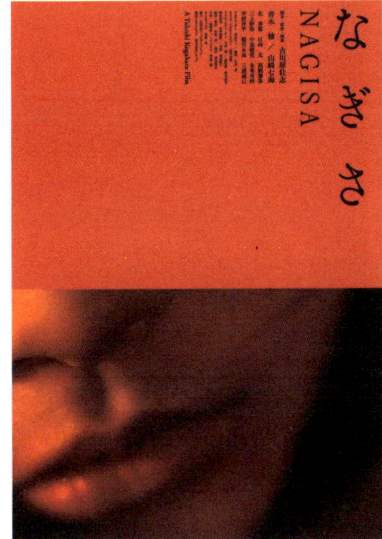

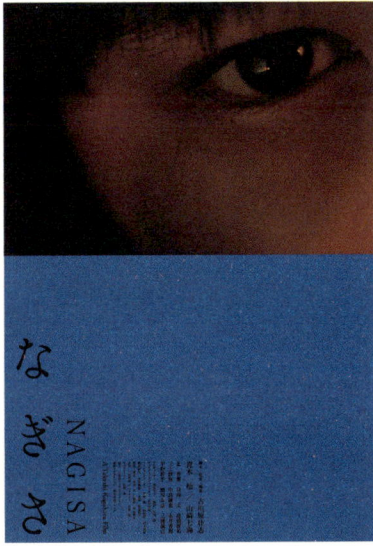

101 Book
TD. Yuan Gao, Wenwen Zhang
CL. Non-commercial work
PT. Custom-made for the project, Clarendon

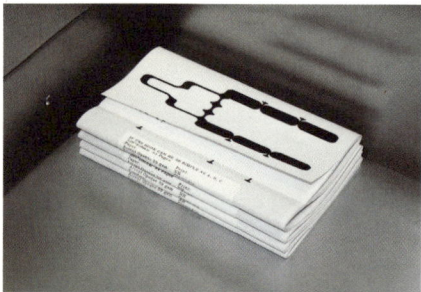
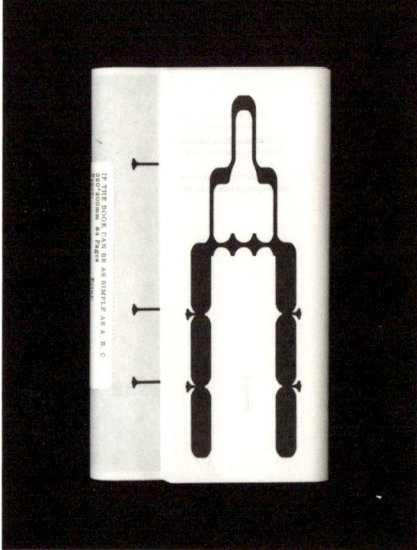
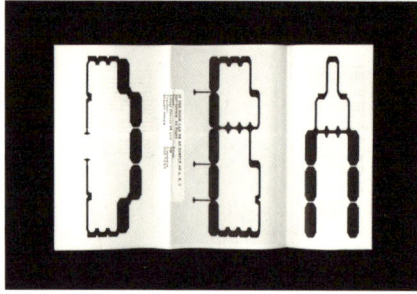

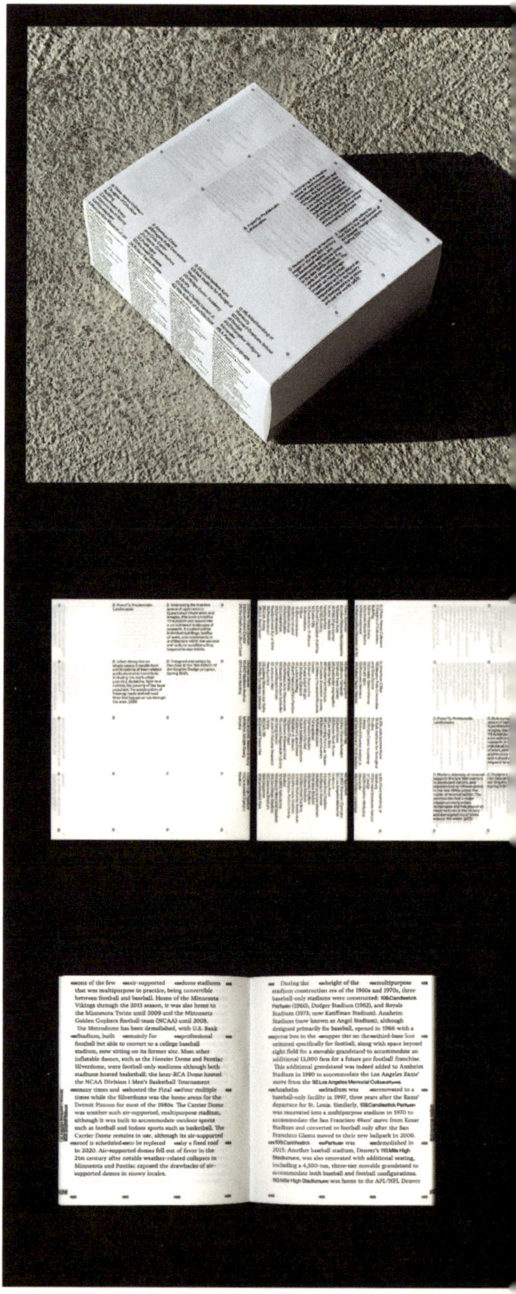

102 Book
TD. Han Gao
CL. T for Typography
PT. Helvetica, Livory

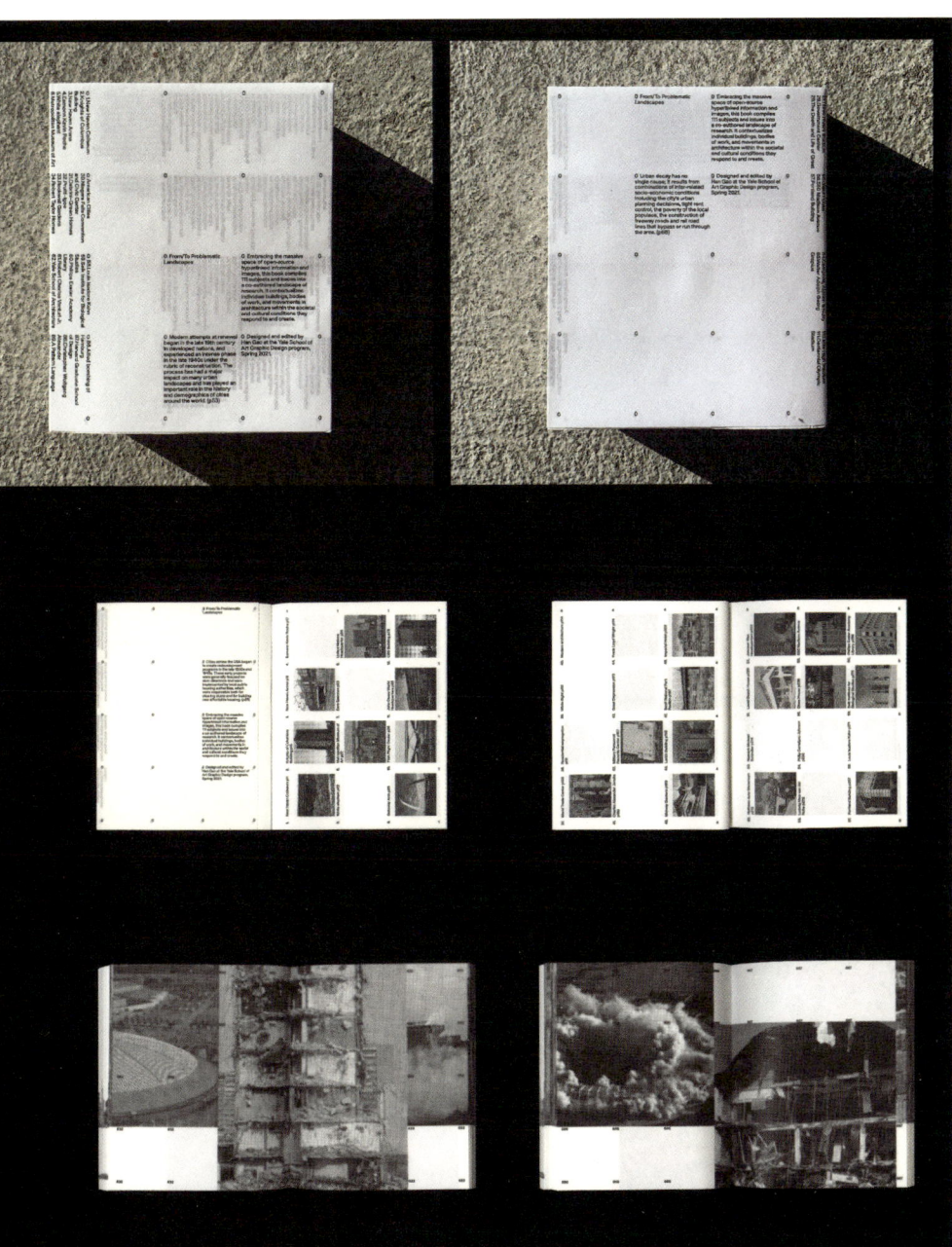

103 Experimental work
TD. D. P. Luo Gan
CL. Multiple Spectrum Project
PT. Custom-made for the project, Helvetica

104 Branding
TD. Han Gao
P. Shilu Wang
CL. Rarely Alike
PT. Custom-made for the project

110

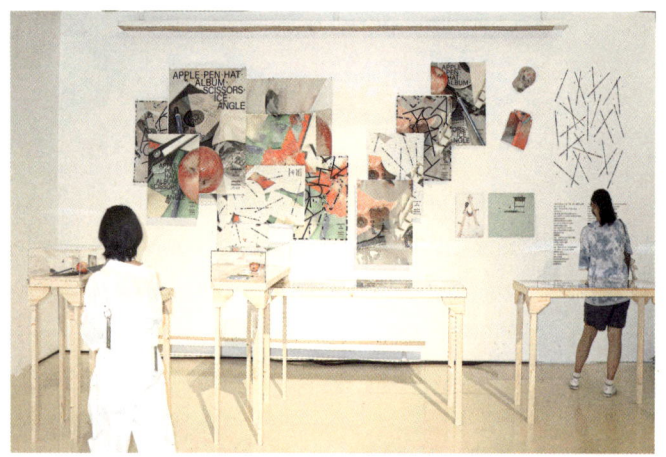

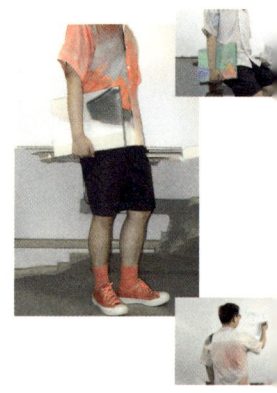

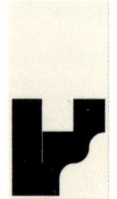 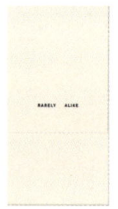 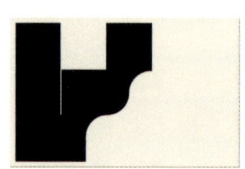

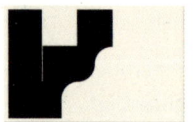 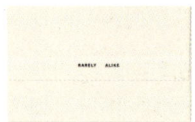 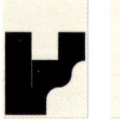 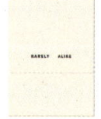

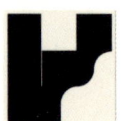  

105 Packaging
TD. Han Gao
P. Shilu Wang
CL. Yours Truly
PT. FZMingChao Regular

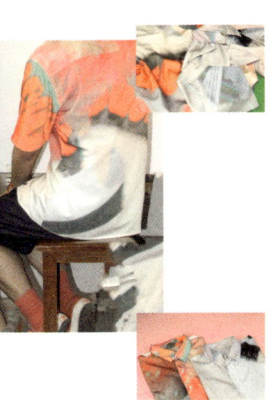

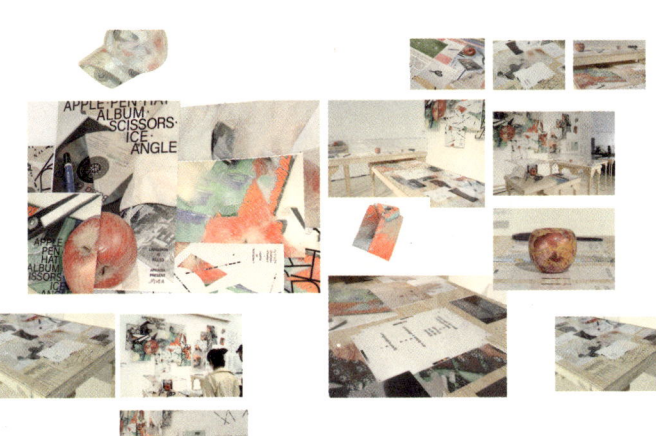

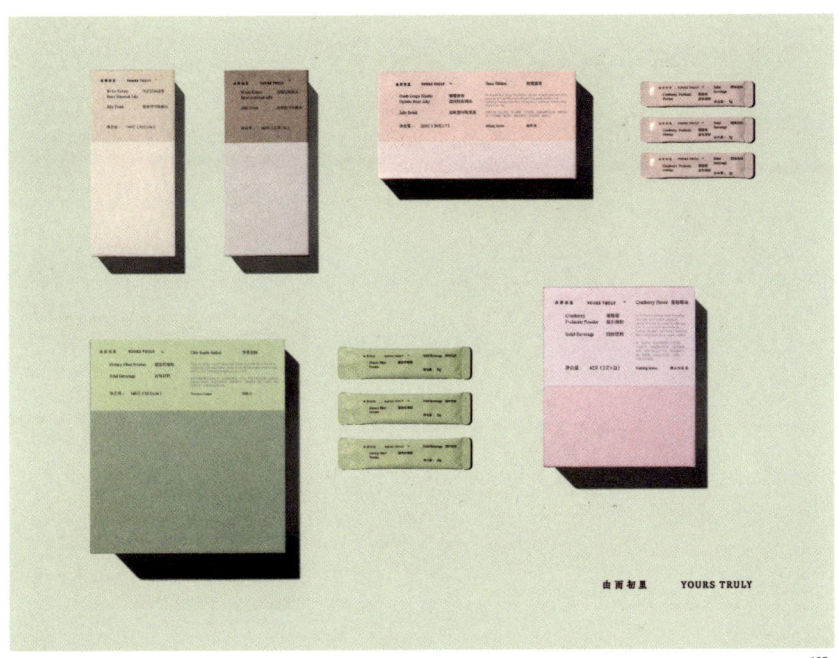

106 Poster
TD. Han Gao
CL. Yale School of Art
PT. Helvetica

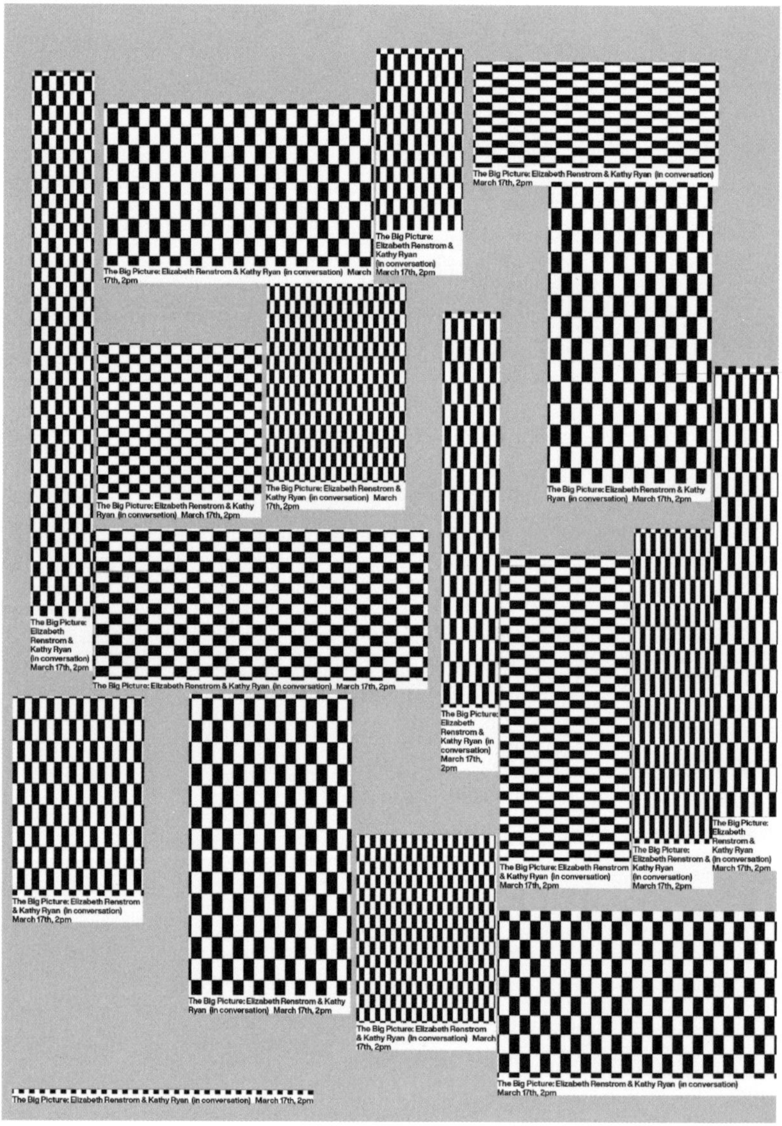

107 Book
TD. Chris Gautschi
E. Olivier Morattel Editeur
CL. Patrick Gilieron Lopreno
PT. Sang Bleu Kingdom

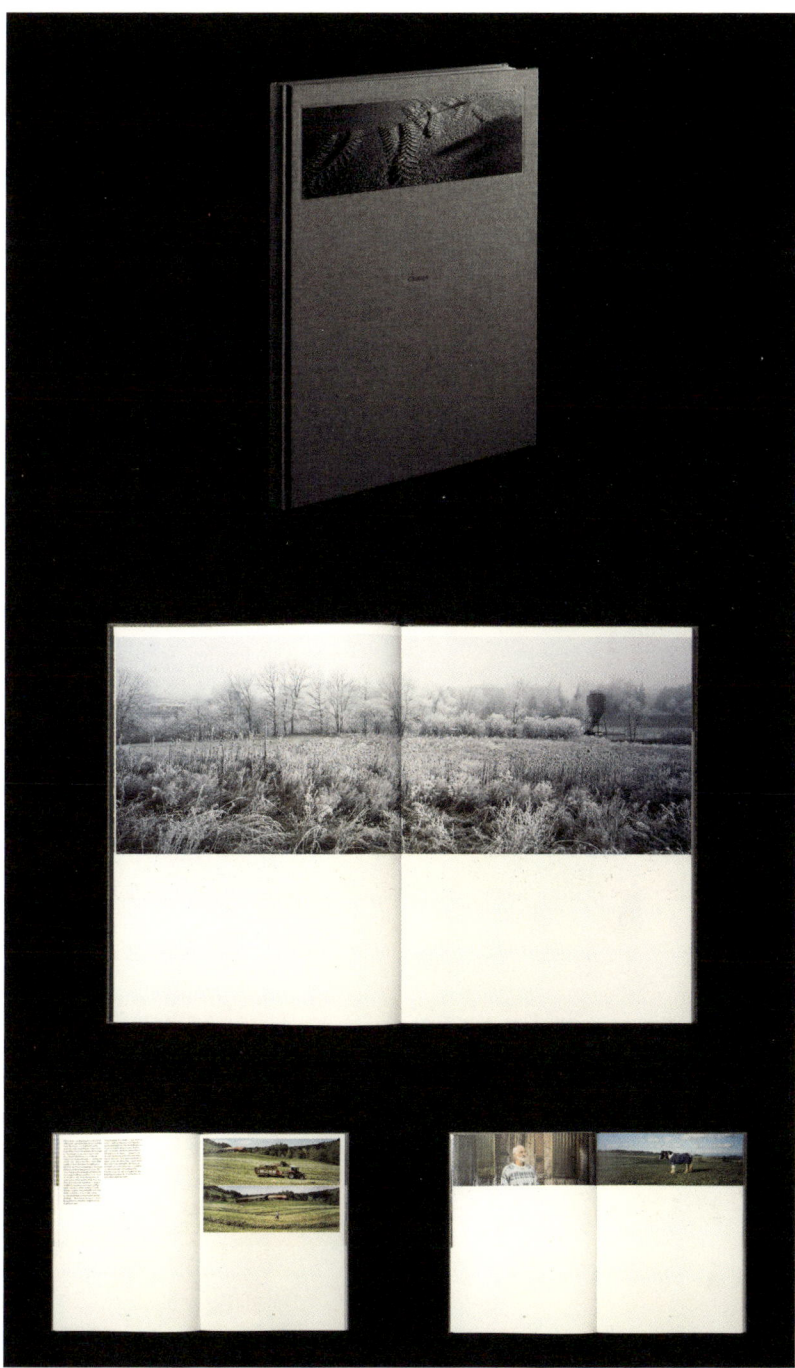

108 Book
TD. Chris Gautschi
P. Filip Dujardin
E. Birkhäuser
CL. Benoit Jacques – Rui Filipe Pinto
PT. Sang Bleu Kingdom, Univers NextPro Bold

109 Logo system
TD. D. Zhao Ge
TD. D. I. Cao Qun
CL. Fayuan Architecture Museum
PT. Original Font, Menlo

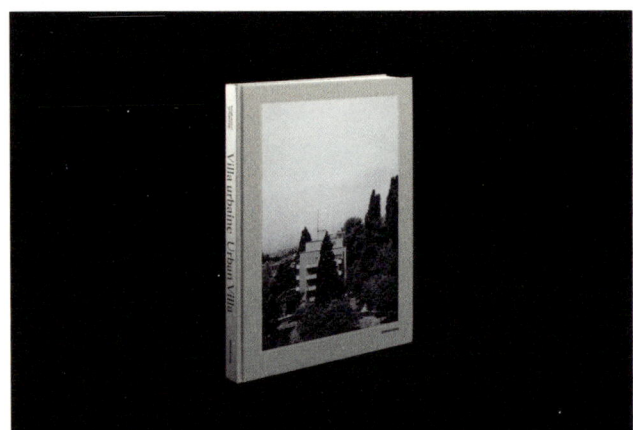

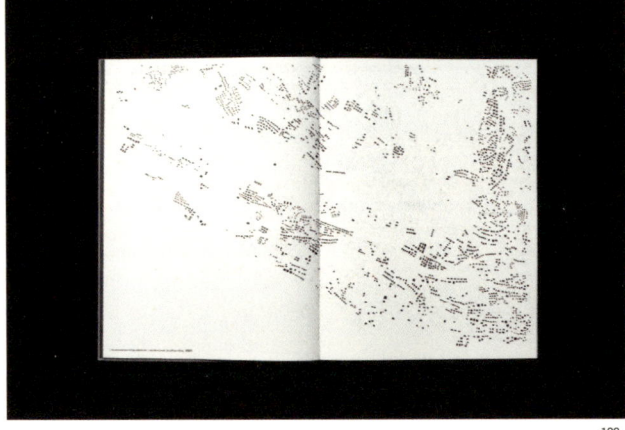

108

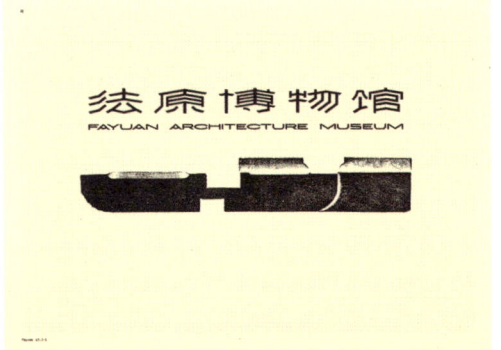

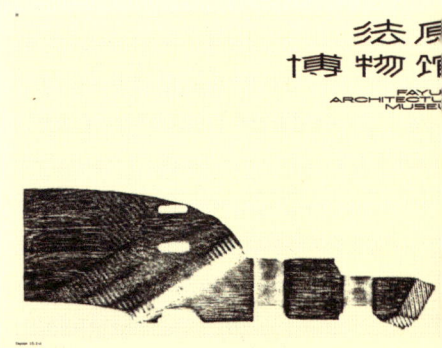

110 Experimental work
TD. GengoRaw: 石橋友也, 新倉健人 GengoRaw: Tomoya Ishibashi, Kento Niikura
CL. Non-commercial work
PT. MS Gothic

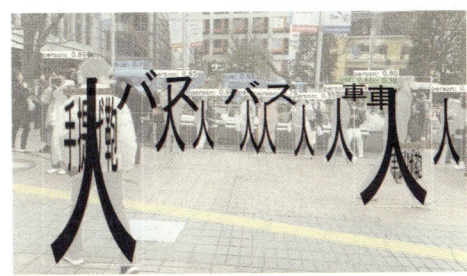

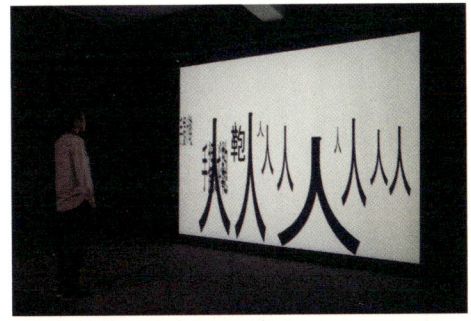

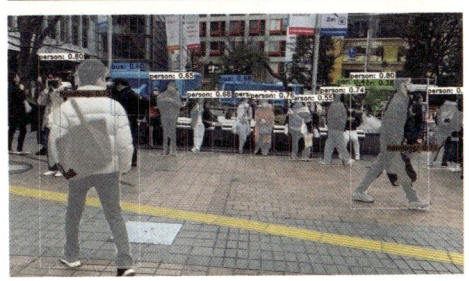

110

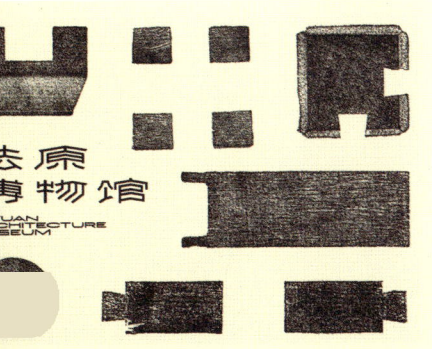

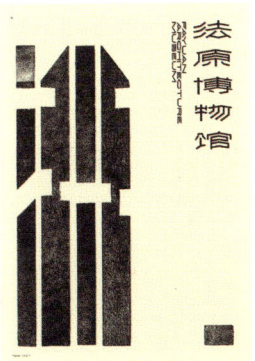

109

Prize Nominee Work

111 Book
TD. Malin Gewinner, Hannes Drißner, Markus Dreßen
AD. Jan Wenzel, Olaf Nicolai
E. Detlef Diedrichsen, Anselm Franke, Katrin Klingan, Daniel Neugebauer, Bernd Scherer
CL. Haus der Kulturen der Welt (HKW), Berlin, Germany
PT. Suisse BP, Lyon Text, FK Raster

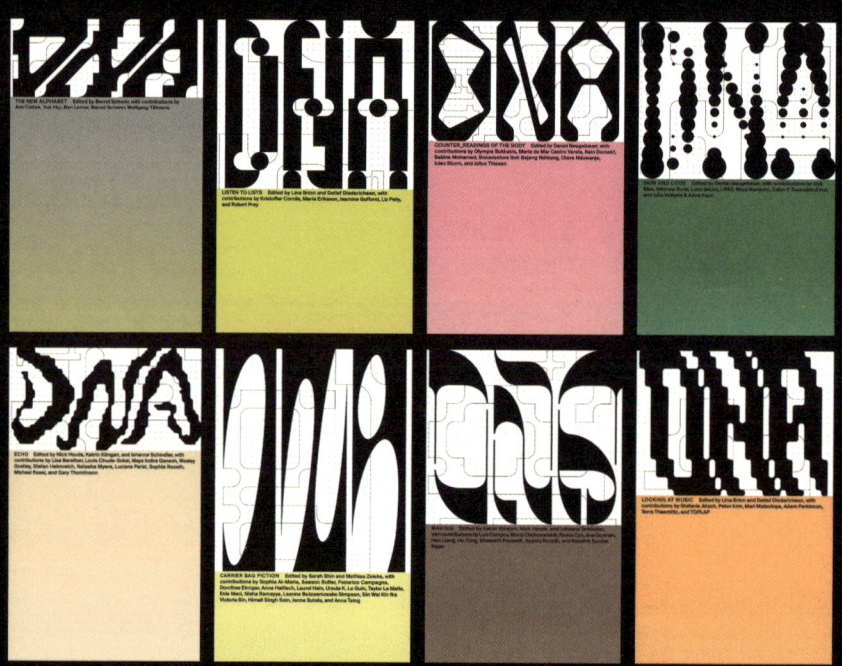

117 112 Book
TD. Dana Gez
E. Rachel Gottesman, Tamar Novick, Iddo Ginat, Dan Hasson, Yonatan Cohen
CL. The Israeli pavilion at the 17th International Architecture Exhibition of the Venice Biennale
PT. Gotham, Minion Pro, Narkiss Block

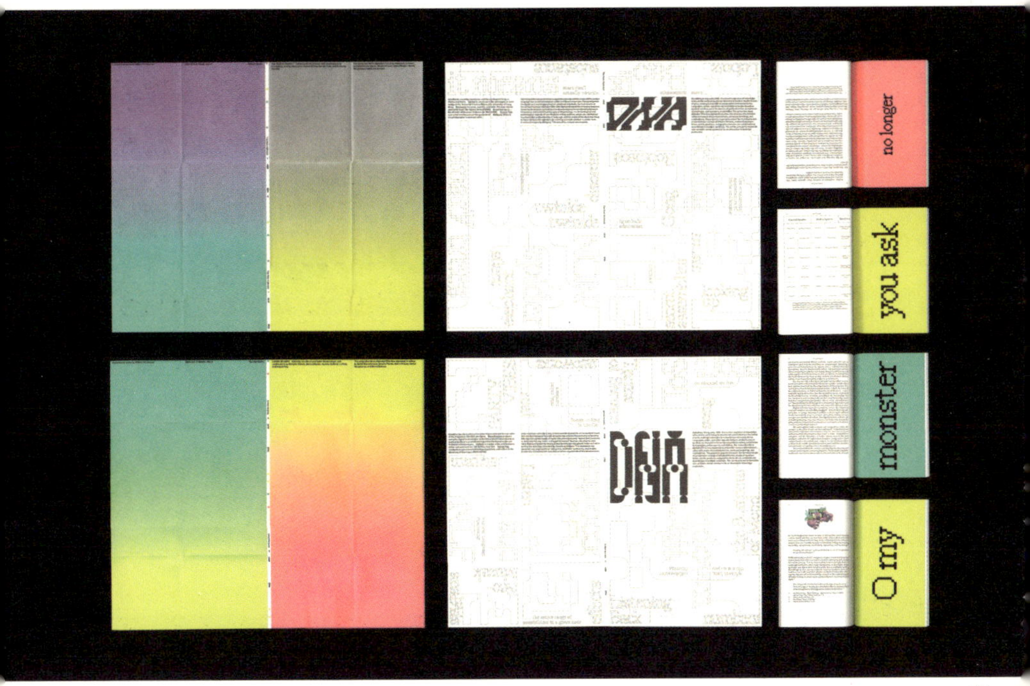

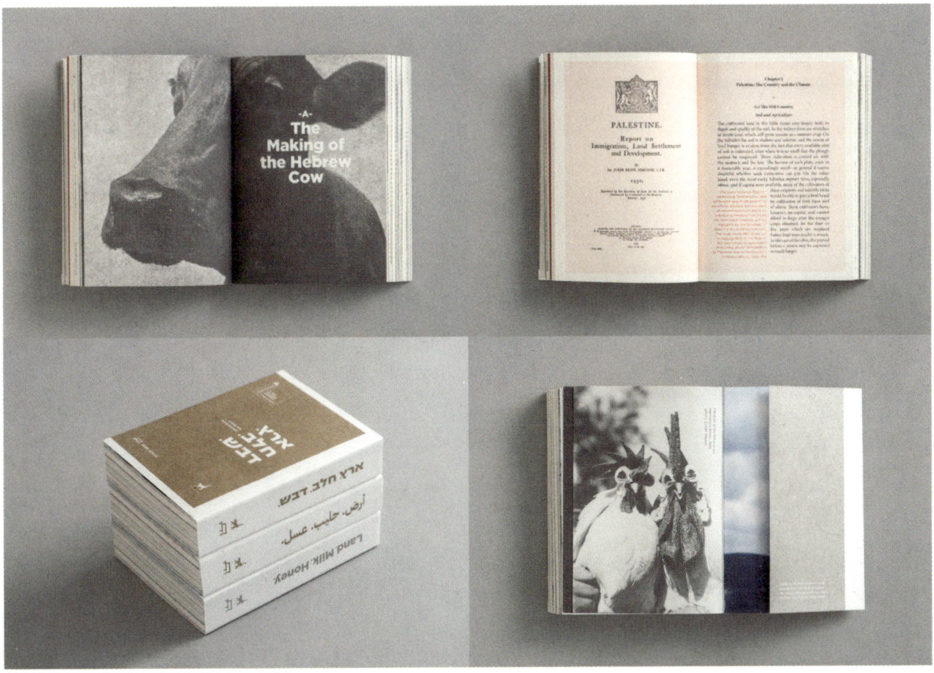

113 Book
TD. D. Bendita Gloria
E. Marc Morro, Alba Rosell, Santi Fuster
CL. Foundawtion
PT. Unica, Brunel with custom punctuation

114 Book
TD. Mark Gowing
CL. Formist Editions

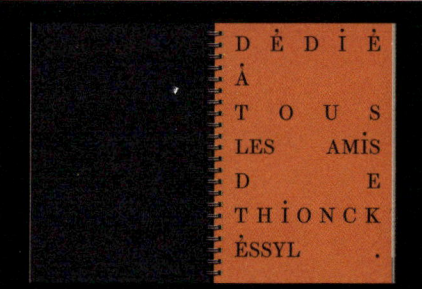

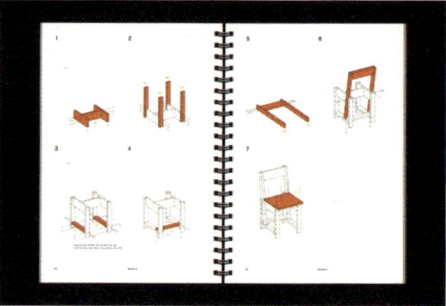

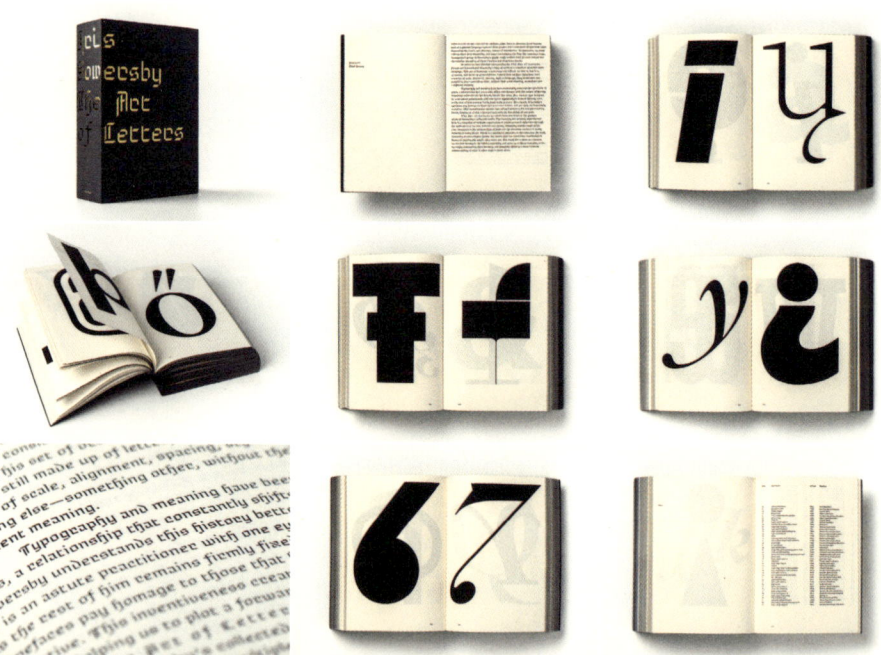

115 Poster
TD. GOO CHOKI PAR
CL. Non-commercial work
PT. Original font

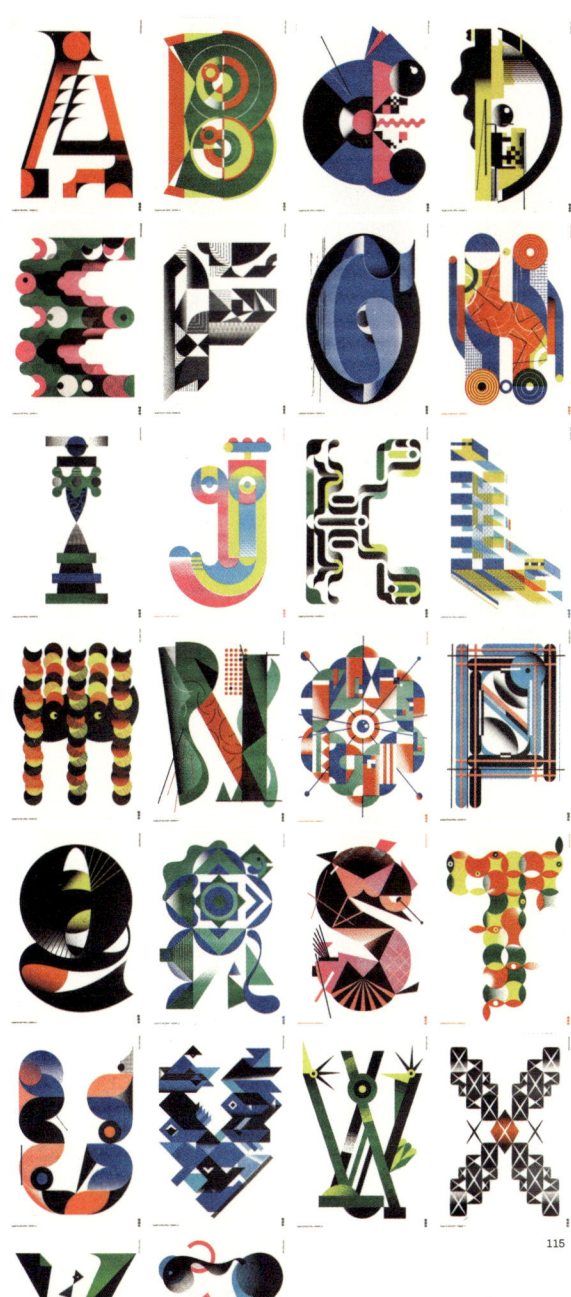

116 Book
TD. Mark Gowing
CL. Formist Editions

117 Record jacket
TD. Martin Grasser
D. Lilly Archer, Jack Burnside, Carina Huynh, Zrinka Buljubašić
P. Daymon Gardner
S. Ted Makarewicz, Gabrielle Muse

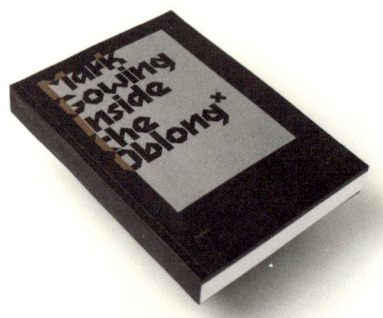
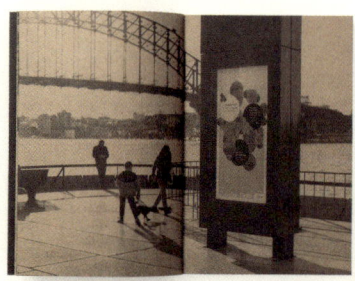
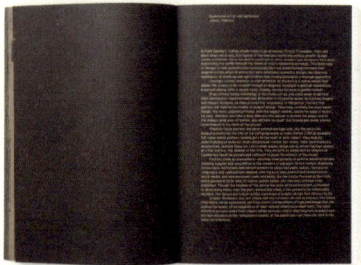
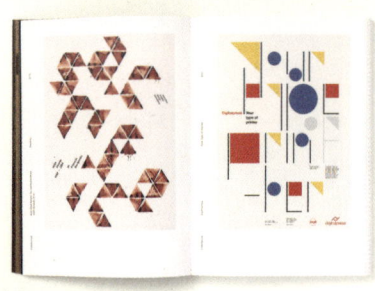

116

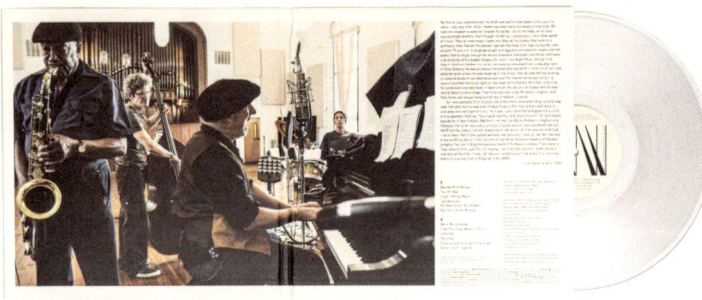

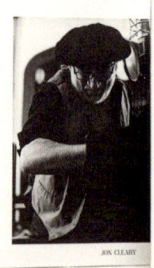
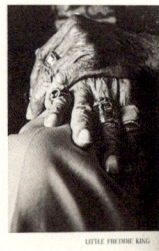
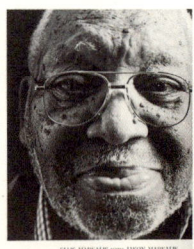
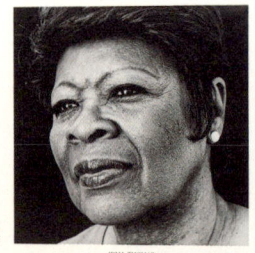

118 Book
TD. Mark Gowing
CL. Formist Editions

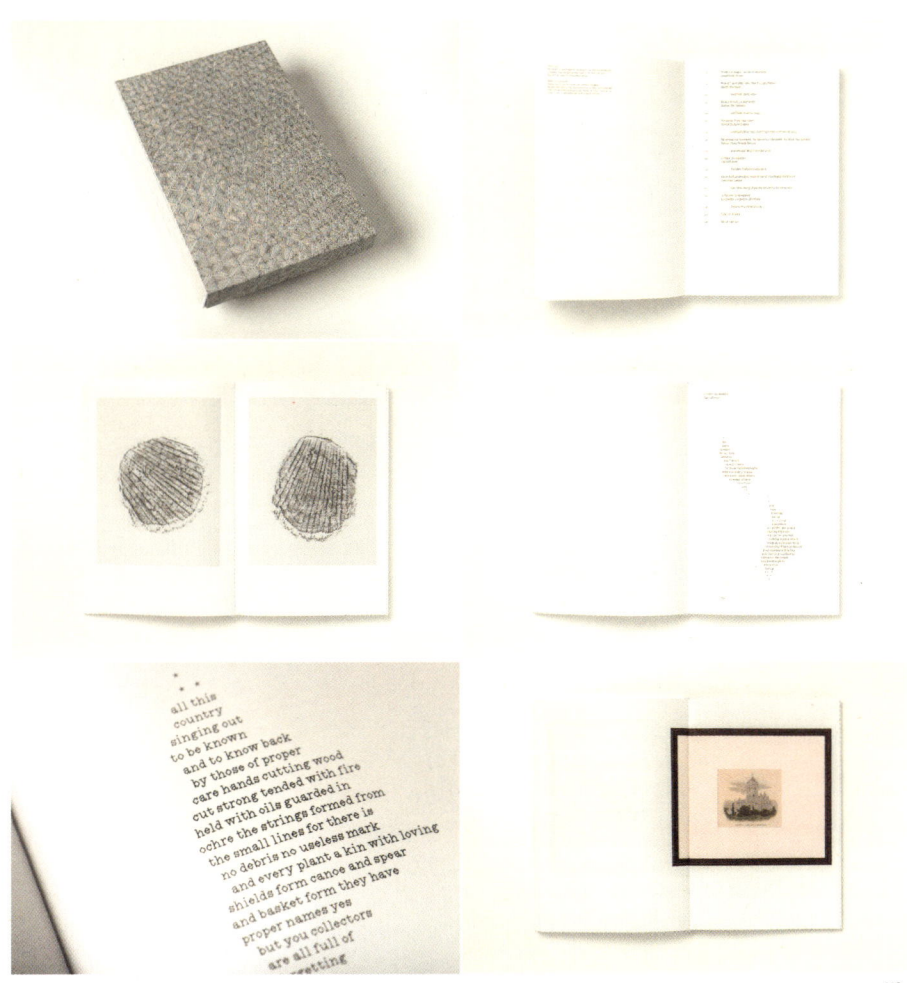

119 Book
TD. Tino Grass
PU. Prestel, London, Munich, New York
CL. Barbican London, Museum Ludwig Cologne, Zentrum Paul Klee Bern
PT. Custom-made for the project, Avenir Next

120 Poster
TD. Xiao Guo
CL. Gallery Sohe
PT. Garamond, Song

122

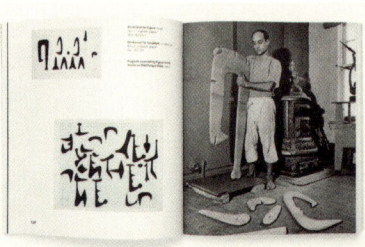

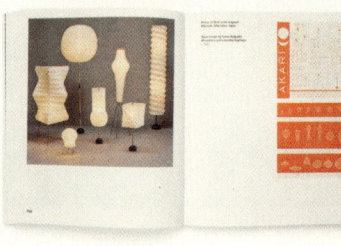

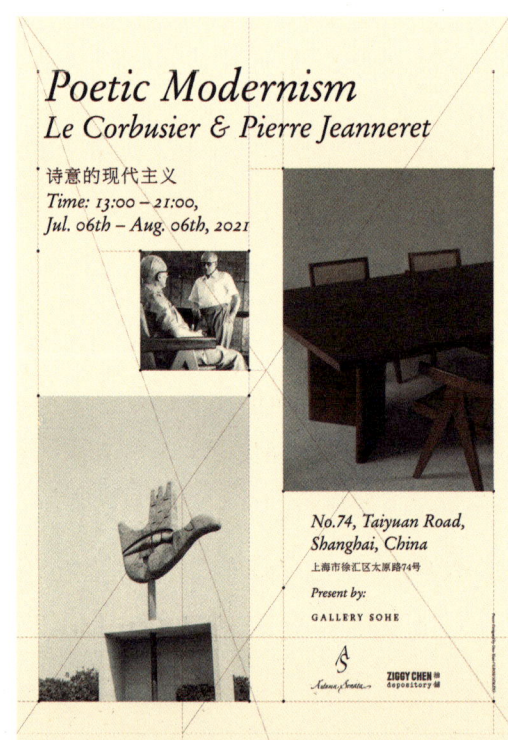

121 Book
TD. Marta Guidotti
SV. Ann Bessemans, María Pérez Mena, Carl Haase
CL. International Master Reading Type & Typography, Readsearch
PT. Noto mono, Times New Roman

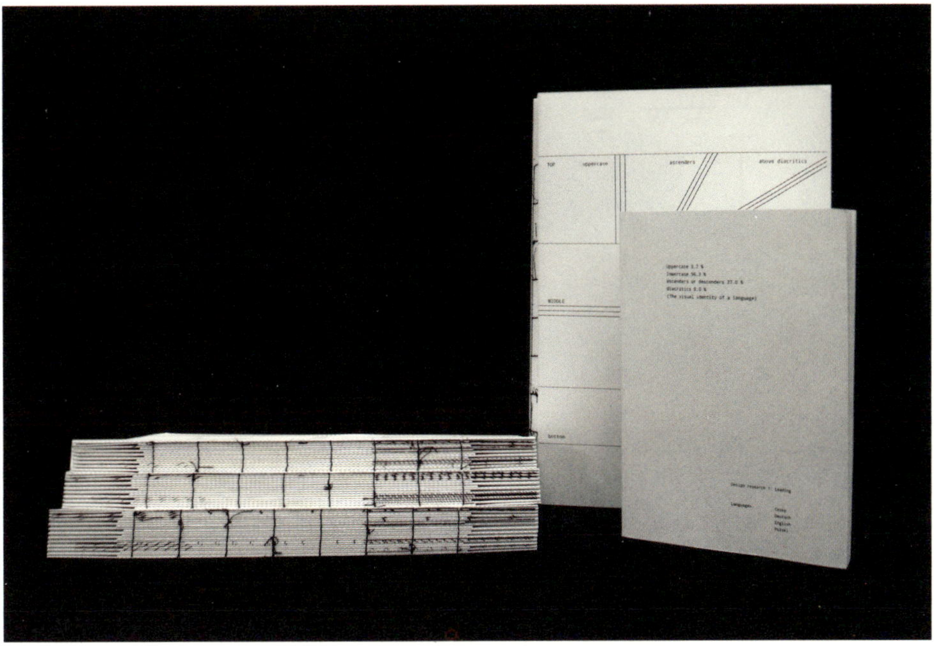

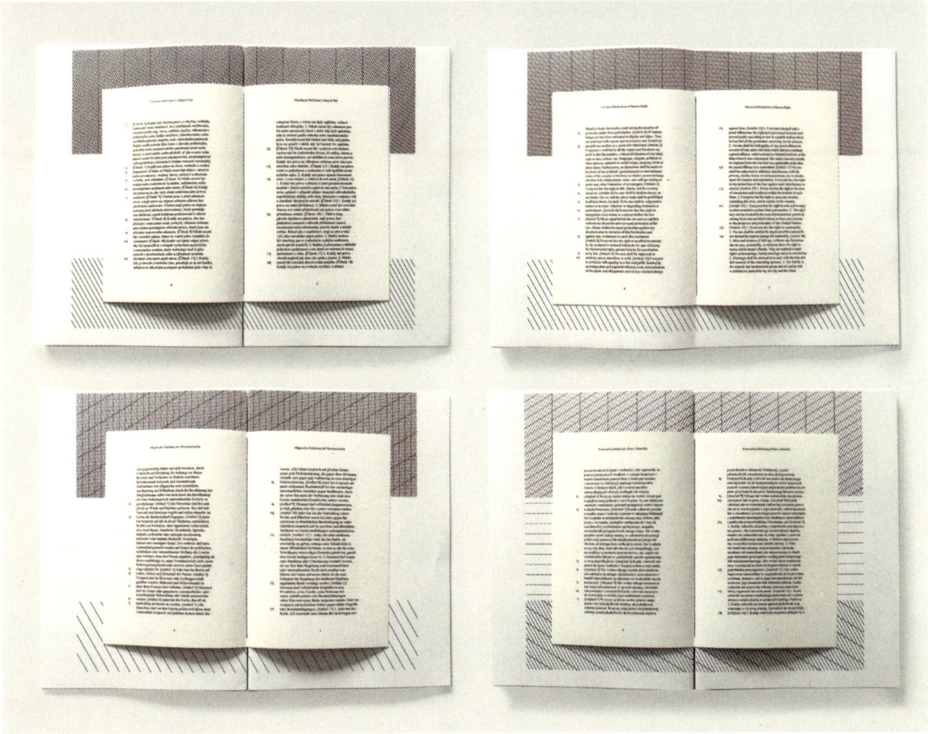

122 Poster
TD. Stefan Guzy, Björn Wiede
CL. Arturo Herrera
PT. Gräbenbach

123 Poster, Cassette tape cover
TD. AD. D. P. Yang Hai
D. Wang Ying
CL. ill lega! Press
PT. Bw Gradual, Noto Sans S Chinese

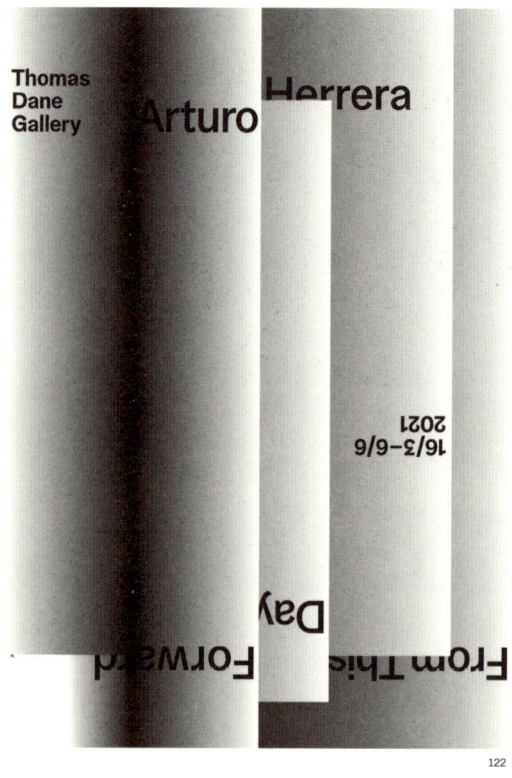

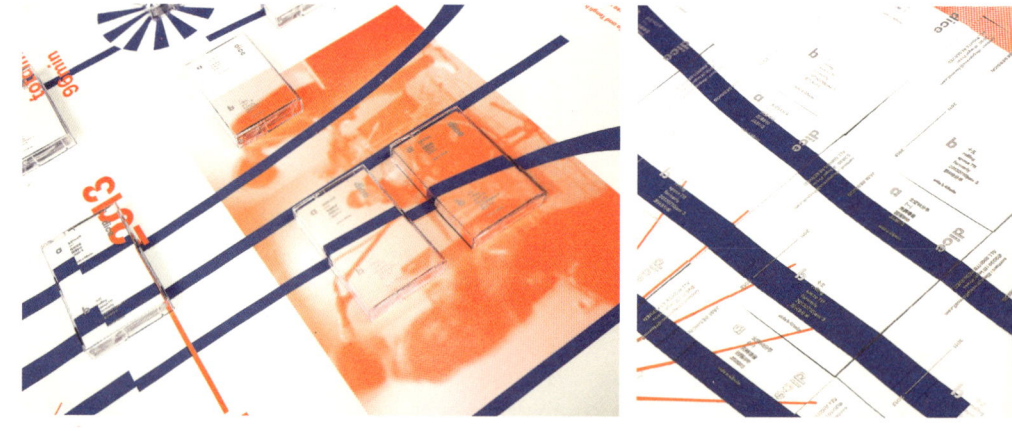

Type design
TD. Xu Han, Huasha Chen, Yin Qiu
CL. China Academy of Art
PT. FZ GuoMeiJinDao Ti

方正国美进道体

天地玄黄宇宙洪荒日月盈昃辰宿列张寒来暑往秋收冬藏闰馀成岁律吕

行居健敬

思古之情求新之念彼此生发古典气息时代精神熔铸一炉介绍西洋艺术整理中国艺术

万物聚于笔端
山水化为符号
典先师
圣有采经
沈勤篁光往思渐上手
机劳在作敬修妙
山居以养敬

汉字是记录汉语的视觉符号也是最日常的沟通工具和最直观的视觉表达汉字具有鲜明的民族文化特性蕴含着先民的智慧与设计哲学充分反映中国人对自身与外

通奇崛沉雄爽豁晴朗追求

山居以养敬
妙机在修篁
劳作勤上手
沈思渐有光
往圣采经典

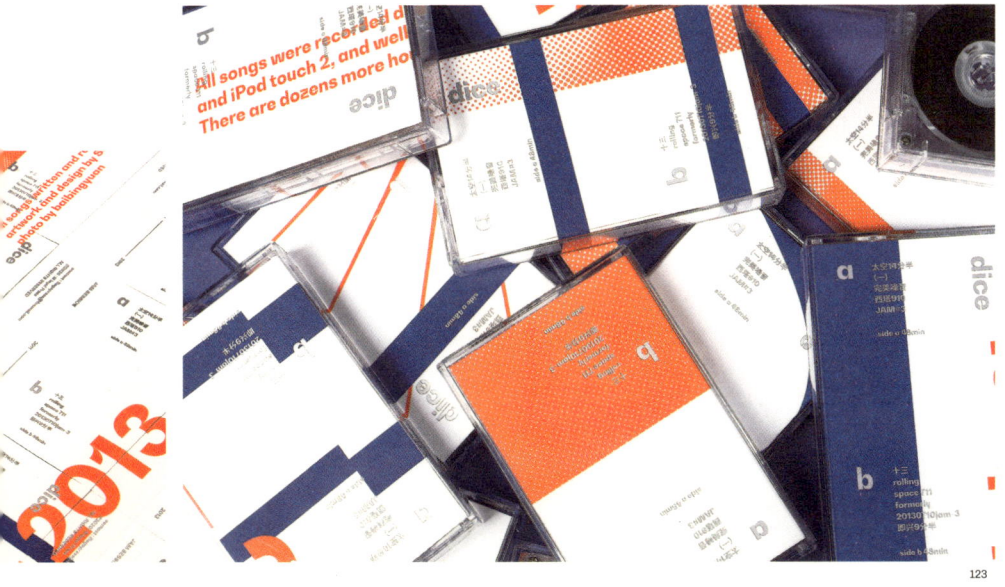

125 Small graphics
TD. 原健三 Kenzo Hara
CL. Non-commercial work

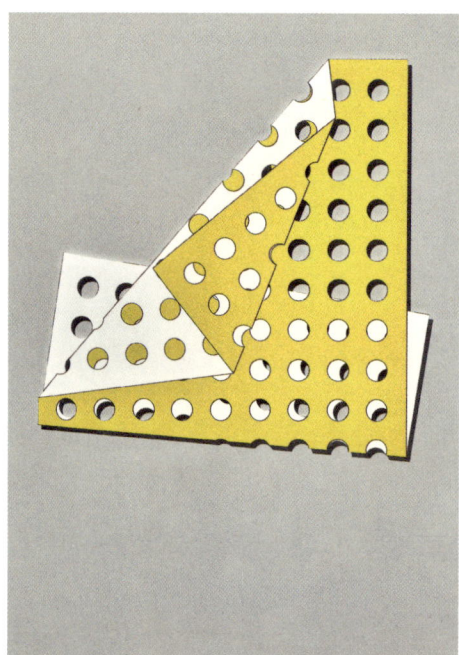
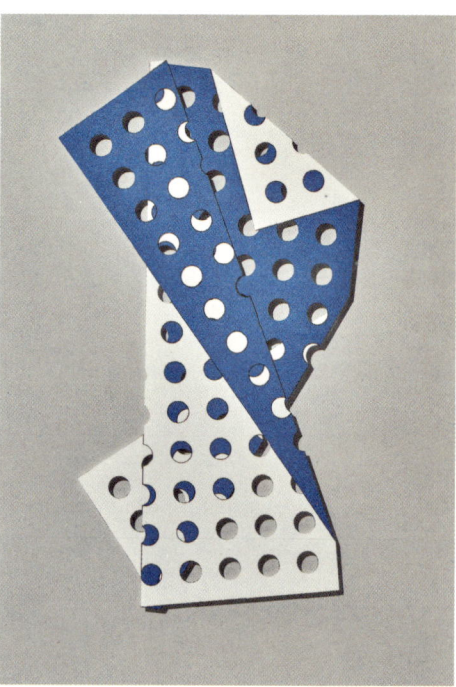
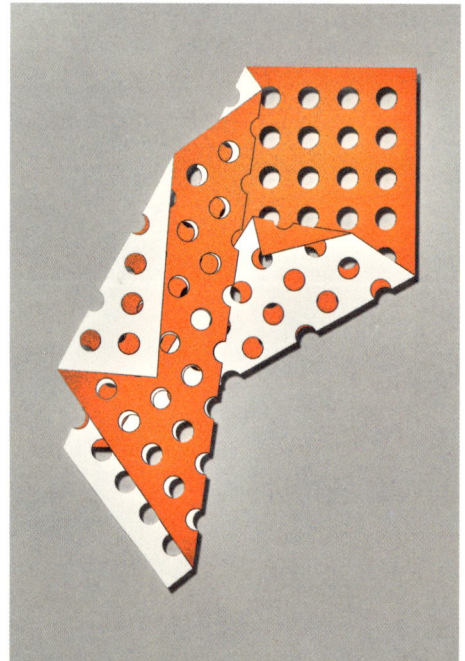
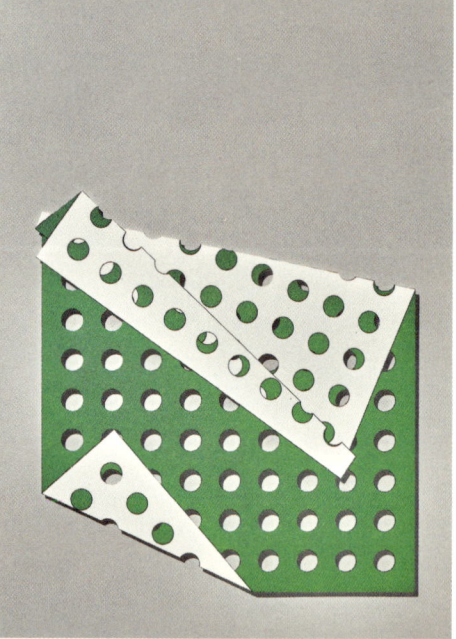

126 Experimental work
TD. 原健三 Kenzo Hara
CL. Non-commercial work

127 Poster
TD. 原健三 Kenzo Hara
CL. Non-commercial work

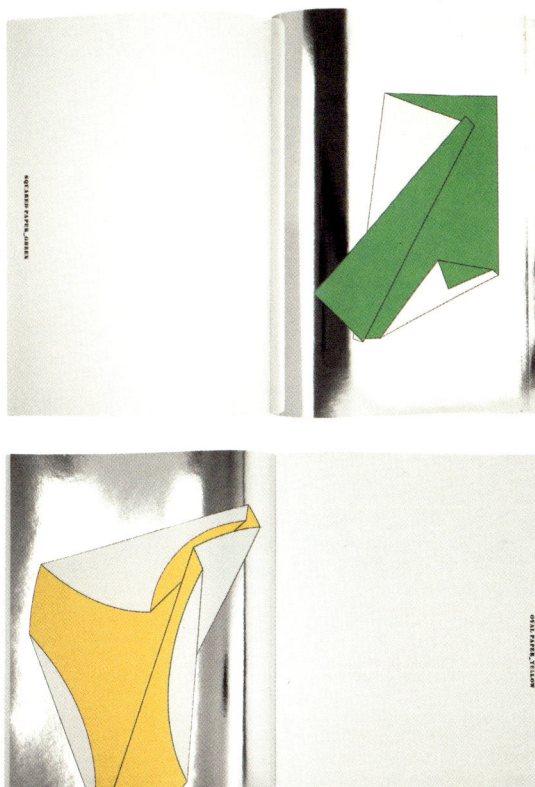

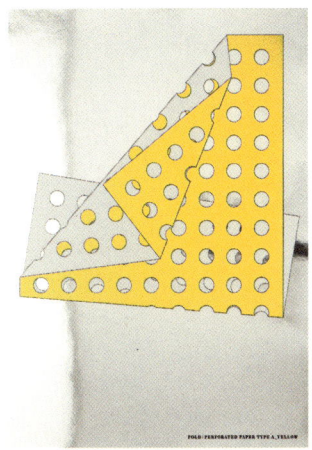 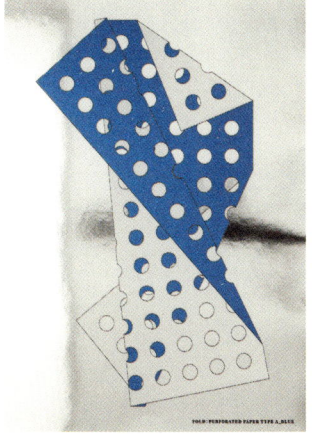 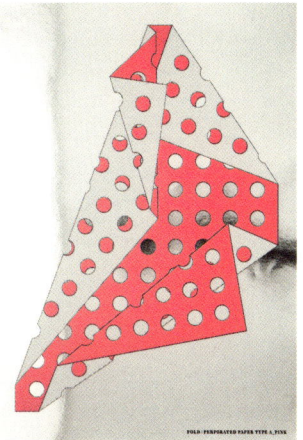

128 Book
AD. D. P. Lye Jia Hao
PT. Poppins, Minion Pro, Objektiv Mk1

129 Building blocks
TD. AD. D. 原田陽奈子 Hinako Harada
CL. Non-commercial work
PT. どうぶつむ字, Futura

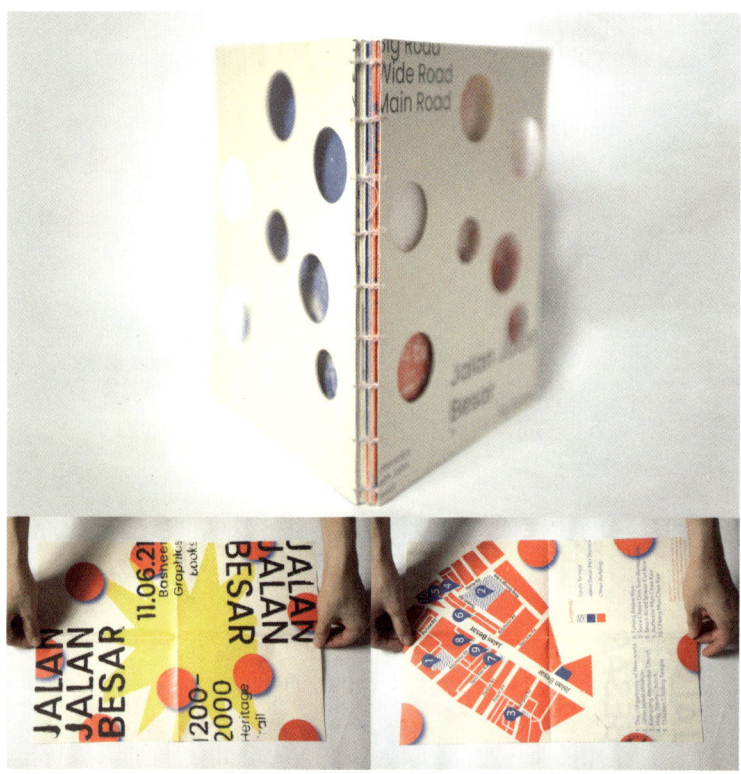

128

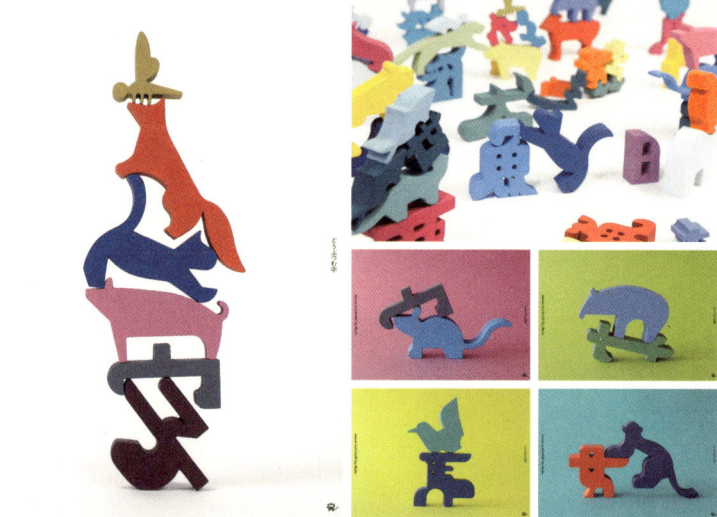

129

130 Book
TD. E. CD. D. DI (publishing). Lars Harmsen
TD. E. CD. D. Marian Misiak
PM. AD. Lisa Panitz
RE. Mahmoud Hamdy, Louis Hunt
E. Clara Weinreich
PM. DI (publishing). Julia Kahl
PU. Slanted Publishers
PT. Di Grotesk, Threedotstype

131 Book
TD. AD. E (V.i.S.d.P.). Lars Harmsen
E. PRR. D. Julia Kahl
E (assistant). D. Lara Zettl
PRR. Jack Dignam
D. Nina Steimel, Clara Weinreich,
D (cover). Crosslucid, Sylwana Zybura, Tomas C. Toth
PU. Slanted Publishers
PT. Apparat Trial, Maison Mono, Suisse Int'l / Neue

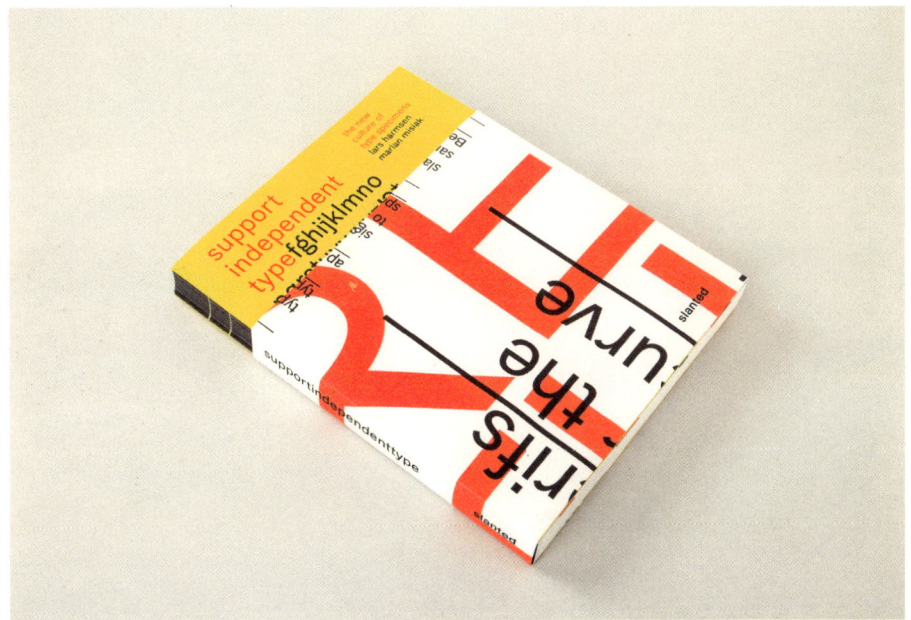

130

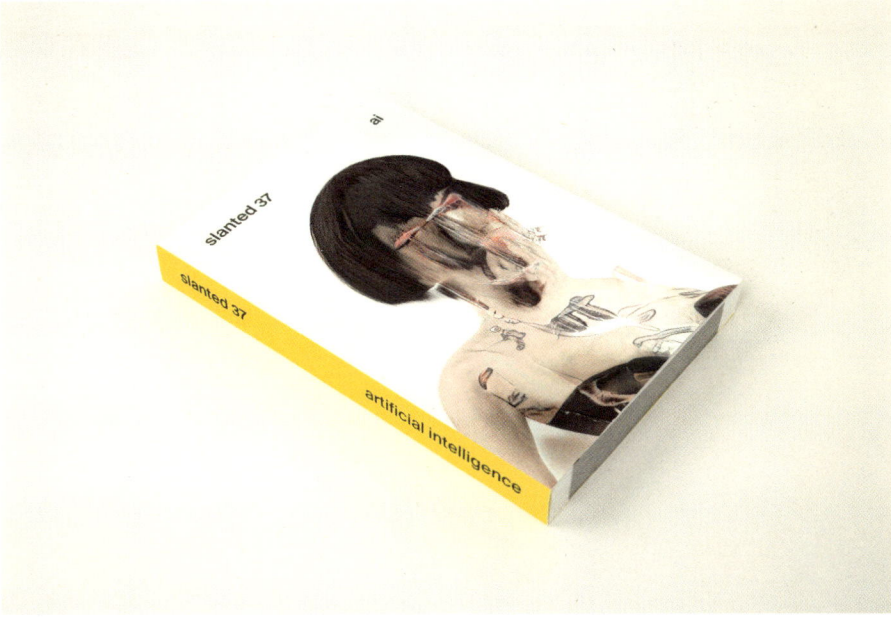

131

Prize Nominee Work

132 Record jacket
TD. AD. D. 服部一成 Kazunari Hattori
P. 大場潤也 Junya Ooba
CL. ビクターエンタテインメント Victor Entertainment Corp.,
（株）JVCケンウッド Jvckenwood Corporation
PT. Futura

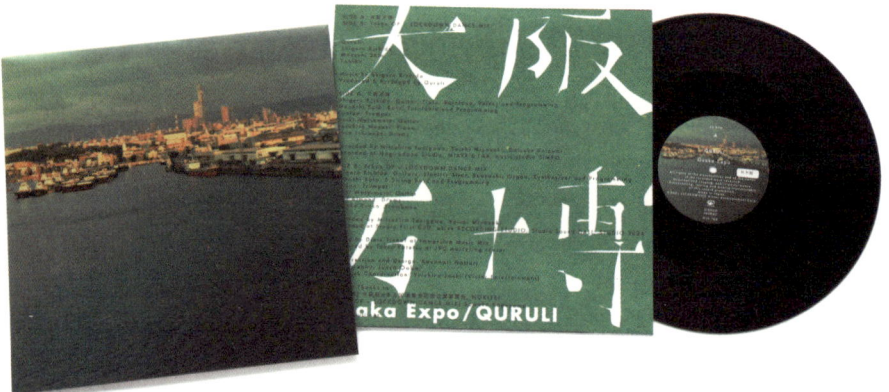

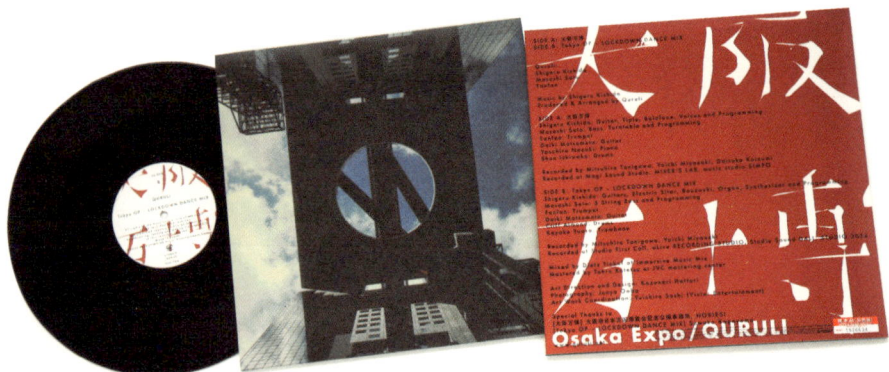

133 Catalogue
TD. AD. D. 服部一成 Kazunari Hattori
I. 泉イネ Ine Izumi
CL. フォーティファイブアールピーエムスタジオ（株）
45rpm studio co., ltd.
PT. 秀英明朝

134 Book
TD. AD. D. 服部一成 Kazunari Hattori
CL. 横尾忠則現代美術館 Yokoo Tadanori Museum of Contemporary Art
PT. 太ゴB101

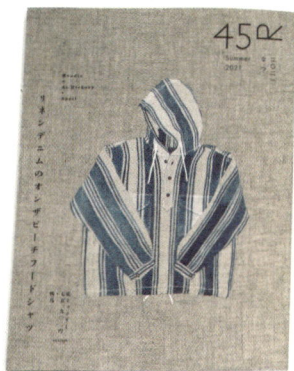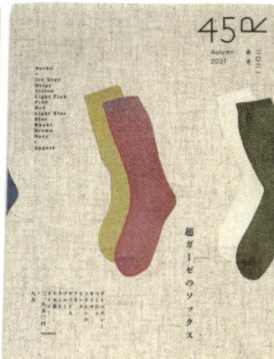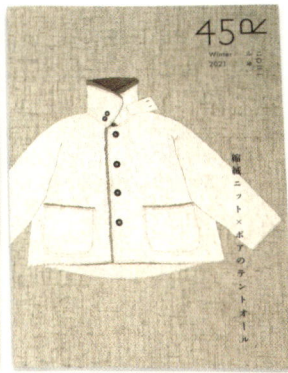

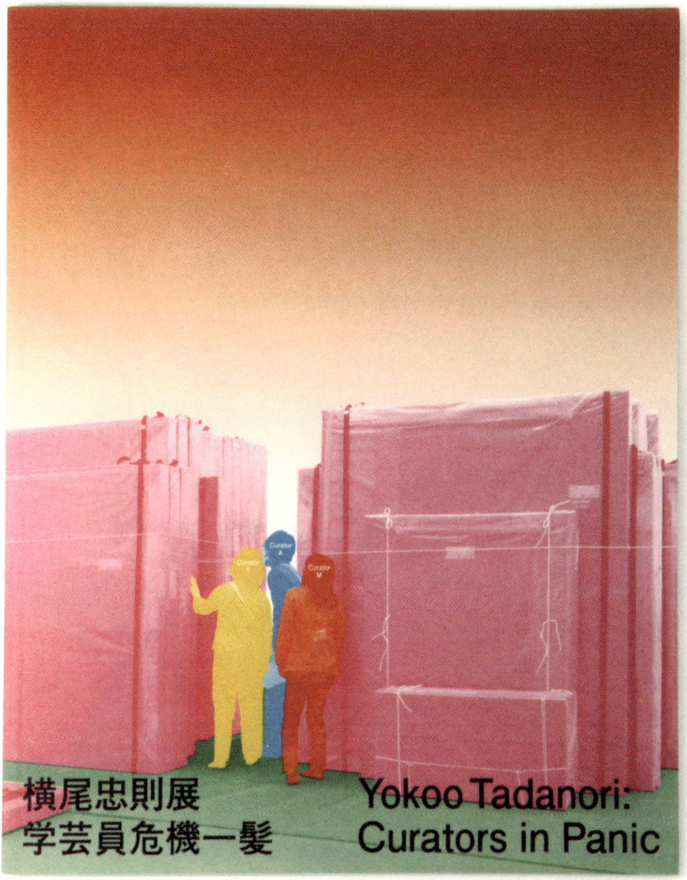

Prize Nominee Work

135 Poster
TD. AD. D. 服部一成 Kazunari Hattori
A. 仲條正義 Masayoshi Nakajo
CL.（株）ADP ADP Company
PT. 太ゴB101

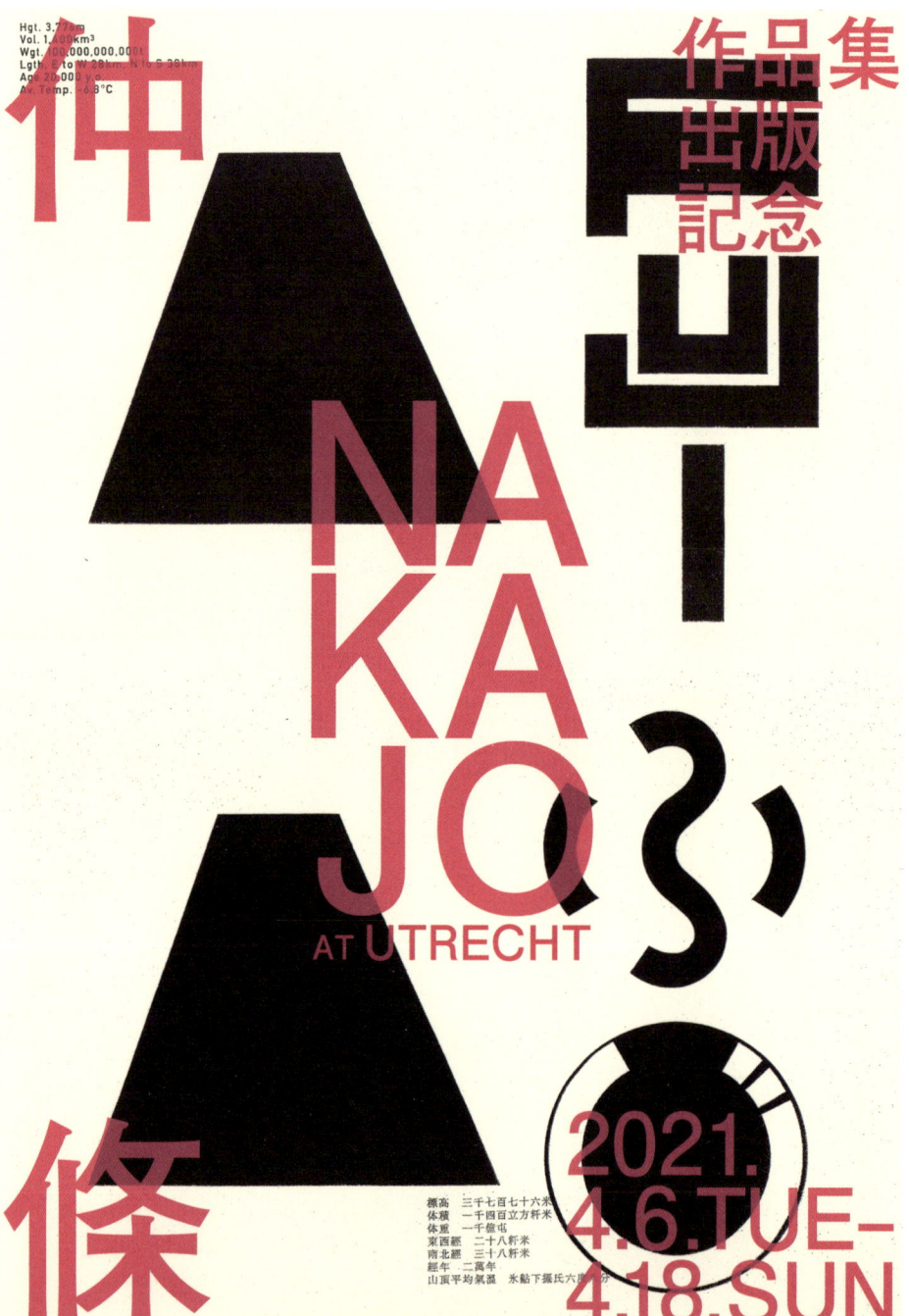

136 Poster

TD. AD. D. 服部一成 Kazunari Hattori
CL.（株）リクルートホールディングス Recruit Holdings Co., Ltd.
PT. School Obrique, Poplar Standard Black, TT Commons

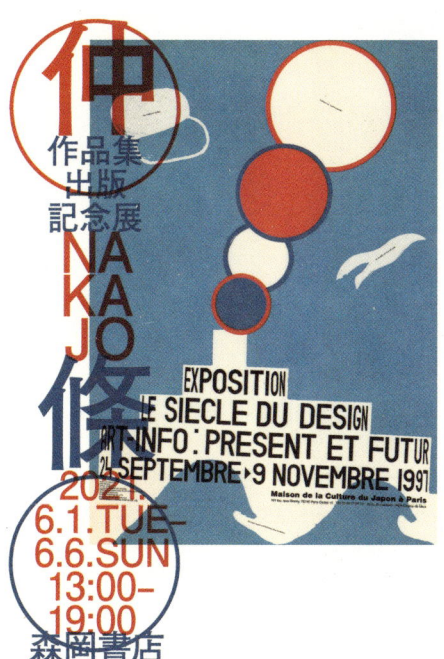
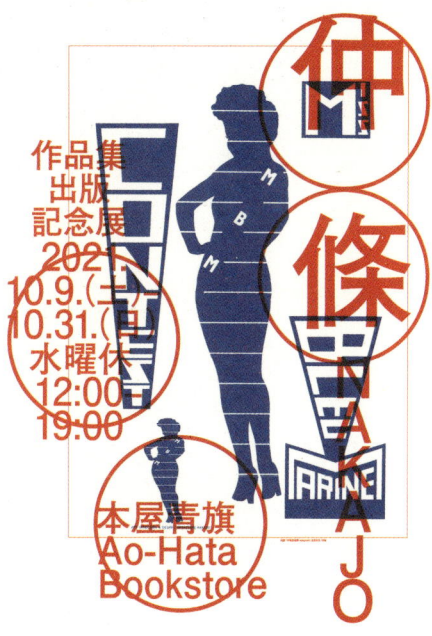
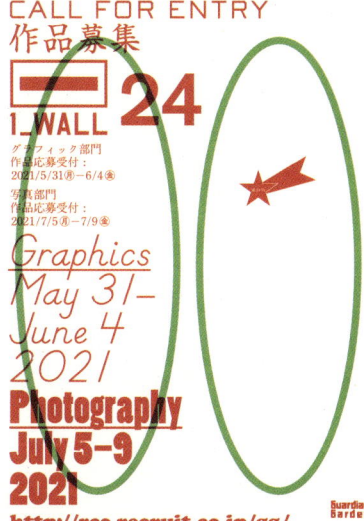

137 Branding
TD. D. Zhihua He
CL. Fun Pot
PT. Neue Plak Wide SemiBold

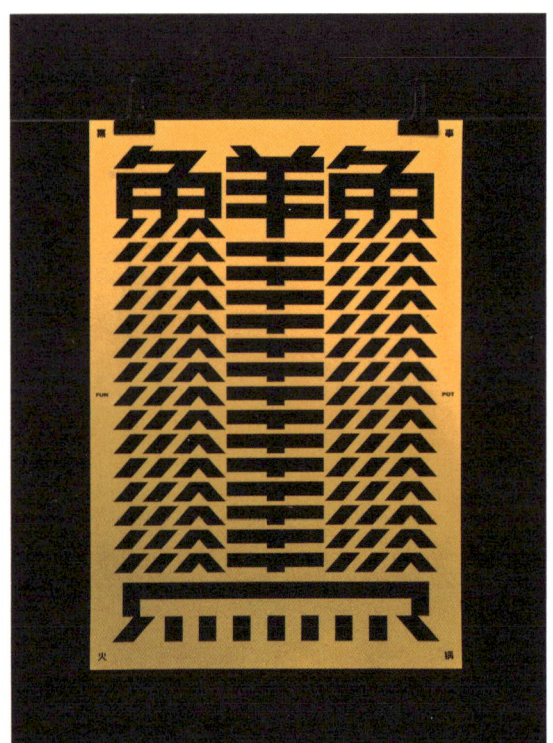

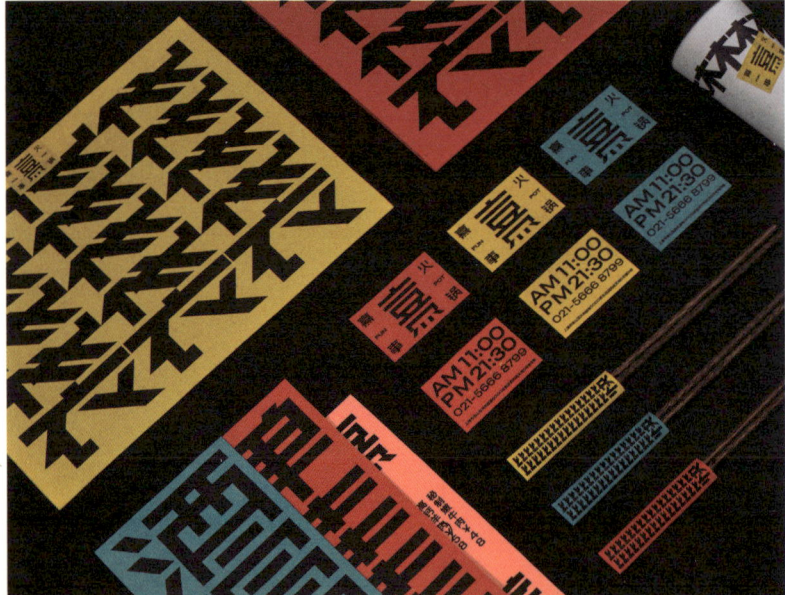

138 Mark & Logotype
TD. Rongkai He
D. Jianing Sui
D (Assistant). Xiyue Zhang
D. P. Hengbin Yang
CL. Center for Balance Architecture, Zhejiang University
PT. Suisse Int'l, Noto Sans S Chinese

139 Book
TD. Fons Hickmann, Fons Hickmann M23
AD. Bjoern Wolf
CT. Anika Neubauer, Gabriele Kiefer
CL. Technische Universität Braunschweig
PT. VAG Rounded

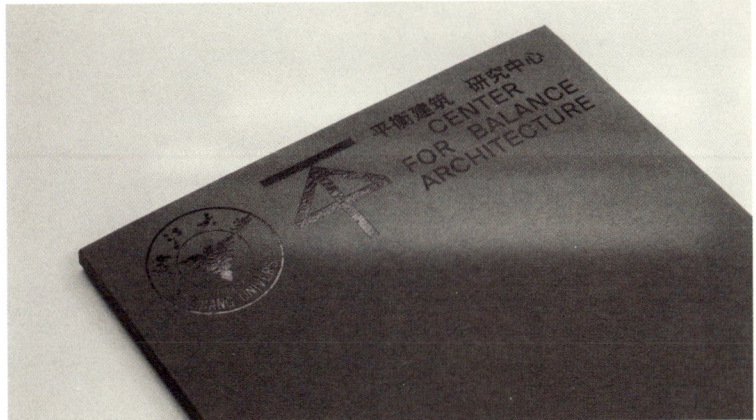

138

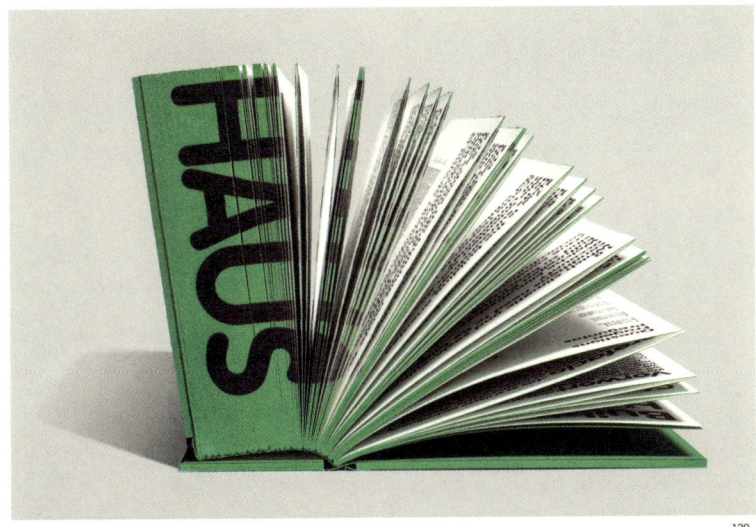

139

140 Poster
TD. AD. Fons Hickmann, Fons Hickmann M23
CL. Cedomir Kostovic, Iwona Rypesc-Kostovic
PT. Custom-made for the project

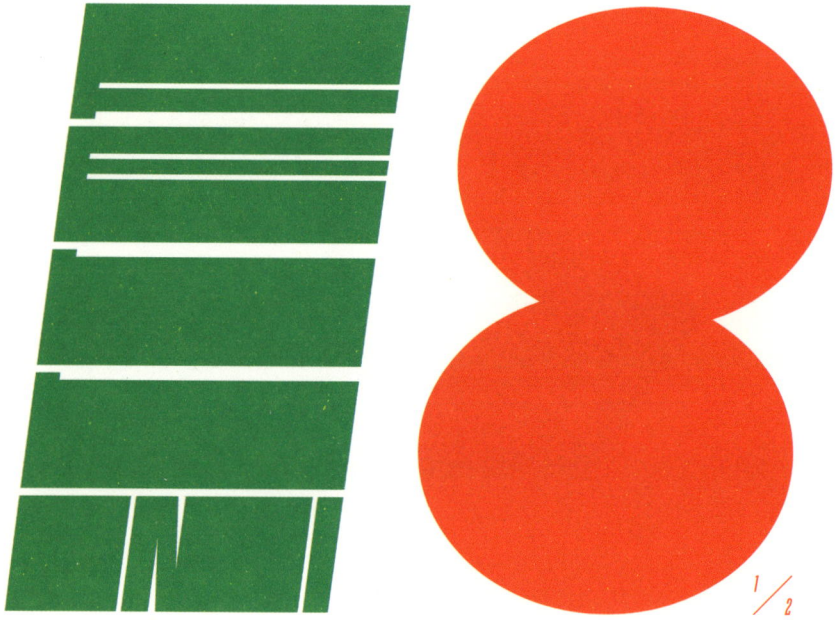

141 Packaging, Wrapping cloth
TD. AD. I. 引地摩里子 Mariko Hikichi
CD. 葛西薫 Kaoru Kasai
CL.（株）虎屋 Toraya Confectionery Co., Ltd.
PT. 本明朝-M新小がな, Adobe Garamond, RA花蓮華

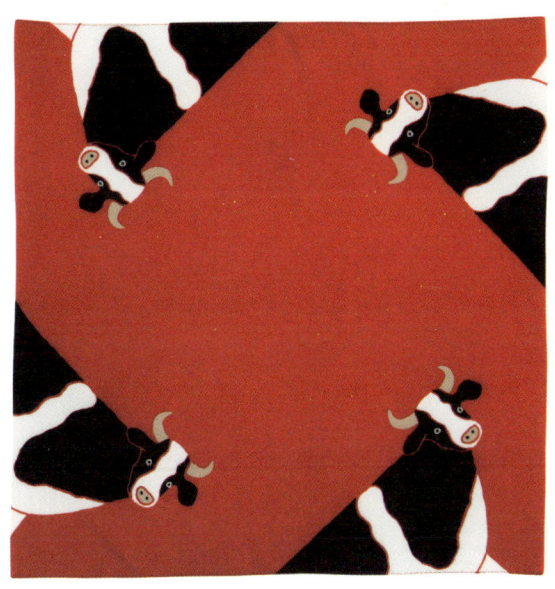

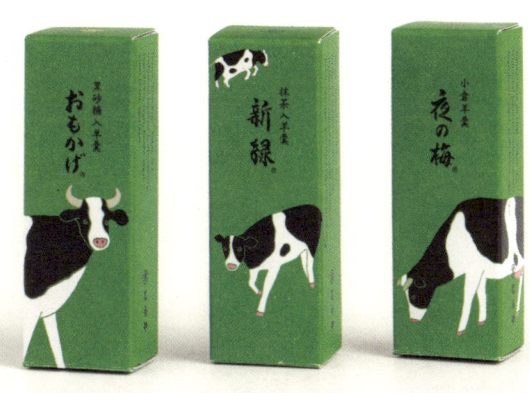

Prize Nominee Work

142 Advertising campaign
TD. AD. Tom Hingston
D. 3DM. AN. Hingston Studio
CL. Victoria & Albert Museum
PT. Custom-made for the project, Coign 47 & 45, Rama Gothic

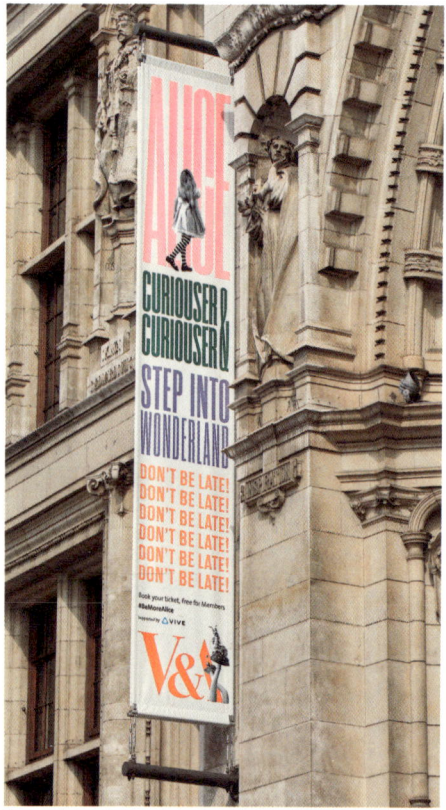
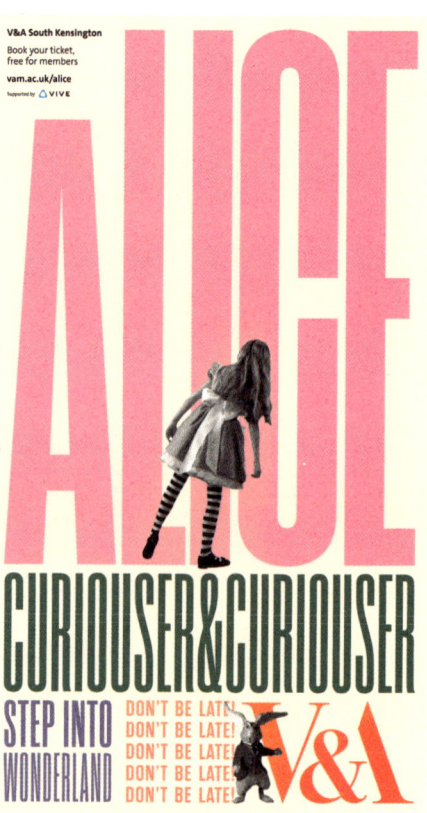
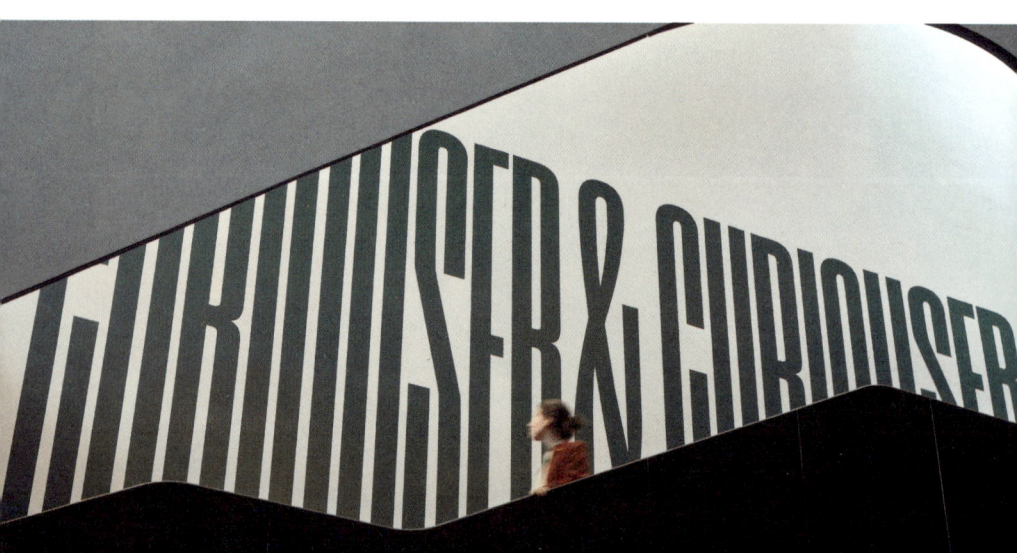

143 Museum VI
TD. Fons Hickmann, Fons Hickmann M23
AD. Bjoern Wolf
CL. Museum für Kunst und Gewerbe Hamburg
PT. Scto Grotesk

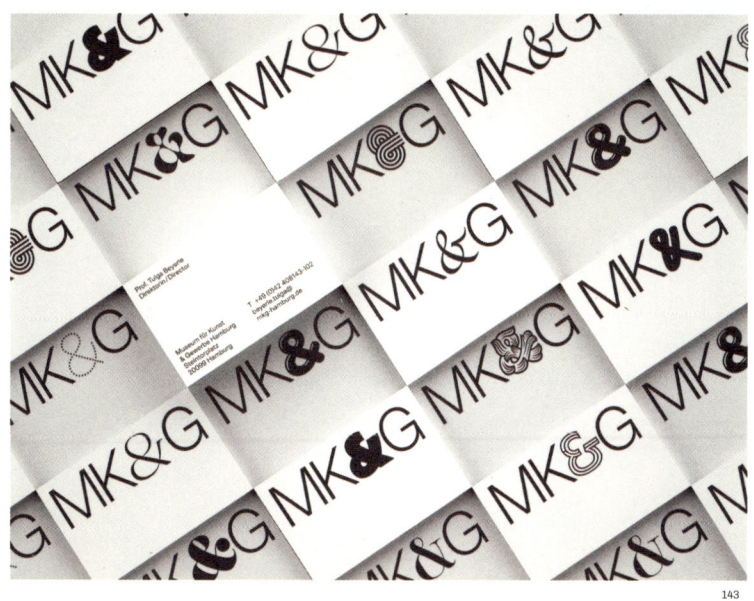

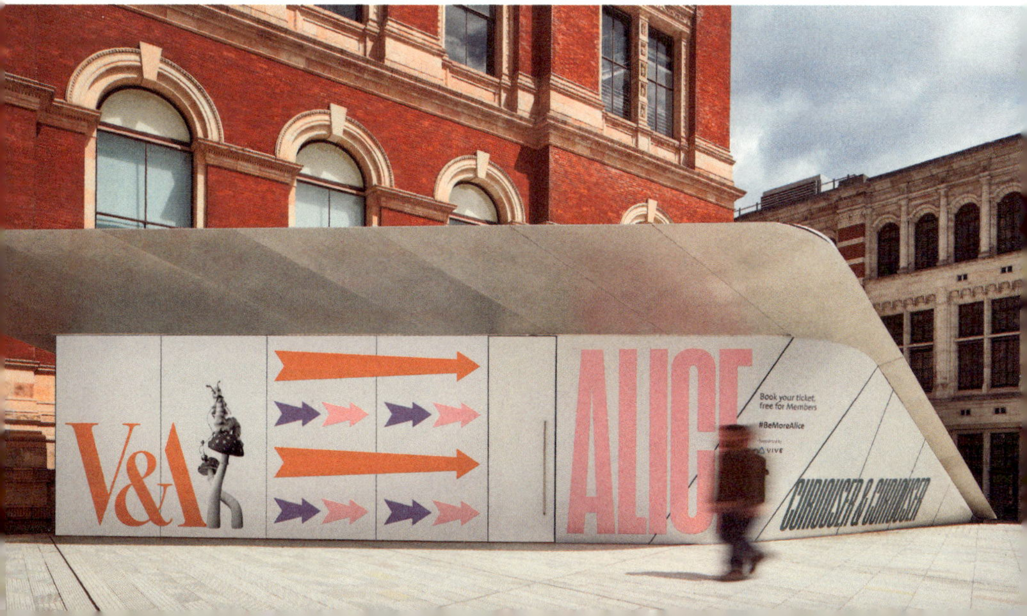

144 Book
TD. AD. D. 平野篤史 Atsushi Hirano
D. 金晃平 Kohei Kim
CL. 東京国立近代美術館 The National Museum of Modern Art, Tokyo
PT. Custom-made for the project, 筑紫A丸ゴシック

145 Exhibition design
TD. AD. D. 平野篤史 Atsushi Hirano
D. 萱沼大喜 Taiki Kayanuma
SPD. Trafu Architecture Office
CL. 東京国立近代美術館 The National Museum of Modern Art, Tokyo
PT. Custom-made for the project, 筑紫A丸ゴシック

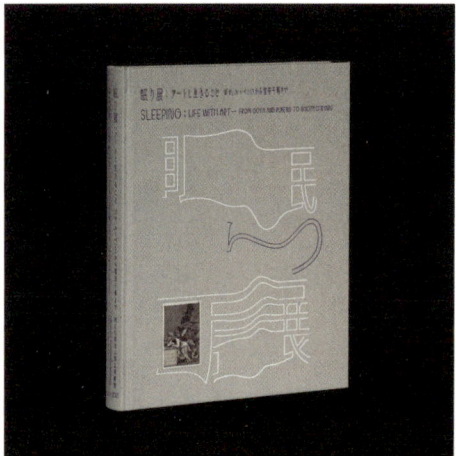
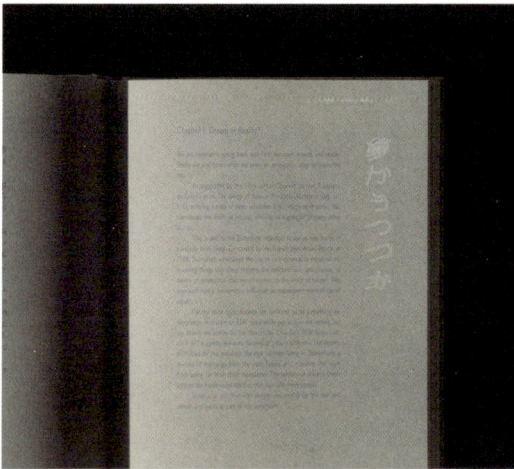

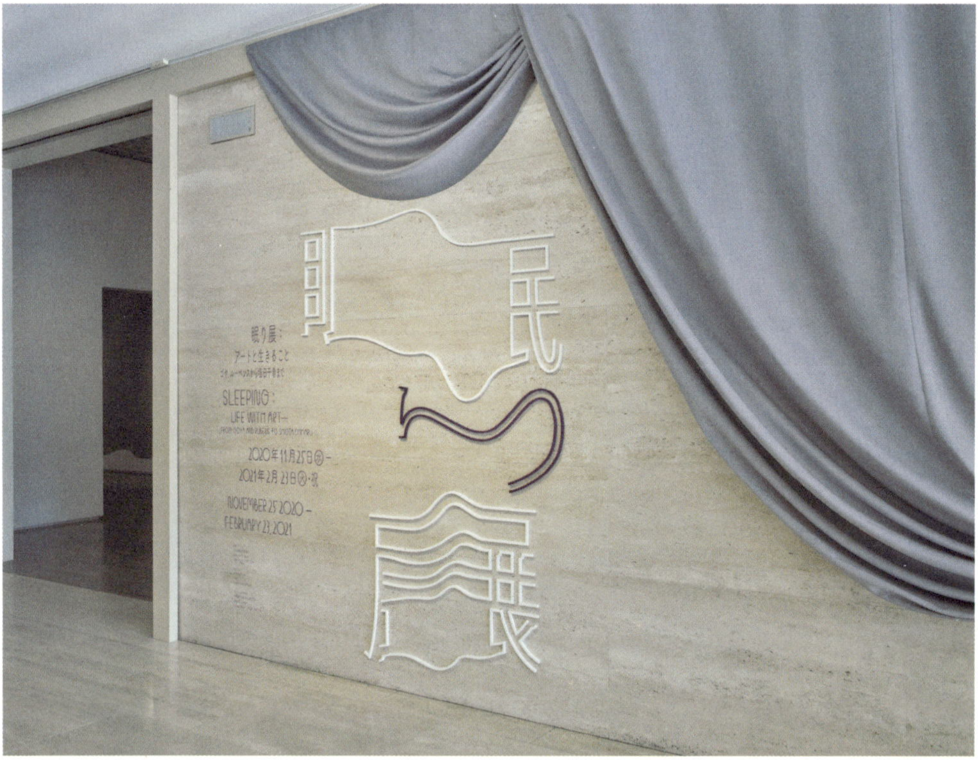

146 Packaging
TD. AD. D. I. 平野篤史 Atsushi Hirano
CL.（株）メリーチョコレートカムパニー Mary Chocolate Co., Ltd.
PT. Custom-made for the project

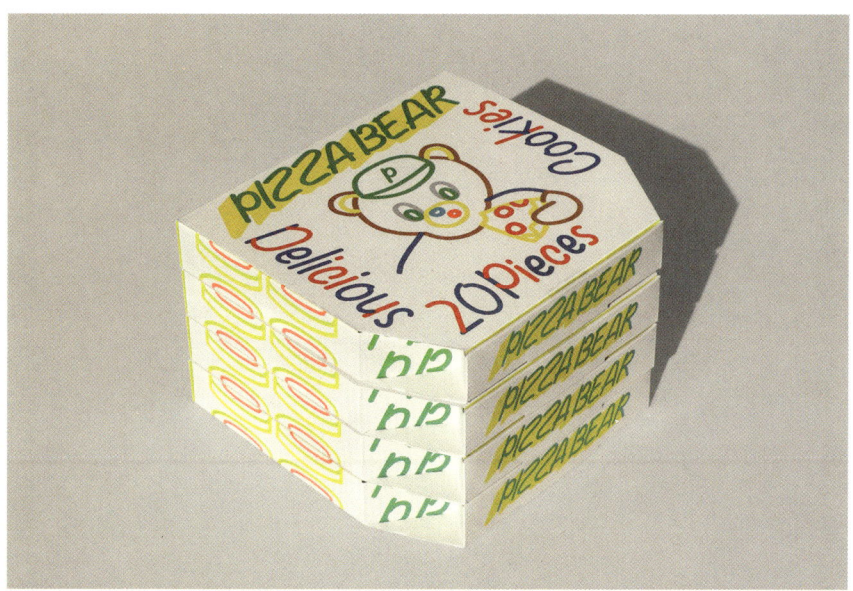

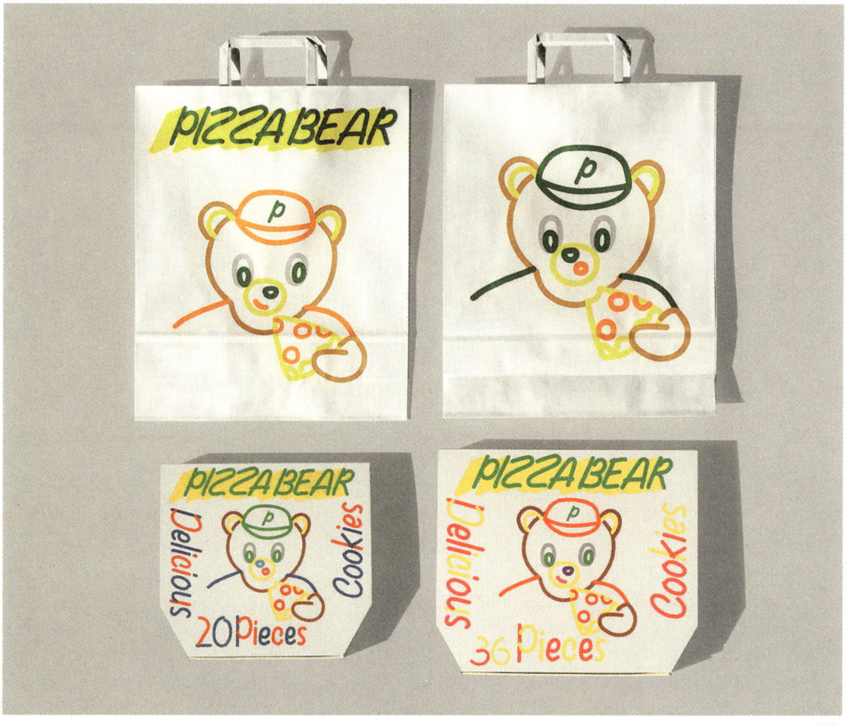

147 Mark & Logo
TD. 平田晴之介 Harunosuke Hirata
CL. bebaragi

148 Poster
TD. AD. Chia-Hsing Ho
T. Yi-Zhi Hu
CL. Taiwan Yueqin Folk Song Association
PT. Custom-made for the project, Ryumin, Tsukushi Old Mincho

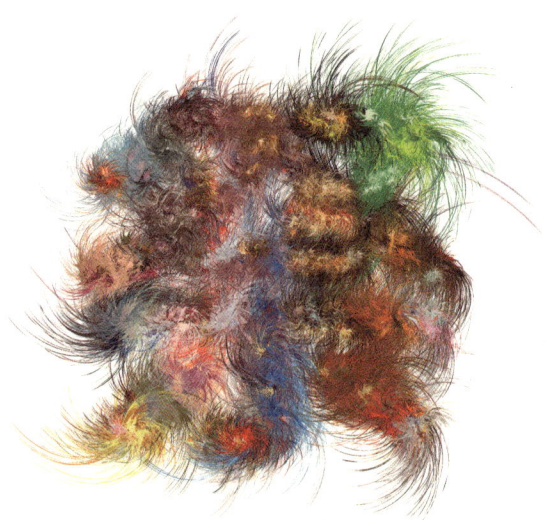

147

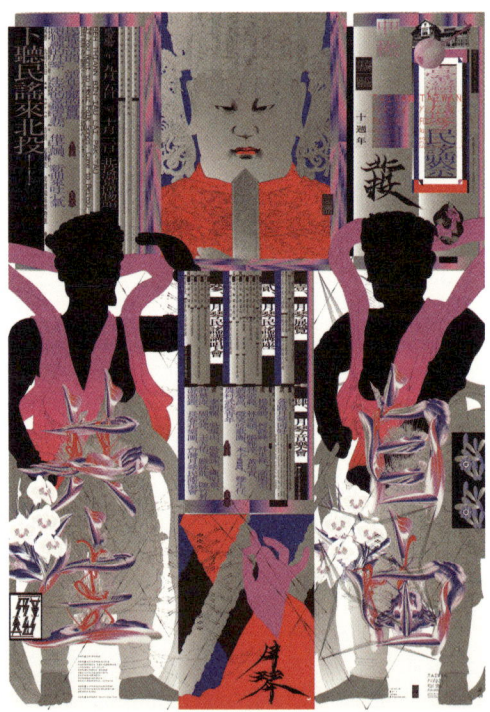

148

149 Packaging
TD. AD. D. Young Ho
CL. A Tea Store
PT. Coppaerplate Gothic, Source Han Serif

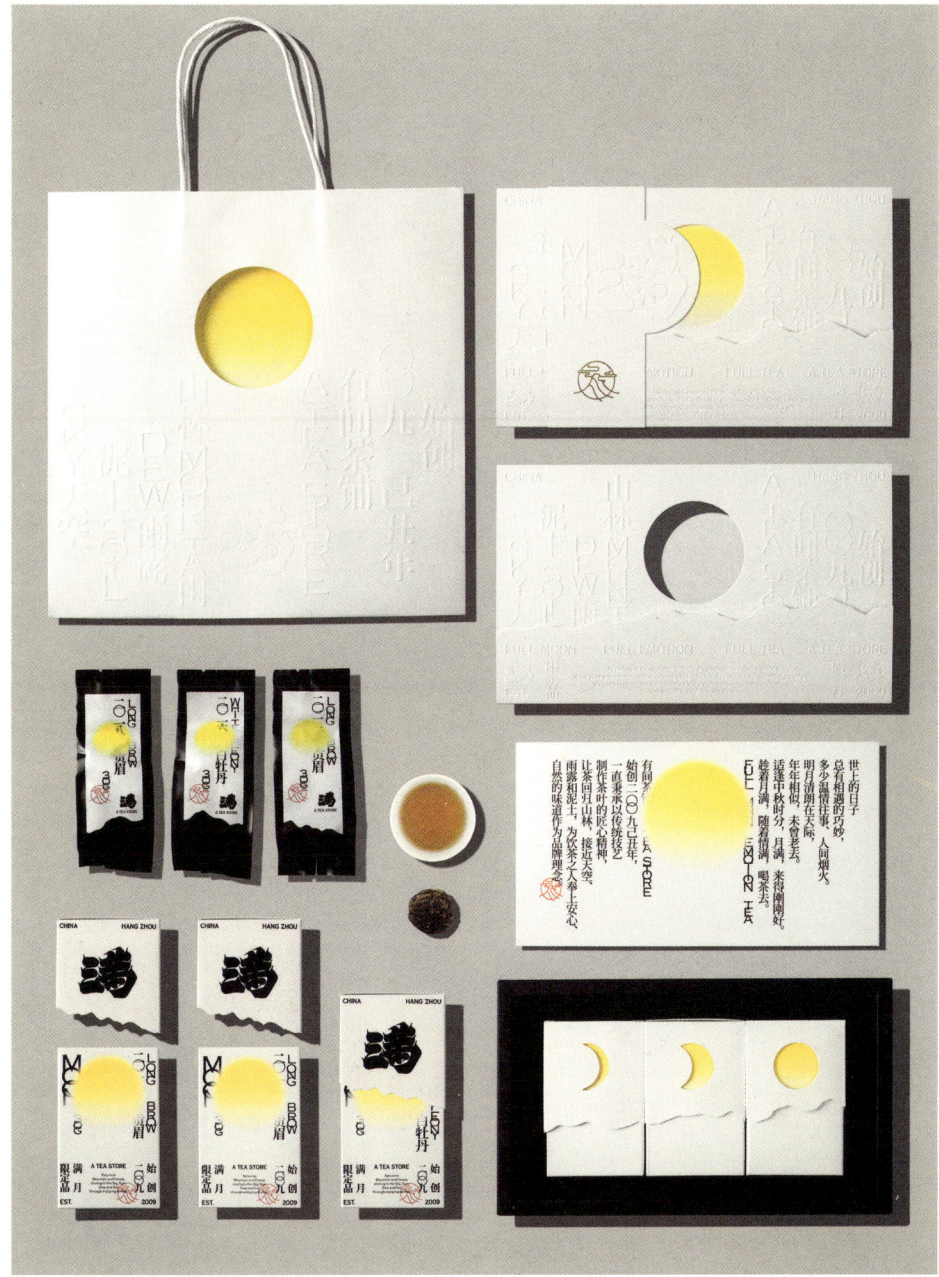

TD. Dominic Hofstede
D. Mucho, AGNSW Creative Studio, Matter of Sorts
CL. Art Gallery of New South Wales
PT. Preston, Syllabus: Custom-made for the project

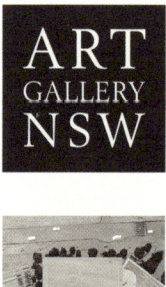

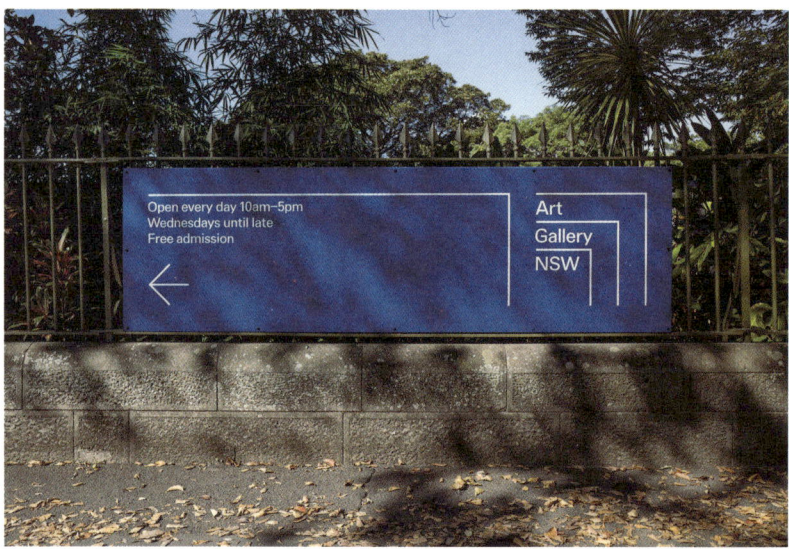

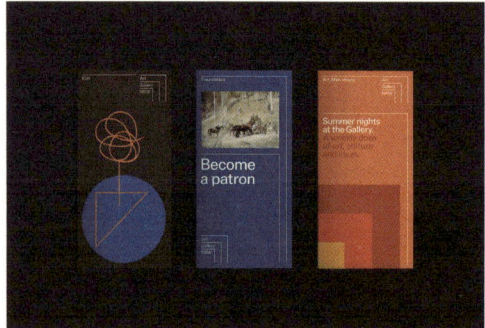

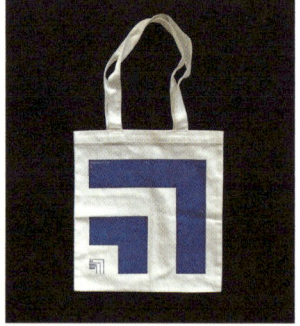

151 Book
TD. AD. Yiu Kwok Ho
CL. Joint Publishing (HK) Co., Ltd.
PT. Plantin MT Pro, Dolly Pro

152 Poster
TD. AD. Wei Hong
CL. Zhuhai Yuzhiming Culture Communication Co., Ltd.

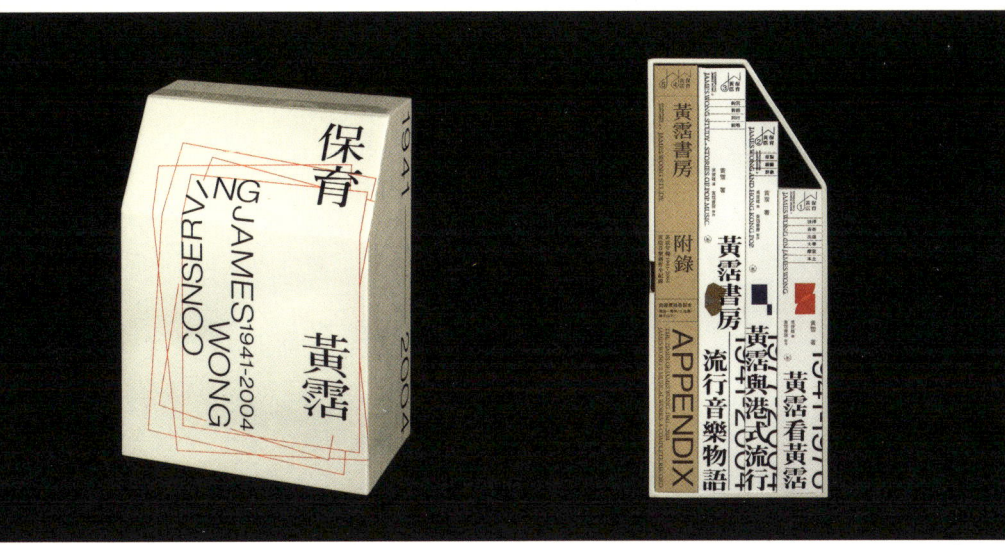

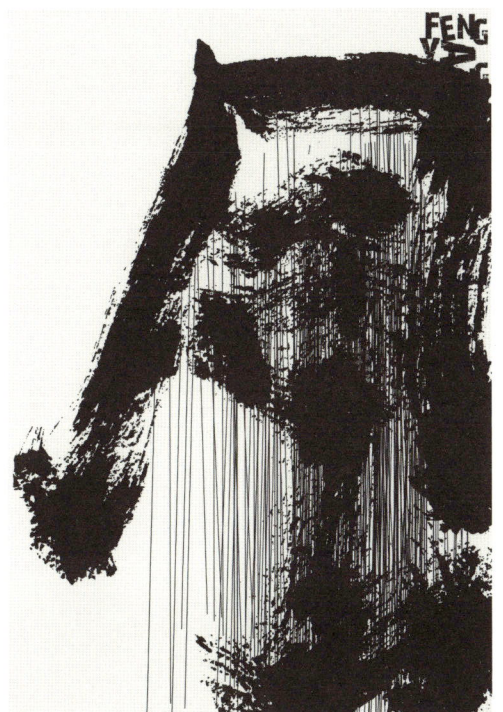

153 Poster
TD. AD. Wei Hong
CL. Day Day Up Design Consultancy

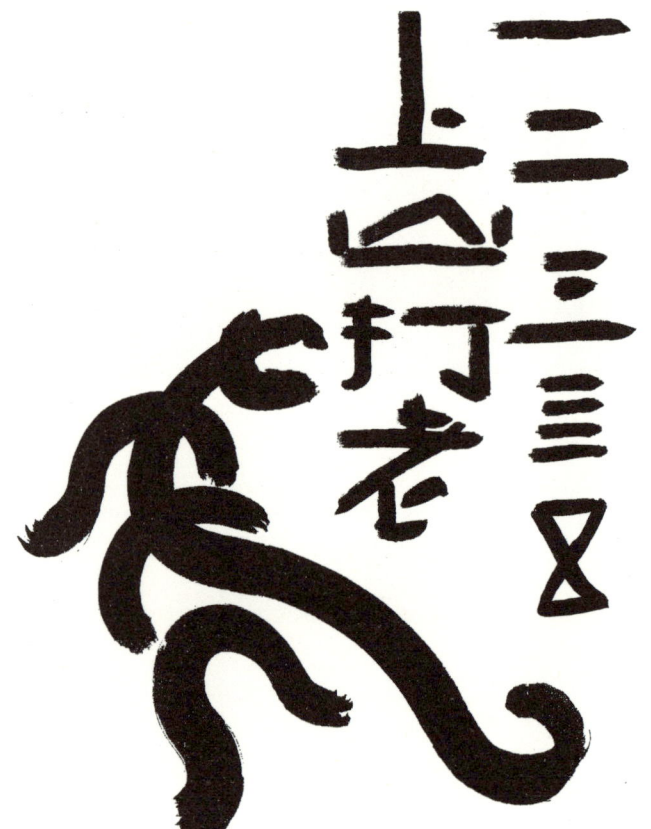
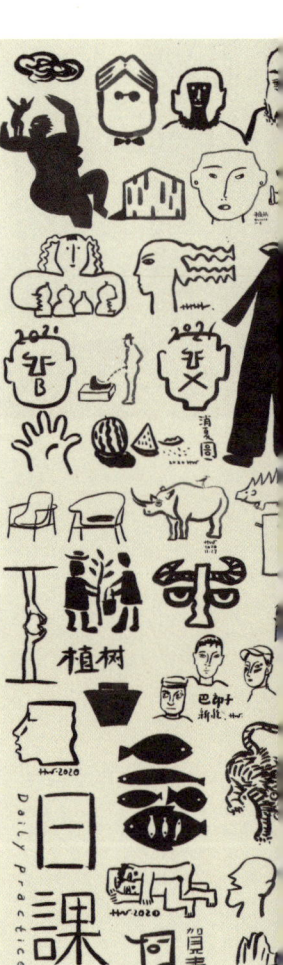

154 Poster
TD. AD. Wei Hong
CL. Day Day Up Design Consultancy

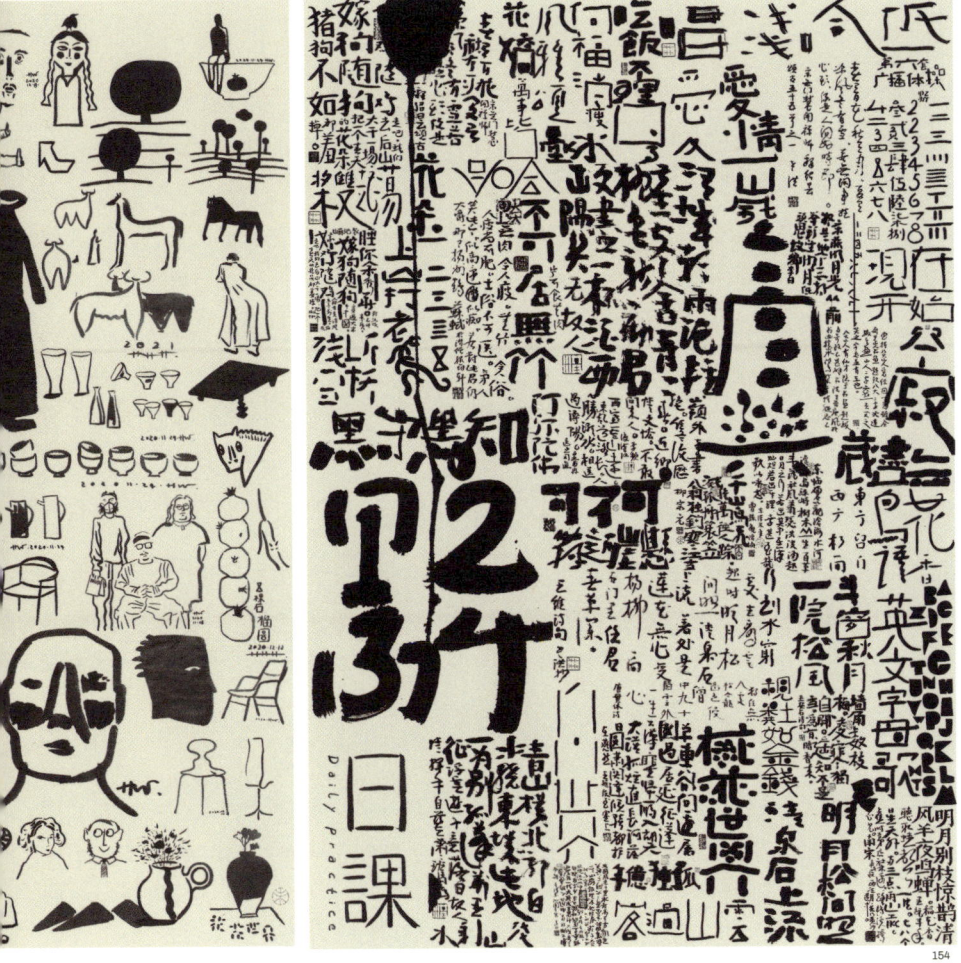

155 Poster
TD. AD. Wei Hong
CL. Zhuhai Ceramic Art Cultural and Creative Industries Ltd.

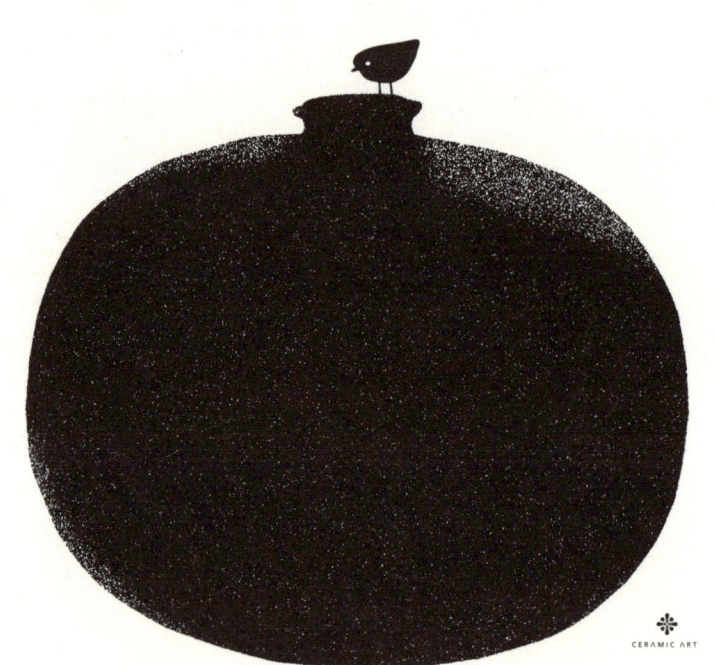

156 Poster
TD. AD. Wei Hong
CL. Day Day Up Design Consultancy

157 Signage
TD. Ying Hou
D. Wang Anan, Zhao Chi, Wang Xingyuan, Wang Xu, Li Zhuo
CL. Jingdezhen Imperial Kiln Museum
PT. Yi Chuan Hei Shui

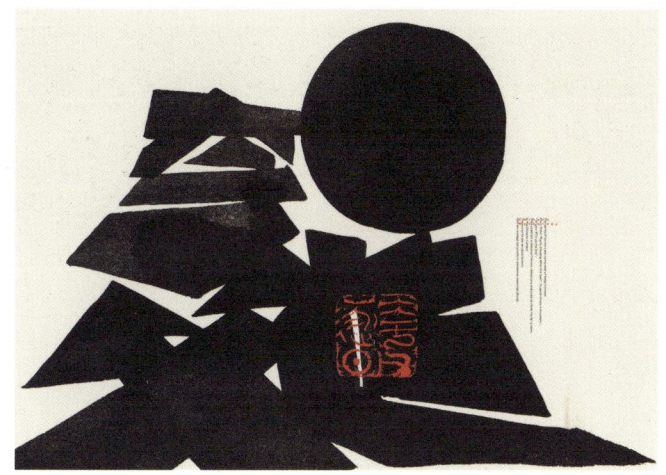

景德镇御窑博物馆↑
主入口♦卸货会议室
展厅入口茶←修复部
办公入口咖啡展陈部
多功能厅遗址藏品部
报告厅→展厅保安部
户外剧场礼品讲解部
交流展厅存衣办公区

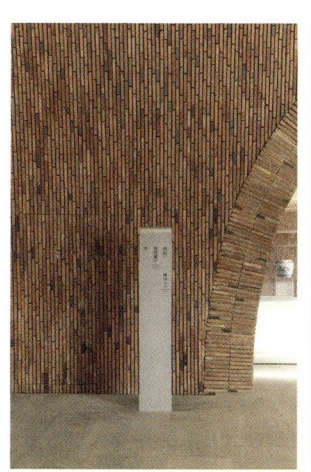
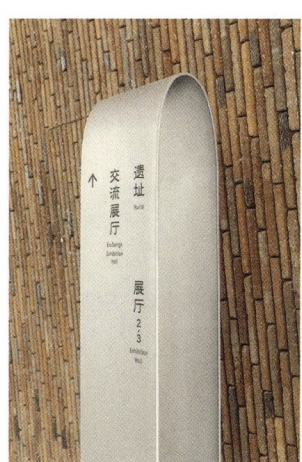
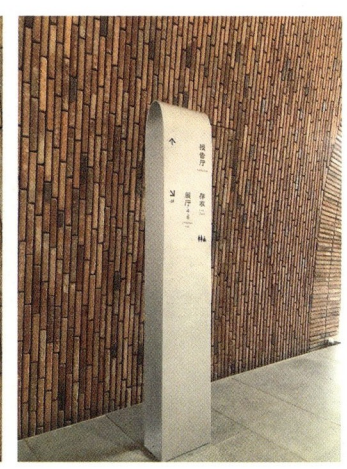

158 Album jacket
TD. AD. D. Hu Zhenchao
CL. Modern Sky
PT. Custom-made for the project, He Sijing

159 Book
TD. D. Yu-Tzu Huang
CL. Kuang-Yi Ku
PT. Custom-made for the project, Neue Machina, Noto Sans TC

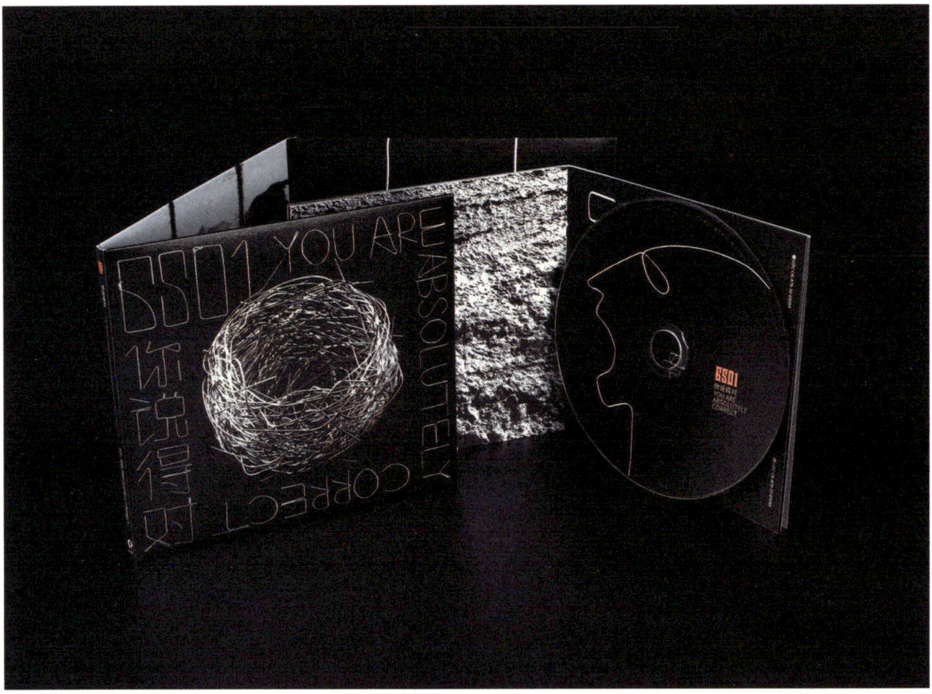

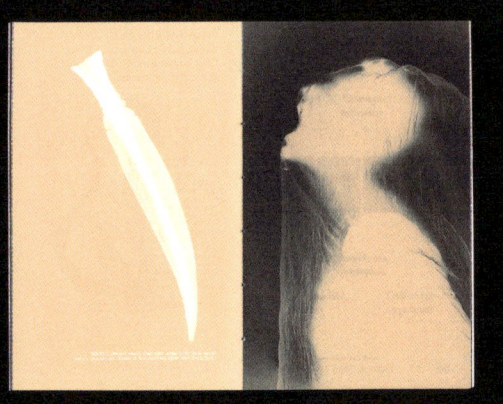

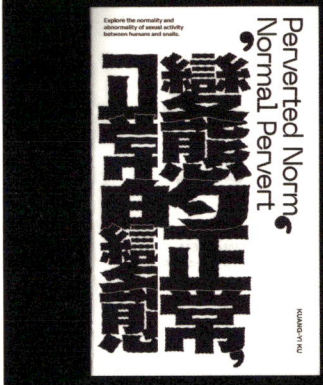

Prize Nominee Work

160 Book
TD. Hubertus Design
AD. Jonas Voegeli
D. Kerstin Landis, Lea Fischlin, Felix Plate, Jonas Voegeli
CL. Collegium Helveticum
PT. Monument Grotesque, ABC Dinamo

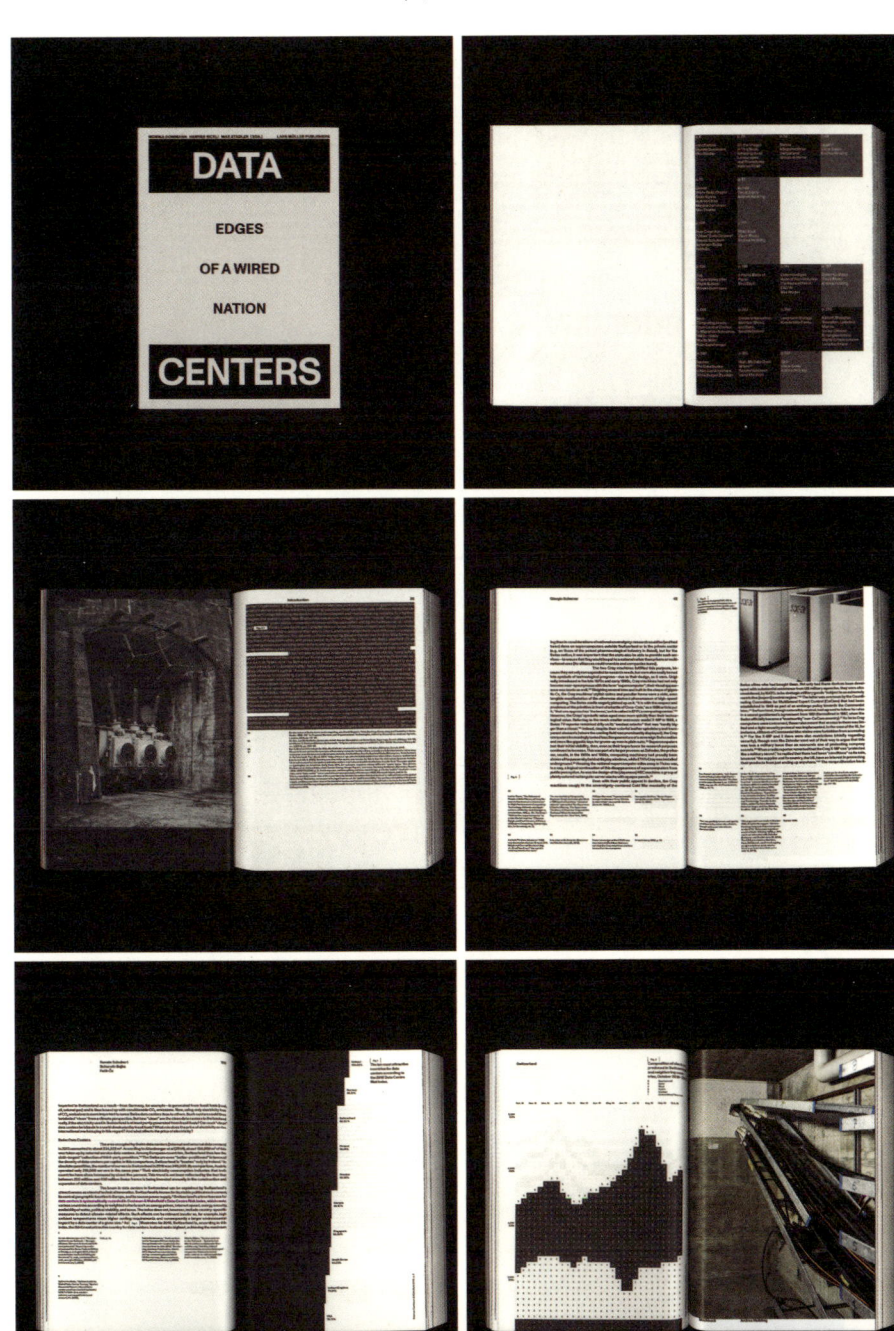

Prize Nominee Work

161 Book
TD. Hubertus Design
AD. Jonas Voegeli
D. Lea Fischlin, Kerstin Landis, Matthias Michel
P. Matthieu Gafsou
CL. Swisstypefaces
PT. Euclid

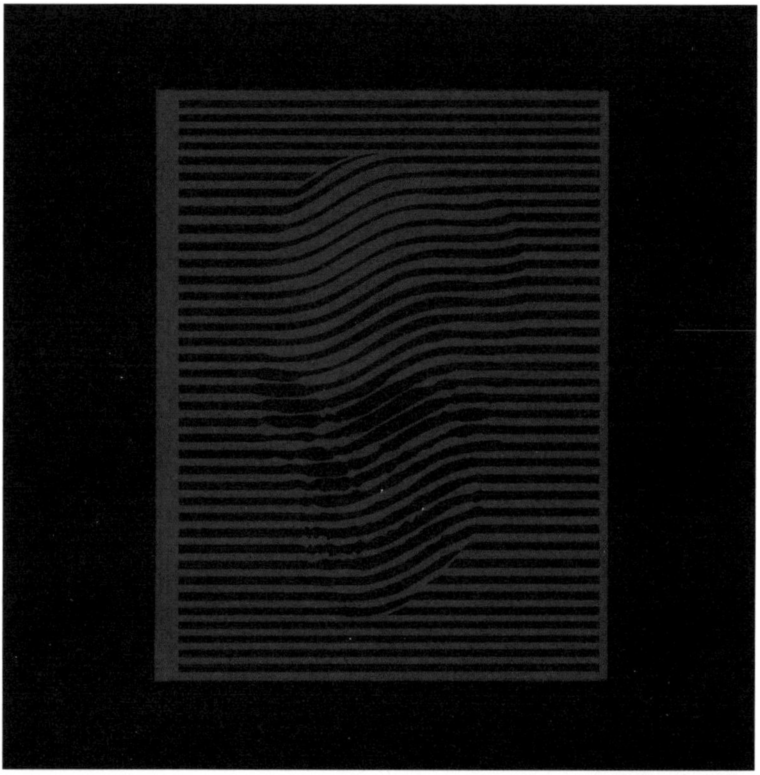

152

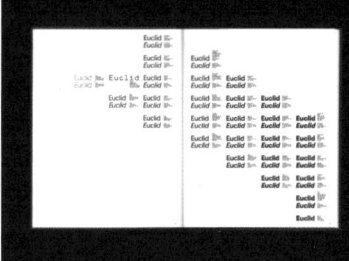
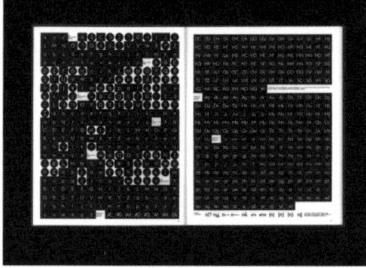
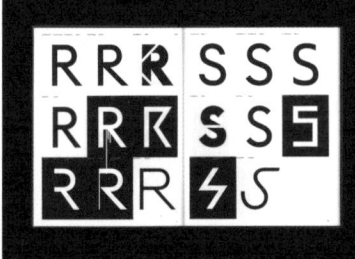
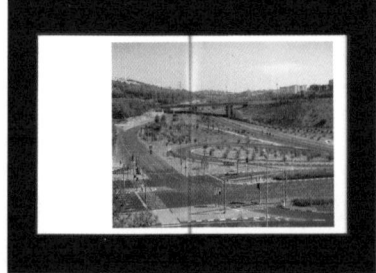

Prize Nominee Work

162 Logotype, Font
TD. Hubertus Design
AD. Jonas Voegeli
D. Kerstin Landis, Lea Fischlin, Felix Plate, Valentin Kaiser, Jonas Voegeli
CL. MAH Musee d'Art et d'Histoire Geneva
PT. Custom Type – MAH-Sans by Hubertus and Scott Vander Zee

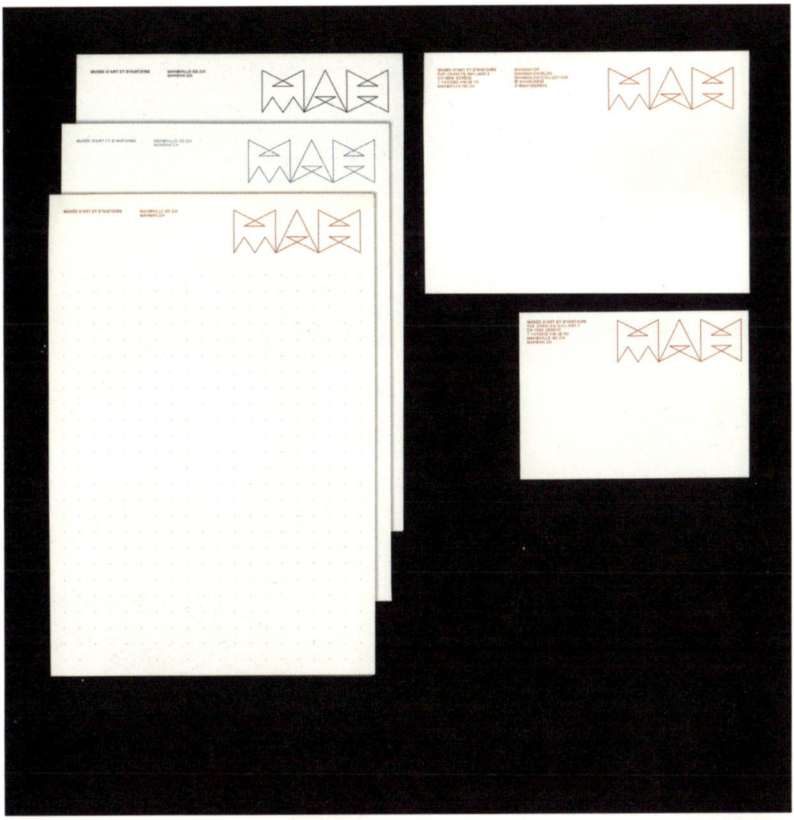

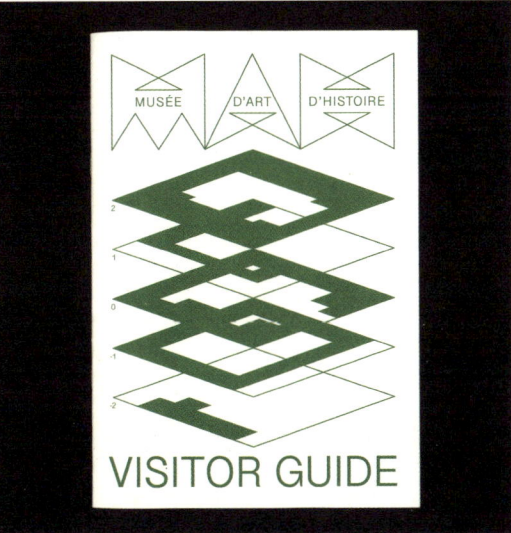
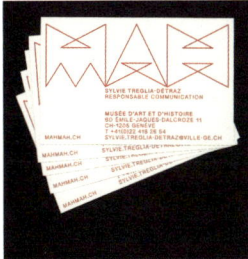
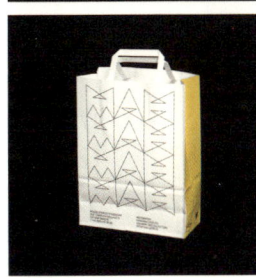

163 BI
TD. Jody Hudson-Powell, Luke Powell
D. Margherita Papini
T. Luke Prowse, NaN
PM. Ceri Stock
MD. Luis Gutiérrez
CL. Frieze. David Lane - Frieze Art Director
PT. Frieze, Sina Nova

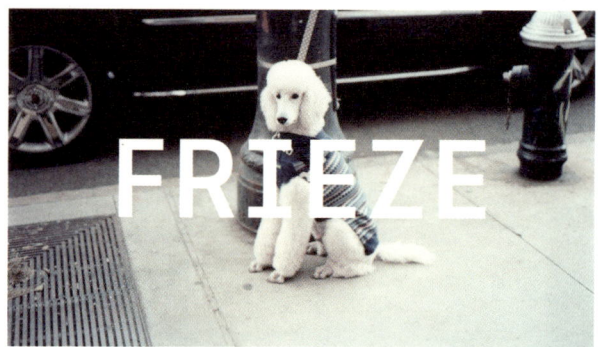
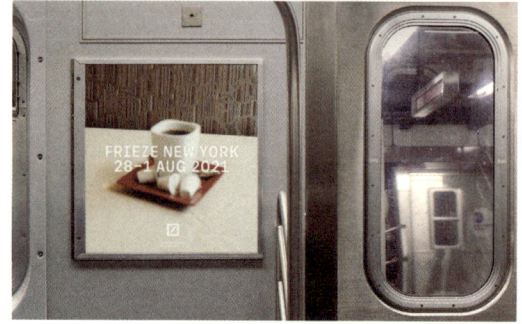
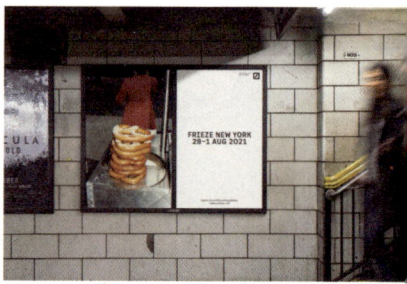
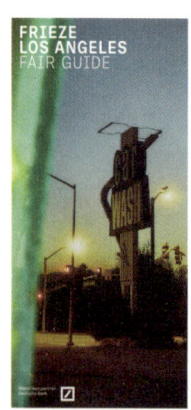
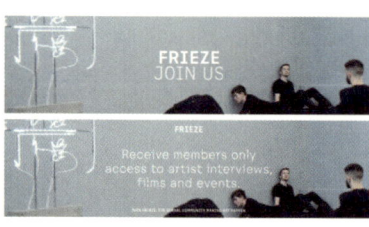
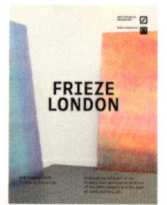
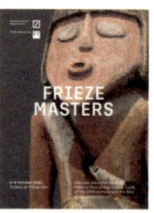
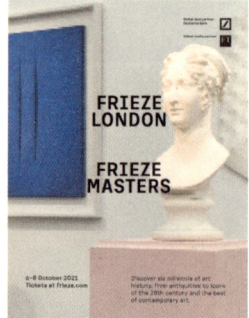

164 Flyer
TD. AD. D. 一橋匠蔵 Shozo Ichihashi
CL. 長谷川大祐 Daisuke Hasegawa
PT. NPGクナド, Neue Haas Grotesk

165 Experimental work
TD. AD. D. 市川良介 Ryosuke Ichikawa
CD. MOODMAN
MD. 黒川瑛紀 Eiki Kurokawa
MU. 佐藤公俊 Kimitoshi Sato
CL. 文化庁 Agency for Cultural Affairs
PT. Custom-made for the project, Roboto
https://asmr.idstr.jp/

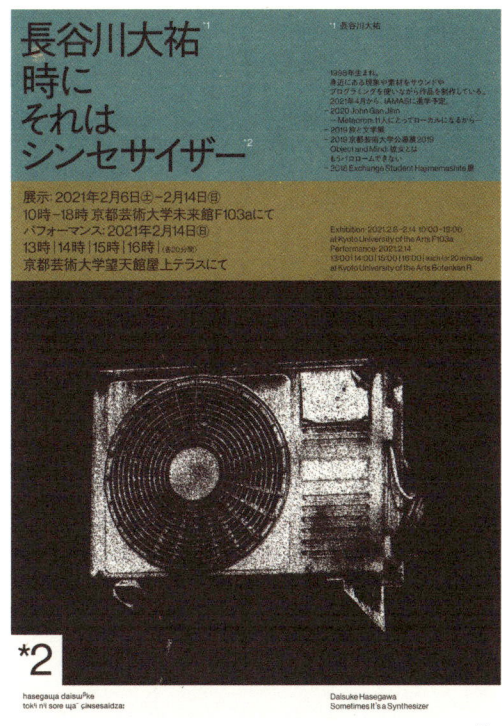

164

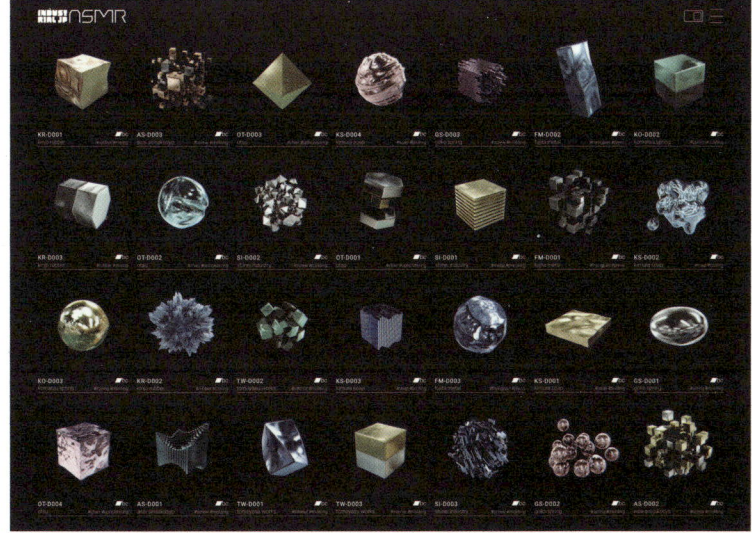

165

Prize Nominee Work

166 Book
TD. AD. D. 井上嗣也 Tsuguya Inoue
D. 稲垣純 Jun Inagaki
P. 西村裕介 Yusuke Nishimura
PR. 孫家邦 Chiapang Sun
CL.（株）リトルモア Little More Co., Ltd.
PT. Futura

156

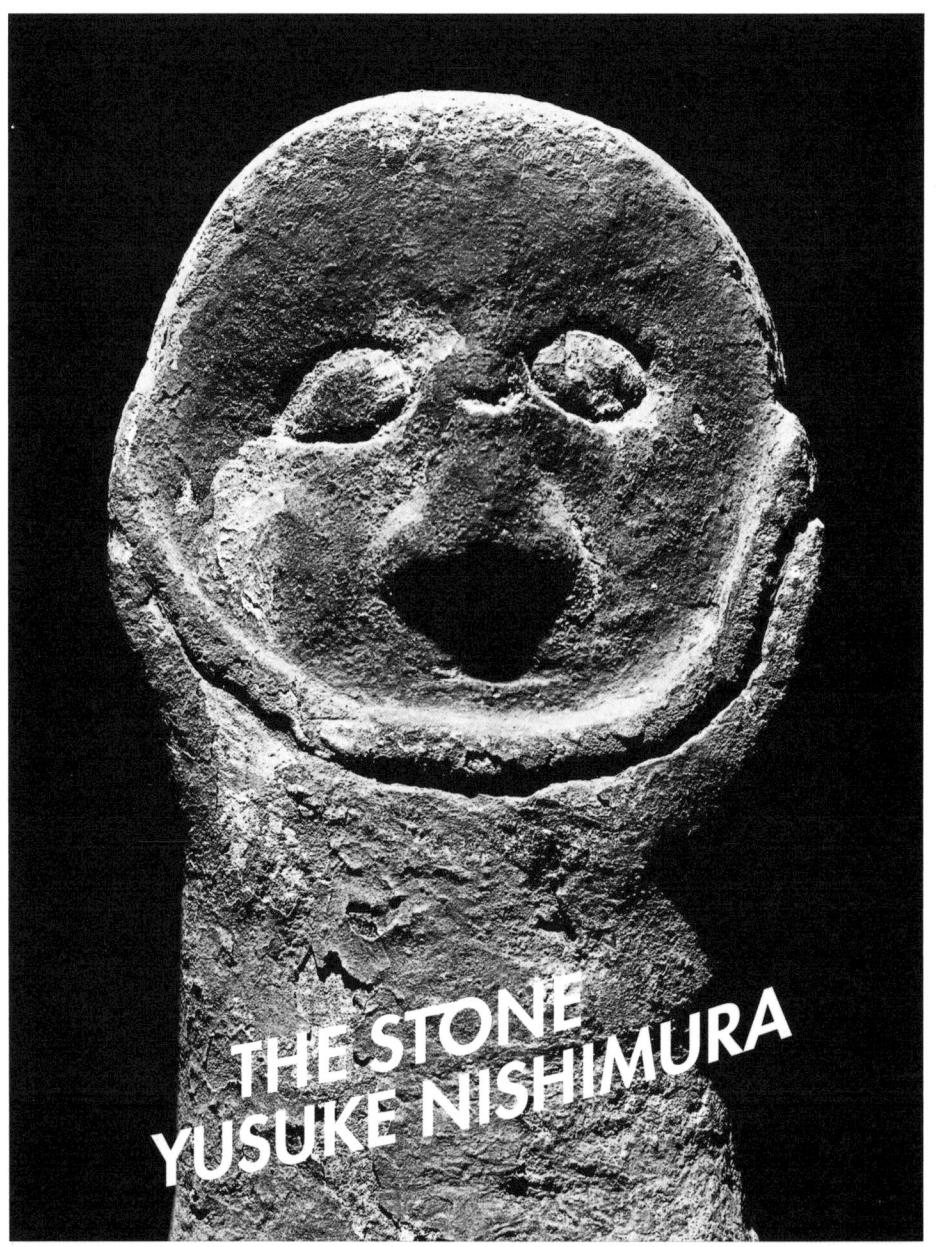

Prize Nominee Work

167 Poster
TD. AD. D. 井上嗣也 Tsuguya Inoue
D. 稲垣純 Jun Inagaki
P. 西村裕介 Yusuke Nishimura
CL. スタジオビービー Studio B.B, 21_21 Design Sight ギャラリー3 21_21 Design Sight Gallery 3
PT. Futura

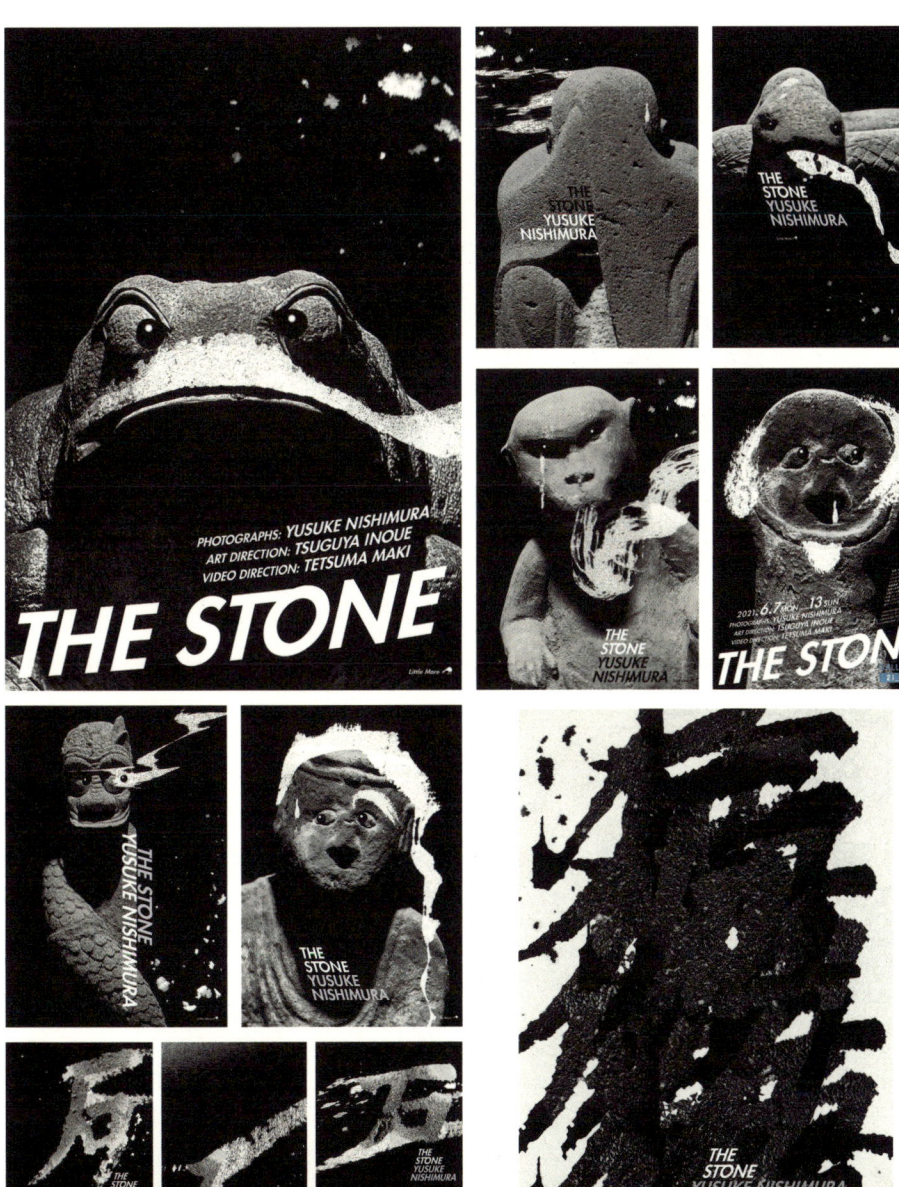

168 Book
TD. AD. D. 井上嗣也 Tsuguya Inoue
D. 稲垣純 Jun Inagaki
CD. P. ウィン・シャ Wing Shya
PR. 古屋言子 Kotoko Koya, アリス・ツェ Alice Tse
CL. サンエンターテインメントカルチャージャパン Sun Entertainment Culture Japan, (株)リトルモア Little More Co., Ltd.
PT. Futura

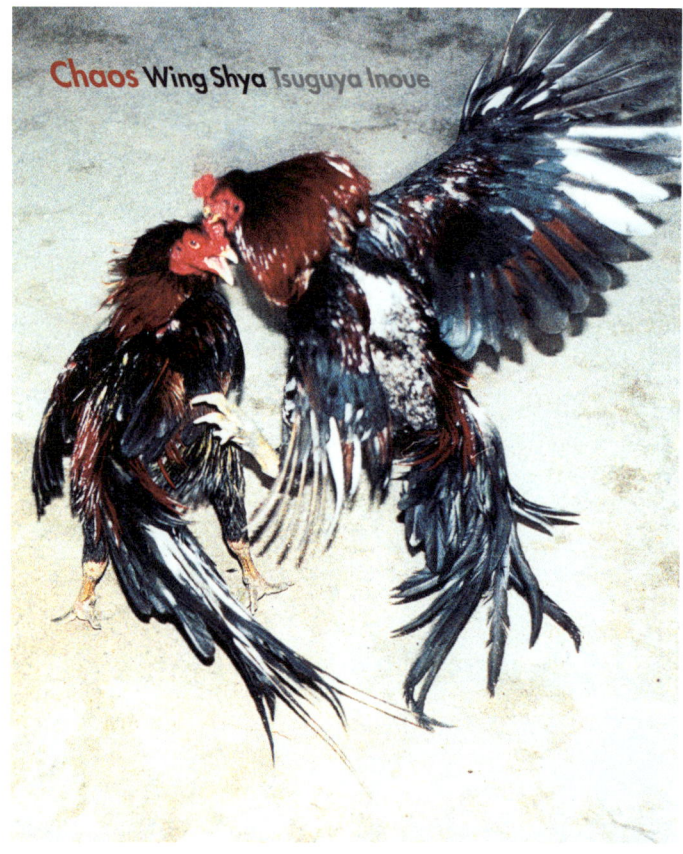

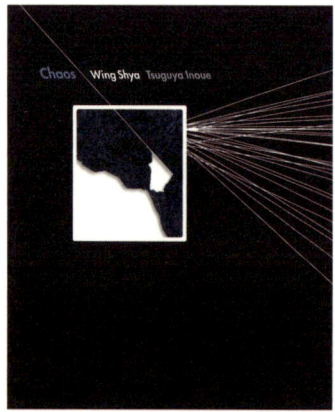

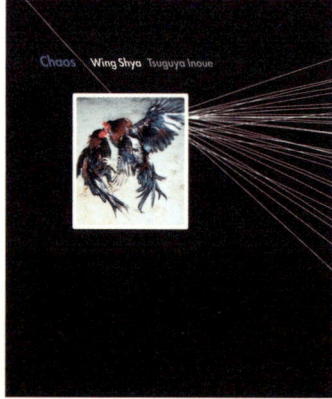

169 Poster
TD. AD. D. 井上嗣也 Tsuguya Inoue
D. 稲垣純 Jun Inagaki
P. レスリー・キー Leslie Kee
ST. 宮増芳明 Yoshi Miyamasu
PR. 丸橋裕史 Hirofumi Maruhashi
CL. 北村写真機店 Kitamura Camera
PT. Futura

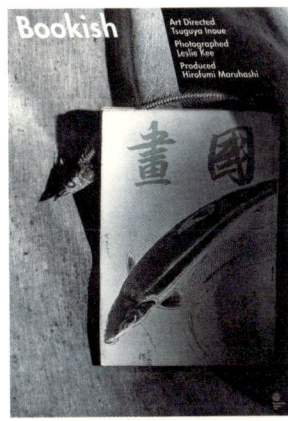
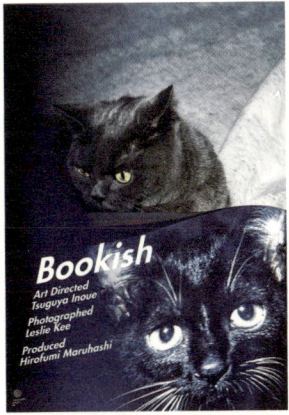
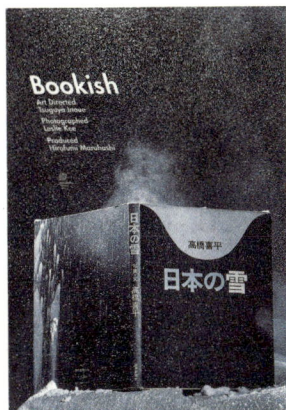
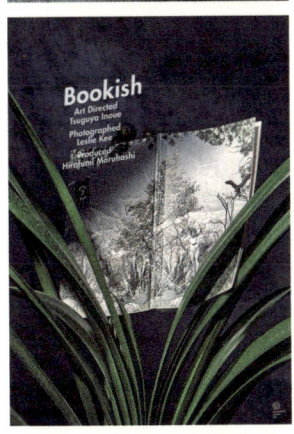
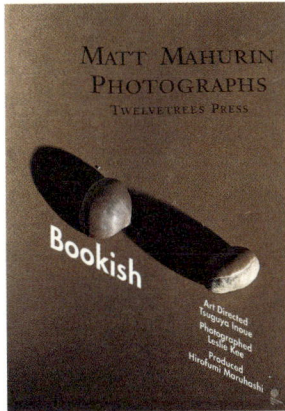
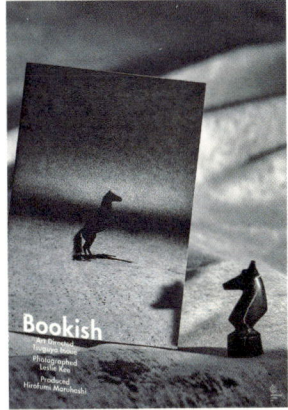
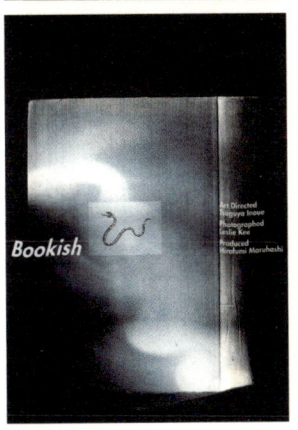
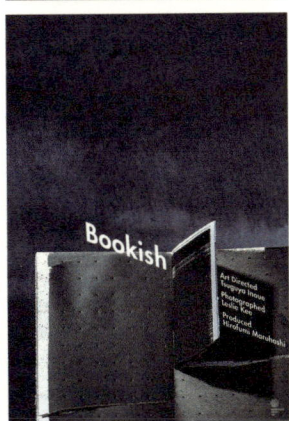
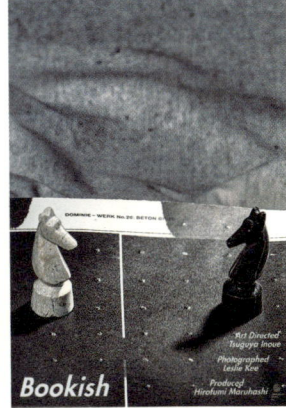

170 Poster
TD. AD. D. 石黒篤史 Atsushi Ishiguro
CL. Buzenbou
PT. 秀英初号明朝

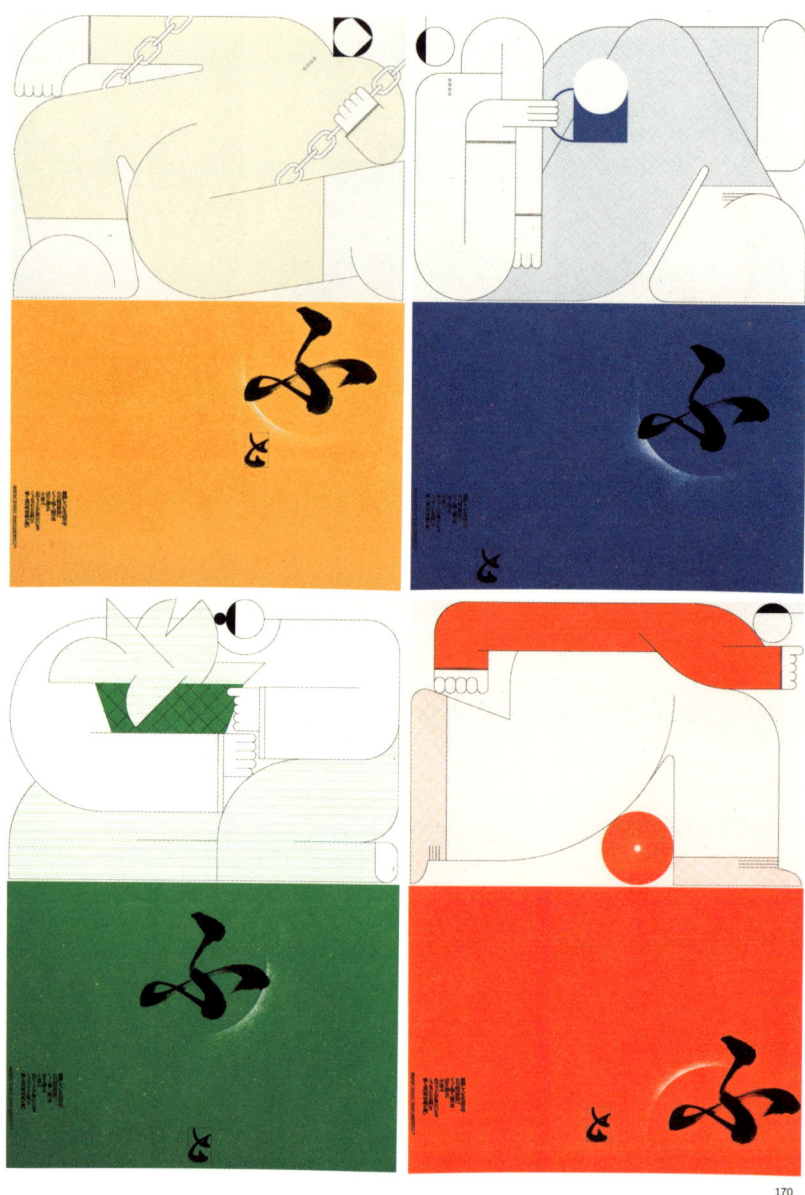

171 Poster
TD. AD. D. 石黒篤史 Atsushi Ishiguro
CL. Non-commercial work
PT. 毎日新聞明朝

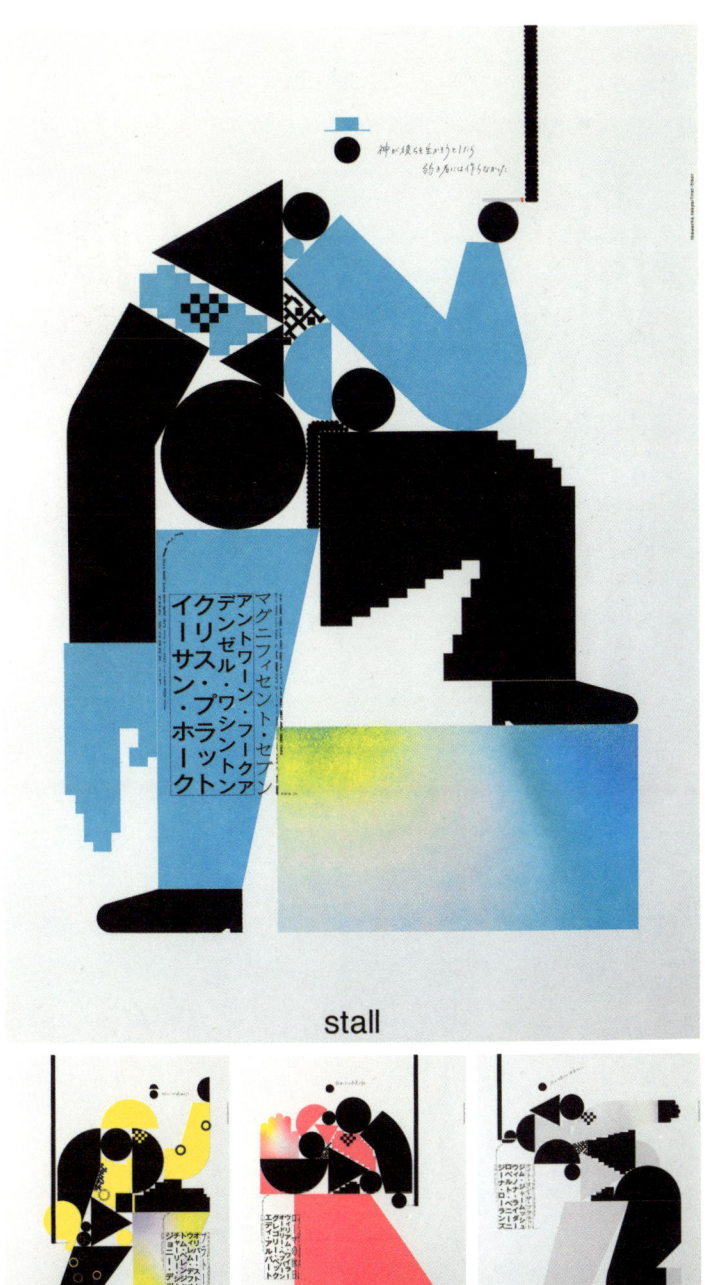

172 Poster
TD. AD. D. 石黒篤史 Atsushi Ishiguro
CL. People and Thought.
PT. 毎日新聞明朝

173 Newspaper ad.
TD. AD. D. 石黒篤史 Atsushi Ishiguro
CL. 阿武の鶴酒造 Abunotsuru
PT. 毎日新聞明朝, ゴシックMB101

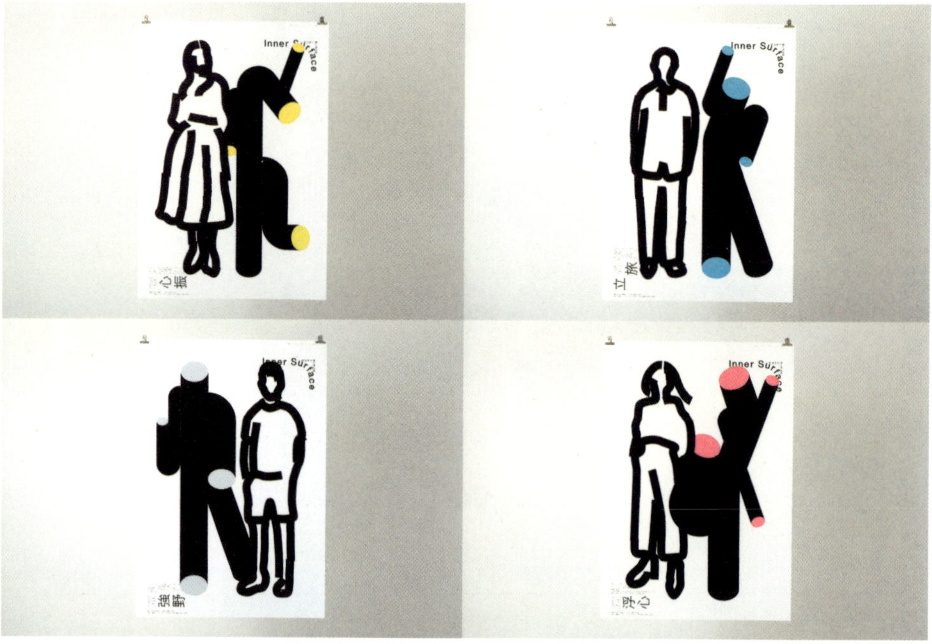

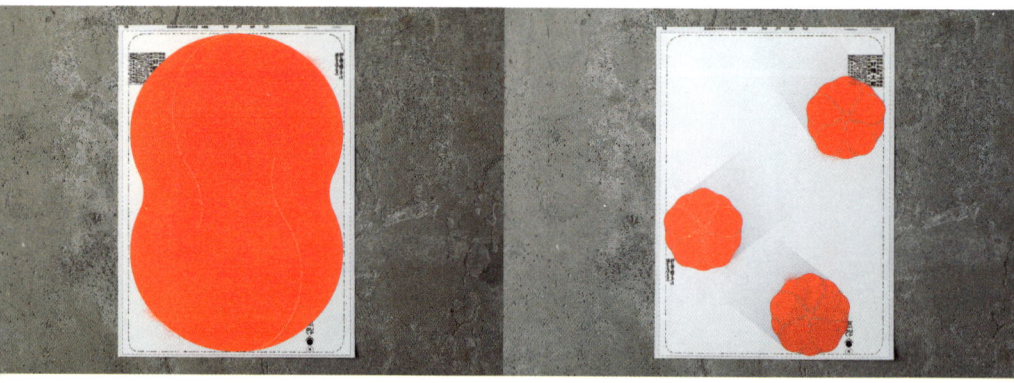

174 Collection of poems
TD. AD. D. 石黒篤史 Atsushi Ishiguro
CL. People and Thought.
PT. PP Eiko Heavy, Leiko Regular, 毎日新聞明朝

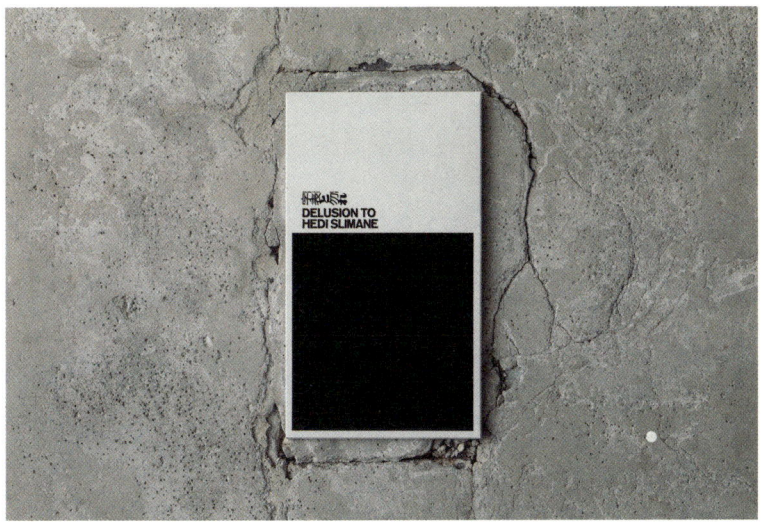

174

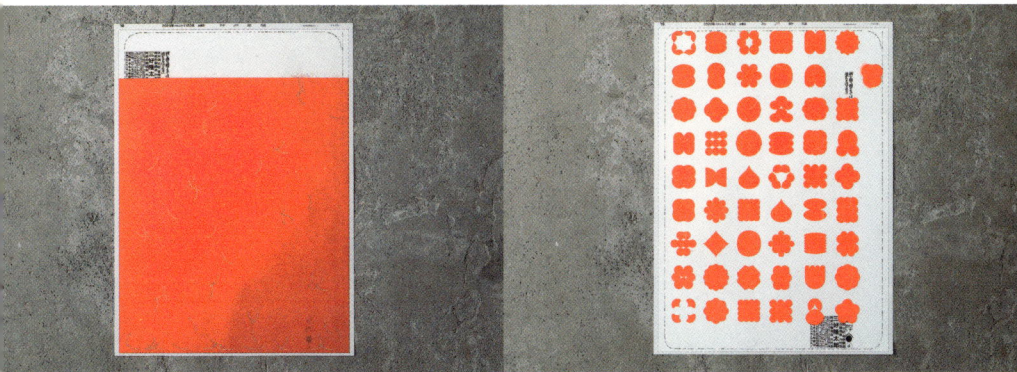

173

175 Poster
TD. AD. D. 稲垣純 Jun Inagaki
P. 新良太 Ryota Atarashi
CL. Tokyo Art and Design

176 Poster
TD. AD. D. 石井玲緒 Reo Ishii
CL. Non-commercial work
PT. Proxima Nova

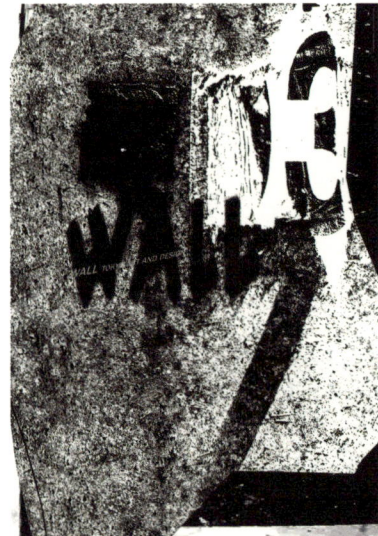
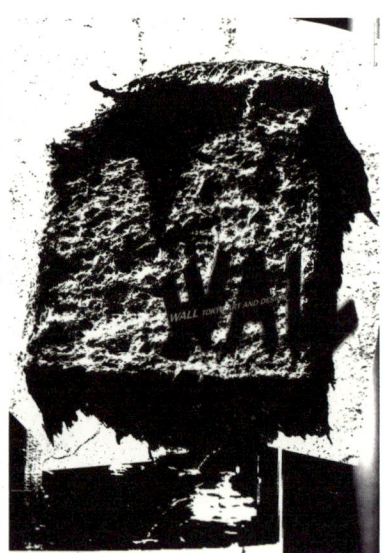

175

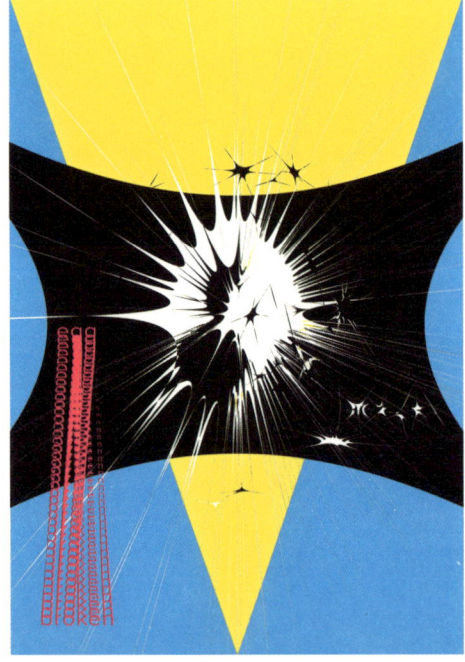

176

177 Experimental work
TD. AD. D. 石川将也 Masaya Ishikawa
D. 言乃田埃 Hokori Iinoda
D (Sound). イトケン Itoken
CL. Non-commercial work
PT. BIELA, Futura Now
https://www.cog.ooo/lol

178 Book
TD. AD. D. 伊藤修一 Nobukazu Ito
D. 後藤寿方 Toshimasa Goto, 神崎美穂 Miho Kanzaki
E. 原瑛莉子 Eriko Hara
CL.（株）パイ インターナショナル PIE International Inc.
PT. Custom-made for the project, 秀英にじみ明朝

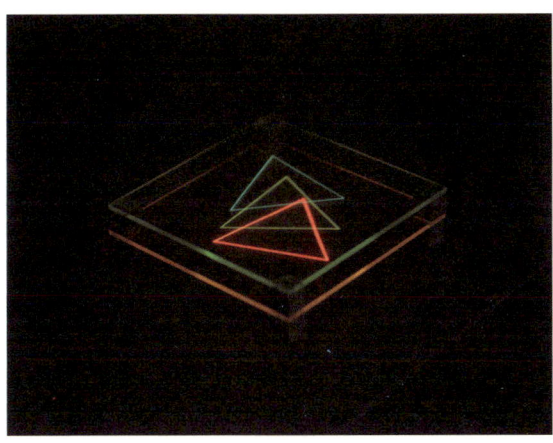
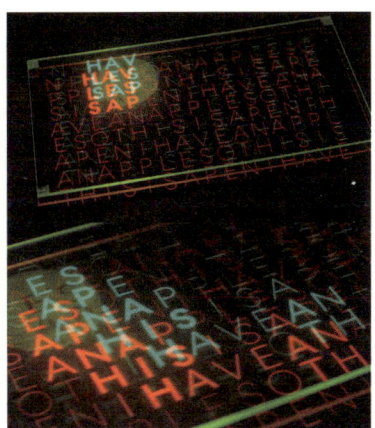

177

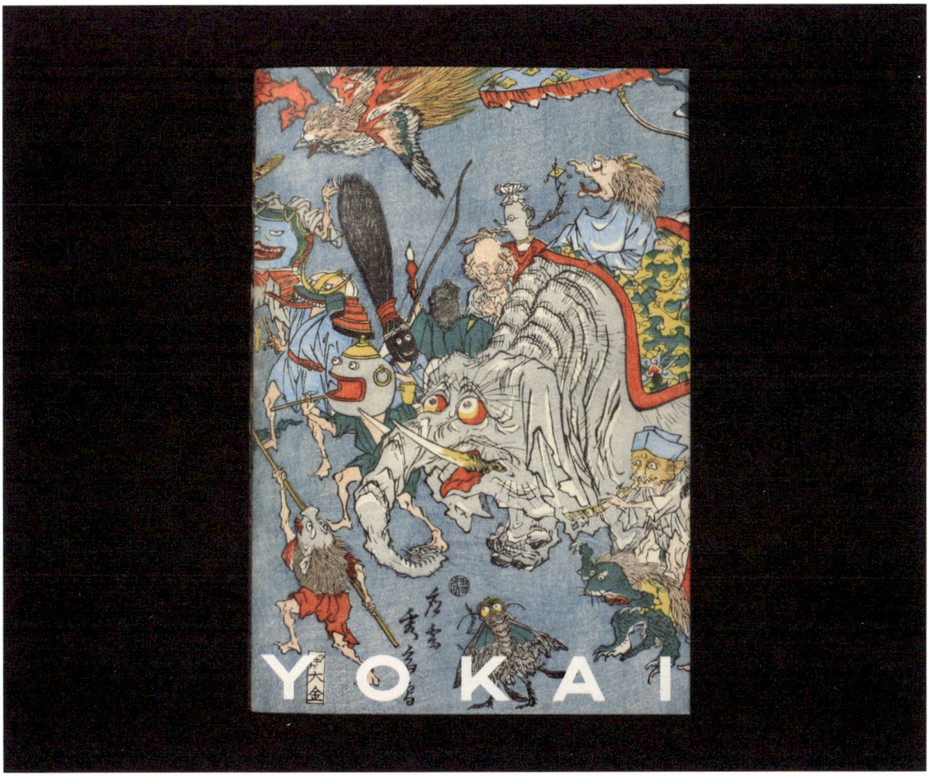

178

Prize Nominee Work

179 Type design
TD. 岩井悠 Hisashi Iwai
CL. Non-commercial work

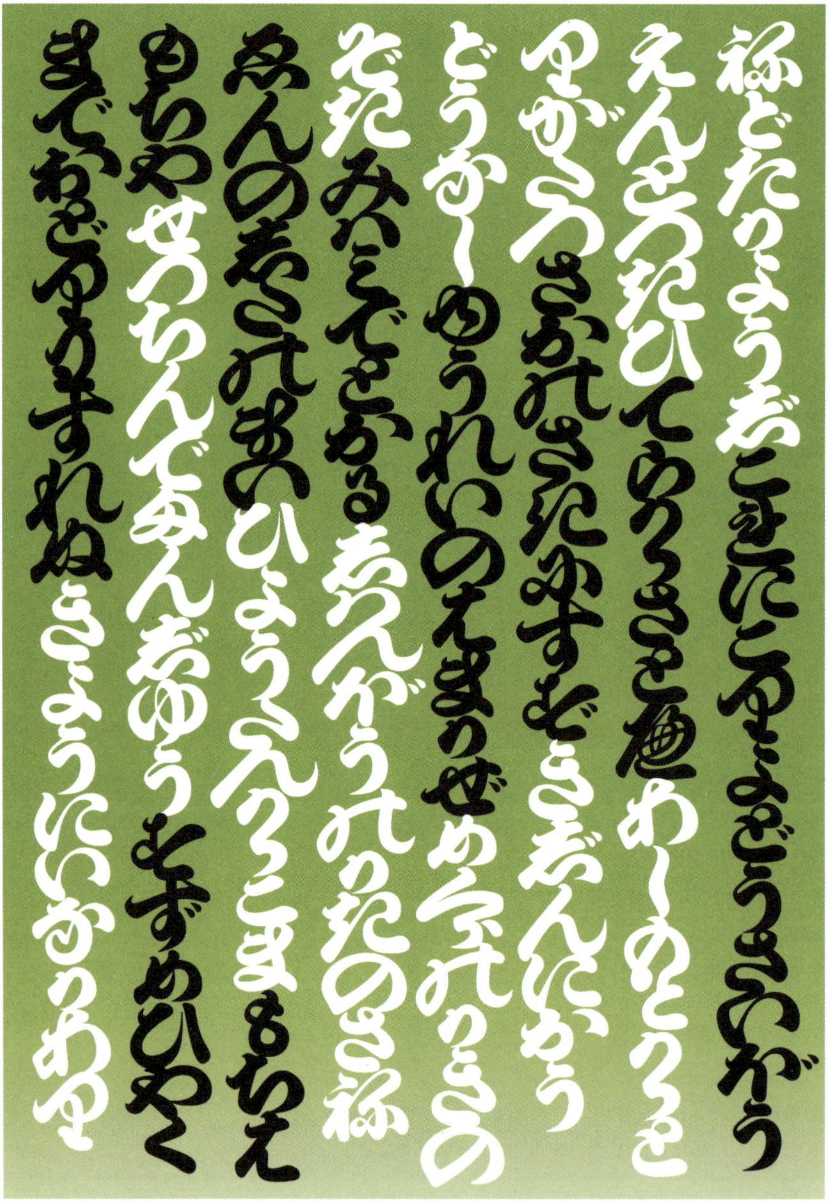

180 Experimental work
TD. D. Dan Jin
CL. Non-commercial work
PT. Qijic

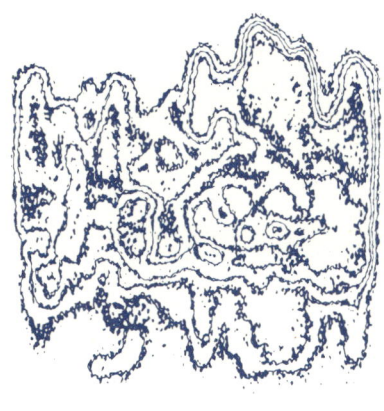

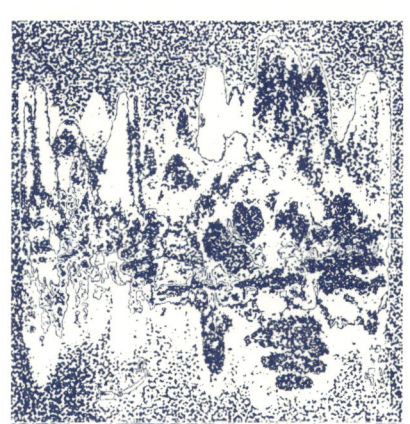

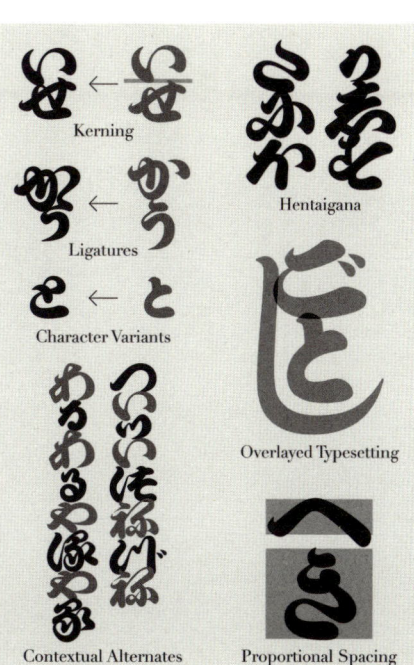

181 Record jacket
TD. 城崎哲郎 Tetsuro Jozaki
CL. World Apart
PT. Neue Haas Grotesk

182 Poster
TD. 城崎哲郎 Tetsuro Jozaki
CL. World Apart
PT. Neue Haas Grotesk

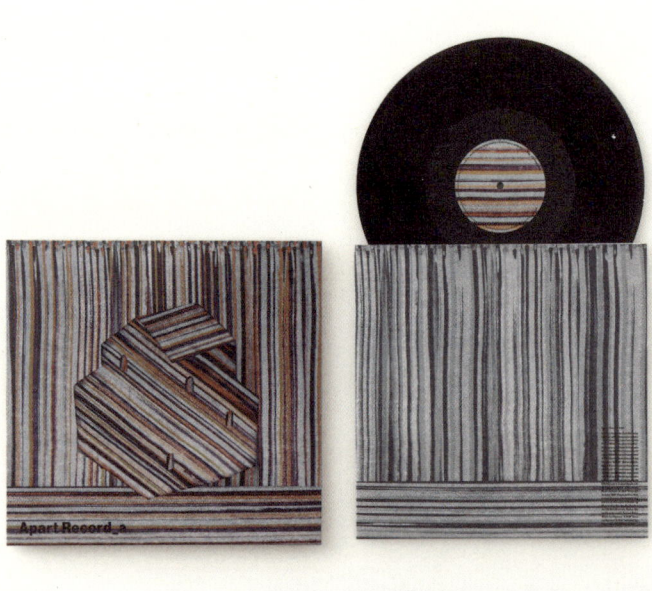

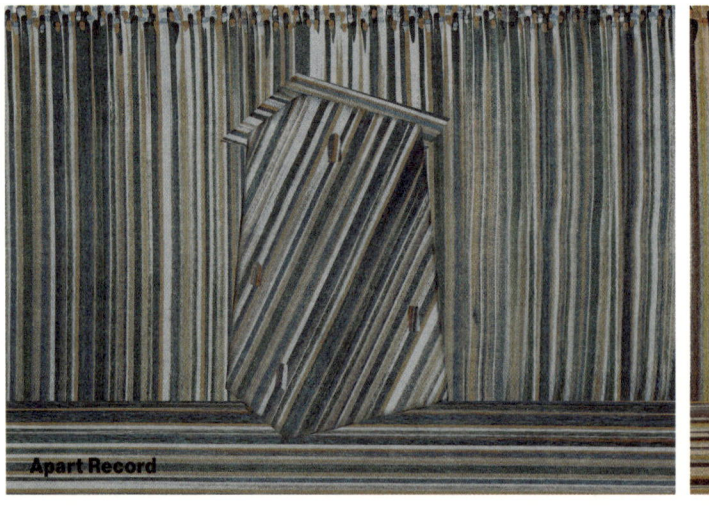

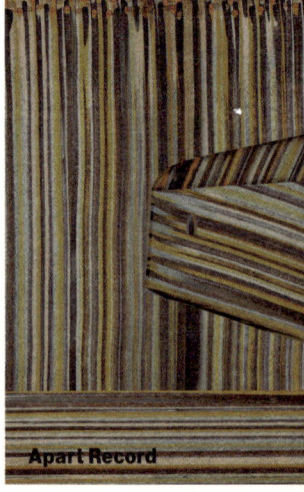

183 Packaging
TD. 城崎哲郎 Tetsuro Jozaki
D. 山口真広 Masahiro Yamaguchi
CL. 朝倉調味料（株）Asakura Chomiryo Ltd.
PT. Custom-made for the project

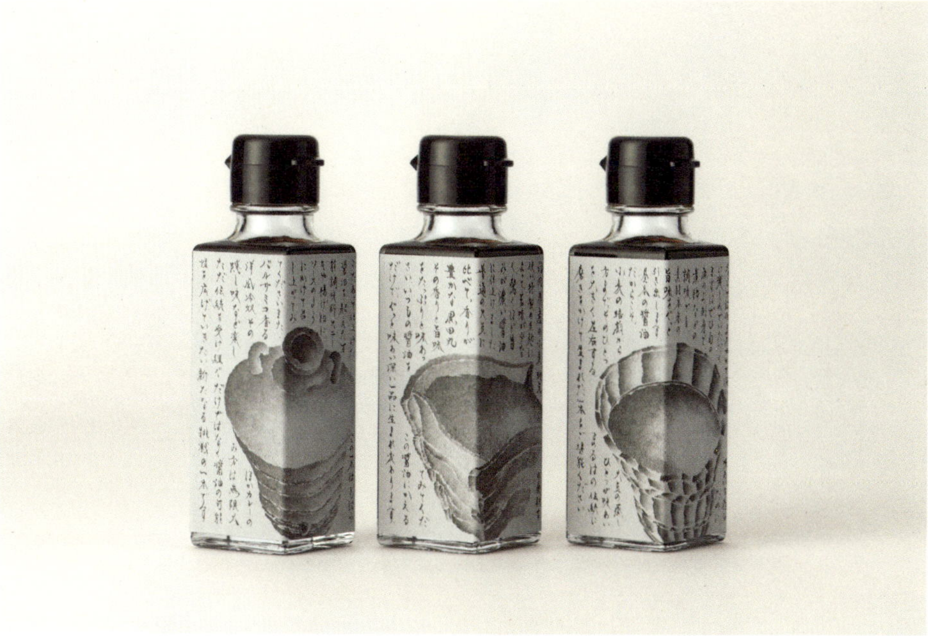

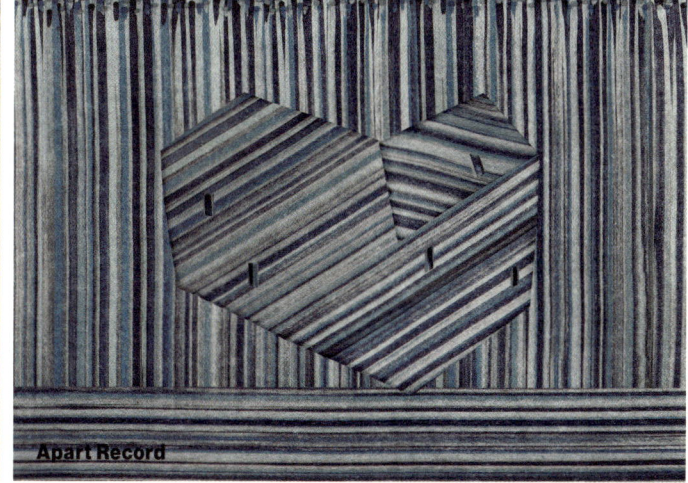

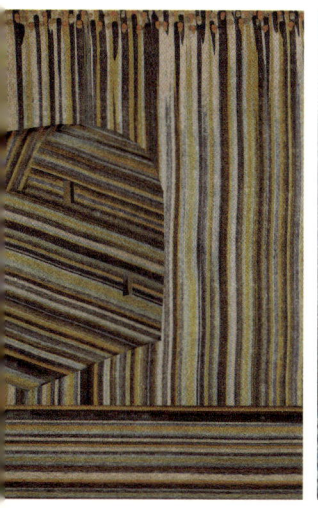

184 Poster
TD. 城崎哲郎 Tetsuro Jozaki
D. 山口真広 Masahiro Yamaguchi
CL. 朝倉調味料（株）Asakura Chomiryo Ltd.
PT. Custom-made for the project

185 Website
TD. 梶垣諒 Ryo Kajigaki
CL. Non-commercial work
PT. リュウミン
https://scrapbox.io/kanji-anima-tion/

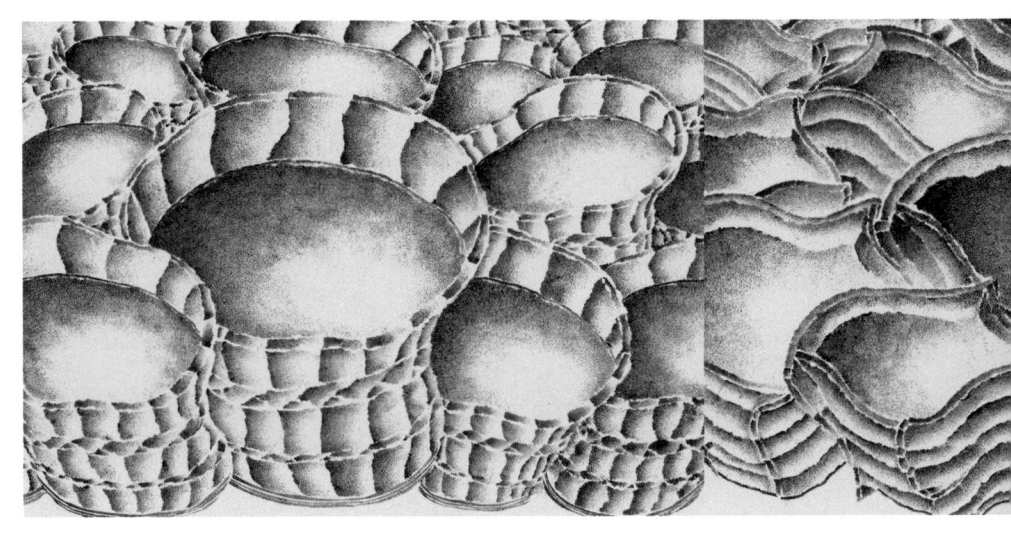

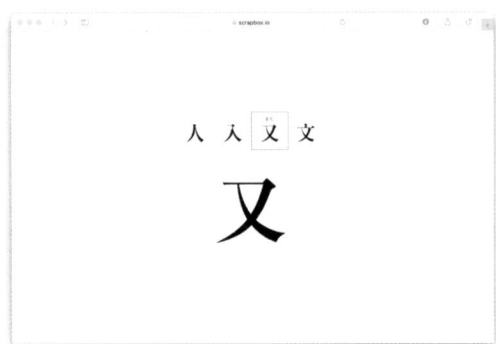

186 Poster
TD. 金坂義之 Yoshiyuki Kanesaka
CL. Office N
PT. Custom-made for the project

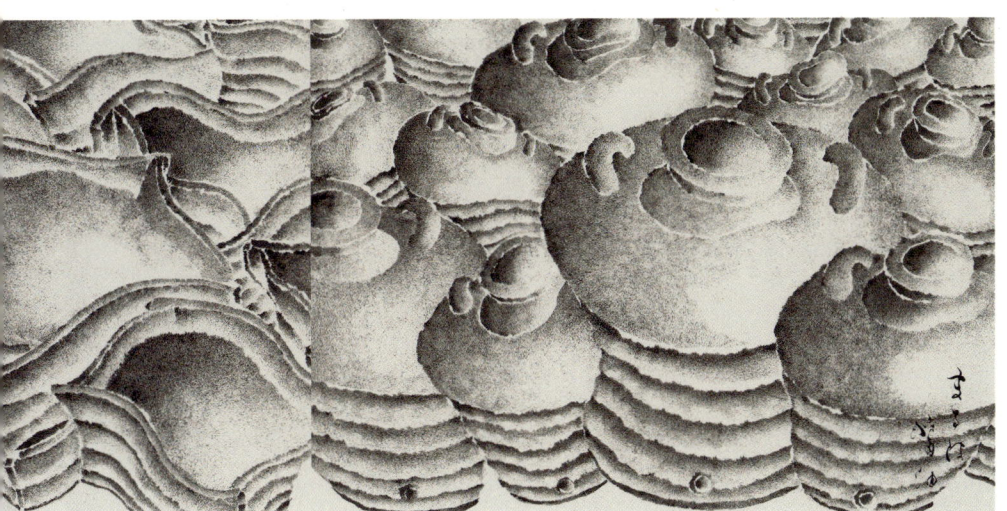

184

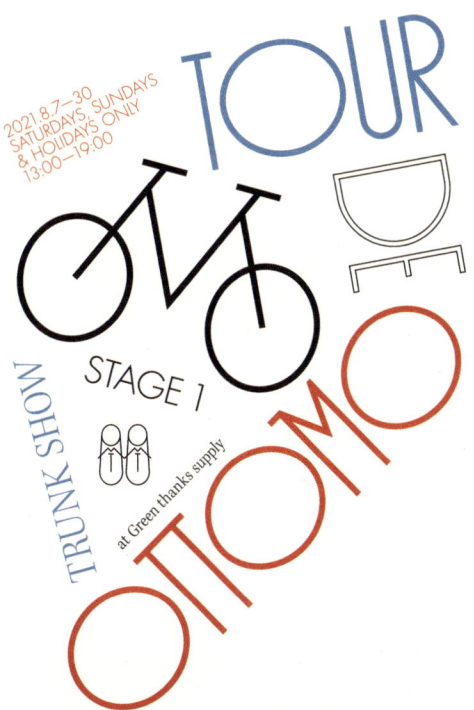

187 Book
TD. AD. 葛西薫 Kaoru Kasai
AD. D. 白井陽平 Yohei Shirai
P. 藤井保 Tamotsu Fujii
CL. Alexis(株) Alexis Co., Ltd.
PT. Eckhart, Helvetica

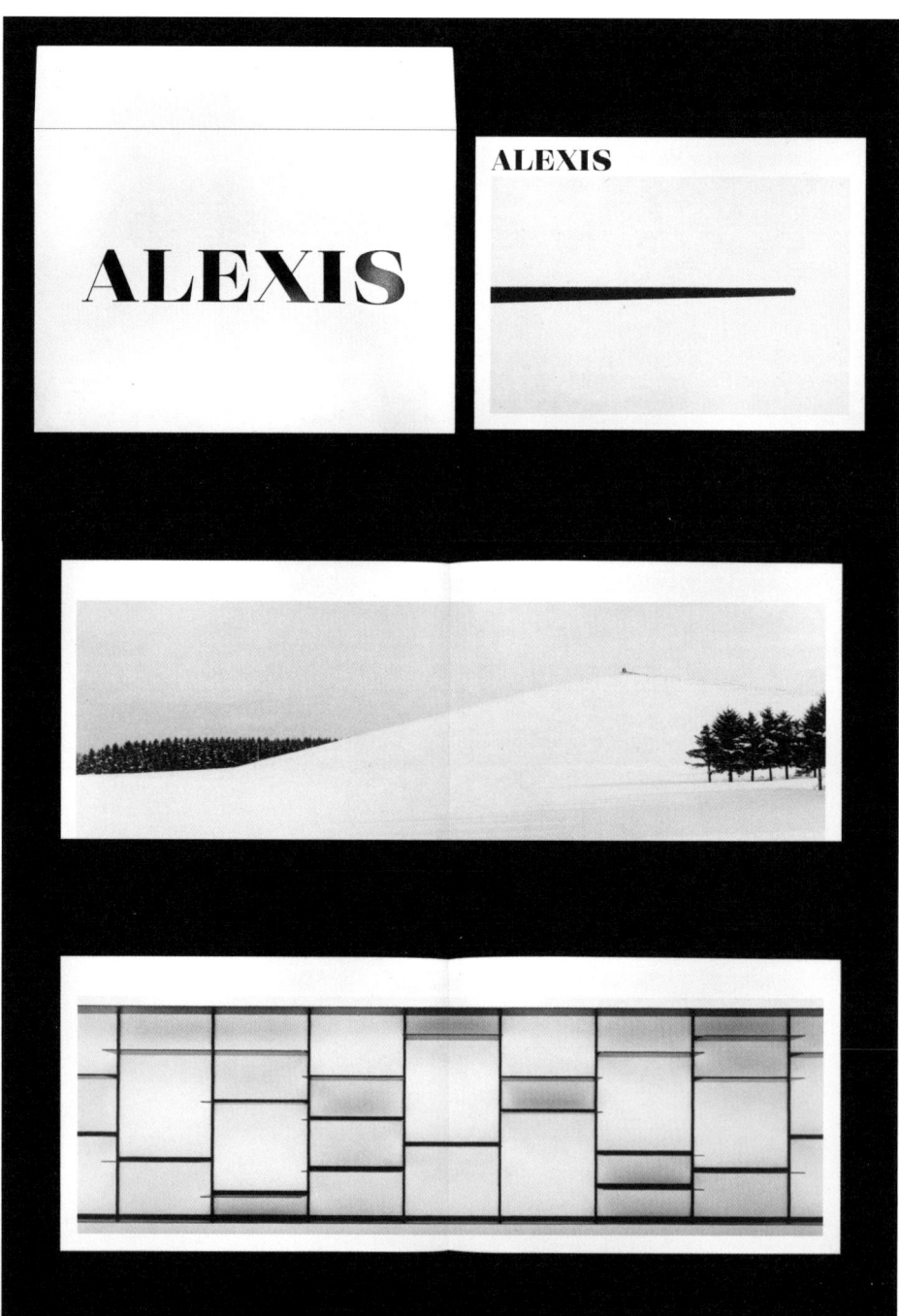

188 Book
TD. AD. 葛西薫 Kaoru Kasai
D. 安達祐貴 Yuki Adachi
P. 奥山由之 Yoshiyuki Okuyama
CL.（株）赤々舎 Akaaka Art Publishing, Inc.
PT. Snell Roundhand

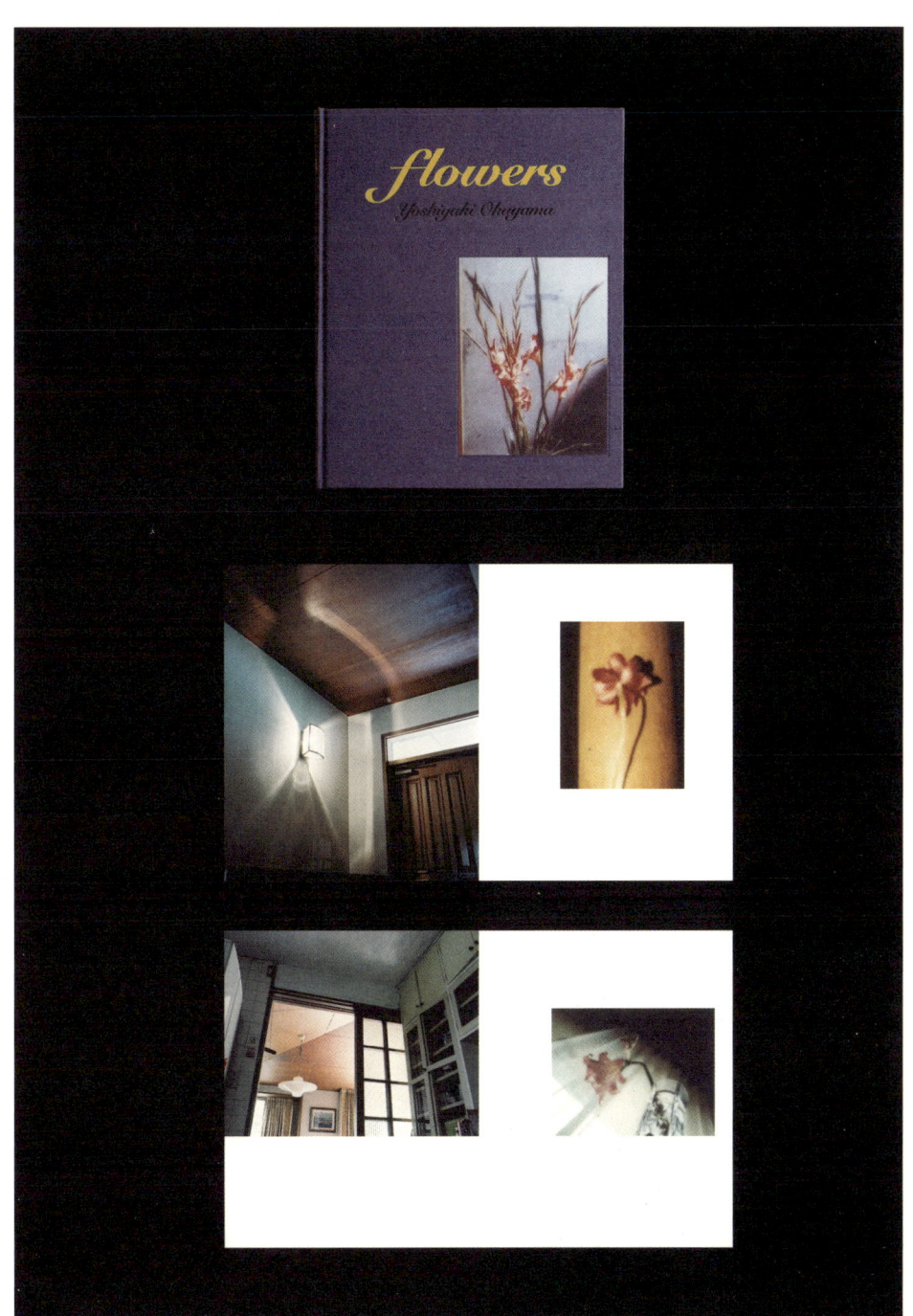

Prize Nominee Work

189 Tapestry
TD. CD. AD. 葛西薫 Kaoru Kasai
D. 増田豊 Yutaka Masuda
A. 仲條正義 Masayoshi Nakajo, 皆川明 Akira Minagawa
CL.（株）虎玄 Kogen Co., Ltd.
PT. Custom-made for the project

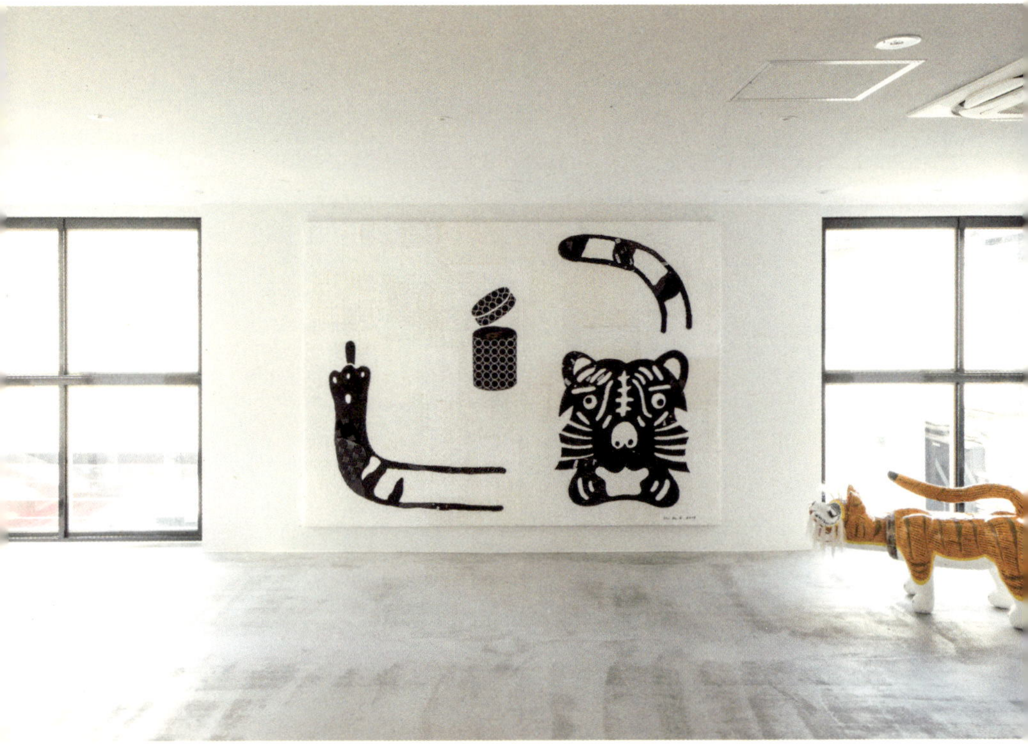

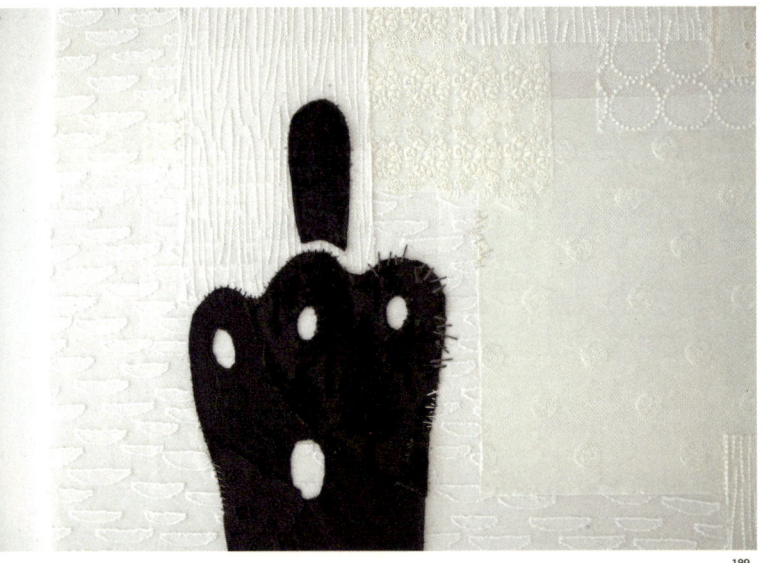

Prize Nominee Work

190 Packaging
TD. CD. AD. 葛西薫 Kaoru Kasai
CD. 山本康一郎 Koichiro Yamamoto
D. 増田豊 Yutaka Masuda, 江藤公昭 Kimiaki Eto
A. 仲條正義 Masayoshi Nakajo
P. 上原勇 Isamu Uehara
CL. (株)虎玄 Kogen Co., Ltd.
PT. Custom-made for the project

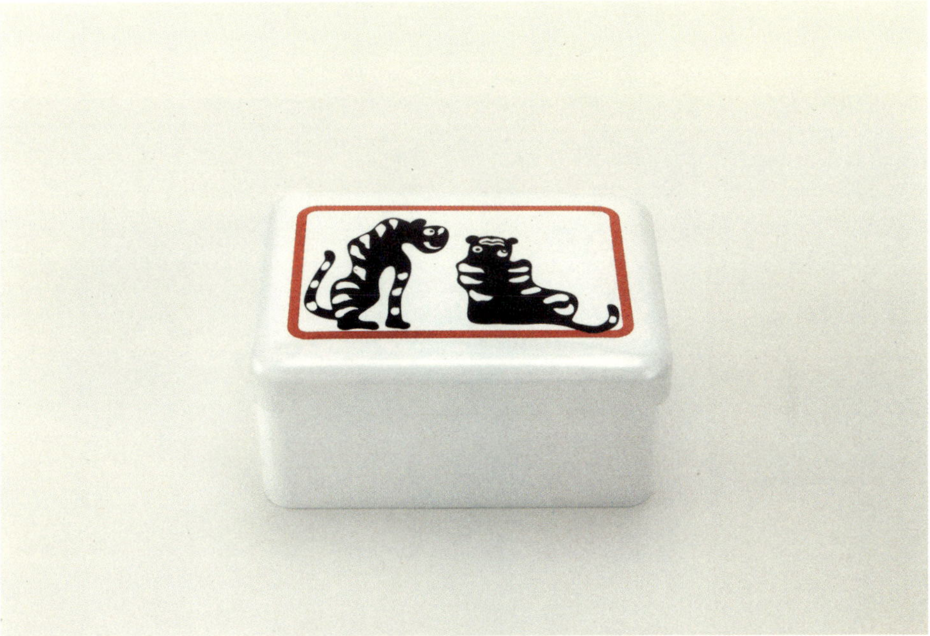

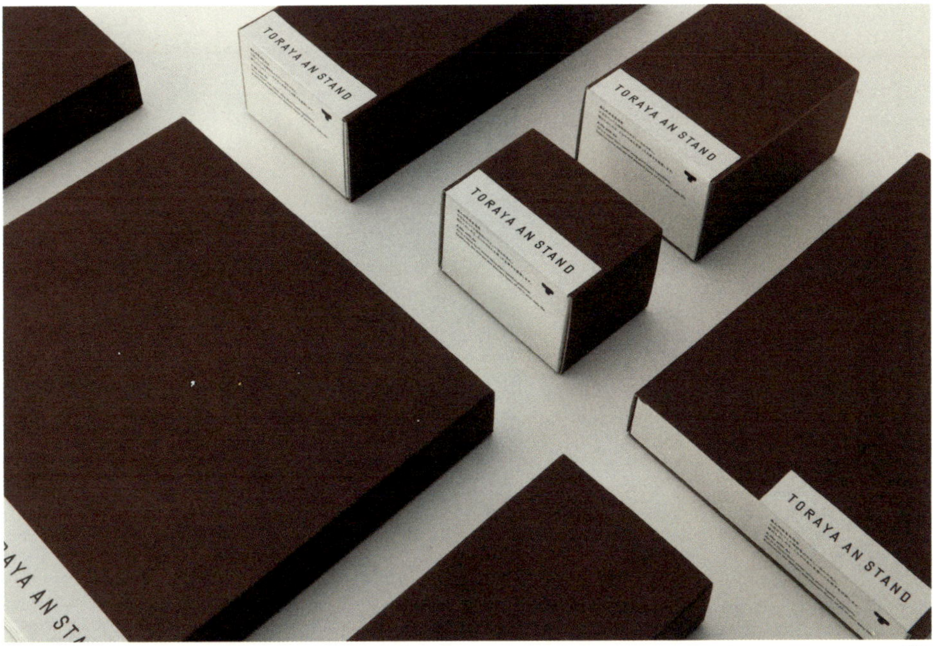

191 Book
TD. AD. I. 葛西薫 Kaoru Kasai
D. 安達祐貴 Yuki Adachi
CL.（株）リトルモア Little More Co., Ltd.
PT. Custom-made for the project

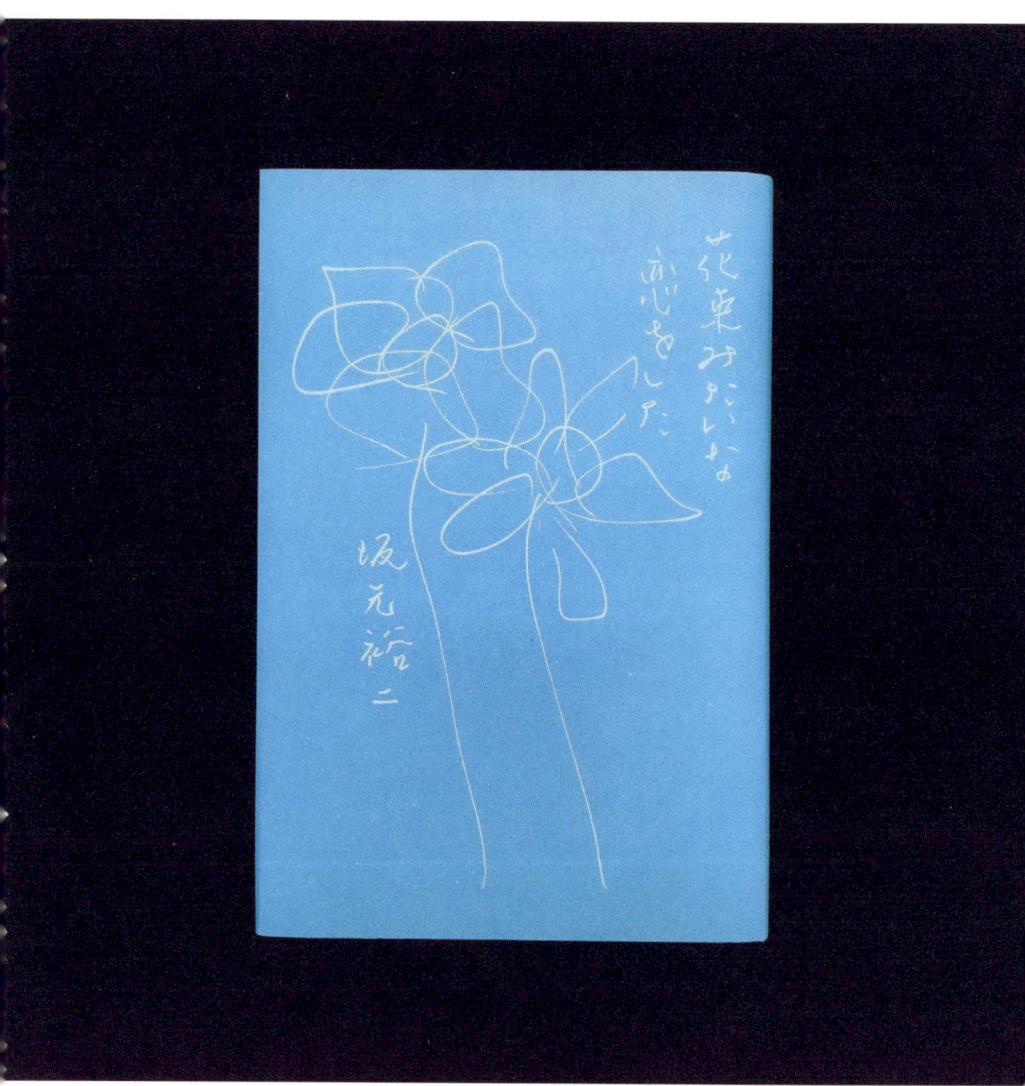

192 Poster
TD. AD. 葛西薫 Kaoru Kasai
D．安達祐貴 Yuki Adachi
CL.（株）フジテレビジョン Fuji Television Network, Inc.,
　　（株）MAパブリッシング M.A Publishing Ltd,
　　（株）サンライズプロモーション Sunrise Promotion
PT. 太ゴB101 Pro Bold, 游明朝体36ポ

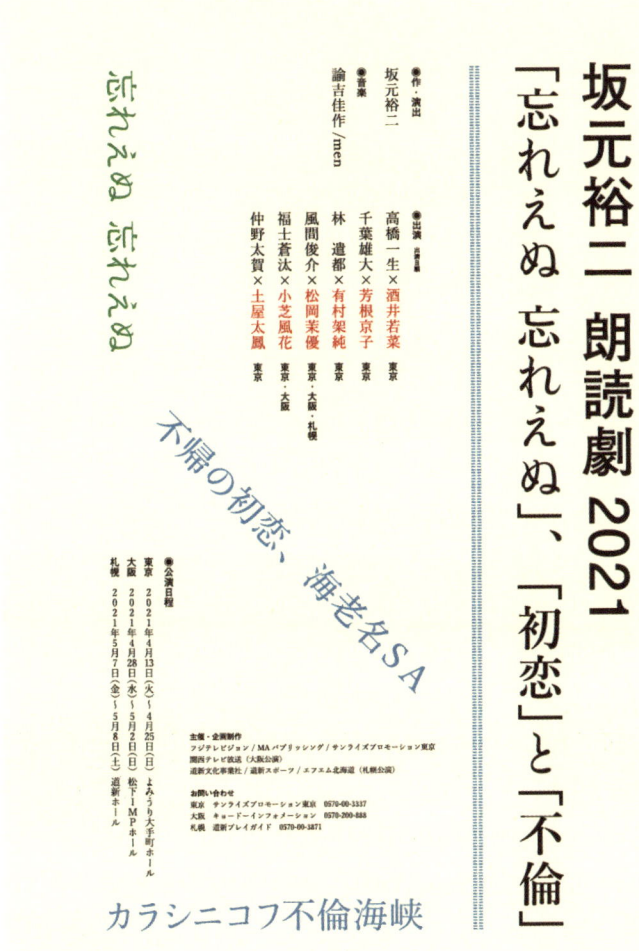

193 Poster
TD. 加瀬透 Toru Kase
CL. Nagi Contemporary Arts Project
PT. たづがね角ゴシック Info

194 Flyer
TD. 加瀬透 Toru Kase
CL.（公社）日本グラフィックデザイン協会
JAGDA Japan Graphic Design Association Inc.
PT. たづがね角ゴシック Info

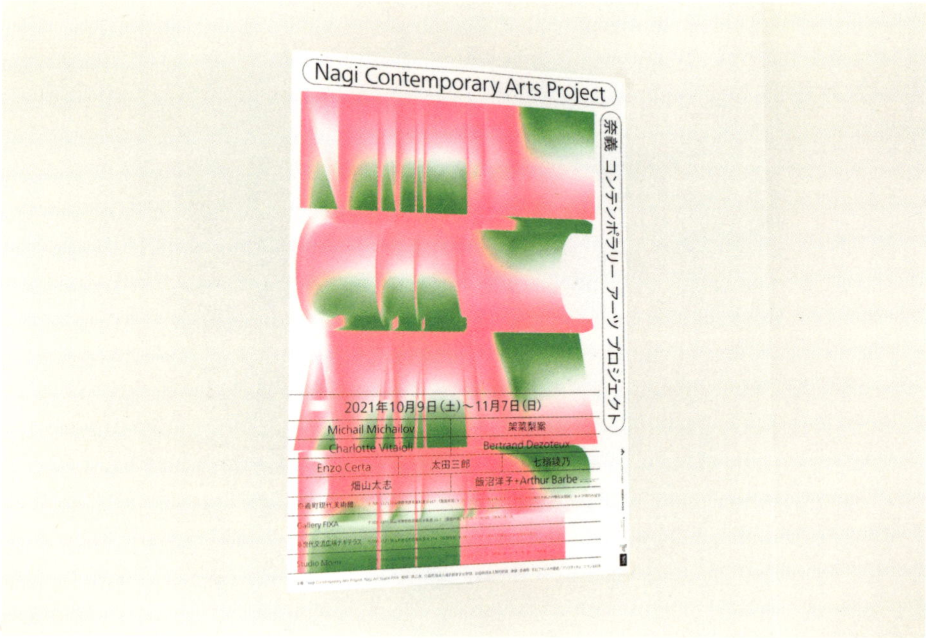

178

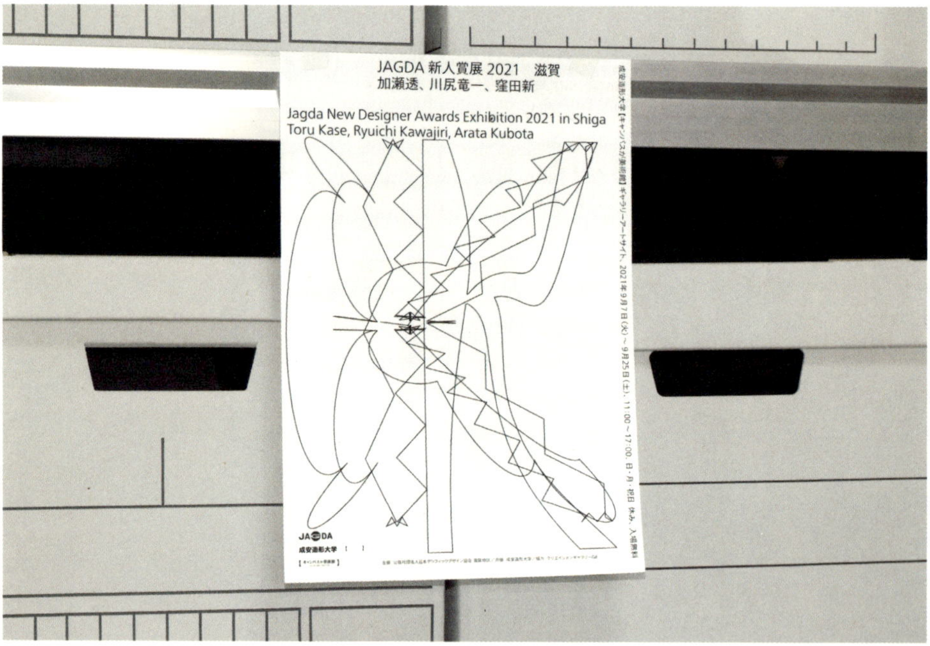

Prize Nominee Work

195 Poster
TD. 加瀬透 Toru Kase
CL. クリエイションギャラリーG8 Creation Gallery G8
PT. Courier New

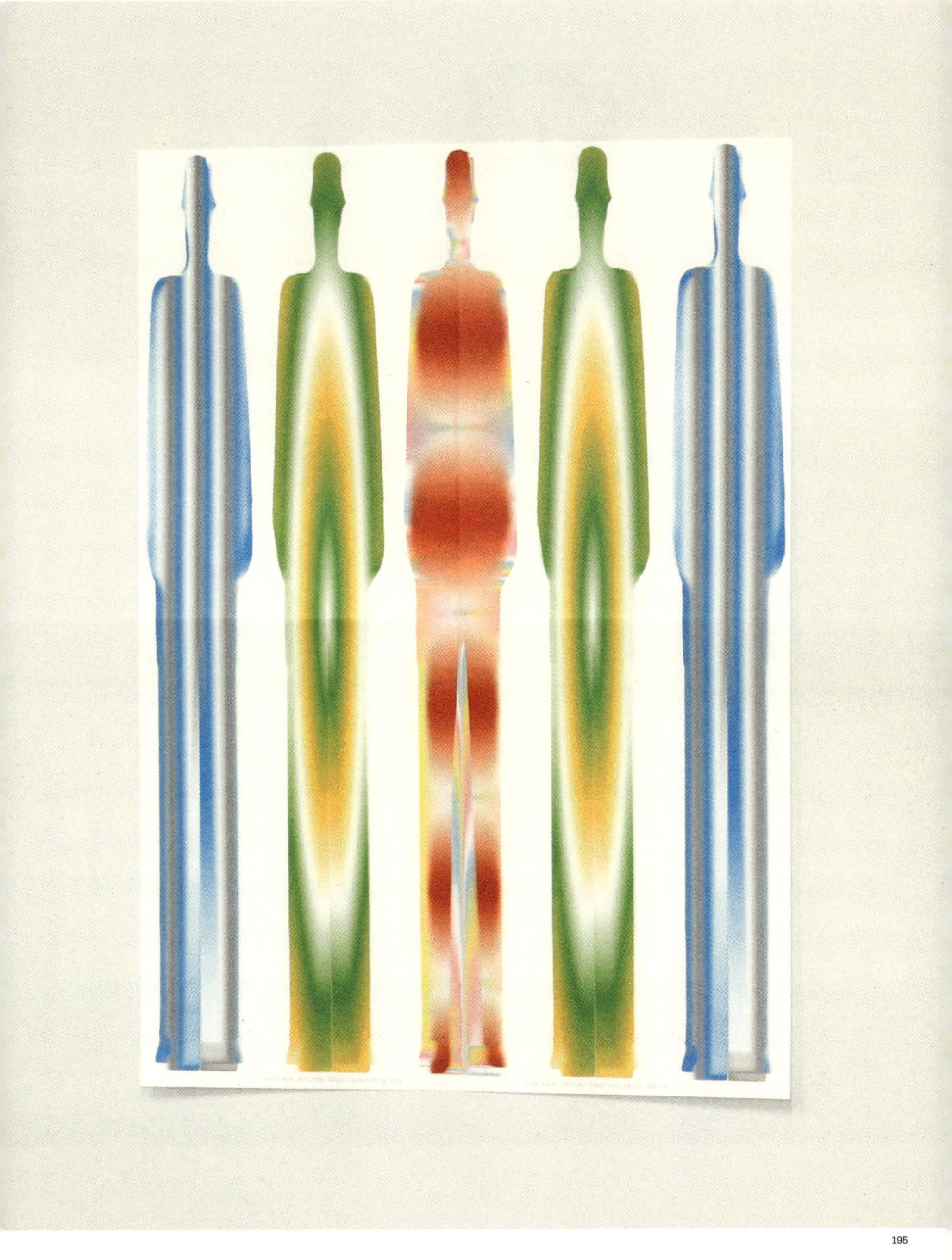

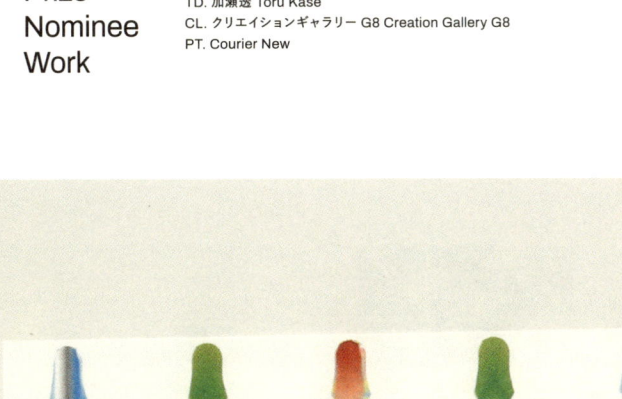

196 Mark & Logo
TD. AD. D. 川尻竜一 Ryuichi Kawajiri
CL. ンチチビル Ntiti Bld.
PT. Custom-made for the project

197 Small graphics
TD. AD. D. 川尻竜一 Ryuichi Kawajiri
CL. 三元社印刷(株) Sangensha Co., Ltd.
PT. MSゴシック, Neue Haas Grotesk Text Pro 56 Italic

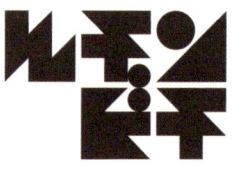

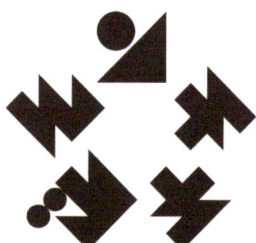

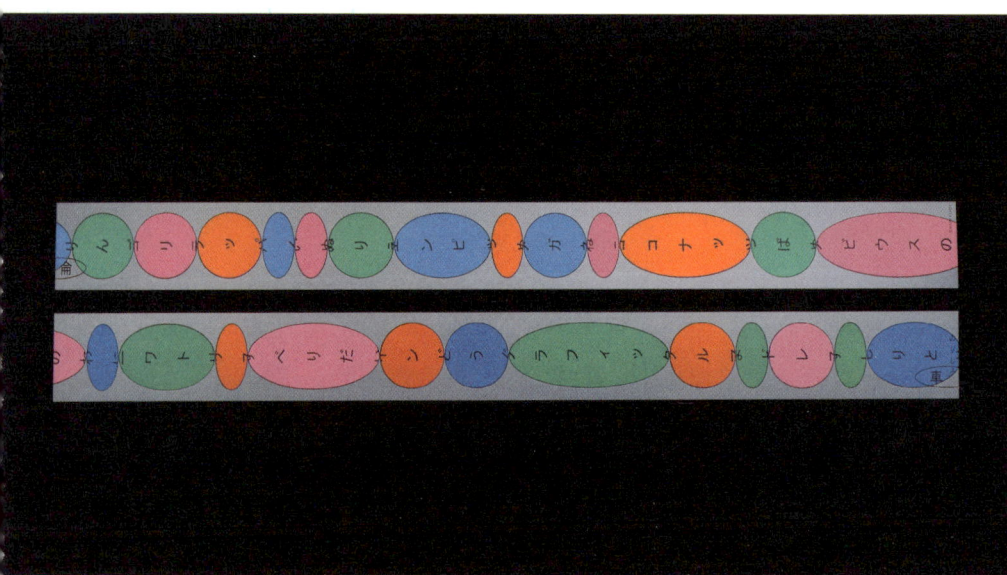

198 Book
TD. AD. D. Nicha Keeratiphanthawong, Tabea Nixdorff
CL. Werkplaatstypografie.org
PT. Ellipsis by Nicha, State by potch.xyz

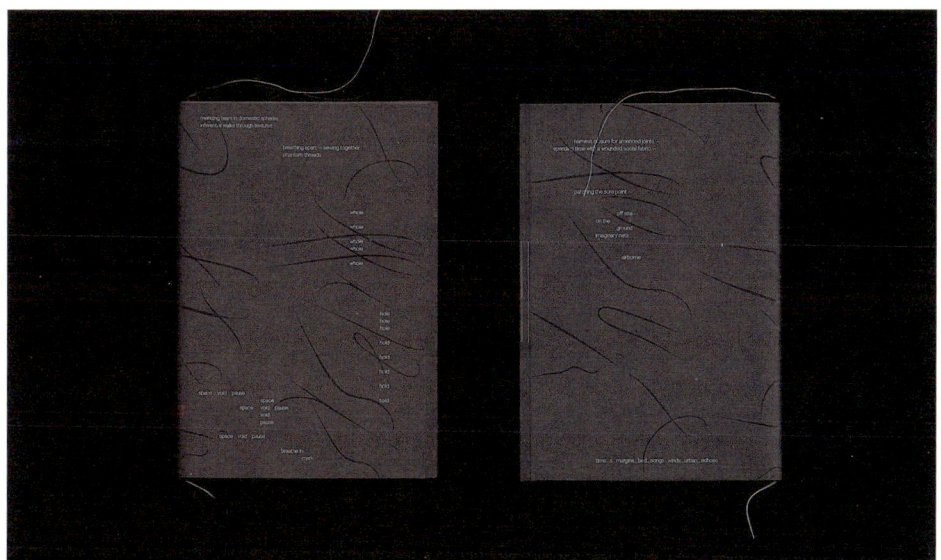

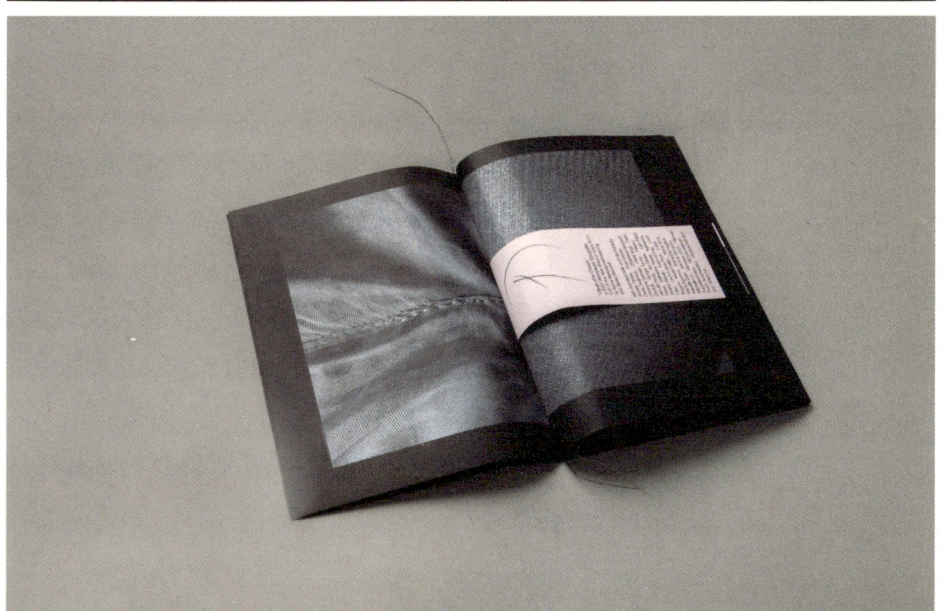

199 Book
TD. Kellenberger–White
CL. Pace
PT. Custom-made KW Sammlung

200 BI
TD. Kellenberger–White
CL. Charleston
PT. Custom-made KW Amorph

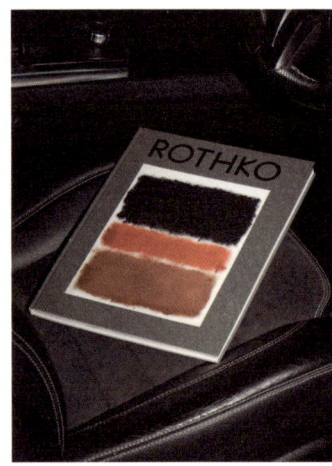

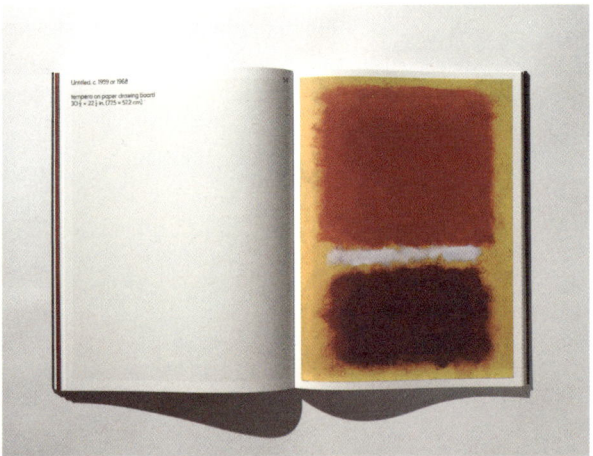

199

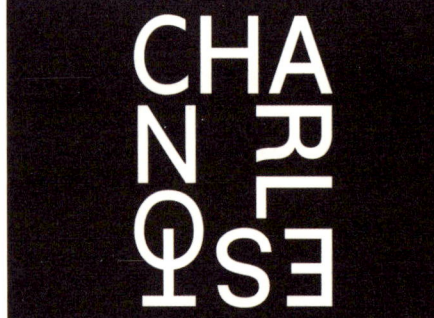

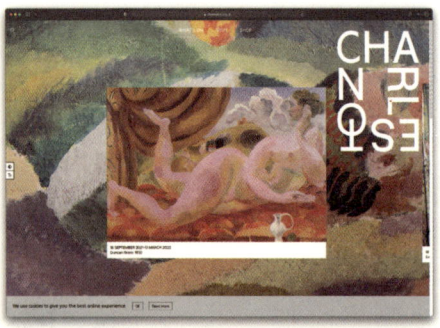

200

201 Exhibition graphics
TD. Kellenberger–White
CL. Barbican Centre
PT. Custom-made KW Sammlung Light, title lettering, wayfinding symbols

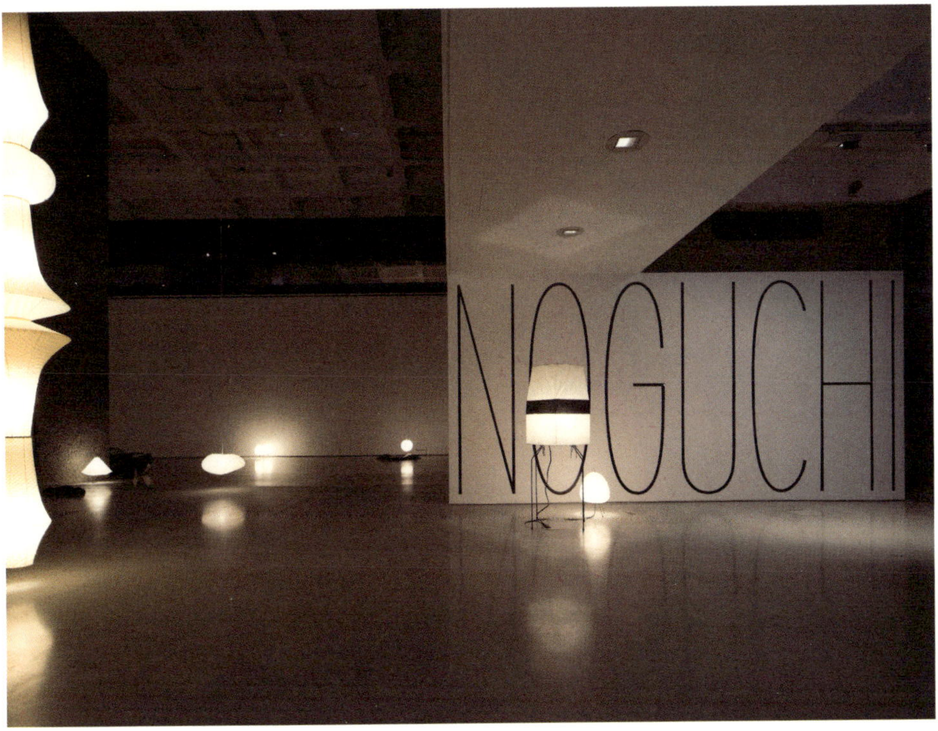

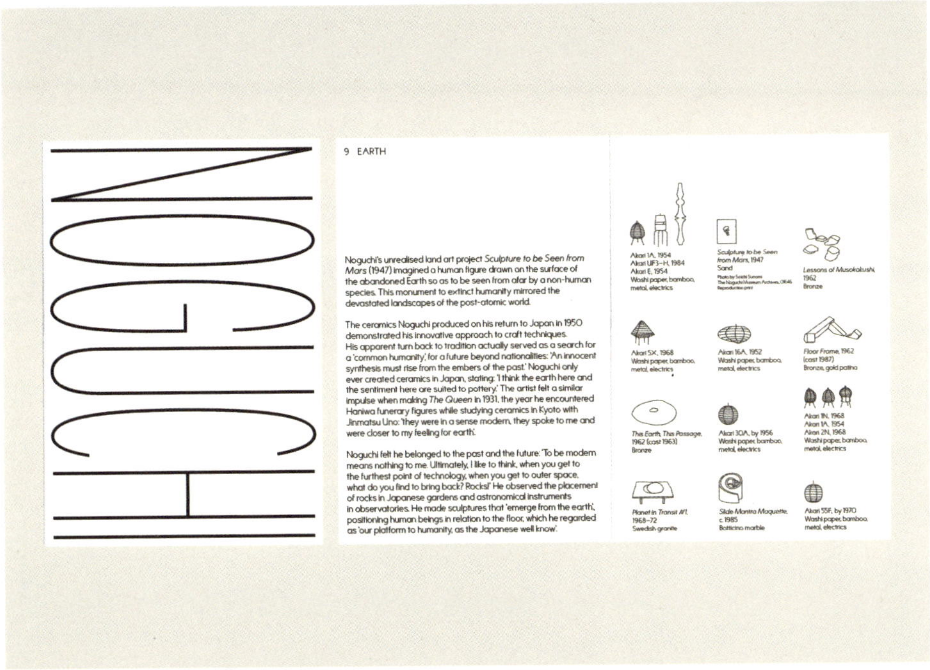

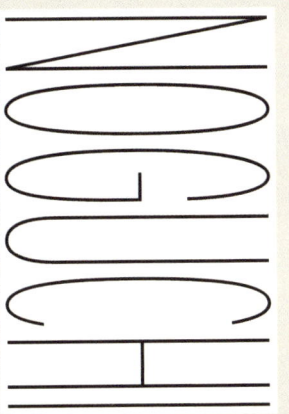

9 EARTH

Noguchi's unrealised land art project *Sculpture to be Seen from Mars* (1947) imagined a human figure drawn on the surface of the abandoned Earth so as to be seen from afar by a non-human species. This monument to extinct humanity mirrored the devastated landscapes of the post-atomic world.

The ceramics Noguchi produced on his return to Japan in 1950 demonstrated his innovative approach to craft techniques. His apparent turn back to tradition actually served as a search for a 'common humanity', for a future beyond nationalities: 'An innocent synthesis must rise from the embers of the past.' Noguchi only ever created ceramics in Japan, stating: 'I think the earth here and the sentiment here are suited to pottery.' The artist felt a similar impulse when making *The Queen* in 1931, the year he encountered Haniwa funerary figures while studying ceramics in Kyoto with Jinmatsu Uno: 'they were in a sense modern, they spoke to me and were closer to my feeling for earth'.

Noguchi felt he belonged to the past and the future. 'To be modern means nothing to me. Ultimately, I like to think, when you get to the furthest point of technology, when you get to outer space, what do you find to bring back? Rocks!' He observed the placement of rocks in Japanese gardens and astronomical instruments in observatories. He made sculptures that 'emerge from the earth', positioning human beings in relation to the floor, which he regarded as 'our platform to humanity, as the Japanese well know'.

Akari 1A, 1954
Akari UF3–H, 1984
Akari E, 1954
Washi paper, bamboo, metal, electrics

Sculpture to be Seen from Mars, 1947
Sand
The Noguchi Museum Archives, 01146. Reproduction print

Lessons of Musokokushi, 1962
Bronze

Akari 5X, 1968
Washi paper, bamboo, metal, electrics

Akari 16A, 1952
Washi paper, bamboo, metal, electrics

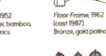
Floor Frame, 1962 (cast 1987)
Bronze, gold patina

This Earth, This Passage, 1962 (cast 1963)
Bronze

Akari 3QA, by 1956
Washi paper, bamboo, metal, electrics

Akari 1N, 1968
Akari 1N, 1954
Akari 2N, 1968
Washi paper, bamboo, metal, electrics

Planet in Transit #1, 1968–72
Swedish granite

Slide-Mantra Maquette, c. 1985
Botticino marble

Akari 15F, by 1970
Washi paper, bamboo, metal, electrics

202 CD jacket
TD. AD. D. 菊地敦己 Atsuki Kikuchi
CL. ユニバーサルミュージック Universal Music LLC
PT. Akzidenz-Grotesk

203 Book
TD. AD. D. E. 菊地敦己 Atsuki Kikuchi
CL. 菊池寛実記念 智美術館 Musée Tomo
PT. 筑紫Aオールド明朝, Bodoni

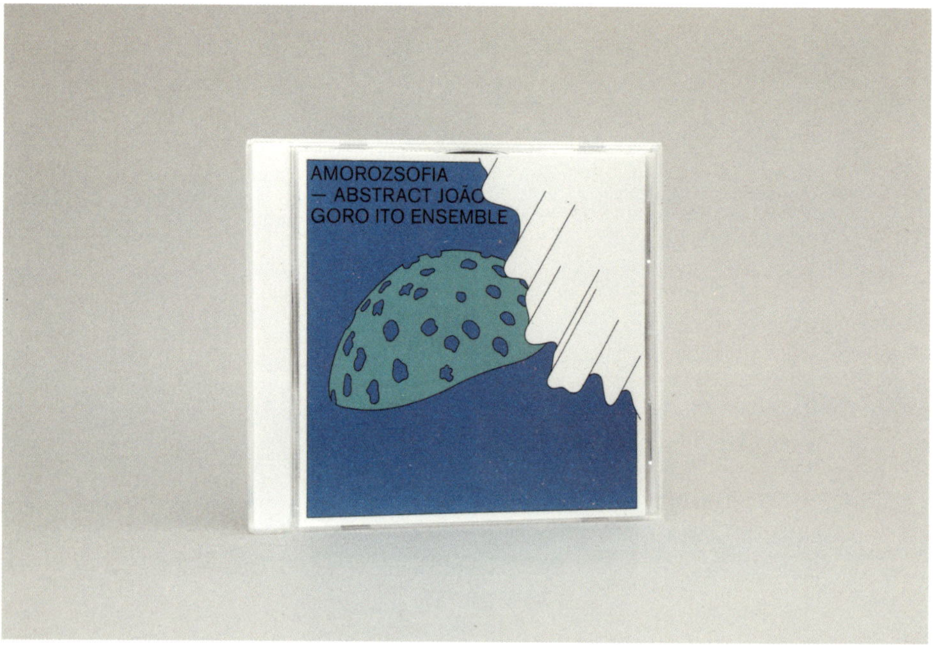

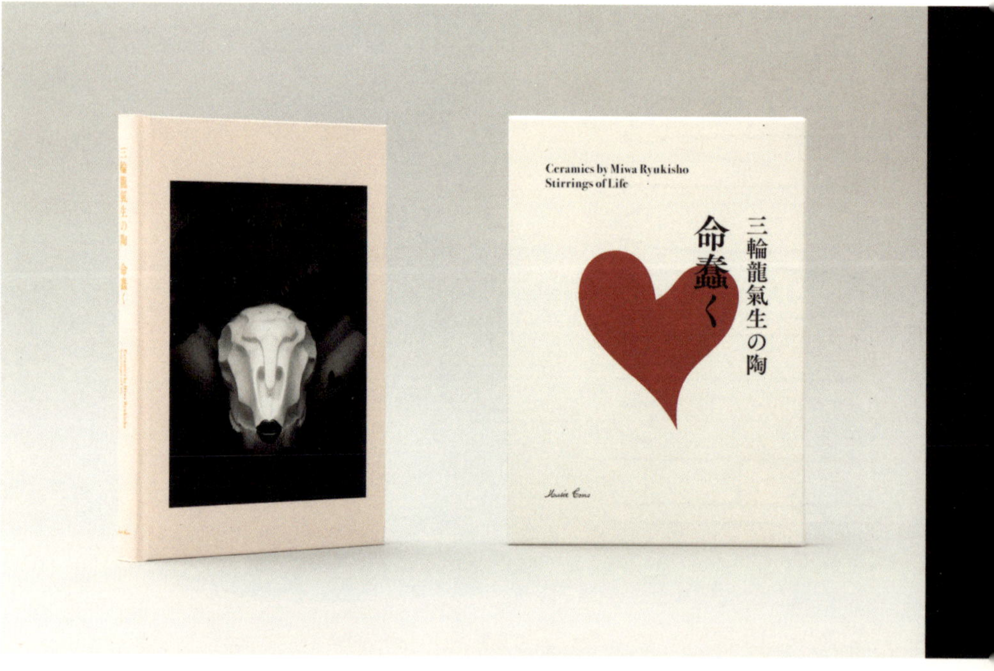

204 Book
TD. AD. D. 菊地敦己 Atsuki Kikuchi
CL.（株）左右社 Sayusha
PT. 游明朝体, Helvetica Neue

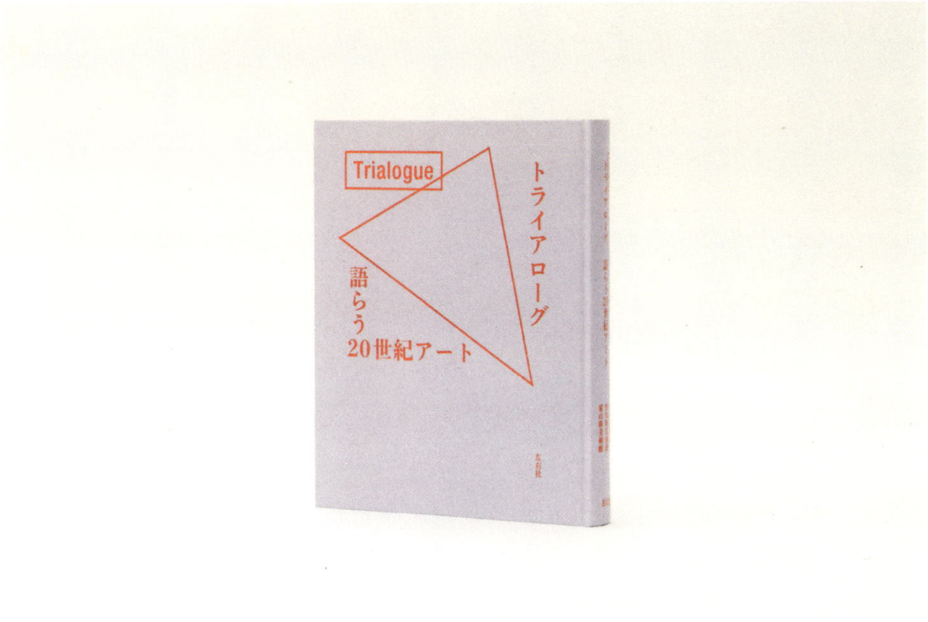

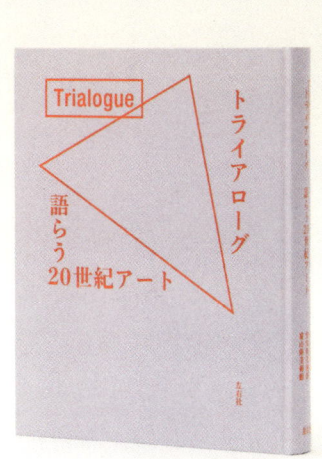

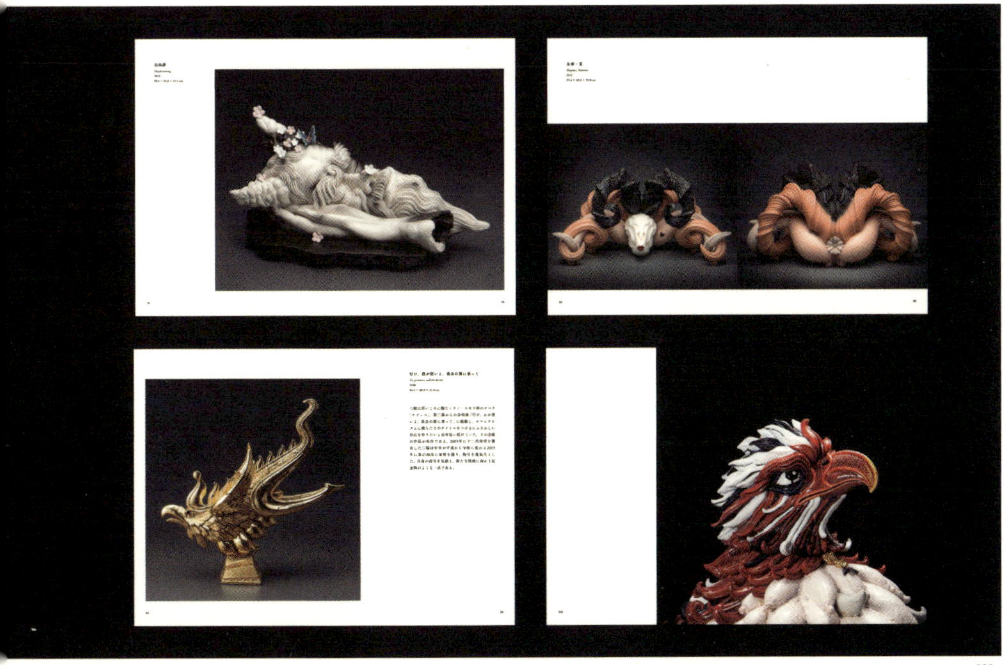

205 Book
TD. AD. D. 菊地敦己 Atsuki Kikuchi
P. 渞忠之 Tadayuki Minamoto
CL.（株）思文閣 Shibunkaku Co., Ltd.
PT. Perpetua

206 Book
TD. AD. D. 菊地敦己 Atsuki Kikuchi
CL.（株）左右社 Sayusha
PT. 太ゴB101

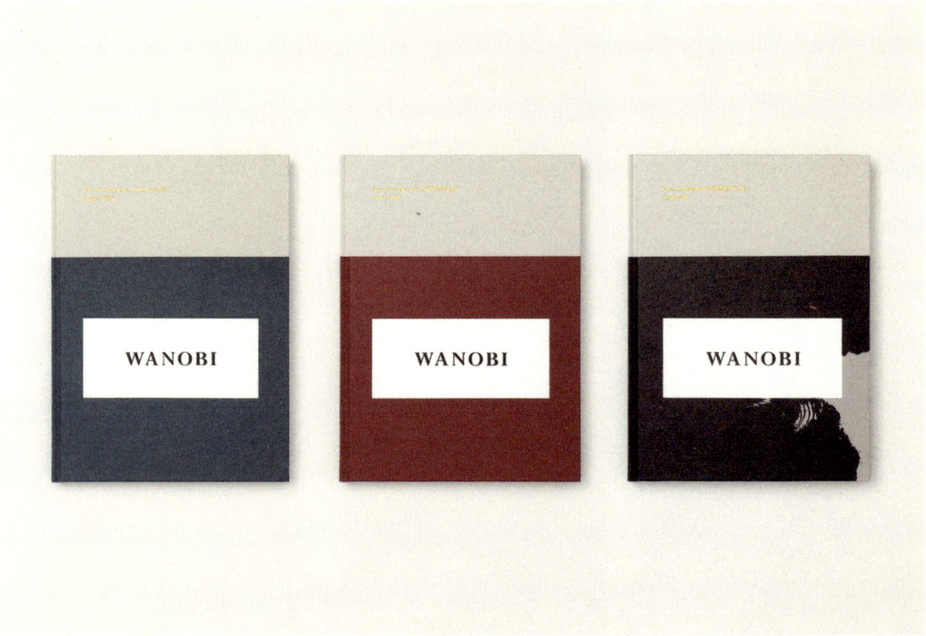

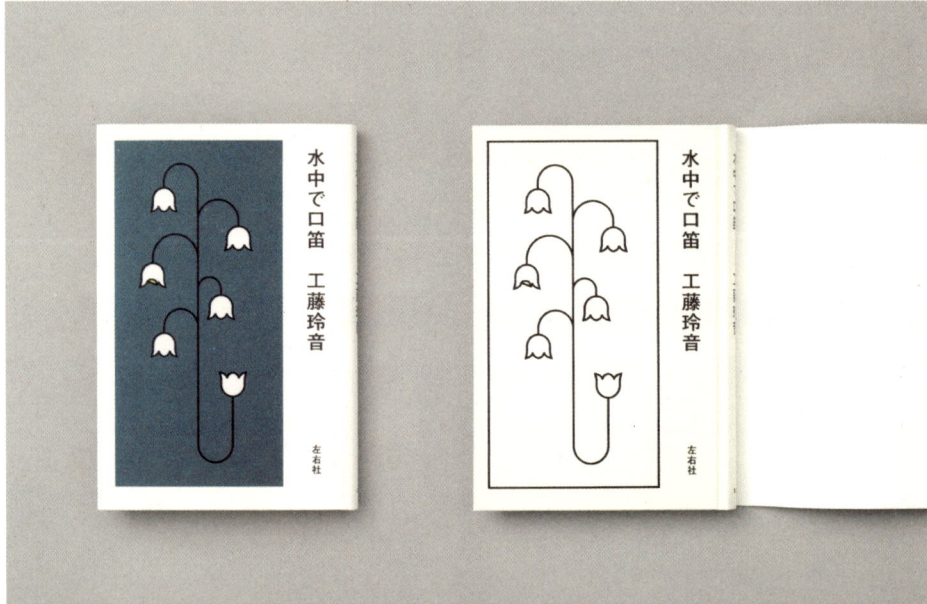

207 Poster
TD. AD. D. 菊地敦己 Atsuki Kikuchi
CL. 京都市京セラ美術館 Kyoto City Kyocera Museum of Art
PT. Akzidenz-Grotesk, 游明朝体

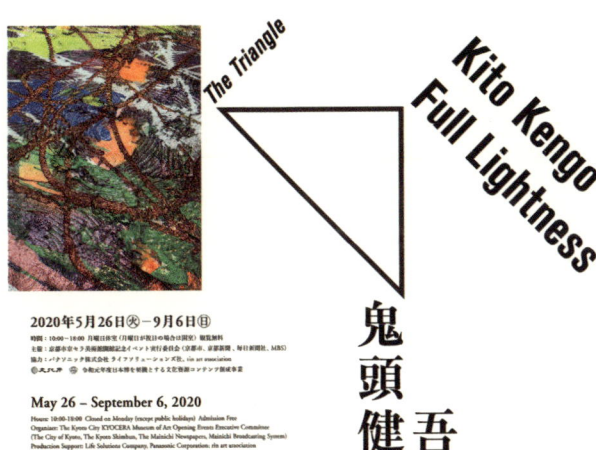
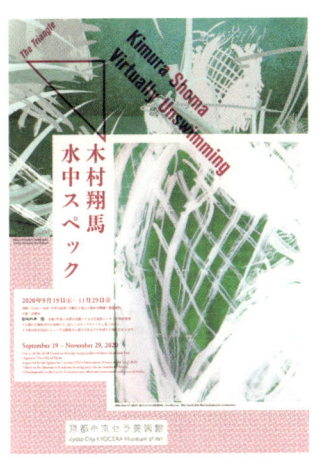
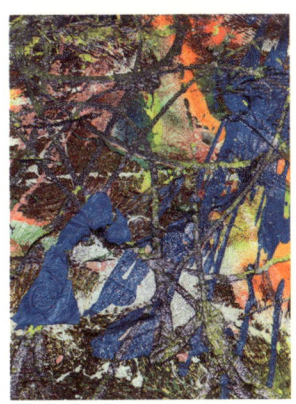
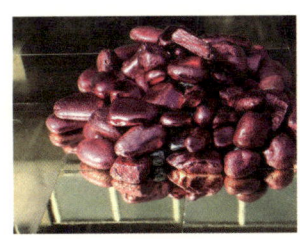
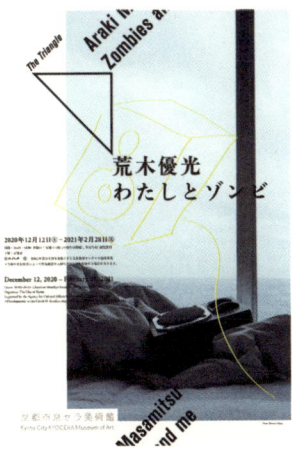
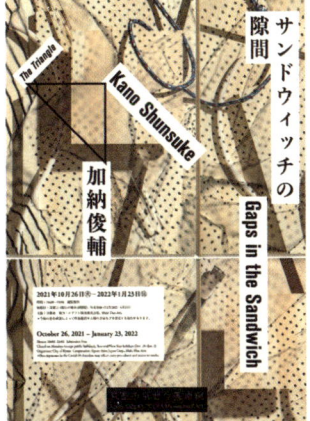
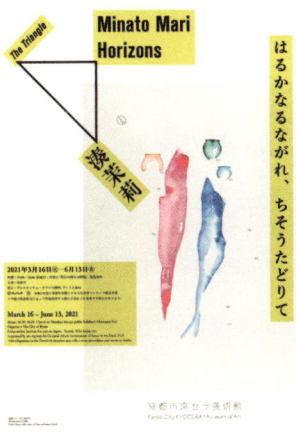
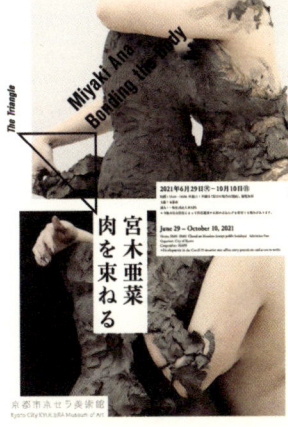

TD. AD. D. 菊地敦己 Atsuki Kikuchi
CL.（株）ジンズホールディングス Jins Holdings Inc.
PT. Helvetica Neue, TBゴシック

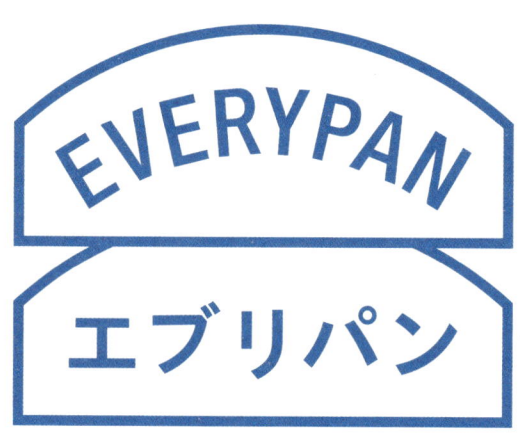

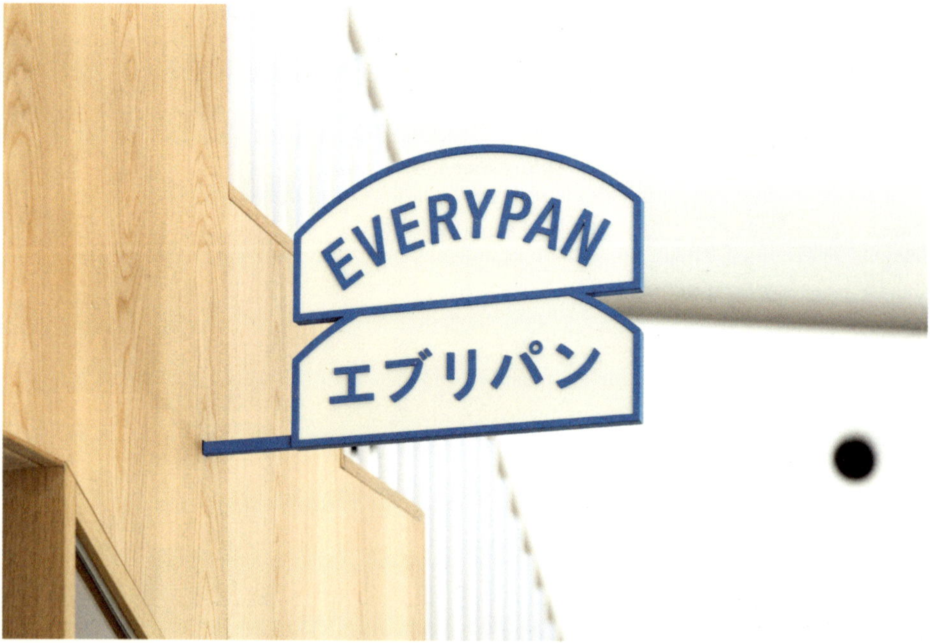

Prize Nominee Work

209 Logotype, Packaging
TD. AD. D. 菊地敦己 Atsuki Kikuchi
CL.（株）ジンズホールディングス Jins Holdings Inc.
PT. Helvetica Neue, TBゴシック

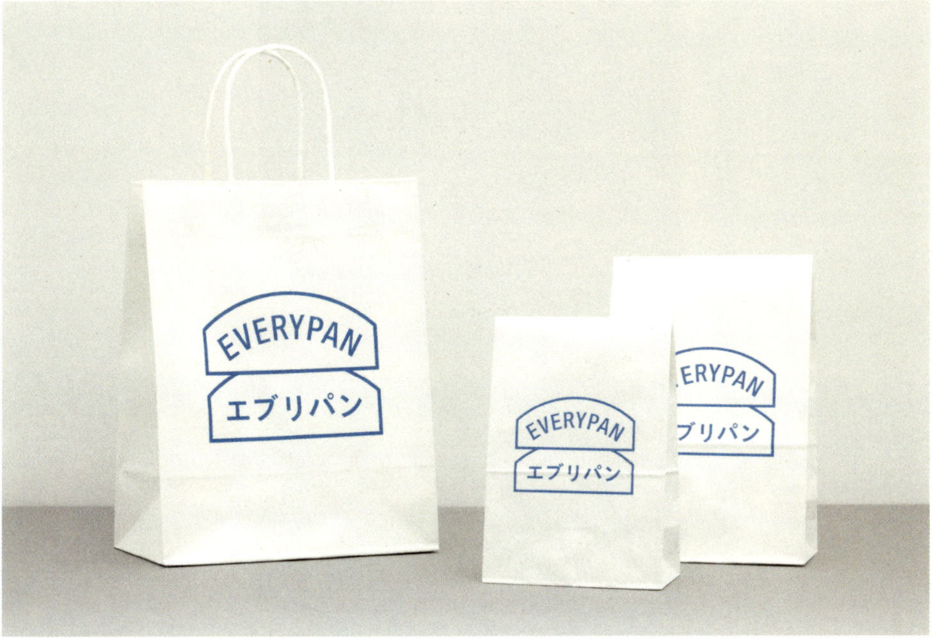

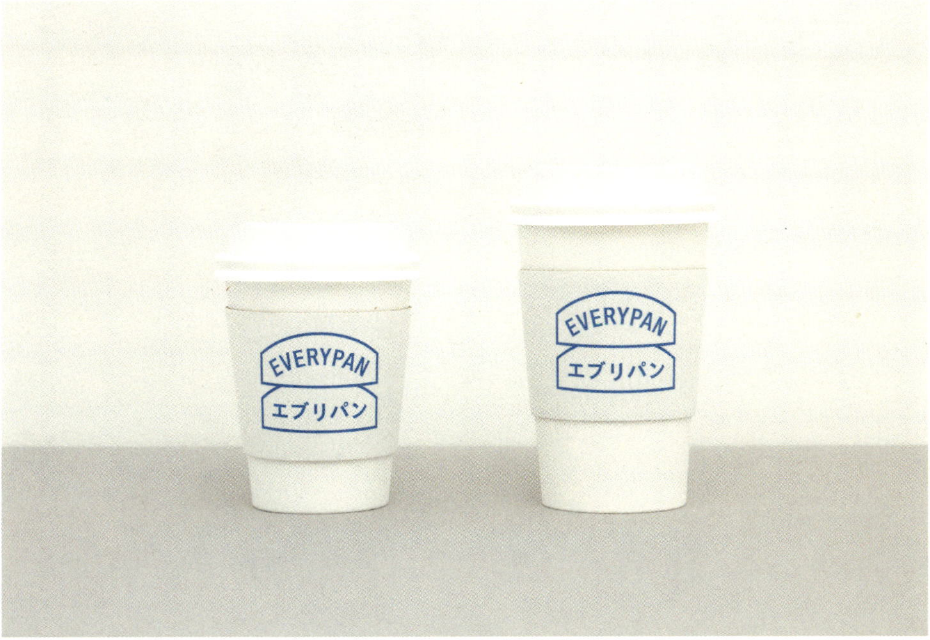

Prize Nominee Work

210 Book
TD. Trisha Kim
CL. Non-commercial work
PT. Akzidenz-Grotesk BQ, Narly OT

211 Poster
TD. AD. D. 木村里奈 Rina Kimura
C. 和田夏実 Natsumi Wada
CL. cocopia

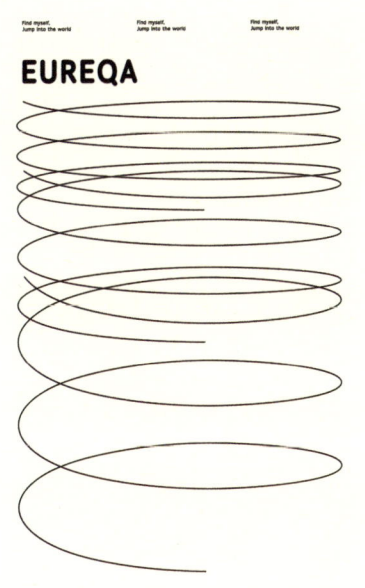

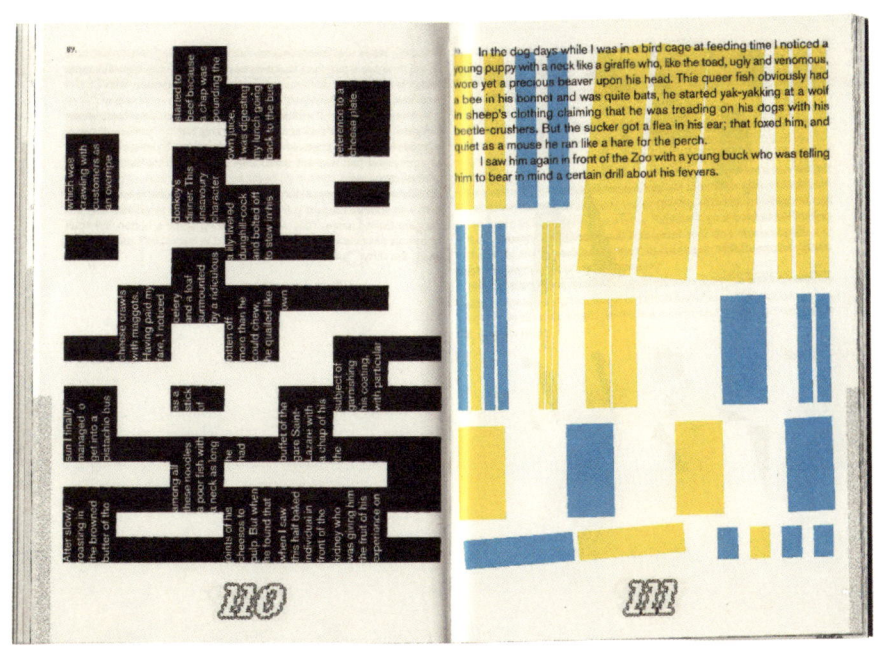

212 Book
TD. AD. W. Gerhard Kirchschlaeger
W. Julia Kirchschlaeger
W. P. CL. Karin Stoettinger
PT. Panama, Steinbeck

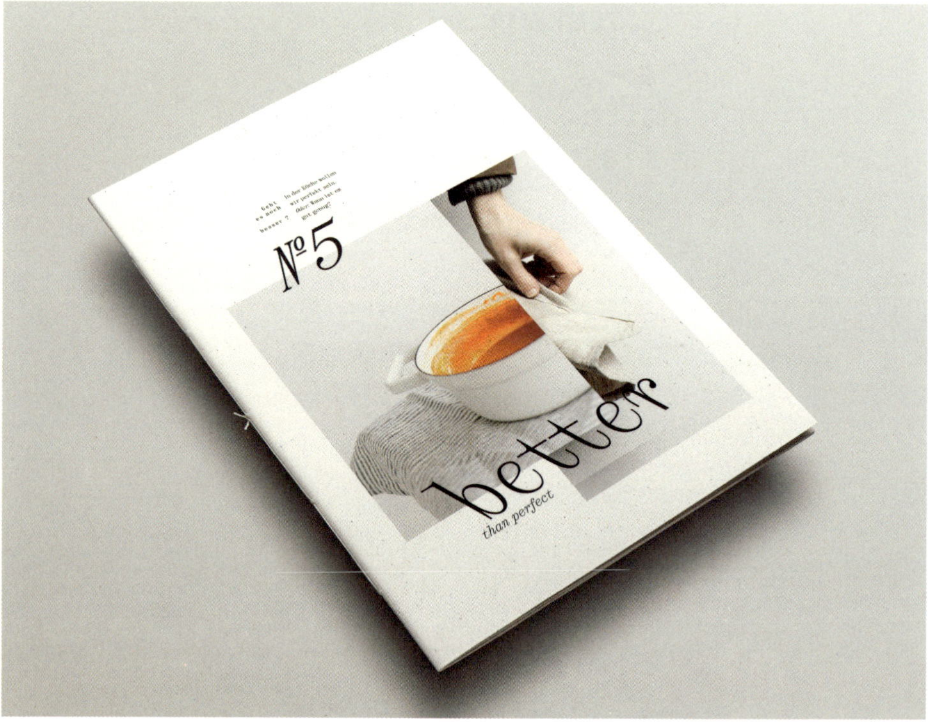

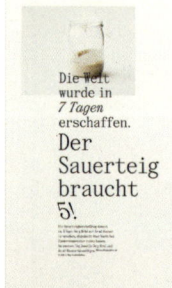
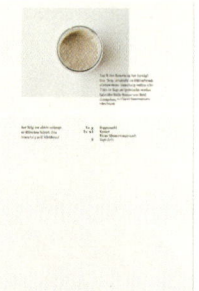
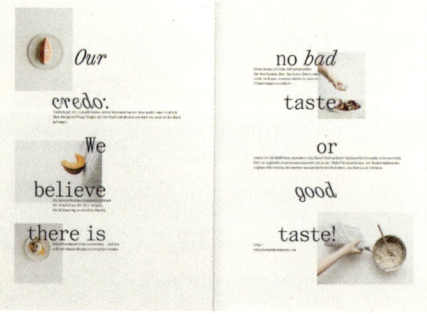

213 Mark & Logo, Branding
TD. 北川一成 Issay Kitagawa
CL. 三菱鉛筆(株) Mitsubishi Pencil Co., Ltd.
PT. Custom-made for the project

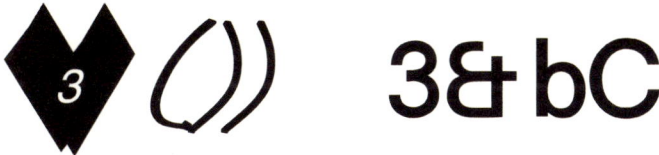

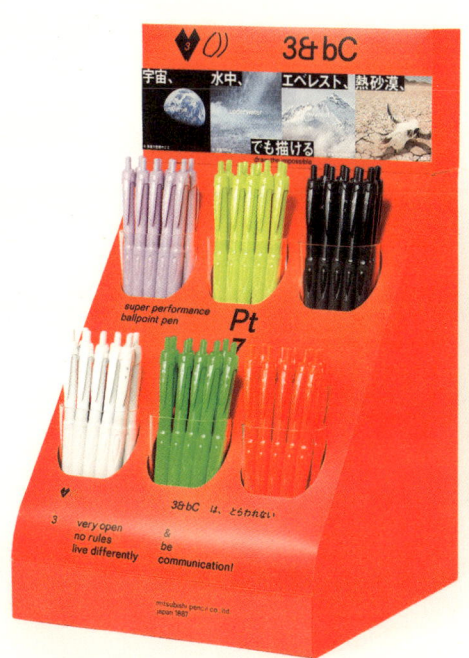

214 BI
TD. AD. 小林昇太 Shota Kobayashi
D. 石田和幸 Kazuyuki Ishida
C. 公庄仁 Hitoshi Gujo, 三浦万裕 Mayu Miura
CA. 古郡達郎 Tatsuro Furugori
I. 牧野伊三夫 Isao Makino
CL. 加納コーポレーション（株）Kano Corporation Co., Ltd.

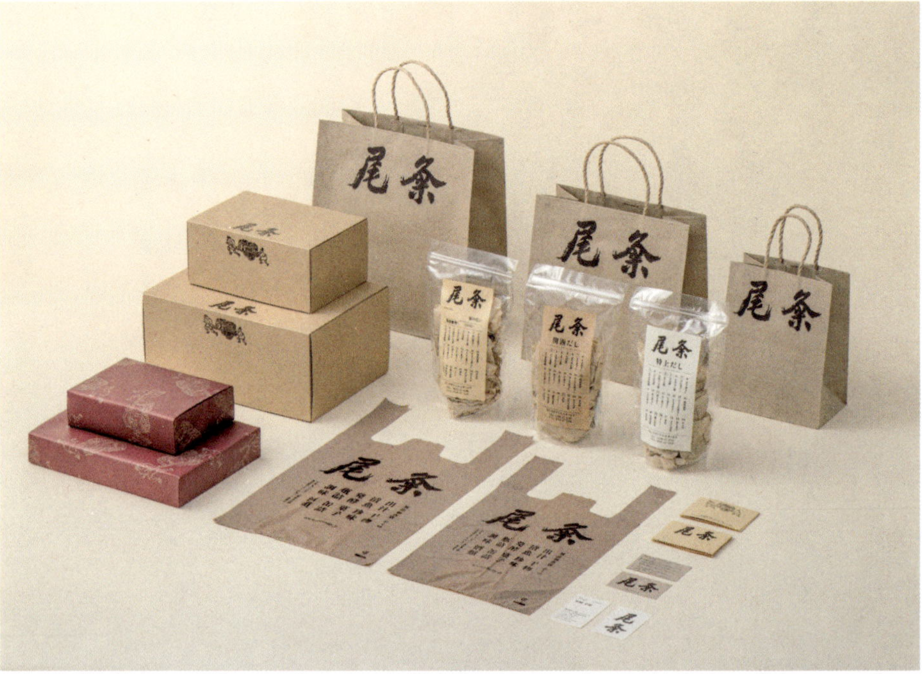

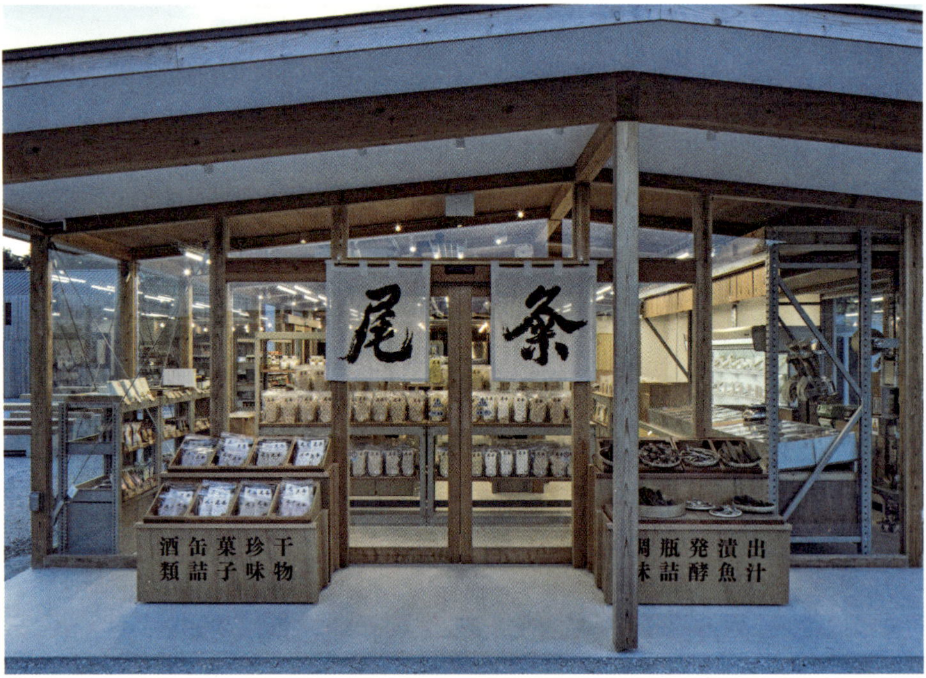

215 Sample book
TD. AD. D. 古平正義 Masayoshi Kodaira
CL.（株）サンゲツ Sangetsu Corporation
PT. Custom-made for the project

216 Campaign
TD. AD. D. 古平正義 Masayoshi Kodaira
P. 薄井一議 Kazuyoshi Usui
CL. ラフォーレ原宿 Laforet Harajuku
PT. Trade Gothic (modified)

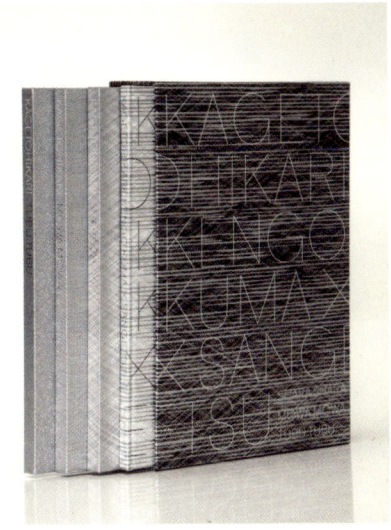
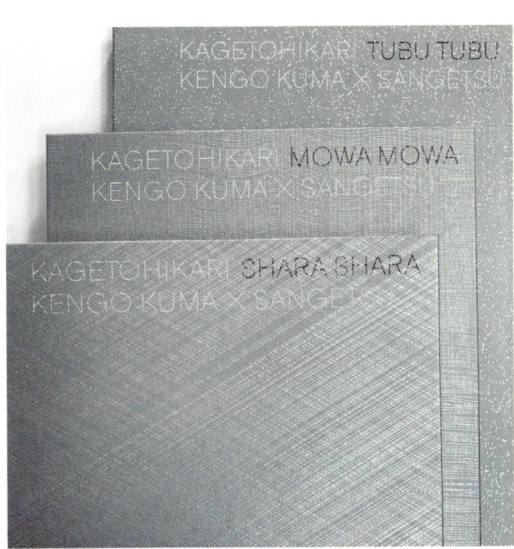

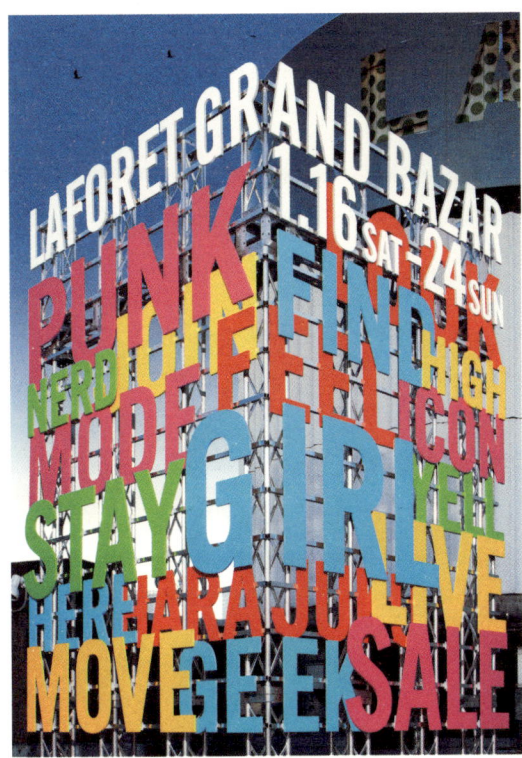

Prize Nominee Work

217 Goods, Promotional item
TD. 小林一毅 Ikki Kobayashi
CL. (株)ワコールアートセンター Wacoal Art Center
PT. Stark Debonair, Erbar Bold Agency, Tiffany light Swash

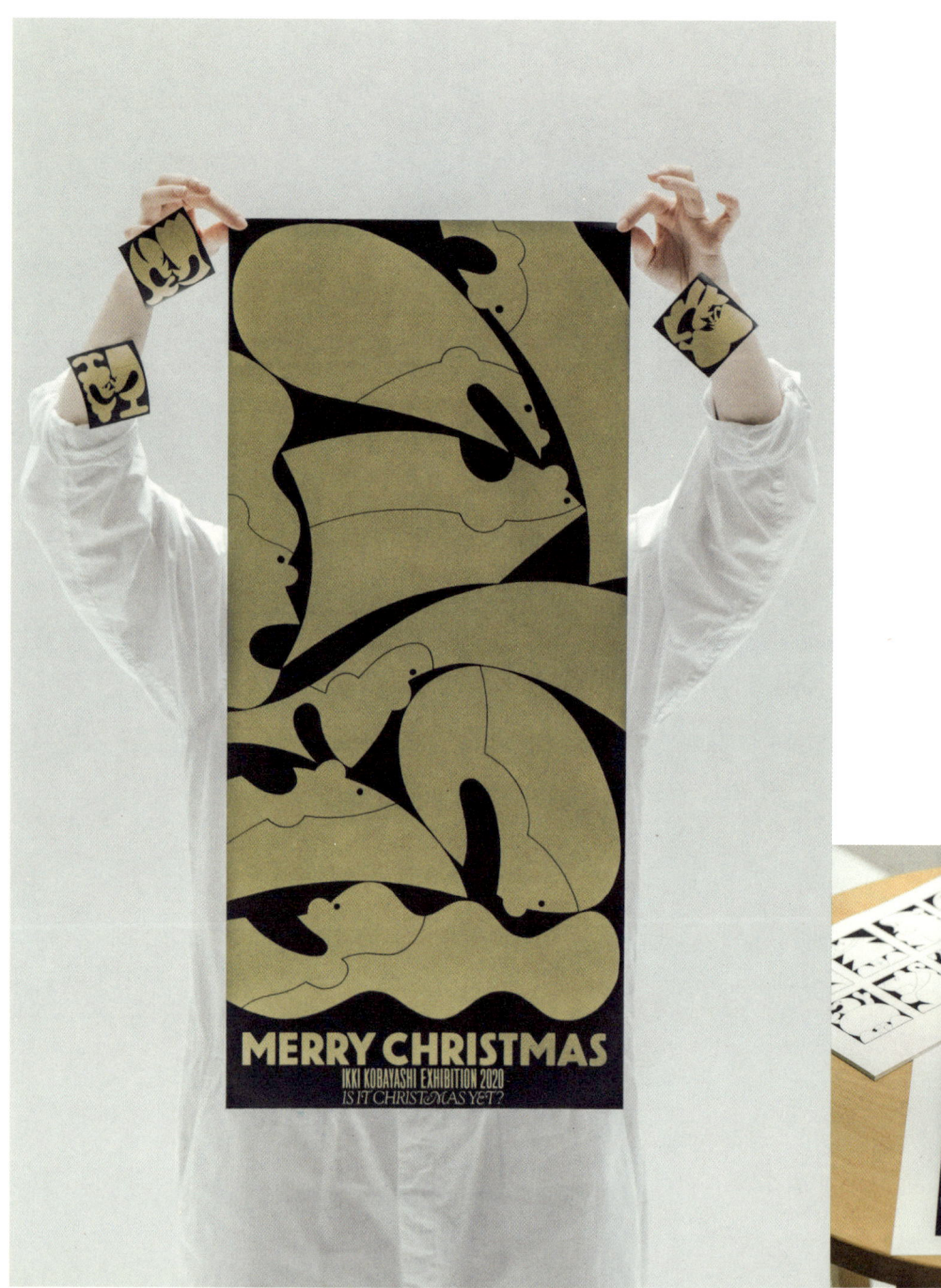

218 Poster
TD. 小林一毅 Ikki Kobayashi
CL. Tokyo Midtown Hibiya
PT. Custom-made for the project

219 Small graphics
TD. 小林一毅 Ikki Kobayashi
CL. 女子美術大学 Joshibi University of Art and Design
PT. Custom-made for the project, Stark Debonair, Nein

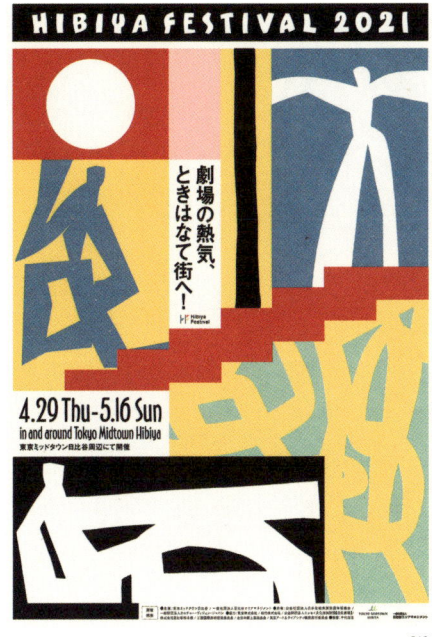

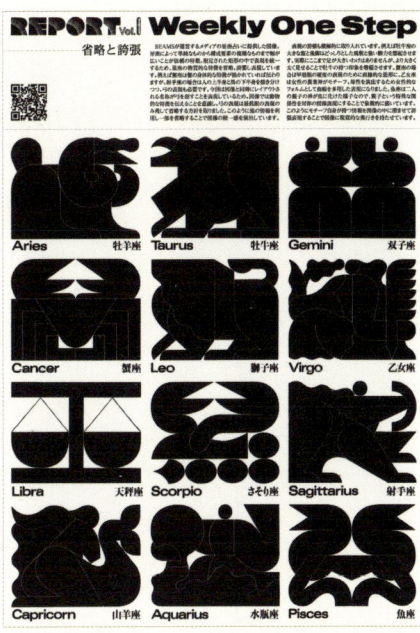

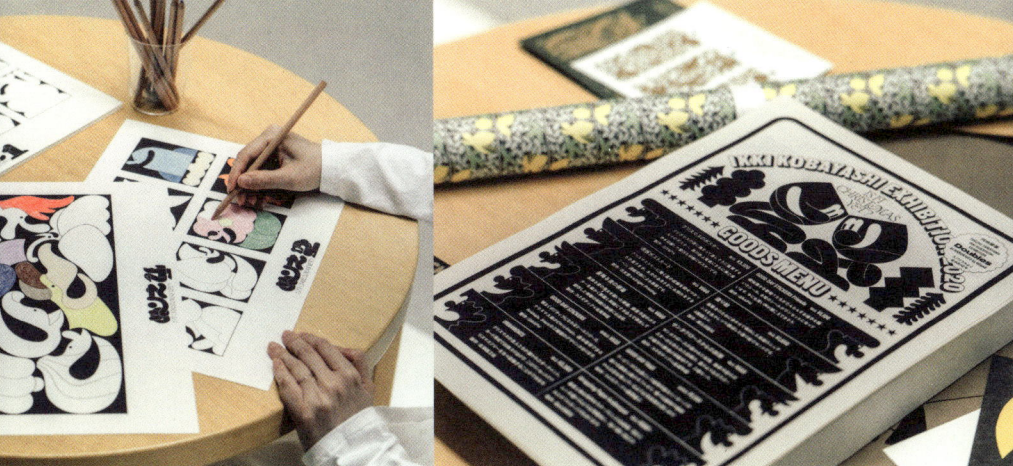

Prize Nominee Work

220 VI
TD. AD. D. P. 小池アイ子 Aiko Koike
CL. Kyoto Experiment 京都国際舞台芸術祭 Kyoto International Performing Arts Festival Executive Committee
PT. 新正楷書, Comic Sans

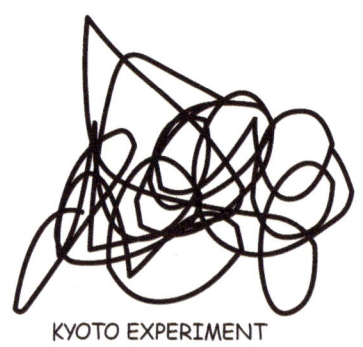

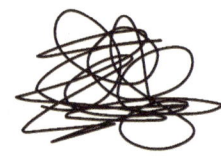

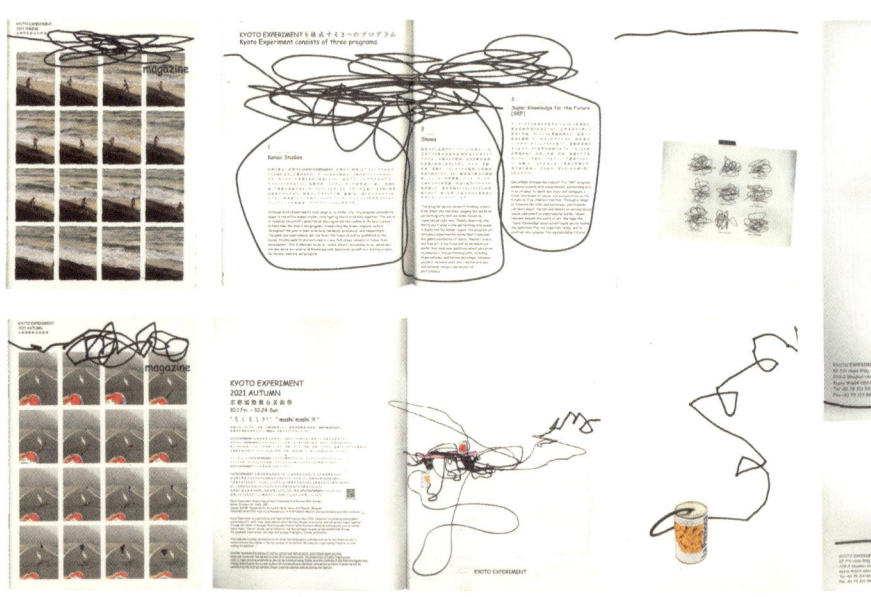

221 Type design
TD. 児玉篤司 Atsushi Kodama
CL. Non-commercial work

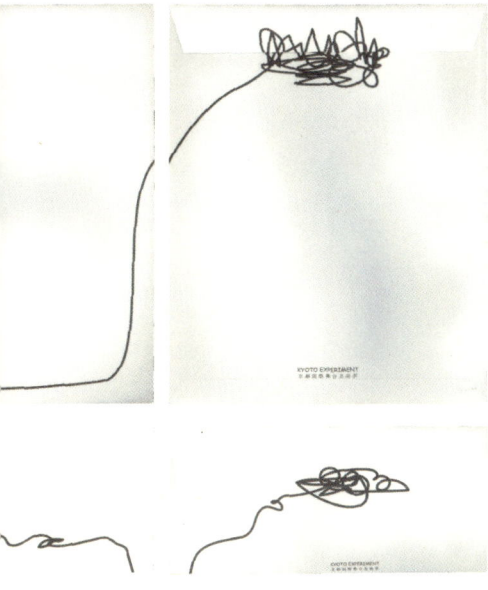

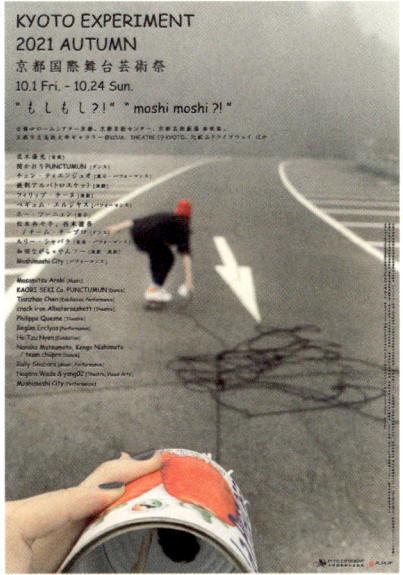

222 Experimental work
TD. AD. 児嶋啓多 Keita Kojima
TDI. 西濱大貴 Daiki Nishihama
CL. Non-commercial work

223 Editorial
TD. Philipp Koller, Lukas Küng, Giulia Schelm, Alessia Meyer
CL. Idolonstudio (Union of European Asian Artists)
PT. Songti SC Light and Self Modern

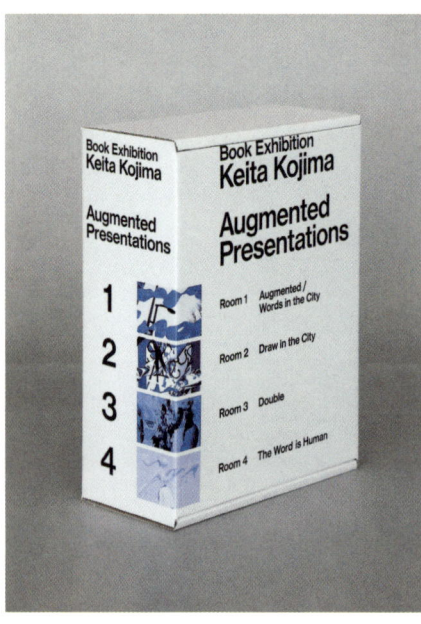
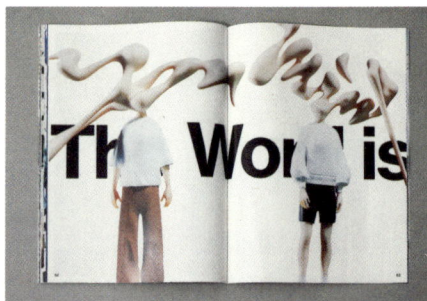
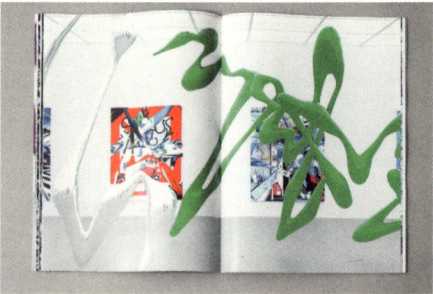

222

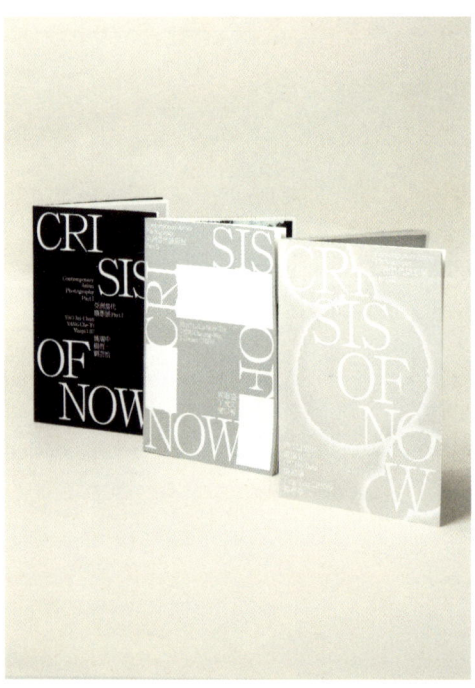
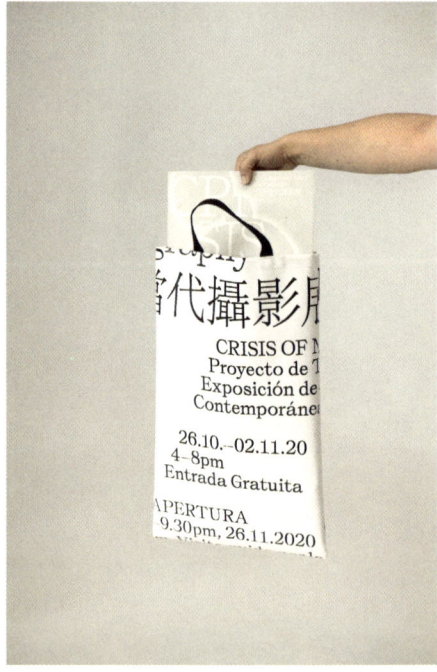

224 Poster
TD. AD. D. Xiangguo Kong
CL. Zhongshan Polytechnic
PT. GeoSlab703 Lt BT

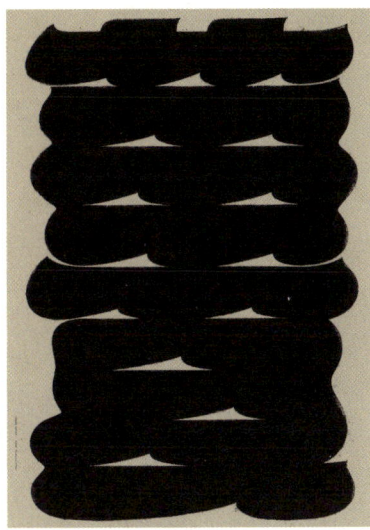
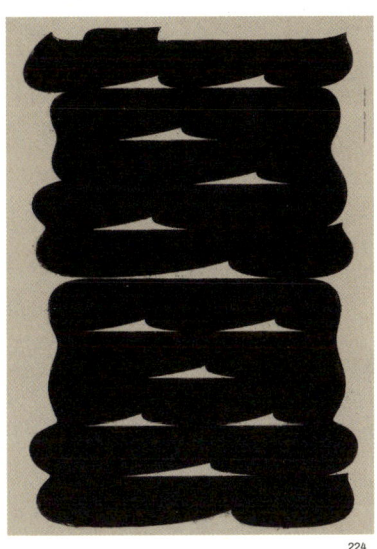

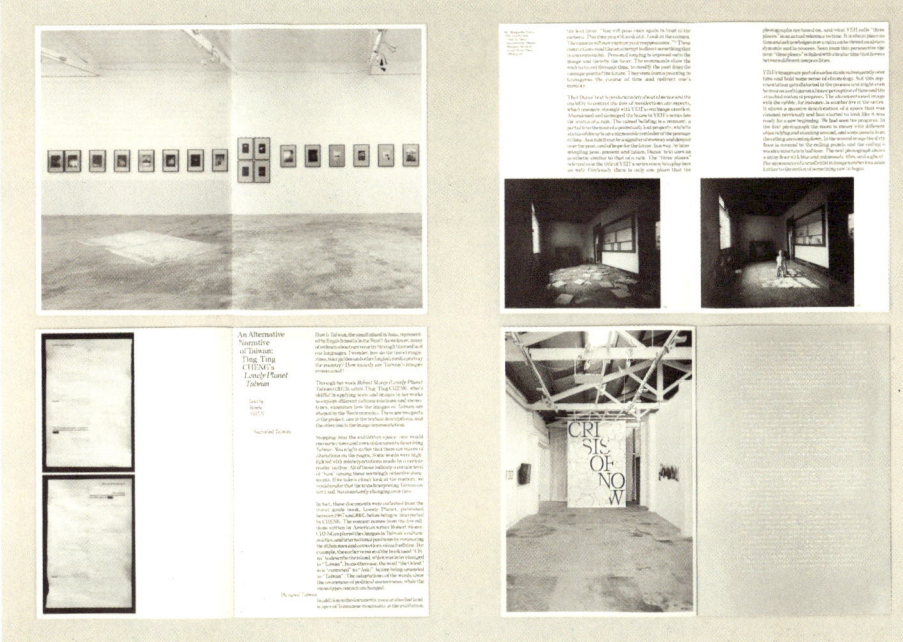

Prize Nominee Work

225 Book
TD. Sophie Kraft
ADV. Gerwin Schmidt
CL. Non-commercial work
PT. Suisse Int'l, Suisse Works

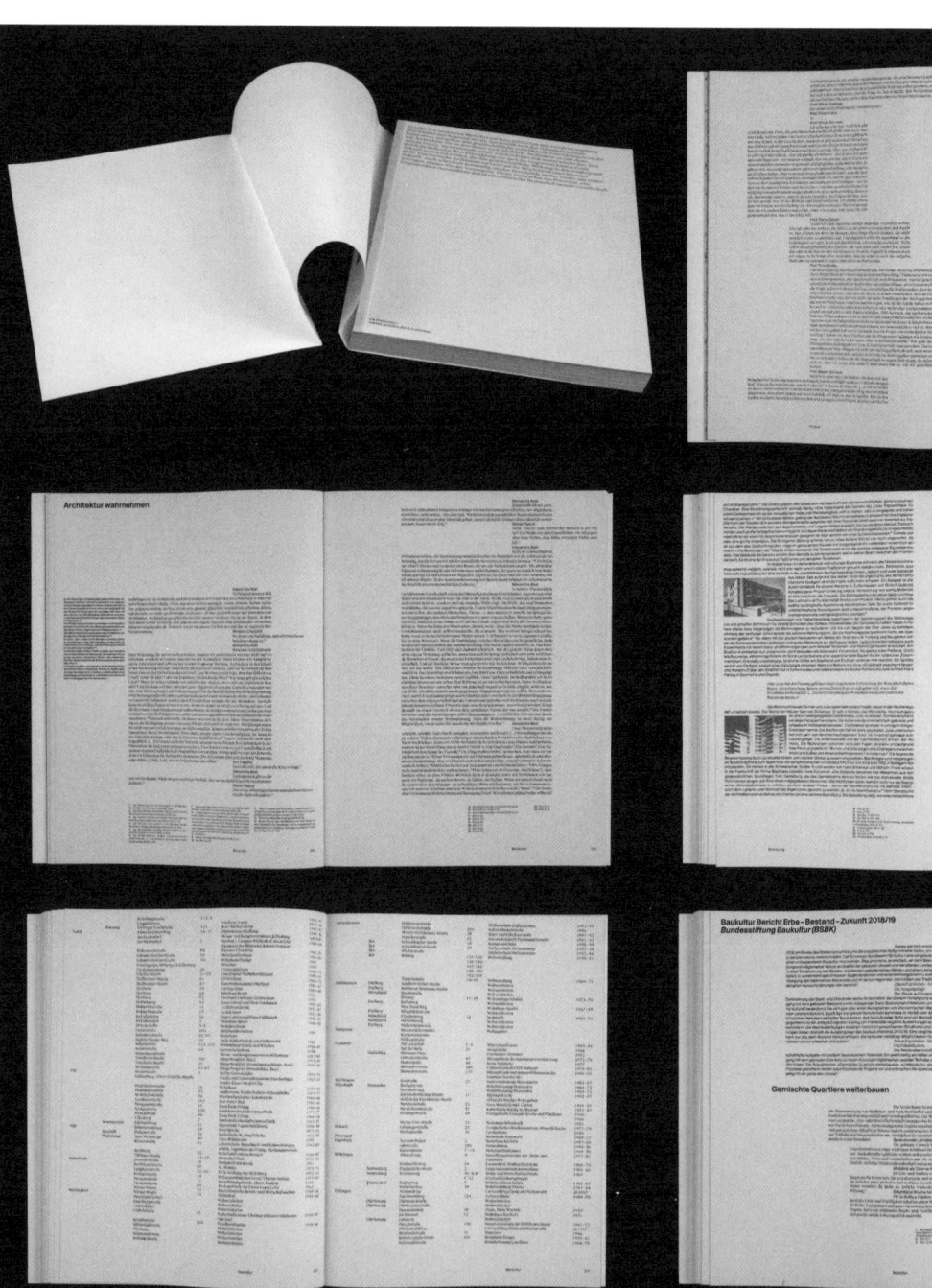

226 Poster
TD. AD. 小杉幸一 Koichi Kosugi
D. 和田伊真 Isana Wada
CL. A-net Inc.

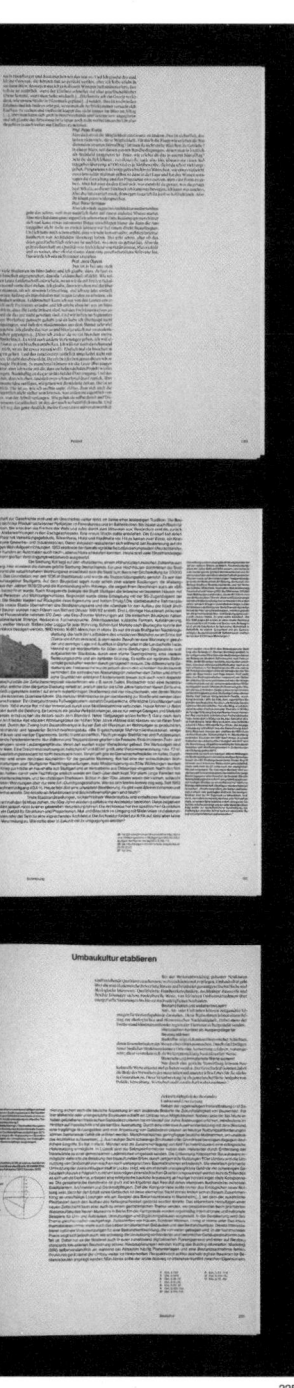

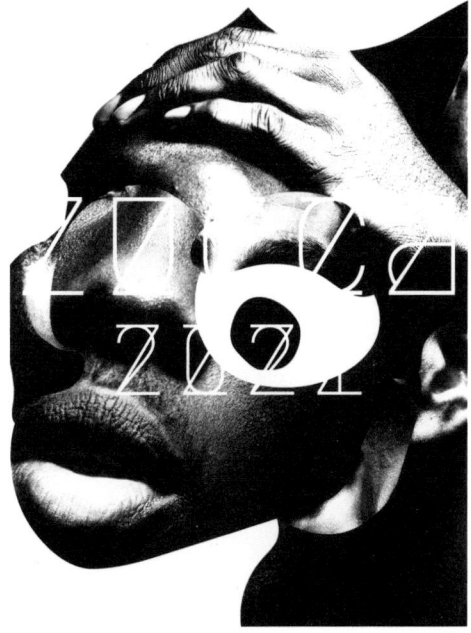

Foundation

A collection of 5 related typefaces

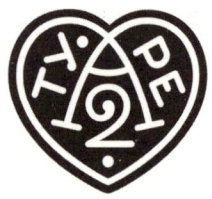

Foundation is a suite of revival typefaces inspired by fonts from historical typeface specimens originating from America, France, and Nordic countries.

The *Foundation* fonts (two serifs and three sans serifs) are eclectic, with their own *unique character* and *distinct history*. Inspiration for the design came from three principal sources: the *Barnhart Brothers & Spindler* specimen No.9 (1907), a *Deberny & Peignot* specimen (1934), and an alphabet sheet from the *Gunnar Biilmann Petersen Archive* (1939). What unites such disparate fonts as a group is that they are all skeletal in form. *To emphasize their barebones, elemental nature, the fonts have been named Foundation.*

228 Type design
TD. Scott Williams, Henrik Kubel
CL. A2-TYPE
PT. Foundation Sans: 44+Condensed+Wide, Foundation Serif+Didot

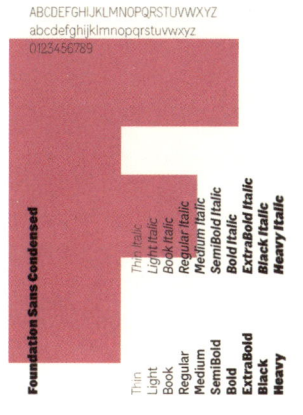

229 Book
TD. Scott Williams, Henrik Kubel
CL. Whitney Museum of American Art,
Philadelphia Museum of Art
PT. A2 Record Gothic

230 Type design
TD. Margaret Calvert, Henrik Kubel
CL. Network Rail
PT. Rail Alphabet 2

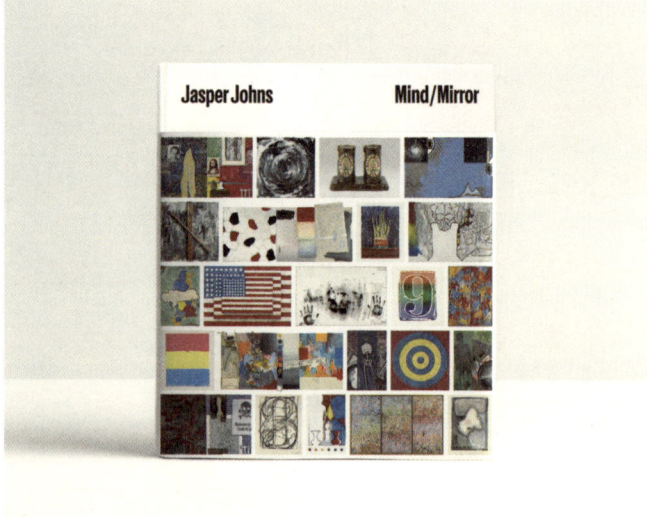

Prize Nominee Work

231 Poster
TD. Dafi Kühne
LP. Sabrina Öttl
PRI (assistance). Laura Porporini, Niclas Funk, Masha Reshetova
CL. City of Zürich, Helmhaus Zürich Switzerland
PT. Berthold Akzidenz Grotesk, Helvetica Bold Extended

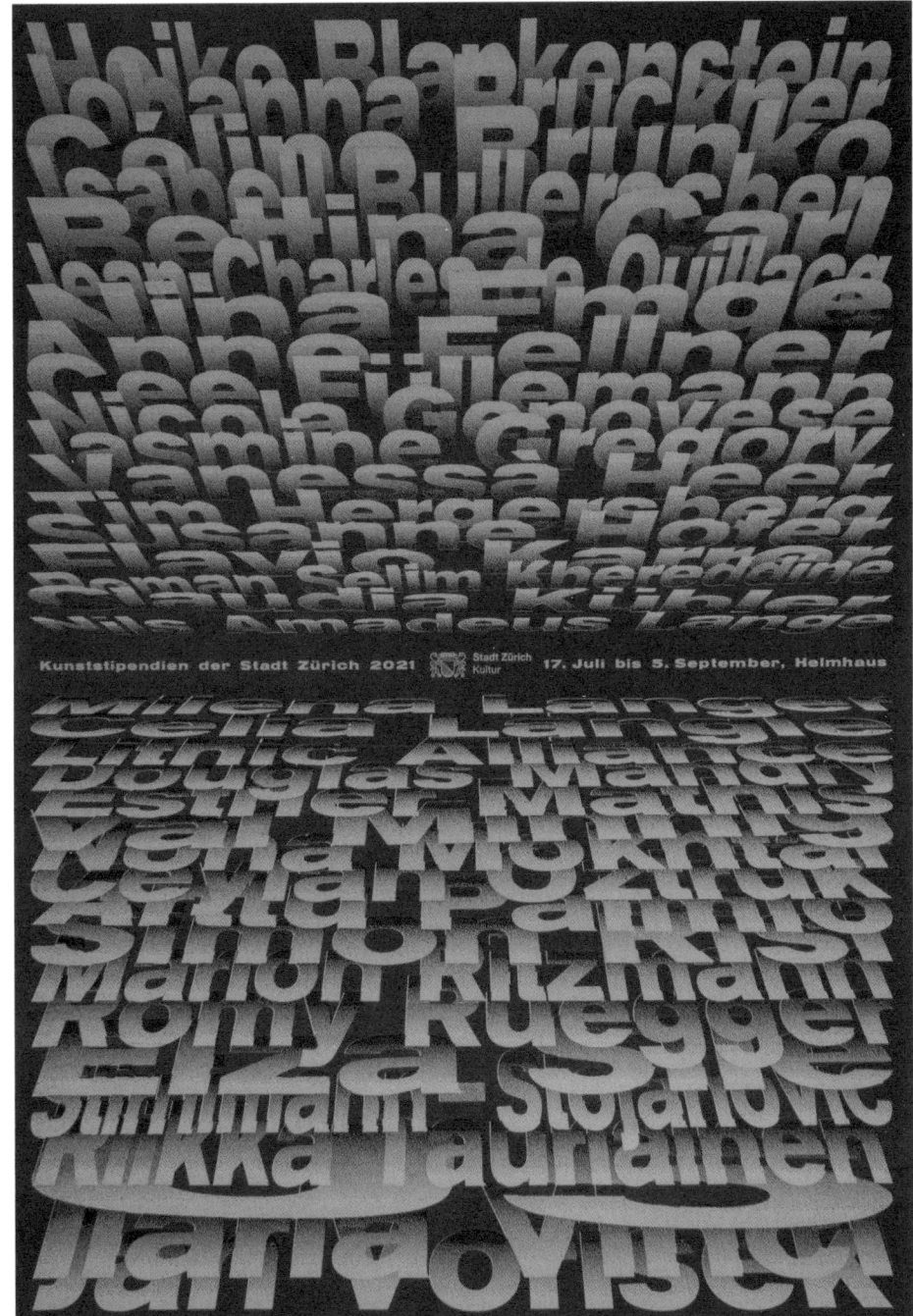

232 Record jacket
TD. AD. D. Jim Kühnel
P. Anton Ginzburg (cover), Postrach, Rothe
(additional photography)
CL. P.A. Hülsenbeck
PT. FK Display

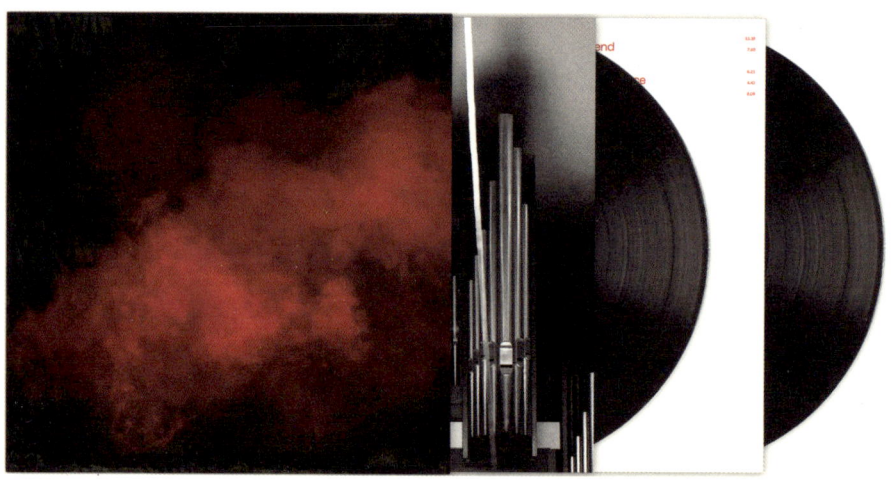

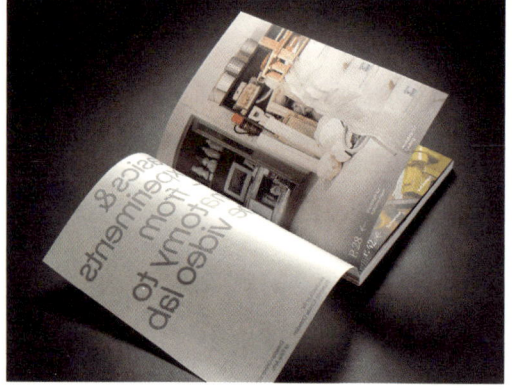

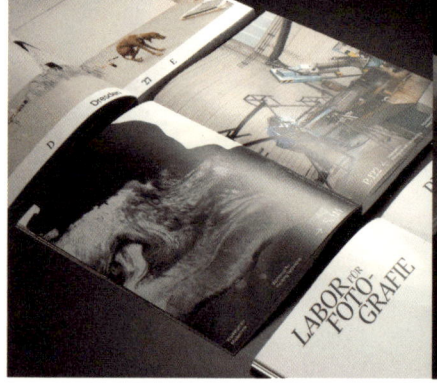

233 Book
TD. AD. D. Jim Kühnel, Roger Lehner
CL. Dresden University of Fine Arts
PT. Routine (Typografische Systeme) & Eliza (Camelot Typefaces)

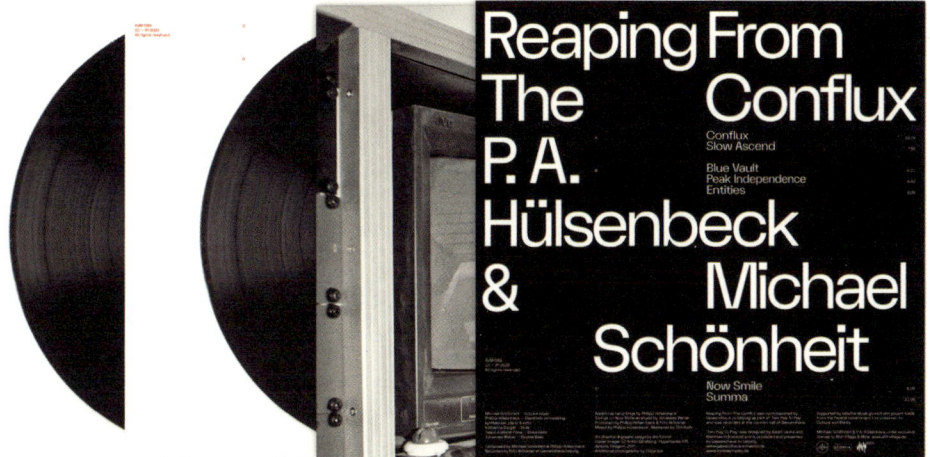

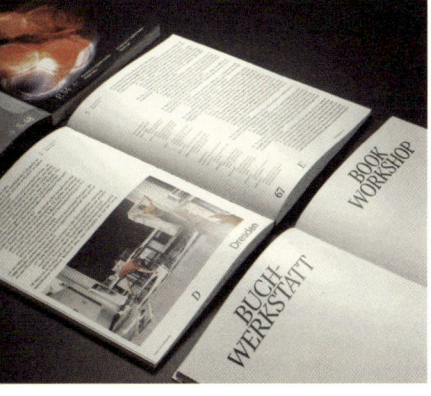

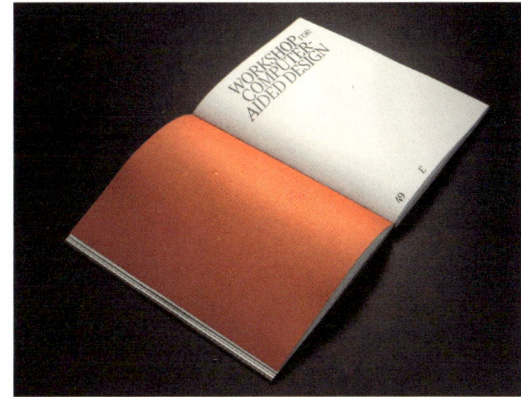

234 Poster
TD. Anna Kulachek
CL. Strelka Bar

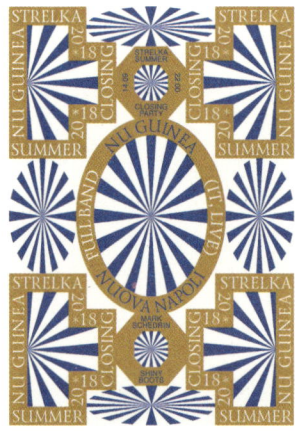
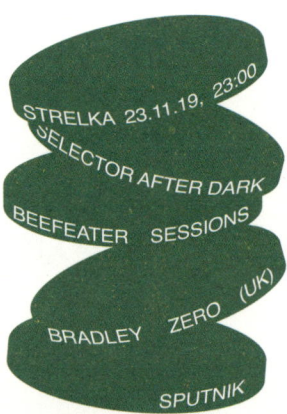
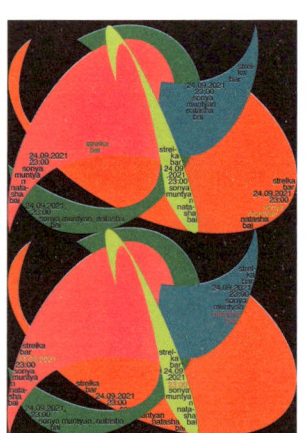
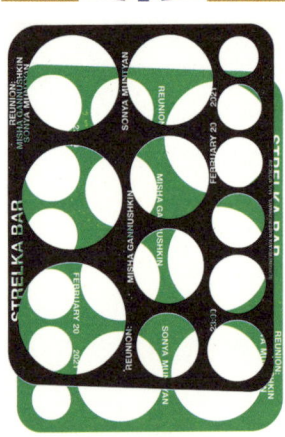
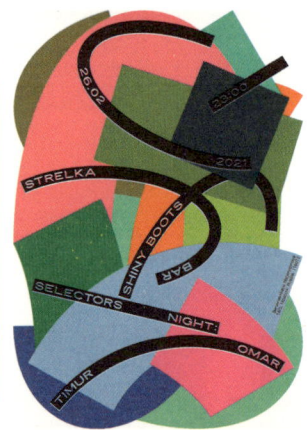
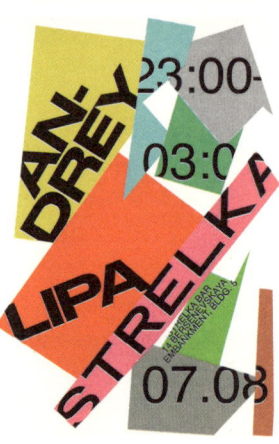
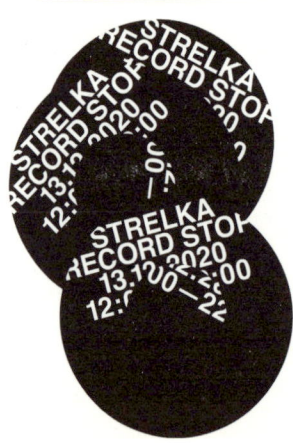
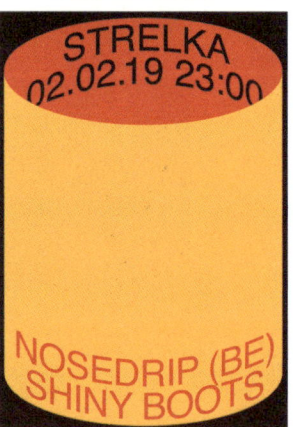
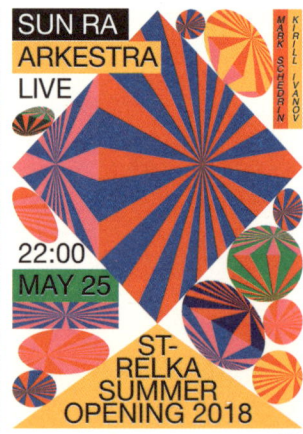

235 Packaging
TD. AD. D. P. 黒野真吾 Shingo Kurono
PM. 加藤潤一 Junichi Kato
CL. (株)Carta Communications Carta Communications Inc.
PT. ABC Favorit

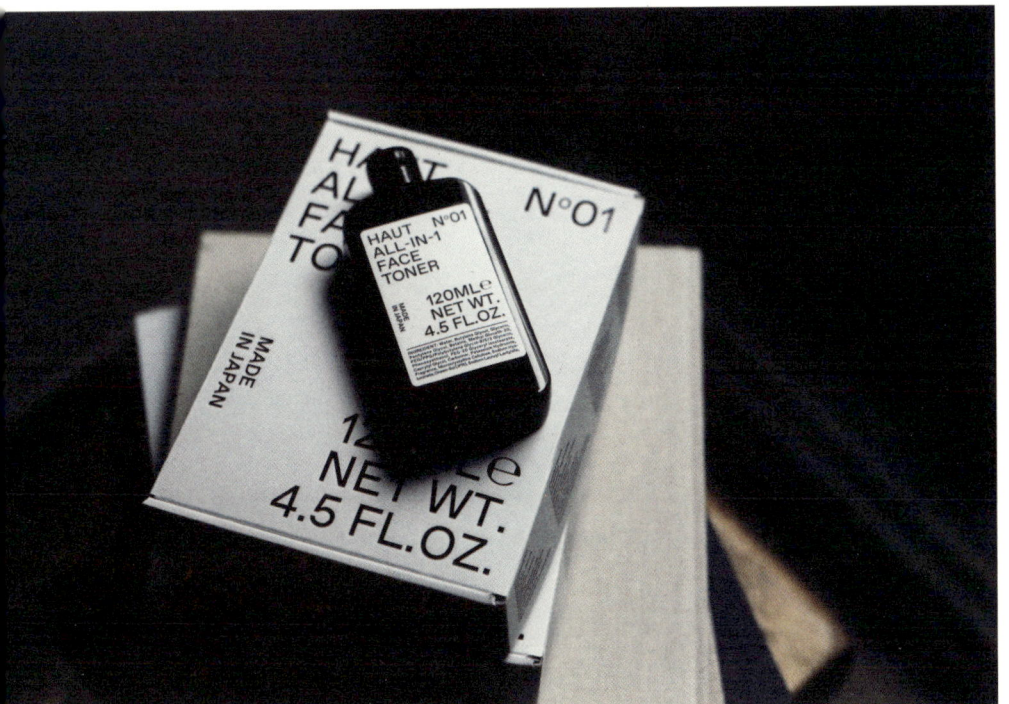

Prize Nominee Work

236 VI
TD. 栗林和夫 Kazuo Kuribayashi
CL. (公財) 福武財団 Fukutake Foundation
PT. Matrix II Hilite OT Extra Bold

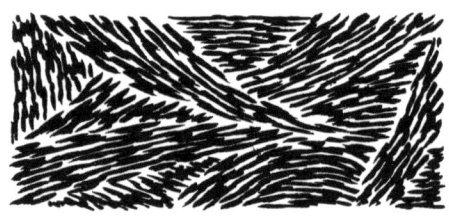

Inujima Life Garden

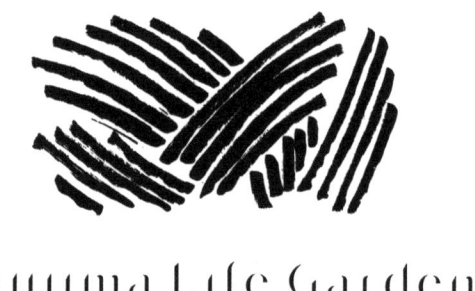

Inujima Life Garden

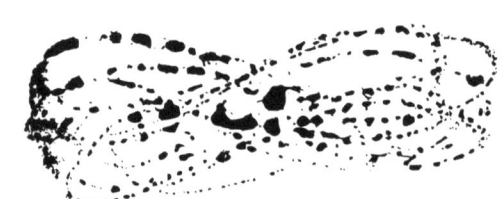

Inujima Life Garden

237 Poster
TD. 栗林和夫 Kazuo Kuribayashi
CL.（公財）福武財団 Fukutake Foundation
PT. Matrix II Hilite OT Extra Bold

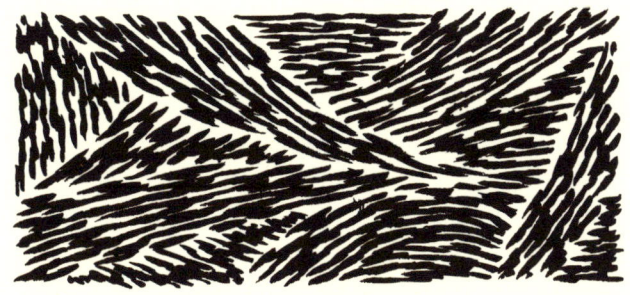

238 Poster
TD. AD. D. Lee Chang Pei
CL. Non-commercial work
PT. Custom-made for the project

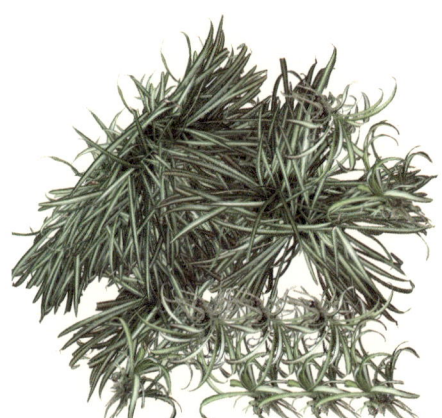
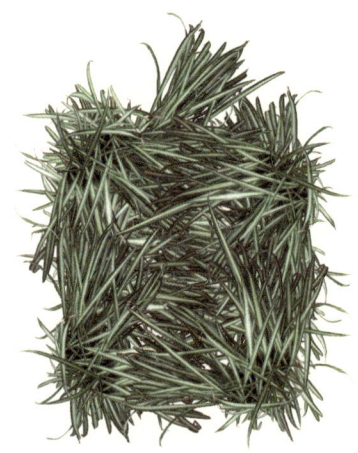
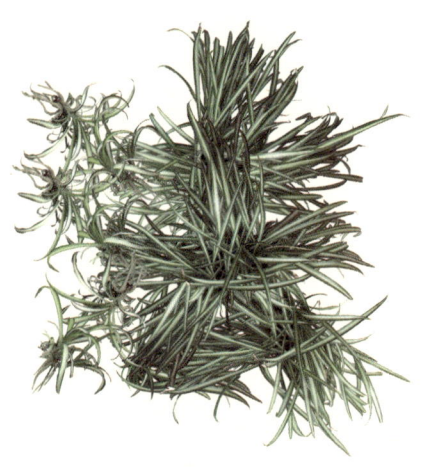
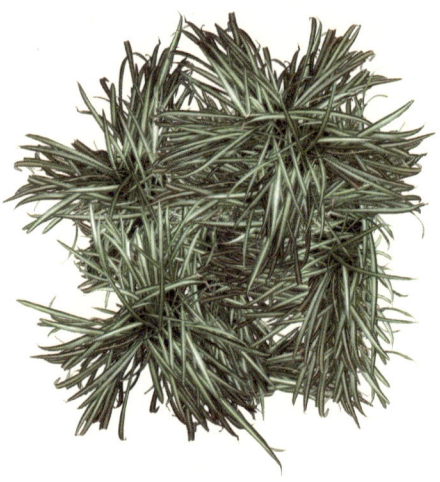

239 Branding
TD. AD. D. Xibin Li
D. Wei Zhang
P. Cong Chen
CL. Boundless
PT. Helvetica, SourceHanSansSC Bold

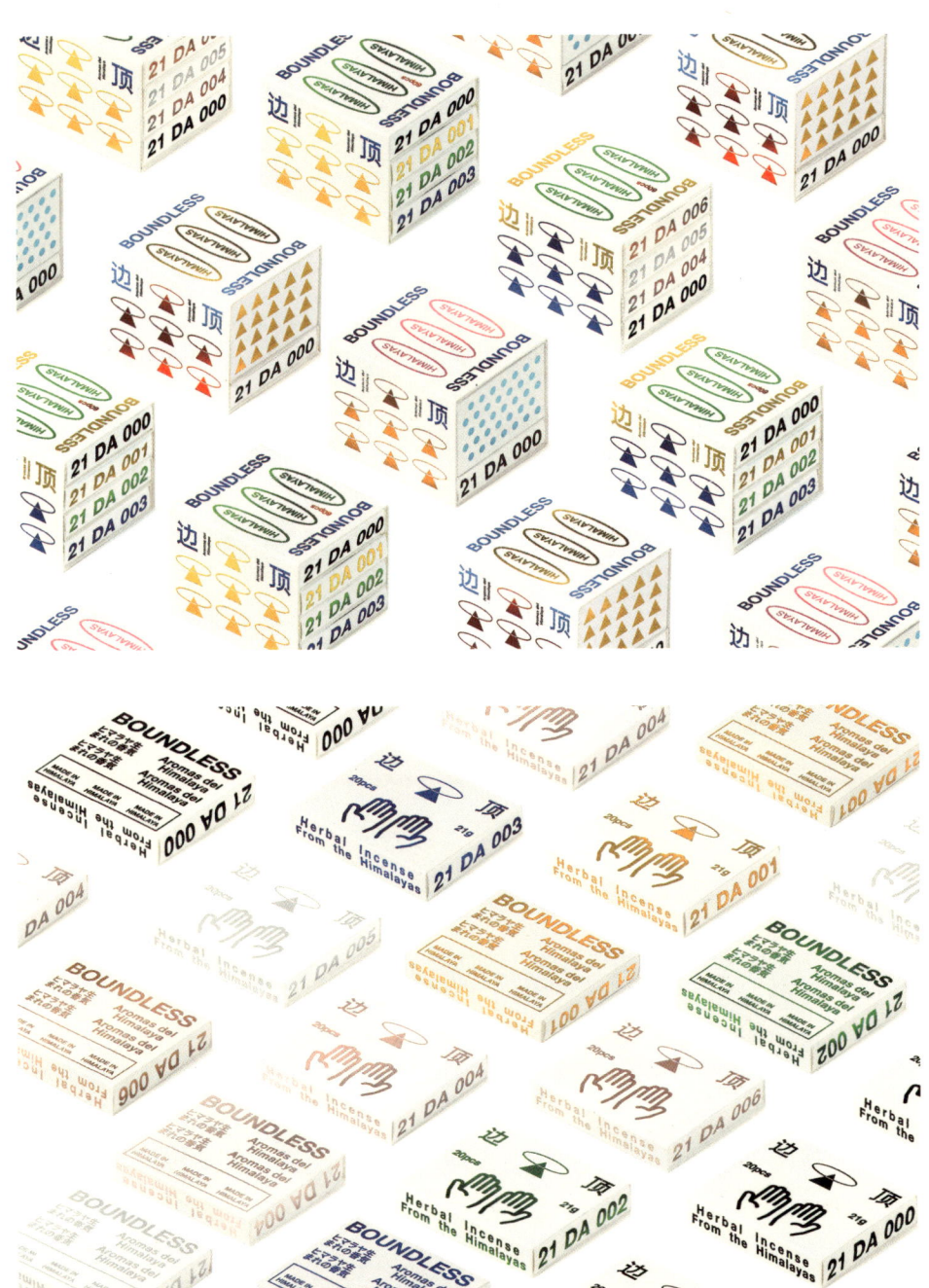

Poster
TD. AD. D. Xibin Li
P. Haojun Zhang, Xiang Feng
CL. Fang Zheng Font
PT. Fang Zheng Xiao Biao Song

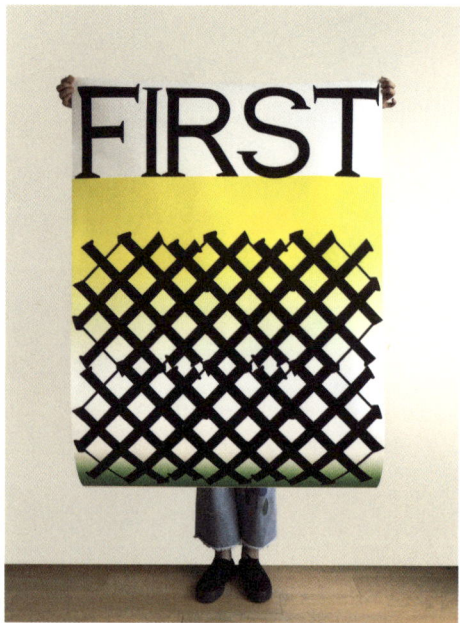
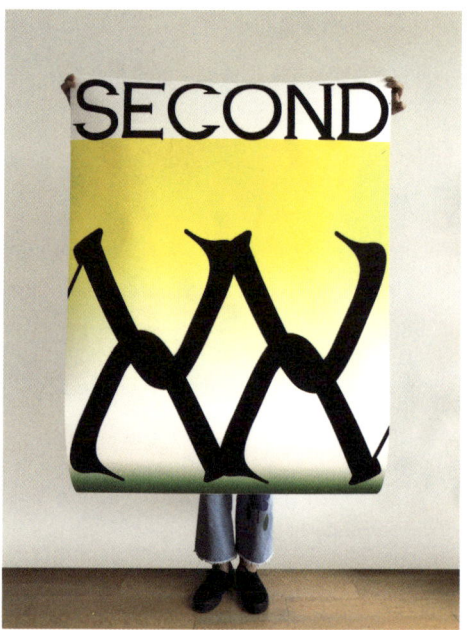
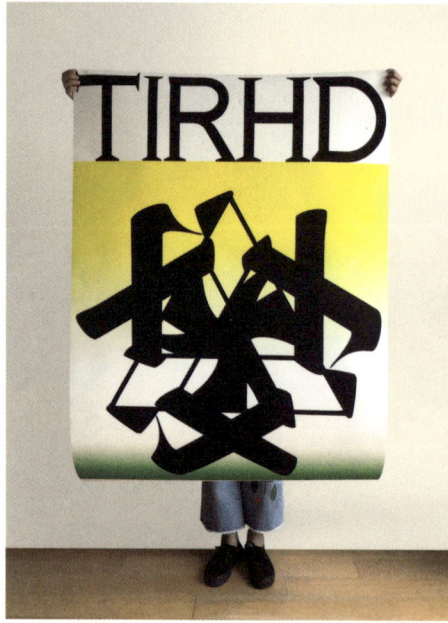
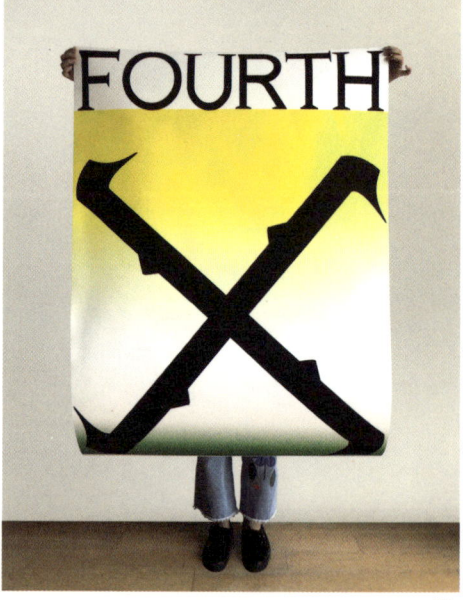

241 Poster
TD. AD. D. Xibin Li
D. P. Haojun Zhang
P. Xiang Feng
CL. Hot Crush
PT. Fang Zheng Lan Ting Hei

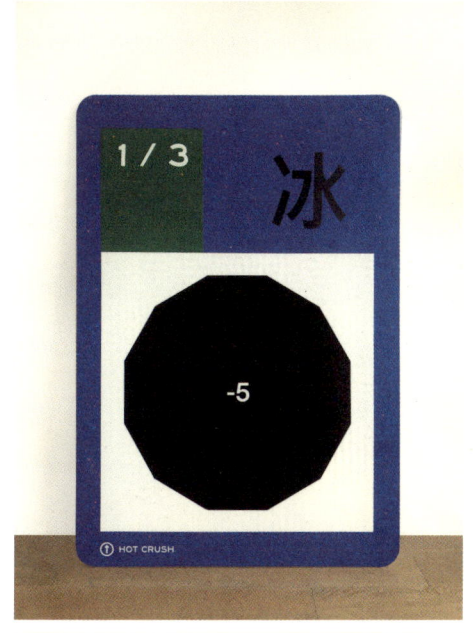
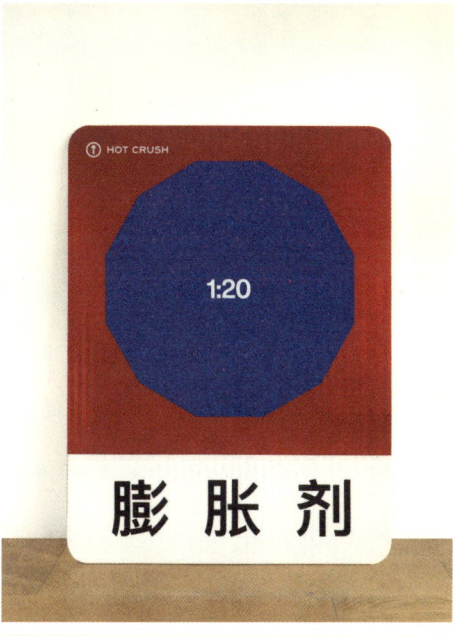
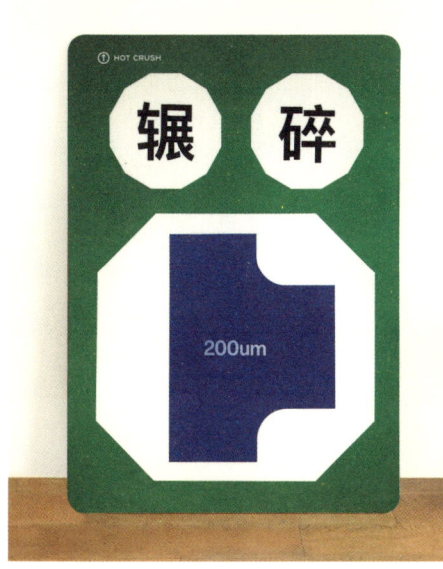
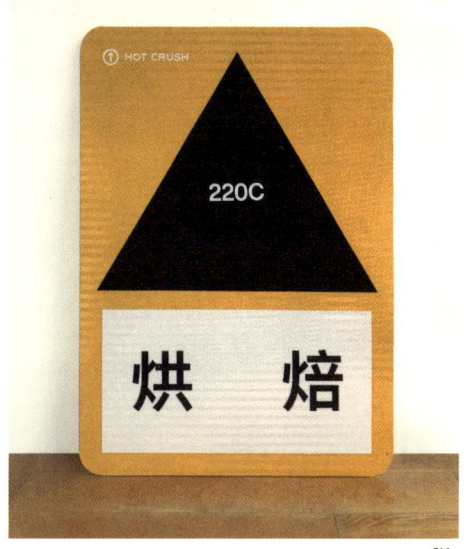

242 VI
TD. AD. D. Che Liang
CL. Chengdu Museum

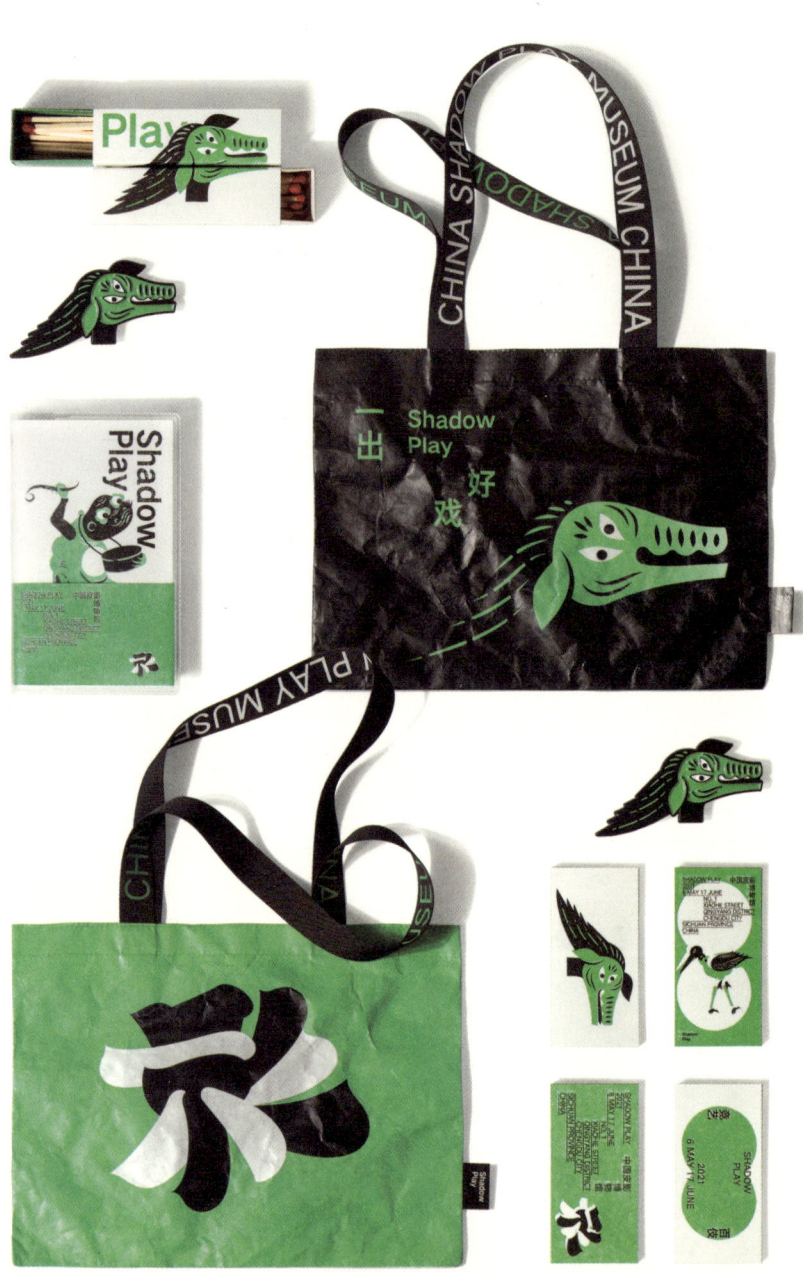

243 Small graphics
TD. Liao Bofeng
I. Liu Xinhua
P. Huang Tao, Huang Yinghua
CL. Lavie Matérielle Bookstore
PT. Helvetica

244 Experimental work
TD. Liao Bofeng
CL. Guangzhou Academy of Fine Arts
PT. Helvetica

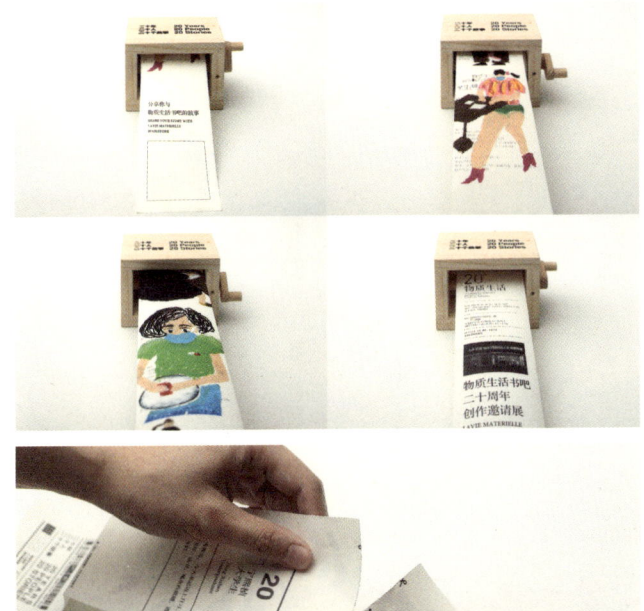

243

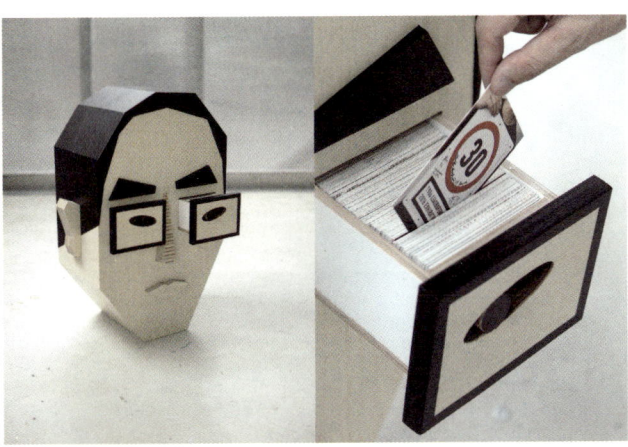

244

Prize Nominee Work

245 Poster
TD. AD. D. Tao Lin
P. Pinlan Zhou
CL. ByNow X Creater
PT. Knockout, Octin Stencil, Holland

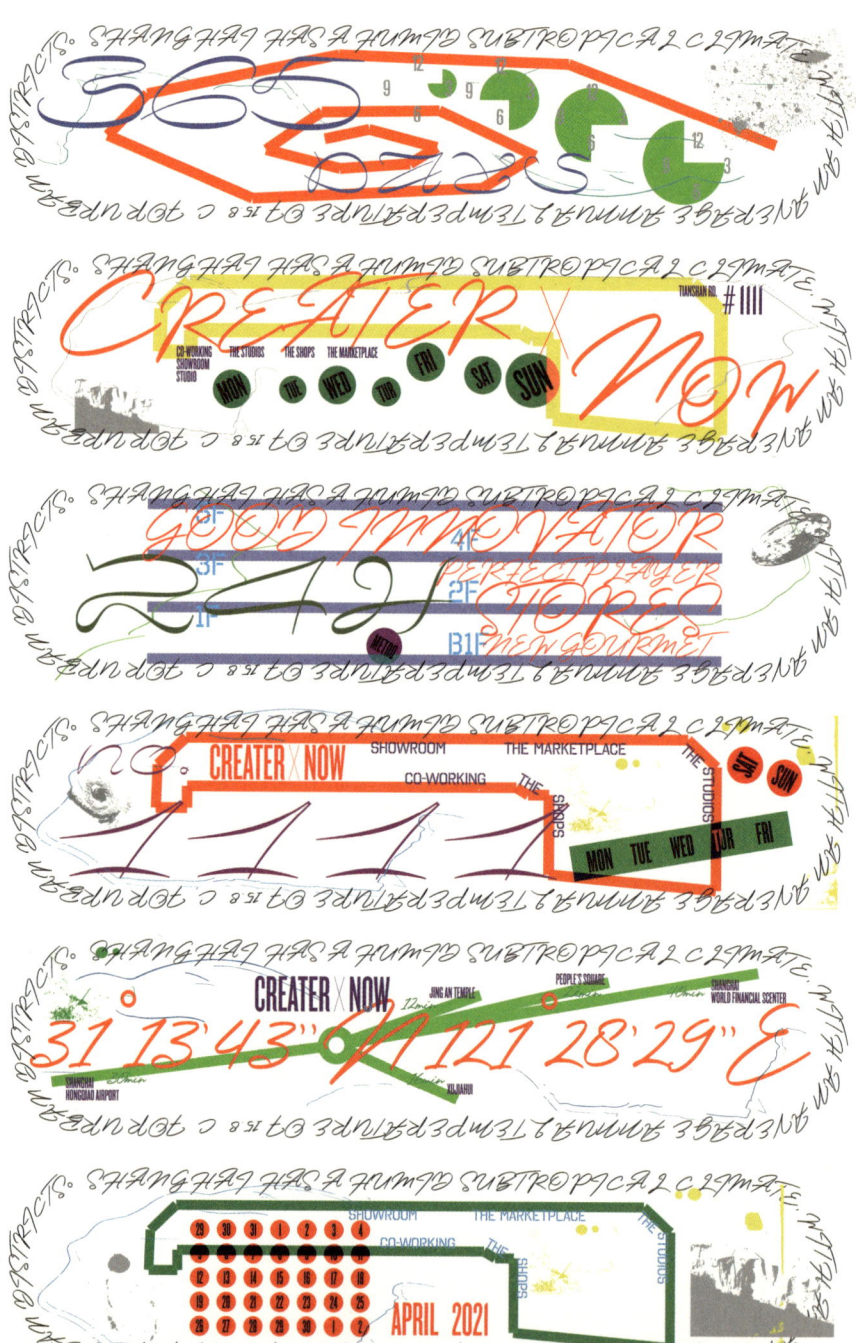

246 Poster
TD. Sven Lindhorst-Emme
CL. R. Raum für drastische Maßnahmen
PT. Melange

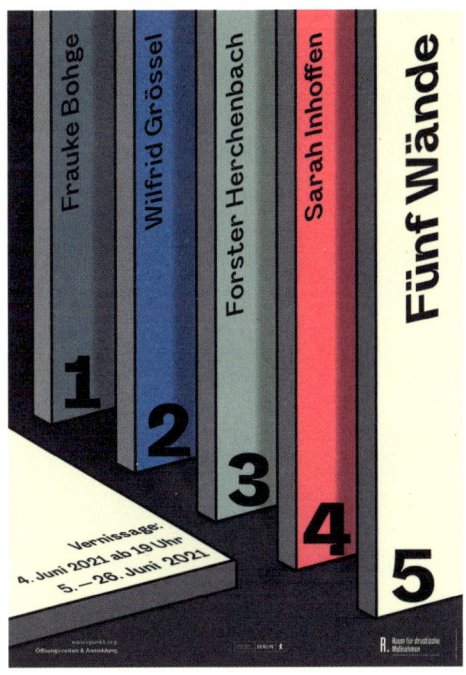

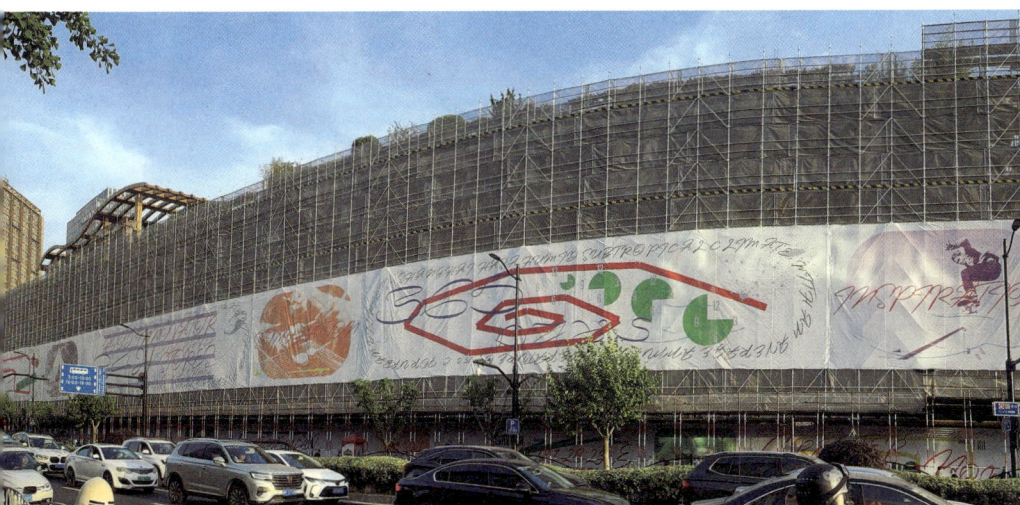

247 Exhibition graphics
TD. AD. D. Big Lin
P. Meng-Tang Chuang
CL. Taipei Artist Village
PT. AR ShuLinMing, Franklin Gothic,
Minion Variable Concept

248 Packaging
TD. D. Cen Liu
CL. Shenyang Jing Gongfang Biological Technology Co., Ltd.
PT. Custom-made for the project, Gatwick Ultrabold

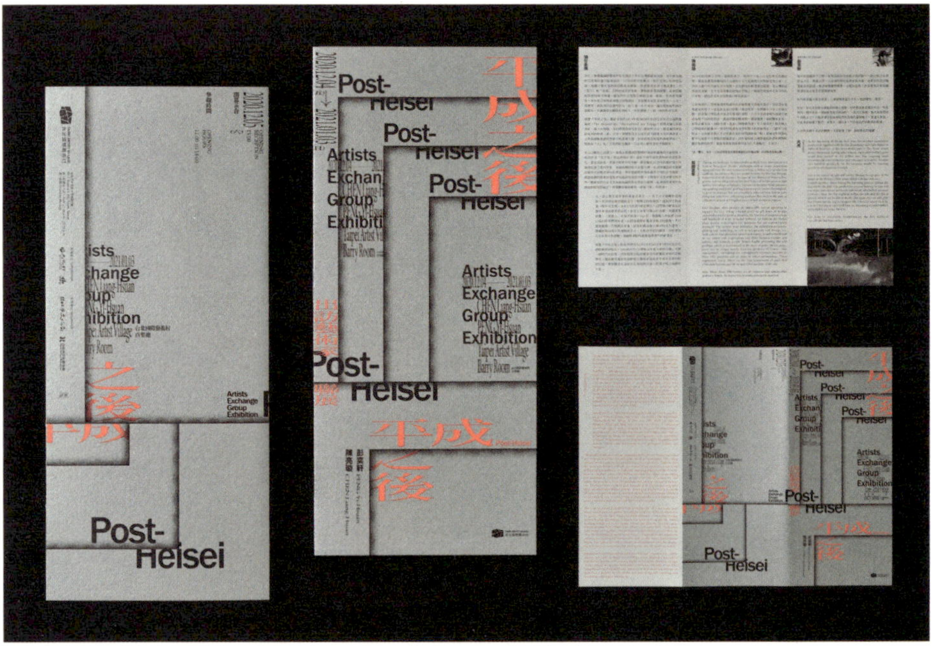

247

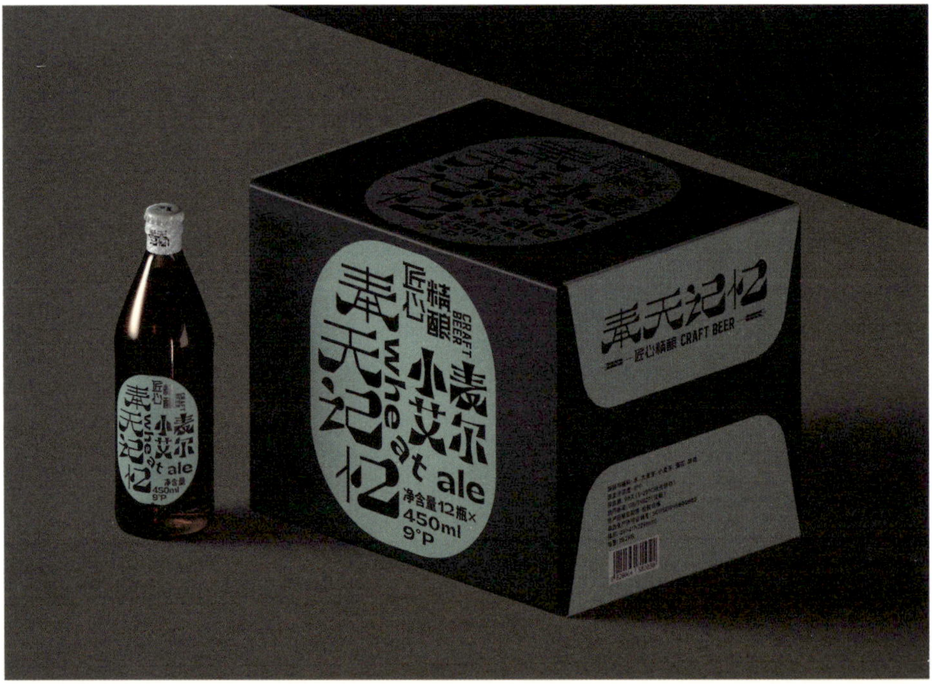

248

249 Type design
TD. Xijiang Liu
CL. Founder
PT. Custom-made for the project, Gaoyuan Minchi

250 Type design
TD. Yunlai Liu
D. Jinqian Liu, Leilei Zhang, Jiajia Li, Meng Hu, Ye Zhuang, Yuhang Zhang
CL. Hanyi Font Library

Prize Nominee Work

251 Calendar
TD. D. W. Lobbin Liu
PRG (+calculation). Junqing Qiao
PB. Songwen Zheng
EE. Sissi Liu
CL. Non-commercial work
PT. Adobe Caslon Pro, Source Serif

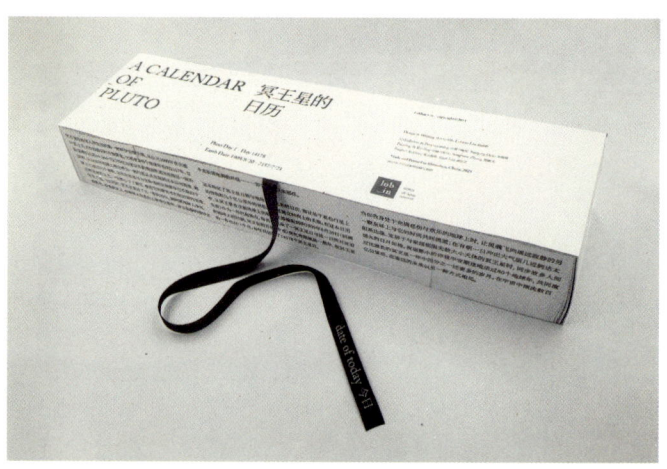

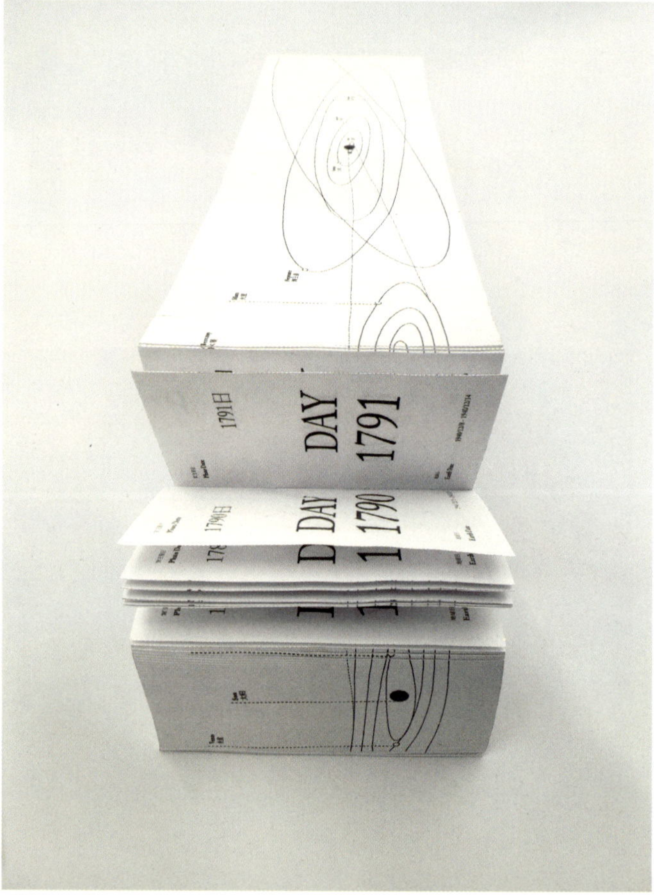

252 VI
TD. CD. AD. Liu Zhao
CD. Zhan Huode
D. Du Xiaojun, Chen Kai, Chen Yuhao, Fu Difan
CL. Guangzhou Sansan Cultural Development Co., Ltd.
PT. ITC

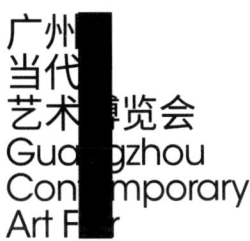

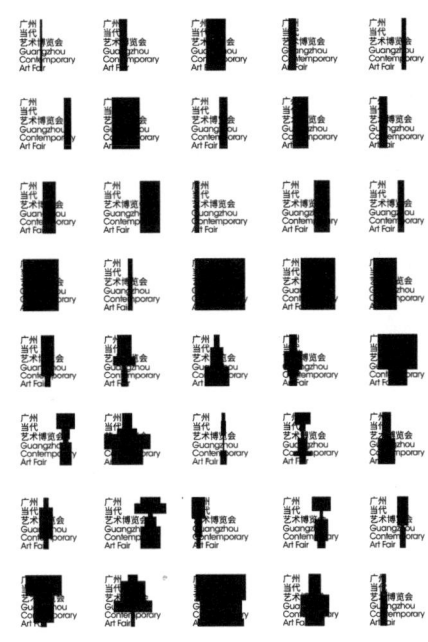

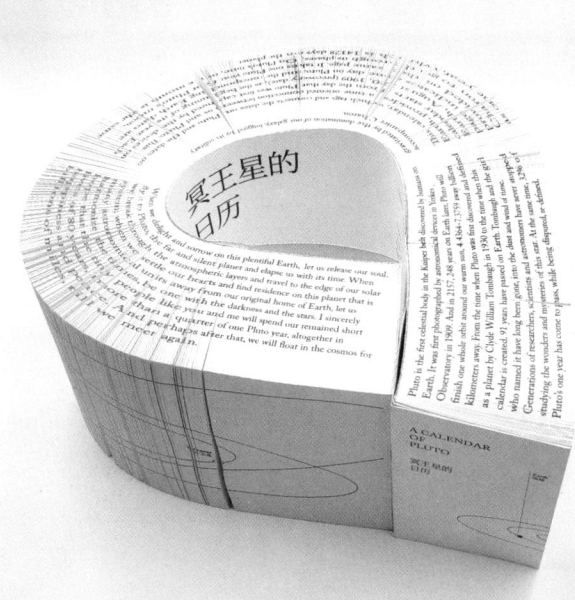

253 Experimental work
TD. AD. Liu Zhao
TD. Zhan Huode
D. Vinci Yang, Gu Jiaxin
CL. Times Museum
PT. Akkurat, Hanyi Qihei

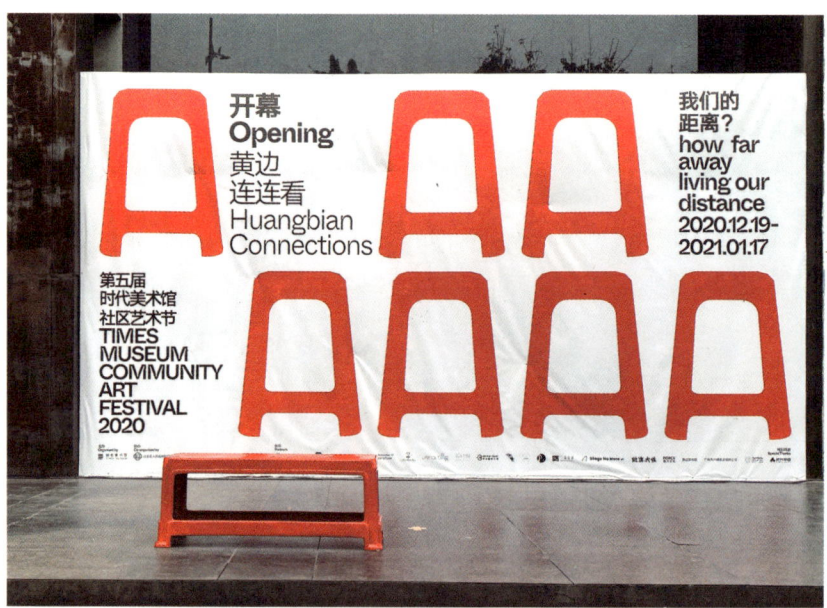

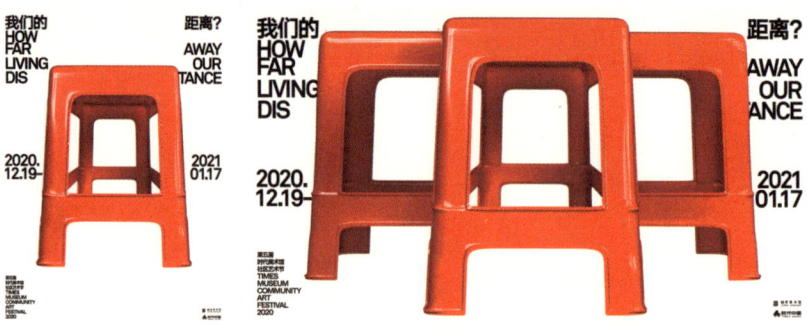

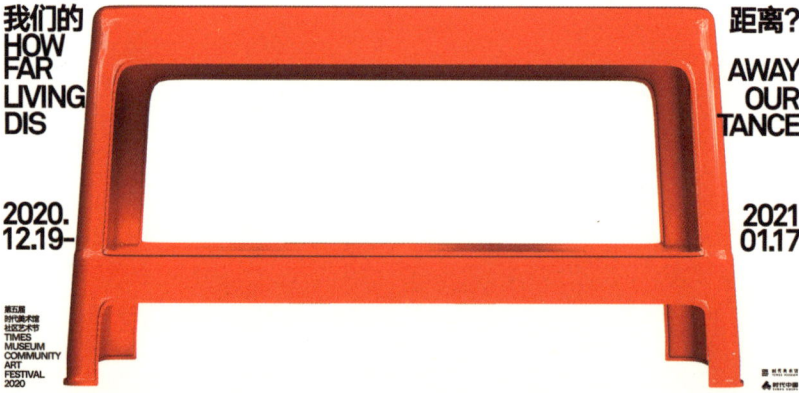

254 Poster
TD. Liu Qingyuan, Liu Zhao
CL. Duende Contemporary Art Museum
PT. Founder Type

255 Logotype
TD. Kelvin Lok
CL. Superdupa
PT. Gotham

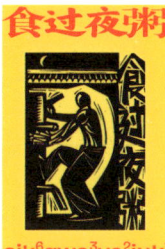
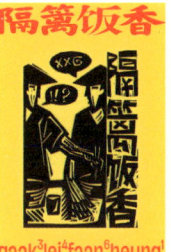
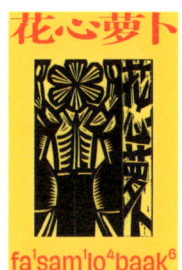
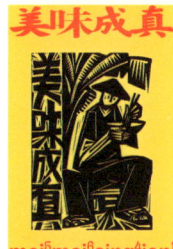
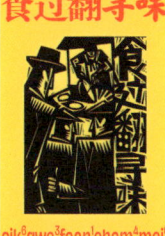
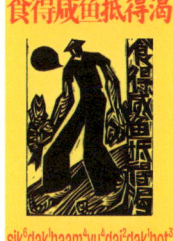
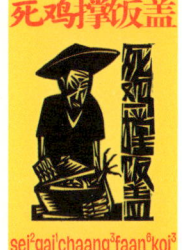
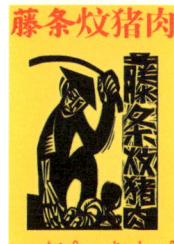
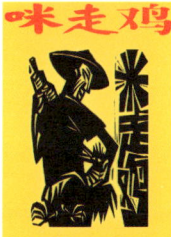
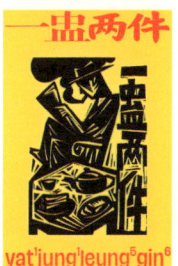
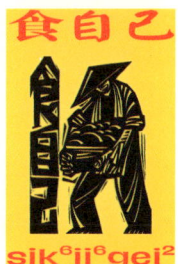
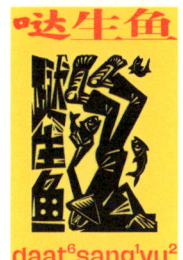
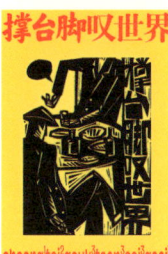
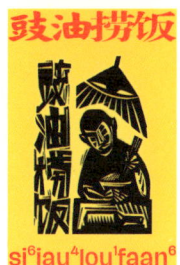
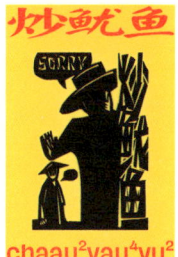

256 Pins, Packaging
TD. loof.design
P. Wang Di
CL. LUNA
PT. Custom-made for the project

257 Record jacket
TD. I. Benedikt Luft
TD. D. Dominik Keller
CL. Kommerz Records
PT. Maison Neue, Empirica Headline

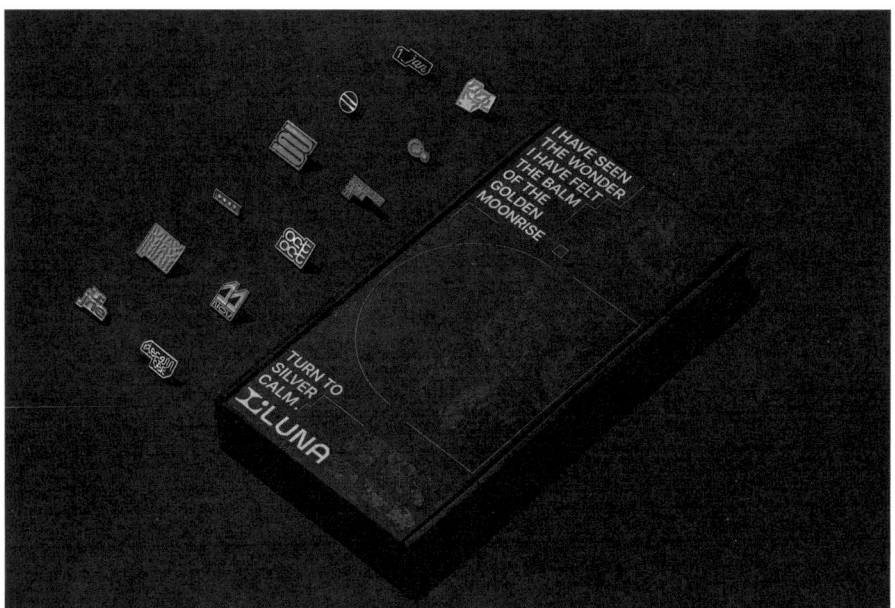

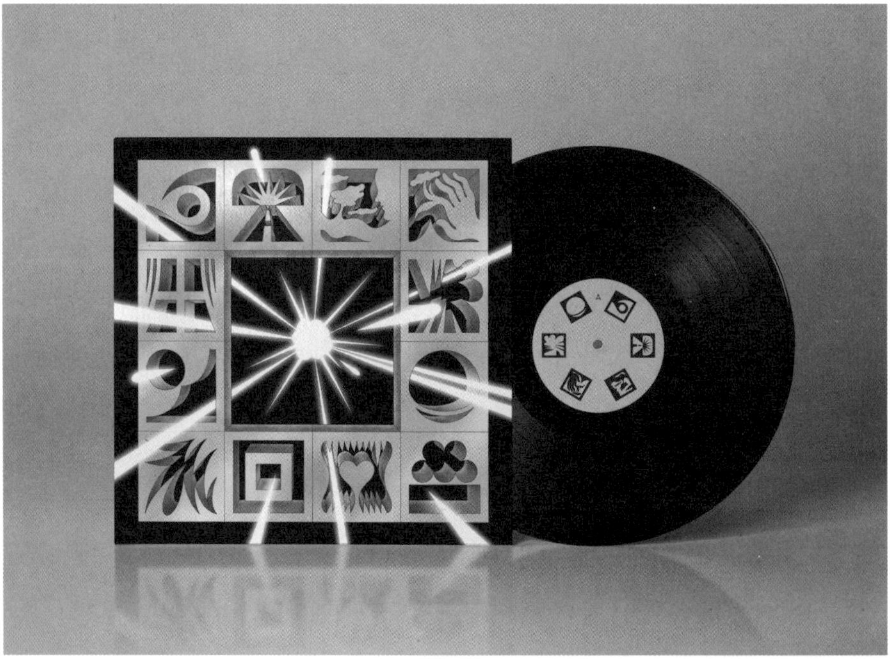

TD. Liu Huan
CL. Special edition Project
PT. Tex Gyre Heros Cn

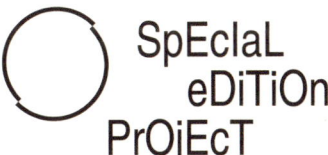

SpEcIaL
eDiTiOn
PrOjEcT

ArT
BoOk
CoFfEe
ExHiBiTiOn
MaGaZiNe
PhOtOgRaPhY
ShOp
WrItInG
by SeP

SpEcIaL
eDiTiOn
PrOjEcT

www.specialeditionproject.com

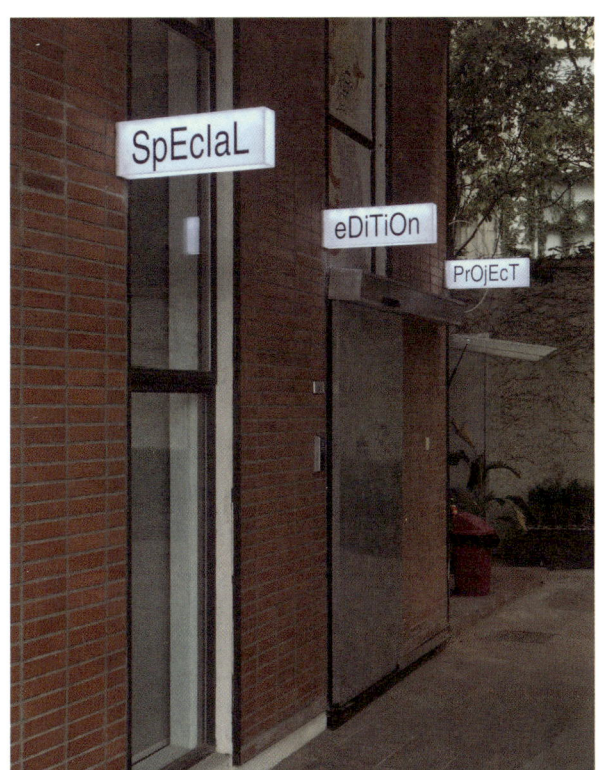

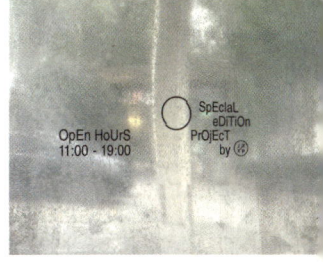

Prize Nominee Work

259 Fashion collection
TD. M/M (Paris)
CL. Loewe

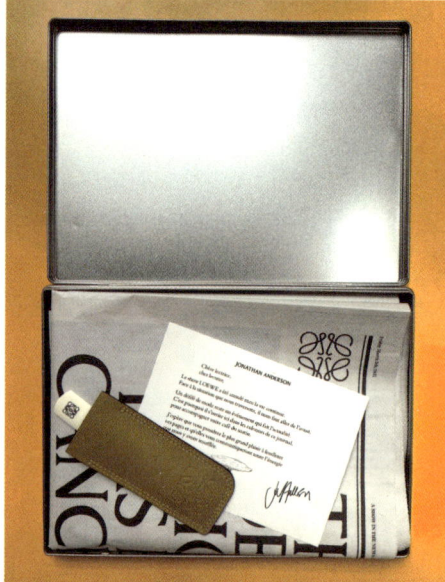
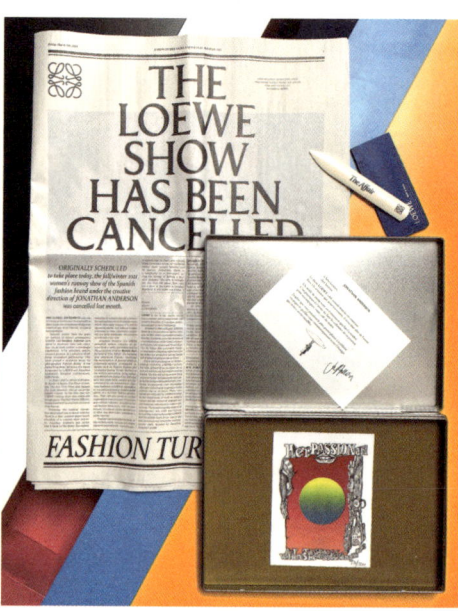

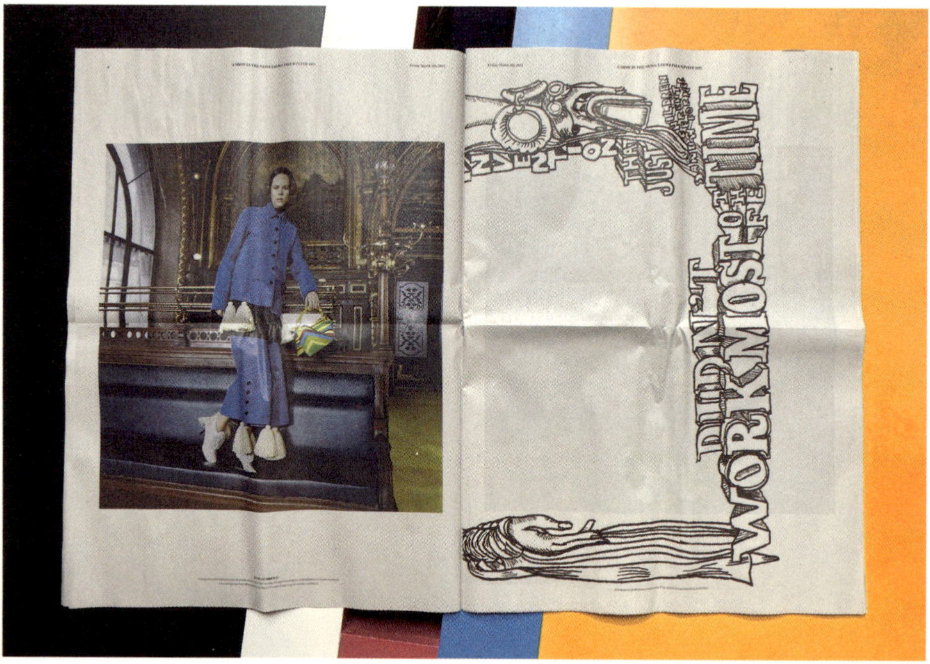

Prize Nominee Work

260 Book, Poster
TD. M/M (Paris)
CL. Château Lafite

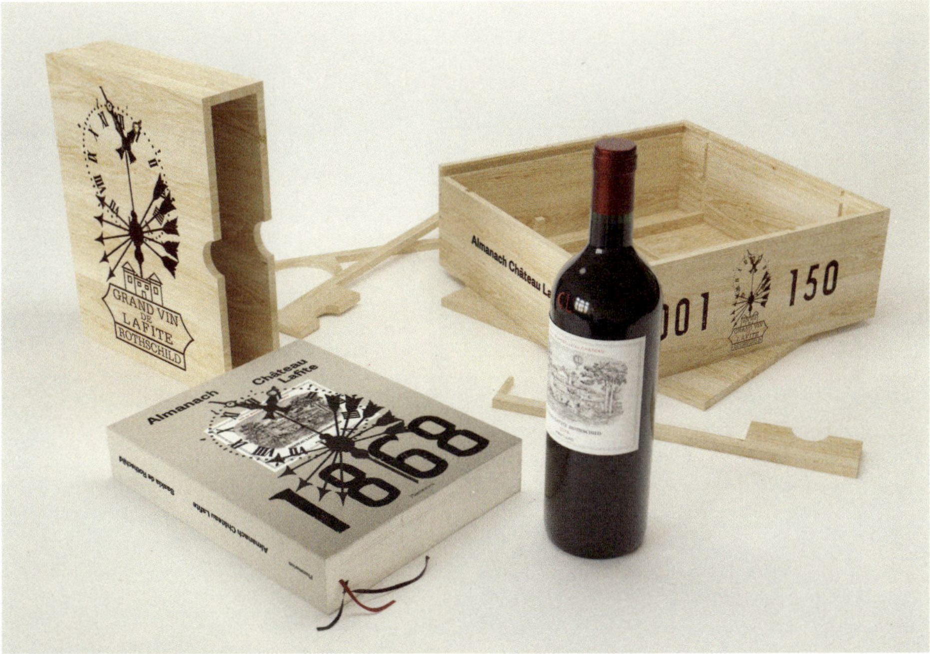

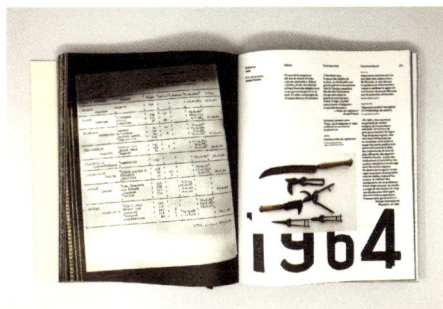

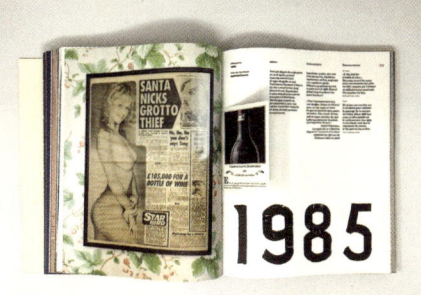

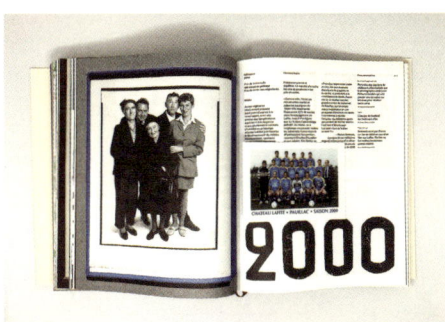

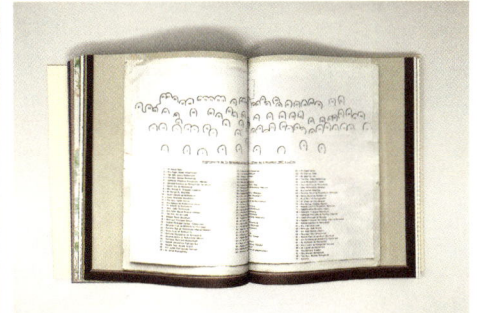

Prize Nominee Work

261 Book, Poster
TD. M/M (Paris)
CL. Centre Pompidou-Metz

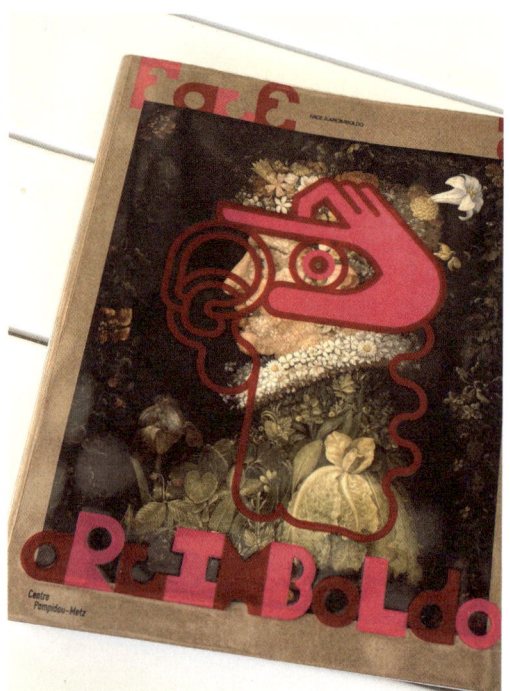
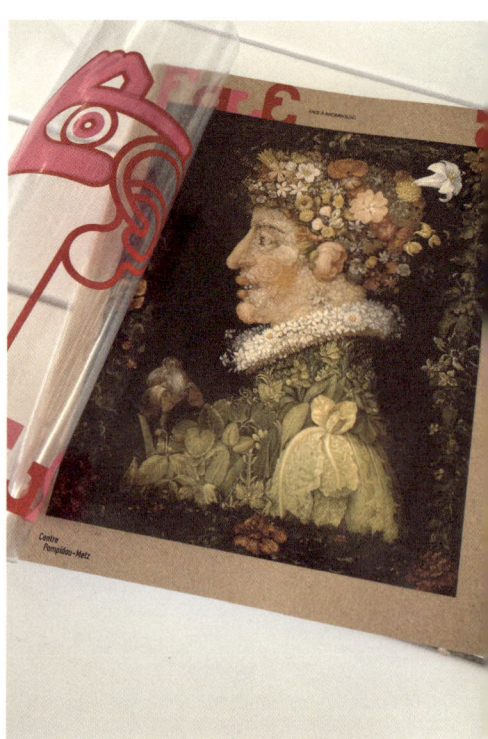

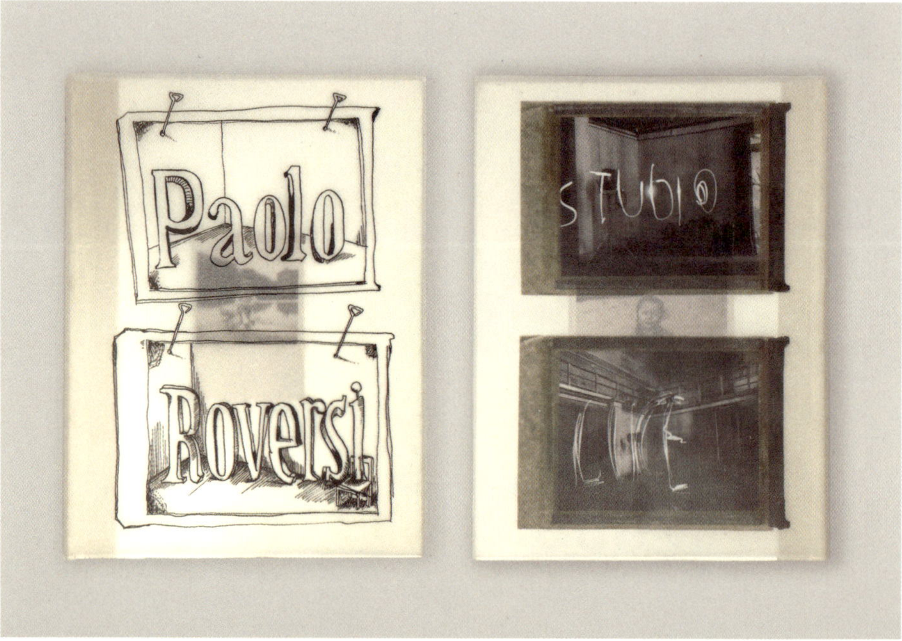

Prize Nominee Work

262 Book
TD. M/M (Paris)
CL. Paolo Roversi

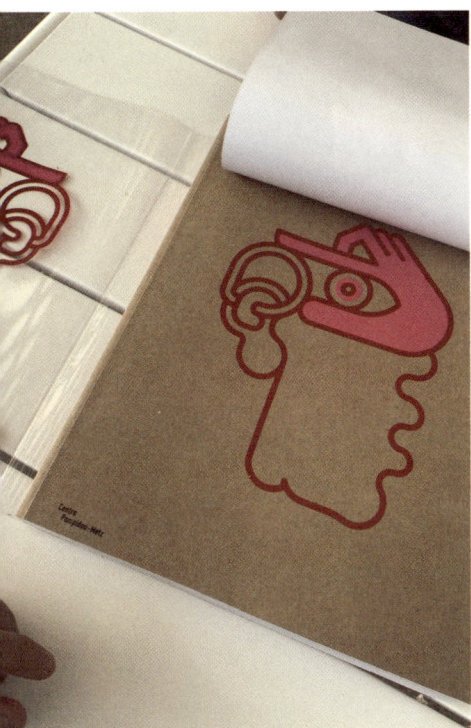
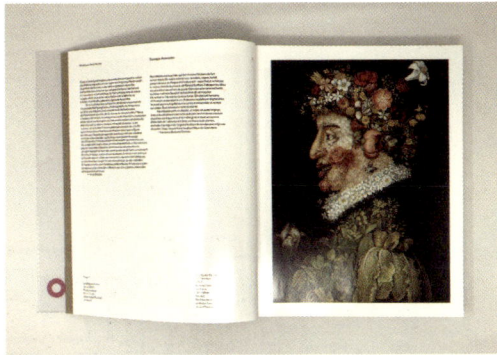
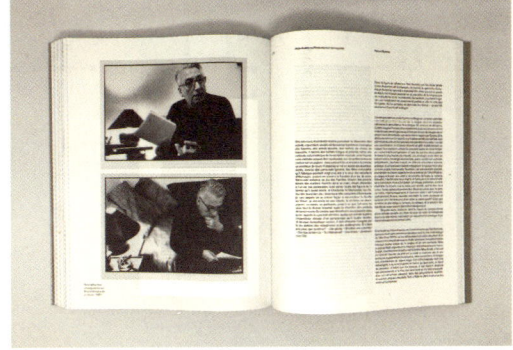
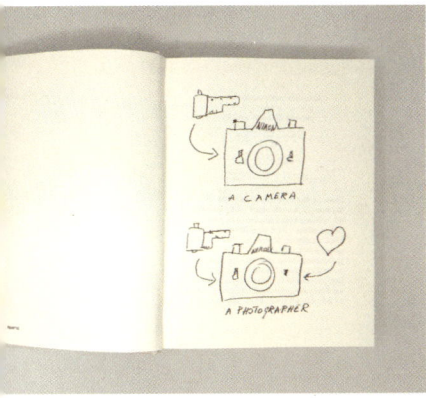
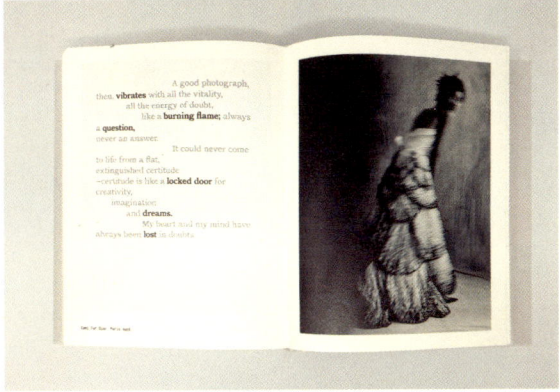

263 Logotype
TD. Shire Ma
AD. D. Ma Shirui
CL. Archipelago Studio
PT. Custom-made for the project

264 Sample book
TD. AD. D. Ma Shirui
CL. Creation Paper
PT. Noto Sans CJK SC, Noto Serif Display

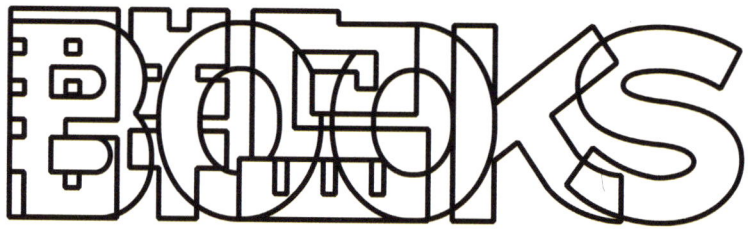

263

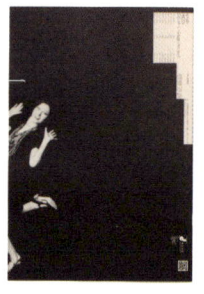 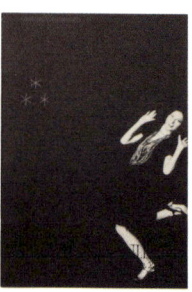  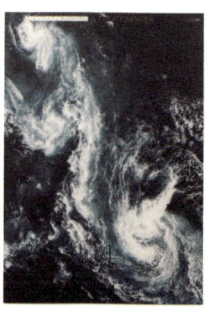

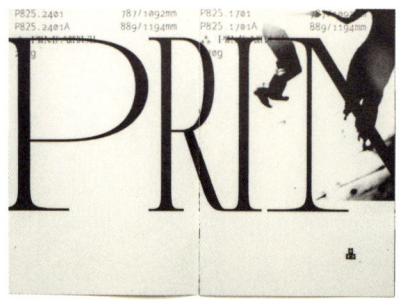 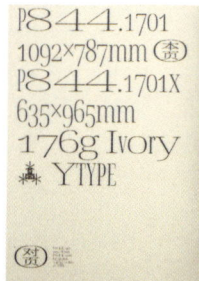 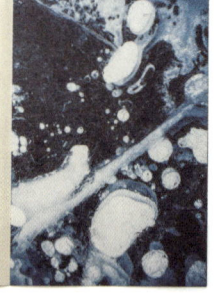

264

265 Calendar
TD. AD. D. P. Lucas Machado
CL. Non-commercial work
PT. Mabry Mono, Colophon Foundry, Benjamin Critton

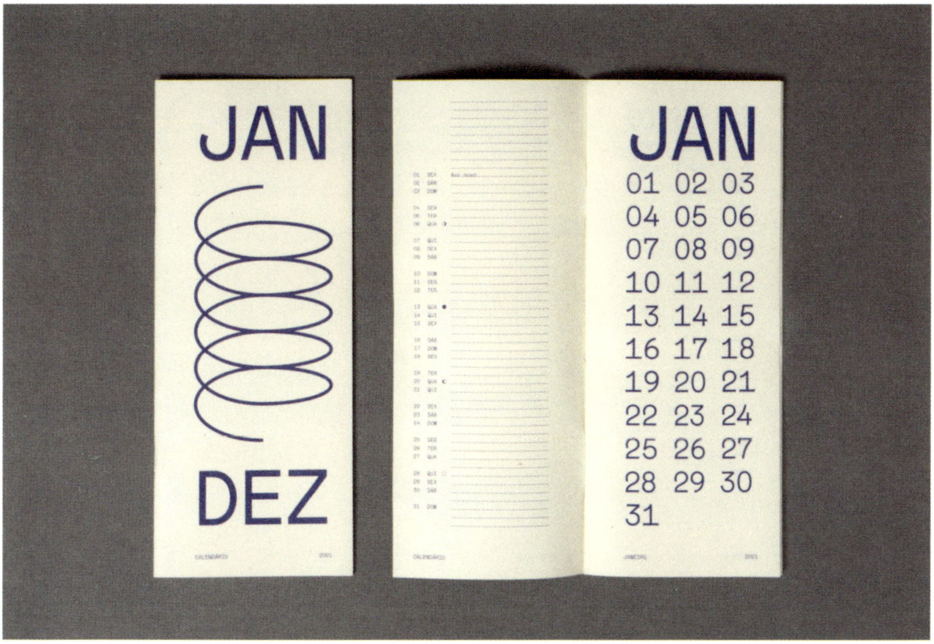

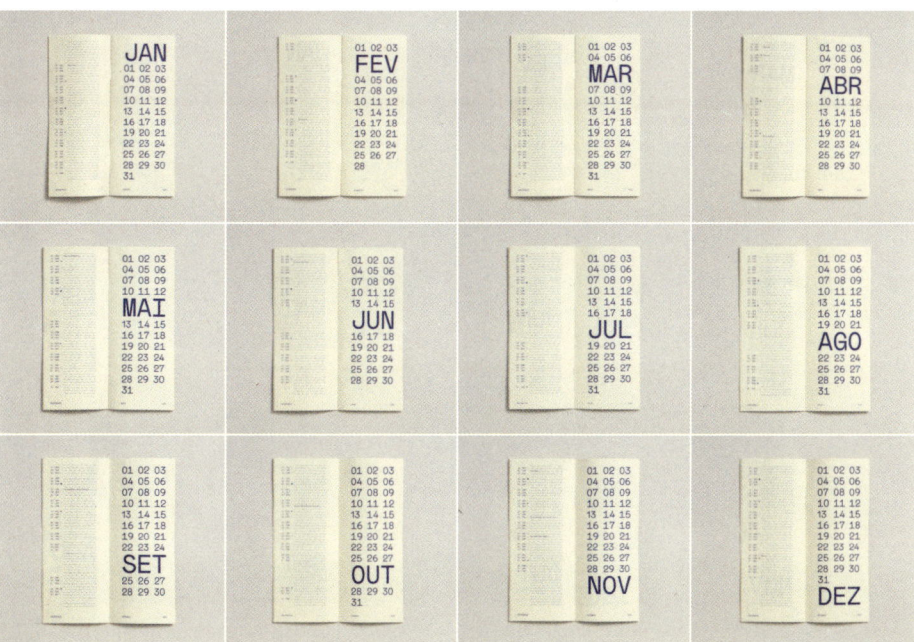

Prize Nominee Work

266 Book
TD. 町口覚 Satoshi Machiguchi
CL. 月曜社 Getsuyosha Ltd., bookshop M

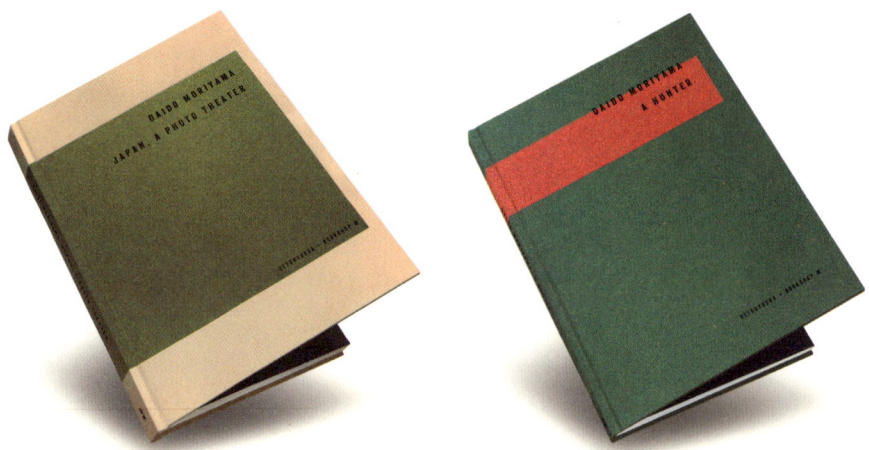

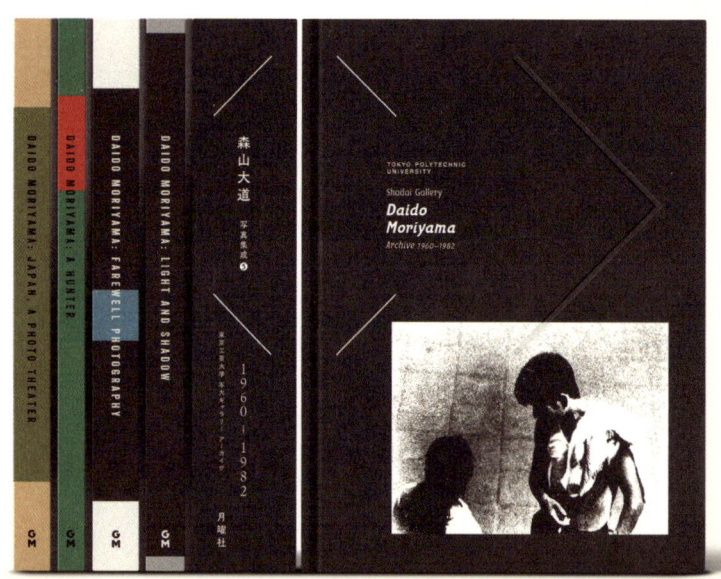

267 Catalogue, Envelopes
TD. AD. Claudio Madella
TD. D. Fabrizio Falcone
CL. Letterpress Workers International
PT. Aurora Galaxy, Sempione Grotesk

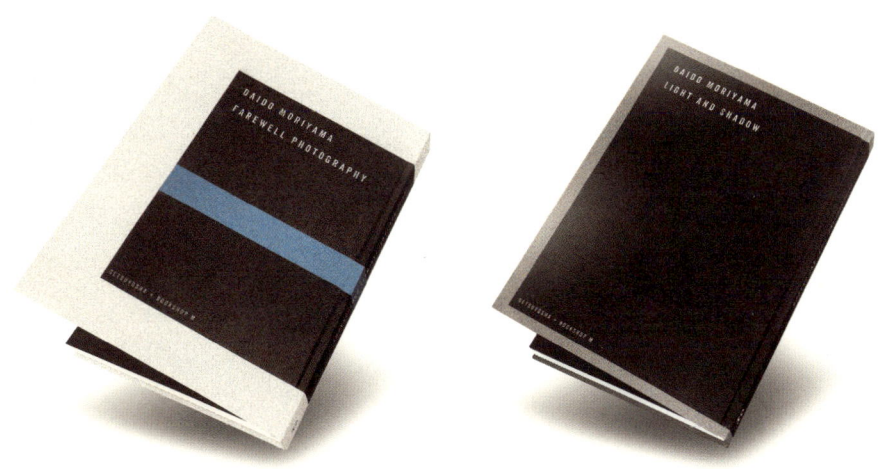

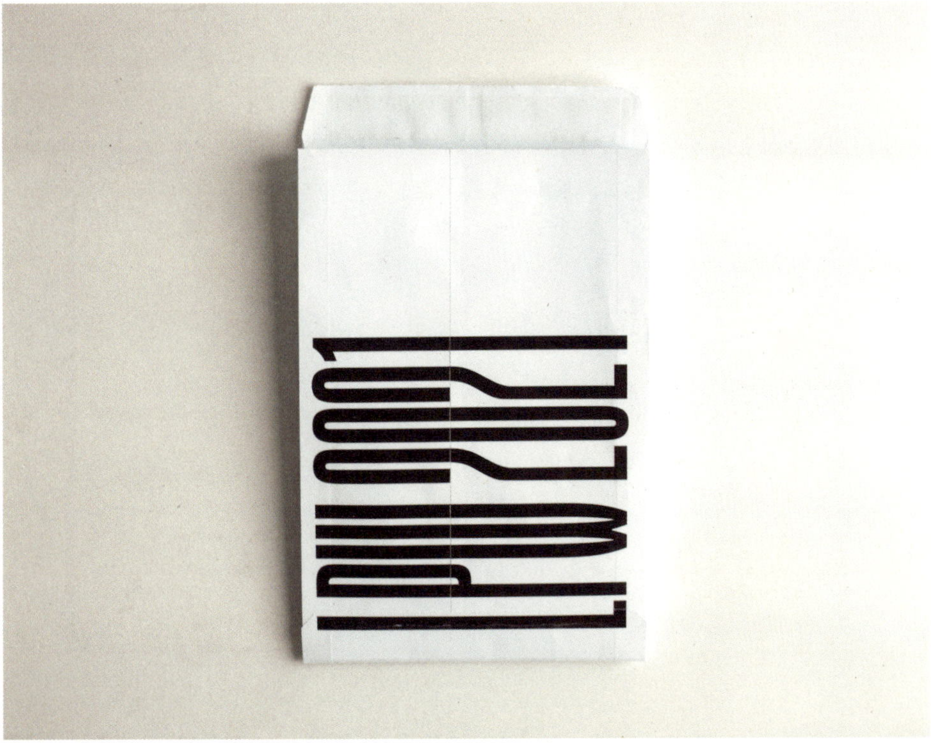

268 Name card
TD. Mak Kai Hang
CL. The Hong Kong Type Foundry Limited

269 Promotion
TD. AD. D. 前田定則 Sadanori Maeda
PRO. ツドイ Tsudoi Inc.
CL. くるり Quruli

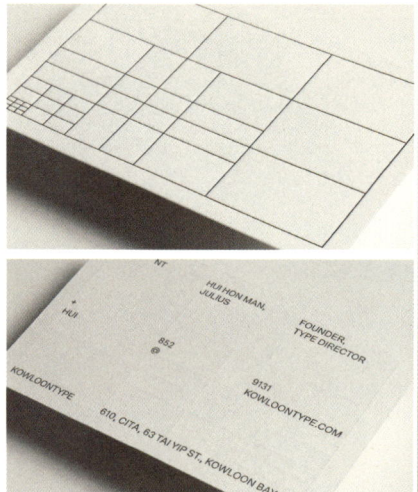
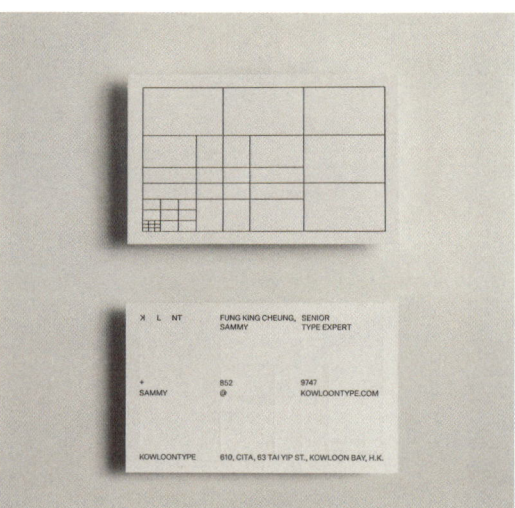

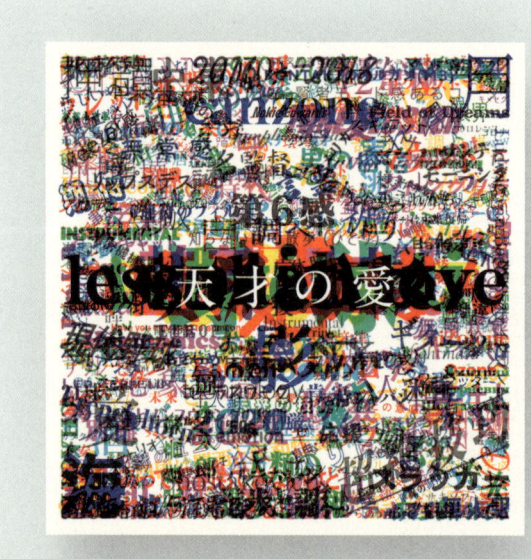
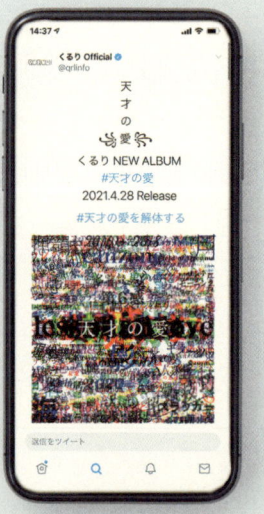

270 Logotype
TD. Mak Kai Hang
CL. Kasei Archive

271 VI
TD. AD. Mak Kai Hang
D. Yeung Yan Shek
MD. Daniel Lam
WD. Simon Chung
CL. Tai Kwun Contemporary

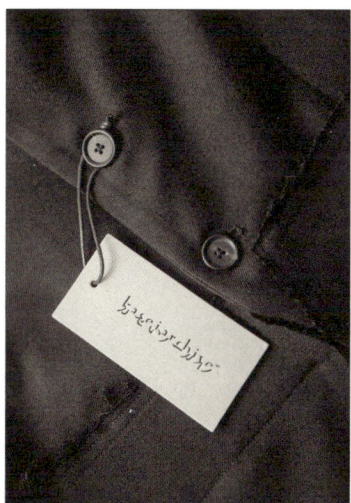
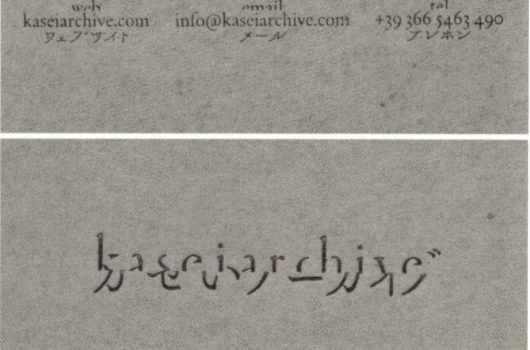

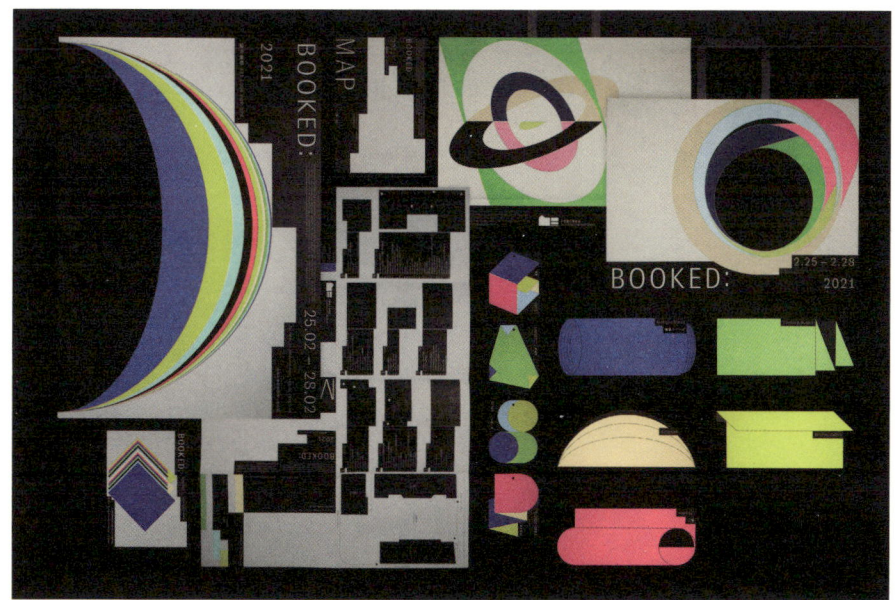

Prize Nominee Work

272 Experimental work
TD. Jannis Maroscheck
CL. Slanted Publishers
PT. Akzidenz Grotesk, Custom-made for the project

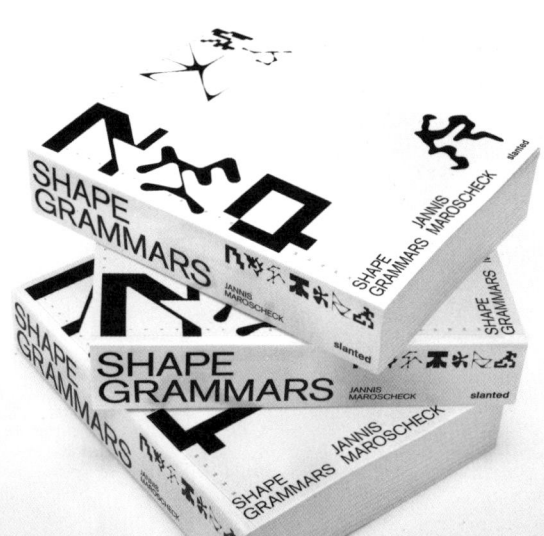

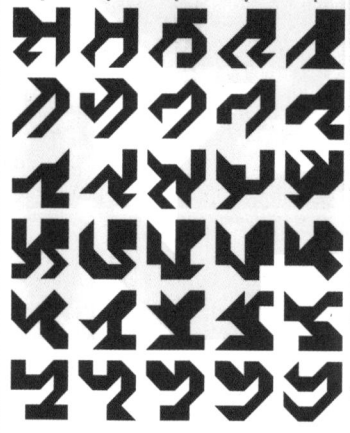

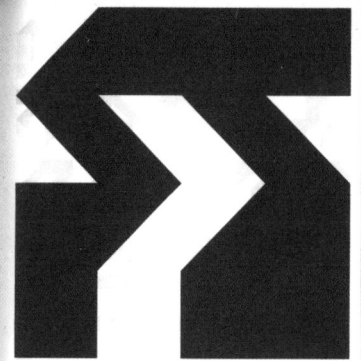

273 Packaging
TD. AD. 松本健一 Kenichi Matsumoto
D. 佐藤千祐 Chihiro Sato
CL. (株)楠城屋商店 Nanjoya Shoten Co., Ltd.
PT. Custom-made for the project

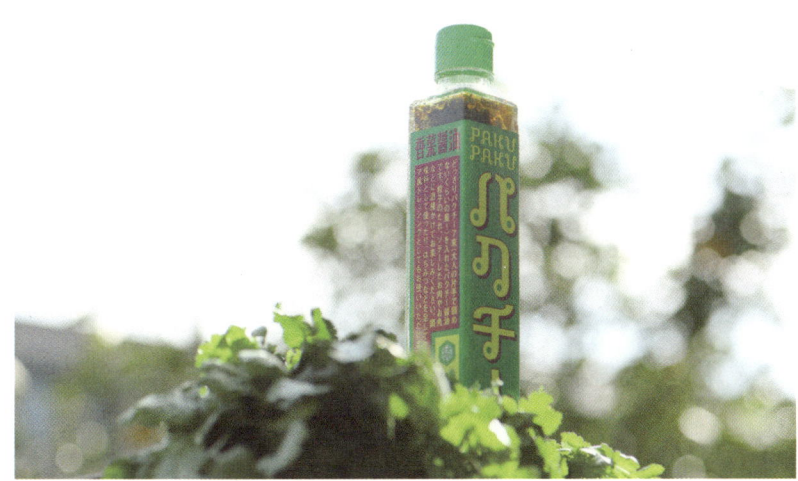

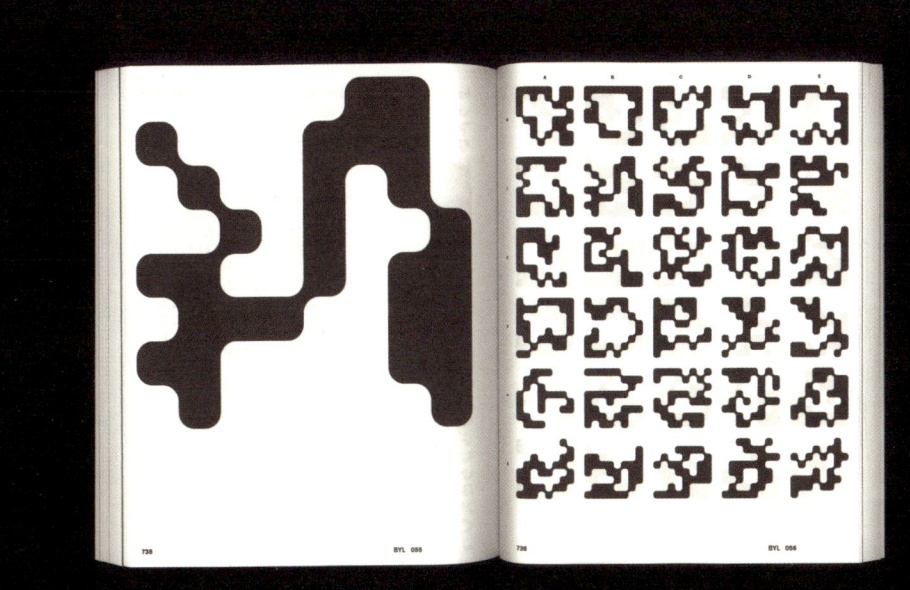

Prize Nominee Work

274 Exhibition design
TD. AD. D. 松本弦人 Gento Matsumoto
P. 木奥恵三 Keizo Kioku
CL. 京都市京セラ美術館 Kyoto City Kyocera Museum of Art
PT. Custom-made for the project

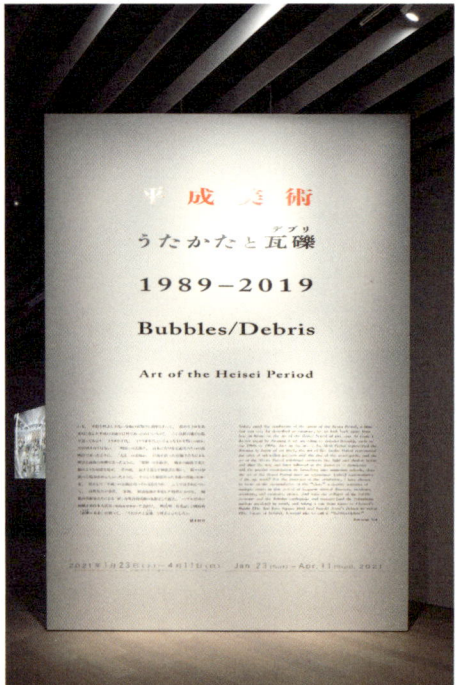
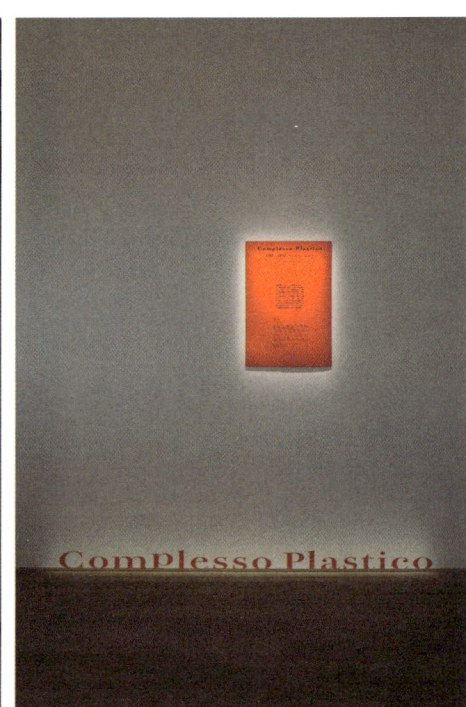

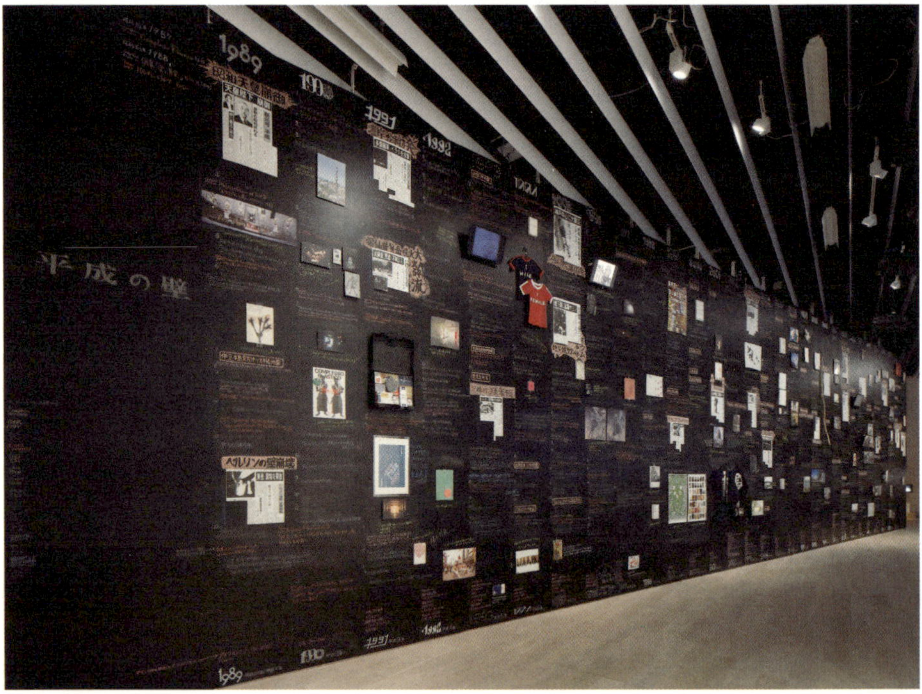

Prize Nominee Work

275 Book
TD. AD. D. 松本弦人 Gento Matsumoto
P. 木奥恵三 Keizo Kioku
CL. 京都市京セラ美術館 Kyoto City Kyocera Museum of Art
PT. Custom-made for the project

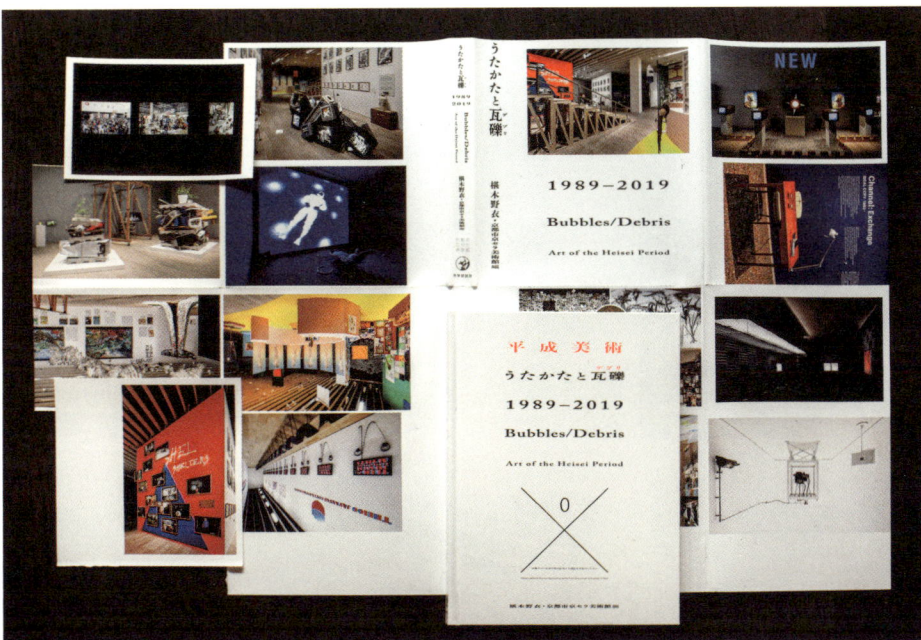

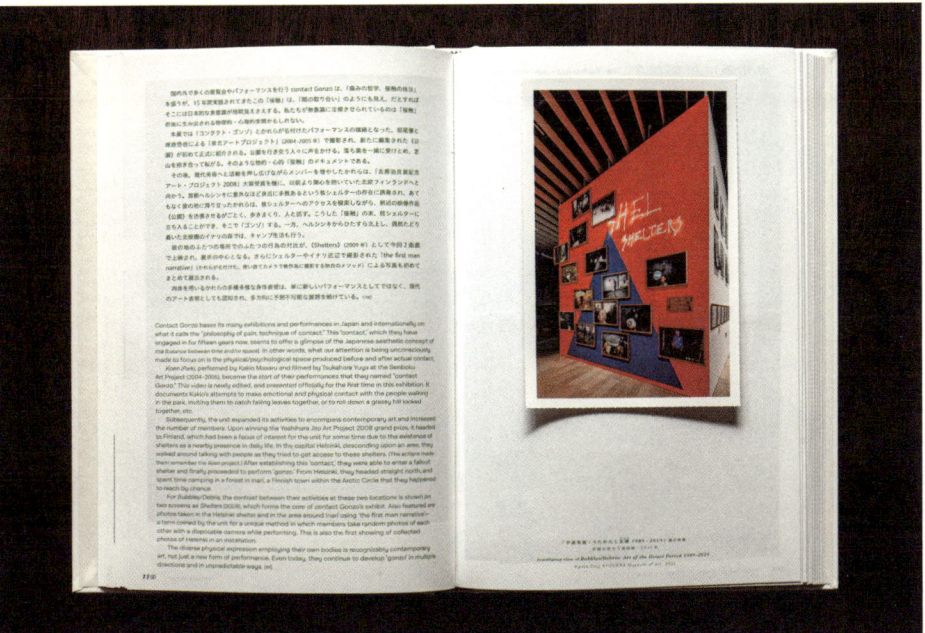

276 Signage
TD. AD. Mazzybox, Liu Zhizhi
D. Chen Chaohao
P. Xing Yun
CL. Icomos China
PT. Custom-made for the project

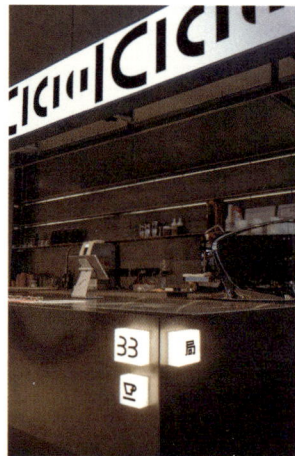
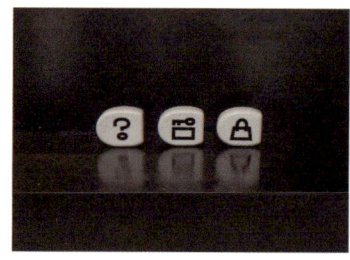
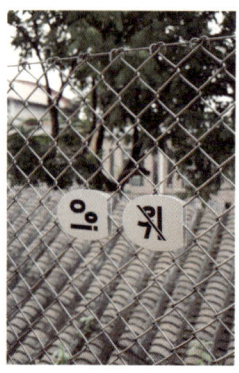
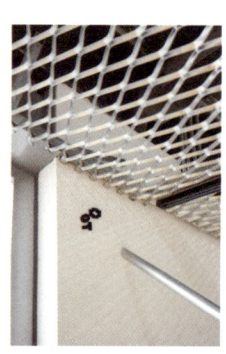
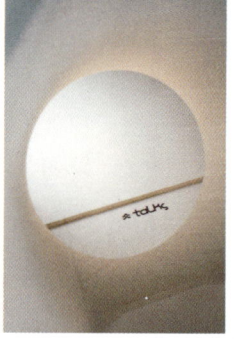
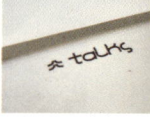
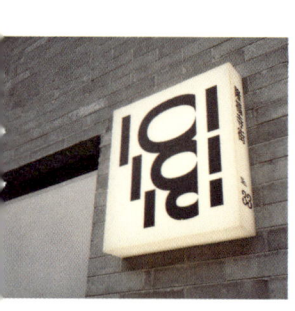
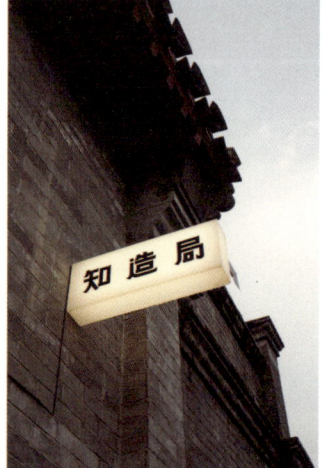
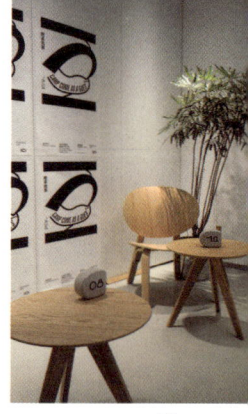

277 VI
TD. AD. Mazzybox, Liu Zhizhi
D. Chen Chaohao
P. Jin Jun
CL. Icomos China
PT. Custom-made for the project

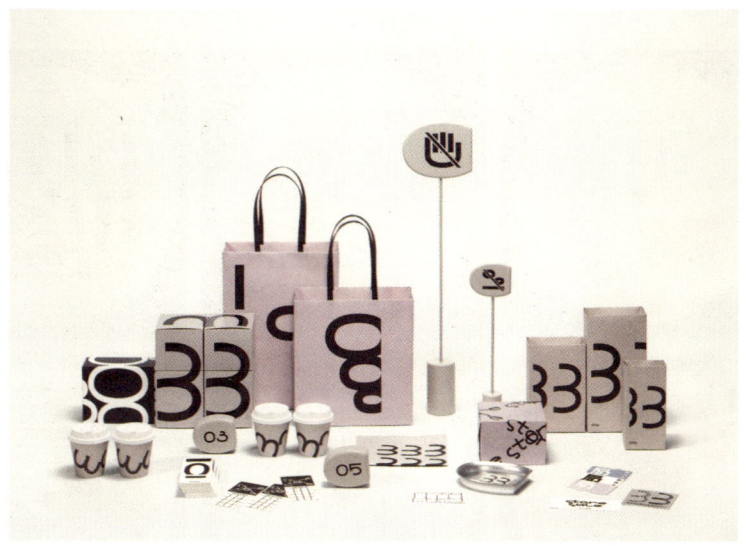
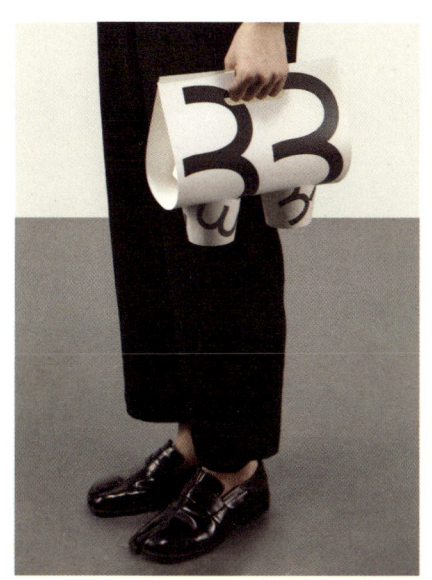
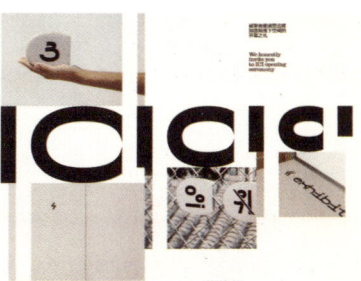
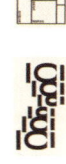
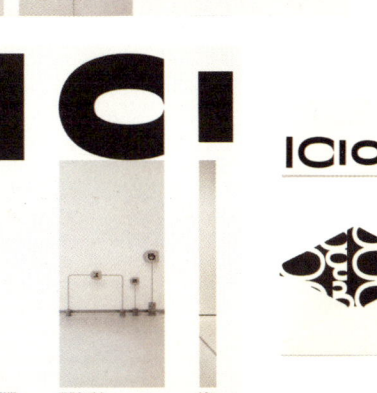

278 Record label
TD. Nathan Meyer
CL. Visions Recordings
PT. Custom-made for the project, Neue Haas Grotesk,
Antique Legacy, Times New Roman, Monument Grotesk

279 Poster
TD. AD. D. 松山智一 Norikazu Matsuyama
CL. Non-commercial work
PT. Custom-made for the project

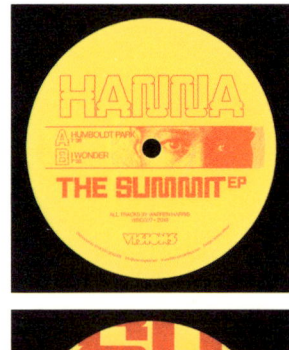
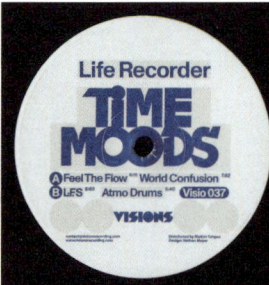
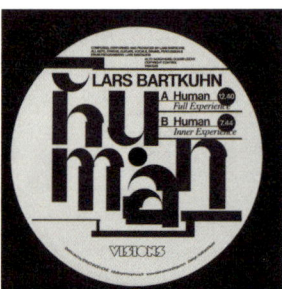
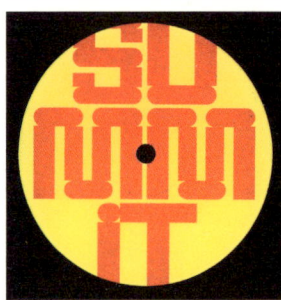
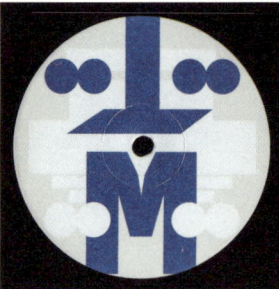
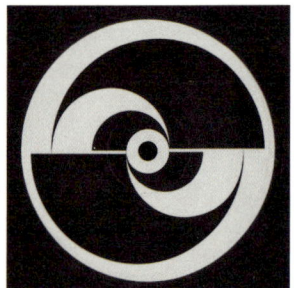

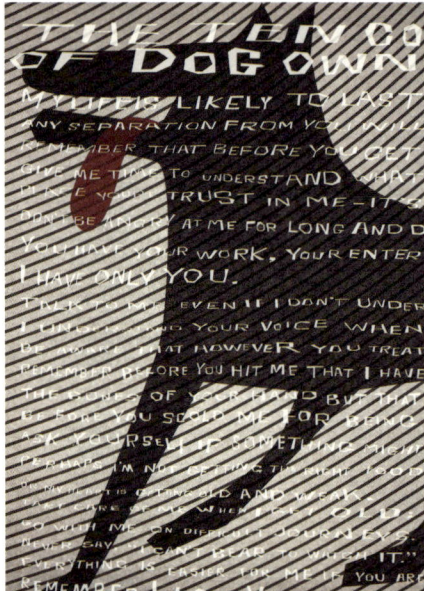
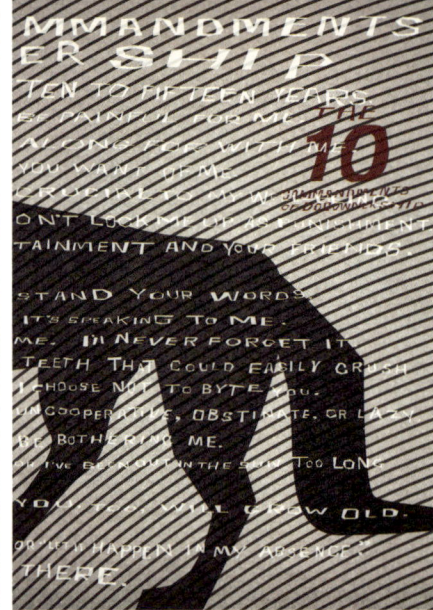

280 Poster
TD. Colin McPartlin
CL. Non-commercial work
PT. Custom-made for the project, Arial

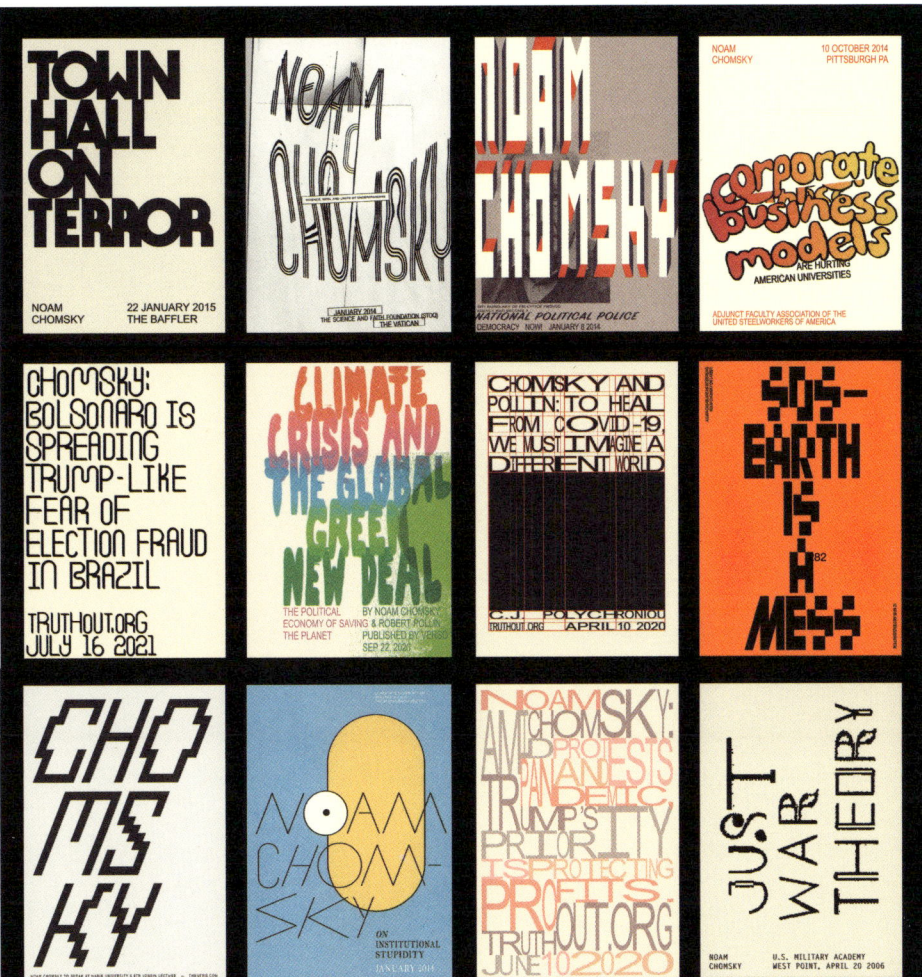

281 Experimental work
TD. 道川雄介 Yusuke Michikawa
CL. Non-commercial work

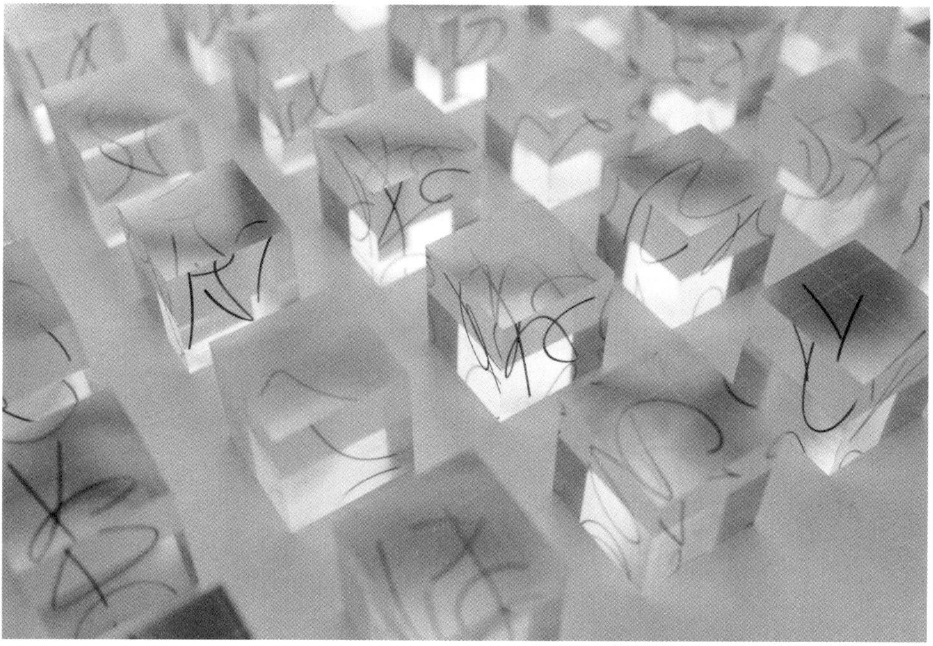

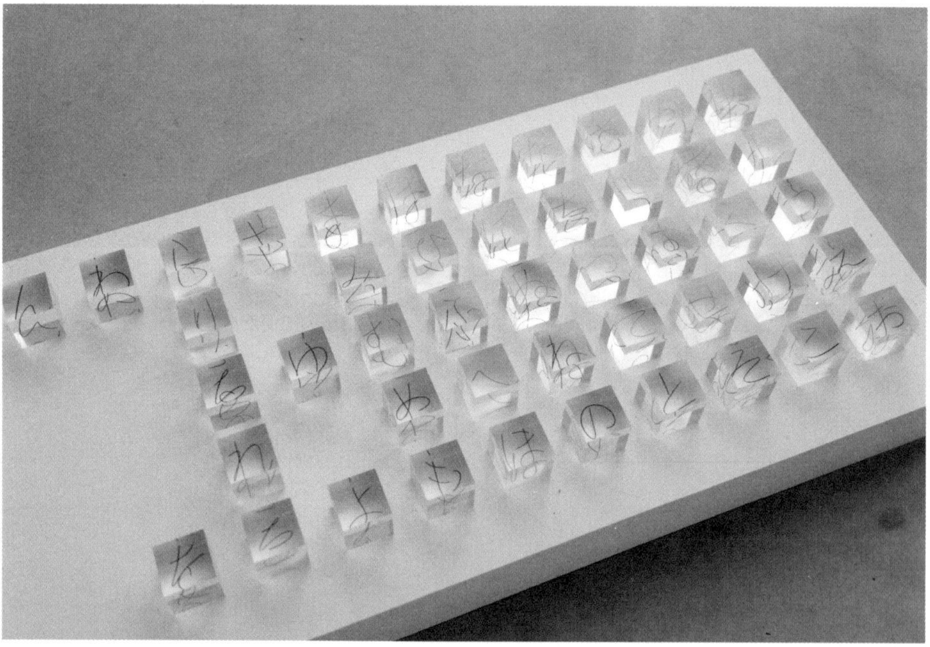

282 Specimen
TD. Varvara Mikhaylova
T. Maria Doreuli, Krista Radoeva
CL. Contrast Foundry
PT. CoFo Sans Mono

283 Poster
TD. AD. D. Mazzybox
D. Chen Shihong
MD. Lv Yixiao
CL. Hiiibrand Awards
PT. Hanyi Qihei, Helvetica Now

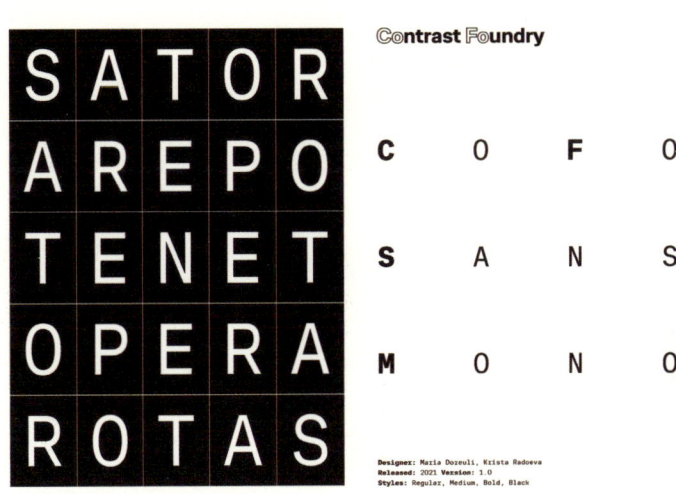

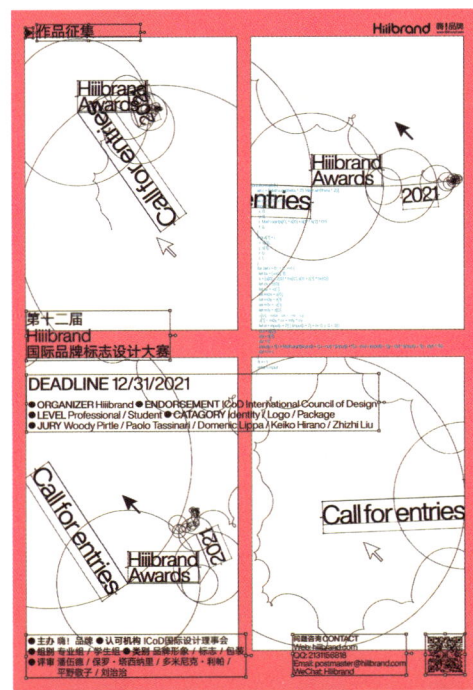

284 Exhibition design
TD. AD. D. 三木健 Ken Miki
D. 犬山蓉子 Yoko Inuyama, 桐原翔子 Shoko Kirihara,
内野阿知花 Achika Uchino, 佐藤健 Takeshi Sato
P. 村上登志彦 Toshihiko Murakami
CL. 兵庫県立美術館 Hyogo Prefectural Museum of Art,
（株）神戸新聞社 The Kobe Shinbun,
（株）日本経済新聞社 Nikkei Inc.

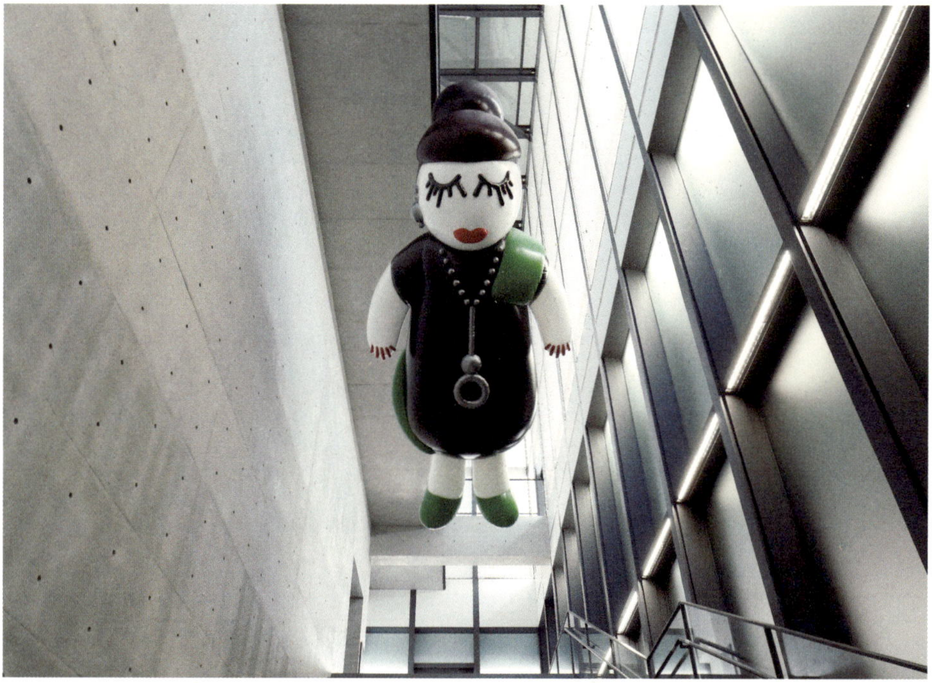

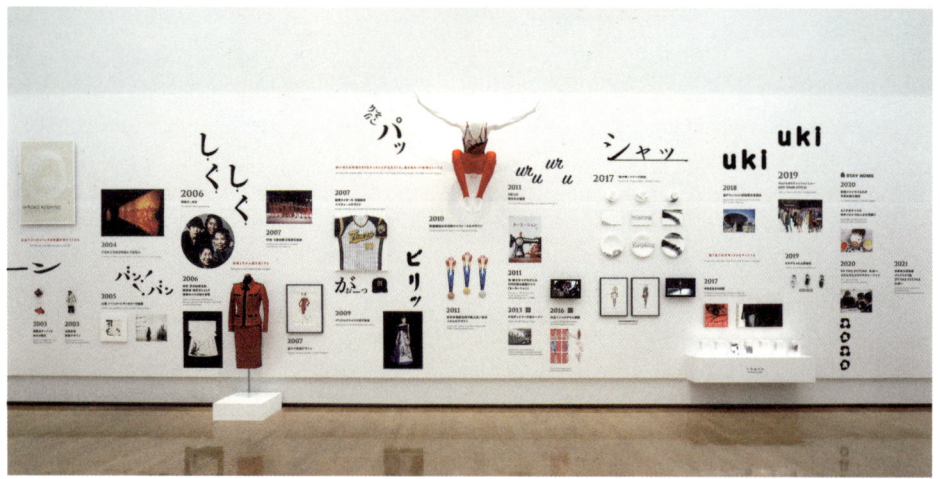

285 Book
TD. Ming Cheung
CL. form & structure
PT. NB International Pro

286 Poster
TD. AD. D. 宮里則徹 Noriaki Miyazato
CL. Non-commercial work

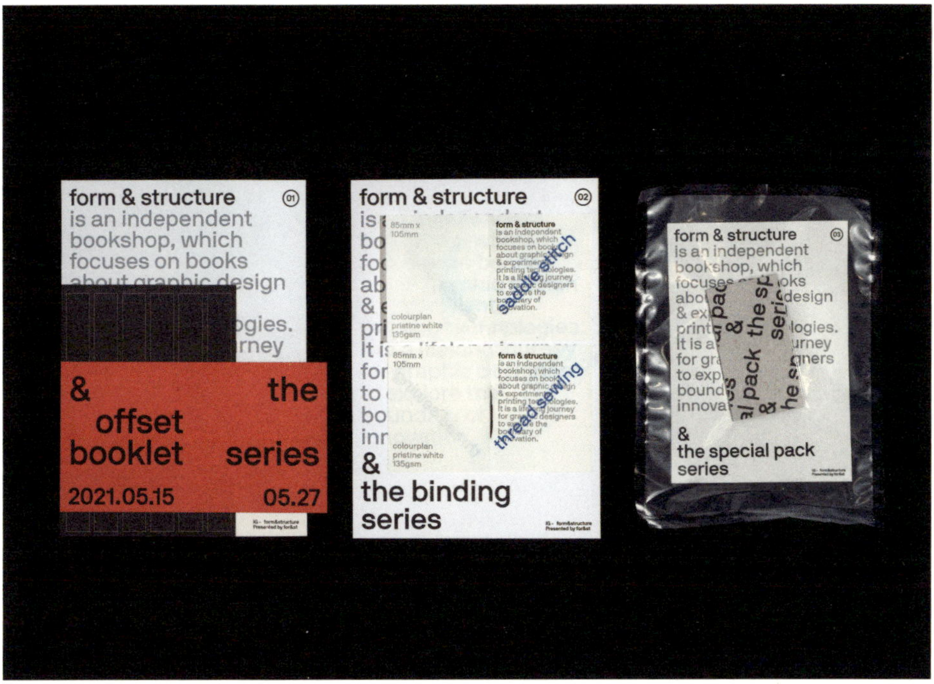

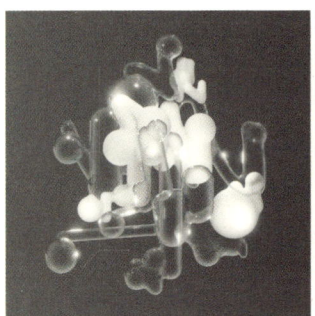
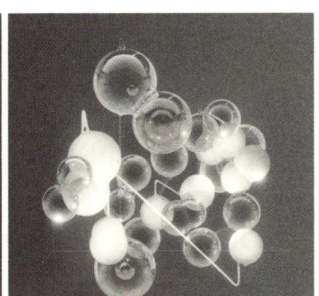
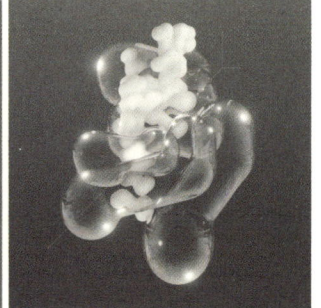

287 Advertising
TD. 水本真帆 Maho Mizumoto
CL.（株）宣伝会議 Sendenkaigi Ltd.

288 Poster
TD. 森川瞬 Shun Morikawa
CL.（公財）札幌市芸術文化財団 Sapporo Cultural Arts Foundation

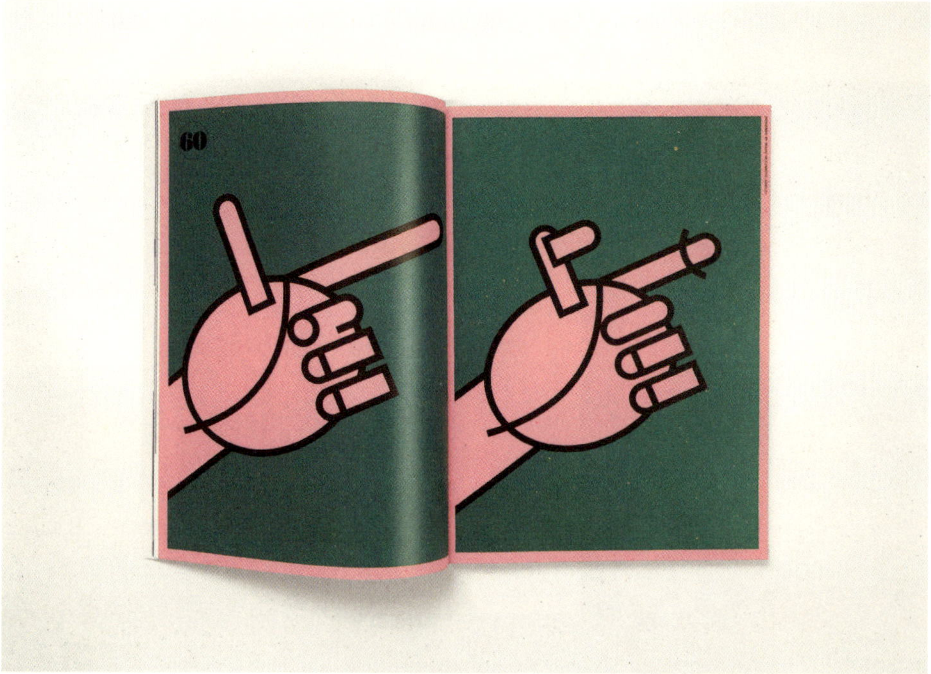

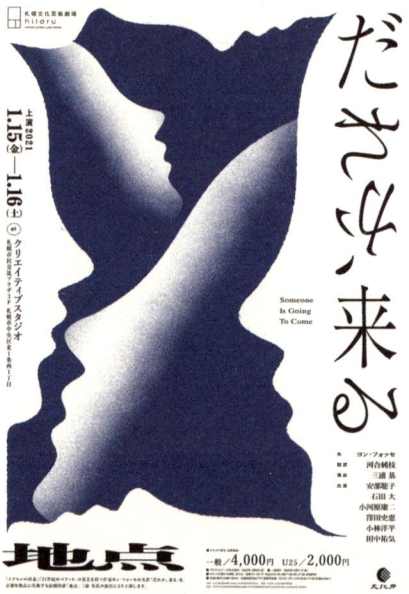

289 Poster
TD. AD. D. 杢谷吉也 Yoshinari Mokutani
A. 小河桃子 Momoko Ogo
CL. 女子美術大学短期大学部 Joshibi University of Art and Design Junior College
PT. Trade Gothic Condensed

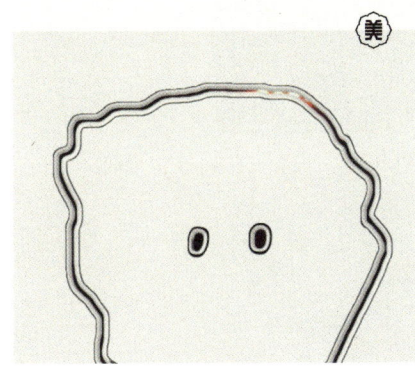

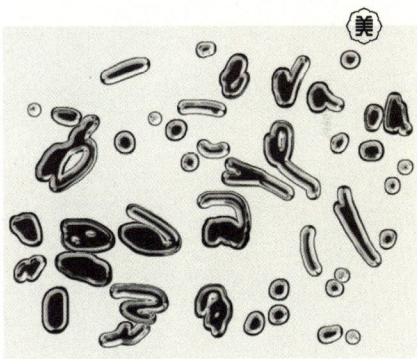

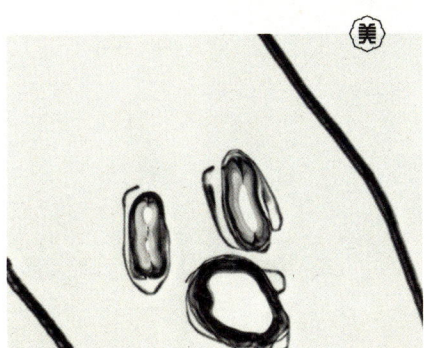

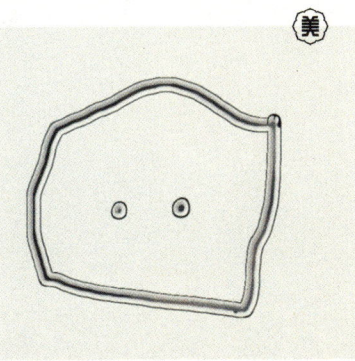

Prize Nominee Work

290 Video
TD. FD. 森翔太 Shota Mori
AD. 鈴木旬 Shun Suzuki
DI (Assistant). 國分智之 Tomoyuki Kokubun
DP. 吉川昌太 Shota Yoshikawa
COMP. とくさしけんご Kengo Tokusashi
A (Manga). やじまり Yajimari
D. 谷川瑛一 Eiichi Tanigawa
CL. Non-commercial work
PT. 源暎アンチック, スーラキャピー, マティス

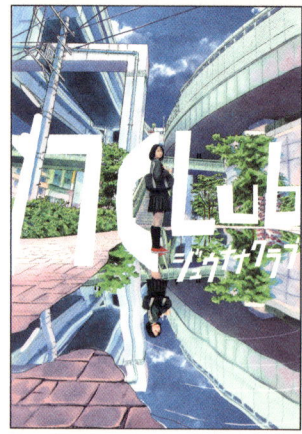
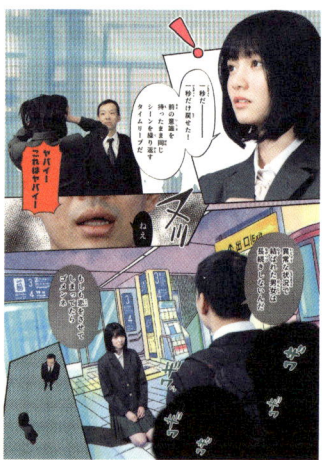
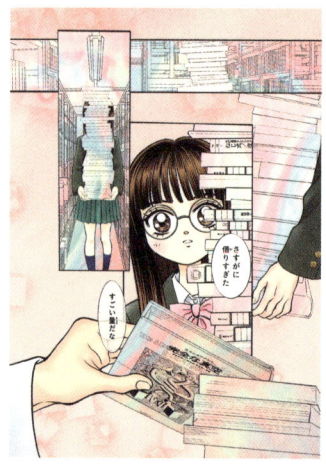
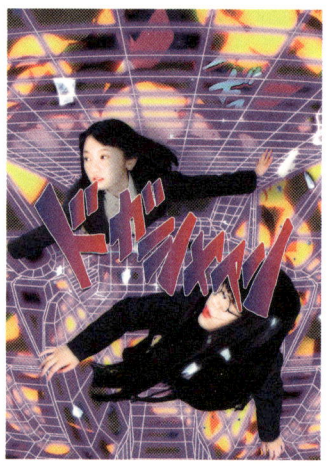
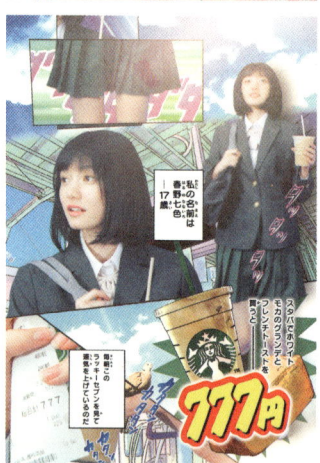
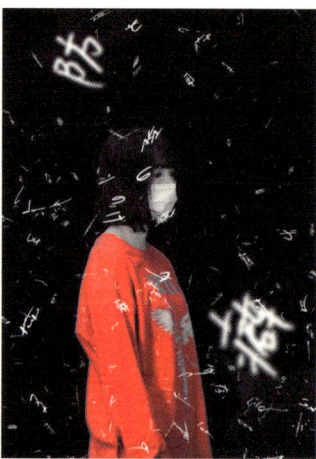
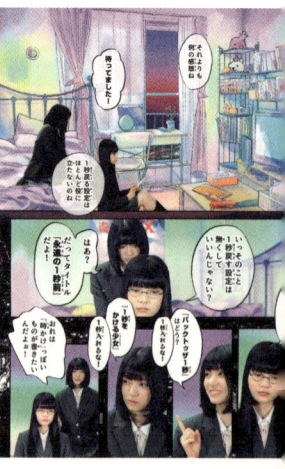

291 Branding
TD. AD. Tian Na
D. Herbr Lin
CL. Momos talk
PT. Custom-made for the project

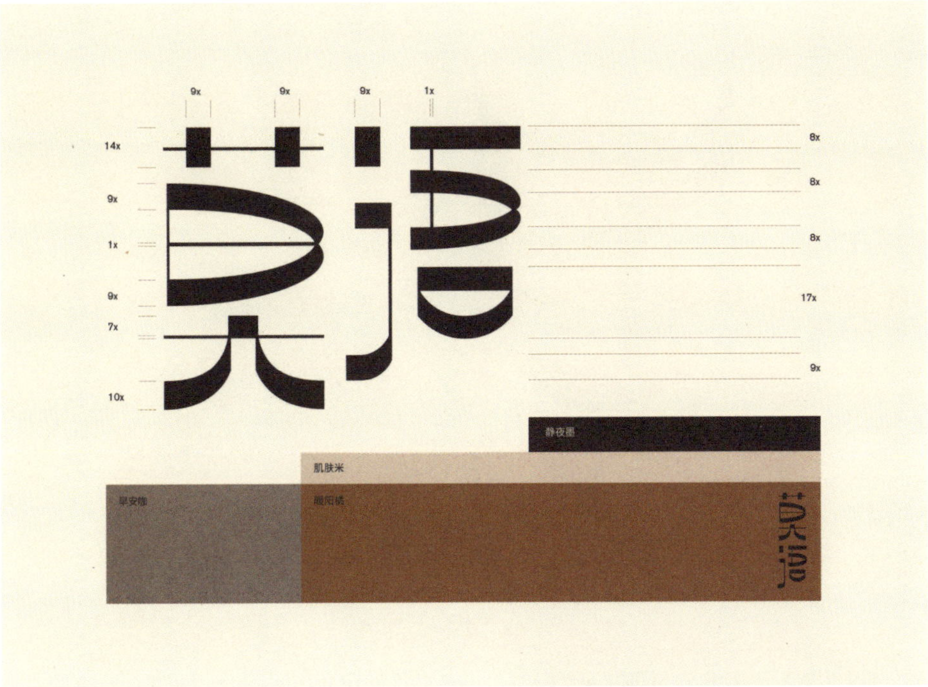

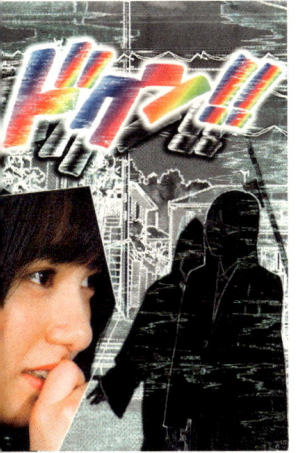

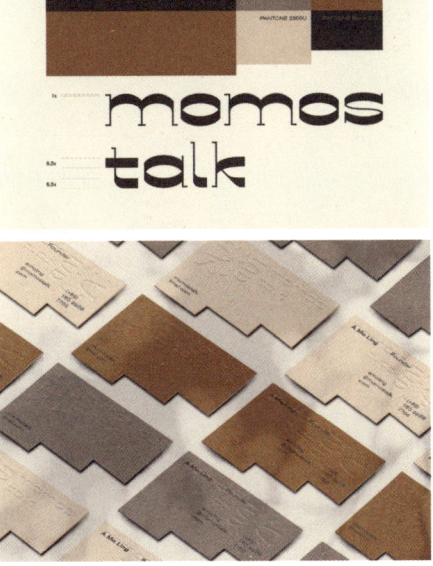

Prize Nominee Work

292 Exhibition Identity
TD. AD. 永井裕明 Hiroaki Nagai
CD. 石岡怜子 Ryoko Ishioka
D. 柏木美月 Mitsuki Kashiwagi
CCO. 堀川玲菜 Rena Horikawa
CL. ギンザ・グラフィック・ギャラリー ginza graphic gallery
PT. Didot, ヒラギノ明朝

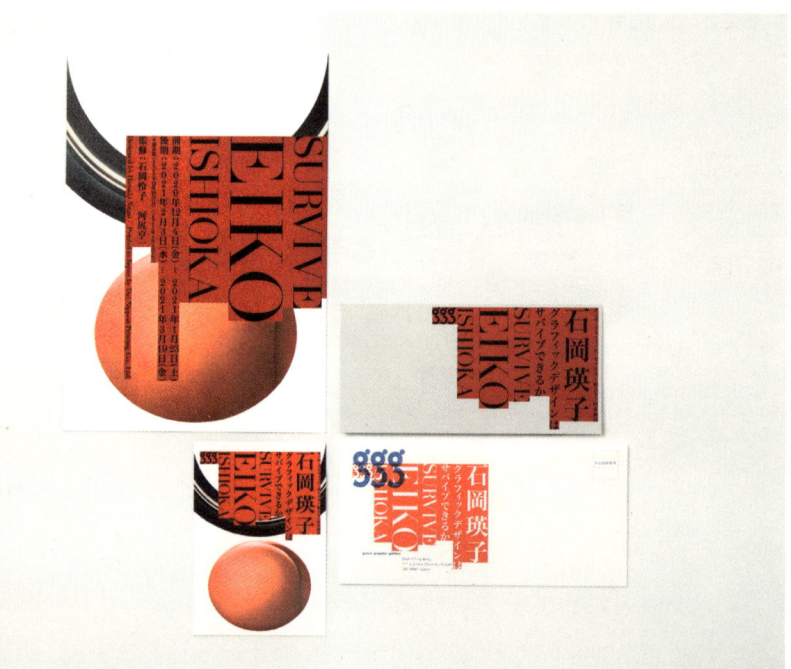

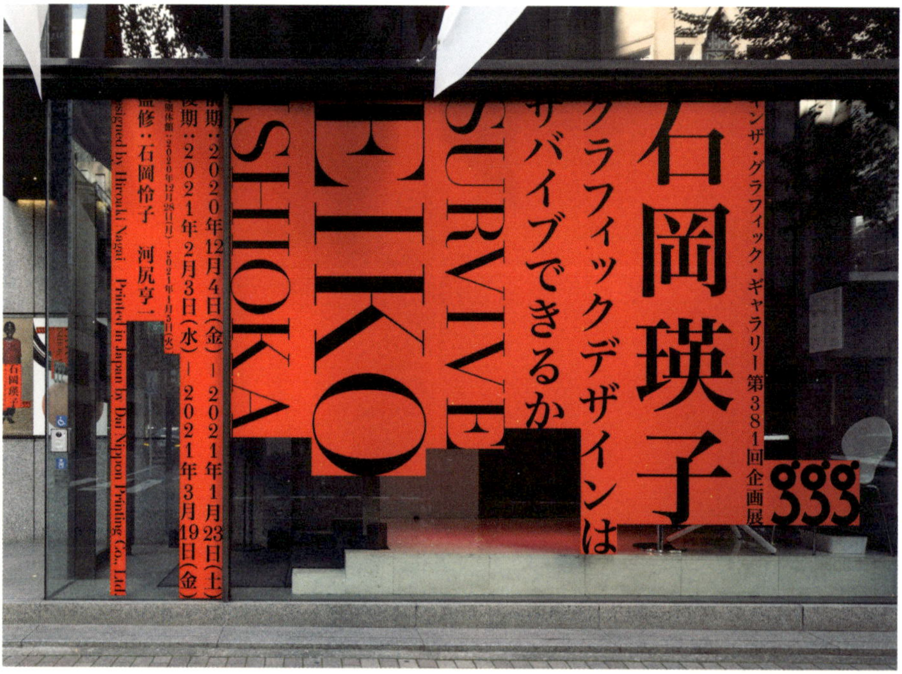

293 Memorial box
TD. AD. D. 永井裕明 Hiroaki Nagai
D. 前田由貴 Yuki Maeda, 柏木美月 Mitsuki Kashiwagi
A. 大平立子 Ritsuko Ohira
CCO. 堀川玲菜 Rena Horikawa
CL. Non-commercial work
PT. Didot

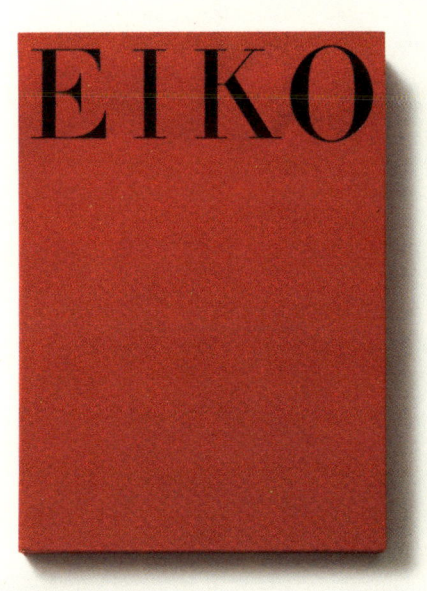
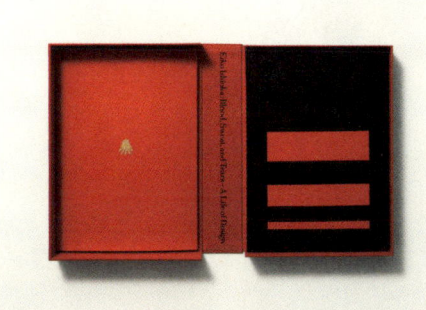
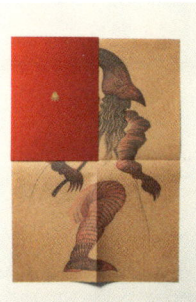
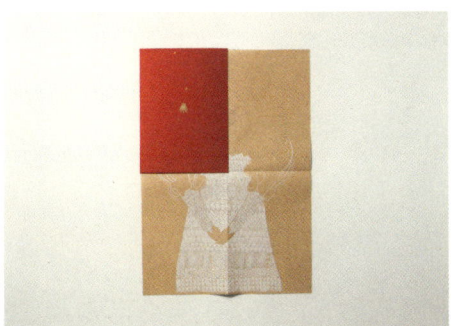
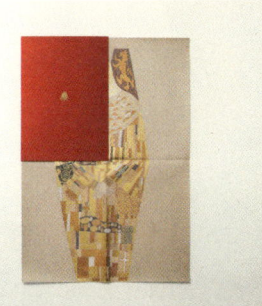

294 VI, Promotional item
TD. MPTY
AD. D. Michelle Yong, Preston Tham
CL. OKOK Services
PT. Custom-made for the project, Fake Receipt

295 Artbook
TD. AD. D. I. 永田傑 Takashi Nagata
CL. 北アルプス展望美術館
North Alps Viewing Museum of Art
PT. Custom-made for the project, Helvetica

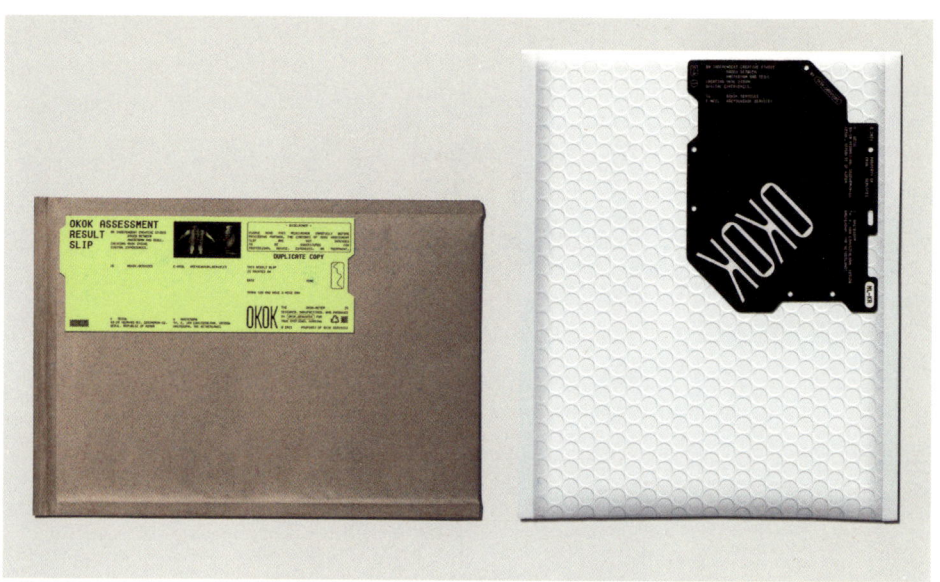

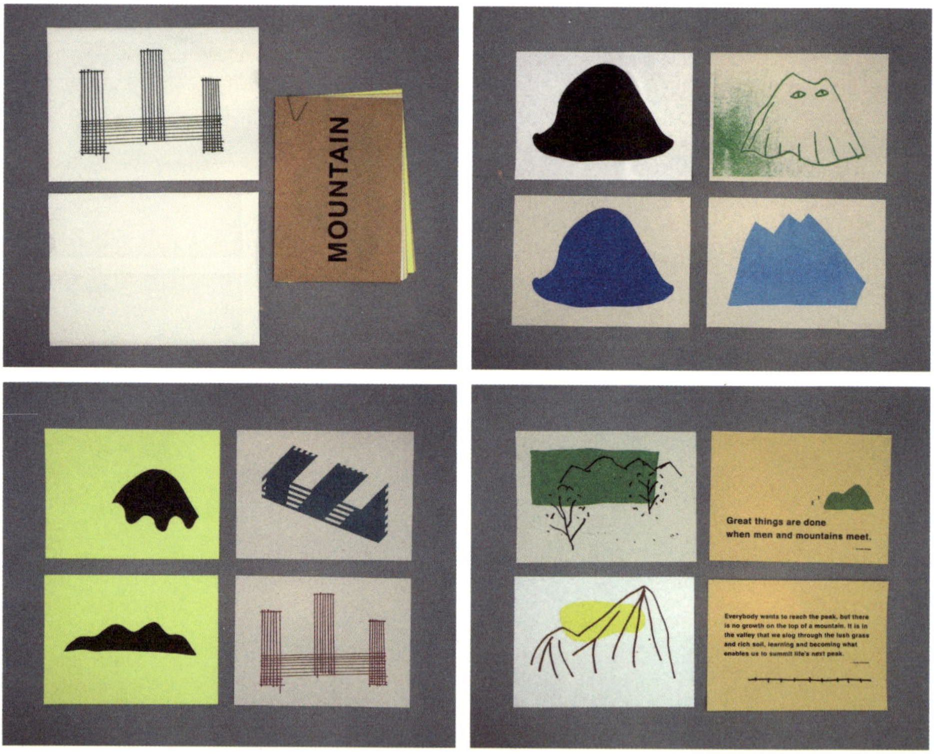

Prize Nominee Work

296 Packaging
TD. AD. D. 中市哲 Satoru Nakaichi
AD. 玉村浩一 Koichi Tamamura
PD. 川村文康 Fumiyasu Kawamura
CL.（株）ヒナタビ Hinatabi Co., Ltd.

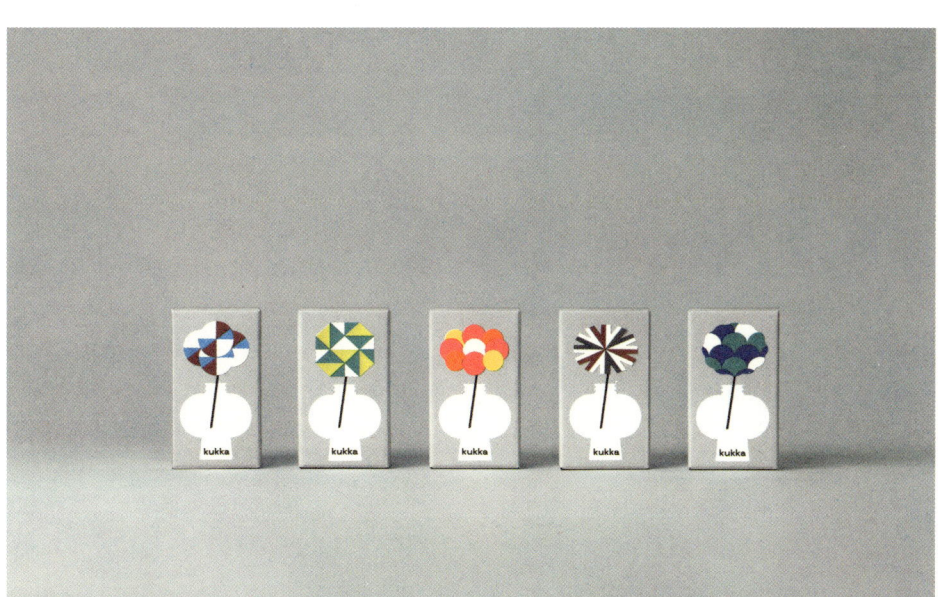

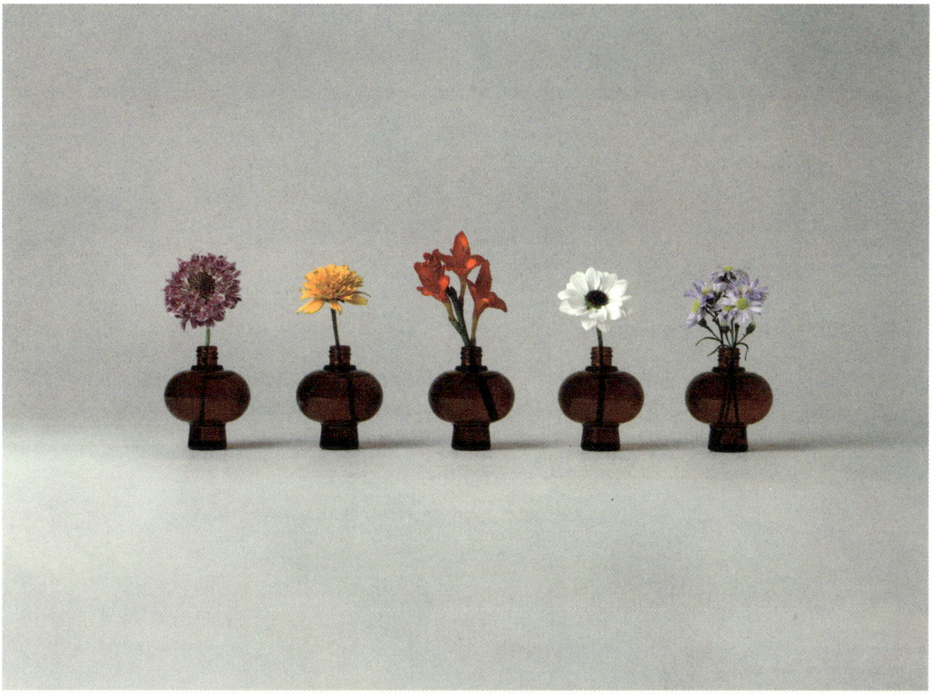

Prize Nominee Work

297 Calendar
TD. 仲條正義 Masayoshi Nakajo
CL. 資生堂パーラー Shiseido Parlour Co., Ltd.

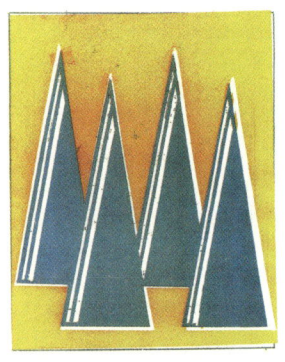

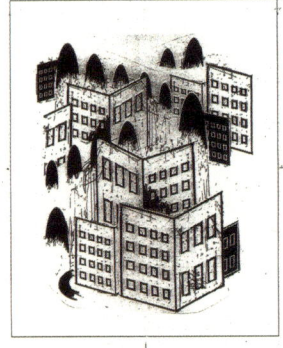

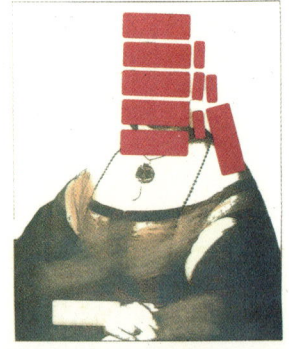

Prize Nominee Work

298 Tabloid
TD. 仲條正義 Masayoshi Nakajo
CL. Punctum

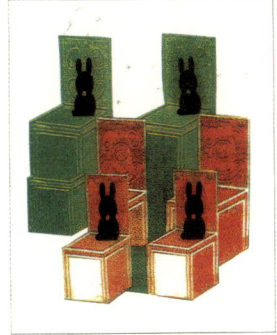
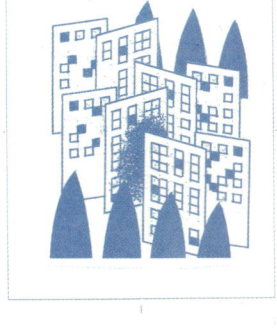
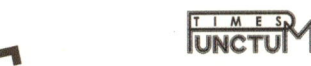
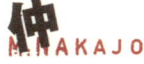
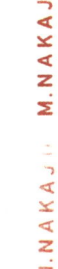
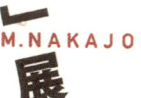
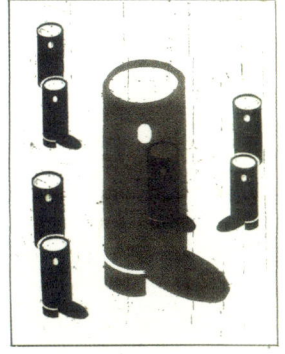
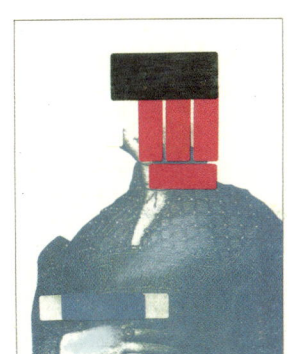
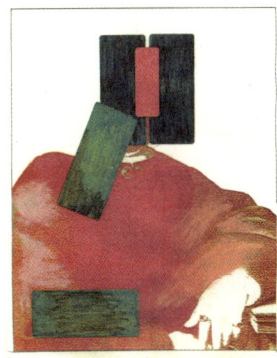

299 Logotype
TD. 仲條正義 Masayoshi Nakajo
CL.「東京タワーで、あいましょう。」計画 TTA Project

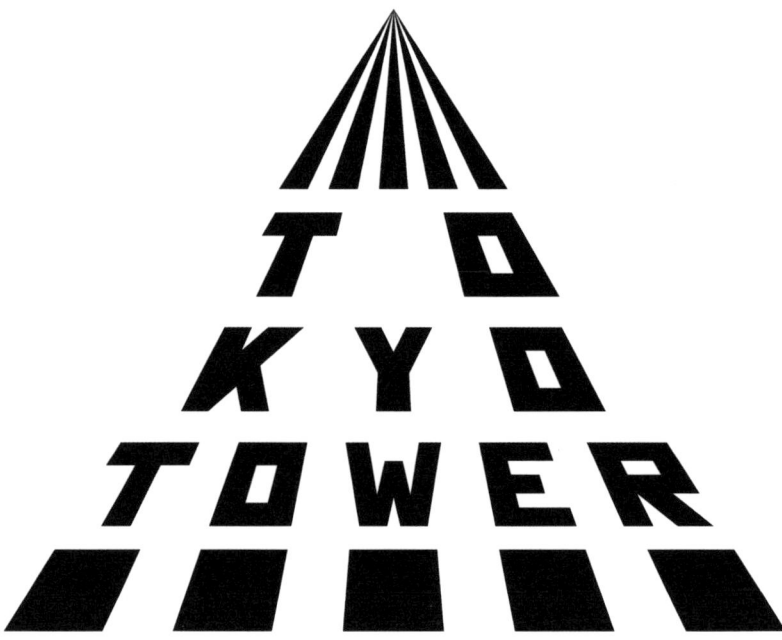

263 **Prize Nominee Work**

300 Poster
TD. 中村至男 Norio Nakamura
CL. Non-commercial work
PT. Futura bold

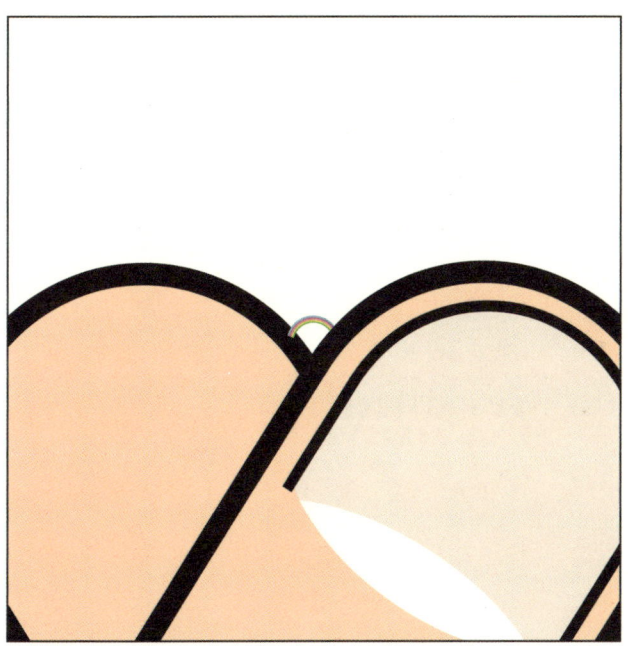

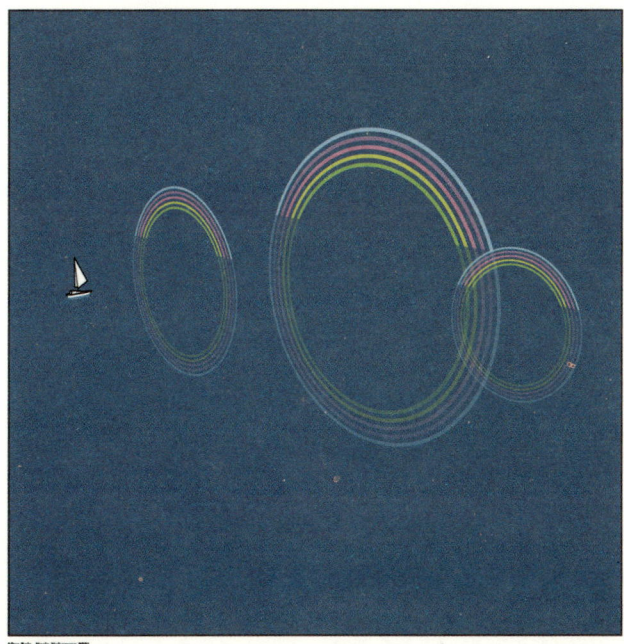

300

301 Poster
TD. 中山智裕 Tomohiro Nakayama
CL. 櫻井充 Mitsuru Sakurai
PT. 筑紫明朝CID

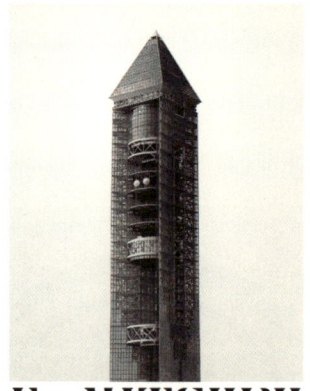
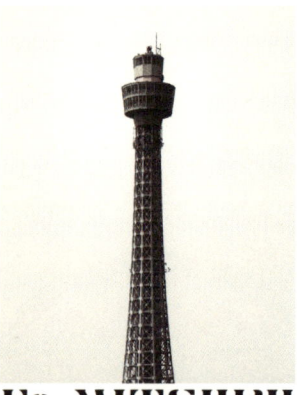
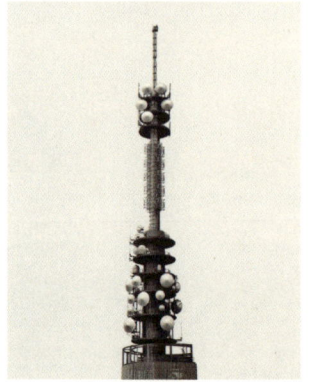
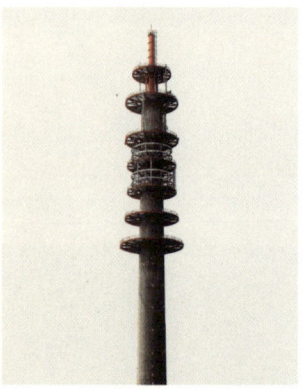
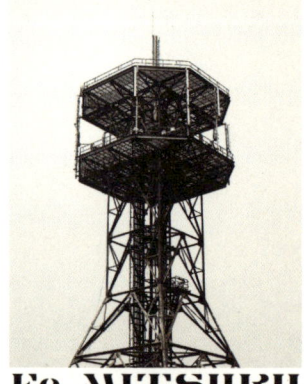
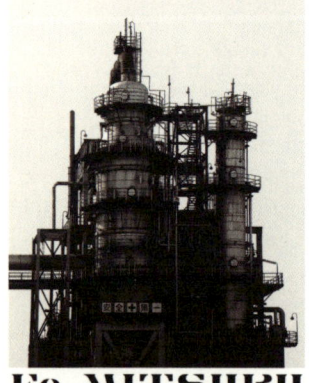

302 Catalogue
TD. D. Toby Ng
D. Ronald Cheung
P. Stephanie Teng
E. Kurt Lin
CL. Optimix
PT. Suisse Int'l, M XiangHe Hei TC

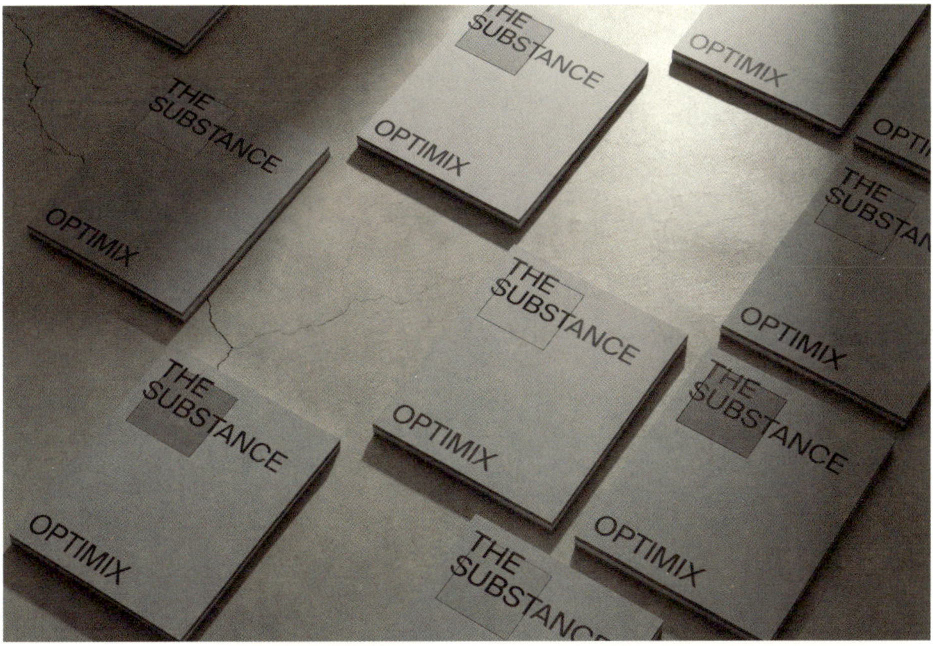

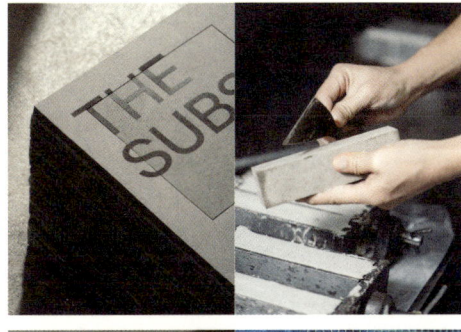
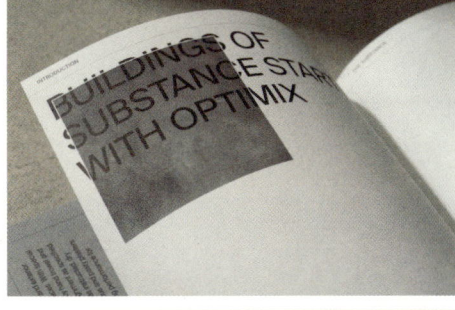
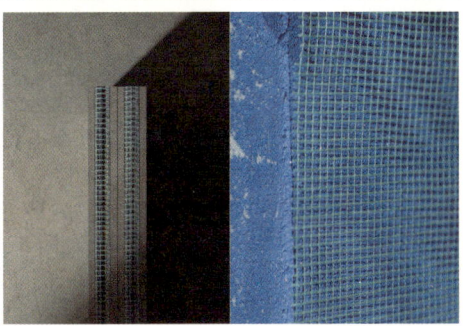
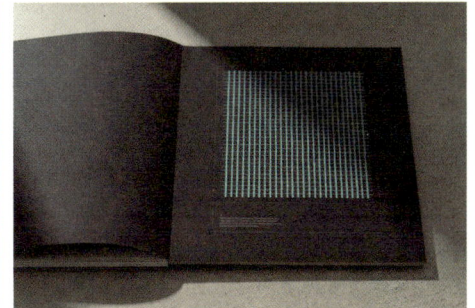

303 Poster
TD. AD. D. Thomas Neeser, Thomas Müller, Jakob Görner
CL. Schule für Gestaltung Basel
PT. Custom-made for the project, Executive

304 Commemorative stamps
TD. AD. D. Aaron Nieh
D. Even Chen
CL. Chunghwa Post
PT. Founders Grotesk

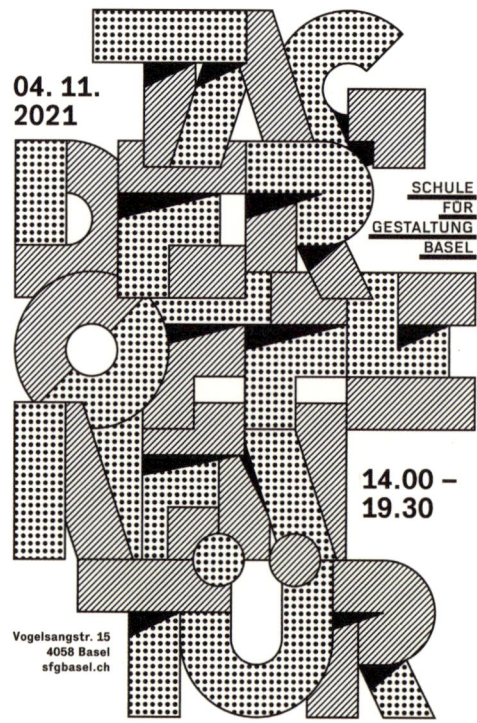

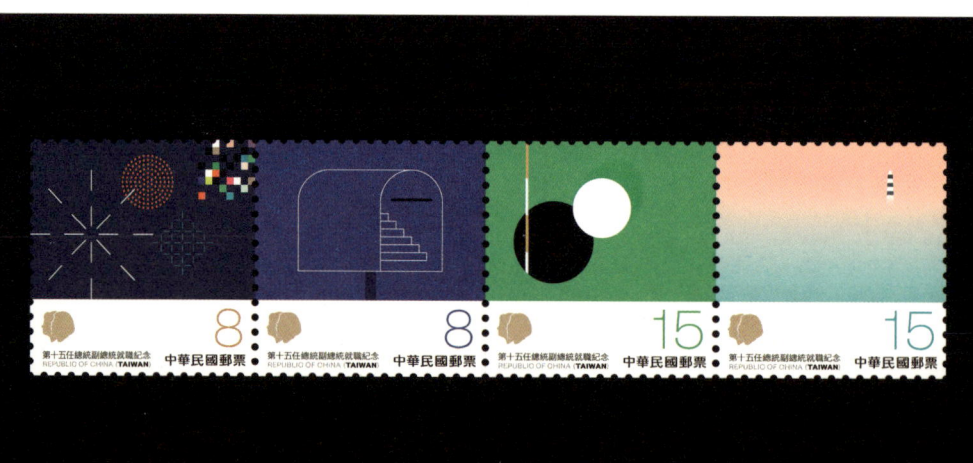

305 VI
TD. AD. D. Aaron Nieh
AD. D. Even Chen
D. Xiang Wei
MD. Pinhsu Chiang
PM. Janice Lin
CL. Taiwan Design Research Institute
PT. Akkurat

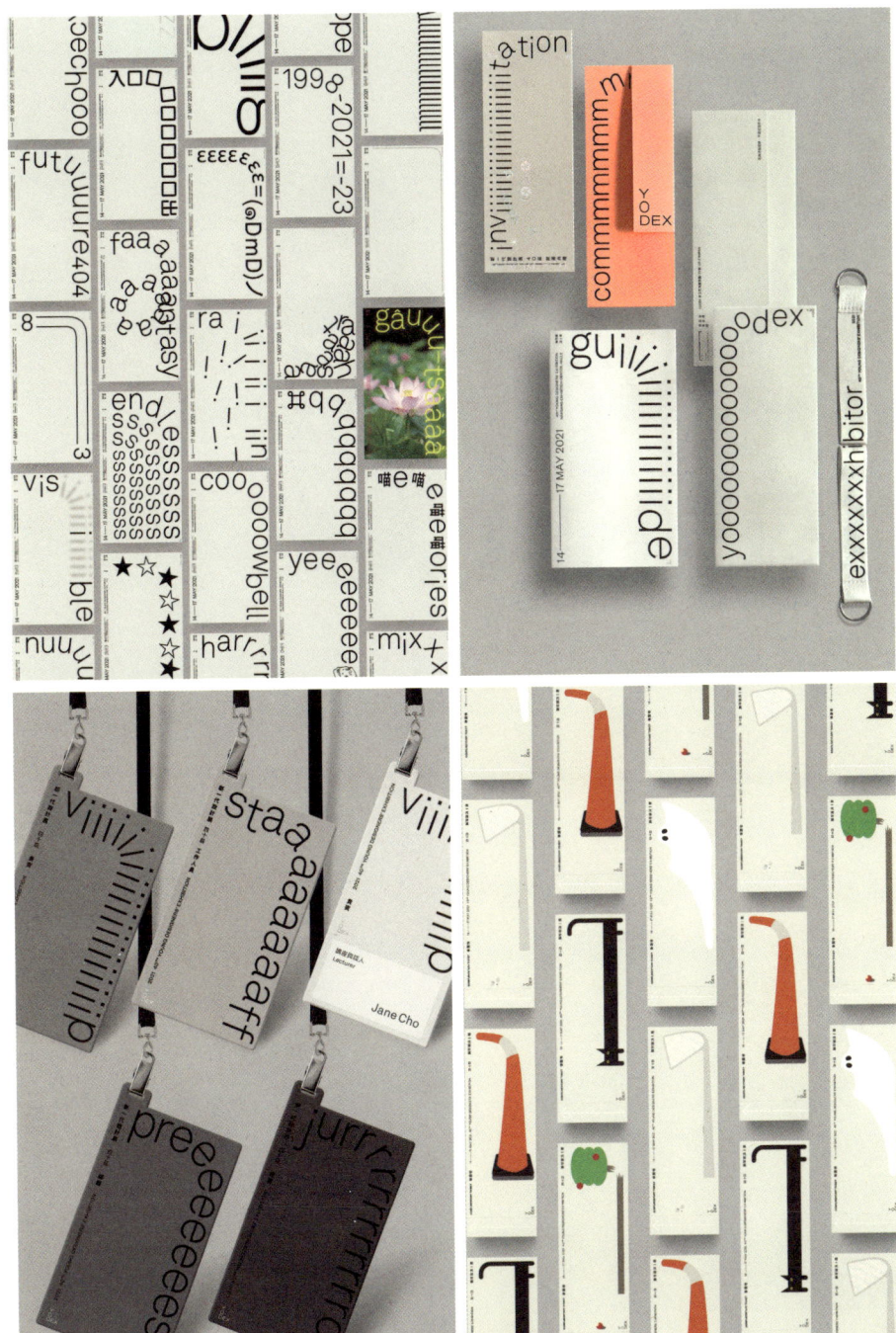

306 Album design
TD. AD. D. Aaron Nieh
AD. D. Even Chen
CL. Sony Music Entertainment Taiwan Ltd.
PT. Custom-made for the project, Founders Grotesk

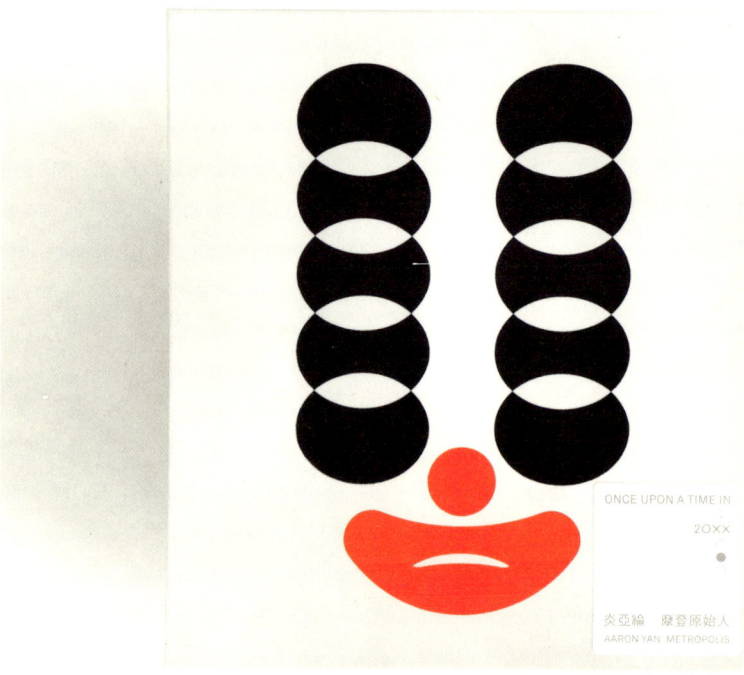

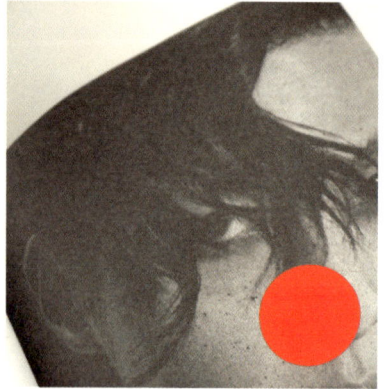

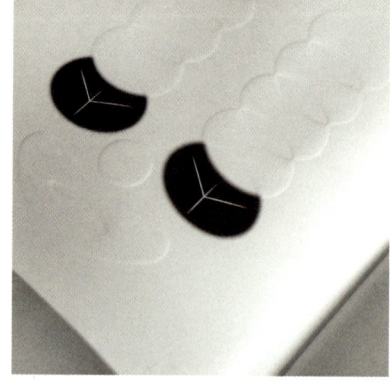

269

307 Poster
TD. AD. D. 西達也 Tatsuya Nishi
CL. 第52回戸隠そば祭り実行委員会 The 52nd Togakushi soba Festival executive committee
PT. Custom-made for the project, 太ゴB101, Rosewood Std Fill

308 Packaging
TD. Aaron Nieh
AD. D. Even Chen
CL. Taiwan Tobacco & Liquor Corporation
PT. Akkurat, Heisei Kaku Gothic

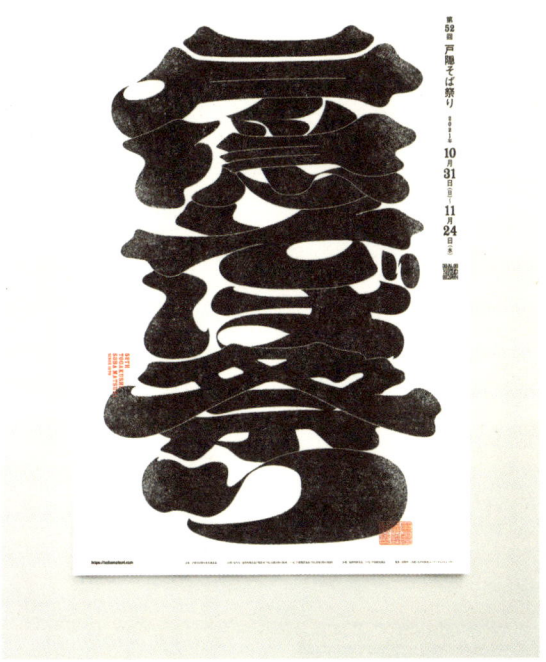

307

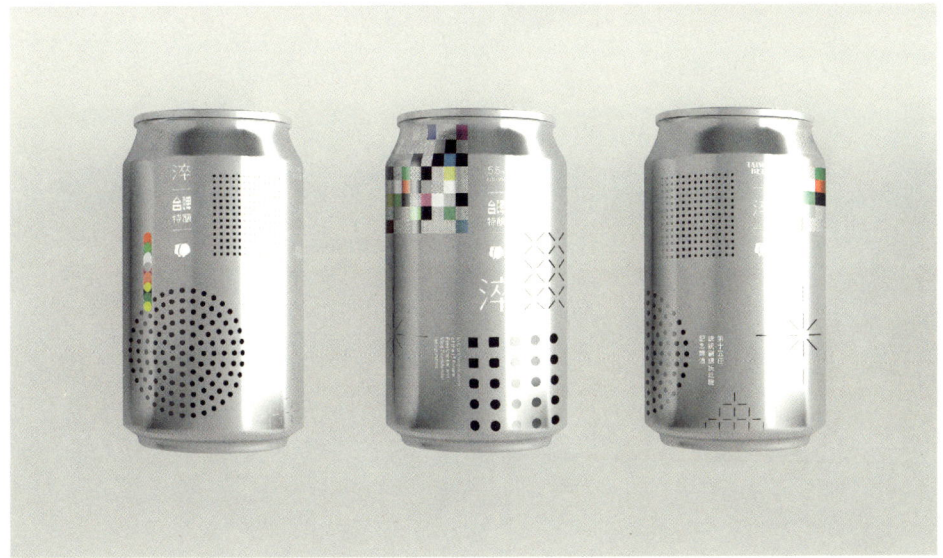

308

309 Signage
TD, BD. 西澤明洋 Akihiro Nishizawa
BD. 橘あずさ Azusa Tachibana
PRO.（株）小林工芸社 Kobayashi Kogeisha Co., Ltd.
P. 谷本裕志 Hiroshi Tanimoto
CL.（株）うぶや Ubuya

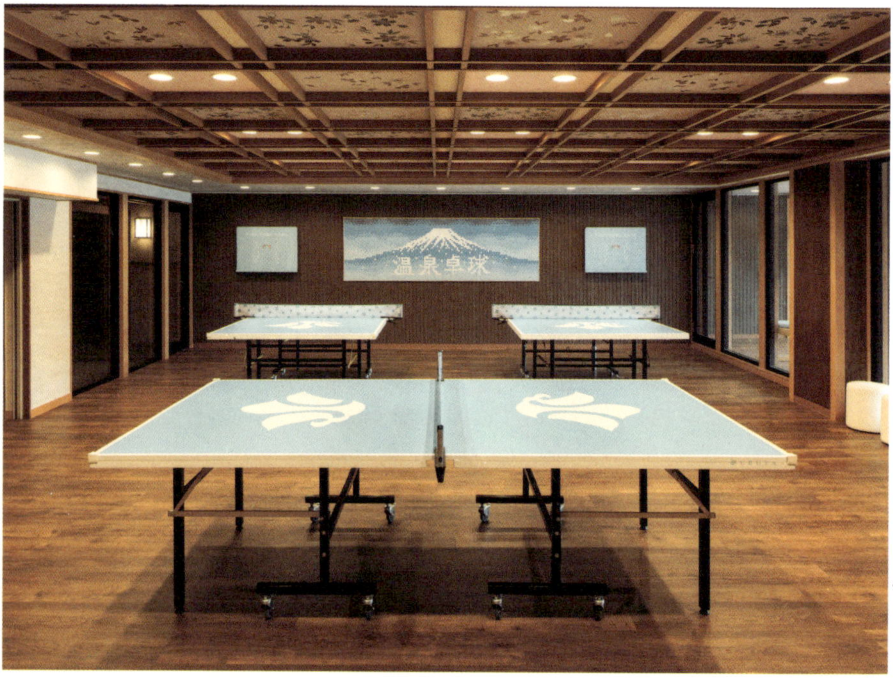

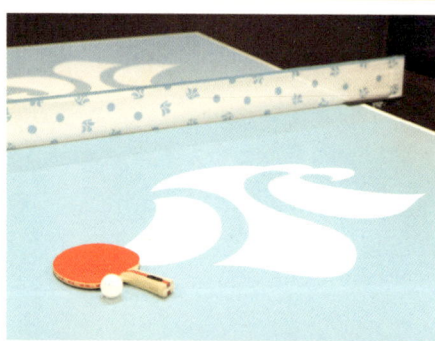
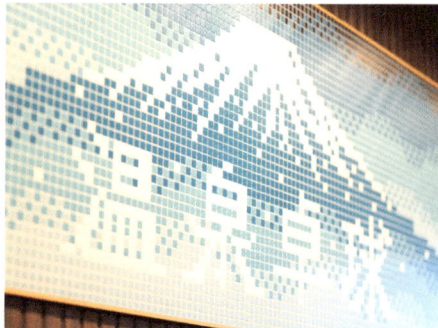
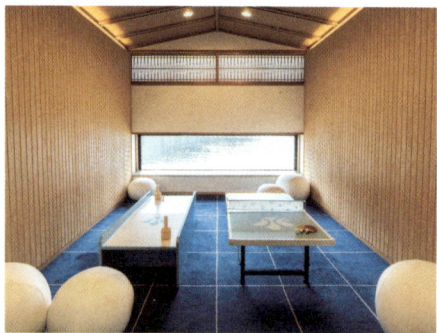
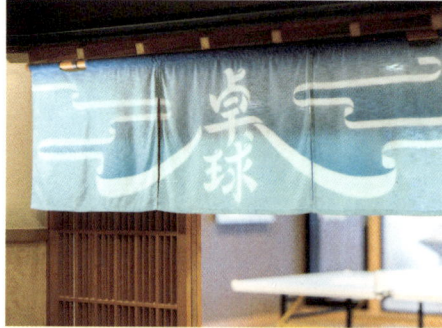

310 Signage
TD. BD. 西澤明洋 Akihiro Nishizawa
BD. 橘あずさ Azusa Tachibana
ID. 吉田昌弘 Masahiro Yoshida
P. 宮本啓介 Keisuke Miyamoto
CL.（株）釜浅商店 Kama-Asa
PT. A1明朝

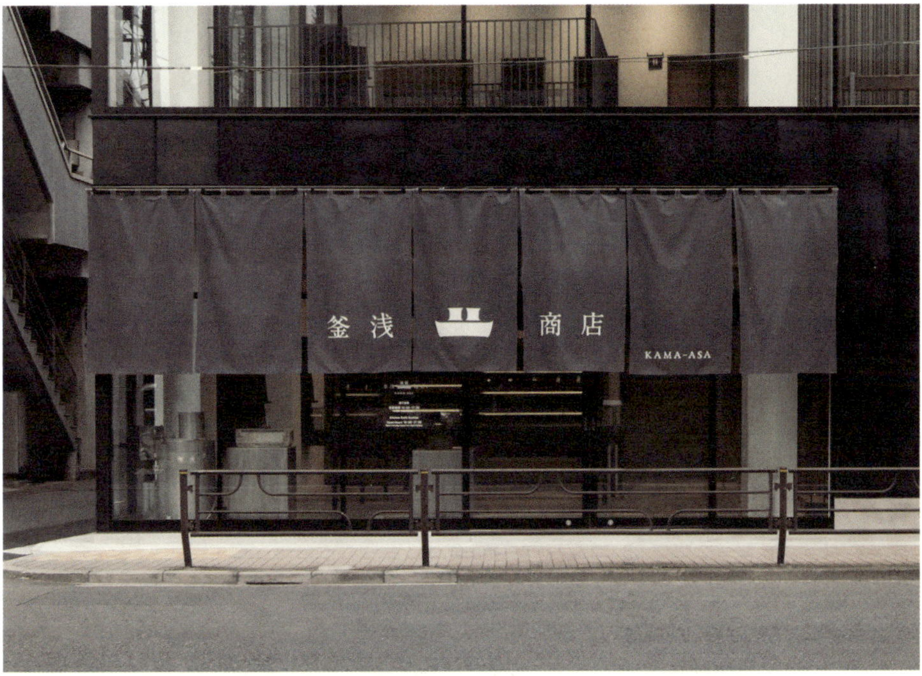

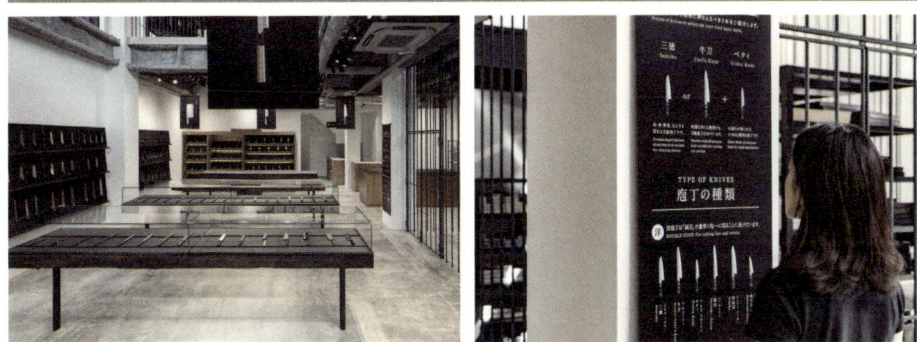

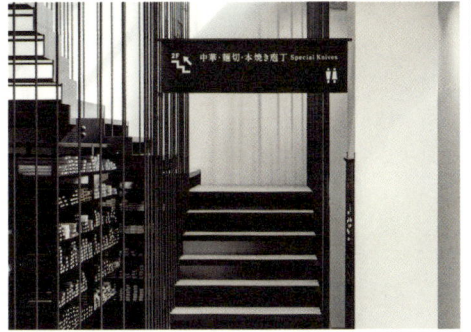

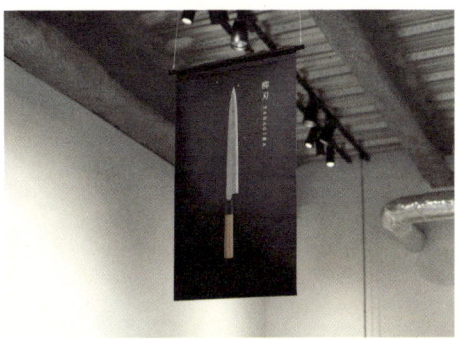

Prize Nominee Work

311 Book
TD. Juliane Nöst
DI (publishing). Lars Harmsen, Julia Kahl
PU. Slanted Publishers
PT. GT America, Minion Pro

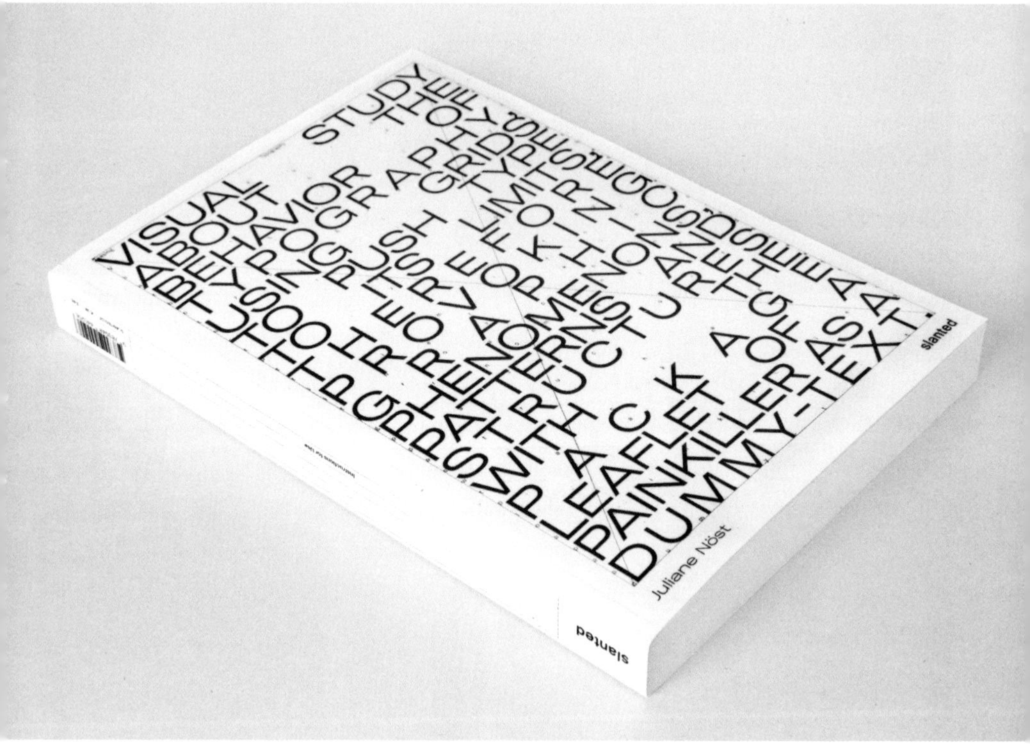

312 Experimental work
TD. 落合翔平 Shohei Ochiai
CL. Non-commercial work

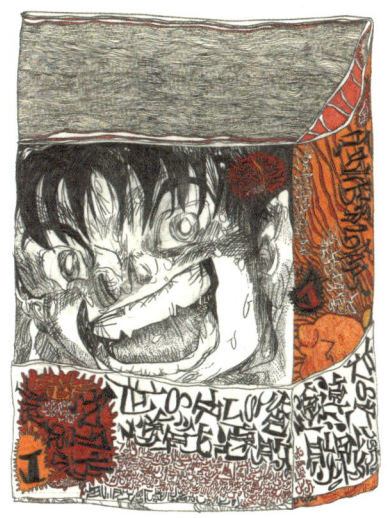
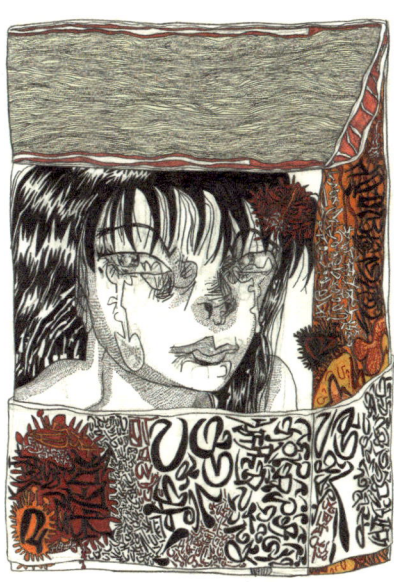
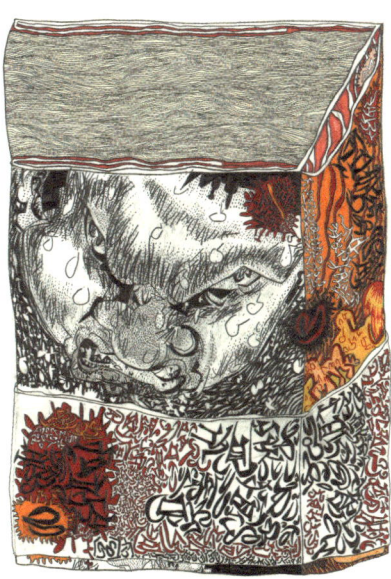
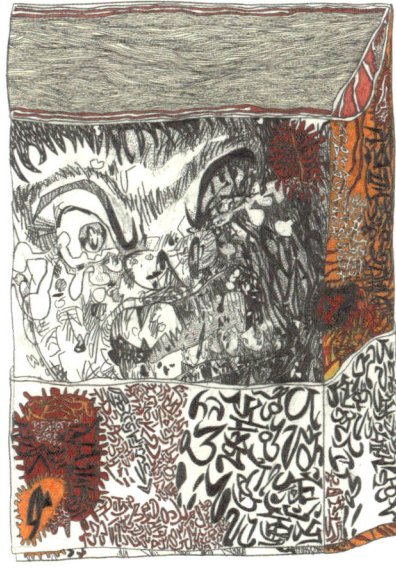

313 Book
TD. CON. CD. D. Tino Nyman, Marina Veziko
D (Logo, FEW display). Jaakko Suomalainen
E. Claudia Cifu, Piia Emilia, Tiina Eronen, Emma Gillespie, Helmi Honkanen, David Jakob, Hanna Jämsenius, Arttu Kokkonen, Unni Leino, Eveliina Lempiäinen, Piia Lempiäinen, Kira Muesa, Sofia Okkonen, Ville Varumo, Mickael Vis, Eve Lahikainen, Taneli Palola, Ione Rawlins

314 Record jacket
TD. D. Non-Format/ANTI: Kjell Ekhorn, Jon Forss
CD. Non-Format/ANTI
I. Zach Lieberman
CL. Lo Recordings
PT. Custom made for the project, Dazzed

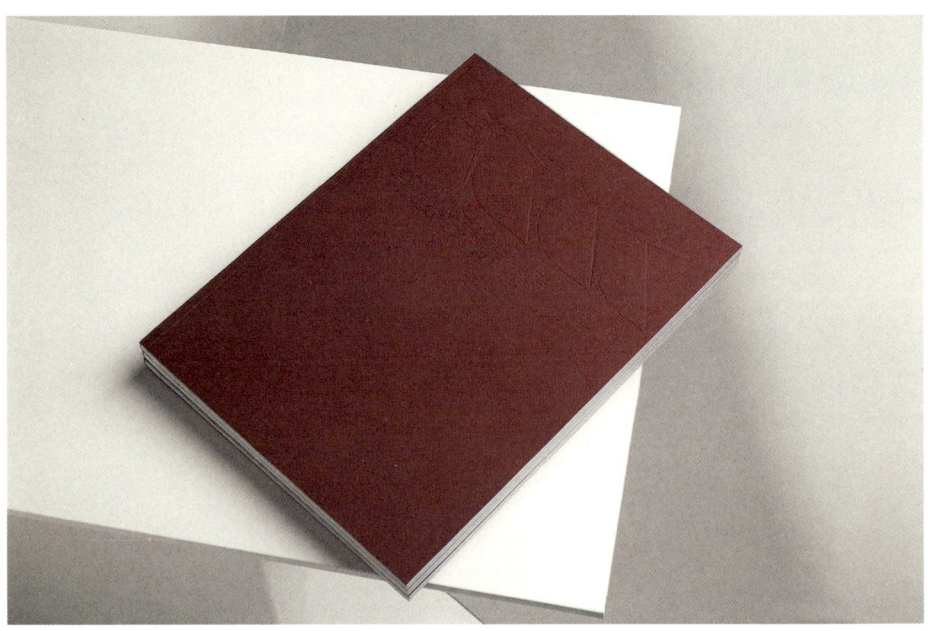

313

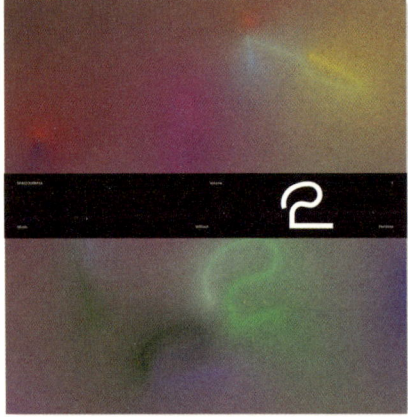

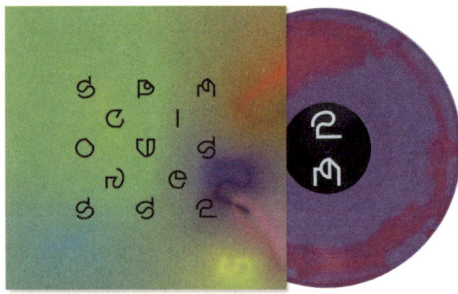

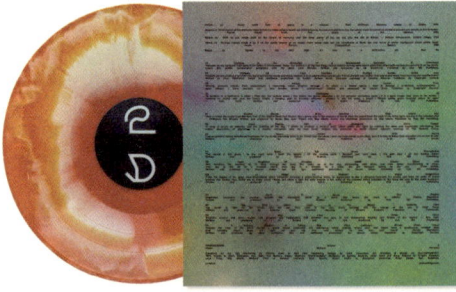

314

275 | Prize Nominee Work | 315 Leaflet, Cards, Envelope
TD. OK-RM: Rory McGrath & Oliver Knight
CL. Maximillian William Gallery, InOtherWords

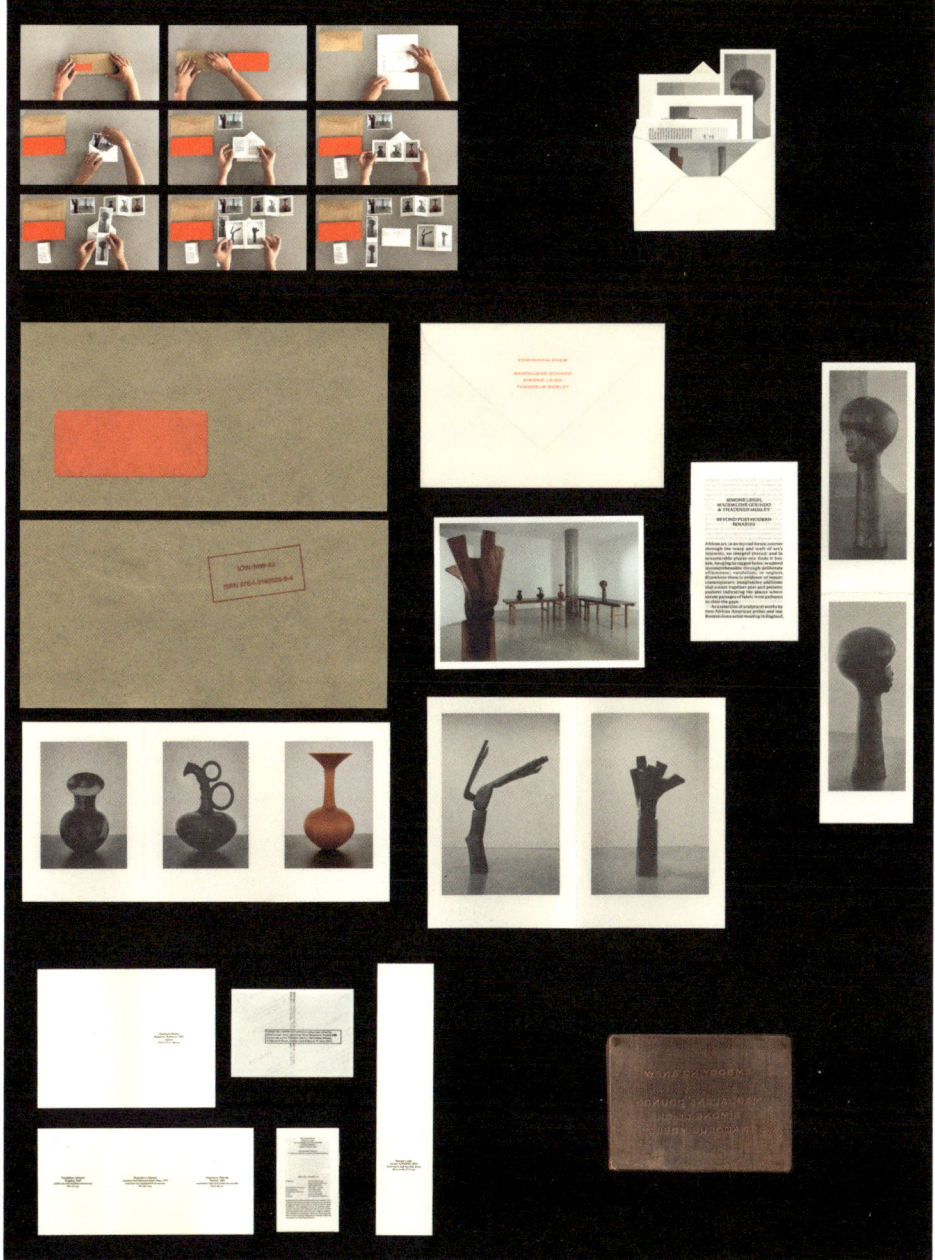

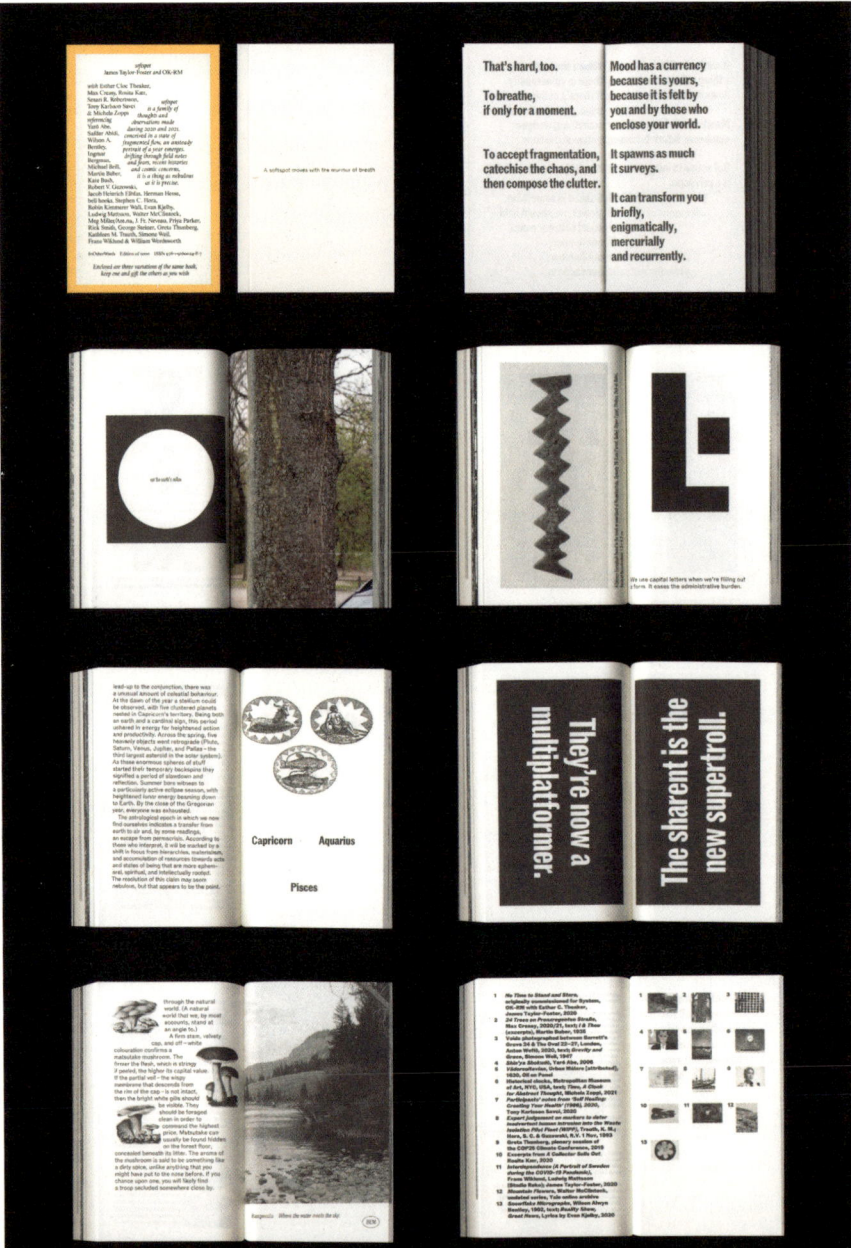

317 Album
TD. OK-RM: Rory McGrath & Oliver Knight
CL. Damon Albarn

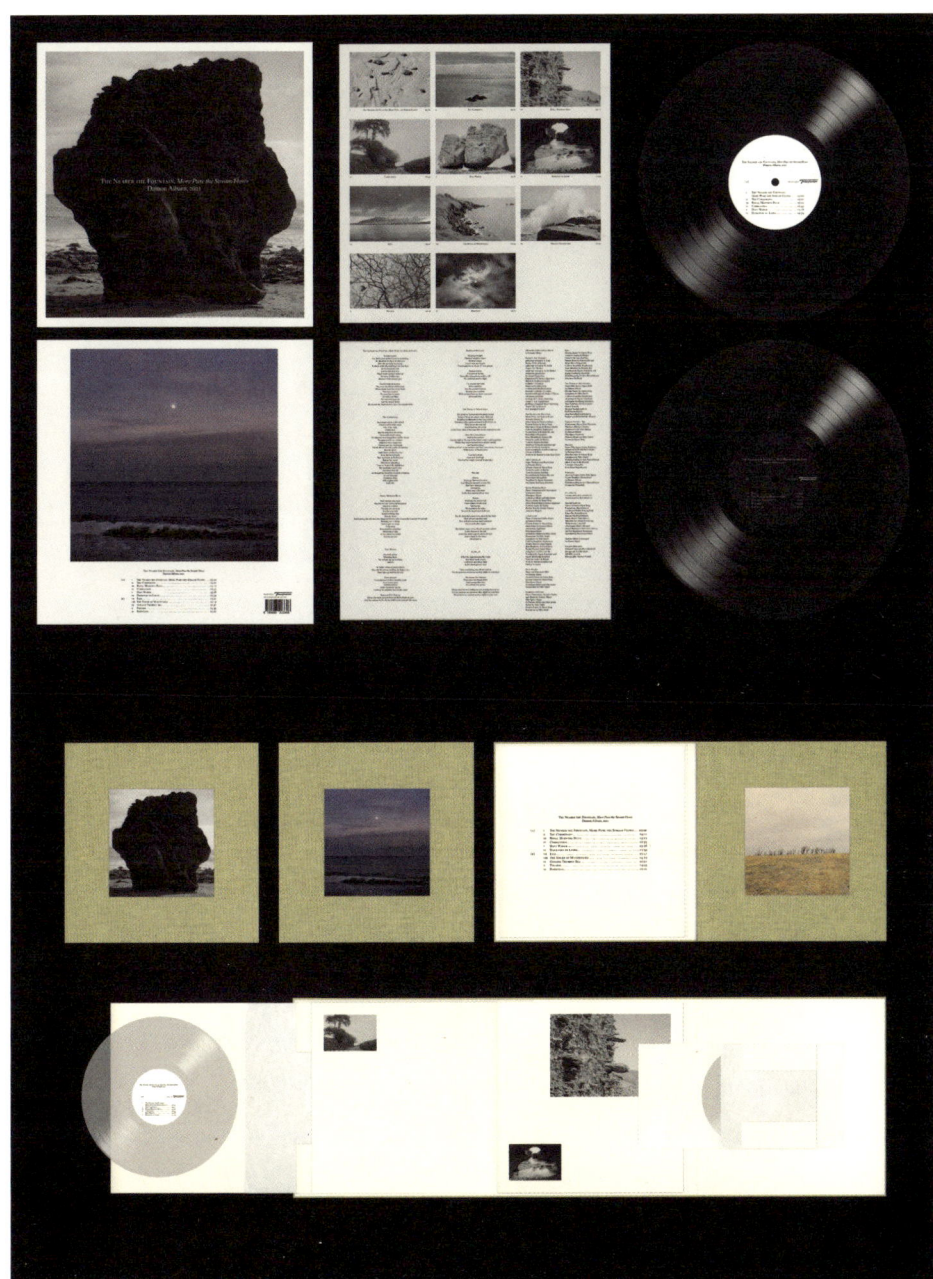

318 DM
TD. 岡本太玖斗 Takuto Okamoto
CL. 筑波大学芸術専門学群 School of Art and Design, University of Tsukuba,
筑波大学大学院人間総合科学研究科博士前期課程芸術専攻 Graduate School of Comprehensive Human Sciences, Master's Program in Art, University of Tsukuba
PT. 太ゴB101

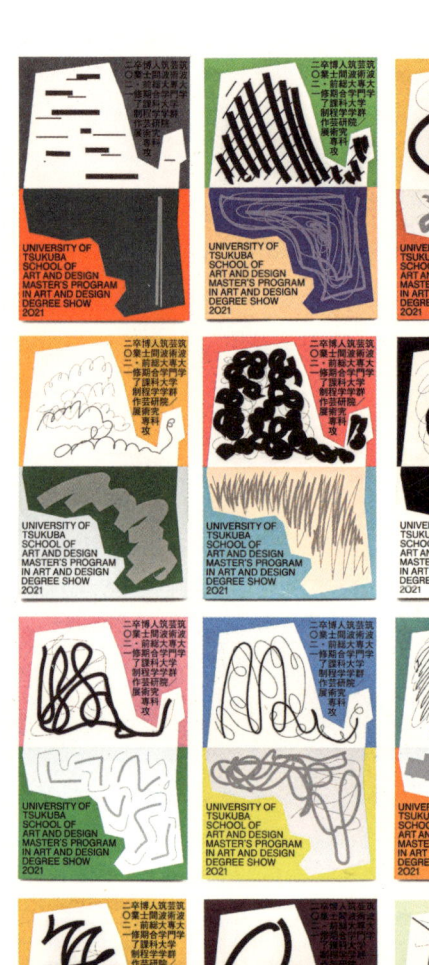
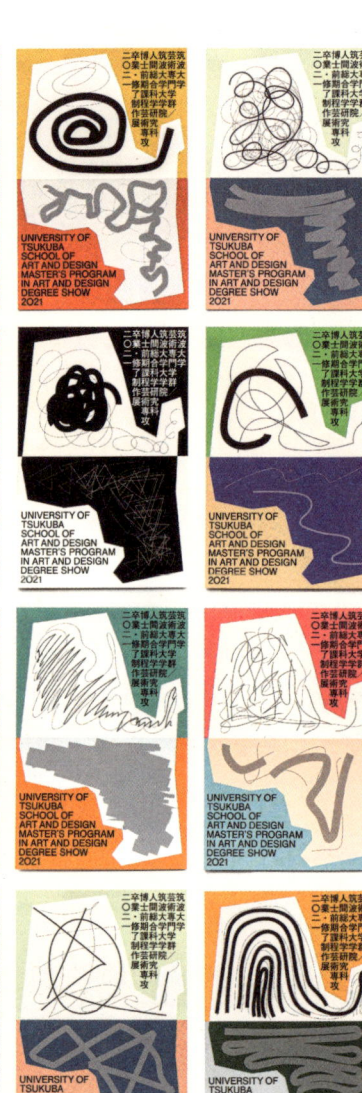

319 Video
TD. 岡大夢 Hiromu Oka
CL. 36 Days of Type
PT. Custom-made for the project

320 Poster
TD. AD. D. P. 岡崎真理子 Mariko Okazaki
CL. Alexandre Taalba, The 5th Floor
PT. 見出しゴMB31, Monument Grotesque

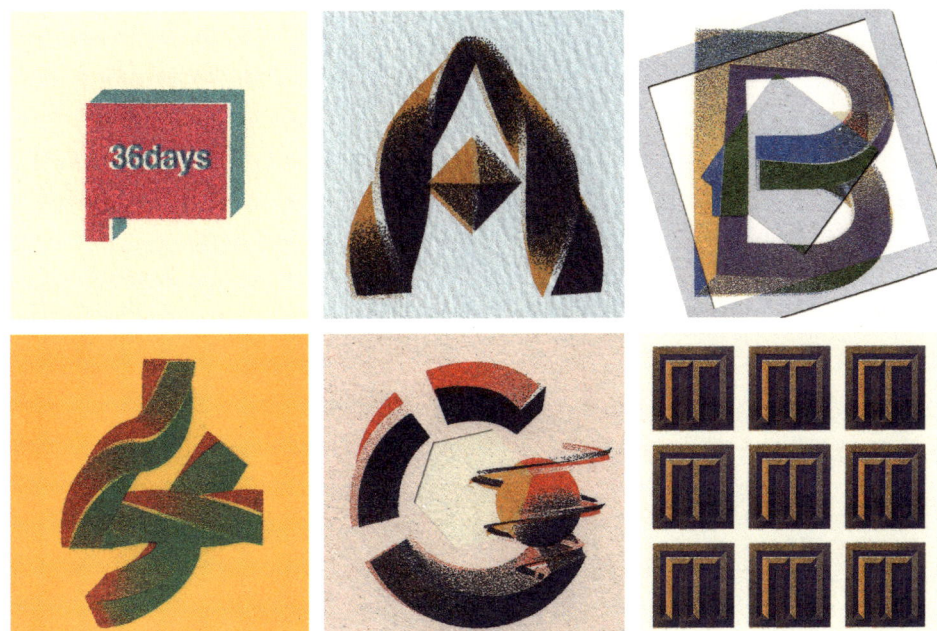

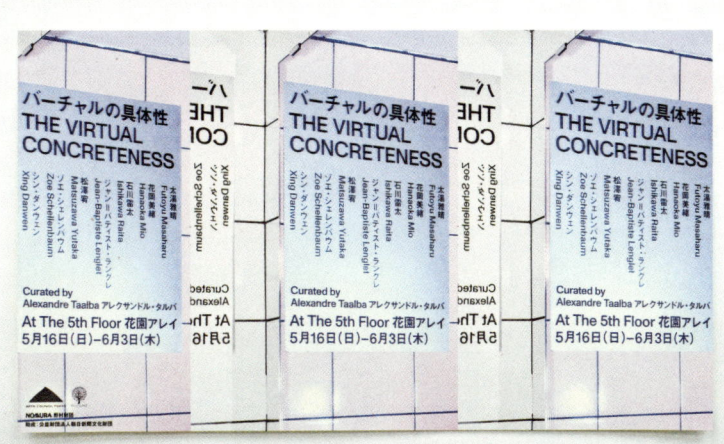

321 Exhibition graphics
TD. AD. D. 岡崎真理子 Mariko Okazaki
D. 後藤尚美 Naomi Goto
CL. 京都国立近代美術館 The National Museum of
 Modern Art, Kyoto, 水戸芸術館 Art Tower Mito
PT. 秀英角ゴシック金, Monument Grotesque,
 Distinct Style Script

322 Catalogue
TD. AD. D. 岡崎真理子 Mariko Okazaki
D. 後藤尚美 Naomi Goto, 泉美菜子 Minako Izumi
CL. 京都国立近代美術館 The National Museum of
 Modern Art, Kyoto, 水戸芸術館 Art Tower Mito
PT. 秀英角ゴシック金, Monument Grotesque,
 Distinct Style Script

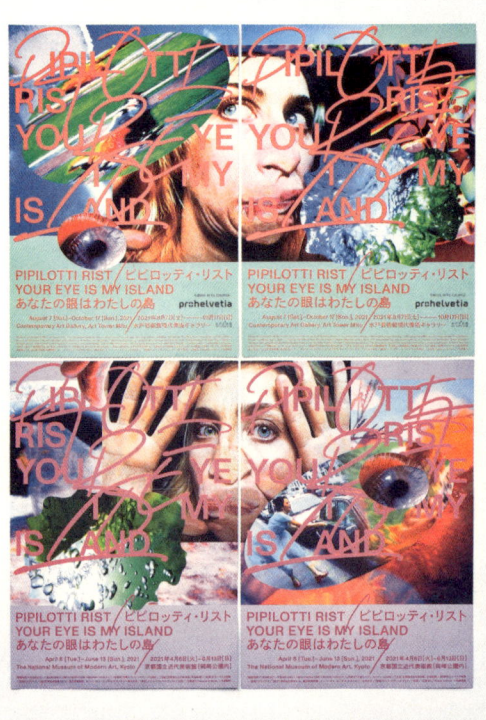
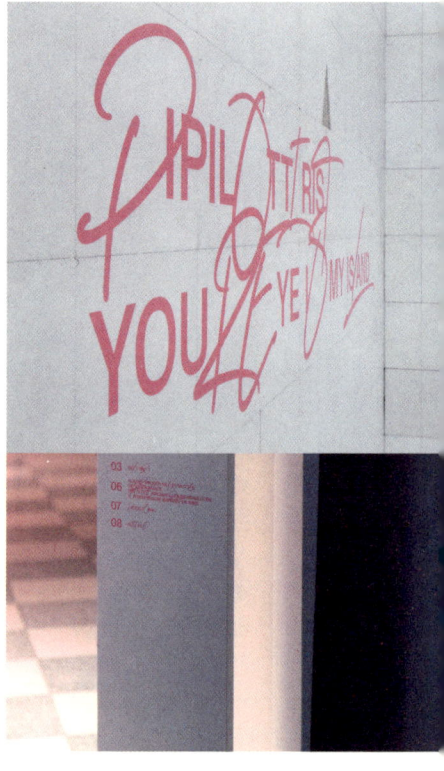

321

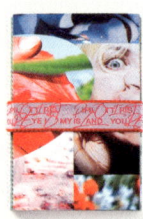
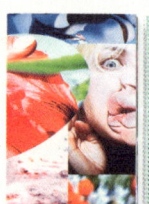
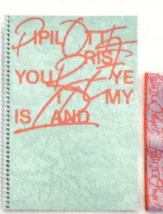
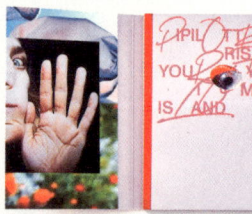
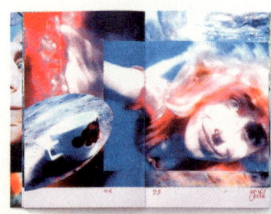
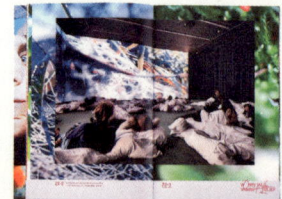
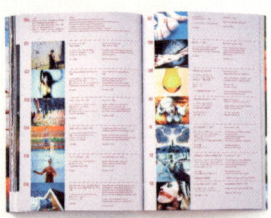

322

323 Signage
TD. AD. D. 岡崎真理子 Mariko Okazaki
D. 後藤尚美 Naomi Goto
CL. 京都国立近代美術館 The National Museum of Modern Art, Kyoto, 水戸芸術館 Art Tower Mito
PT. 秀英角ゴシック金, Monument Grotesque, Distinct Style Script

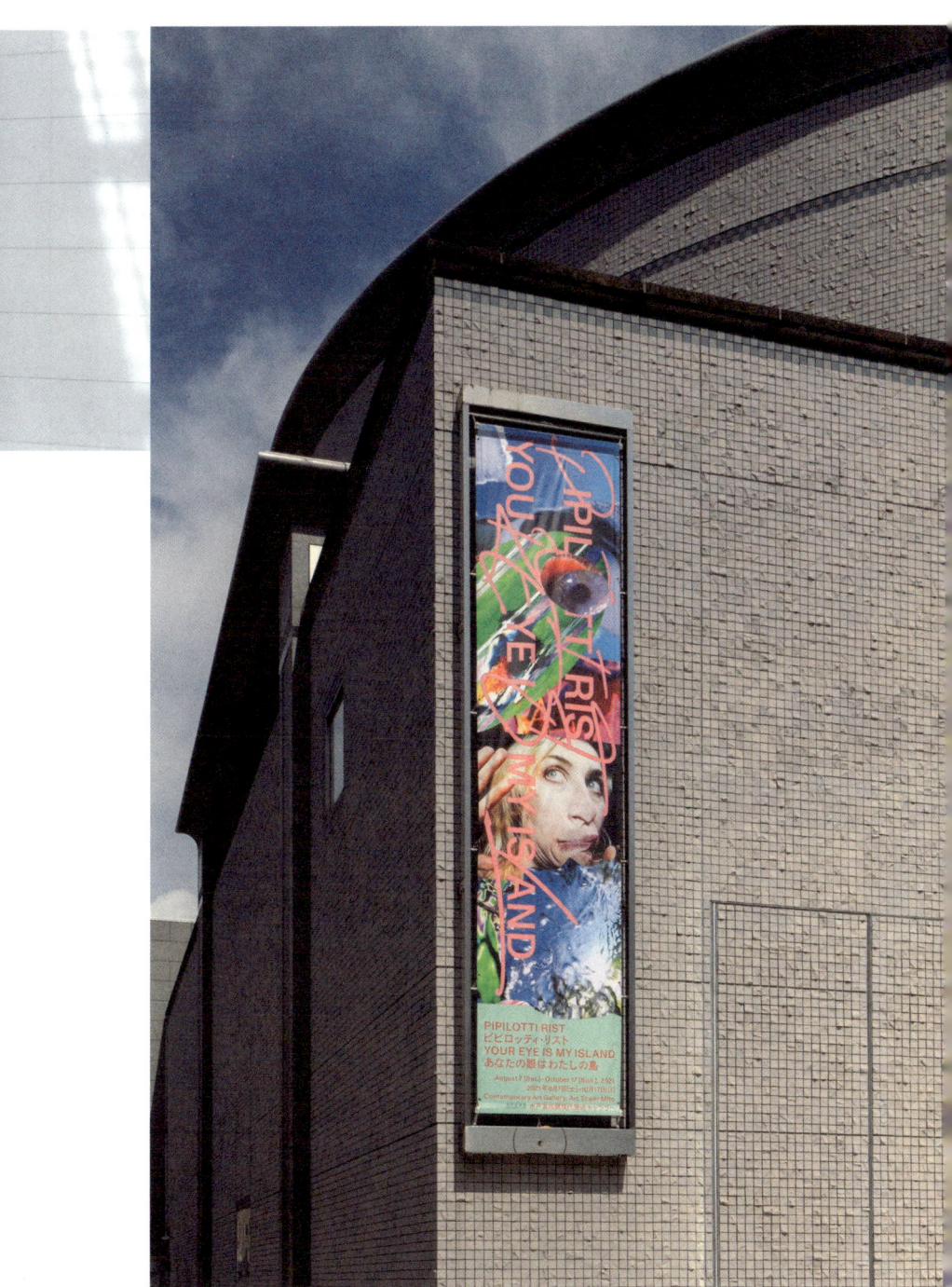

324 VI
TD. Gregory Page
CL. Milkshake, Sony Music
PT. Custom-made for the project, Inferi

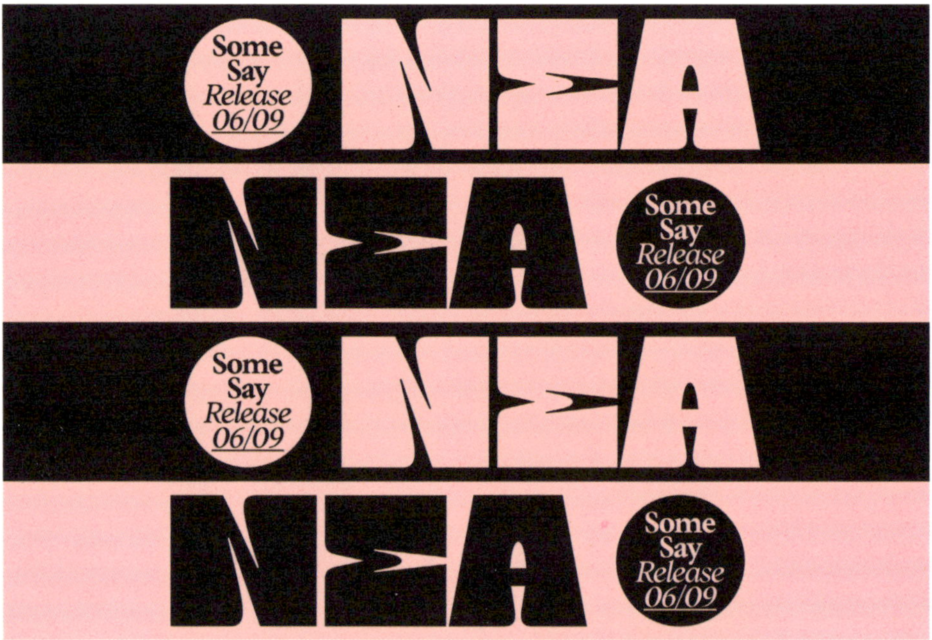

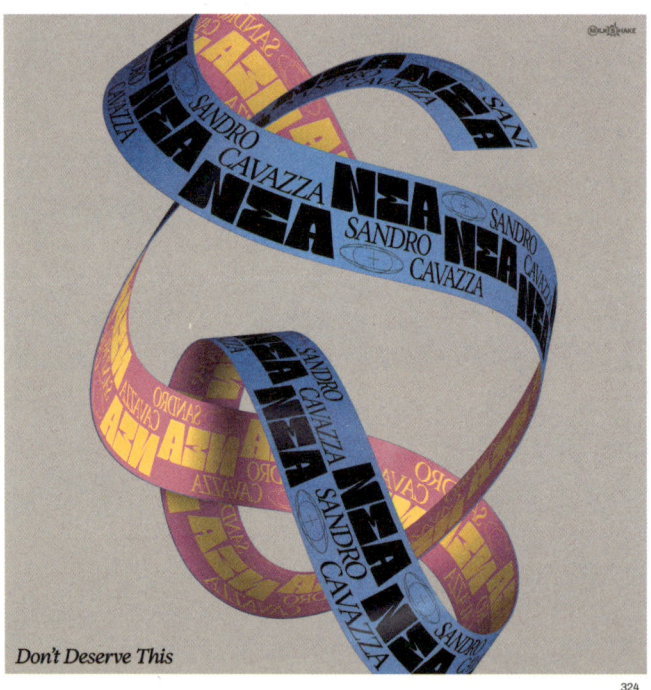

Don't Deserve This

325 Flyer, Booklet
TD. 大島慶一郎 Keiichiro Oshima
A. ちゃんしげ Chen Shige
CL.（株）リクルートホールディングス Recruit Holdings Co., Ltd.
PT. イワタ明朝-細N, イワタ明朝オールド

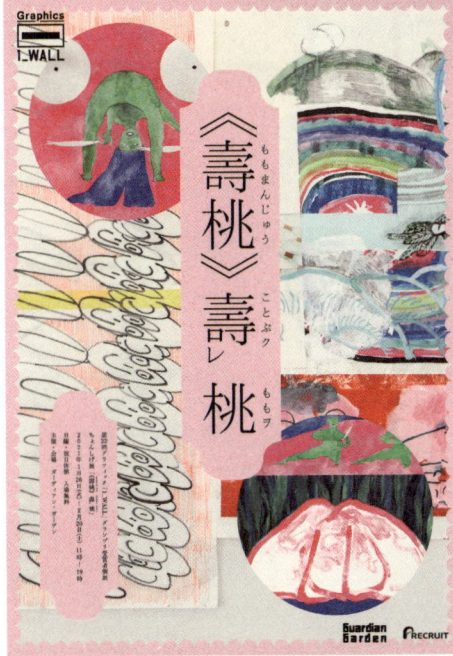
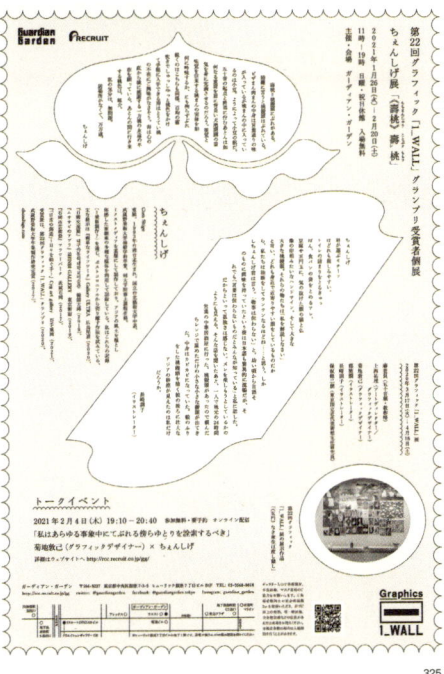

326 Poster
TD. AD. D. P. 奥山太貴 Taiki Okuyama
MO. 億なつき Natsuki Oku, ミネユキ Yuki Mine
OR. 吉田史織 Shiori Yoshida
CL. PASfeS
PT. Harmond

327 Packaging
TD. AD. D. 押見健太郎 Kentaro Oshimi
CD. 長谷川昭雄 Akio Hasegawa
CL. Nautica Japan
PT. Roboto Condensed

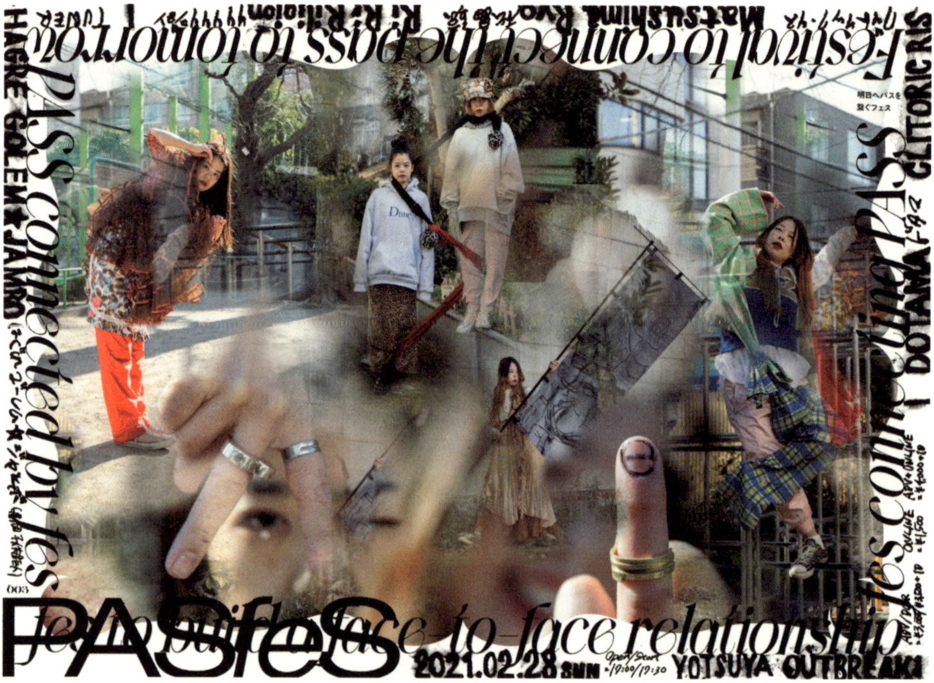

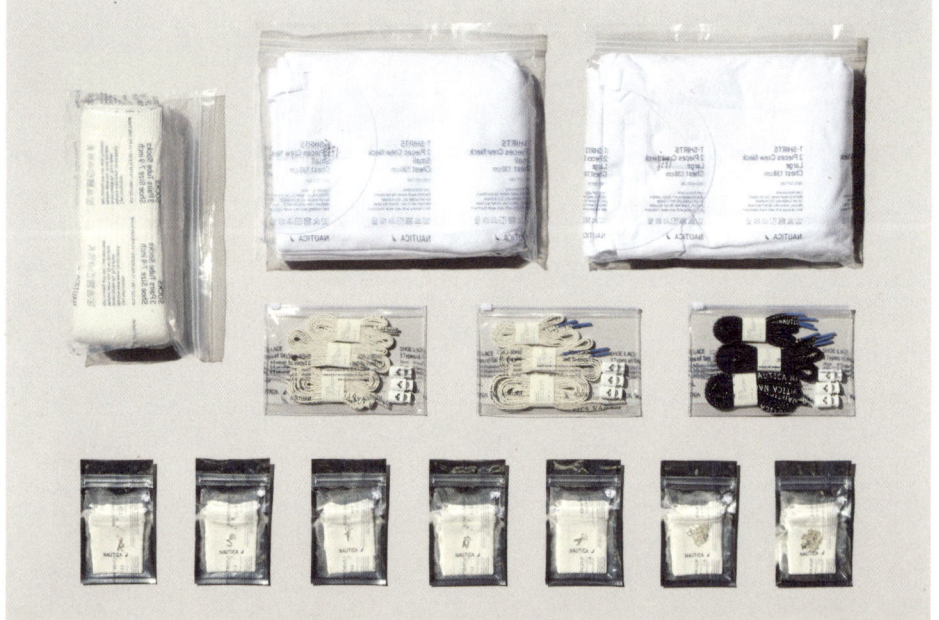

328 Record jacket
TD. 大澤悠大 Yudai Osawa
I. 坂内拓 Taku Bannai
CL. マーライオン Maarion
PT. Custom-made for the project

329 Poster
TD. 大山大介 Daisuke Oyama
C. 安達岳 Gaku Adachi
CL. 岩波ホール Iwanami Hall

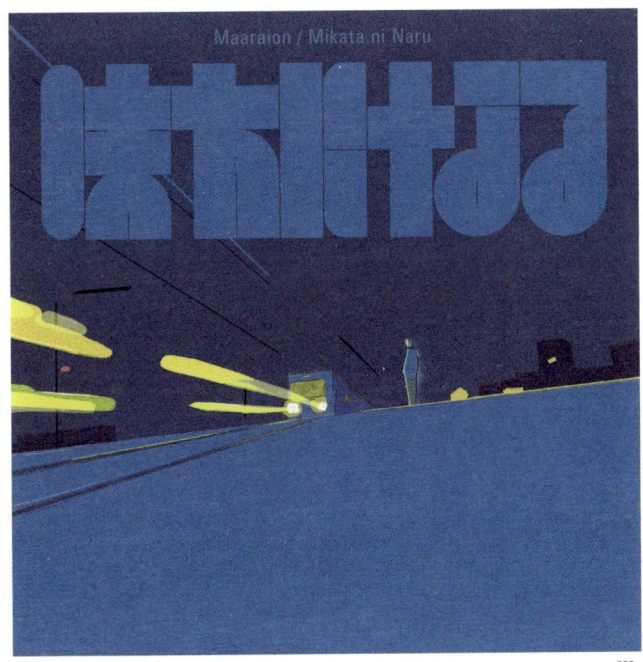

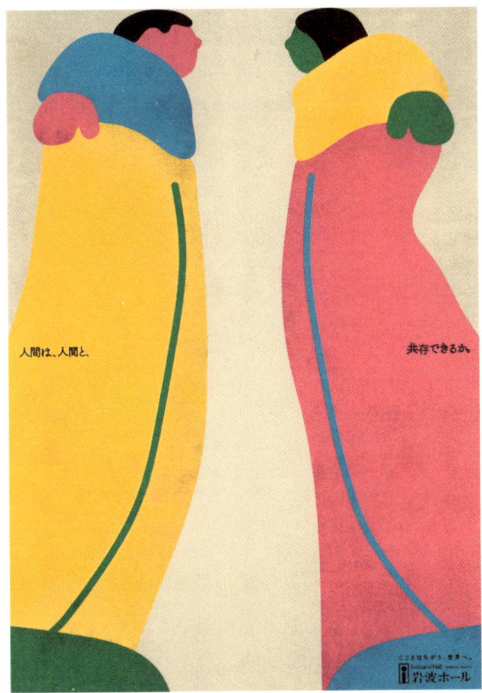

330 Book
TD. Yanrong Pan
CL. Zizai movable type studio
PT. Custom-made for the project

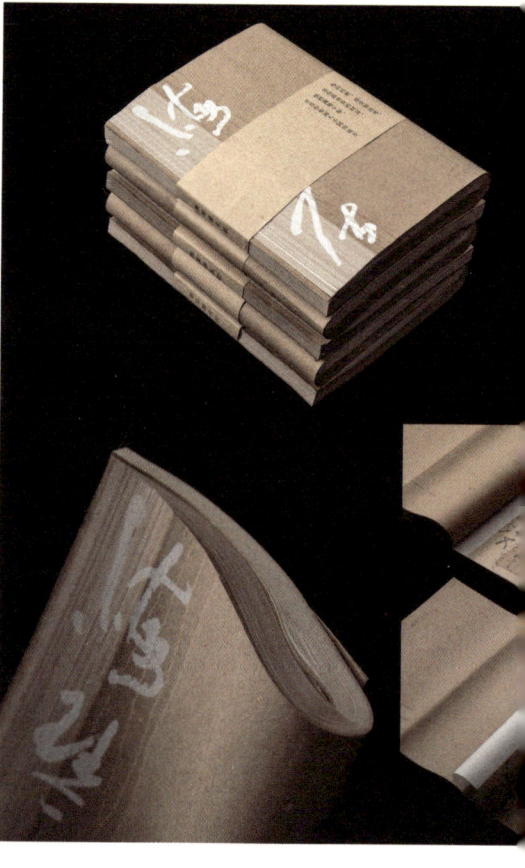

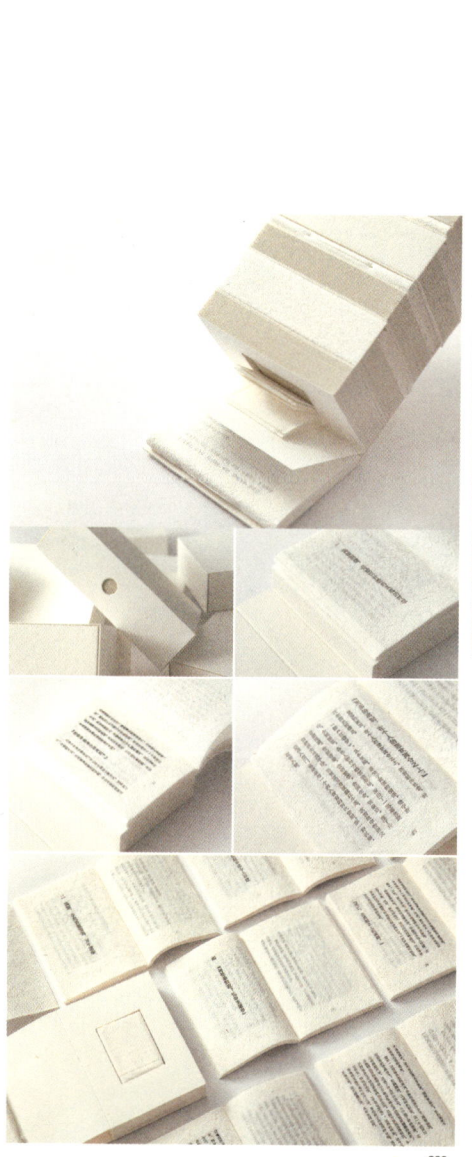

Prize Nominee Work

331 Book
TD. Yanrong Pan
CL. Xiling Seal-Engravers' Society
PT. Founder Susong

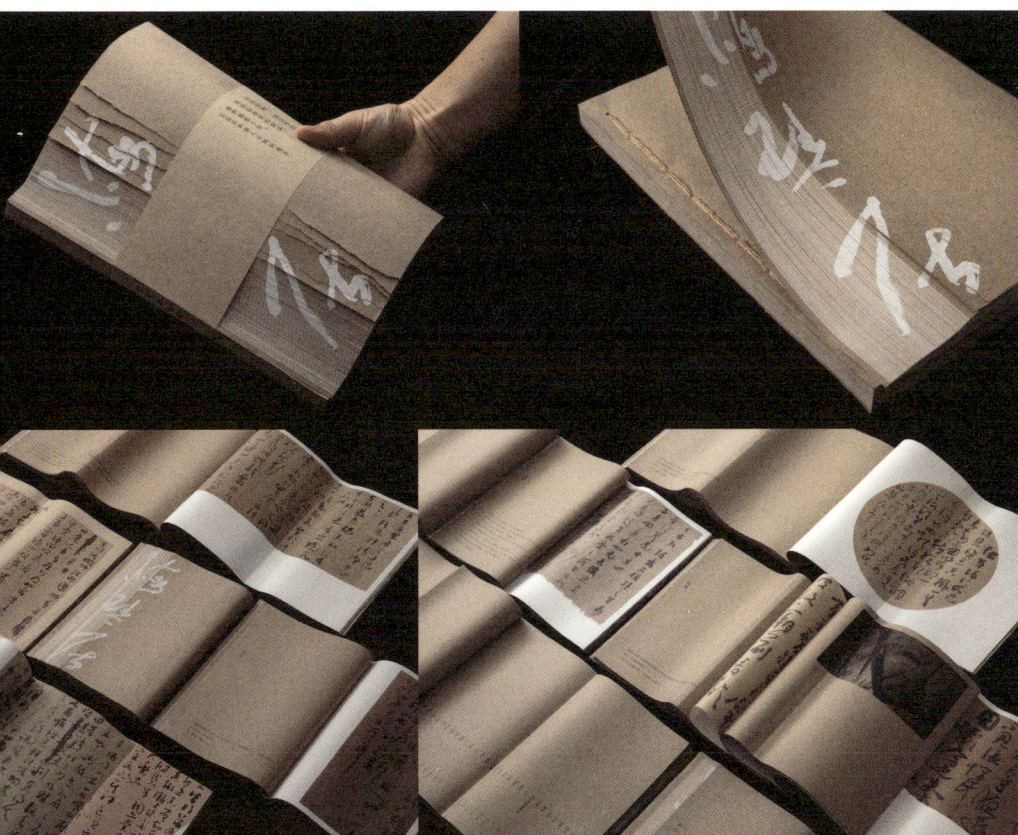

Prize Nominee Work

332 Specimen
TD. Pierre Pané-Farré
CL. Non-commercial work
PT. Library, Film, Amateur

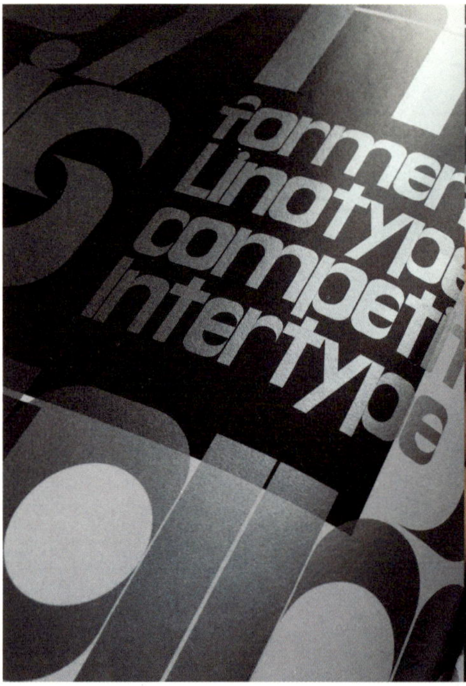

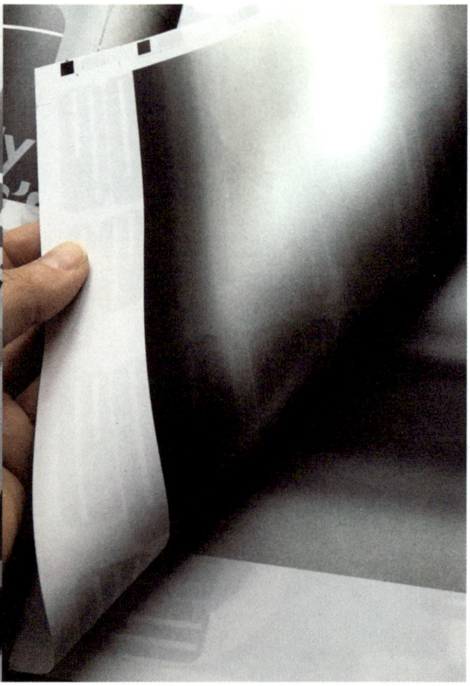

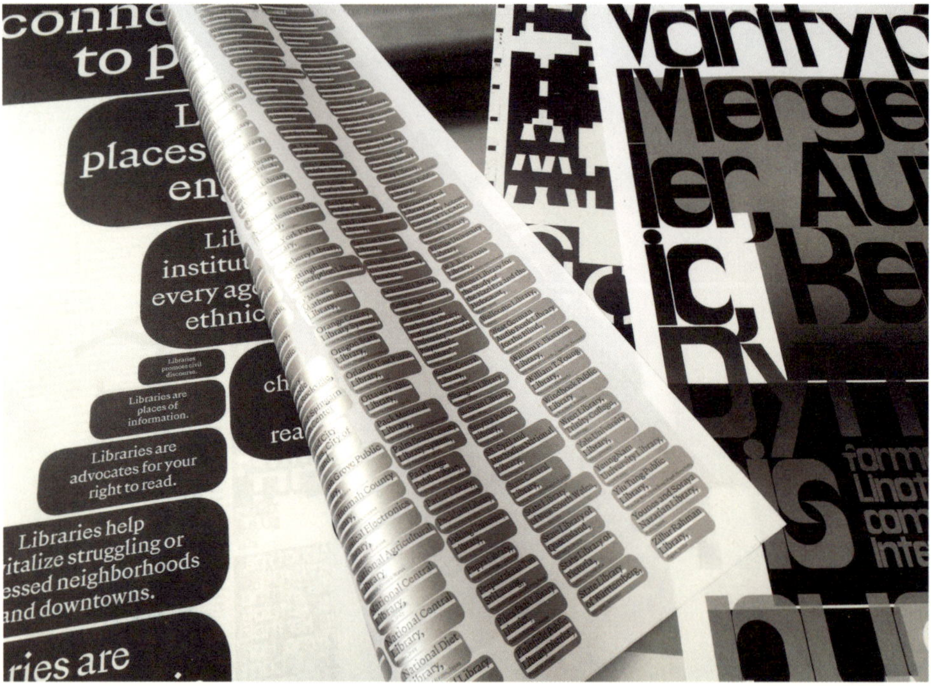

333 Type design
TD. Pierre Pané-Farré
CL. Non-commercial work
PT. Library, Film, Amateur

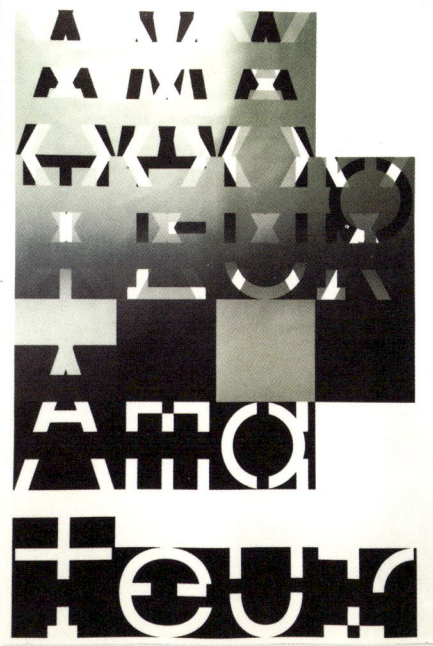

334 Book
TD. AD. D. P. Yunqi Peng
CL. Non-commercial work
PT. Custom-made for the project, Times New Roman, Source Han Sans

335 Book
TD. AD. D. P. Yunqi Peng
CL. Non-commercial work
PT. Custom-made for the project, Helvetica, Source Han Sans

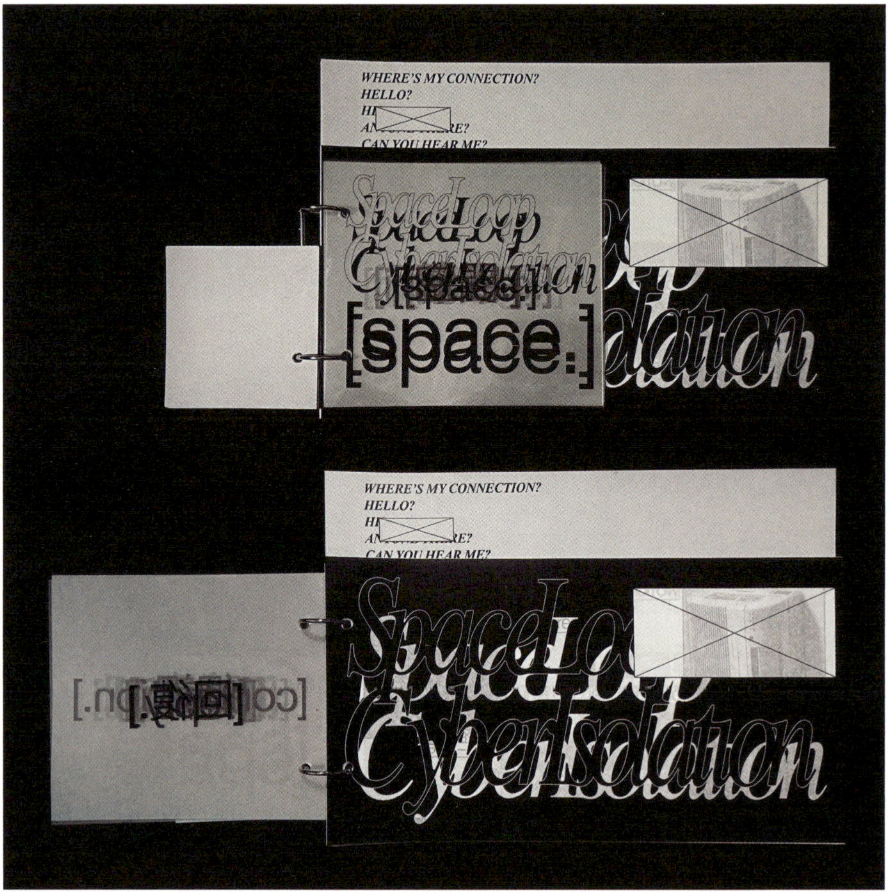

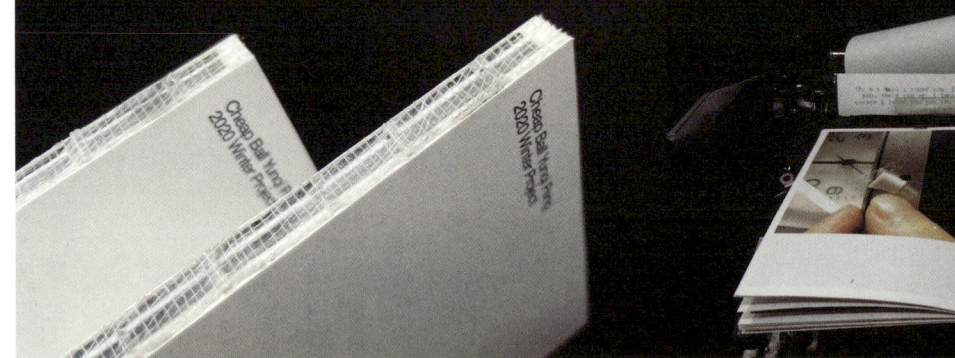

336 Booklet
TD. Xuejing Weng
CL. Non-commercial work
PT. Custom-made for the project, Source Han Sans

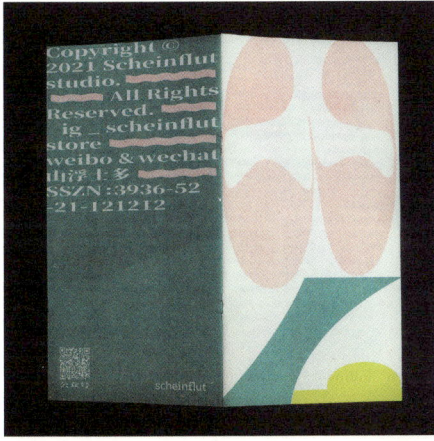
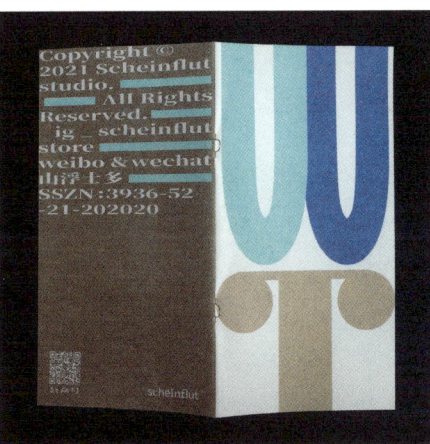
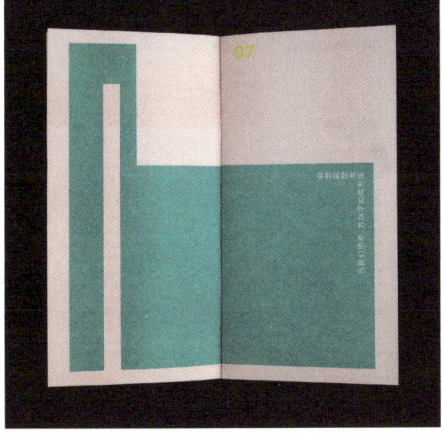
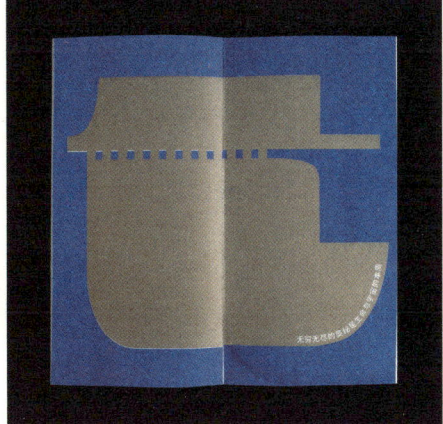
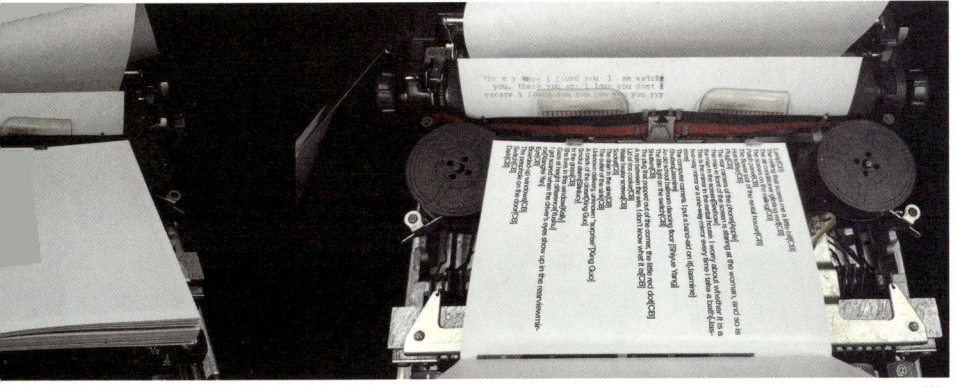

337 Magazine cover
TD. AD. D. Jay Guan-Jie Peng
CL. Shopping Design Magazine
PT. Custom-made for the project, Sages 02

338 Type design
TD. Jean François Porchez
D. Joachim Vu, Benjamin Blaess, Pauline Fourest, Fanny Hamelin, Morgane Pambrun
CL. Typofonderie

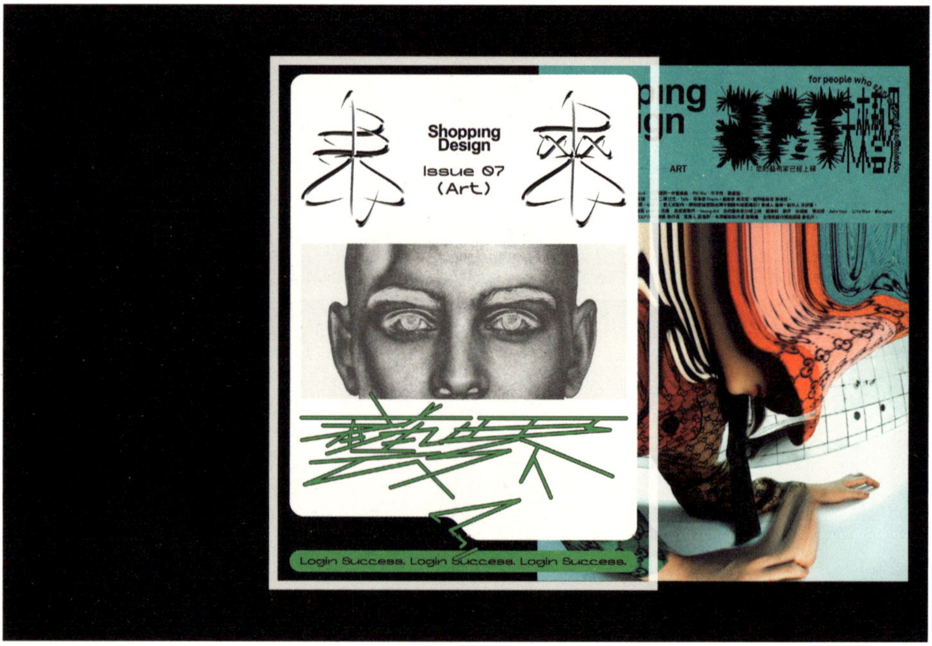

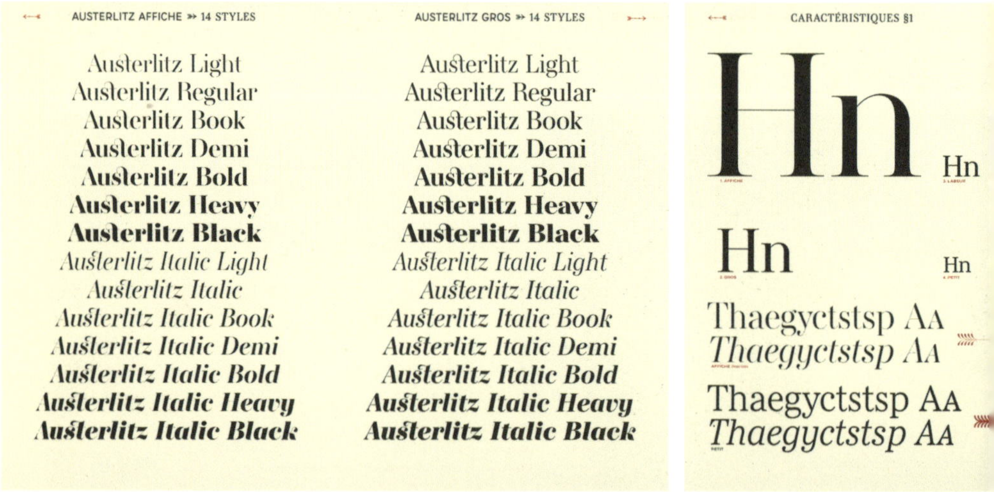

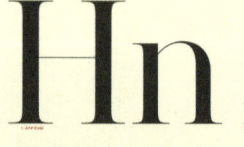

339 Book
TD. Margherita Porrà
D. Rachel Sanvido, Lindsey Hampton
PM. Elizabeth Vegh
CL. Westbank
PT. Calibre, Temeraire, Domaine Text, Cholla, Monument Grotesk

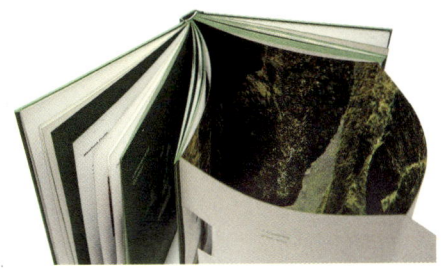

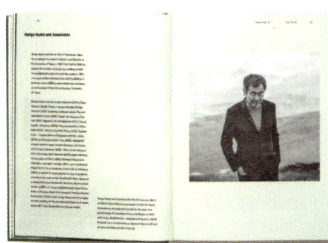

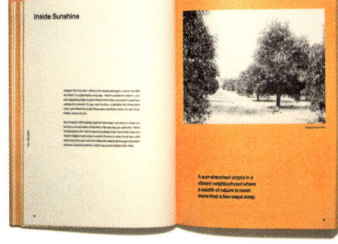

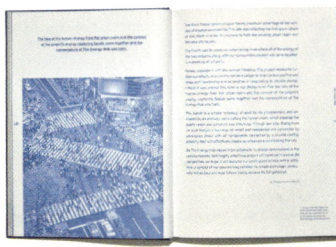

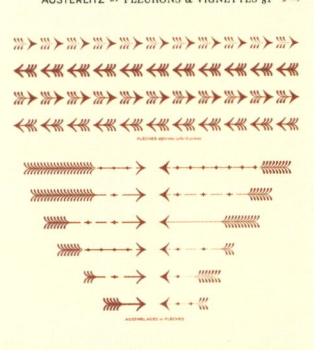

Prize Nominee Work

340 Book
TD. Qu Minmin, Jiang Qian
CL. Wang Muyuu
PT. Fangzheng Longzhua, Fangzheng Fangsong, Garamond

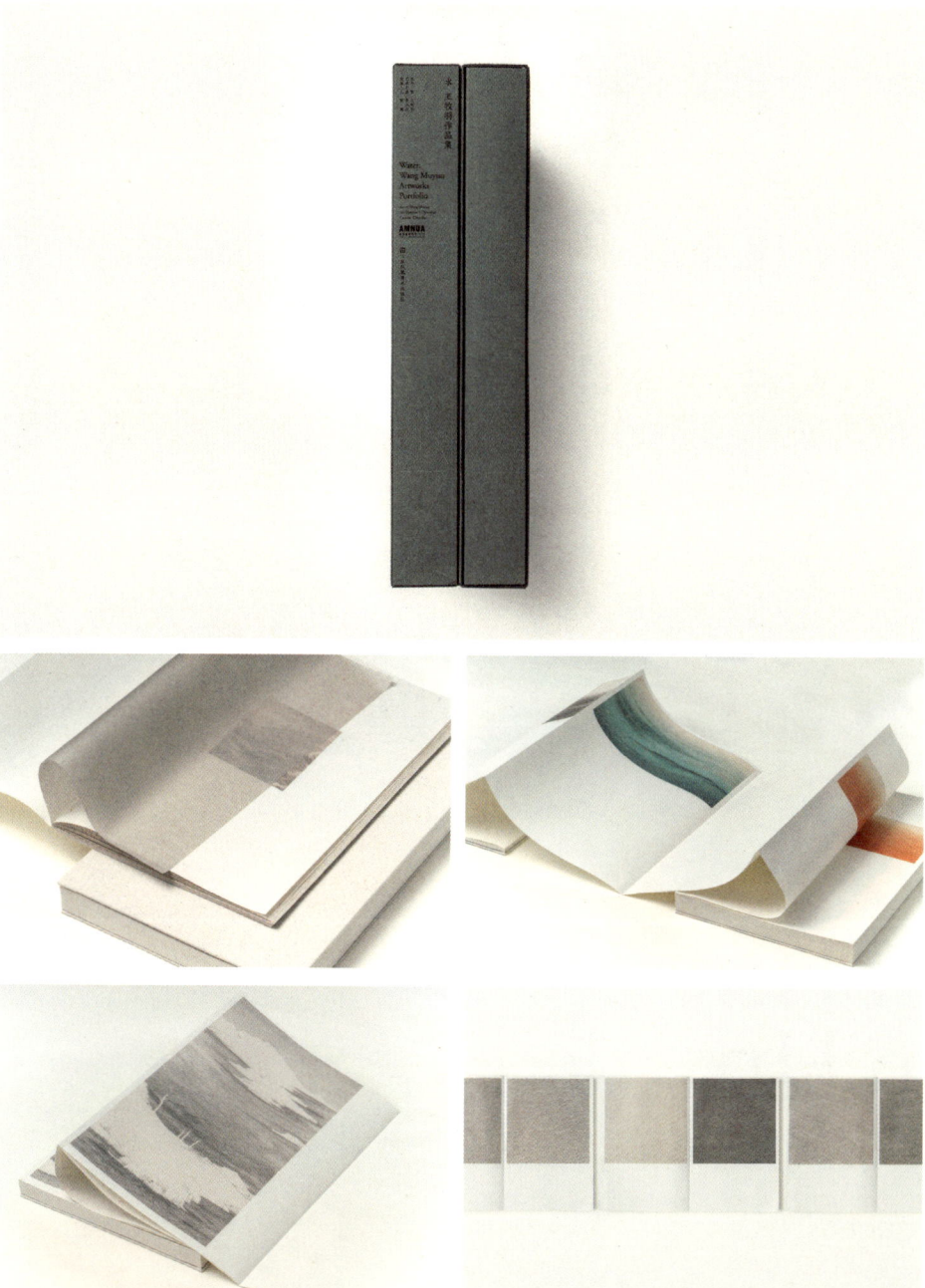

341 Packaging
TD. AD. D. Qianqian Ren
P. Jiaxu Hu
PRM. Wenfei Ma
E. Wei Wang
CL. pidan
PT. Neue Haas Grotesk Display, Hanyi Qihei

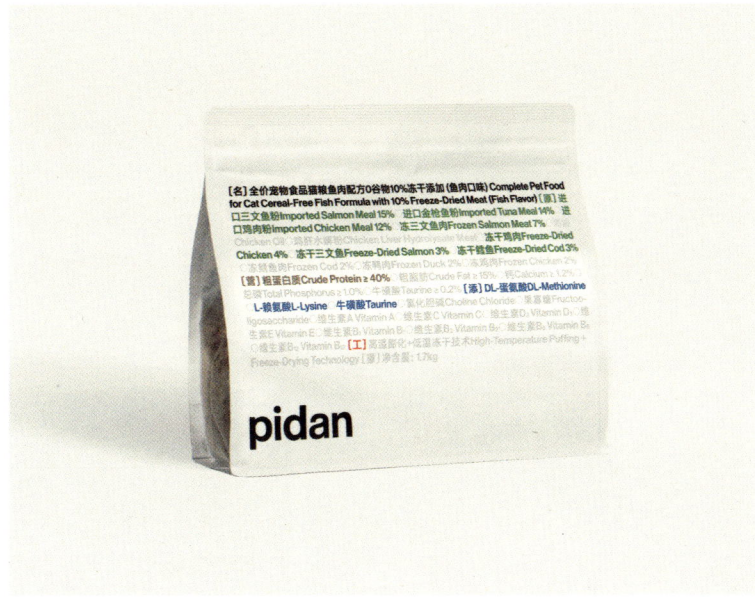

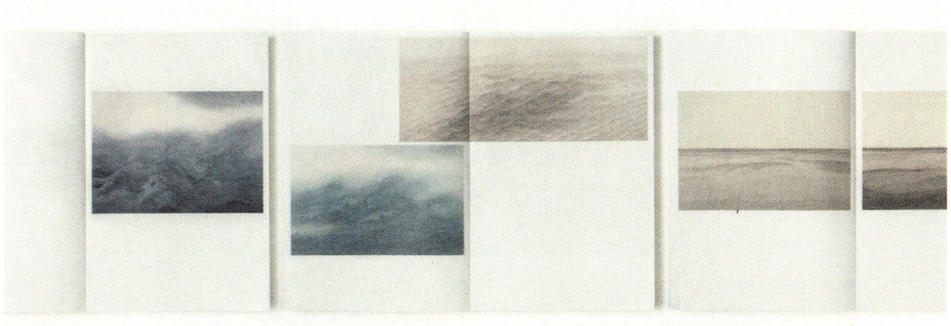

342 Campaign poster
TD. AD. Jamie Reid
D. Jack Sachs
P. Johnny Dufort
CL. Parco
PT. Custom-made for the project

343 BI, Packaging
TD. Grace Robinson-Leo, Rob Matthews
D. Will Kortum
I. Lulu Lin, Pete Gamlen
P. Anemone Works
CL. Soft Services
PT. GT Eesti Regular, Bell MT

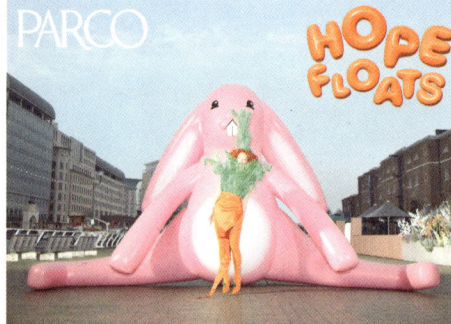
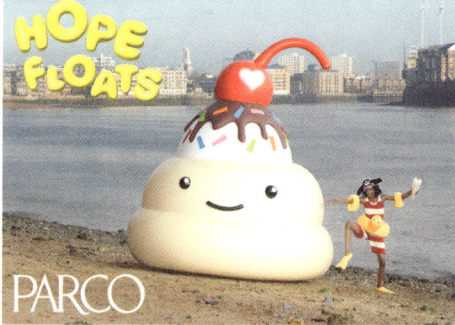
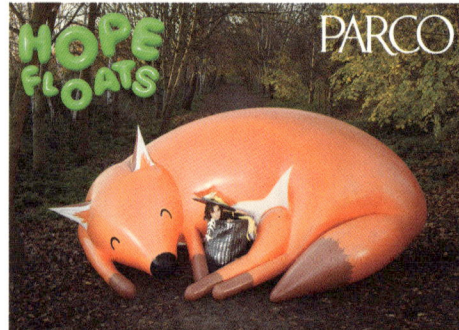
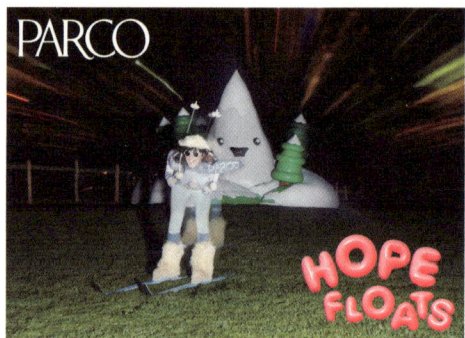

342

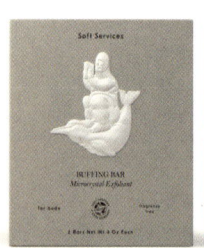
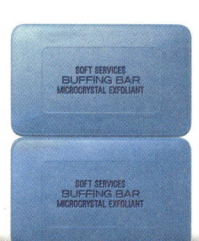

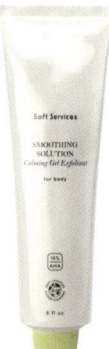
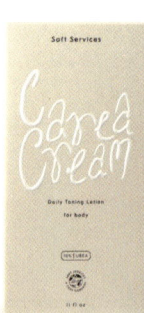
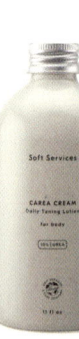

297

344 Experimental work
TD. Grace Robinson-Leo, Rob Matthews
D. Will Kortum
CL. Non-commercial work
PT. Times Dot, Mabry

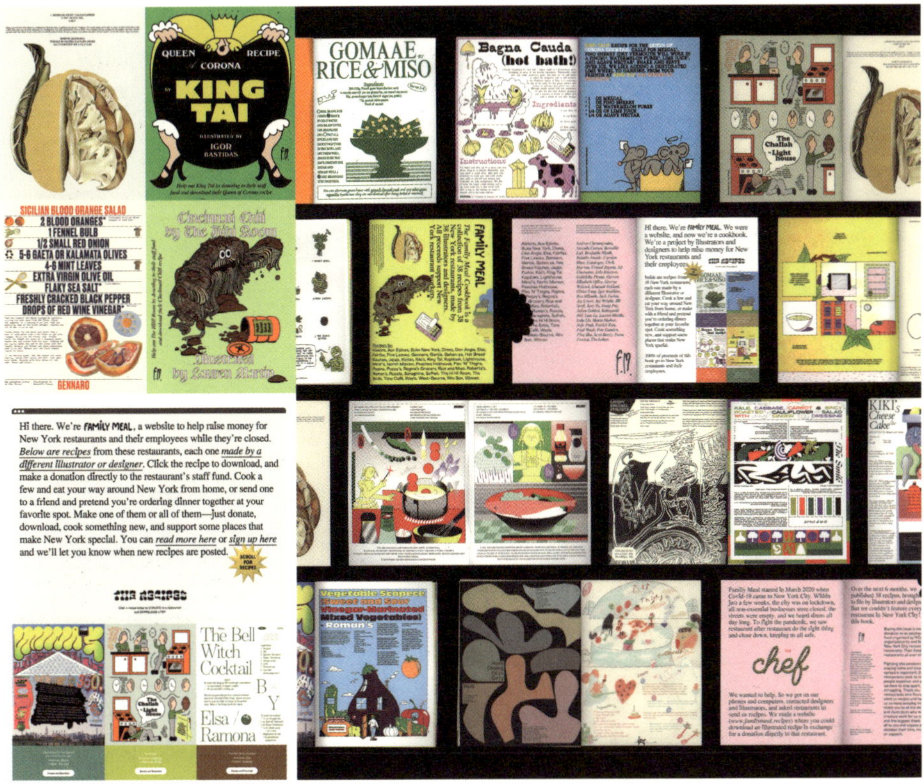

344

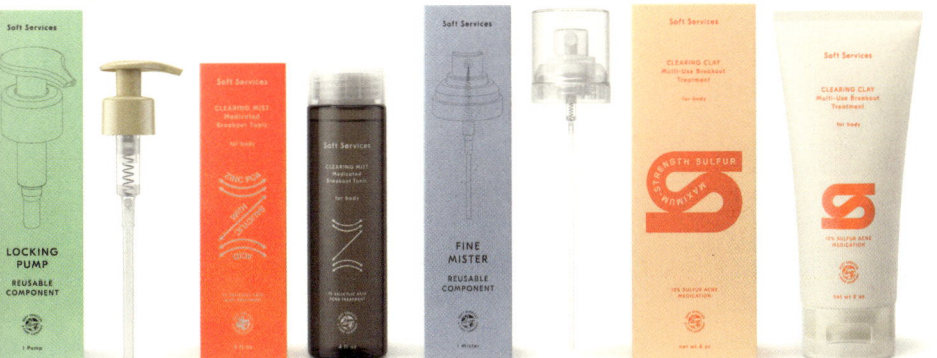

343

345 Poster
TD. AD. 相楽賢太郎 Kentaro Sagara
D. 清水艦期 Kango Shimizu, 千葉陸矢 Rikuya Chiba
I. 佐貫絢郁 Ayaka Sanuki
PR. 稲貫護 Mamoru Inagaki
CL. (株)アミューズ Amuse Inc.
PT. 太ゴシック体B1, Custom-made for the project

346 Website
TD. AD. 相楽賢太郎 Kentaro Sagara
D. 林久純 Hisayoshi Hayashi, 小澤愛実 Manami Ozawa
CL. 石田真澄 Masumi Ishida
PT. Helvetica Neue
http://masumiishida.com/

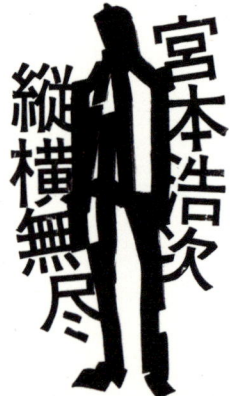
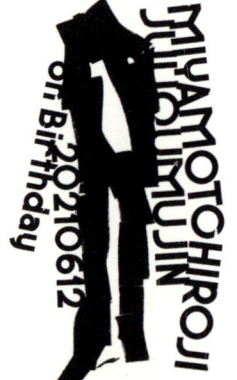
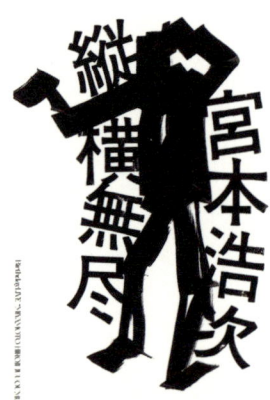
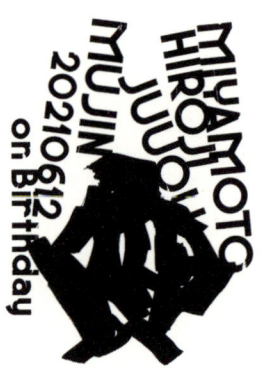
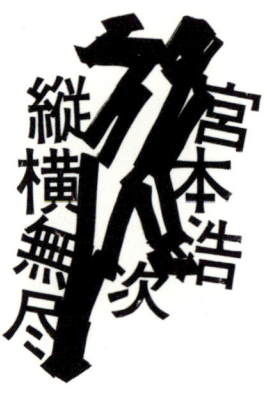
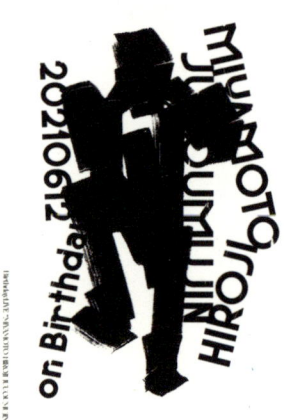

345

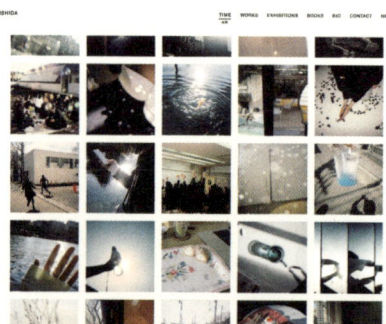
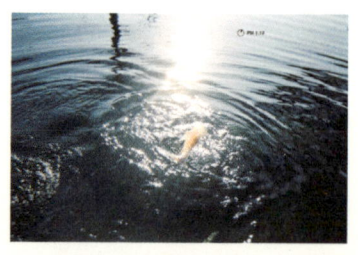

347 Advertising
TD. AD. D. 佐古田英一 Eiichi Sakota
D. 川上利男 Toshio Kawakami
CD. C. 田中有史 Yuji Tanaka
CL. 神戸親和女子大学 Kobe Shinwa Women's University.
PT. Custom-made for the project, 中ゴシックBBB

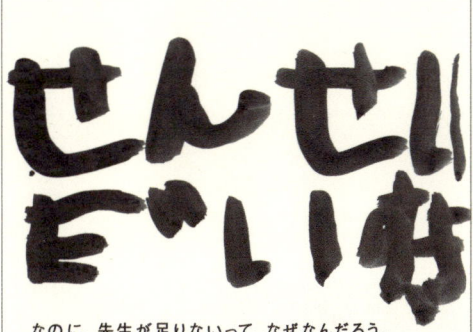

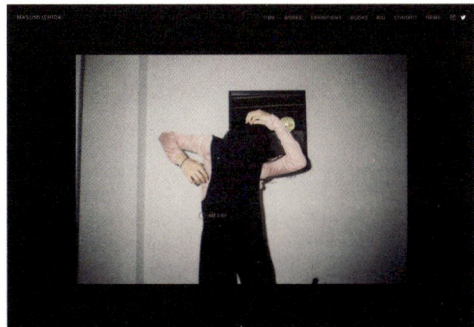

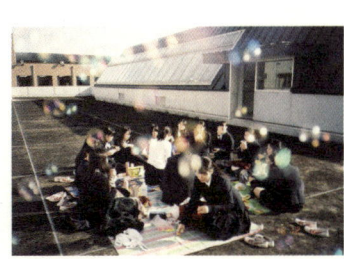

348 Exhibition
TD. D. Stefan Sagmeister
PR. Ting Yih, Tine Kindermann, Robert Kalka,
Alex Whyte, Eric Porter, Matteo Pani
CL. Thomas Erben Gallery
PT. Not applicable

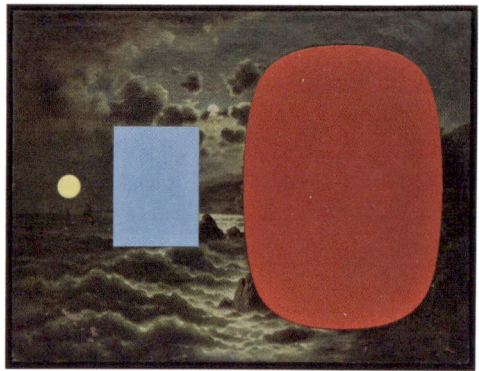
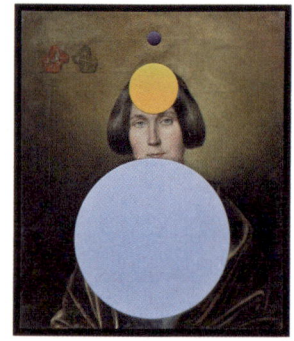
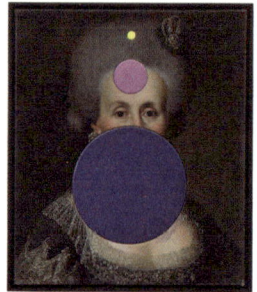
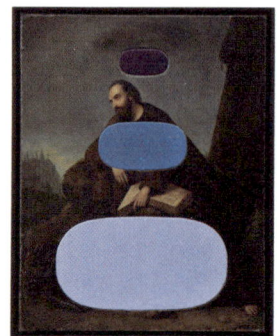
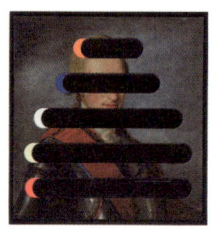

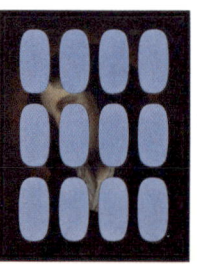

349 Website
TD. 佐々木遊太 Yuta Sasaki
CON. 中野信子 Nobuko Nakano
COO. 佐々木慶子 Keiko Sasaki
CL. Non-commercial work
PT. Helvetica Neue, Custom-made for the project
https://alive.salon

350 Signage
TD. AD. D. 佐々木拓 Taku Sasaki, 金井あき Aki Kanai
D (sign). 汐田瀬里菜 Serina Shiota
CL. コクヨ（株） Kokuyo Co., Ltd.
PT. Din Next

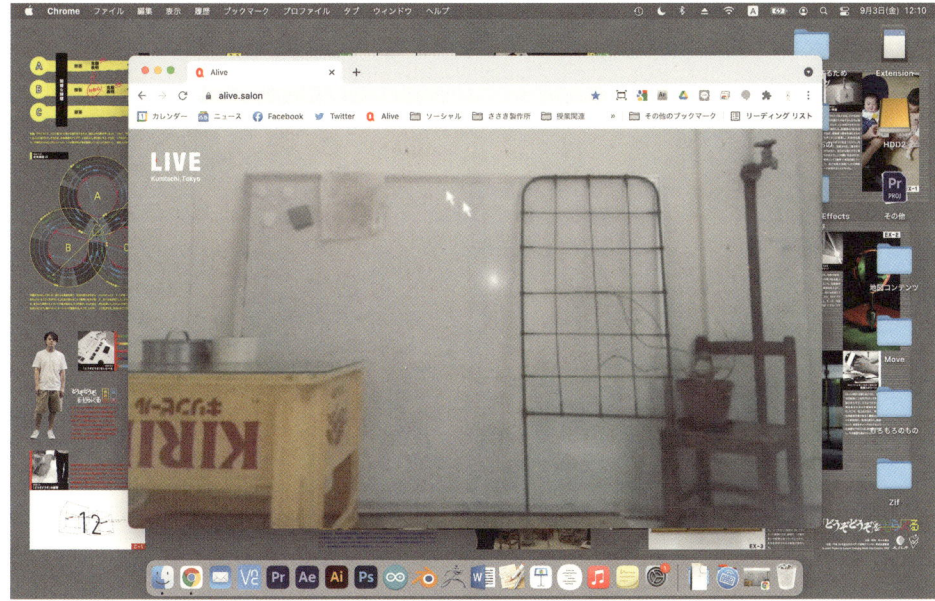

349

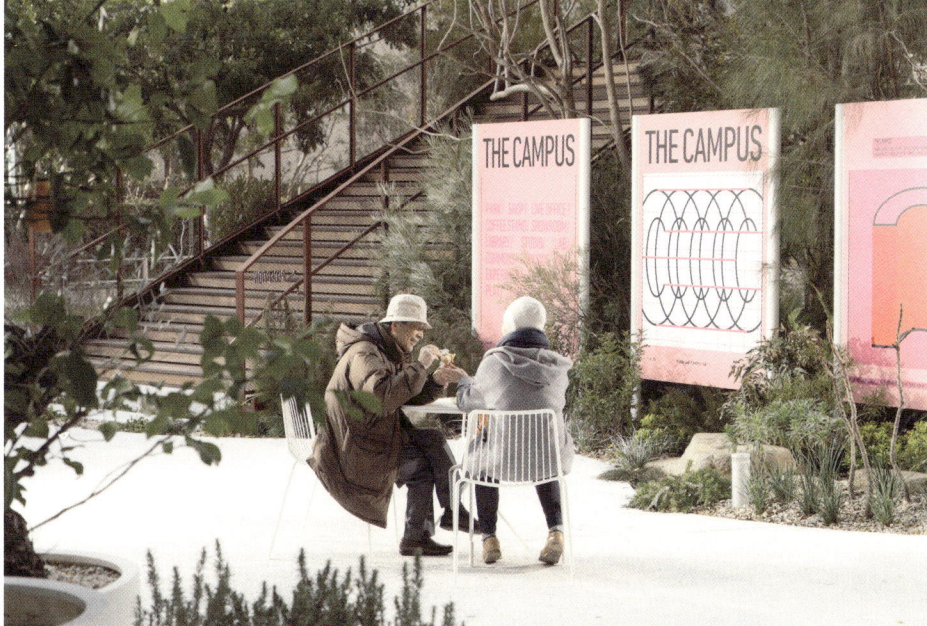

350

351 Goods
TD. AD. D. 佐々木拓 Taku Sasaki, 金井あき Aki Kanai
PM. 星剛 Go Hoshi
CL. コクヨ(株) Kokuyo Co., Ltd.
PT. Din Next

352 Website
TD. AD. 佐々木拓 Taku Sasaki, 金井あき Aki Kanai
WD. 田中良治 Ryoji Tanaka, 有本誠司 Seiji Arimoto
MD. 井口皓太 Kota Iguchi
PR. 安永哲朗 Tetsuro Yasunaga
CL. コクヨ(株) Kokuyo Co., Ltd.
PT. Din Next, FF Good, 遊ゴシック
https://the-campus.net/

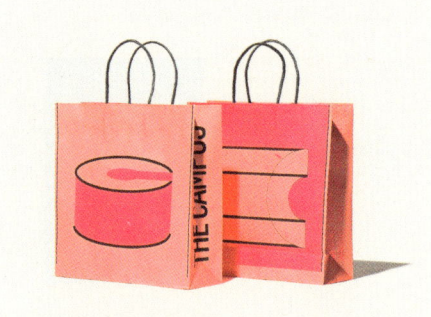
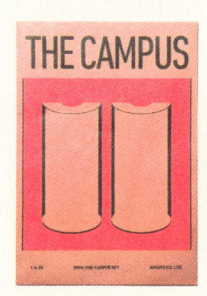
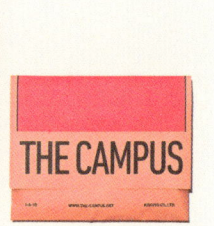
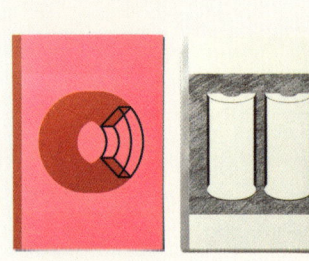
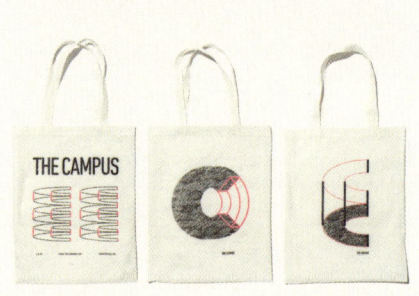
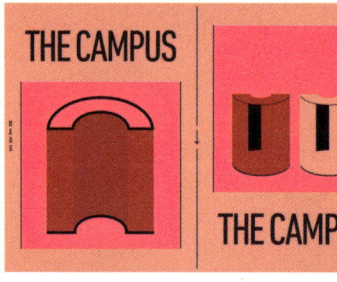
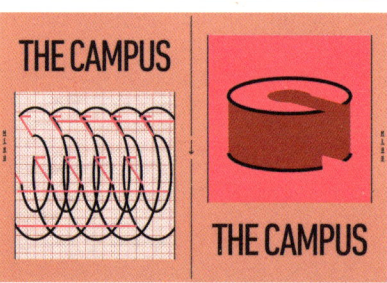
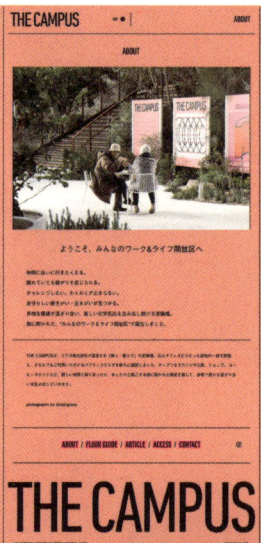
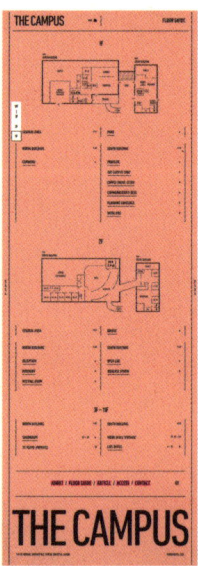

353 Poster
TD. AD. D. 佐々木拓 Taku Sasaki, 金井あき Aki Kanai
CL. コクヨ(株) Kokuyo Co., Ltd.
PT. Din Next

354 Poster
TD. AD. D. 佐々木拓 Taku Sasaki, 金井あき Aki Kanai
P. ゴッティンガム Gottingham
CL. コクヨ(株) Kokuyo Co., Ltd.
PT. Din Next

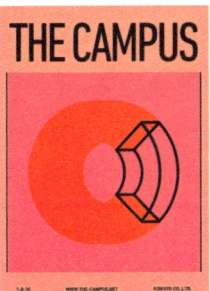
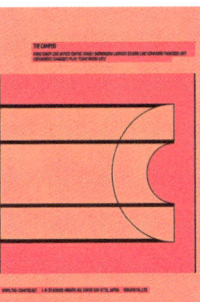
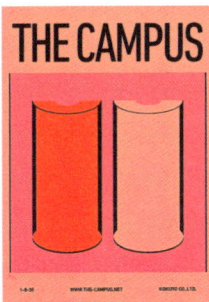
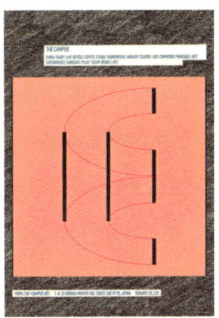
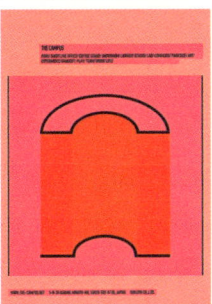
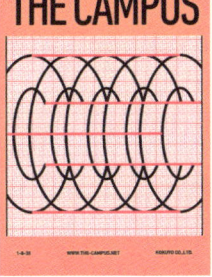
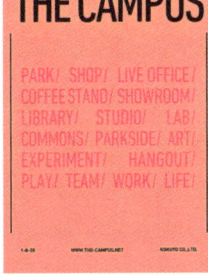
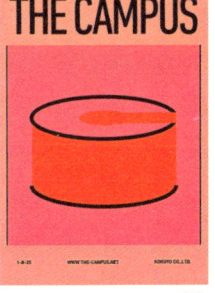

353

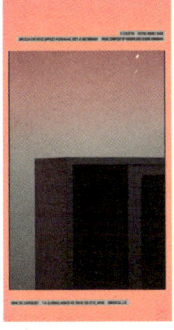
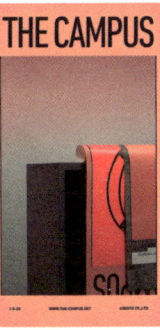
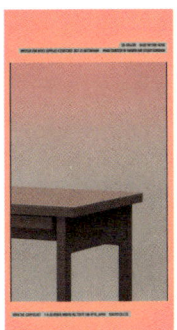
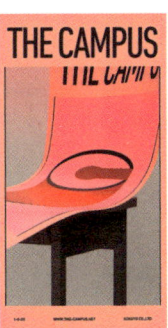
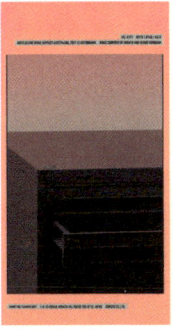
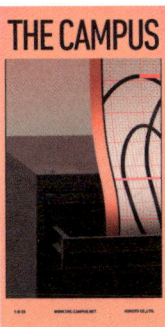
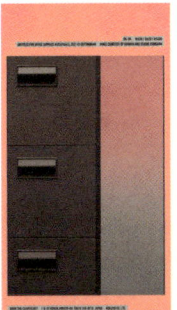
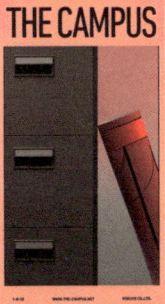

354

355 Envelope
TD. 佐野研二郎 Kenjiro Sano, 香取有美 Yumi Katori, 村松弘友紀 Hiroyuki Muramatsu
CL. 大洋印刷(株) Taiyo Printing Co., Ltd.

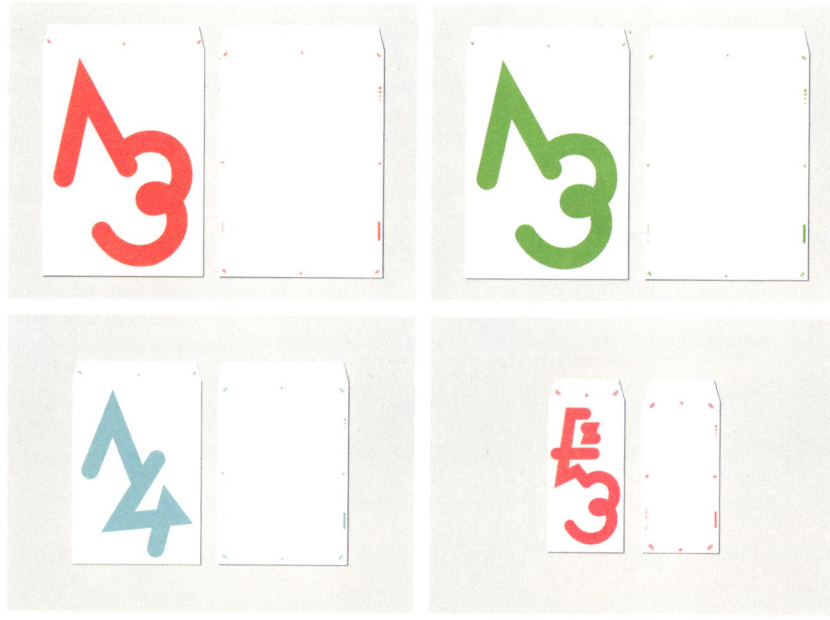

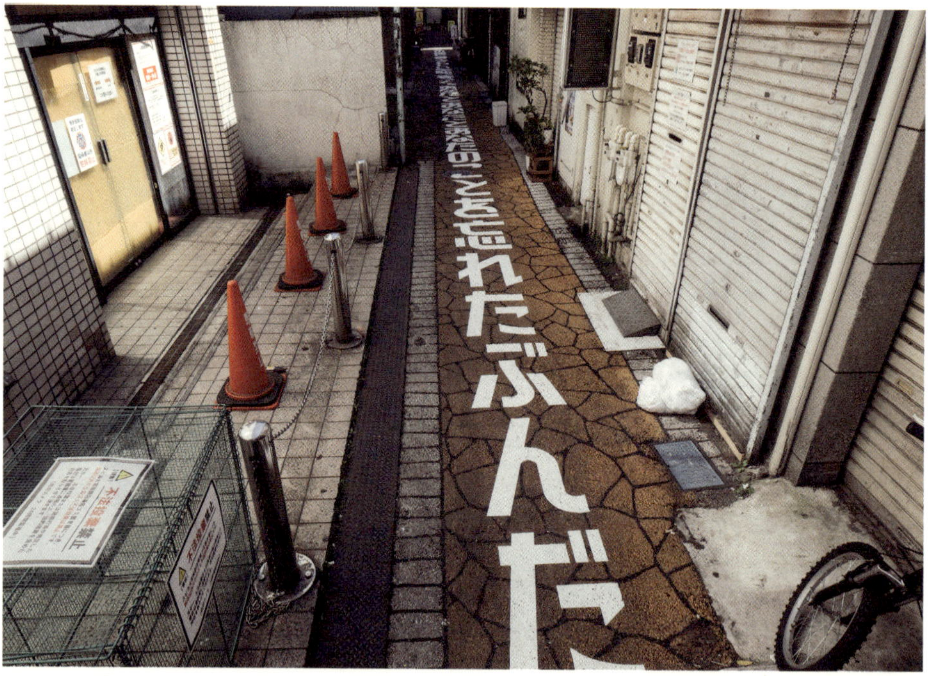

Prize Nominee Work

356 Experimental work
TD. 佐々木俊 Shun Sasaki
W (Poet). 最果タヒ Tahi Saihate
P. 鴨川一也 Kazuya Kamogawa, 松尾宇人 Ujin Matsuo, 丸尾隆一 Ryuichi Maruo
CL. さいたま国際芸術祭2020 Saitama Triennale 2020
PT. Custom-made for the project

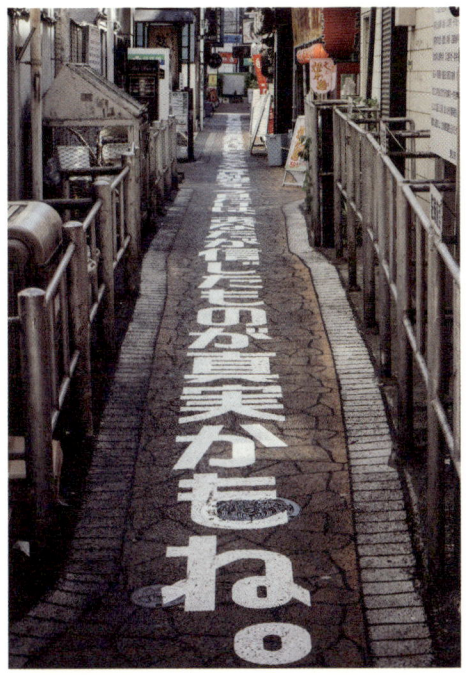
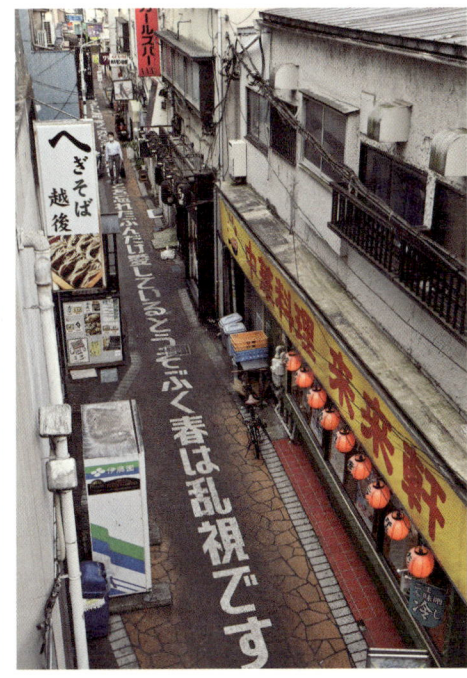
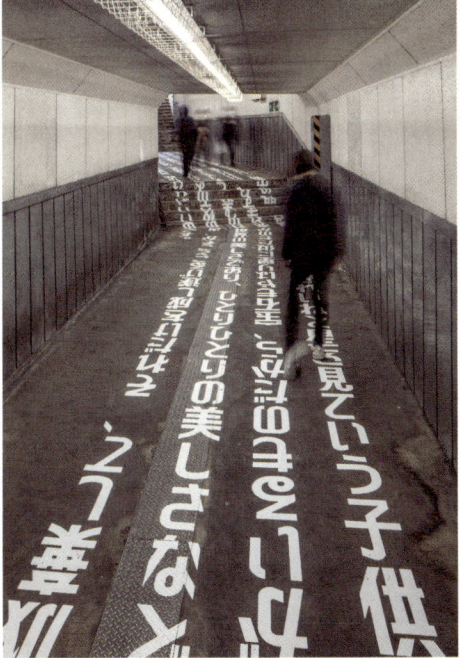
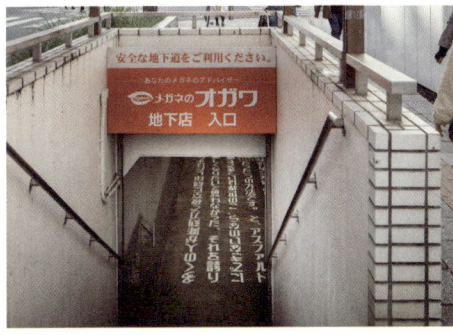
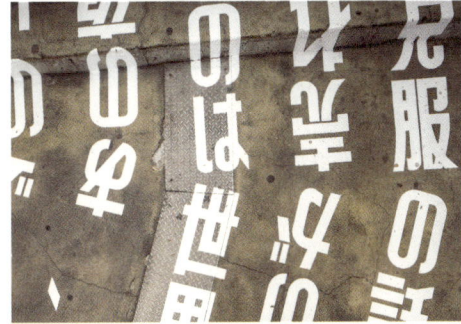

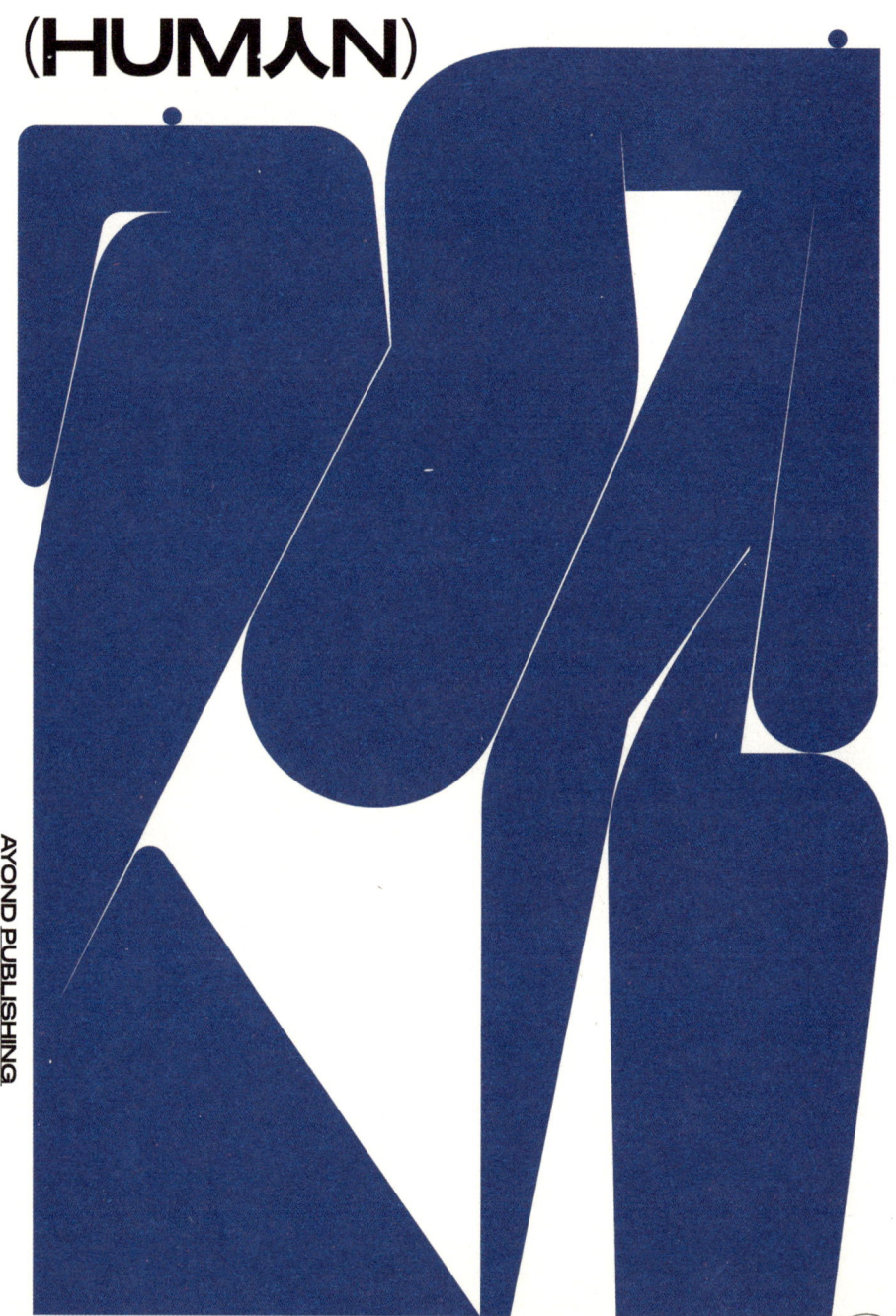

358 Poster
TD. 佐々木俊 Shun Sasaki
CL. 三菱地所アルティアム Mitsubishi Estate Artium
PT. モトヤ新聞明朝, 秀英角ゴシック銀

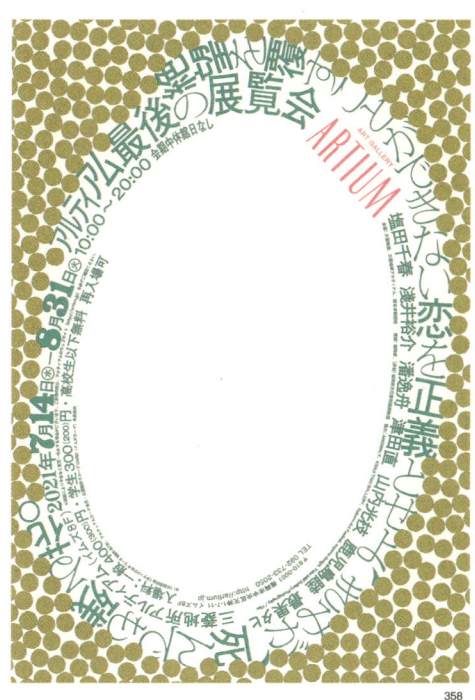

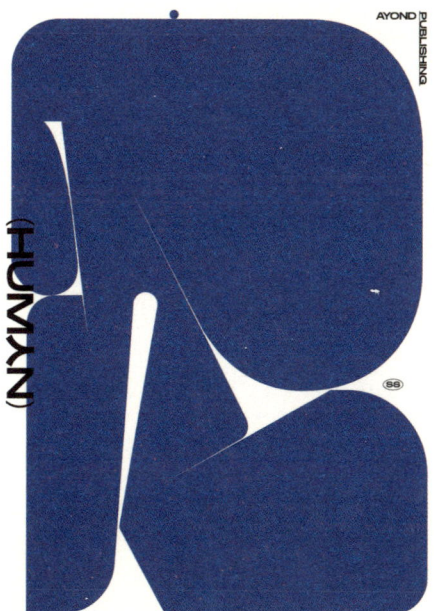

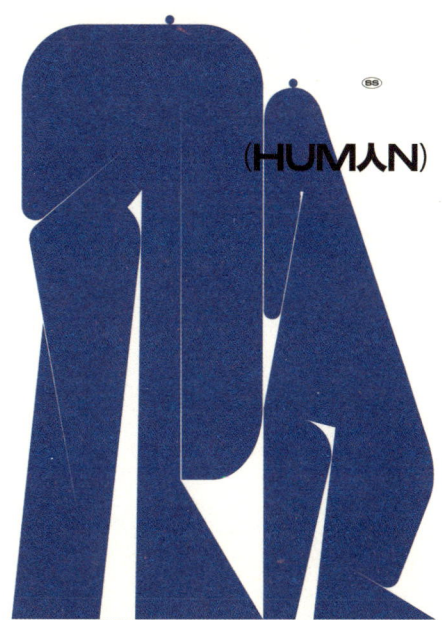

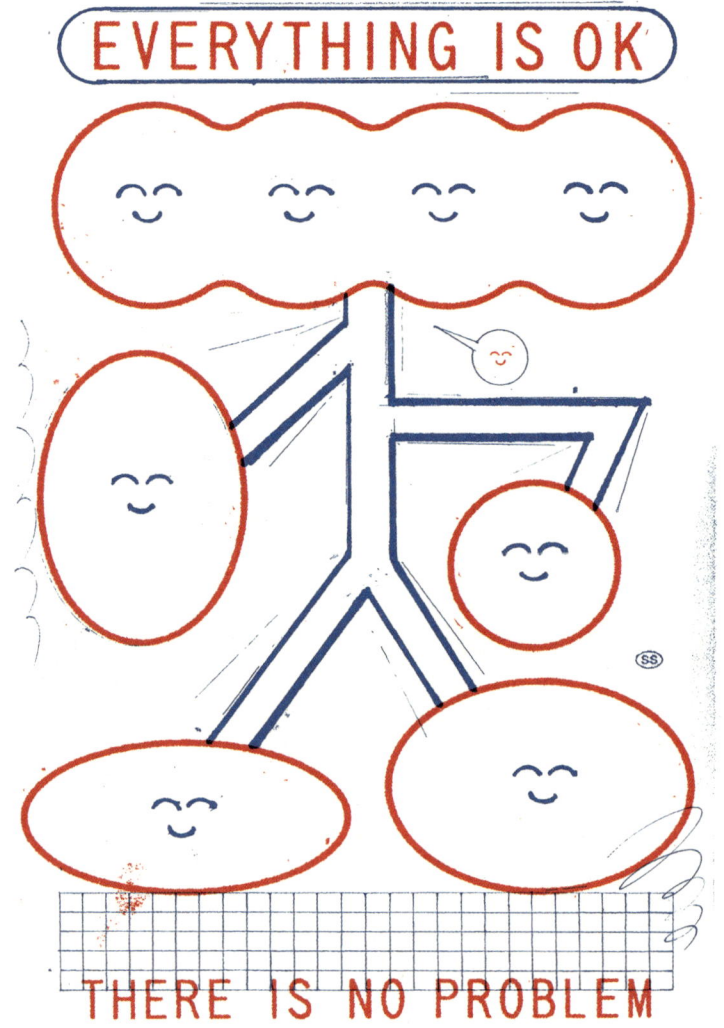

360 Poster
TD. 佐々木俊 Shun Sasaki
CL. 金沢21世紀美術館 21st Century Museum of Contemporary Art, Kanazawa
PT. 太ゴB101, Grot10

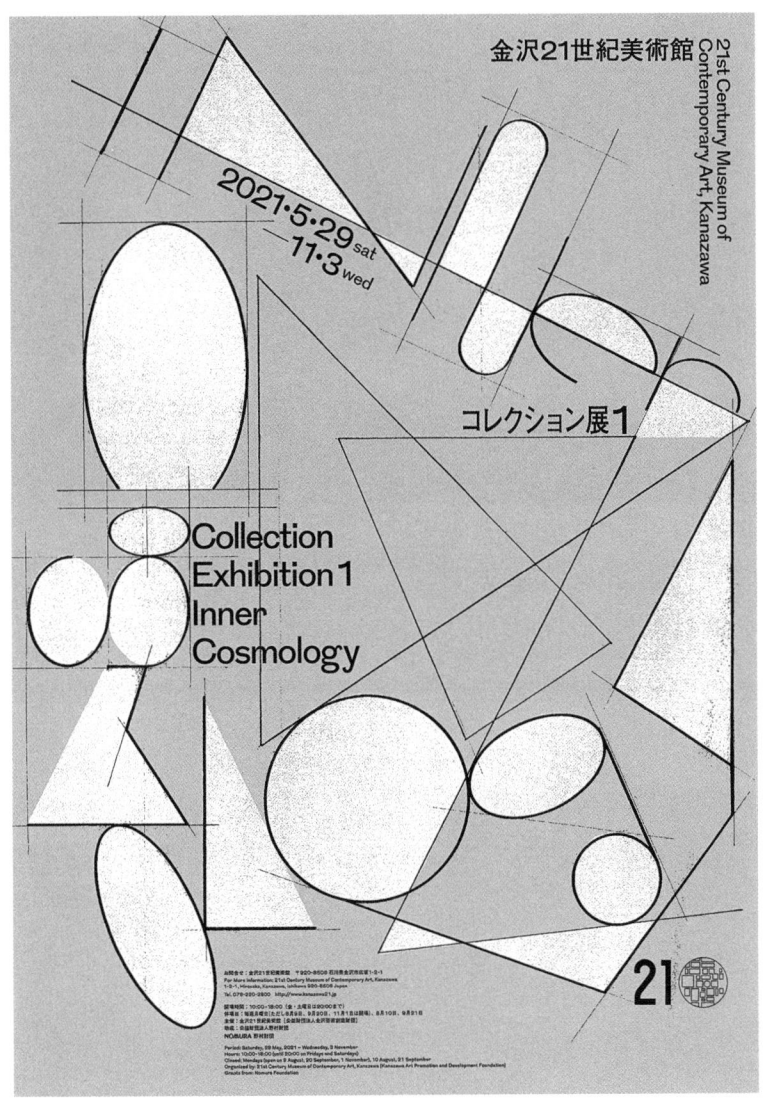

361 Space design
TD. 佐藤可士和 Kashiwa Sato, 楽天デザインラボ Rakuten Design Lab,
楽天技術研究所 Rakuten Institute of Technology, Dalton Maag Ltd.
CL. 楽天グループ(株) Rakuten Group, Inc.
PT. Rakuten Sans Semi Bold, UD新ゴNT Pro B

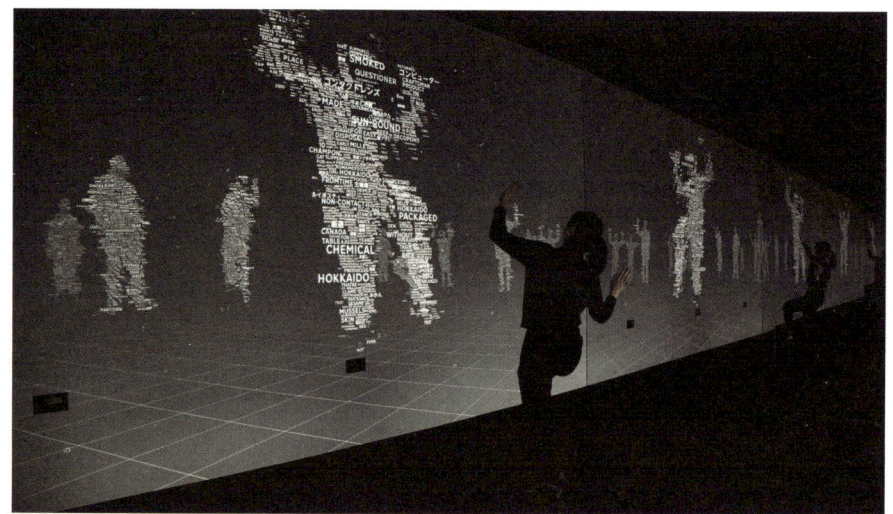

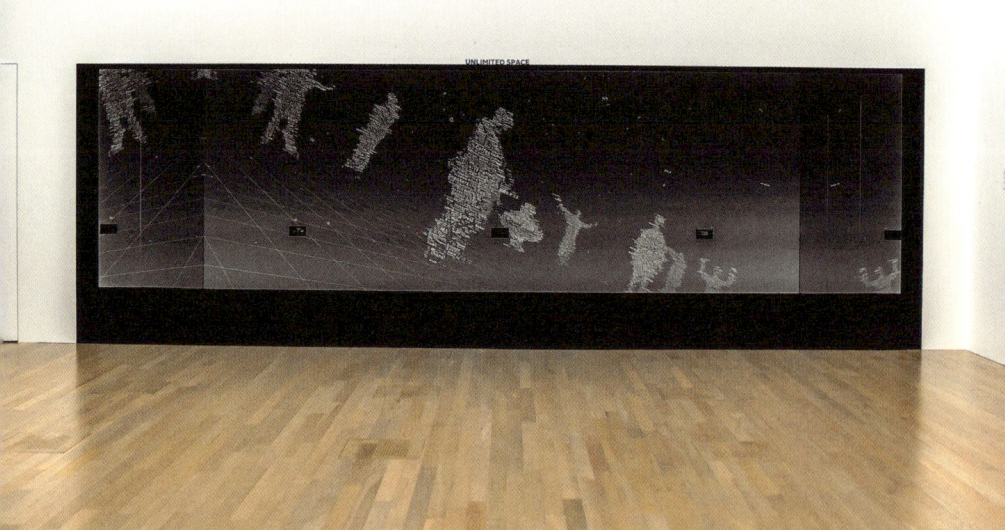

362 Exhibition catalogue
TD. CD. 佐藤可士和 Kashiwa Sato
TD. AD. 糟谷義人 Yoshihito Kasuya
CL. 国立新美術館 The National Art Center, Tokyo
PT. Custom-made for the project, こぶりなゴシック, Mark Pro

363 Packaging
TD. CD. 佐藤可士和 Kashiwa Sato
TD. AD. 糟谷義人 Yoshihito Kasuya
D (Bottle). 土屋恵里 Eri Tsuchiya
PRO (Bottle). キハラ Kihara Inc.
P. 村田昇 Noboru Murata
PR. 幅允孝 Yoshitaka Haba
CA. Samurai
CL. 青木酒造（株）Aokishuzo The Sake Brewery Co., Ltd.
国立新美術館 The National Art Center, Tokyo
PT. Custom-made for the project, ヒラギノ明朝

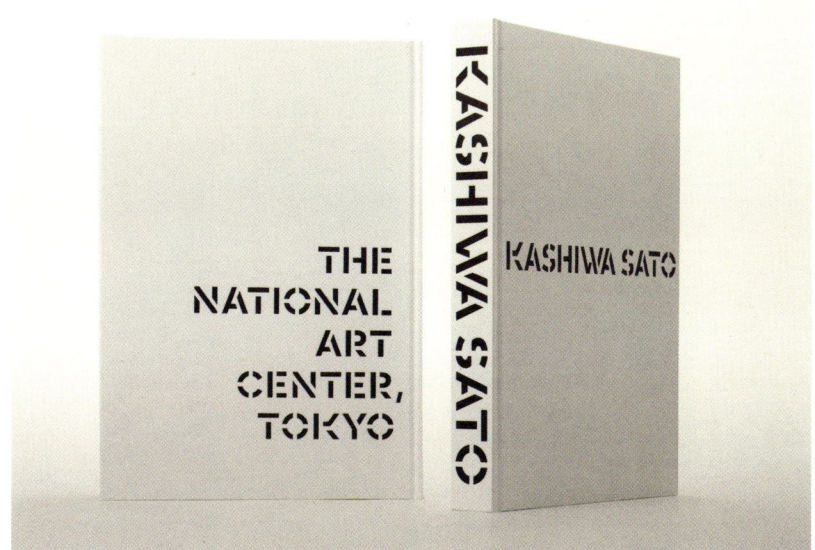

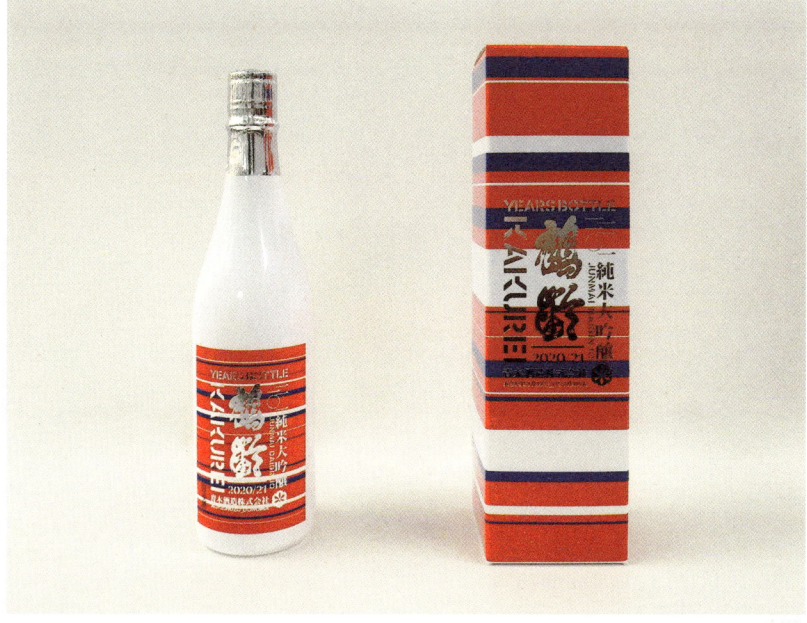

364 Poster
TD. CD. 佐藤可士和 Kashiwa Sato
TD. AD. 糟谷義人 Yoshihito Kasuya
CL. 国立新美術館 The National Art Center, Tokyo
PT. Custom-made for the project, ヒラギノ明朝

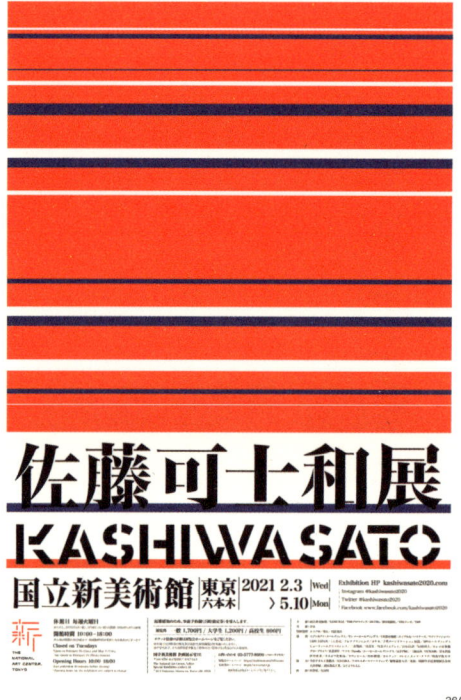

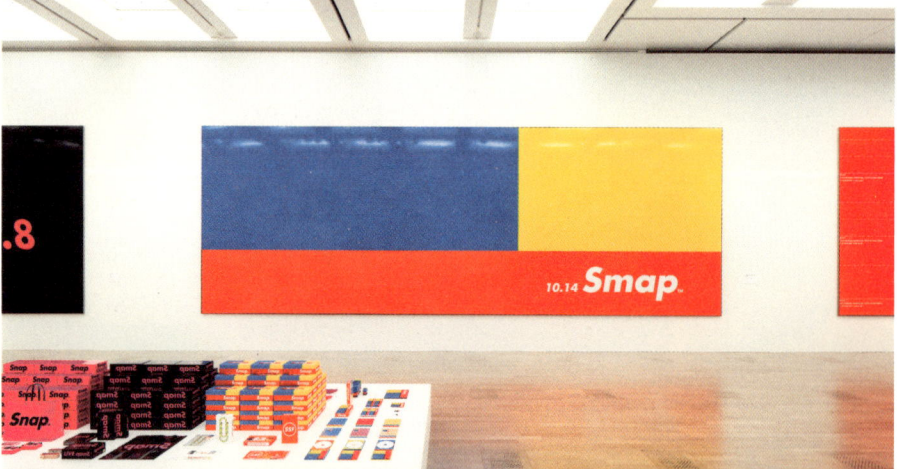

Prize Nominee Work

365 Exhibition
TD. CD. 佐藤可士和 Kashiwa Sato
CU. 宮島綾子 Ayako Miyajima
PR. 佐藤麻理子 Mariko Sato
D. Samurai
P. 太田拓実 Takumi Ota

CL. 国立新美術館 The National Art CenterTokyo, Samurari, （株）TBS グロウディア TBS Glowdia, Inc., （株）BS-TBS BS-TBS, INC., （株）朝日新聞社 The Asahi Shimbun Company, （株）TBS ラジオ TBS Radio Inc., （株）TBS Tokyo Broadcasting System Television, Inc., ぴあ（株）PIA Corporation
PT. Custom-made for the project

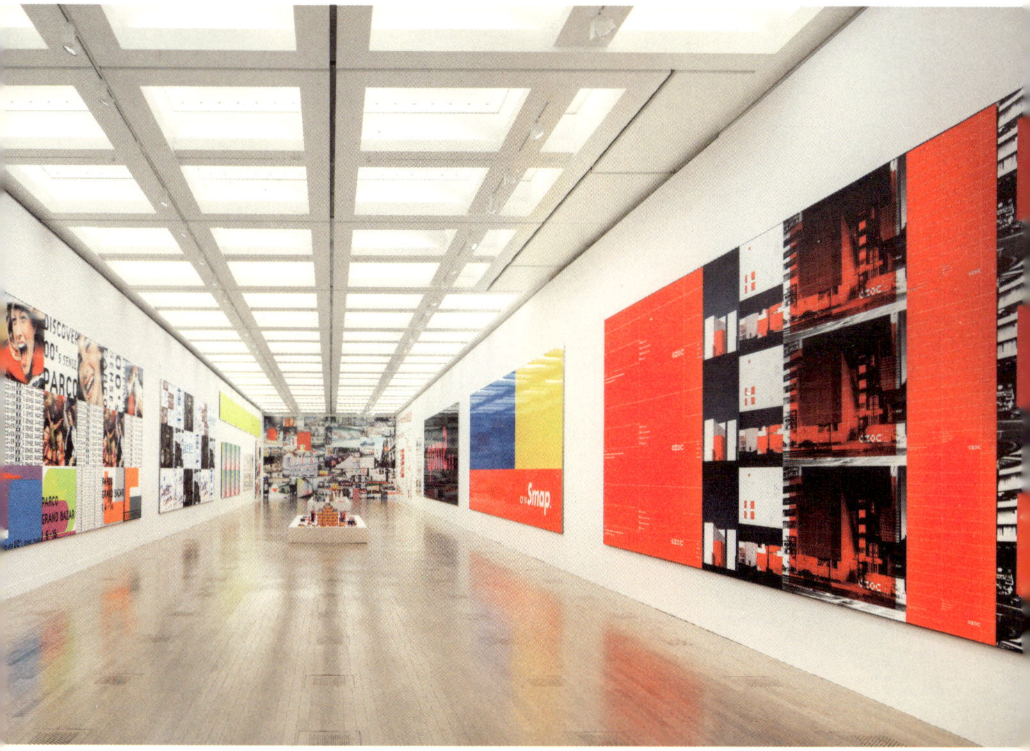

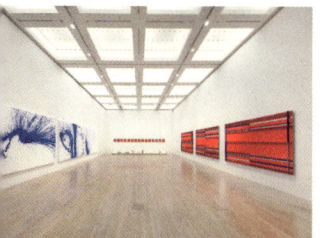
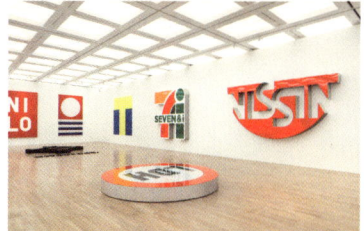
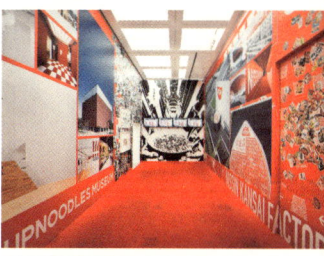
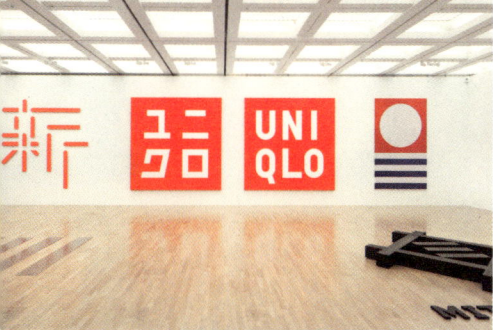
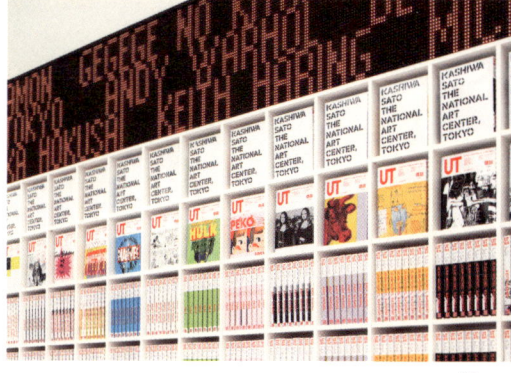

366 Poster
TD. 佐藤卓 Taku Satoh
D. 向井翠 Sui Mukai
CL. 巷房 Kobo
PT. Custom-made for the project

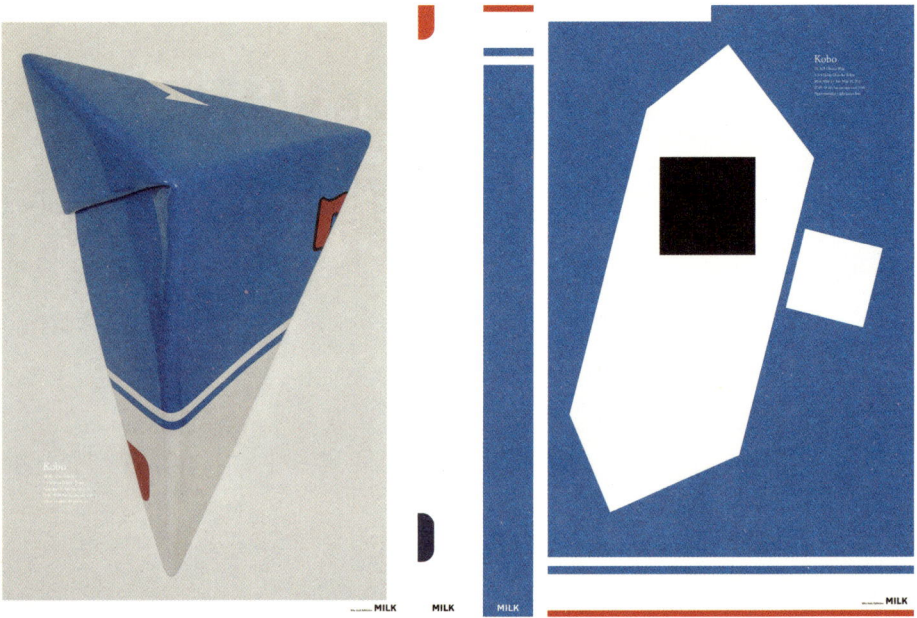

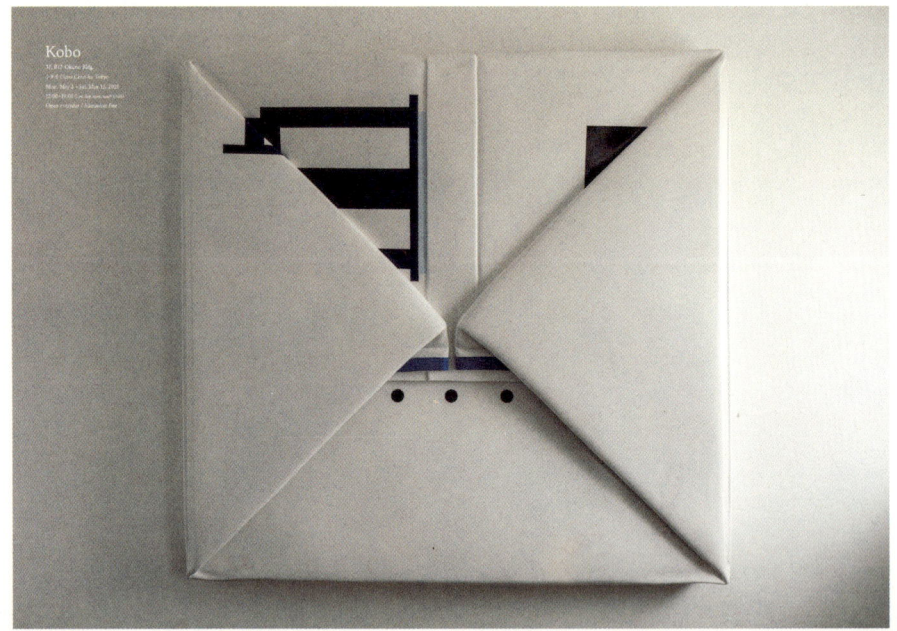

367 Poster
TD. 佐藤卓 Taku Satoh
D. 向井翠 Sui Mukai
CL. 巷房 Kobo
PT. Custom-made for the project

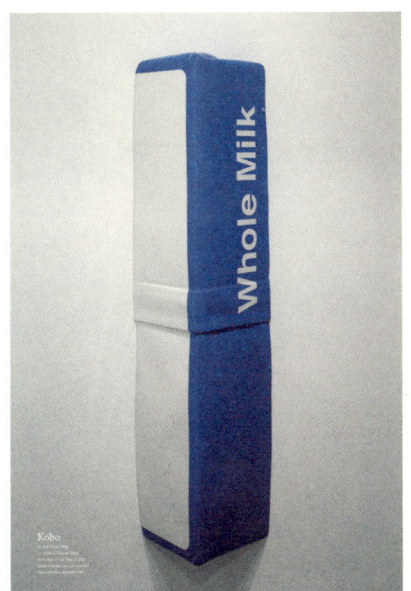
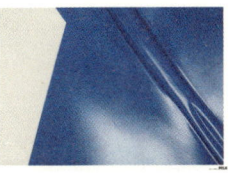
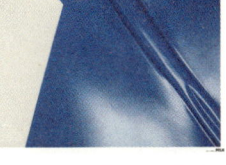
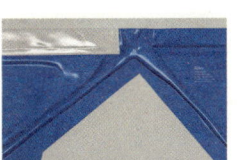
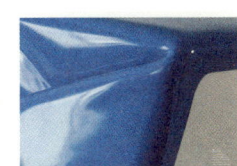
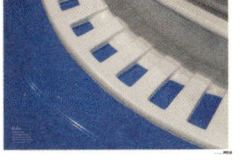
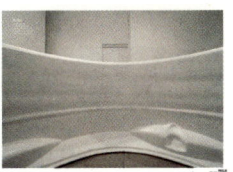
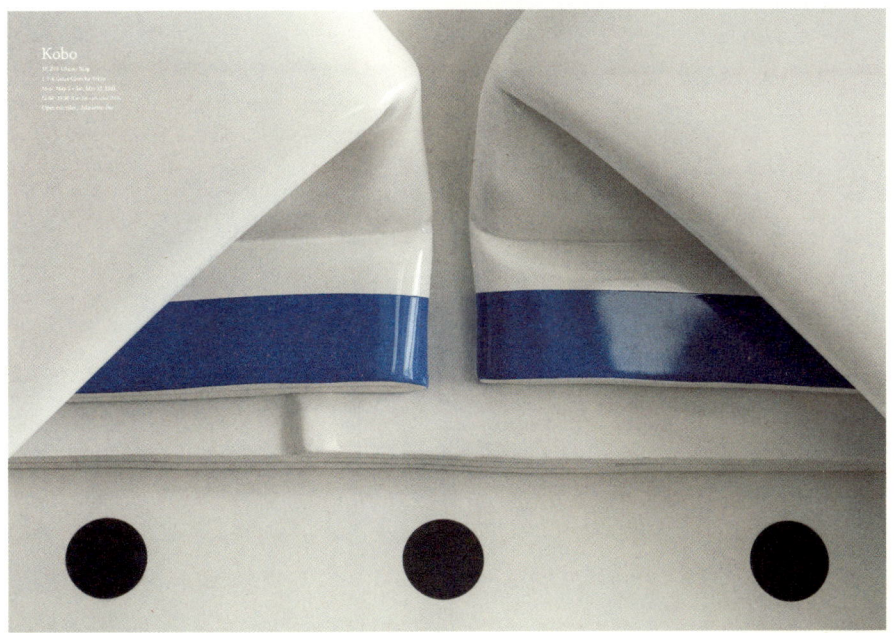

368 DM
TD. 佐藤卓 Taku Satoh
D. 向井翠 Sui Mukai
CL. 巷房 Kobo
PT. RoGaramond, Custom-made for the project

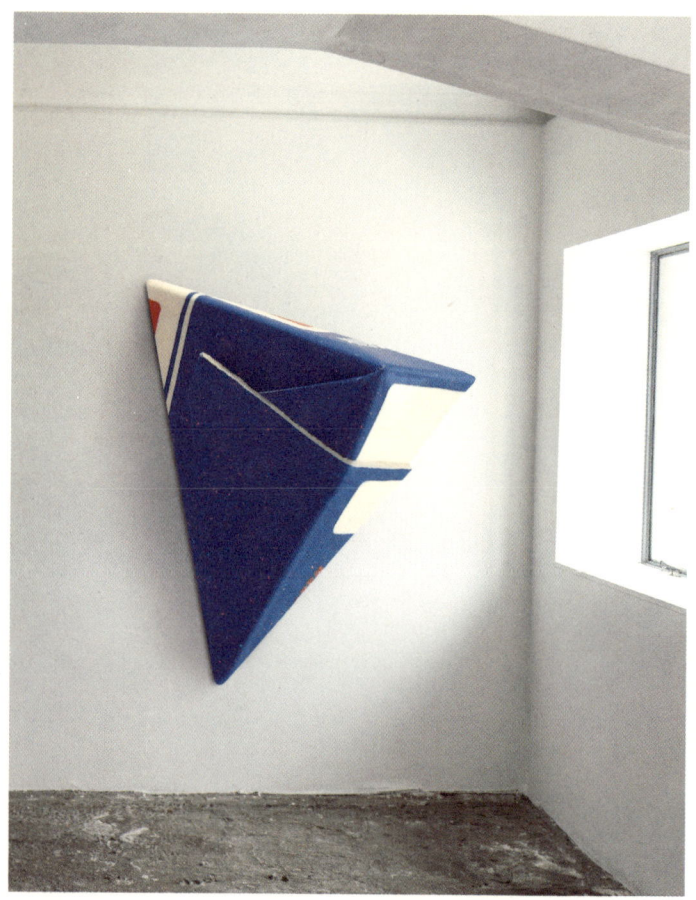

Taku Satoh Exhibition Mon. May 3 – Sat. May 15 Gallery Kobo
MILK 12:00-19:00 (Last day: open until 17:00) 3F, B1F Okuno Bldg.
Open everyday / Admission free 1-9-8 Ginza Chuo-ku Tokyo

369 Mark & Logo
TD. D. 佐藤卓 Taku Satoh
D. 白石卓也 Takuya Shiraishi, 山崎良弥 Ryoya Yamazaki
CL. 21_21 Design Sight
PT. Custom-made for the project

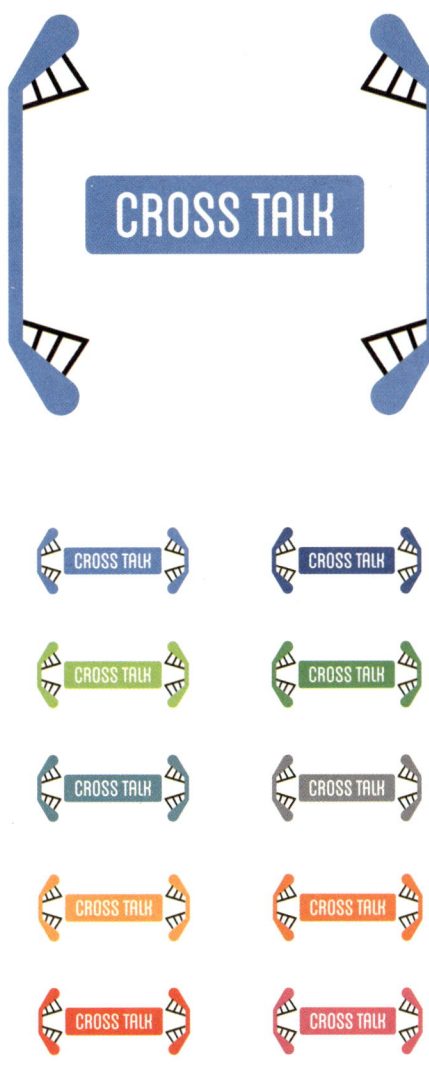

370 Book
TD. AD. 佐藤祐太郎 Yutaro Sato
CL. Non-commercial work
PT. U-OTF リュウミン Upr

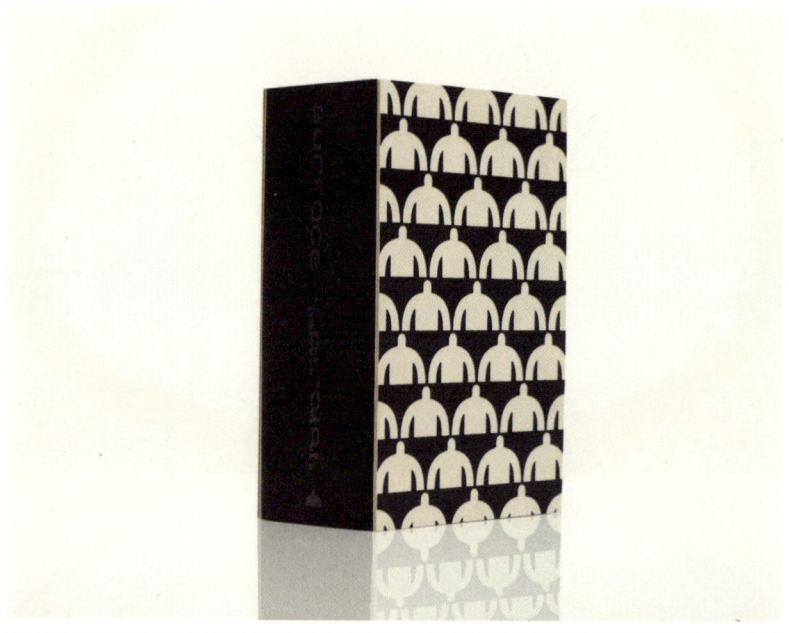

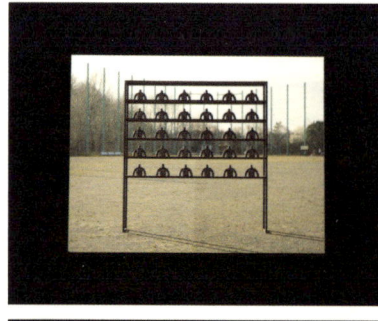
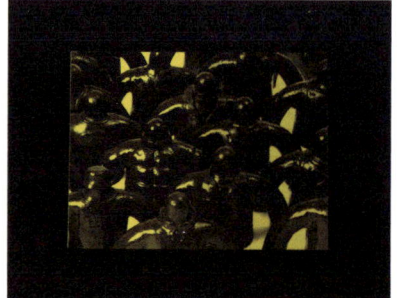
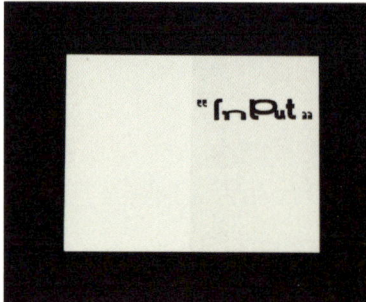
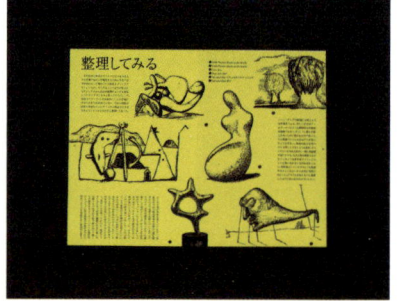

371 Poster
TD. Stefanie Schwarz
CL. Künstlerhaus Stuttgart
PT. Weissenhof Grotesk

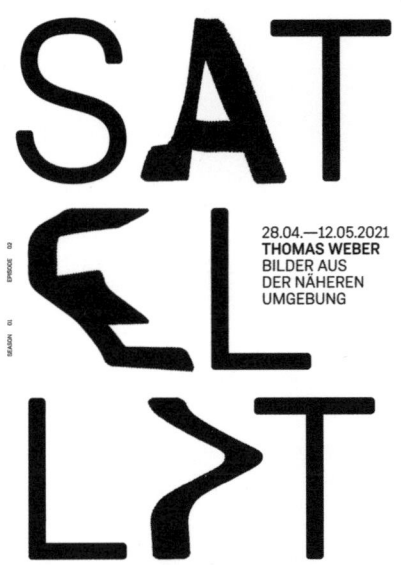
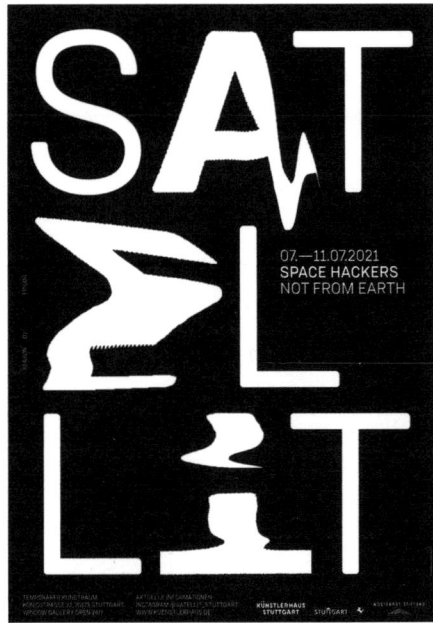
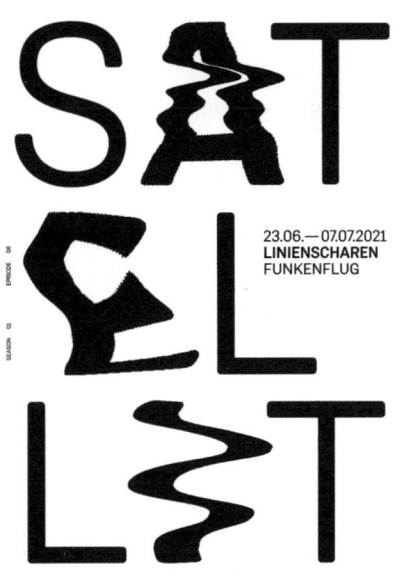

Prize Nominee Work

372 BI
TD. Paula Scher
D. Emily Atwood
CL. Berkeley Rep
PT. Obviously

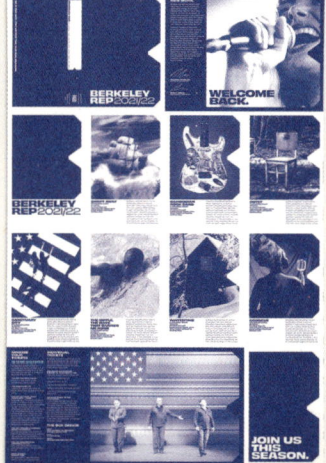

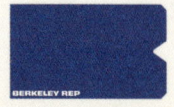
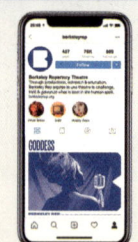
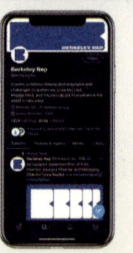

373 Mark & Logo
TD. 清水艦期 Kango Shimizu
CL.（株）BFF

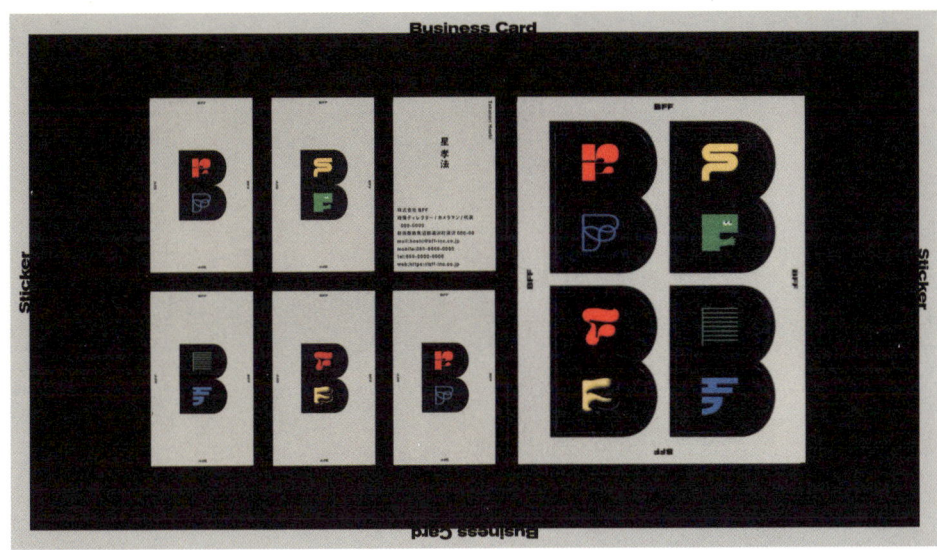

373

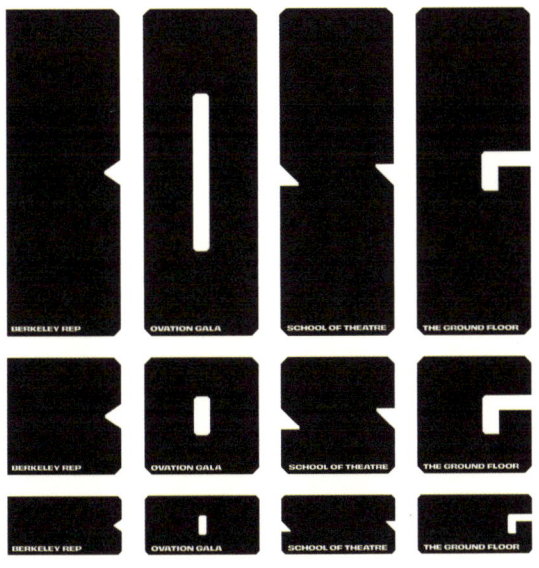

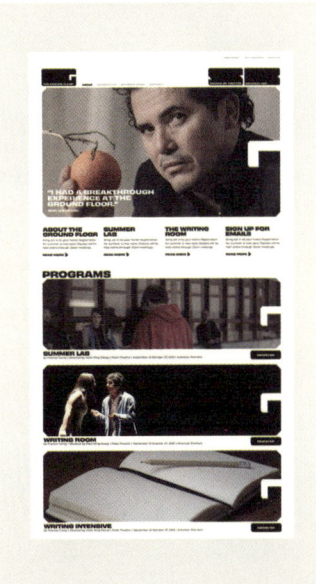

372

374 Online album covers
TD. 702design
AD. Mei Shuzhi
CL. Line Park
PT. Akkurat-Mono

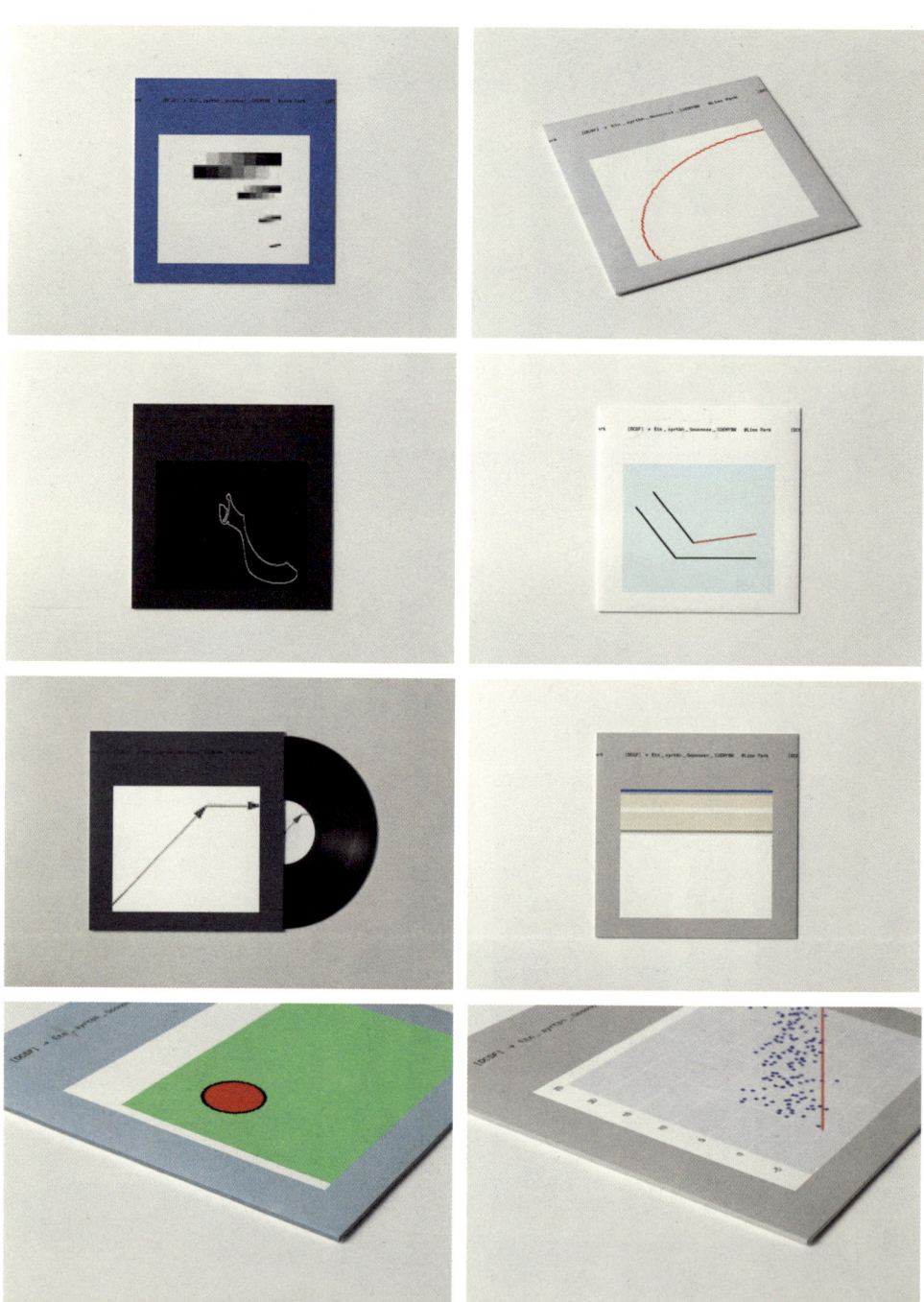

375 Branding
TD. 702design
AD. Mei Shuzhi
D. Li Jingjie, Chen Yijia
CL. Rich Whisky Bar
PT. Source Han Sans CN, FrutigerCE UltraBlack

376 Branding
TD. 702design
AD. Mei Shuzhi
D. Yao Kailun, Xie Qizhang
CL. TTS
PT. Custom-made for the project

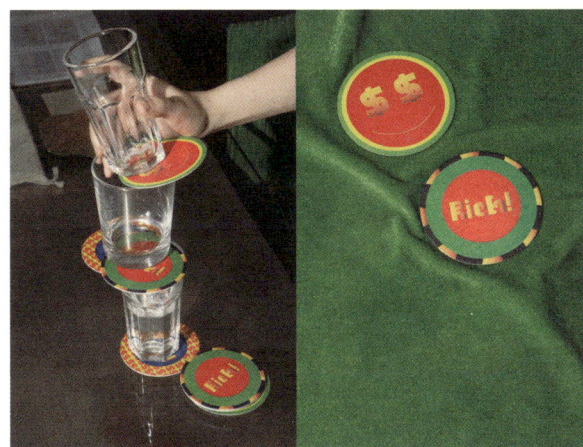
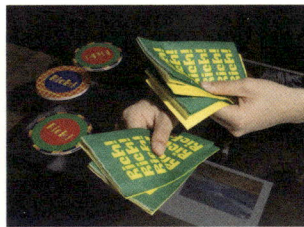
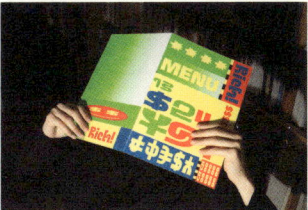

375

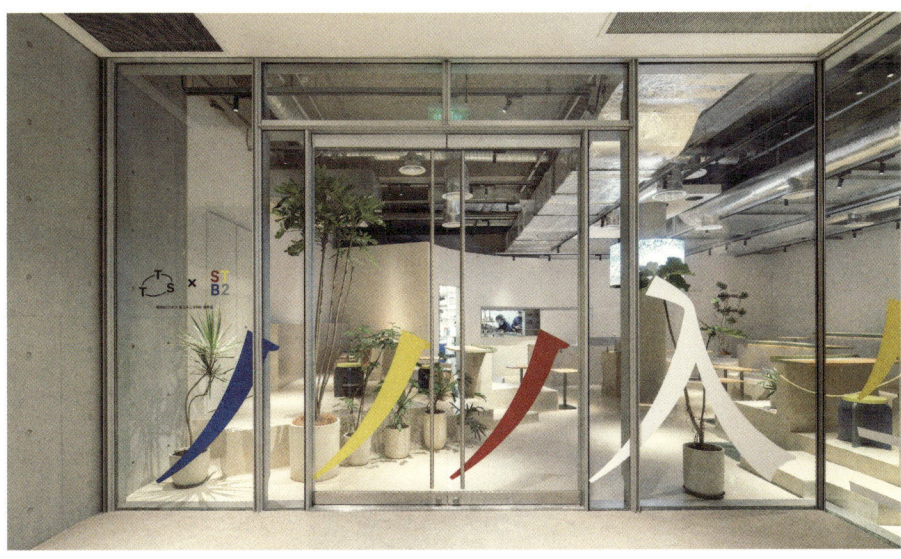
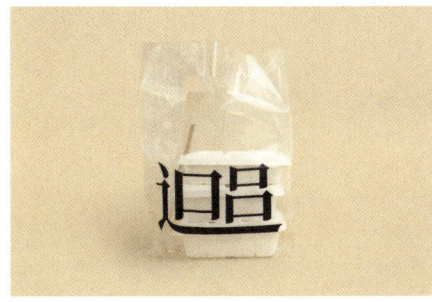
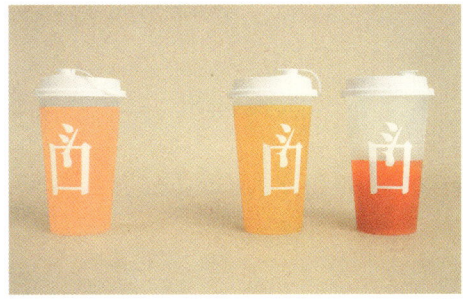

376

377 Signage
TD. 702design
AD. Mei Shuzhi
D. Chen Chenxia
CL. Xixi Live
PT. Custom-made for the project

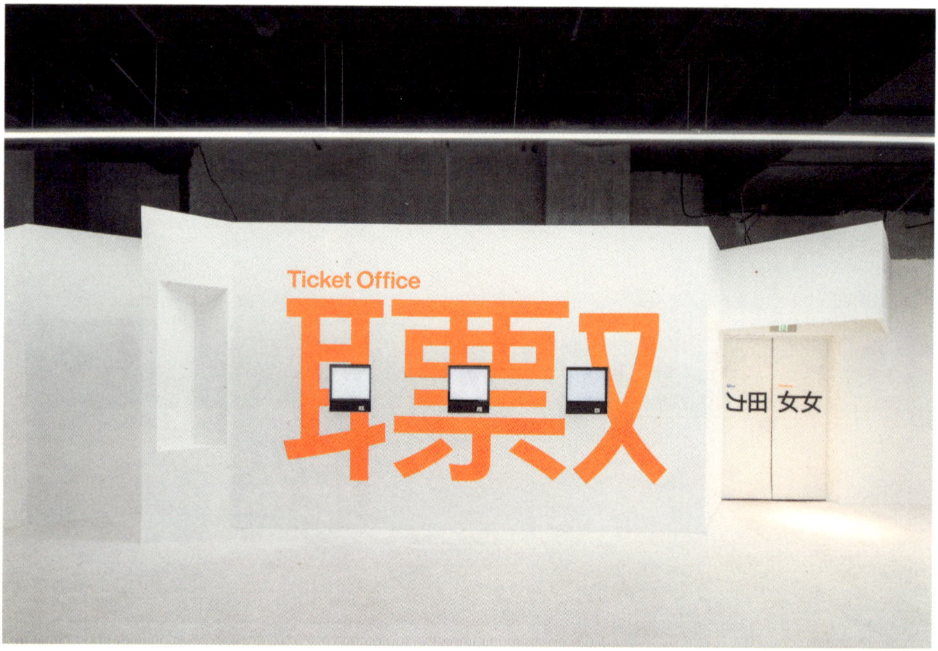

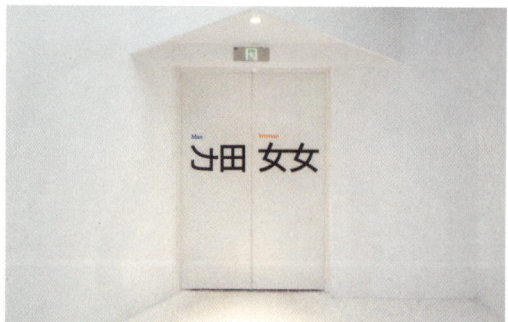
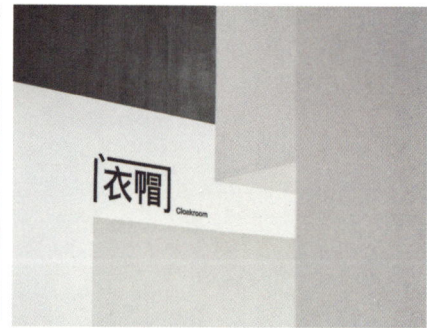
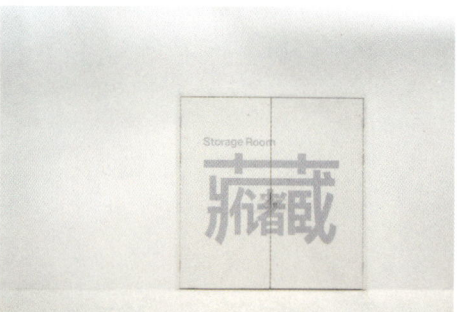
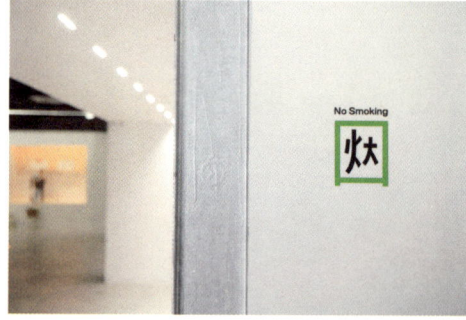

378 VI
TD. Paula Scher
D. Emily Atwood, Jack Roizental
CL. YoungArts
PT. Degular

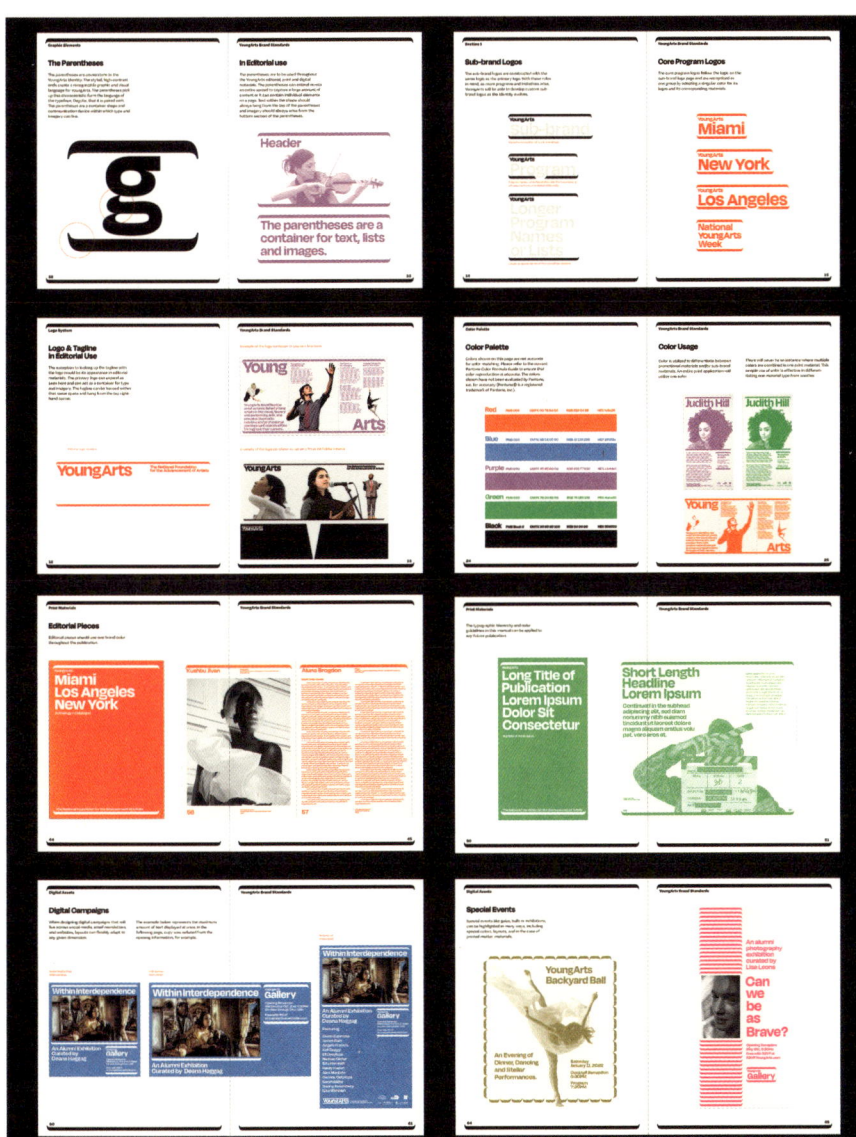

Prize Nominee Work

379 Diary (cards)
TD. AD. Zhuohan Shao
CL. Non-commercial work
PT. Custom-made for the project

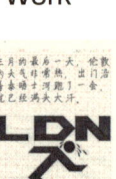
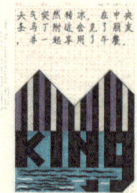
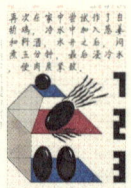
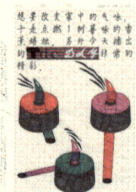
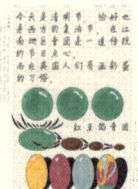
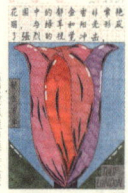
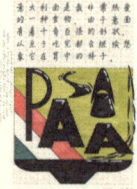
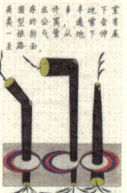
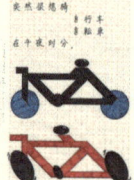
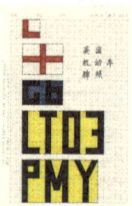
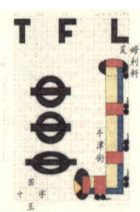
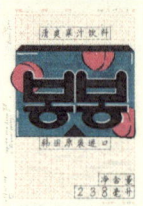
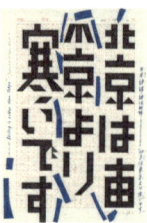
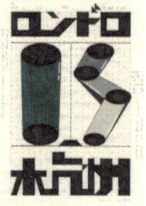
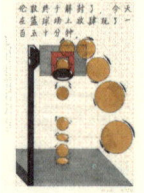
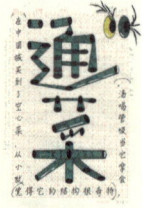
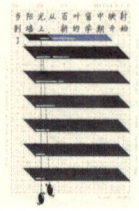
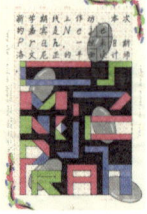
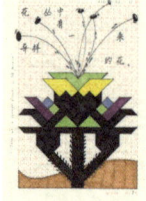
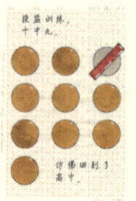
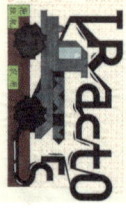
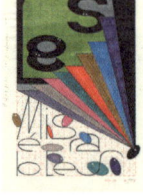
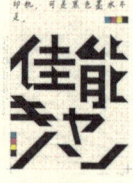
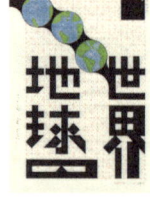
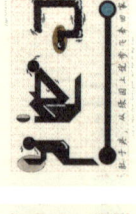
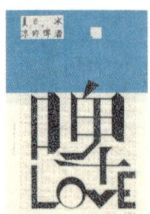
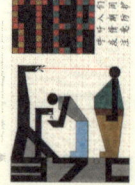
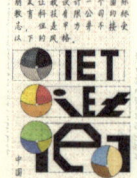
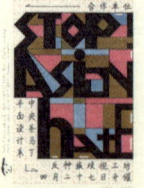

Prize Nominee Work

380 Diary (book)
TD. AD. Zhuohan Shao
P. Qianwen Wang
CL. Non-commercial work
PT. Custom-made for the project, Hiragino Sans GB

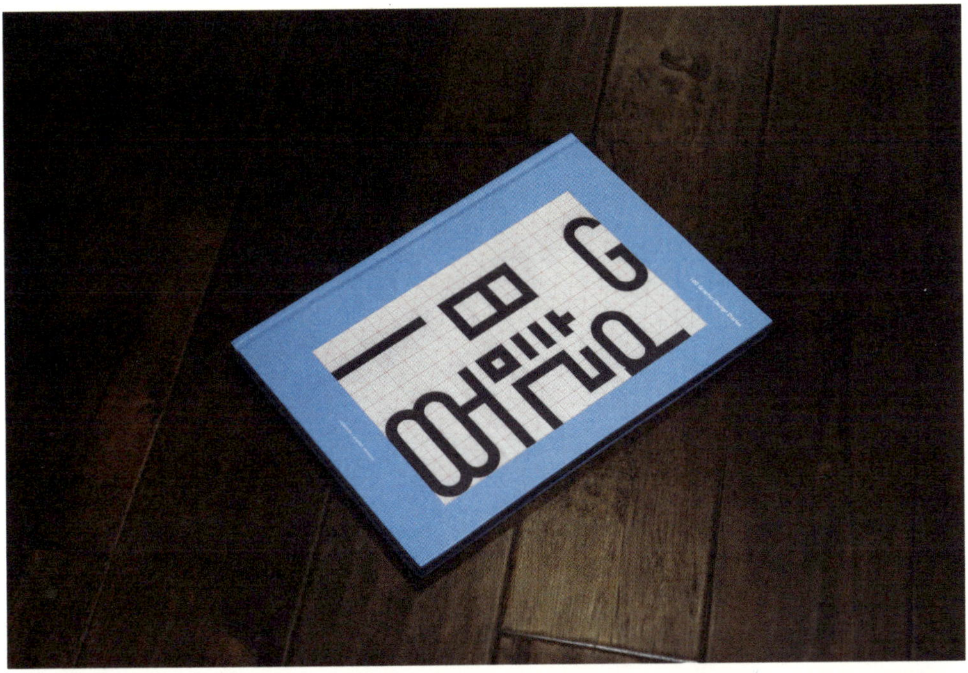

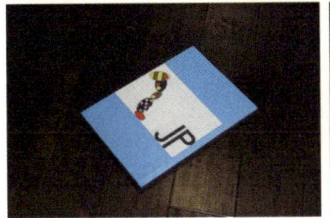
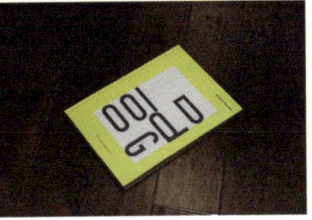
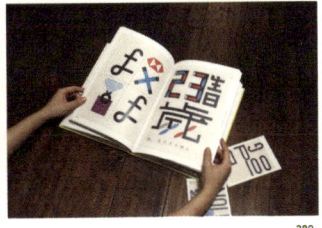

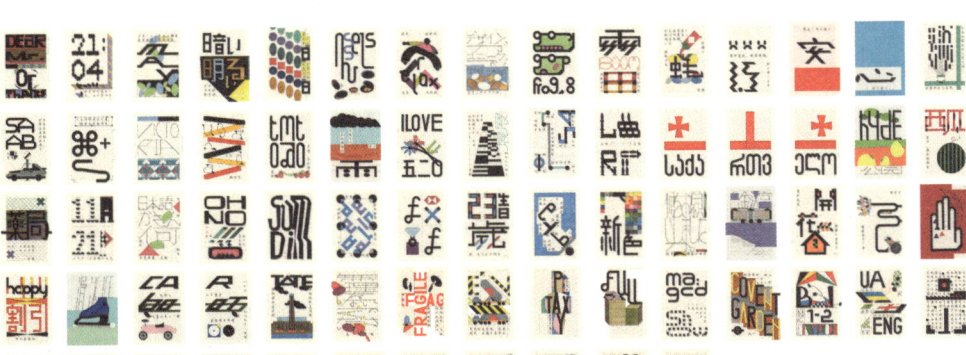

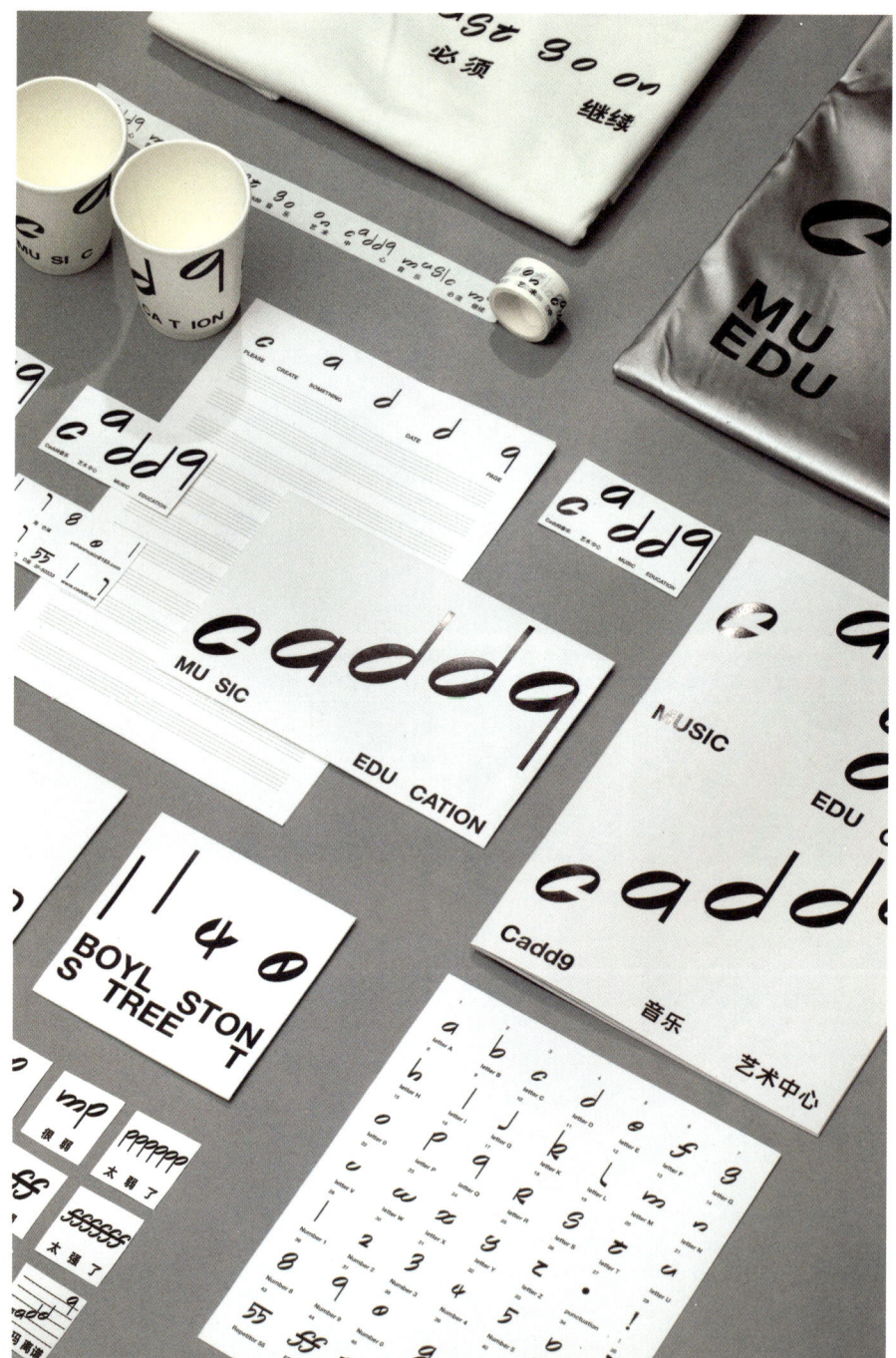

382 CD jacket
TD. 清水鑑期 Kango Shimizu
CL.（株）トイズファクトリー Toy's Factory

383 Packaging
TD. Oliver Siegenthaler
AD. Felipe Osorio
D. Nicolas Galeano
P. Espacio Crudo
CL. Masa
PT. Cactus & Studio Feixen Sans

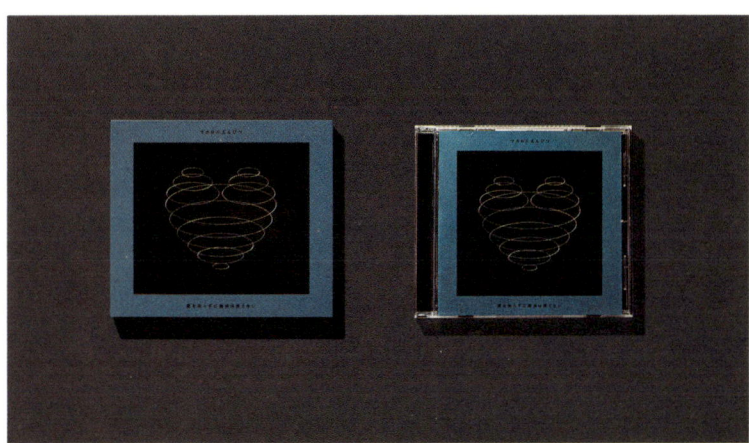

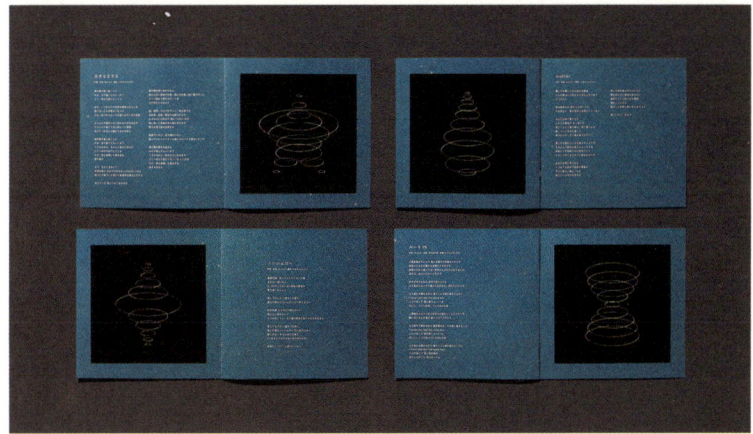

382

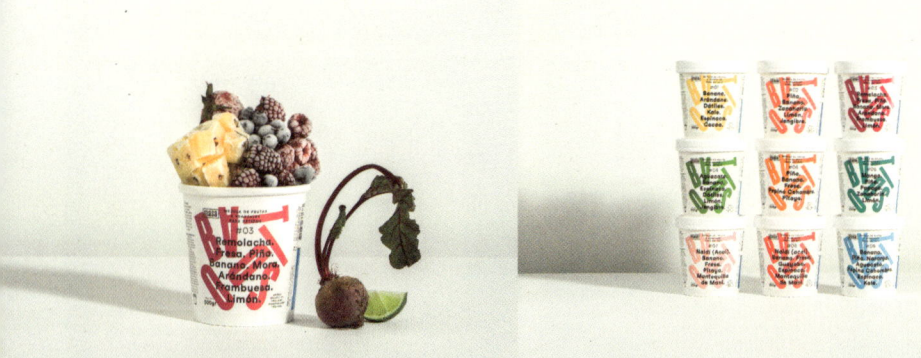

383

Book
TD. AD. D. 塩谷嘉章 Yoshiaki Shioya
E. 栗村卓生 Takuo Kurimura
CL. TOTO出版 TOTO Publishing
PT. Neue Haas Grotesk

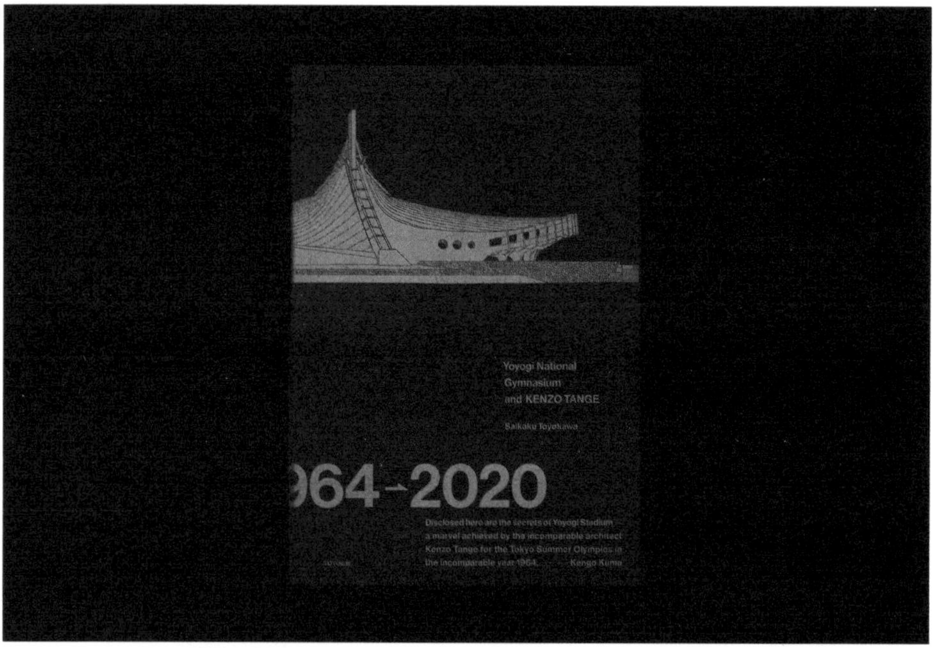

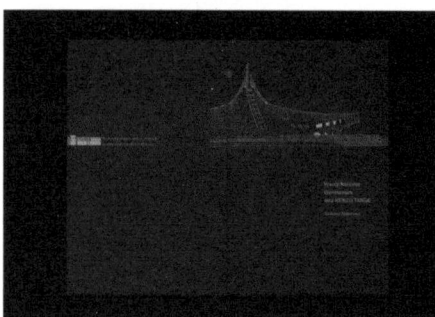
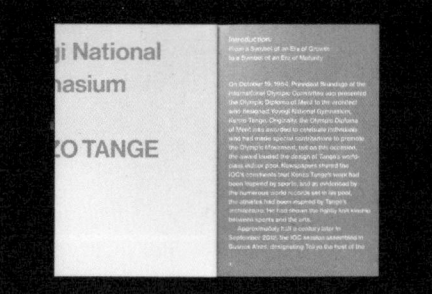
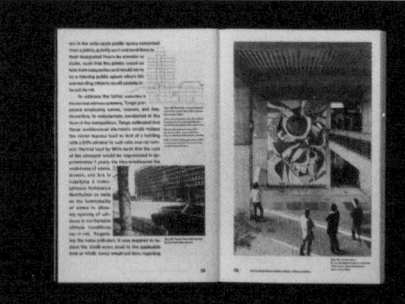
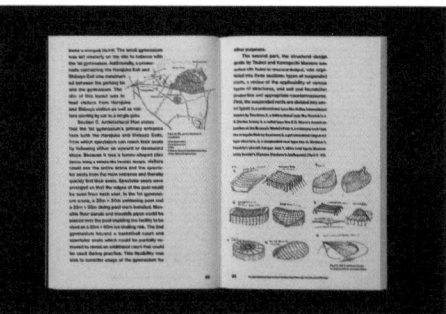

385 Poster
TD. 白澤真生 Masao Shirasawa
CL. Non-commercial work
PT. Helvetica Neue

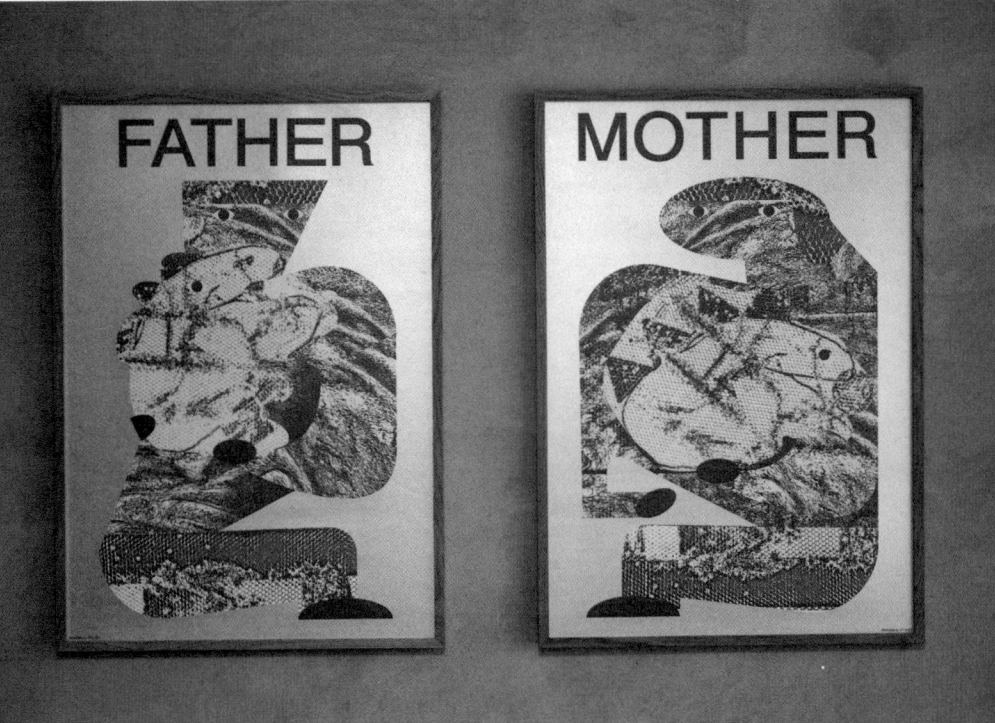

Prize Nominee Work

386 Exhibition design
TD. AD. 祖父江慎 Shin Sobue
D. 藤井瑶 Haruka Fujii
CL. 凸版印刷（株）Toppan Inc.
PT. TBゴシック, 游築初号ゴシックかな, Vastago Grotesk

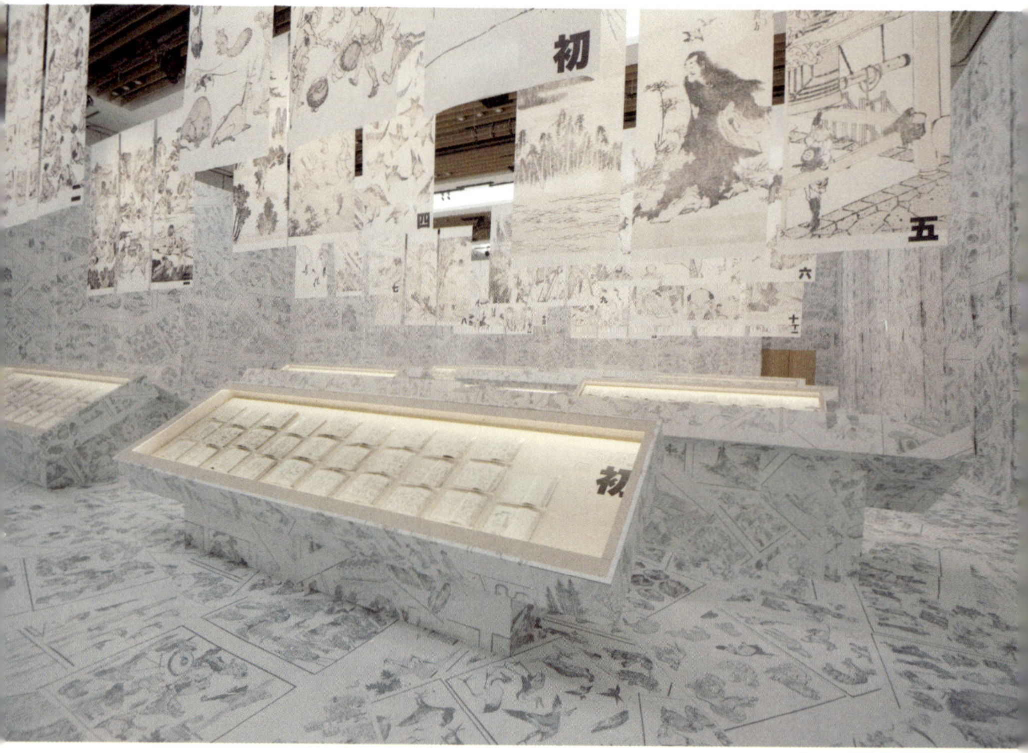

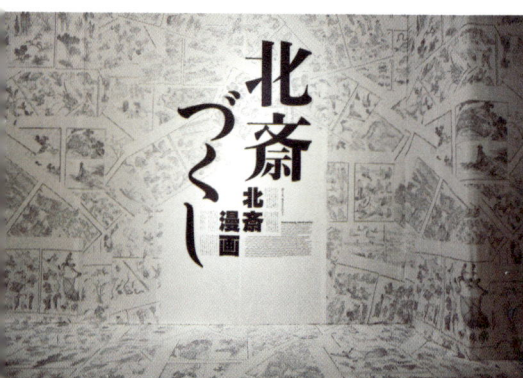
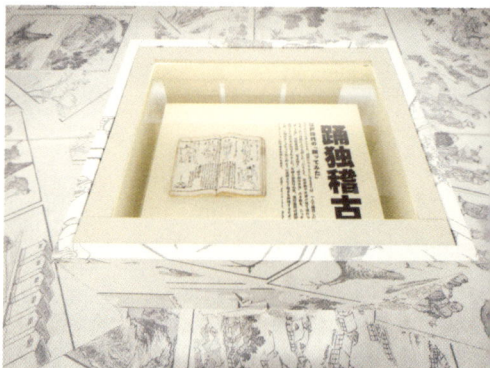
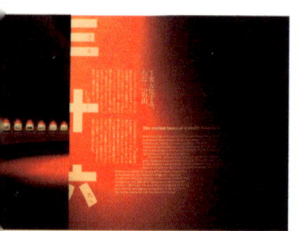
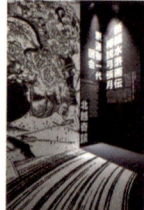
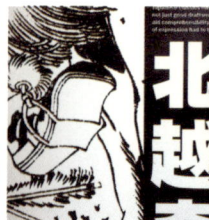
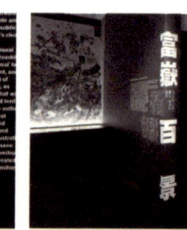

Prize Nominee Work

387 Exhibition catalogue
TD. AD. 祖父江慎 Shin Sobue
D. 藤井瑶 Haruka Fujii
CL. (株)青幻舎 Seigensha Art Publishing, Inc.
PT. TBゴシック, 游築初号ゴシックかな, Vastago Grotesk

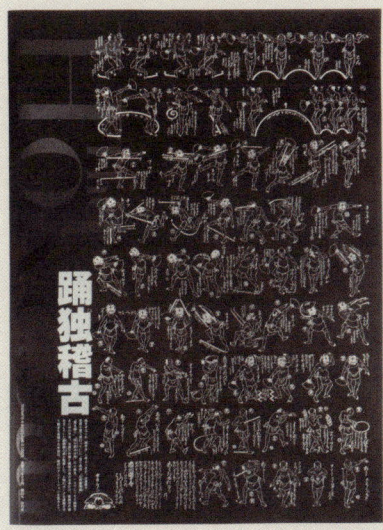
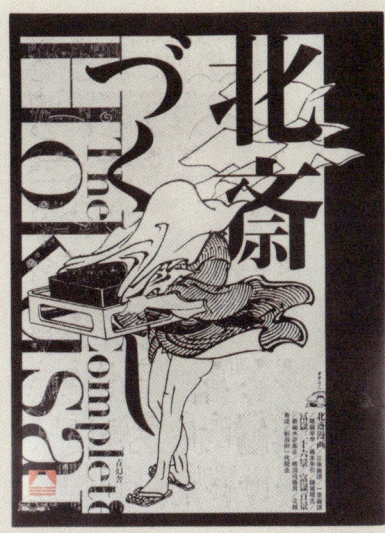
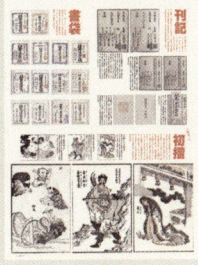
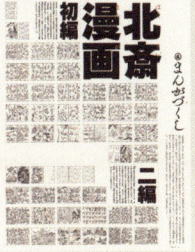
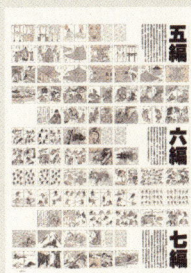
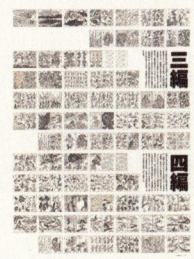
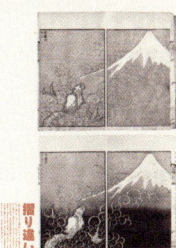
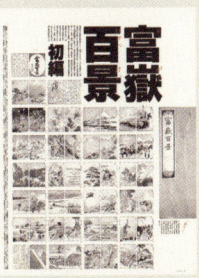
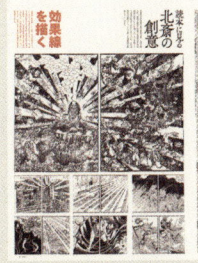
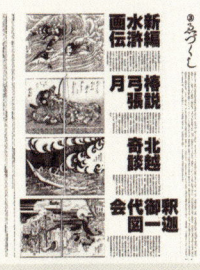
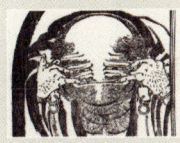
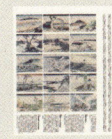
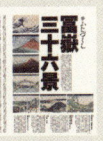
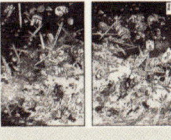
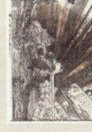
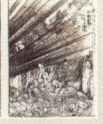

388 Book
TD. AD. 祖父江慎 Shin Sobue
D. 藤井瑶 Haruka Fujii, 志間かれん Karen Shima
CL. 888 Books
PT. UD新聞明朝, A1ゴシック, Bureau Grot

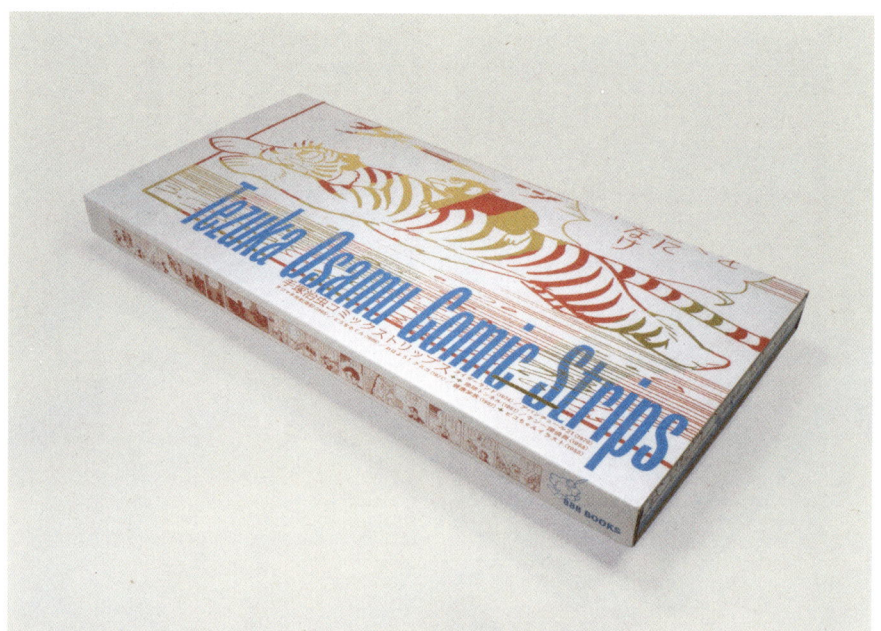

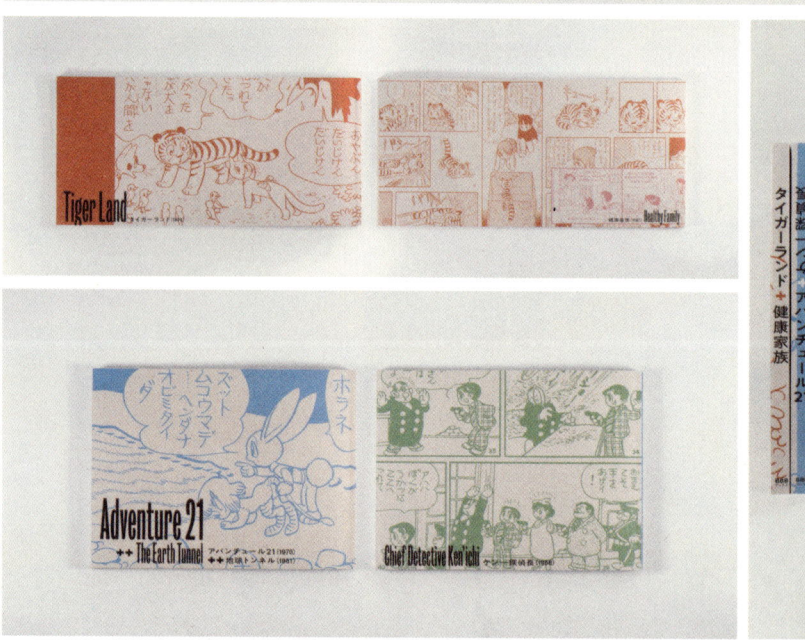

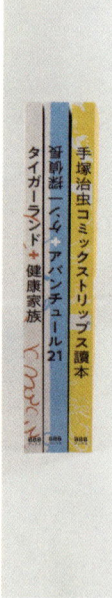

389 Book
TD. AD. 祖父江慎 Shin Sobue
D. 脇田あすか Asuka Wakida
CL. Tokyo Art Book Fair 事務局 Tokyo Art Book Fair Secretariat
PT. こぶりなゴシック, Dawnton

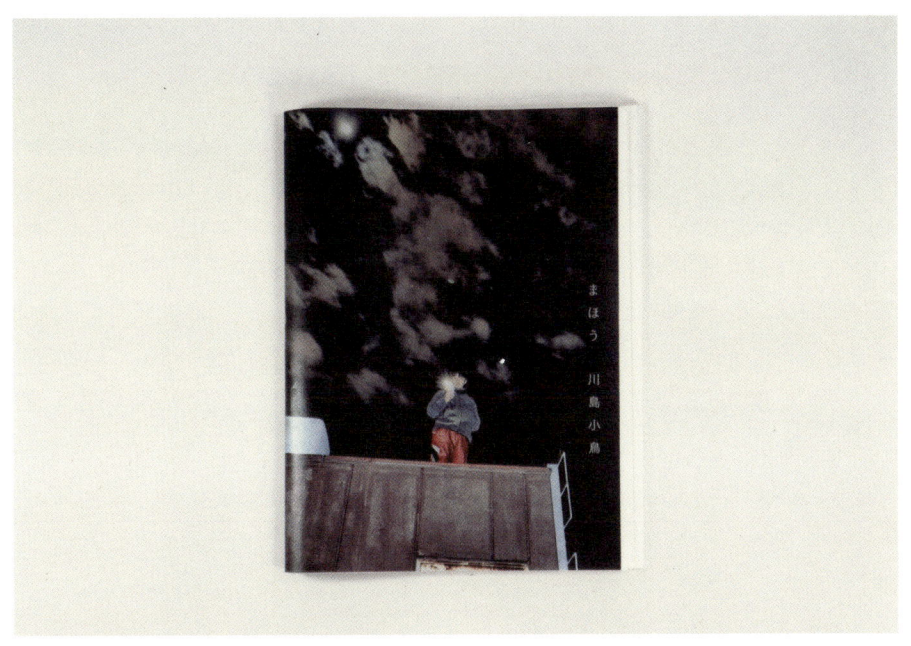
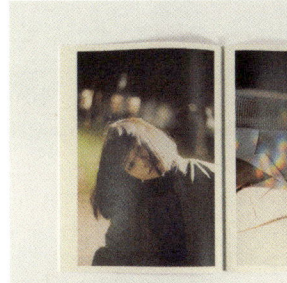
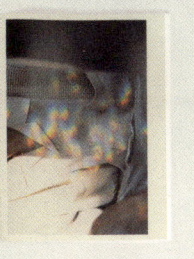
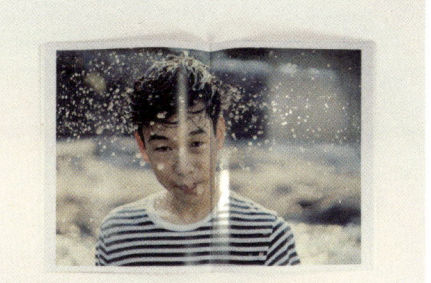
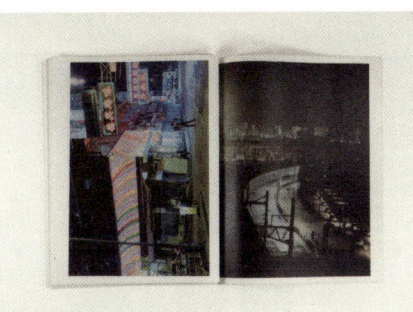
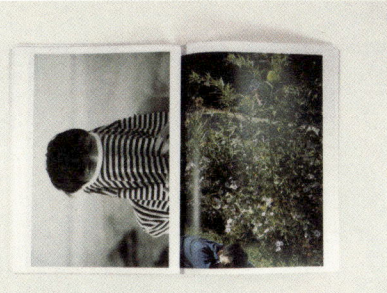

390 Poster
TD. Something Moon Design
D. Chiwai Cheang
CL. Transnation
PT. Interface Regular

391 Website
TD. Ayong Son
CL. SAA, Screen Art Agency
PT. Helvetica Now, Spoqa Han Sans
http://screenartagency.com

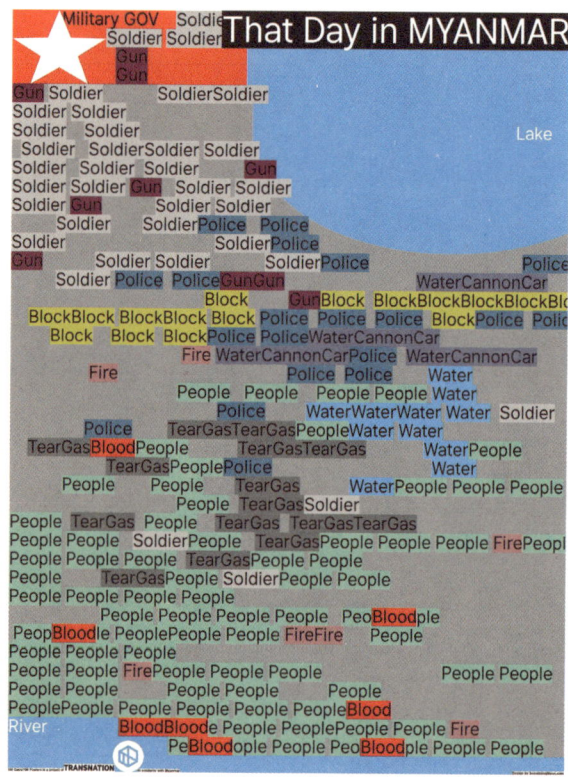

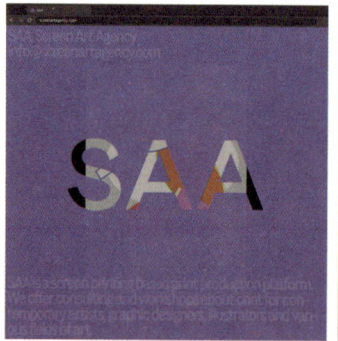
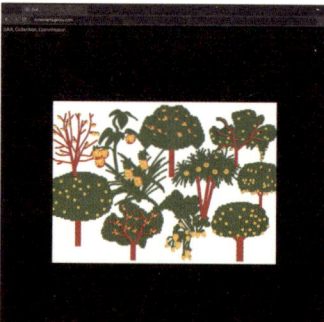
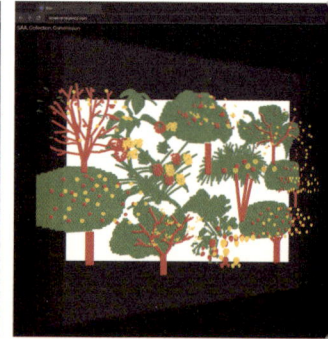

392 Book
TD. Alessandro Sommer
D. Denise Albrecht, Katharina Sellier
P. Jan Düfelsiek, Julia Autz
CL. Bielefeld University of Applied Sciences
PT. Maxima Now Pro, Antique Olive

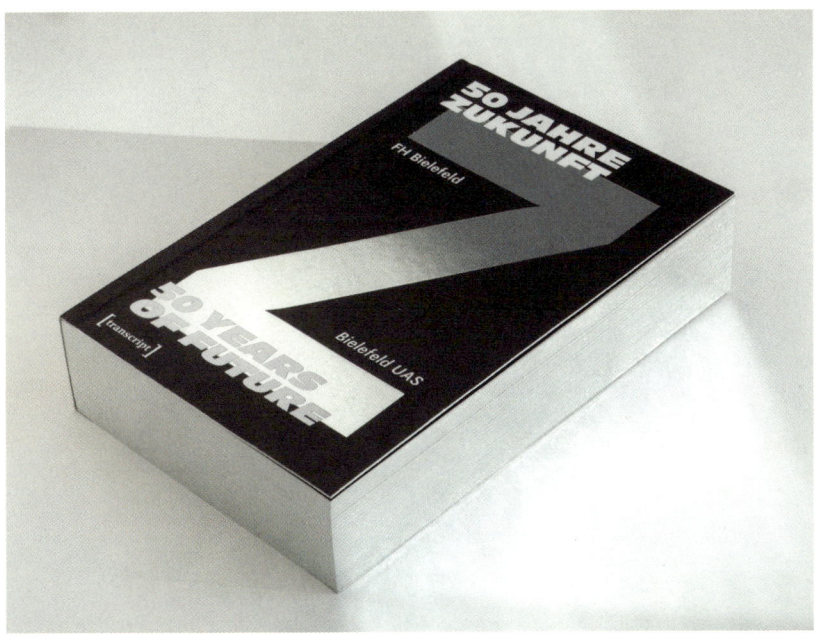

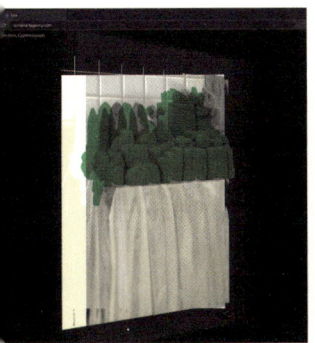
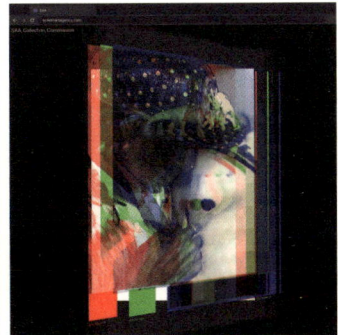
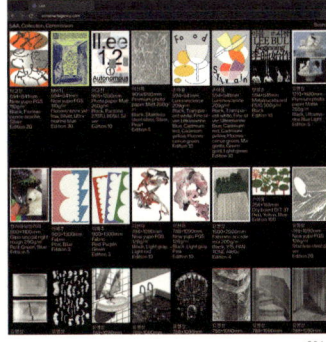

393 Book
TD. AD. Jiang Song
CL. Suzhou Museum
PT. Song, Times New Roman

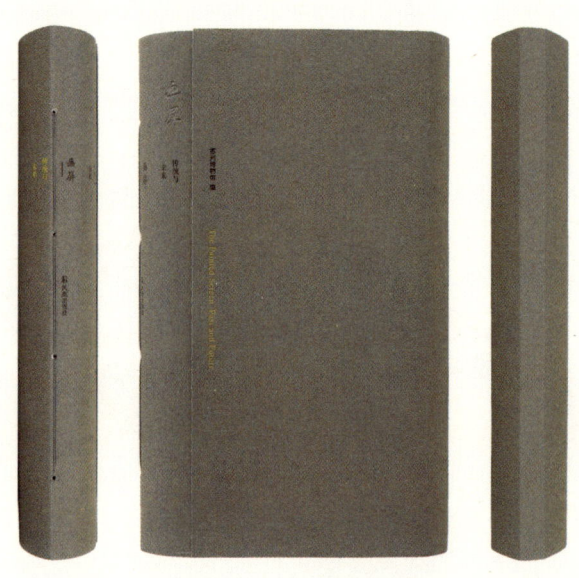

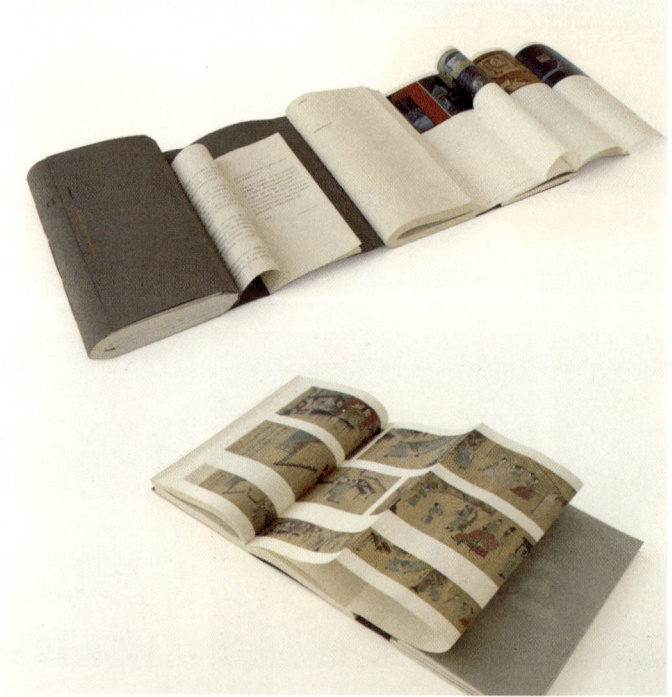

394 Graphic Installation
TD. AD. Leonardo Sonnoli
CL. MAXXI, National Museum of 21st Century Arts, Rome
PT. Custom-made for the project, Founders Grotesk

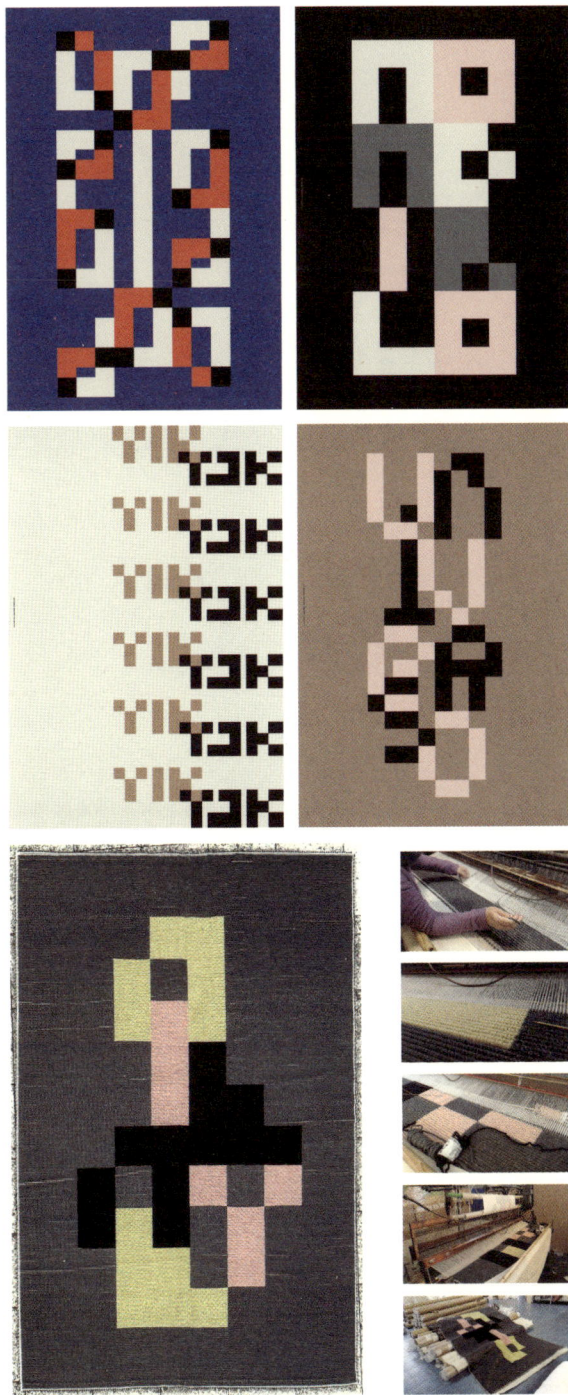

Prize	395 Type design
Nominee	TD. AD. Kris Sowersby
Work	D. Dave Foster
	EN. Noe Blanco
	CL. Klim Type Foundry
	PT. Signifier

R g *fl* r
a sk & £
5 N G n

Structuralism **Nonuniform**
Psychological **Comparison**
Classification *Misclassification*
Highlighting *Shadowgraphist*
Scientifiques *Crystallization*

396 Type design
TD. AD. Kris Sowersby
D. Dave Foster
EN. Noe Blanco
CL. Klim Type Foundry
PT. Söhne

Söhne
—Collection.

Families

Söhne.
Extraleicht Extraleicht Kursiv Leicht Leicht Kursiv Buch Buch Kursiv
Kräftig Kräftig Kursiv Halbfett Halbfett Kursiv Dreiviertelfett
Dreiviertelfett Kursiv Fett Fett Kursiv Extrafett Extrafett Kursiv

Söhne Mono.
Extraleicht Extraleicht Kursiv Leicht Leicht Kursiv
Buch Buch Kursiv Kräftig Kräftig Kursiv Halbfett
Halbfett Kursiv Dreiviertelfett Dreiviertelfett Kursiv
Fett Fett Kursiv Extrafett Extrafett Kursiv

Söhne Schmal.
Extraleicht Extraleicht Kursiv Leicht Leicht Kursiv Buch Buch Kursiv Kräftig Kräftig Kursiv Halbfett
Halbfett Kursiv Dreiviertelfett Dreiviertelfett Kursiv Fett Fett Kursiv
Extrafett Extrafett Kursiv

Söhne Breit.
Extraleicht Extraleicht Kursiv Leicht Leicht Kursiv Buch
Buch Kursiv Kräftig Kräftig Kursiv Halbfett Halbfett Kursiv
Dreiviertelfett Dreiviertelfett Kursiv Fett Fett Kursiv
Extrafett Extrafett Kursiv

Information
Söhne is the memory of Akzidenz-Grotesk framed through the reality of Helvetica. It captures the analogue materiality of "Standard Medium" used in Unimark's legendary wayfinding system for the NYC Subway.

Schriftgießerei
Commonplace
Didot Systems
Anwendungen
Royal-Grotesk
Typografische
Punchcutters
Galvanotypie

Approximately
Seine Gießerei
Developments
Catastrophical
Idiosyncrasies
Monatsblätter
Draughtsmen
Bibliographie

Historians, consciously or unconsciously, must go through some filtering processes.

When Jan Tschichold's Die neue Typographie appeared in 1928 it was also composed entirely with sans serifs.

For decades, if not for a century, Akzidenz-Grotesk was not attributed to any single designer, engraver, or punchcutter.

Forming conclusions after only consulting some of the total available historical data can lead one into trouble.

In what way does it matter who designed Akzidenz-Grotesk, for which typefoundry, and in which year?

Compositors, graphic designers & typographers between the 1890s and the 1990s were not aware of any exact individual behind the types' appearance.

36pt Black Italic

The idea that both the signifier & the signified are inseparable is explained by Saussure's diagram, which shows how both components coincide to create the sign.

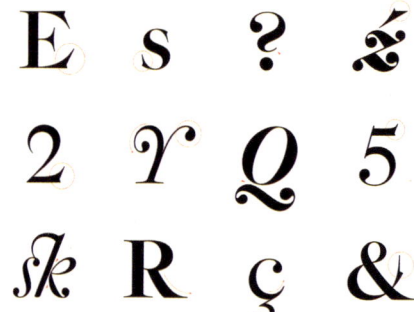

Grappillémes Skeletonization
Degenerately Aufklaubendes
Roosterwerk Klapperkruid
Angoisserais Échenillaient
Epistolatory Zuckrigstem

THE BAROQUE STYLE used contrast, movement, exuberant detail, deep colour, grandeur and surprise to achieve a sense of awe. The style began at the start of the 17th century in Rome, then spread rapidly to France, northern Italy, Spain and Portugal, then to Austria, southern Germany and Russia. By the 1730s, it had evolved into an even more flamboyant style, called *rocaille* or *Rococo*, which appeared in France and Central Europe until the mid to late 18th century. In the decorative arts there is an excess of ornamentation. The departure from Renaissance classicism has its own ways in each country. But a general feature is that everywhere the starting point is the ornamental elements introduced by the Renaissance. The classical repertoire is crowded, dense, overlapping, loaded, in order to provoke shock effects. New motifs introduced by Baroque are: the cartouche, trophies and weapons, baskets of fruit or flowers, and others, made in marquetry, stucco, or carved. The English word

EL BARROCO fue un período de la historia en la cultura occidental originado por una nueva forma de concebir el arte (el «estilo barroco») y que, partiendo desde diferentes contextos histórico-culturales, produjo obras en numerosos campos artísticos: literatura, arquitectura, escultura, pintura, música, ópera, danza, teatro, etc. Se manifestó principalmente en la Europa occidental, aunque debido al colonialismo también se dio en numerosas colonias de las potencias europeas, principalmente en Latinoamérica. Cronológicamente, abarcó todo el siglo XVII y principios del XVIII, con mayor o menor prolongación en el tiempo dependiendo de cada país. Se suele situar entre el Manierismo y el Rococó, en una época caracterizada por fuertes disputas religiosas entre países católicos y protestantes, así como marcadas diferencias políticas entre los Estados absolutistas y los parlamentarios, donde una incipiente burguesía empezaba a poner los cimientos del capitalismo. Como estilo artístico, el

DE BAROK is een Europese stijlperiode die aan het begin van de 17e eeuw in Italië tot ontwikkeling kwam en tot in de eerste helft van de 18e eeuw voortduurde, en die zich kenmerkt door overdaad van vorm en heftigheid van gevoelsuitdrukking. De barok kwam tot uiting op alle terreinen van de cultuur, zoals architectuur, tuinarchitectuur, schilderkunst, beeldhouwkunst, literatuur en muziek. Er wordt een onderscheid gemaakt tussen vroeg-, hoog- en laatbarok. De laatbarok wordt ook wel rococo genoemd. Het woord barok komt van het Portugese barroco, wat 'onregelmatig gevormde parel' betekent. Er wordt ook verondersteld dat het uiteindelijk terug te voeren is op het Italiaanse barocco, een term waarmee middeleeuwse filosofen een obstakel in de logica beschreven. De barok ontstond aan het eind van de 16e eeuw in Italië, met name in Rome, als onderdeel van de contrareformatie. Bij het Concilie van Trente was besloten dat kunst een

The dome was one of the central symbolic features of Baroque architecture illustrating the union between the heavens and the earth.

In the 18th century the term began to be used to describe music, and not in a flattering way.

French philosopher Michel de Montaigne (1533–1592) associated the term baroco with "Bizarre and uselessly complicated."

The style began at the start of the 17th century in Rome, then spread rapidly to France.

Costumes of the personages were blown by the wind, or moved by their own gestures.

LES HISTORIENS DE L'ART, souvent protestants, ont traditionnellement accentué le fait que le style baroque évoluait à une époque où l'Église catholique romaine réagissait face à plusieurs mouvements culturels produisant une nouvelle science et de nouvelles formes de religions—la Réforme. On a dit que le baroque monumental était un style que la papauté pouvait instrumentaliser, comme le firent les monarchies absolues, en imposant une voie d'expression à même de restaurer son prestige, au point de commencement symbolique de la Contre-Réforme catholique. Que ce fût ou non le cas, son développement eut du succès à Rome où l'architecture baroque renouvela largement le centre-ville ; peut-être la plus importante rénovation urbanistique. Le terme « baroque » dans son sens actuel, comme la plupart des périodes ou désignations stylistiques, a été inventé postérieurement par la critique d'art (c'est Heinrich Wölfflin qui

DER BEGRIFF WURDE IM FRANZÖSISCHEN Raum zuerst abwertend im Sinne von „merkwürdig" für Kunstformen gebraucht, die nicht dem schlichteren Geschmack des classicisme unter Ludwig XIV. entsprachen. Ein wesentliches Gestaltungselement des Barock und Rokoko sind Stuck (siehe auch Stuckateur) und Schnitzereien, die zu oft reichem und geschwungenem Ornamentschmuck geformt wurden. Seit 1855 wurde der Begriff von Jacob Burckhardt — zunächst in seinem Werk Cicerone noch mit abwertender, später mit freundlich-neutraler Bedeutung — genutzt. Der Begriff wurde dann auf die Musik und Literatur der Zeit übertragen und wird heute als allgemeiner historischer Epochenbegriff verwendet, auch über den Bereich der Kunst hinausgehend. Die Bedeutungserweiterung ist auch daran erkennbar, dass sich das Wort Barock auf ganz verschiedene Erscheinungen des

398 Signage
TD. AD. Andrew Stevens
D. Hyunil Shin
P. Louise Melchior
CL. Alumno Group
PT. Founders Grotesk

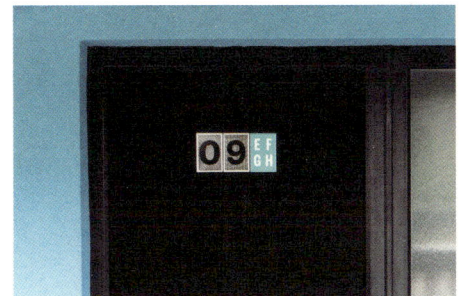
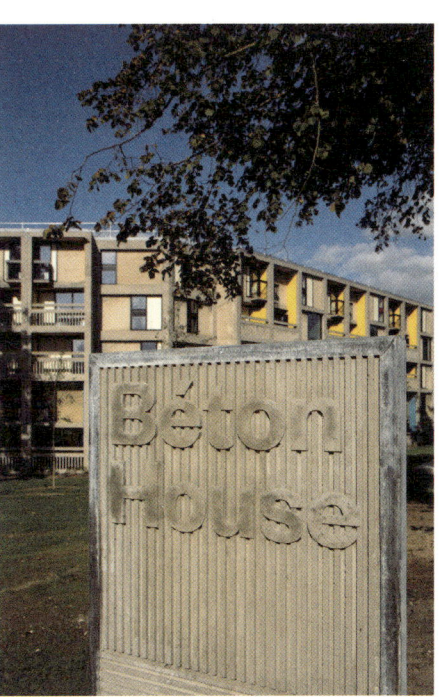
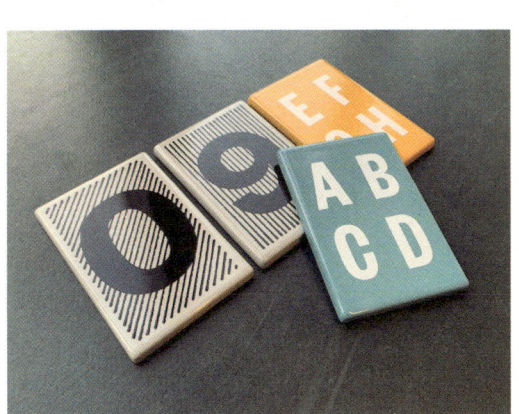
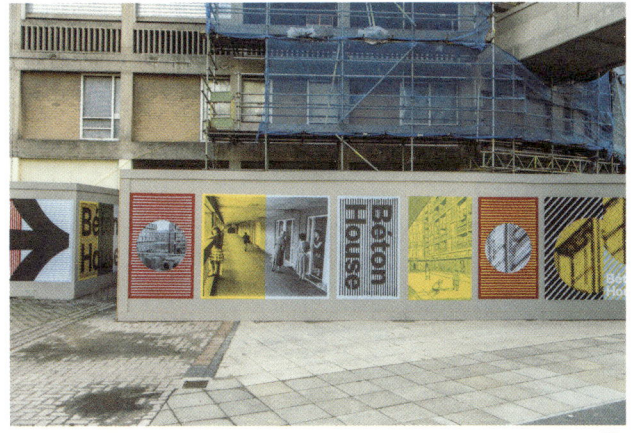

Prize Nominee Work

399 VI
TD. Studio Ljudje & Studio Nejc Prah
D. I. Nejc Prah
D. Miha Artnak, Emil Kozole, Urška Stariha
AN. Jure Lavrin
CL. Celtra
PT. Nitro, Favorit

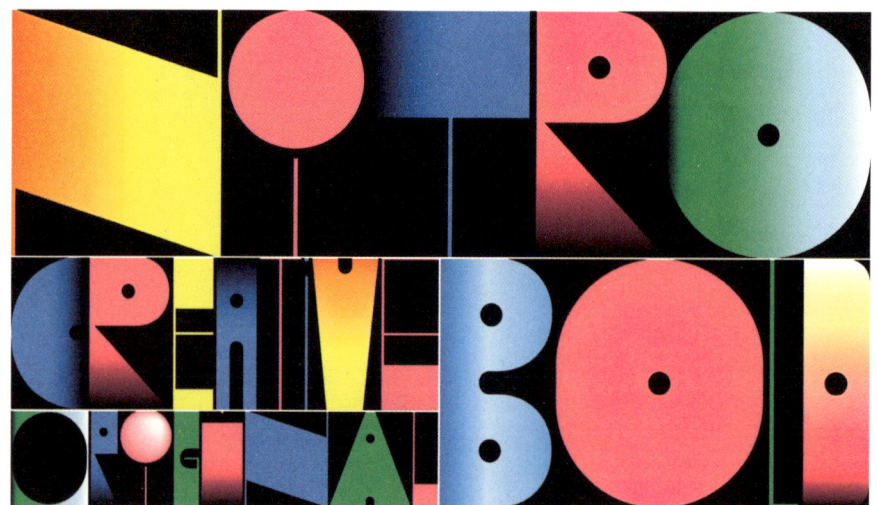
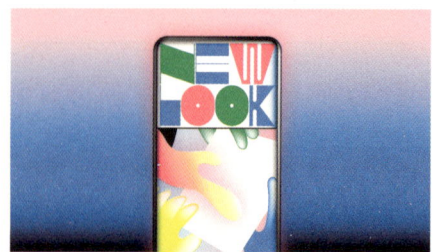
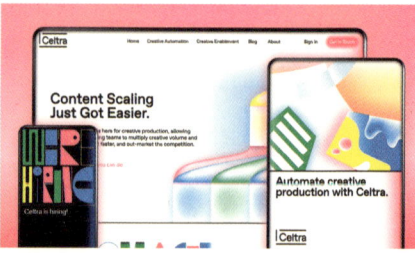
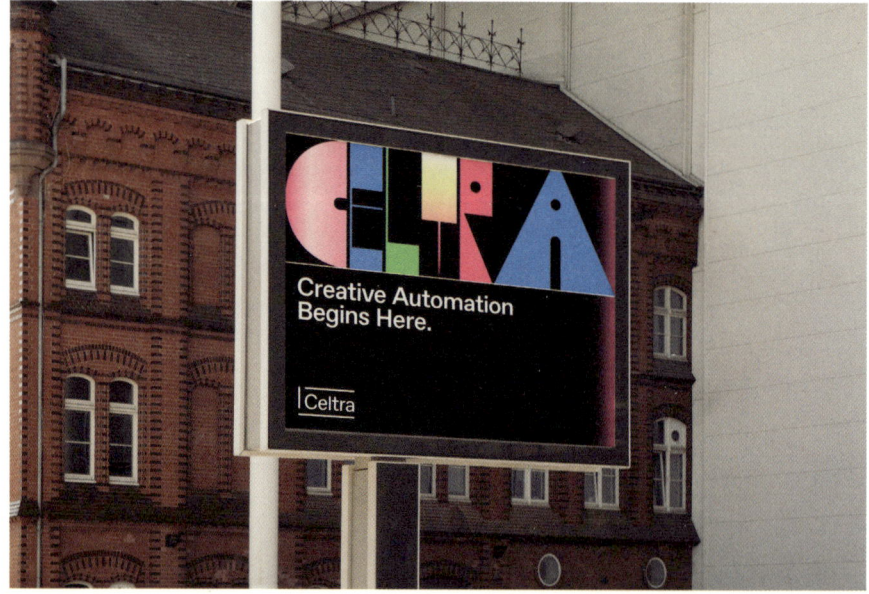

400 Packaging
TD. AD. 杉山紘一 Koichi Sugiyama
TD. D. 遠藤美奈子 Minako Endo
C. 成瀬雄太 Yuta Naruse
PR. 北野拓 Taku Kitano
CL. かどや Kadoya
PT. Custom-made for the project, Bodoni, 游明朝体, 中ゴシックBBB

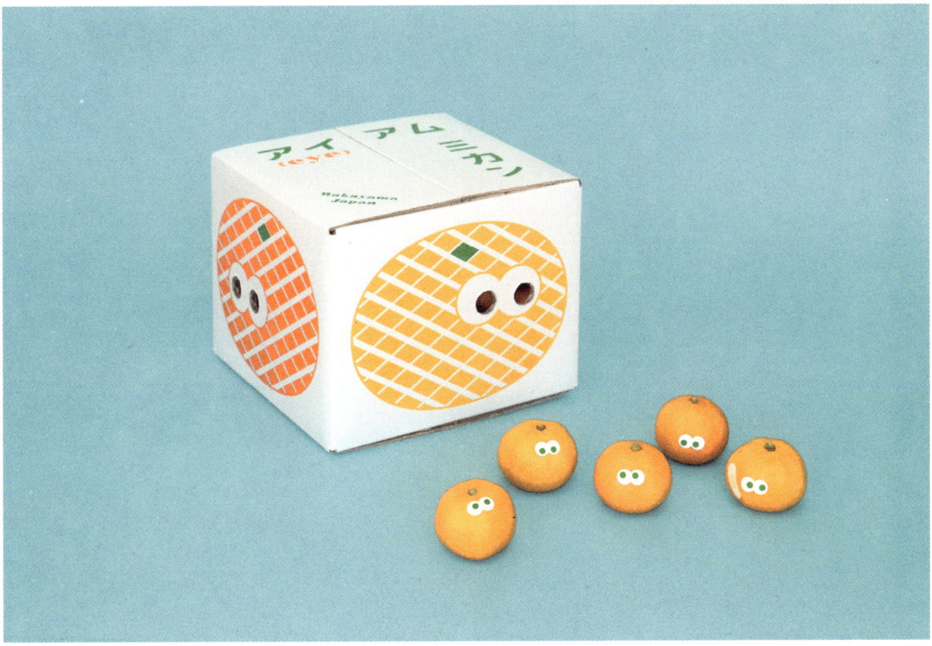

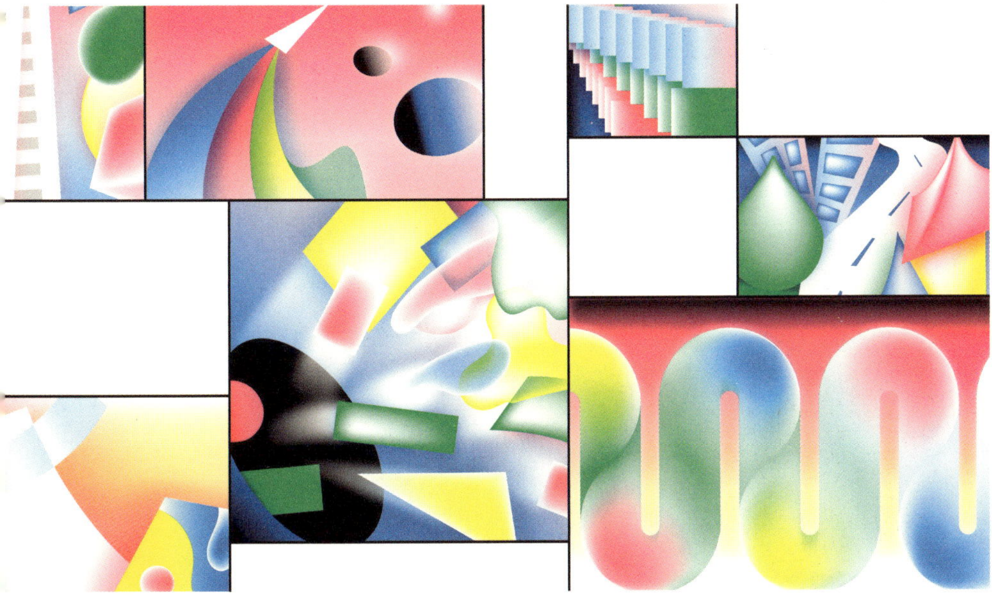

401 Book
TD. Studio Woork
AD. P. Io Woo
D. Gita Sulistiyo
CL. Studio Woorkzzz
PT. Suisse Int'l Regular

A Guide to Measure Life in Points.

(pt)

48 pages
6 height
22,5 width
2 thickness
200-3 pt

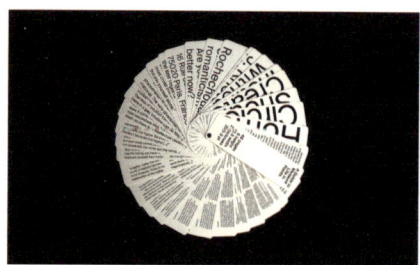
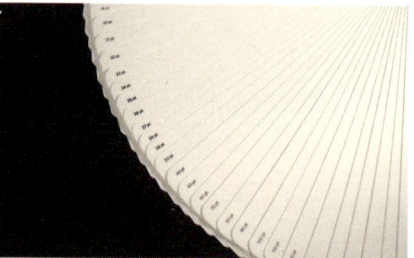

402 Poster
TD. AD. D. 杉山陽平 Yohei Sugiyama
CL. Non-commercial work
PT. Original

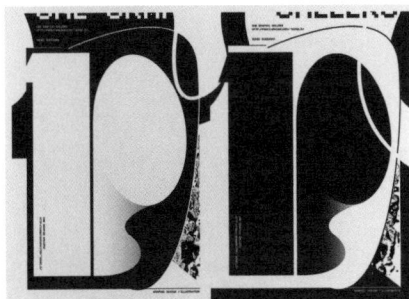
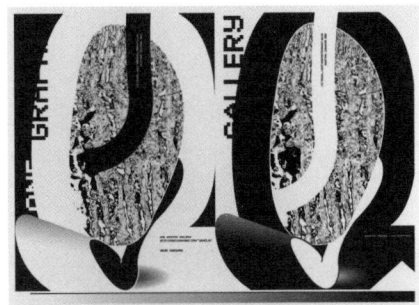
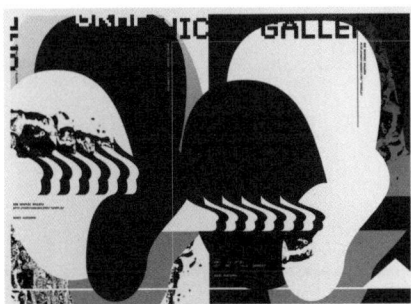
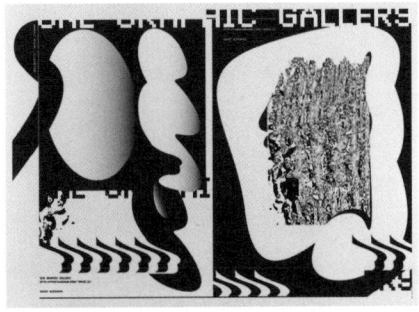
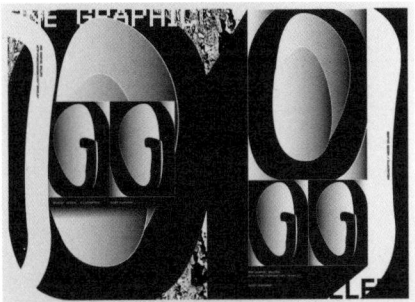
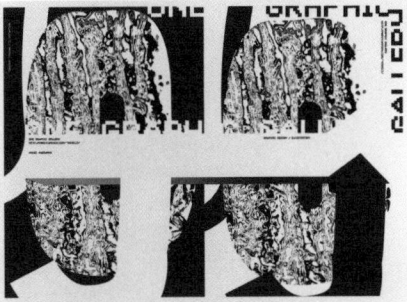

403 Book
TD. 杉園はるな Haruna Sugizono
CL. Non-commercial work

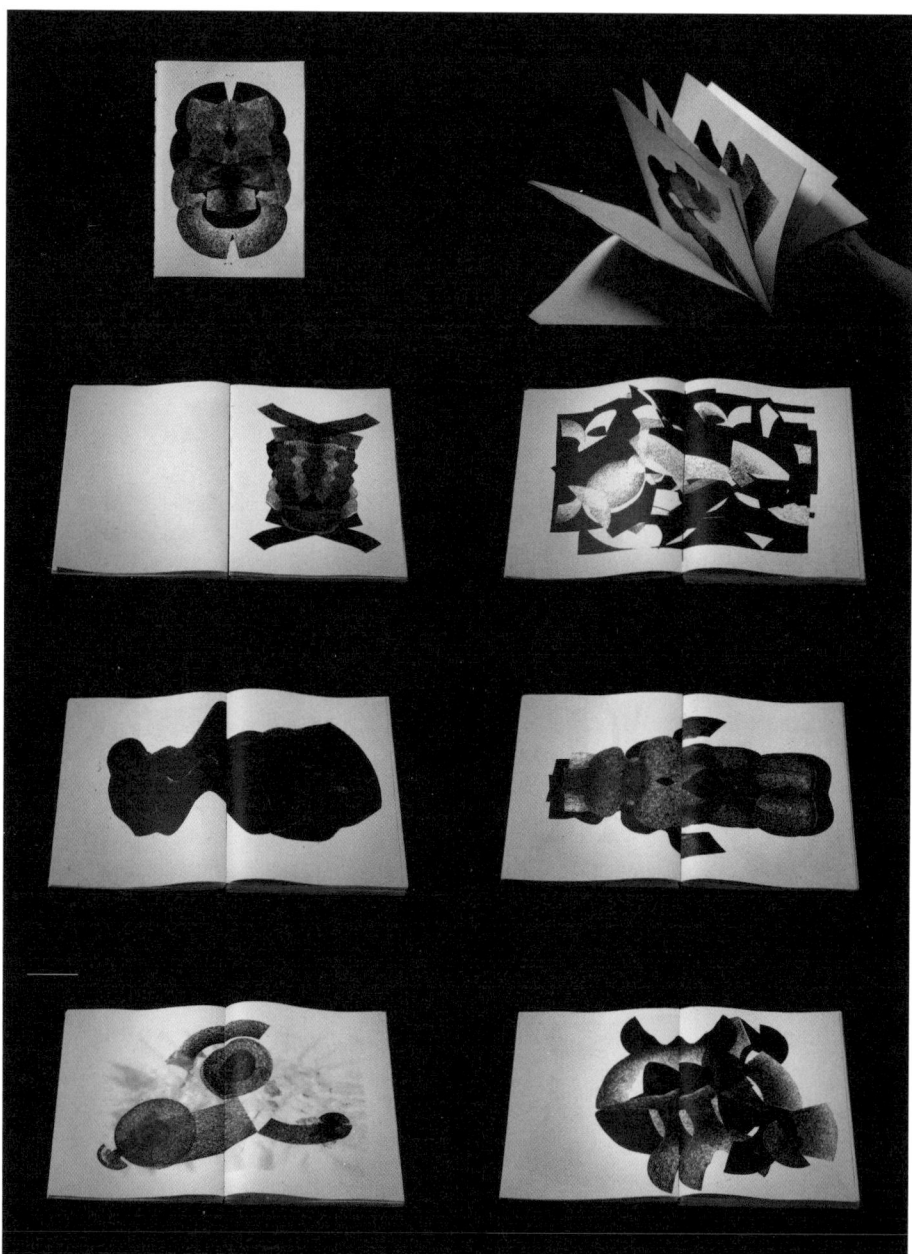

404 Postcard
TD. 助川誠 Makoto Sukegawa
D. 門野由華 Yuka Kadono
CL. 大日本印刷（株）Dai Nippon Printing Co., Ltd.

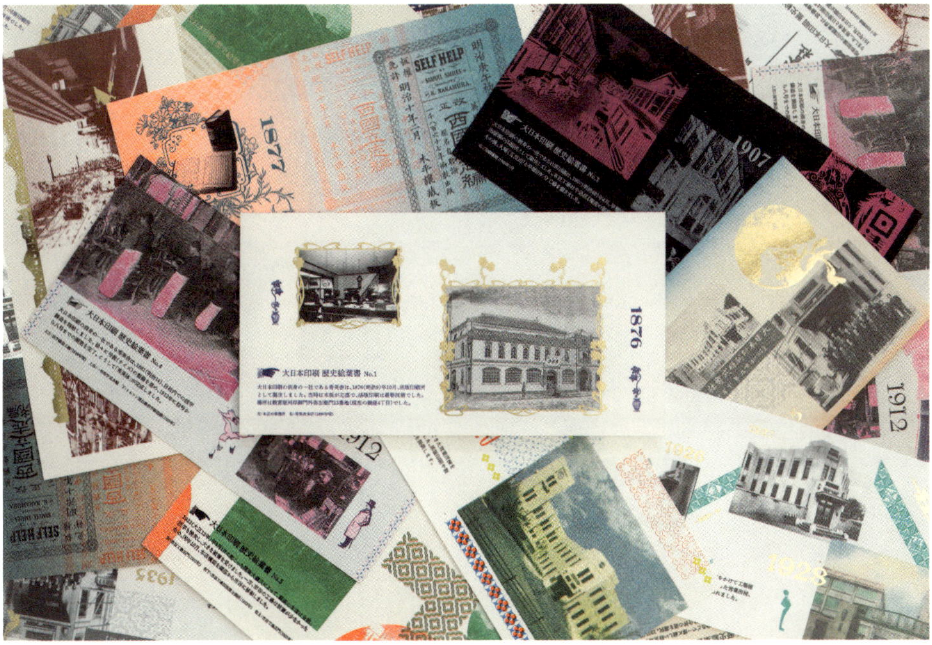

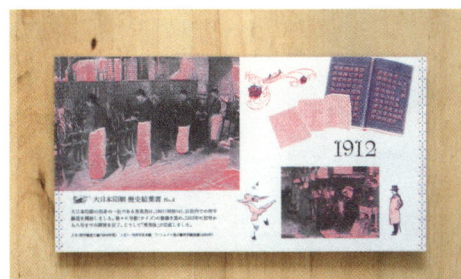
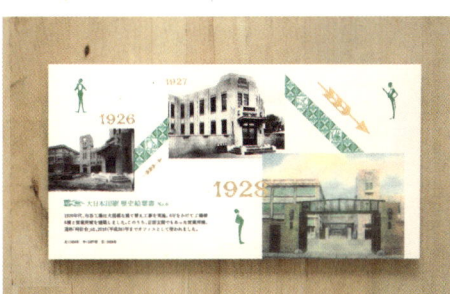
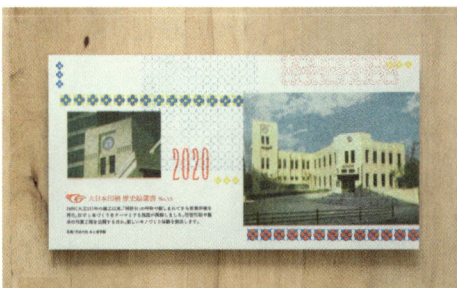
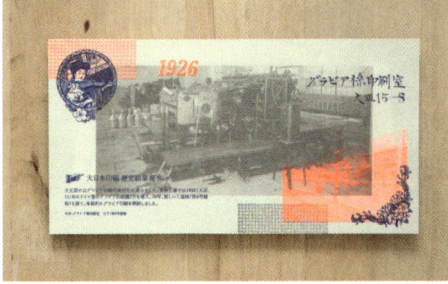

Prize Nominee Work

405 Editorial
TD. 助川誠 Makoto Sukagawa
P. 上野則宏 Norihiro Ueno
CL. (一社) 日本機械学会 Japan Society of Mechanical Engineers
PT. Axis Compressed ProN L

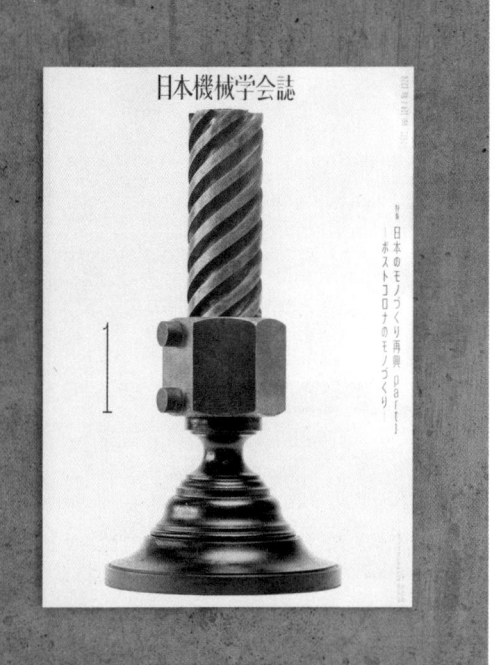
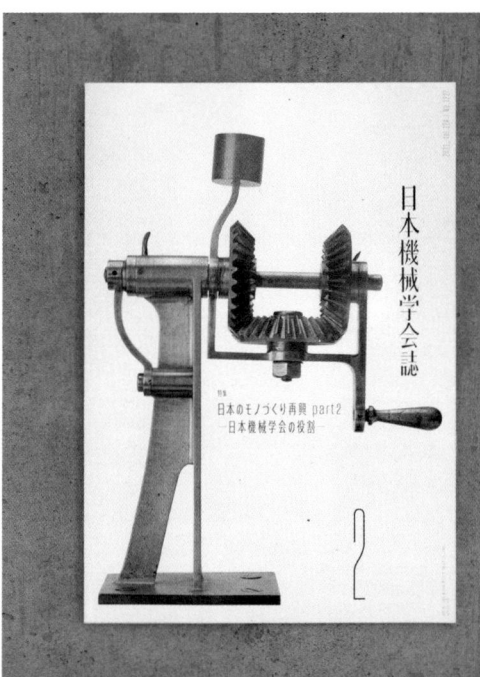
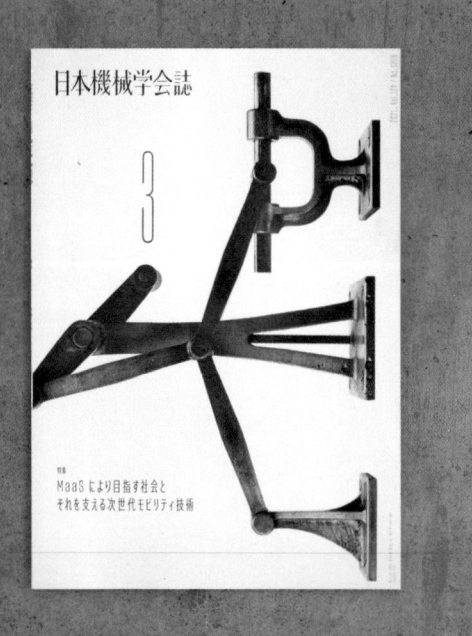
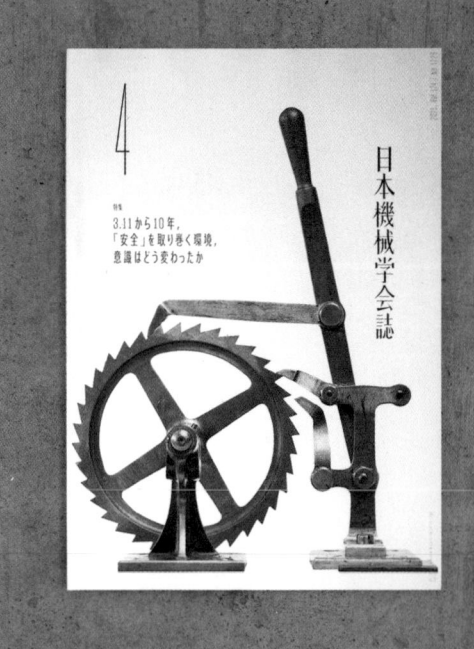

406 Exhibition poster
TD. D. Dawang Sun
AD. Hui Pan
P. Fei Wei
CL. Tongji University
PT. CooperHewitt-Bold

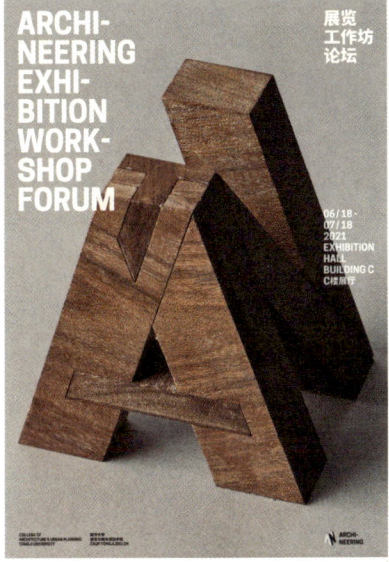
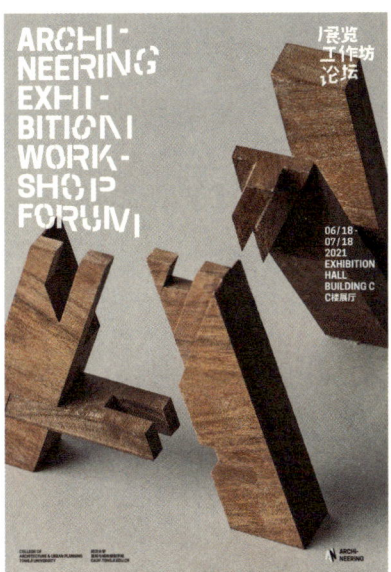

406

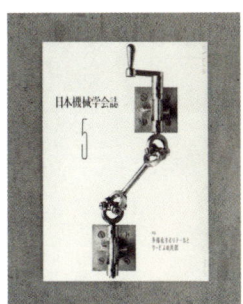
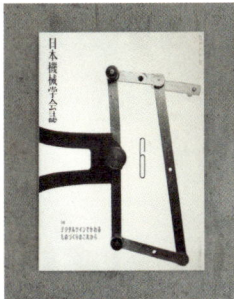
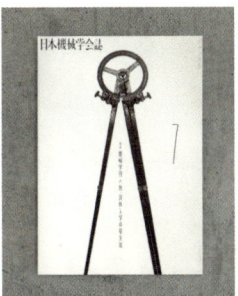
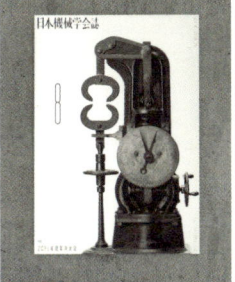

408 Exhibition graphics
TD. D. Dawang Sun
AD. Hui Pan
P. May Meng
CL. May Art Foundation
PT. Display Dots

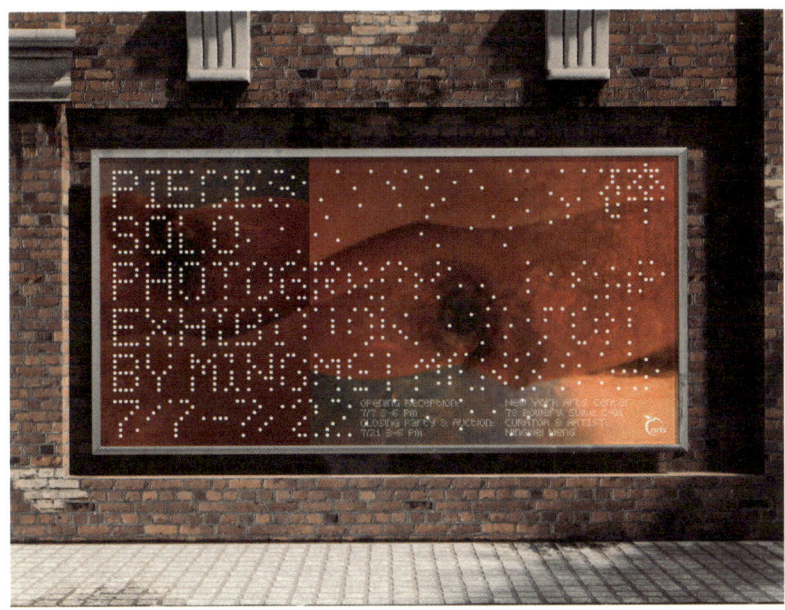

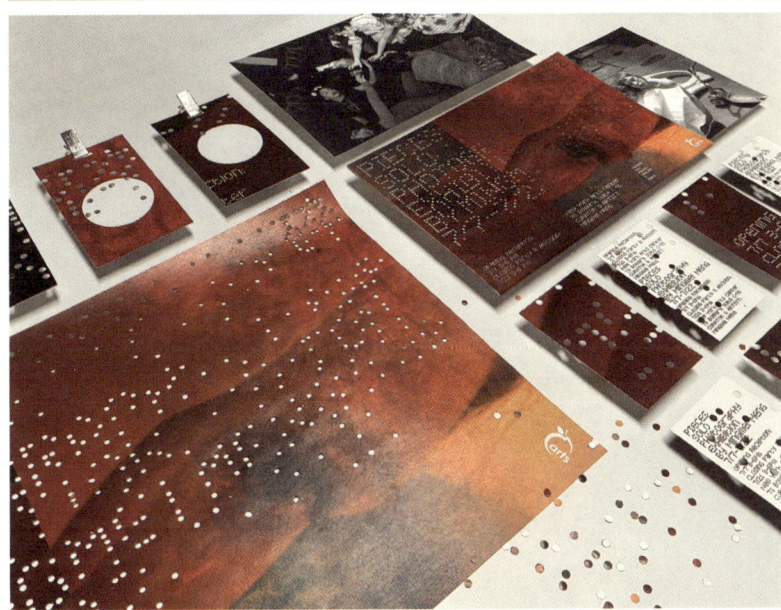

Prize Nominee Work

409 Poster
TD. Sun Jianyu
CL. Individual

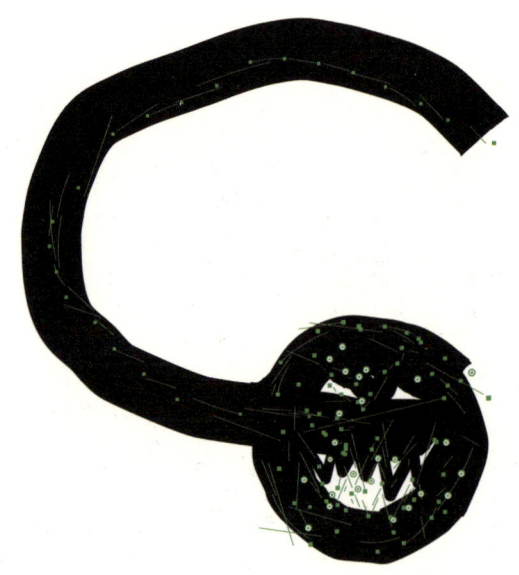

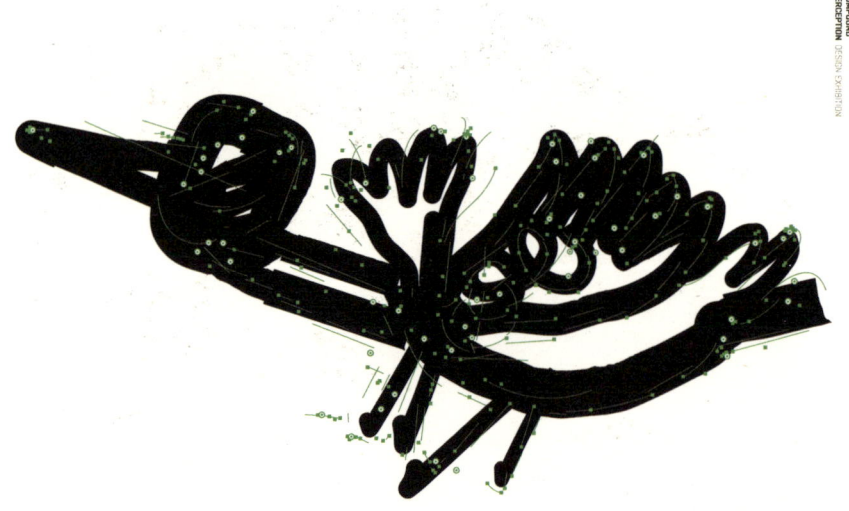

410 Exhibition Identity
TD. Sun Jianyu
CL. Canton Fair

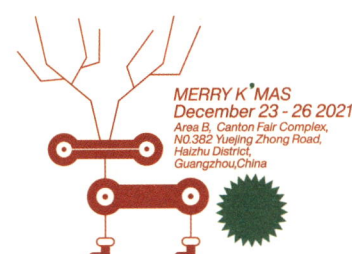

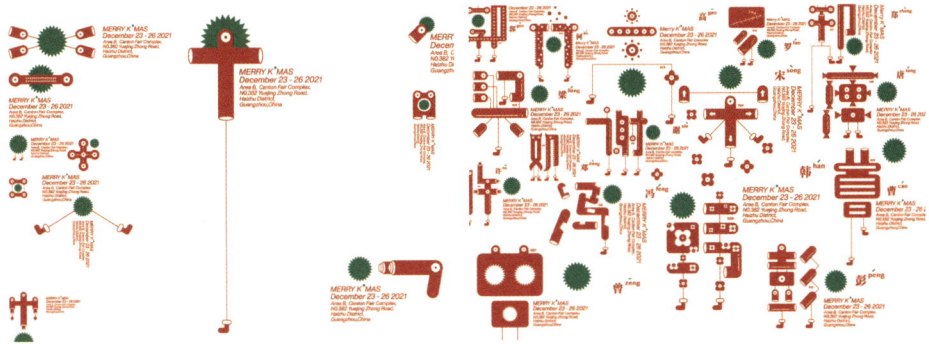

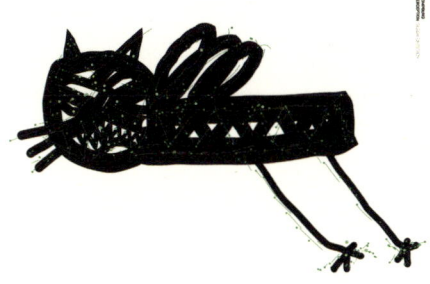

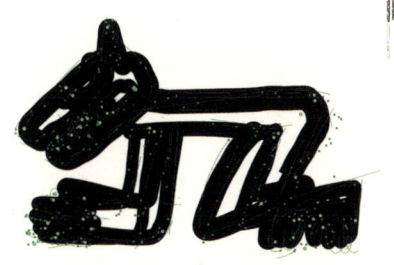

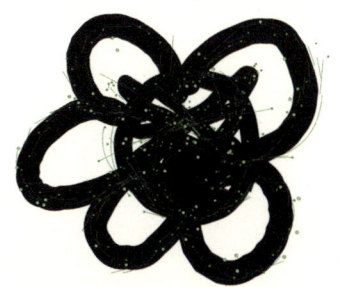

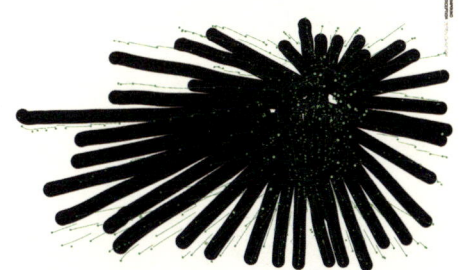

411 Branding
TD. 鈴木聡史 Satoshi Suzuki
PL. 黒田天兵 Tenpei Kuroda
CD. 古田啓祐 Keisuke Furuta
PR. 應本幸紀 Koki Omoto
AD. 名古屋豊 Yutaka Nagoya
D. 近藤海空 Misora Kondo, 篠原美由 Miyu Shinohara
CL. 三井物産（株）Mitsui & Co., Ltd.
PT. Avenir Next, 游ゴシック

412 Image visual
TD. 田部井美奈 Mina Tabei
P. 小川真輝 Masaki Ogawa
CL. 武蔵野美術大学 Musashino Art University
PT. Suisse Int'l Light

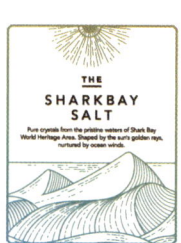
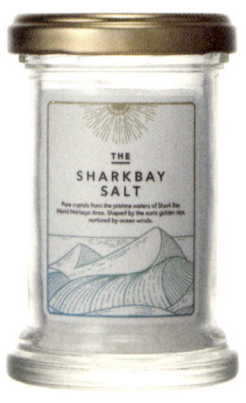

411

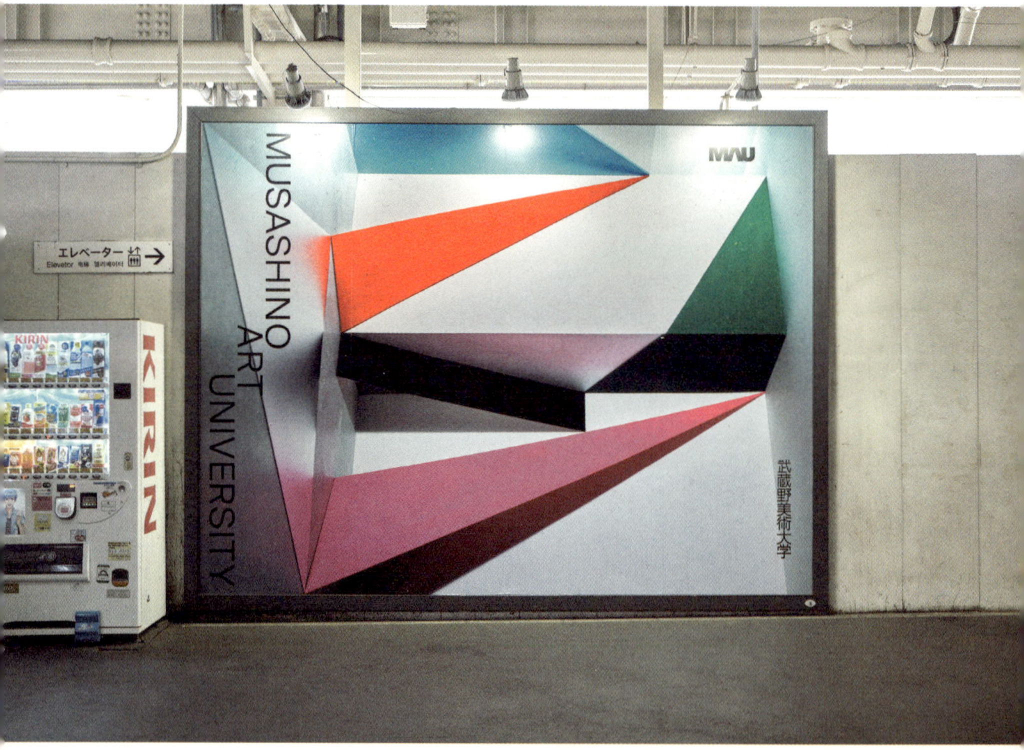

412

413 Poster
TD. 田部井美奈 Mina Tabei
P. 小川真輝 Masaki Ogawa
CL. 武蔵野美術大学 Musashino Art University
PT. Suisse Int'l Light

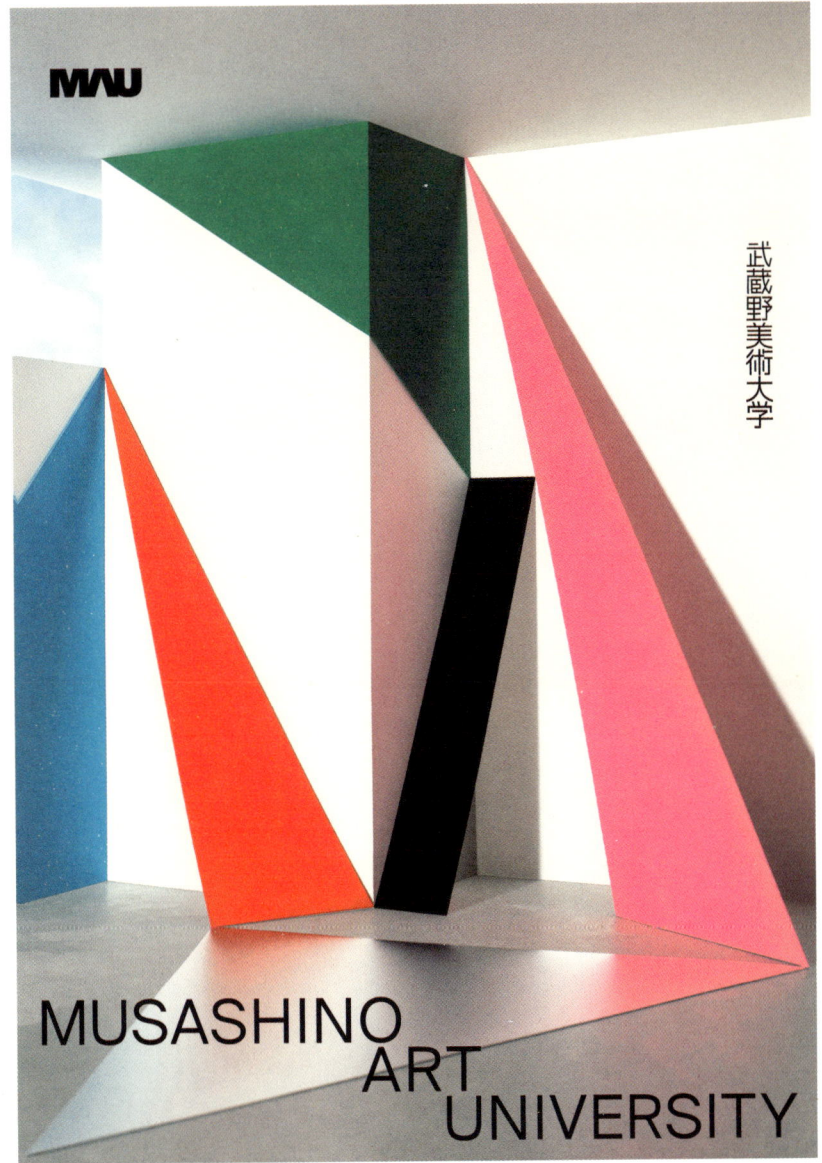

414 Mark & Logo
TD. 髙田唯 Yui Takada
D. 齋藤拓実 Takumi Saito
DCO. 髙田舞 Mai Takada
I. Akina Haga
CL. フェスティバル/トーキョー Festival/Tokyo

415 Motion graphics
TD. 髙田唯 Yui Takada
AW. Wenliang.C
MG. Wang Ruiyu
CL. Picnic Art Festival

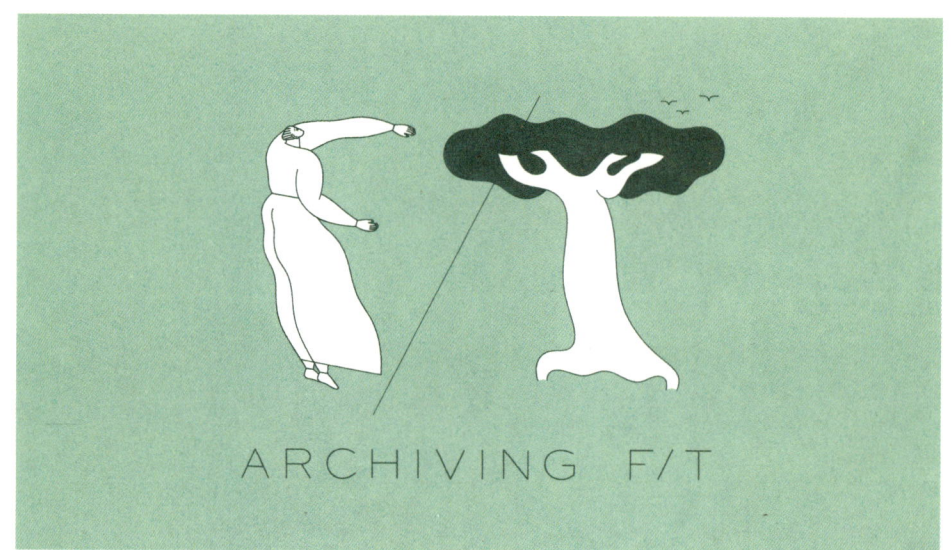

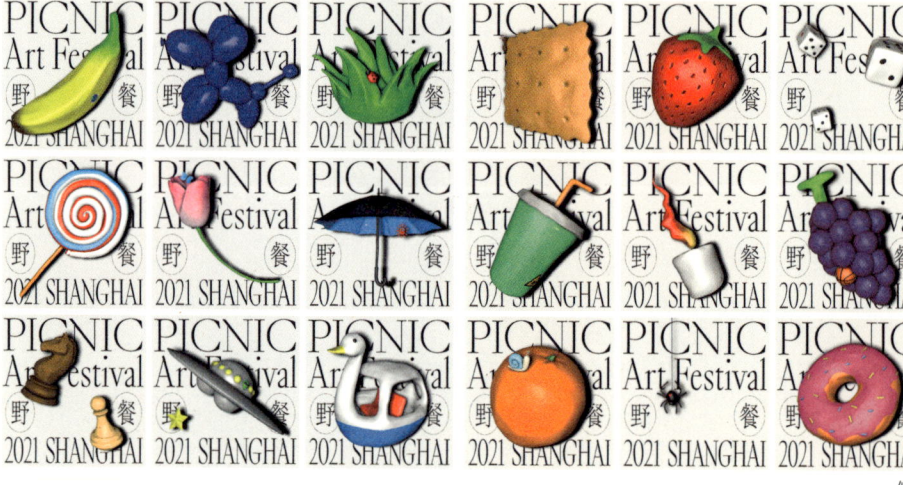

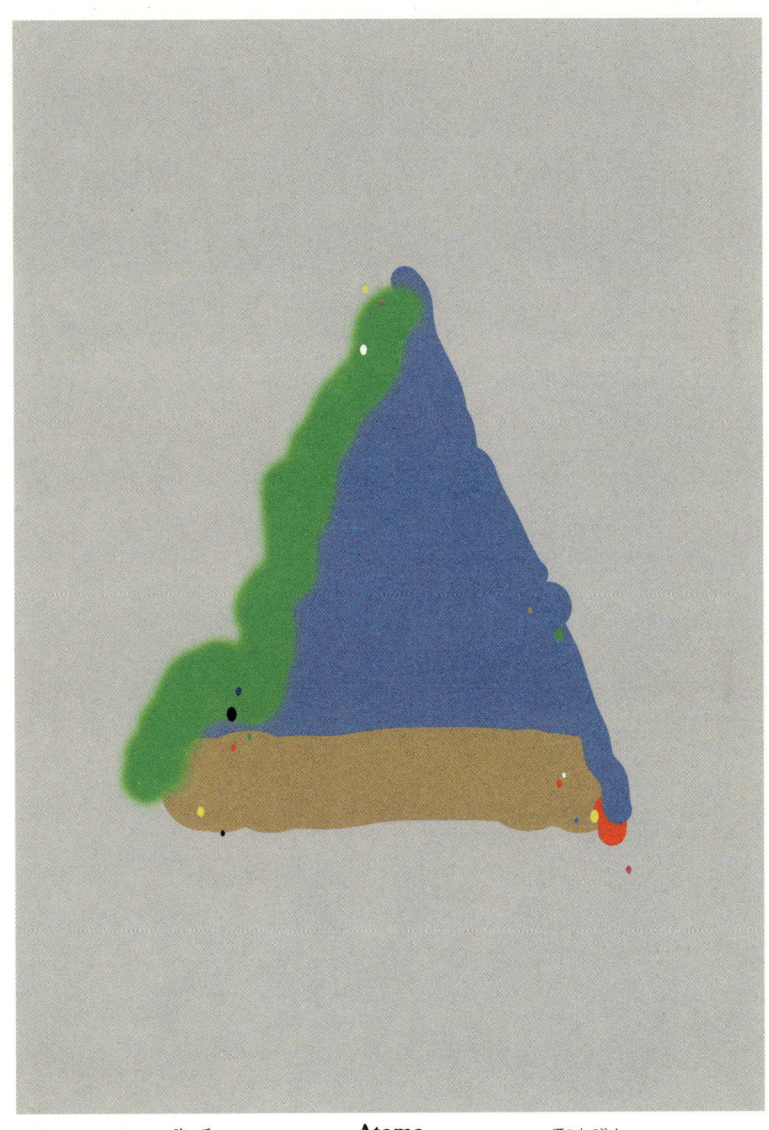

417 Key visual
TD. 竹林一茂 Kazushige Takebayashi, 伊佐奈月 Natsuki Isa, 渡邊晃己 Kohki Watanabe
TD. PRG. 北千住デザイン Kitasenju Design
CL. FabCafe
https://kitasenjudesign.com/youfab/

418 Advertising
TD. AD. 瀧澤章太郎 Shotaro Takizawa
CD. 関遼 Ryo Seki
D. 浅岡敬太 Keita Asaoka
CA. 下村奈那 Nana Shimomura
CL. (株)四国新聞社 The Shikoku Shimbun

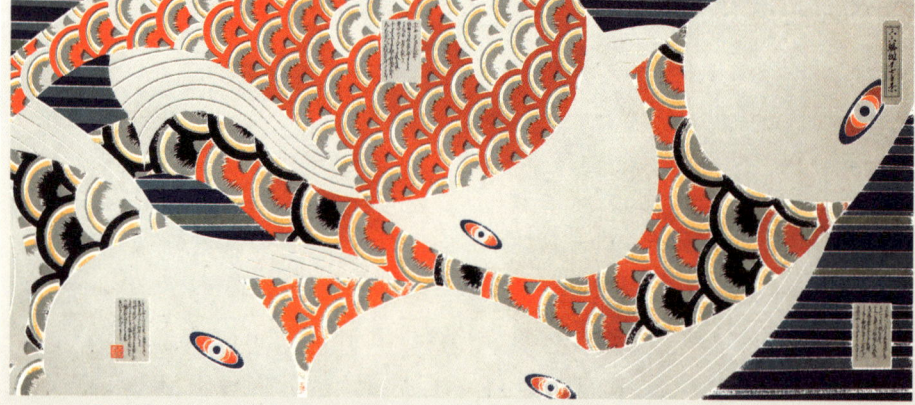

419 Packaging
TD. AD. 田中せり Seri Tanaka
P. Masaya Yoshimura, Copist (shop), 藤川直矢 Naoya Fujikawa (package)
CL.（株）イッセイ ミヤケ Issey Miyake Inc.
PT. Helvetica

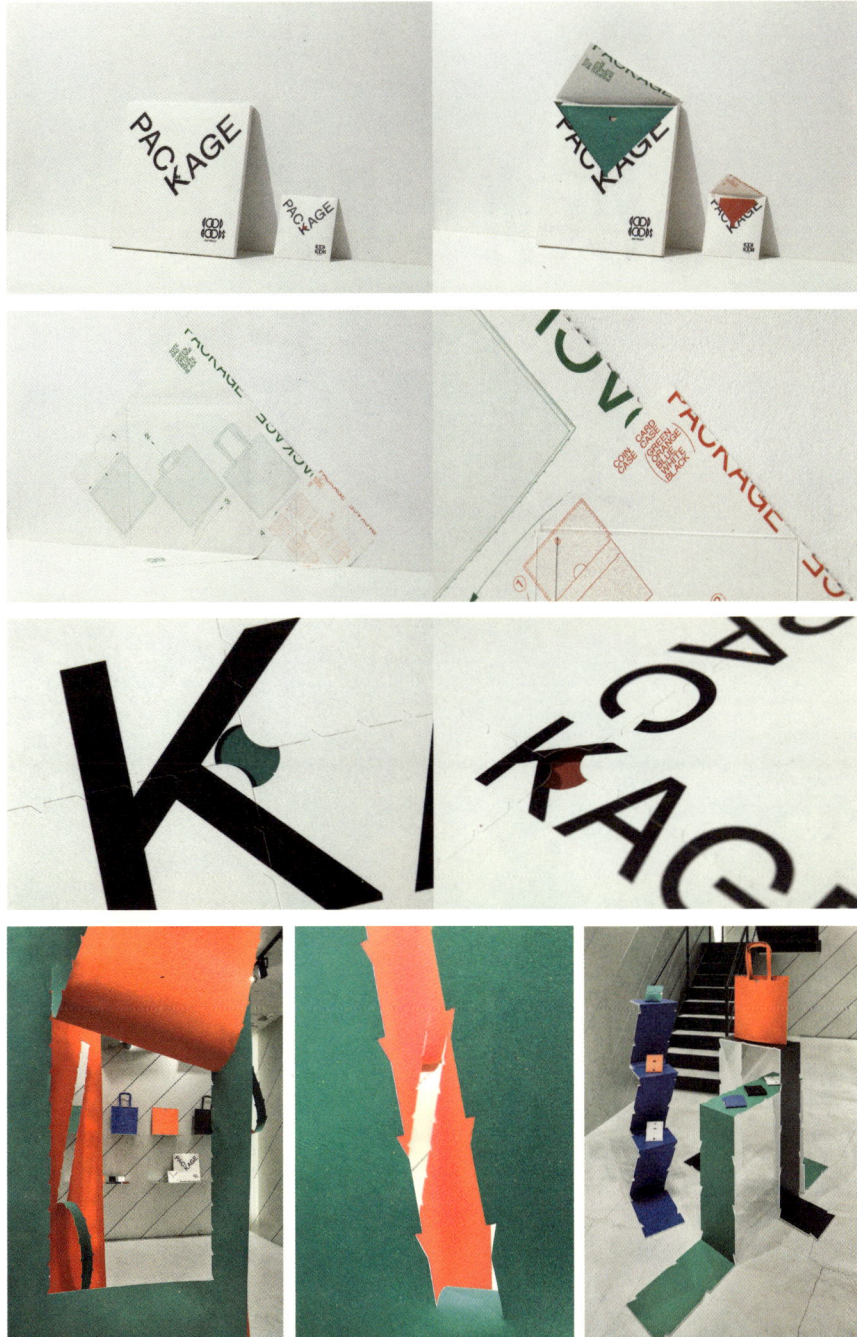

420 Motion logo
TD. AD. 田中せり Seri Tanaka
P. 後藤武浩 Takehiro Goto
CL. 蓮沼執太フィル Shuta Hasunuma Philharmonic Orchestra
PT. 秀英初号明朝, Arial Rounded MT

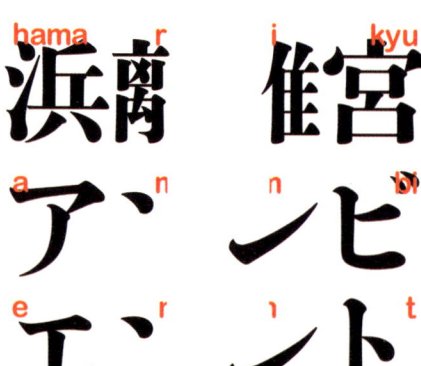

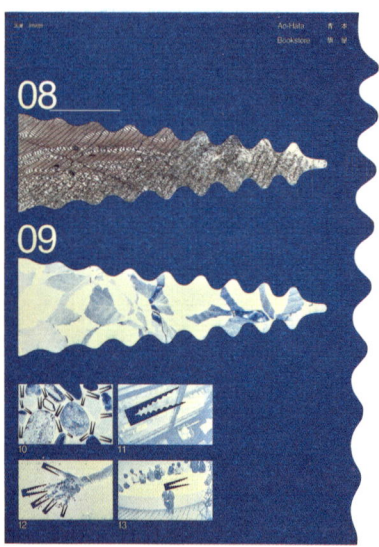

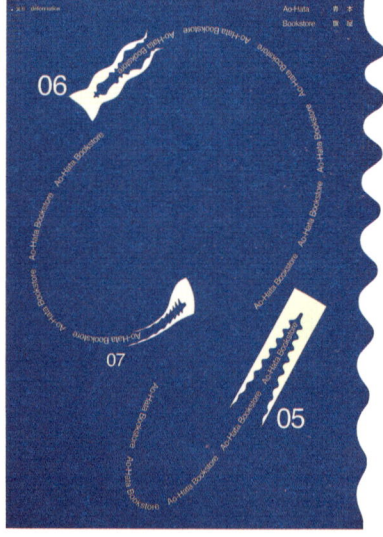

421 Poster
TD. AD. P. 田中せり Seri Tanaka
CL. 本屋青旗 Ao-Hata Bookstore
PT. Helvetica, 游ゴシック

422 Poster
TD. 田中良治 Ryoji Tanaka
CL. クリエイションギャラリー G8 Creation Gallery G8,
（公社）日本グラフィックデザイナー協会 Japan Graphic Design Association Inc.
PT. 筑紫明朝体, Editorial New

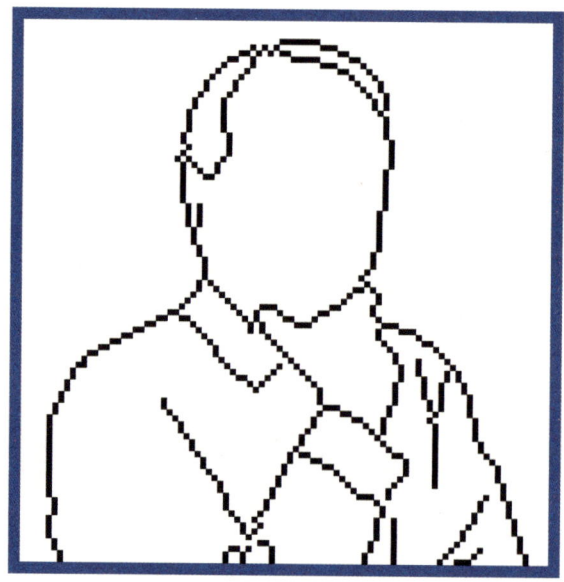
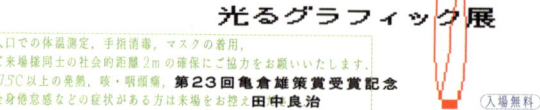
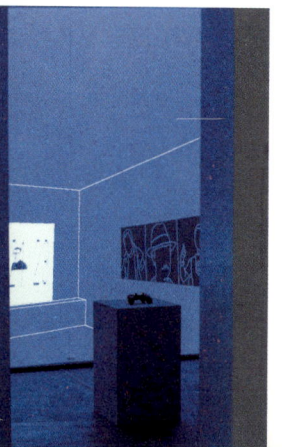
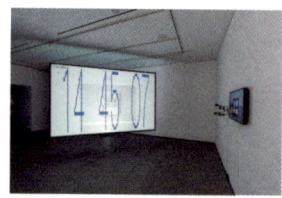
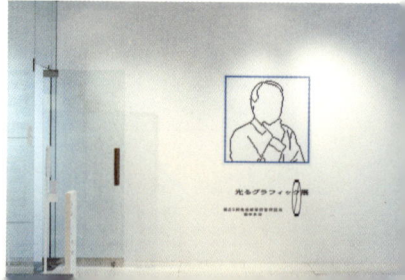

Prize Nominee Work

423 Exhibition
TD. 田中良治 Ryoji Tanaka
PRG. 郡司和也 Kazuya Gunji
CL. クリエイションギャラリー G8 Creation Gallery G8,
（公社）日本グラフィックデザイン協会 Japan Graphic Design Association Inc.
PT. 筑紫明朝体, Editorial New

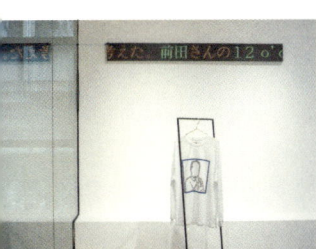
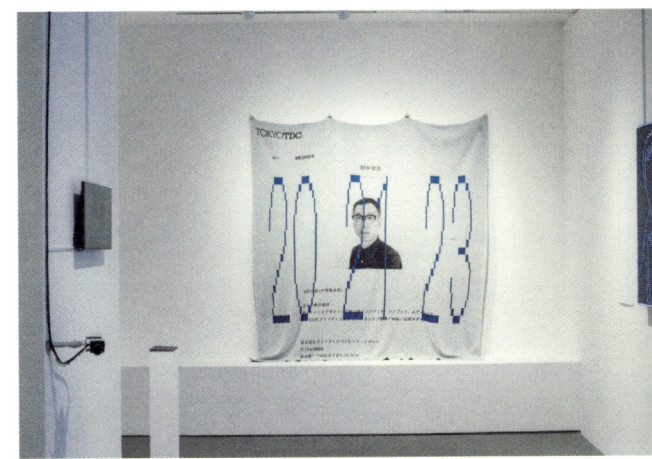
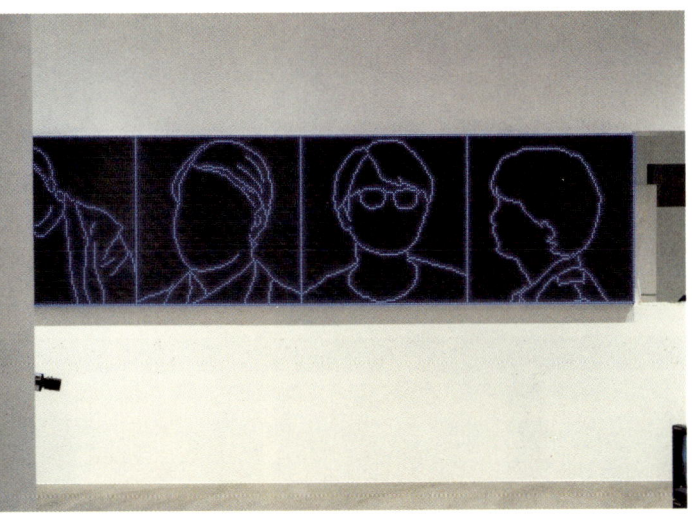
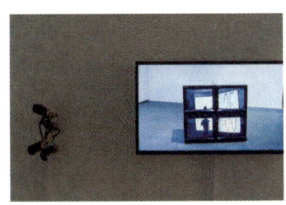

423

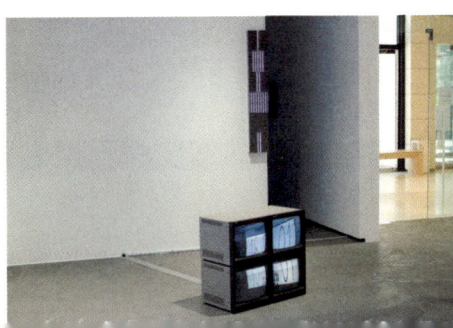

424 Type design
TD. Andrea Tartarelli
CL. Zetafonts

425 Pamphlet
TD. AD. D. Antonia Terhedebrügge, Silvia Terhedebrügge
CL. Künstlerhaus Stuttgart, Eric Golo Stone
PT. Monument Grotesk-Medium, Ultra,
ABC Dinamo Chapter-Bold, Good Type Foundry

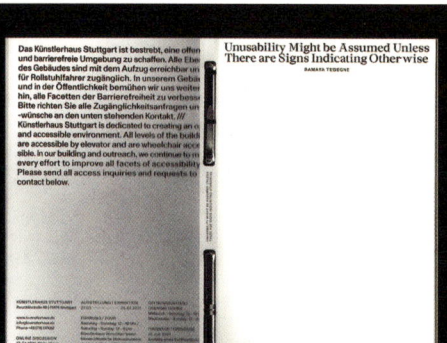

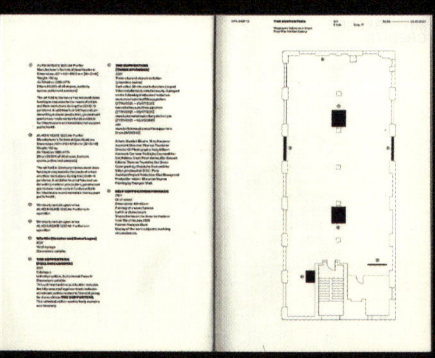

426 Book
TD. AD. D. 田代祐美子 Yumiko Tashiro
CL. Non-commercial work
PT. Custom-made for the project

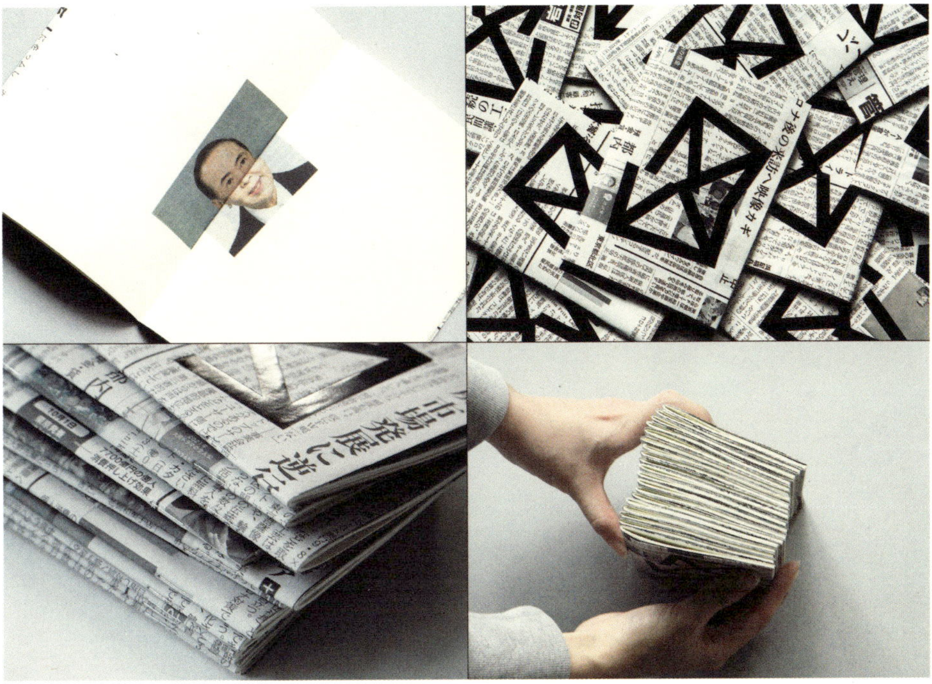

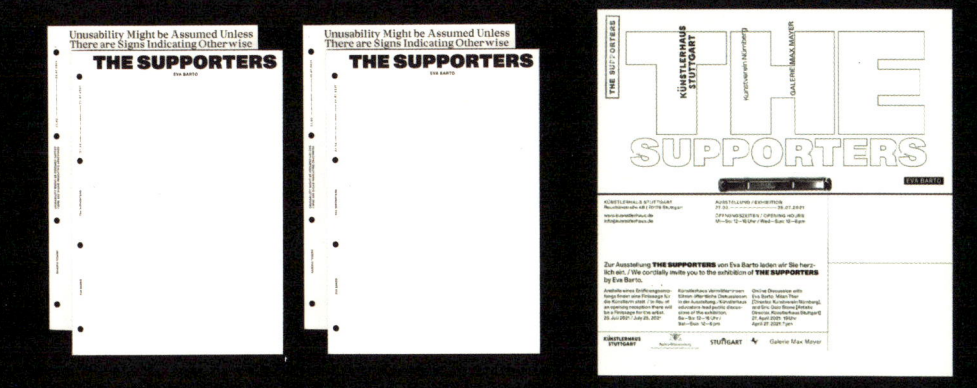

TD. AD. D. Tian Bo
CL. Guangzhou Academy of Fine Arts
PT. Hanyi Qihei, Resist Sans Text

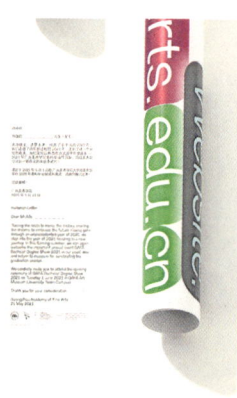
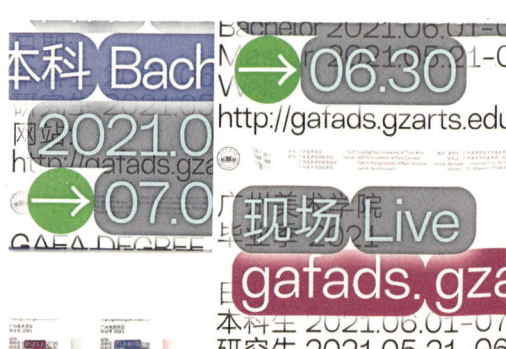
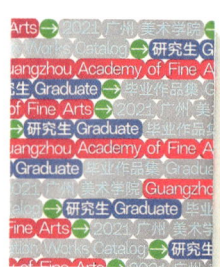
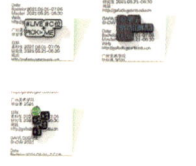
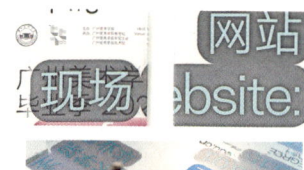
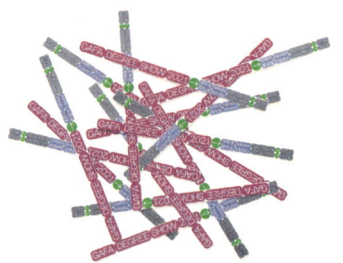
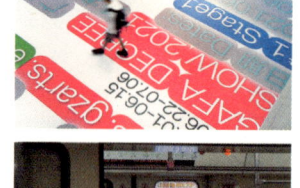
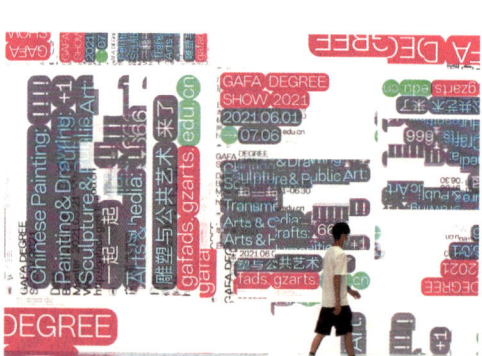
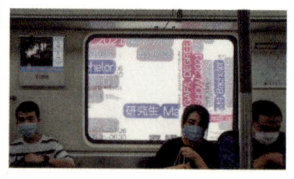
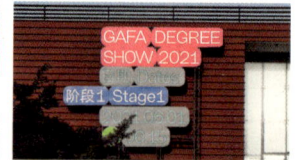

428 Mark & Logo
TD. AD. D. 藤堂智子 Tomoko Todo
CL. 東京しゃも生産組合 Tokyo Shamo Poultry Farmers Union
PT. Sabon, Garamond, Custom-made for the project

429 Book
TD. AD. D. Tsai Chia-Hao
CL. New Rain Publishing
PT. Custom-made for the project, Century Gothic

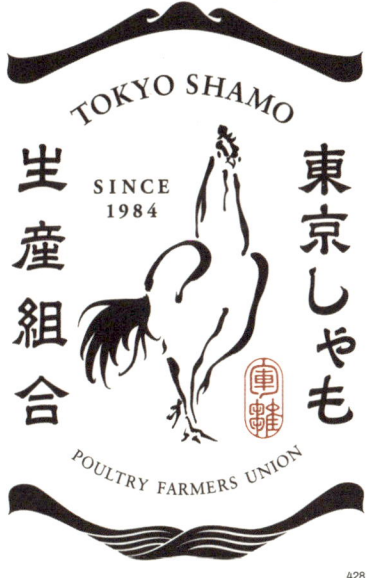

428

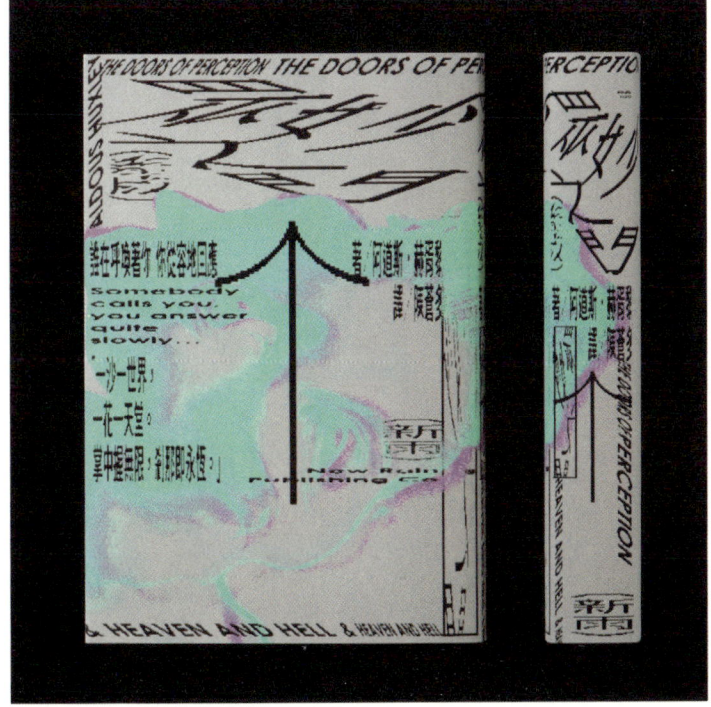

429

Prize Nominee Work

430 Book
TD. AD. E. 富田光浩 Mitsuhiro Tomita
I. E. 牧野伊三夫 Isao Makino
E. 佐野由佳 Yuka Sano, 瀬戸山玄 Fukashi Setoyama, 髙橋亜弥子 Ayako Takahashi
CL. 飛騨産業(株) Hida Sangyo Co., Ltd.
PT. 岩田明朝オールド

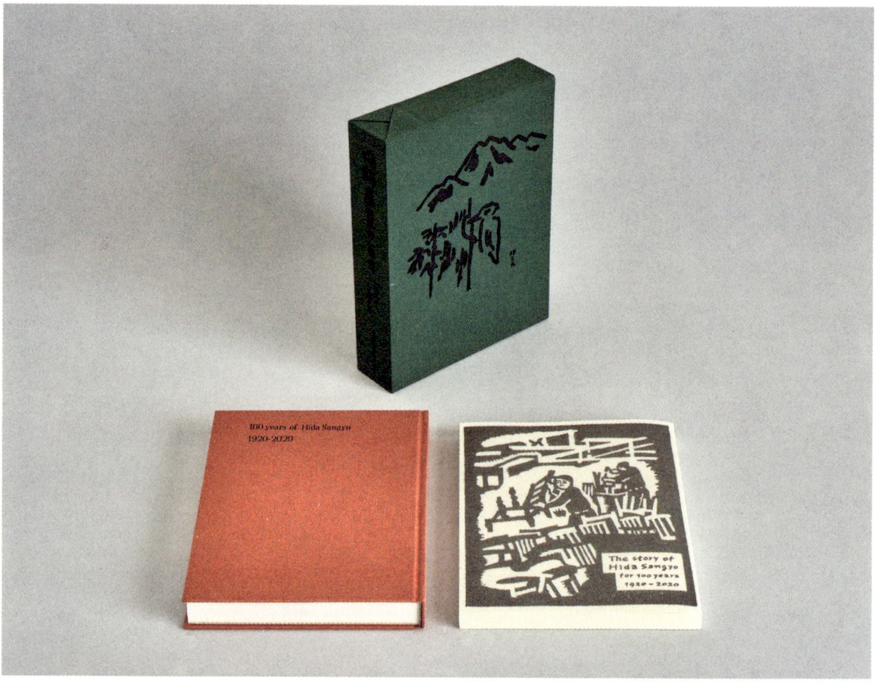

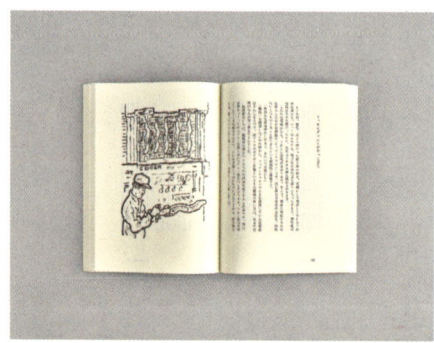
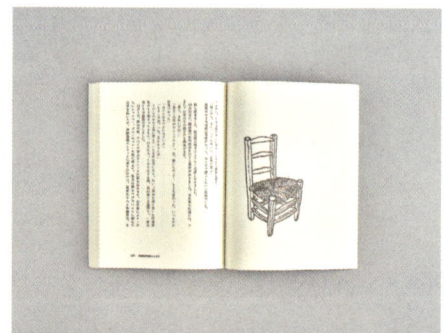
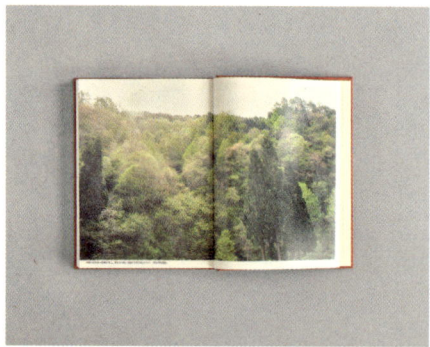
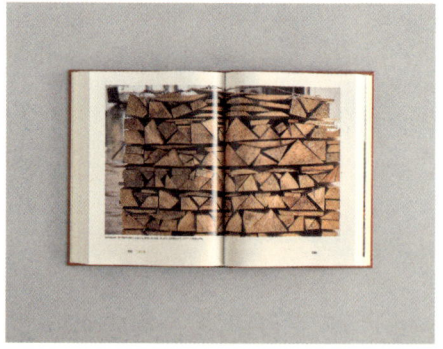

Prize Nominee Work

431 Poster
TD. AD. D. Tsai Chia-Hao
CL. Non-commercial work
PT. Custom-made for the project, Century Gothic

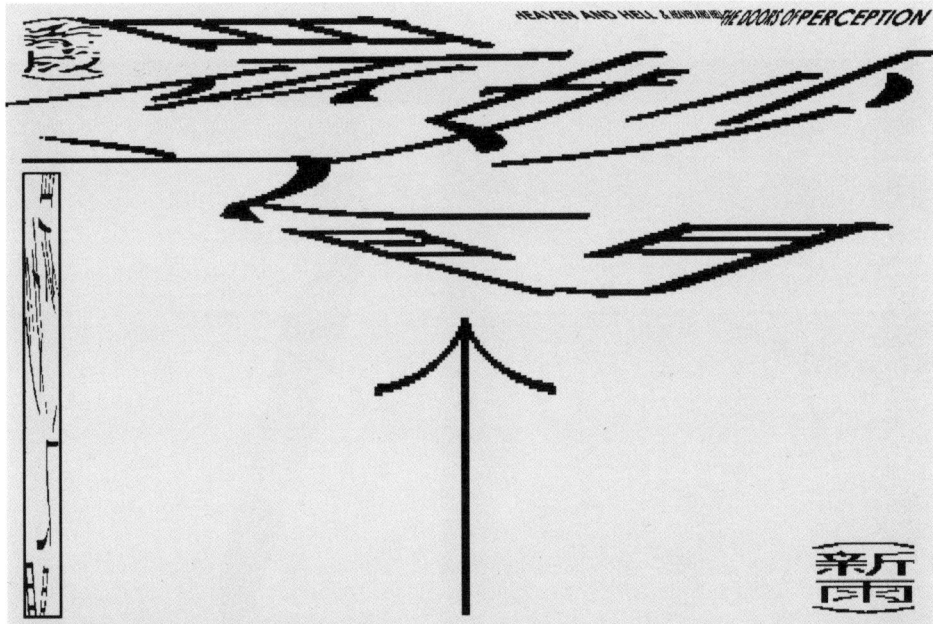

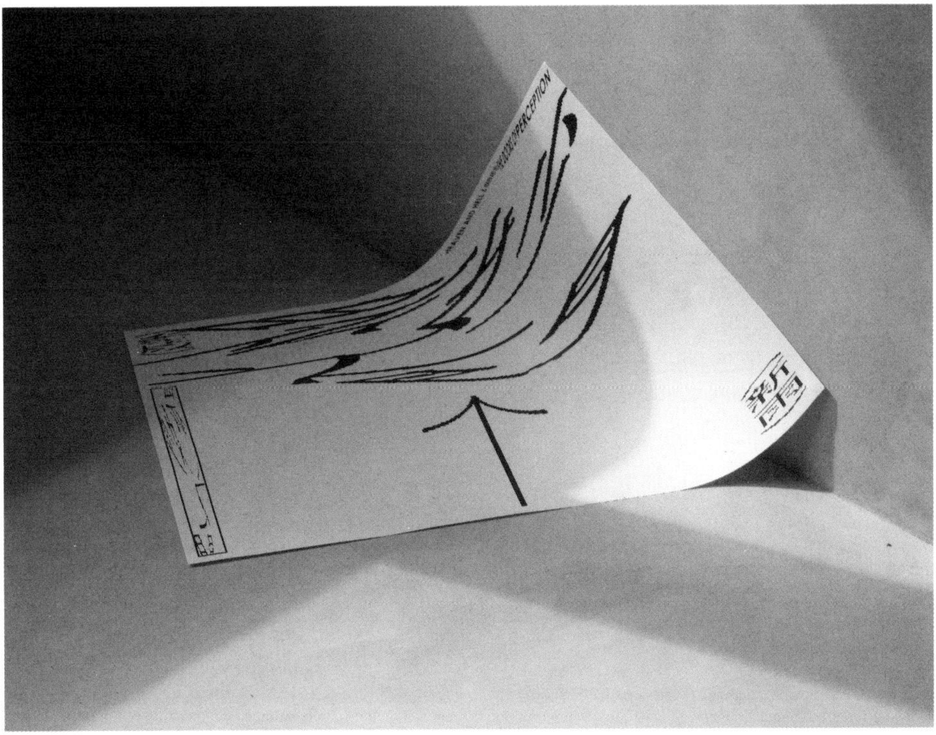

432 Small graphics
TD. AD. D. 鶴沢咲子 Sakiko Tsurusawa
CL. Non-commercial work
PT. Custom-made for the project

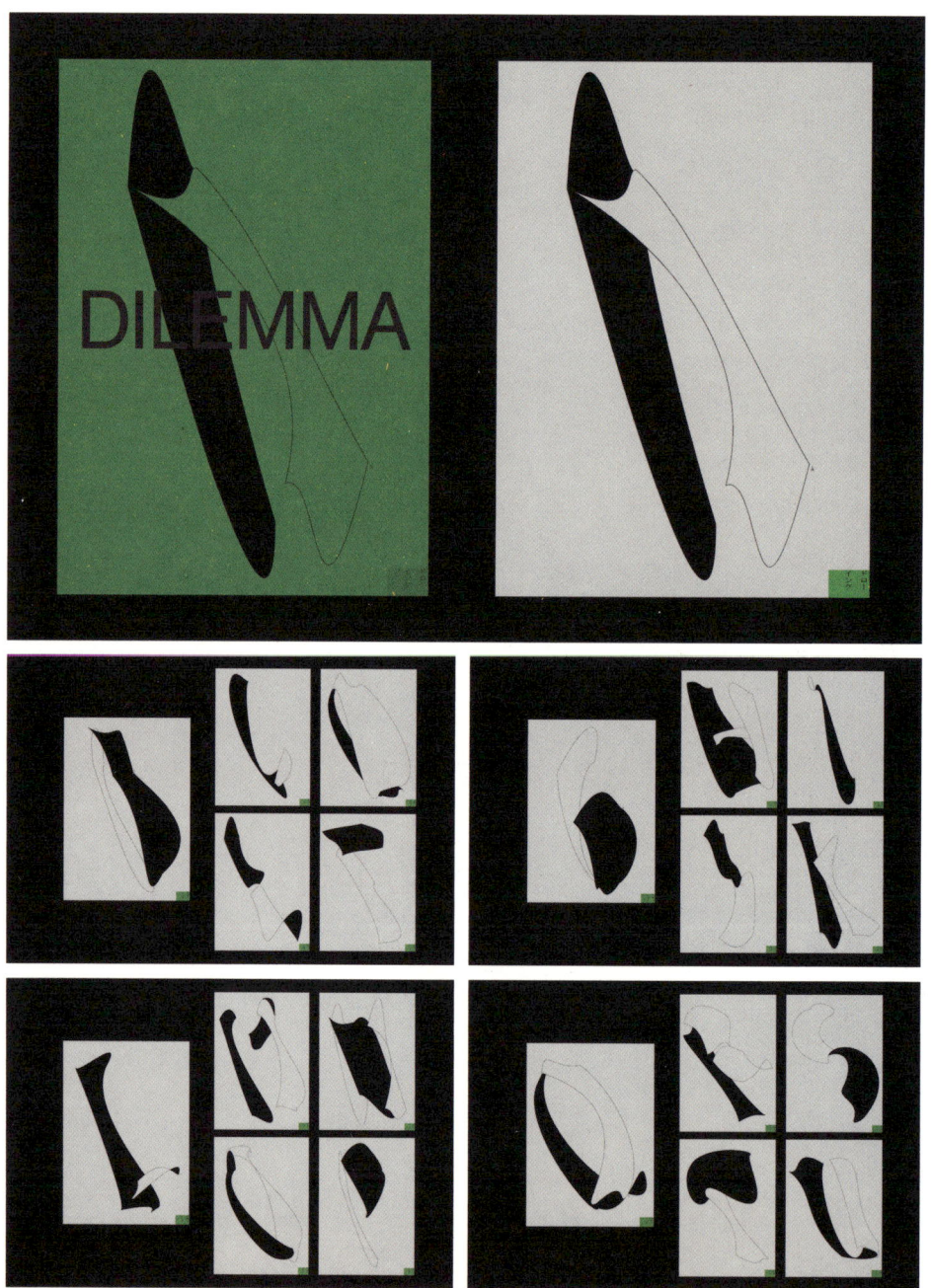

433 Competition tool
TD. CD. AD. 植原亮輔 Ryosuke Uehara
CD. 渡邊良重 Yoshie Watanabe
D. 前田怜右馬 Ryoma Maeda, 森本麻友 Mayu Morimoto
P. 小野慶輔 Keisuke Ono
CL. コクヨ(株) Kokuyo Co., Ltd.
PT. Helvetica Neue, Custom-made for the project

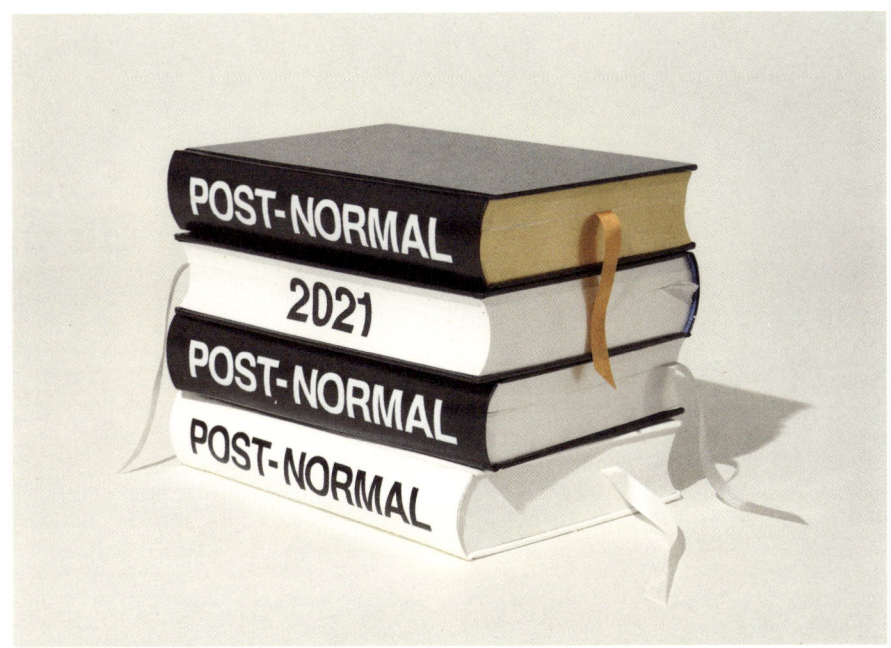

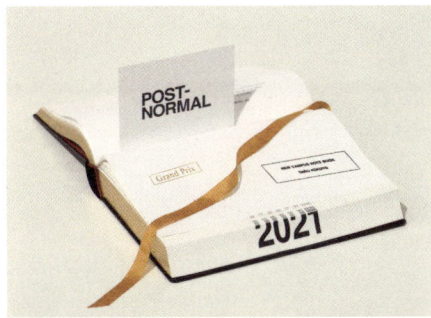

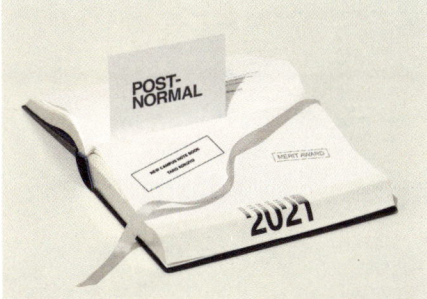

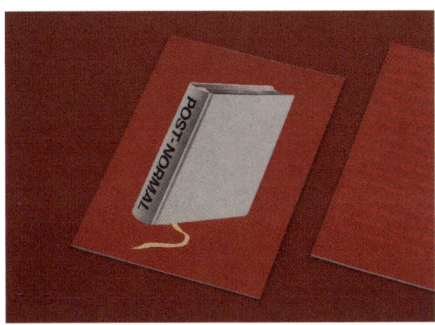

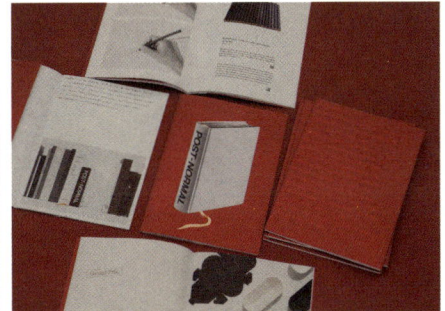

434 Packaging
TD. AD. 植原亮輔 Ryosuke Uehara
D. サリーン・チェン Sarene Chan
CL. Our Favorite Shop
PT. 毎日新聞明朝

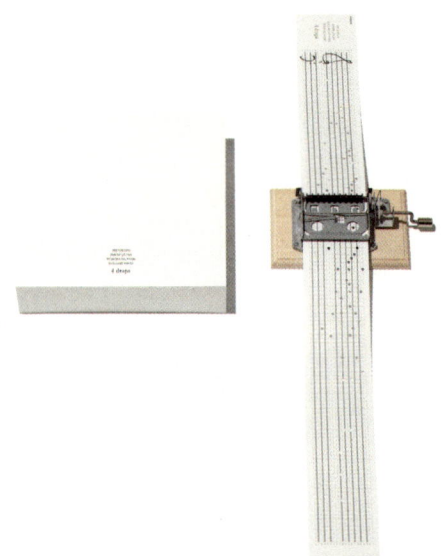

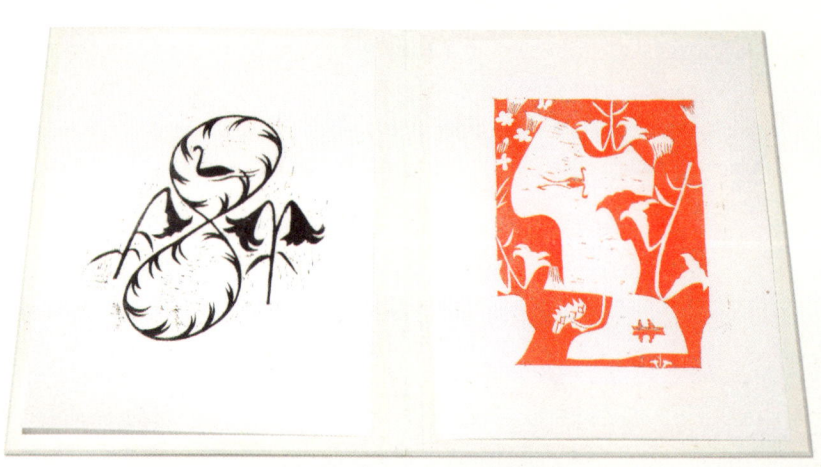

435 Booklet
TD. AD. 植原亮輔 Ryosuke Uehara
D. 森本麻友 Mayu Morimoto
CL. (公財)DNP文化振興財団 DNP Foundation for Cultural Promotion
PT. Logic MT, Custom-made for the project

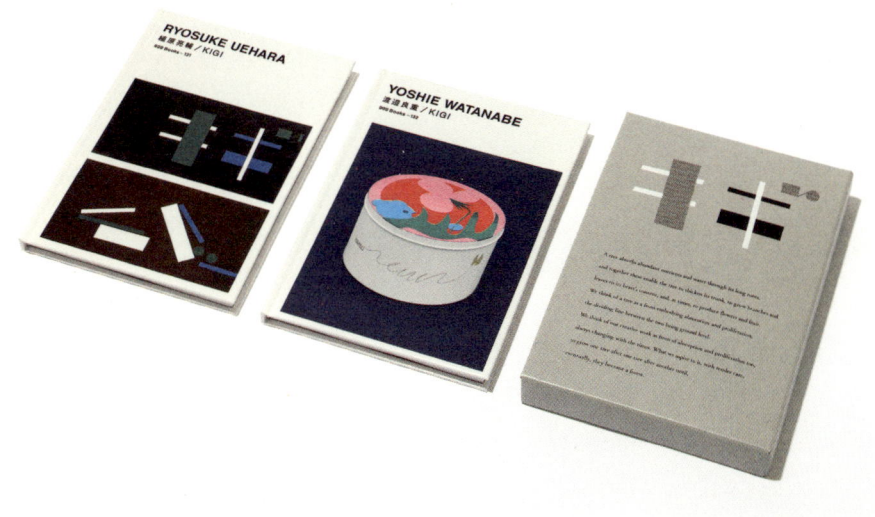

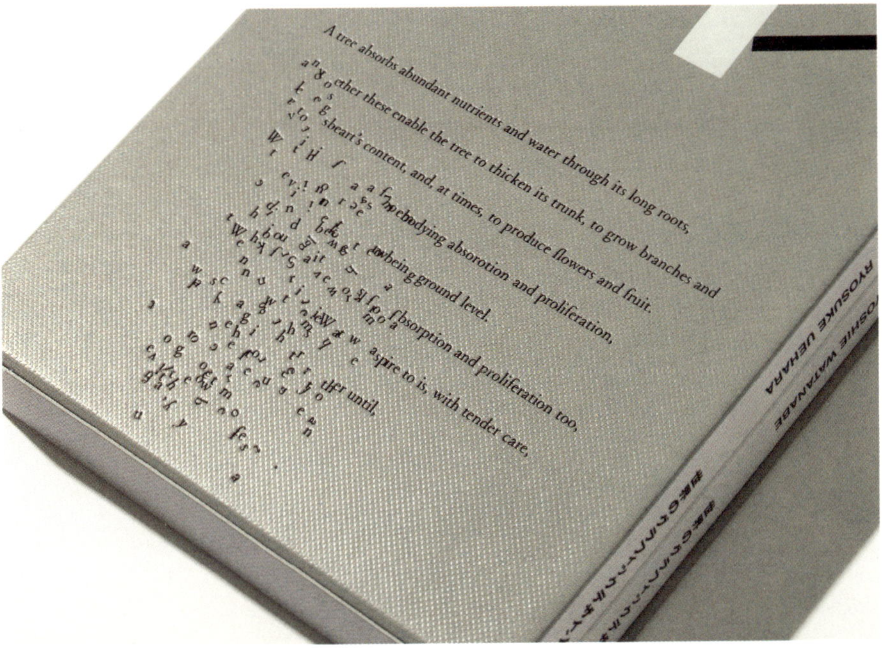

436 Calendar
TD. AD. 植原亮輔 Ryosuke Uehara
CD. 宮田識 Satoru Miyata
D. サリーン・チェン Sarene Chan
CL. ディーブロス D-Bros
PT. 筑紫B明朝, Custom-made for the project

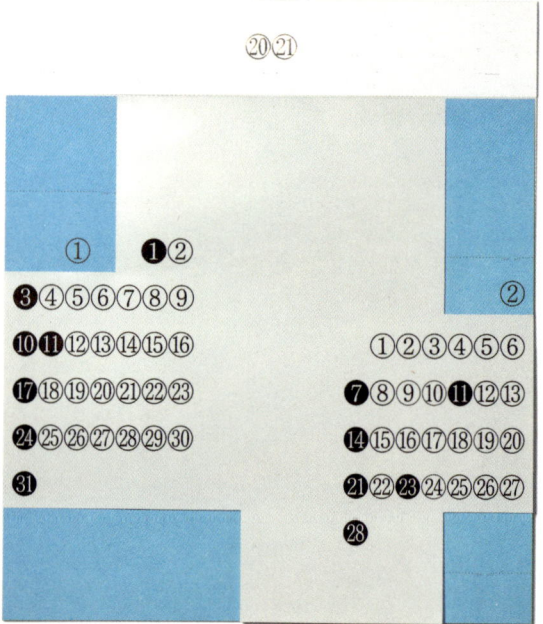

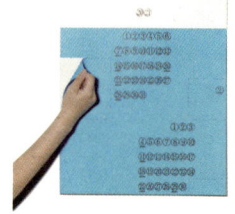
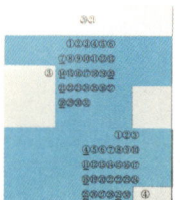
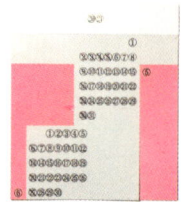
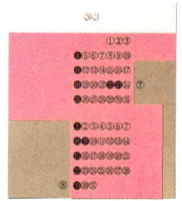

437 Record jacket, Goods
TD. CD. AD. 植原亮輔 Ryosuke Uehara
CD. I. 渡邊良重 Yoshie Watanabe
D. 齋藤春香 Haruka Saito, シケン・ゲン Siken Gen
CL. Theatre Musica
PT. Baskerville, Snell Roundhand, Bosque

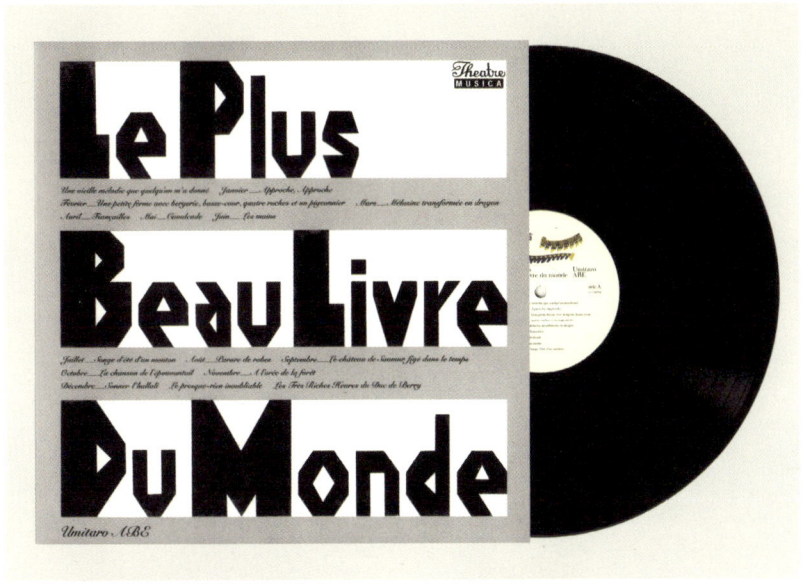

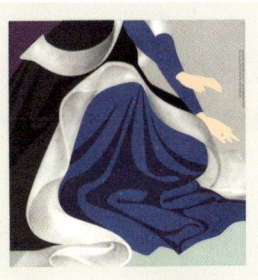

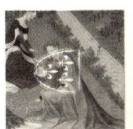
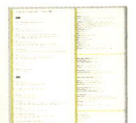
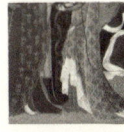

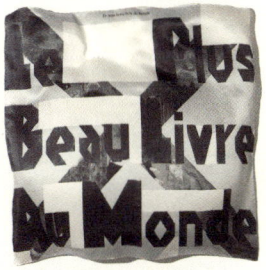
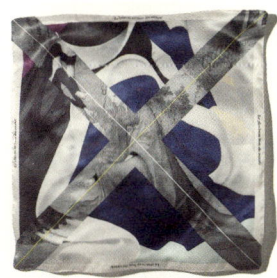

Prize Nominee Work

438 Products, Packaging
TD. CD. AD. 植原亮輔 Ryosuke Uehara
TD. AD. 渡邊良重 Yoshie Watanabe
D. サリーン・チェン Sarene Chan
CL. Kikof
PT. Custom-made for the project

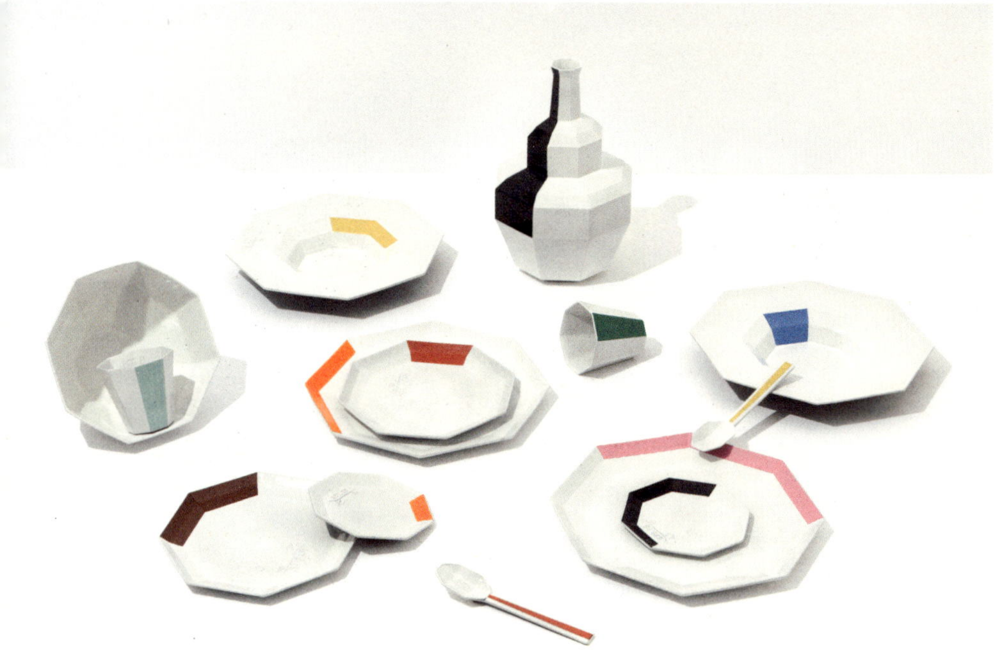

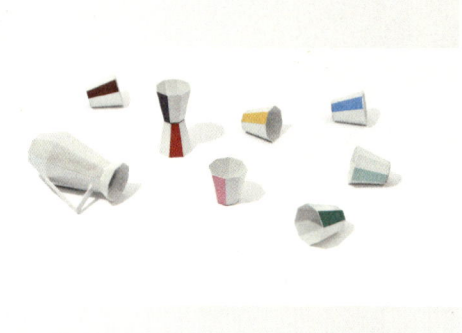
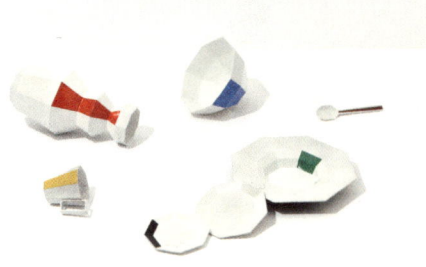
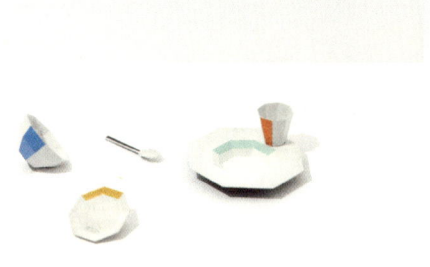
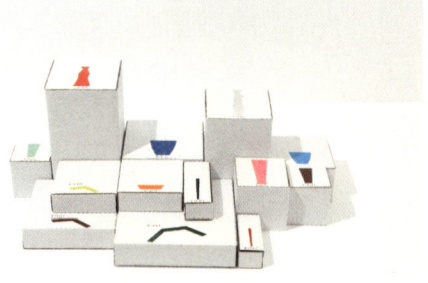

439 Poster
TD. CD. AD. 植原亮輔 Ryosuke Uehara
TD. AD. 渡邊良重 Yoshie Watanabe
D. サリーン・チェン Sarene Chan
P. 小野慶輔 Keisuke Ono
CL. Kikof
PT. Apercu, Custom-made for the project

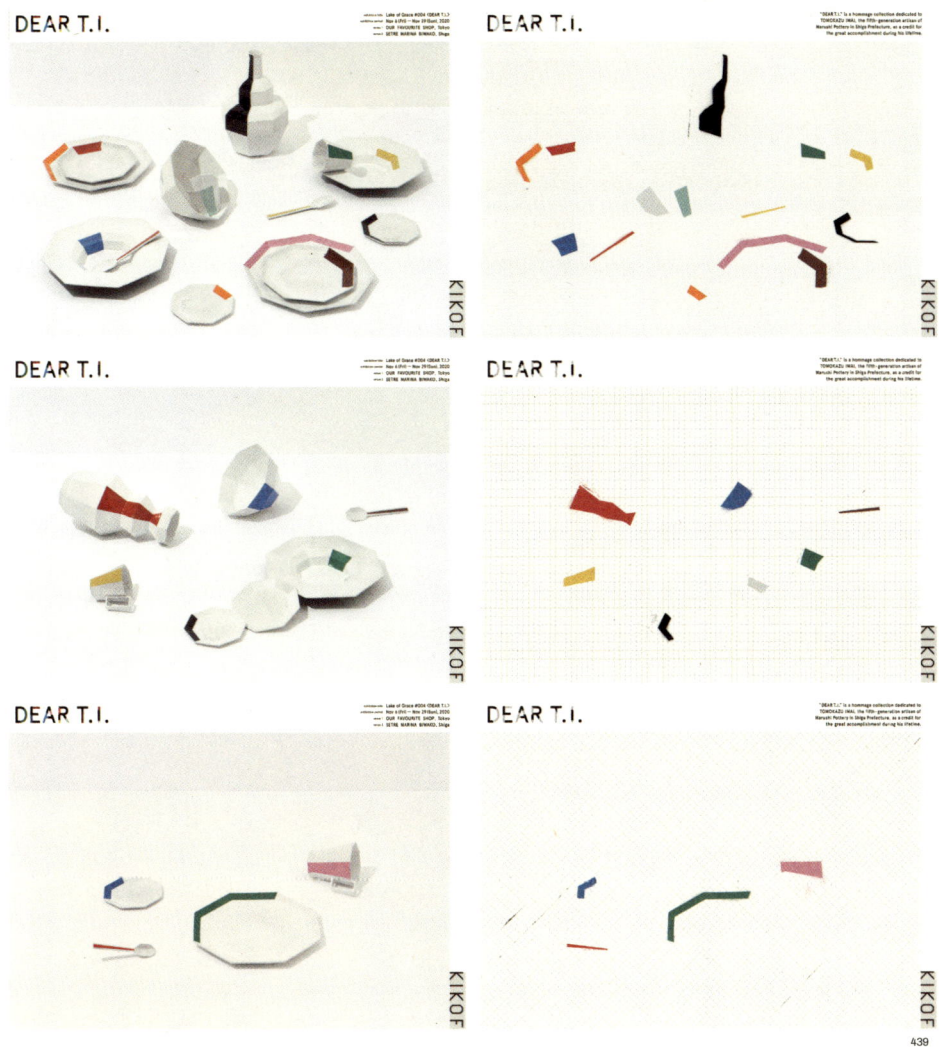

440 Promotional tools
TD. CD. AD. 植原亮輔 Ryosuke Uehara
CD. 渡邉良重 Yoshie Watanabe
D. サリーン・チェン Sarene Chan
CL. The Ginza
PT. 凸版文久ゴシック, 游ゴシック体

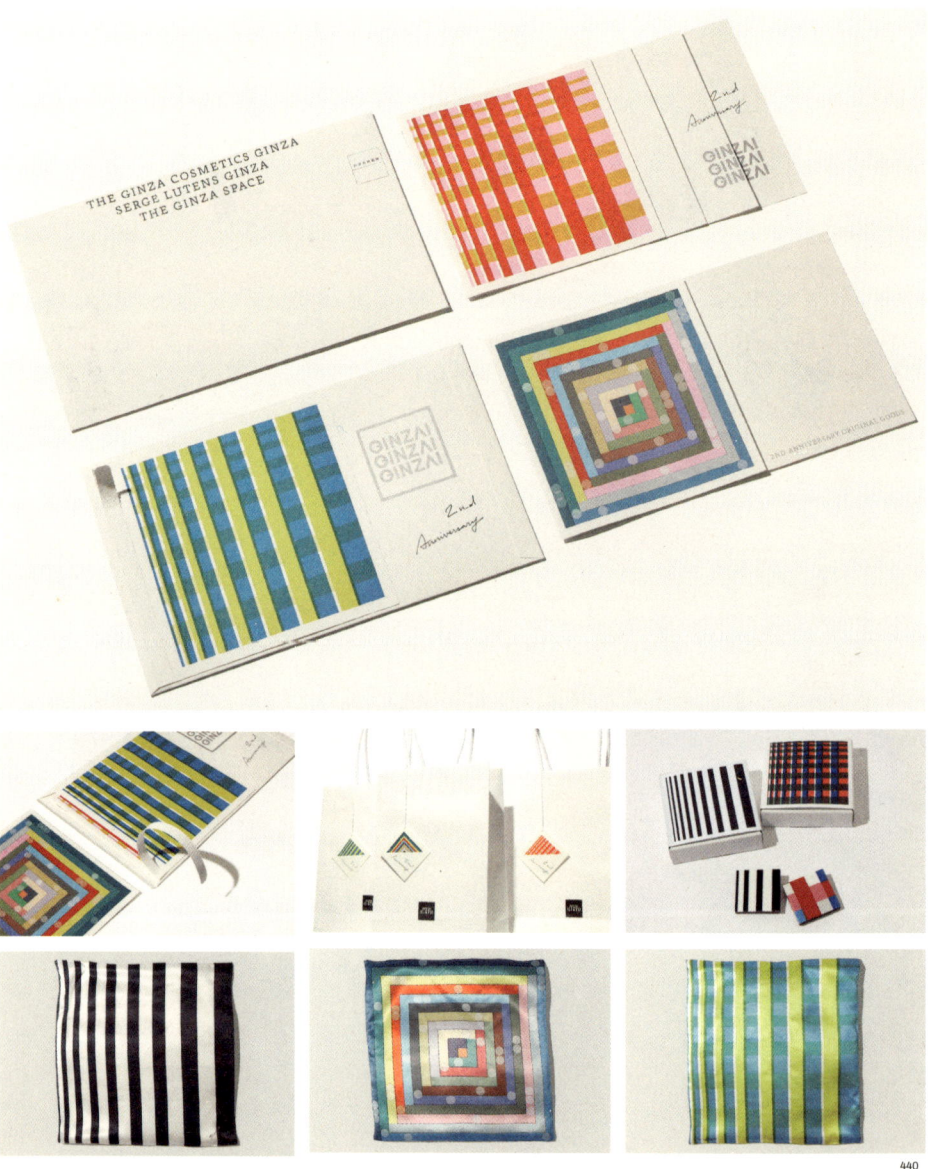

441 Packaging
TD. CD. 植原亮輔 Ryosuke Uehara
TD. AD. 渡邊良重 Yoshie Watanabe
D. 森本麻友 Mayu Morimoto
CL.（株）Zaxfox
PT. Custom-made for the project

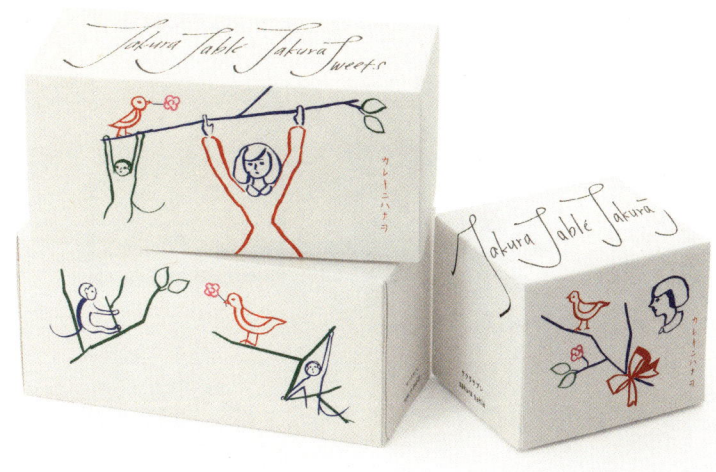

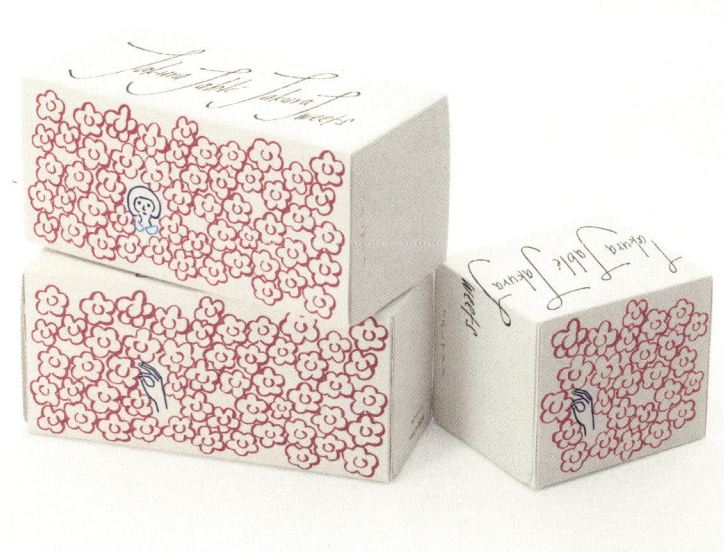

442 VI
TD. AD. 植原亮輔 Ryosuke Uehara
D. 小泉勁介 Keisuke Koizumi
I. 渡邊良重 Yoshie Watanabe
CL. 風と湖 kaze to umi
PT. Helvetica Neue, 游ゴシック体 Std

443 Packaging
TD. CD AD. 植原亮輔 Ryosuke Uehara
TD. CD AD. I 渡邊良重 Yoshie Watanabe
D. 大坪メイ Mei Otsubo
CL. ラフラ・ジャパン(株) Rafra Japan Co., Ltd.
PT. Custom-made for the project, BodoniFLF

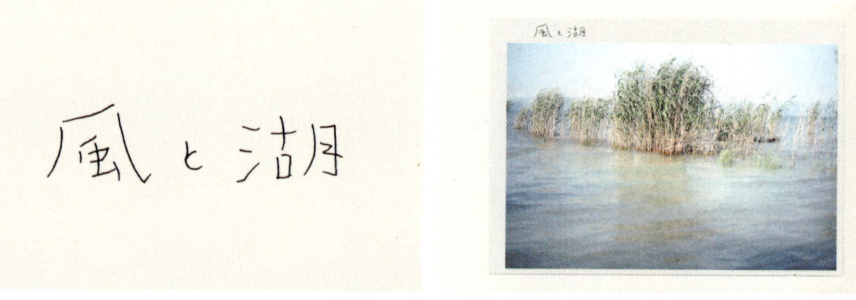
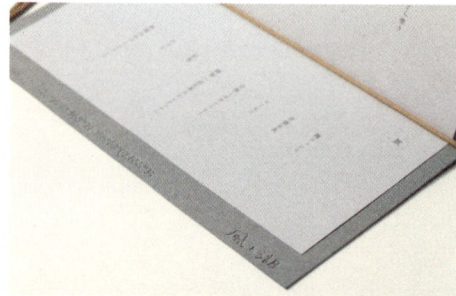
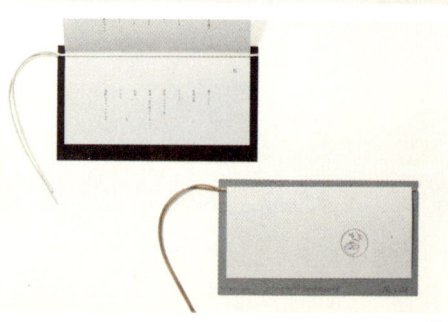
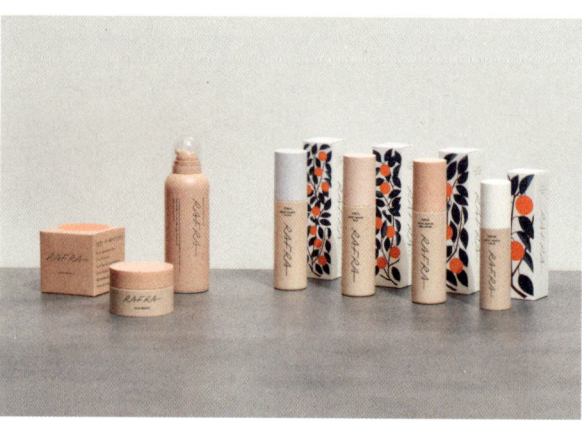
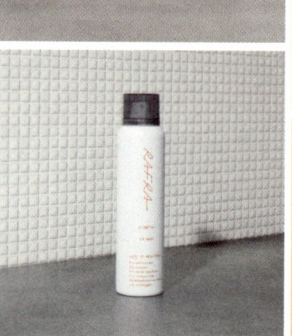
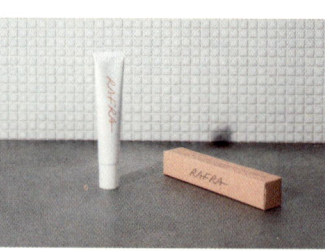
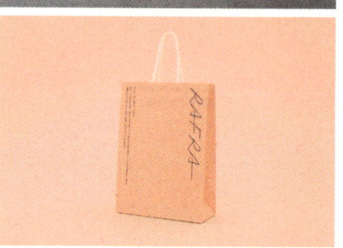
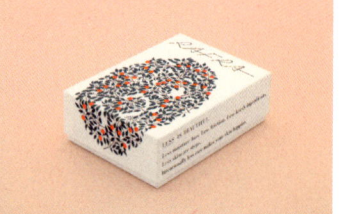

444 Experimental work
TD. AD. 植原亮輔 Ryosuke Uehara, 渡邉良重 Yoshie Watanabe
D. サリーン・チェン Sarene Chan
CL. 没後40年向田邦子カケル会
Committee for Kuniko Mukoda 40th anniversary of her death
PT. 太ゴB101, 秀英横太明朝

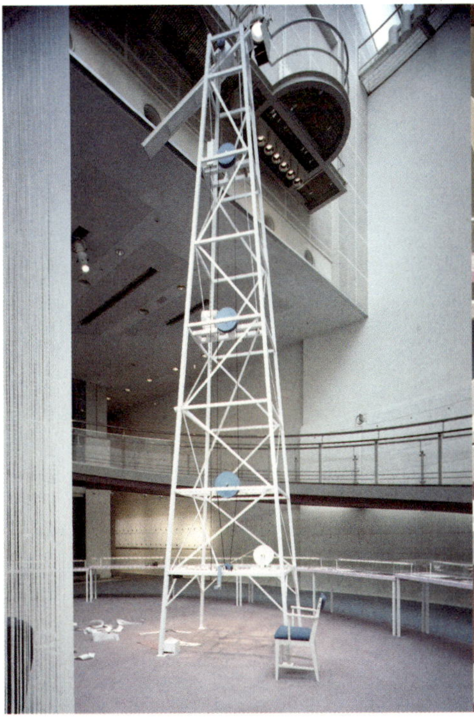

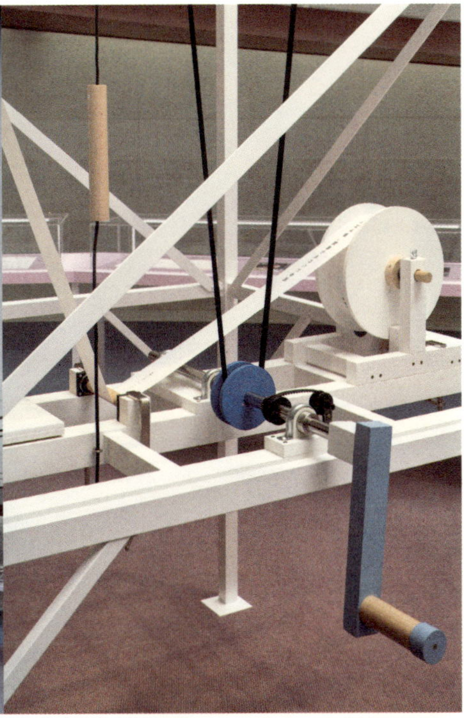

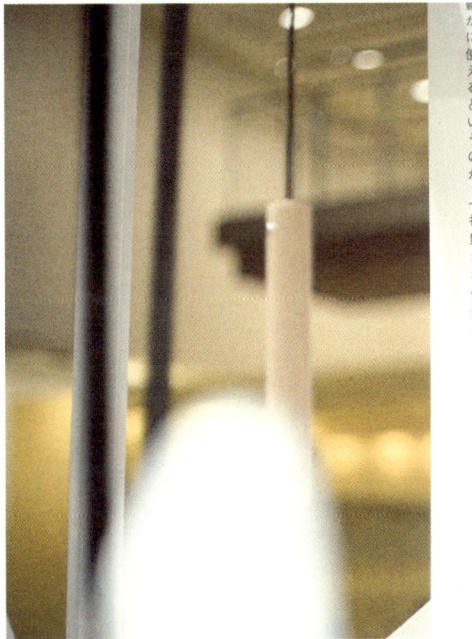
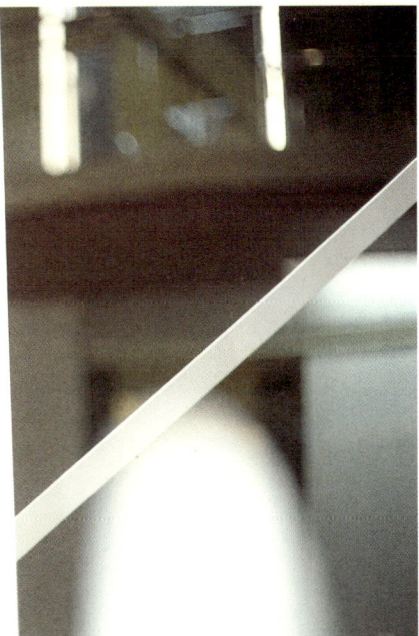

445 Poster
TD. AD. 植原亮輔 Ryosuke Uehara
TD. AD. I. 渡邊良重 Yoshie Watanabe
D. サリーン・チェン Sarene Chan
CL. 没後40年向田邦子カケル会
Committee for Kuniko Mukoda 40th anniversary of her death
PT. 太ゴB101, Custom-made for the project

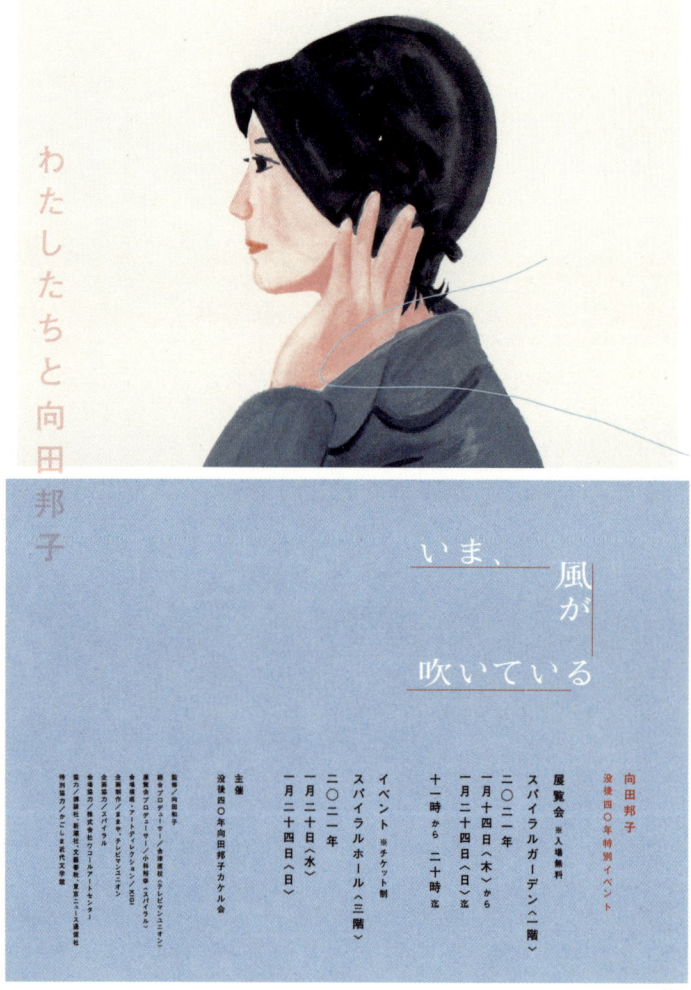

446 Poster
TD. 上西祐理 Yuri Uenishi
CL. ラフォーレ原宿 Laforet Harajuku

447 Mark & Logo
TD. 上杉滝 Taki Uesugi
CL. 太陽ホエール Taiyo Whale
PT. Custom-made font for the project

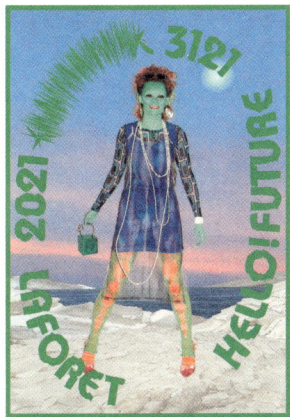
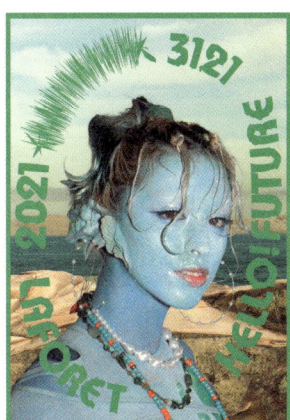
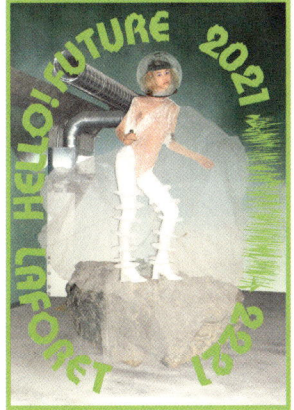
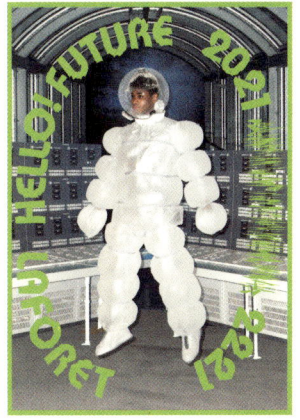

446

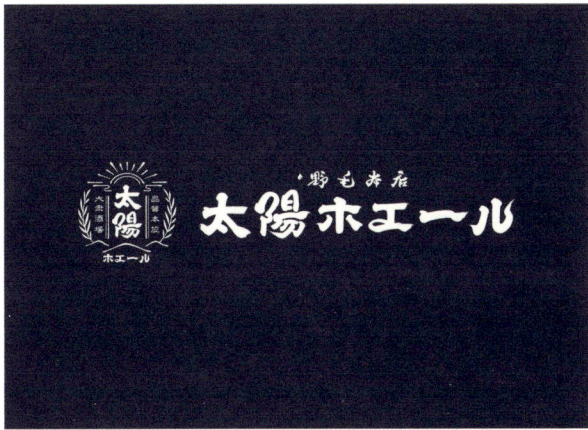

447

Prize Nominee Work

448 Book
TD. D. Hagen Verleger
AU. Koen Bulckens, Václav Janoščík, Paul de Lange
CL. Sharon Van Overmeiren, Damien & The Love Guru
PT. Custom-made for the project, Baskerville, Futura

386

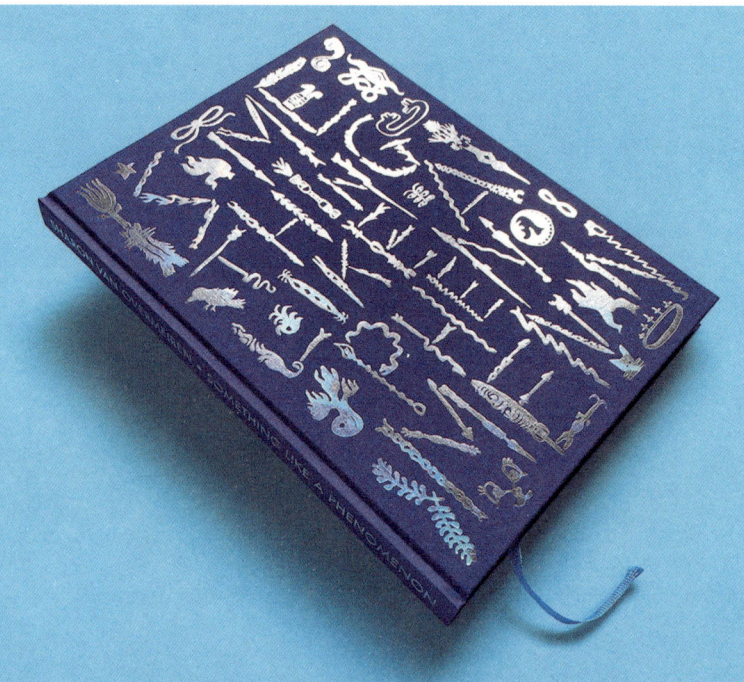

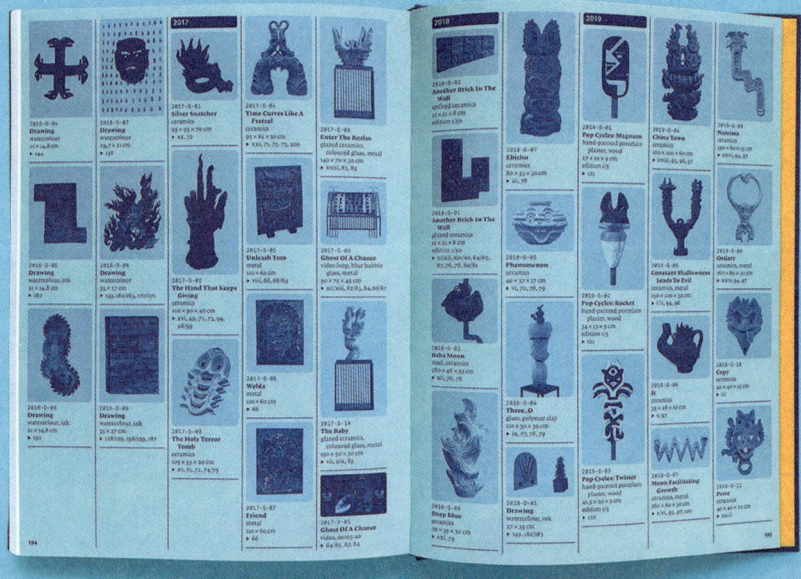

449 Branding
TD. D. C. 宇都勝宏 Katsuhiro Uto
CL. Cord Inc.
PT. Original, Trade Gothic LH Bold Extended :Custom-made for the project

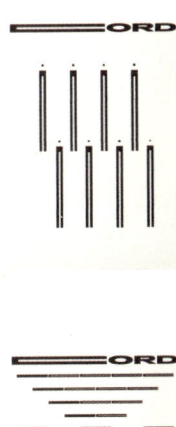

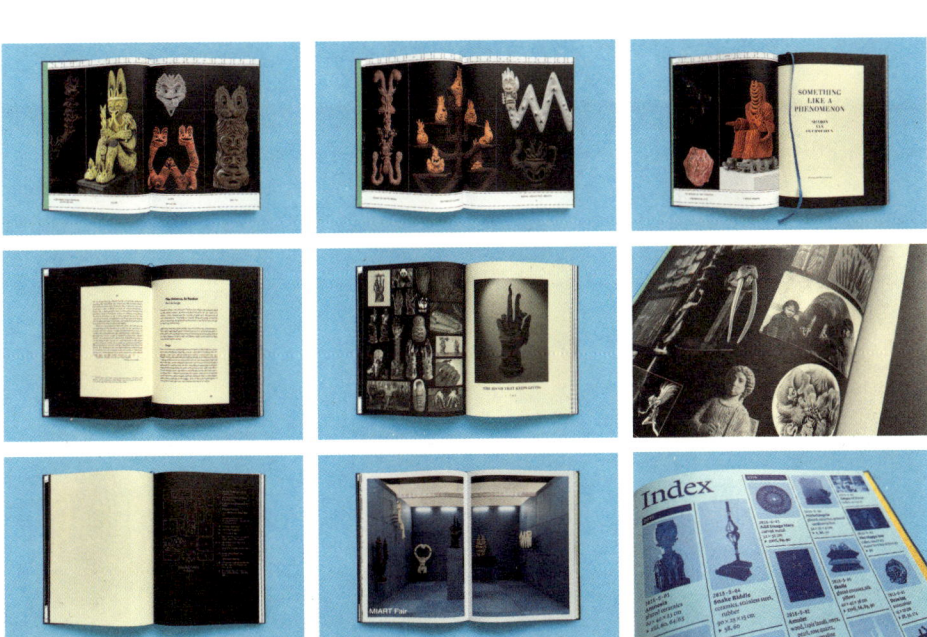

450 Book
TD. D. Hagen Verleger
AU. Petra Maria Meyer
CL. Wilhelm Fink
PT. Paradox, Folio

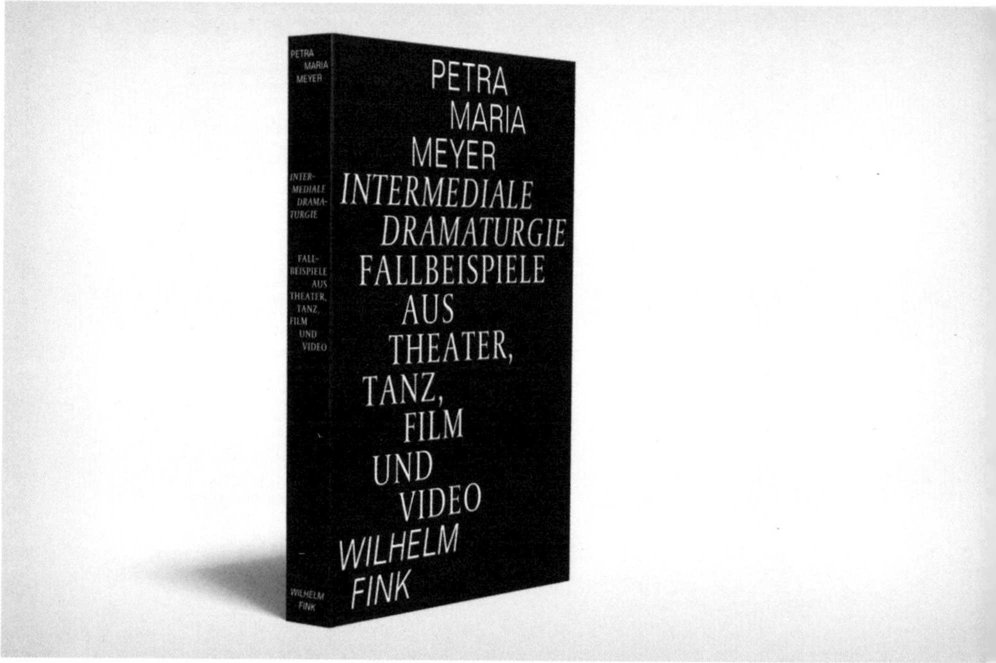

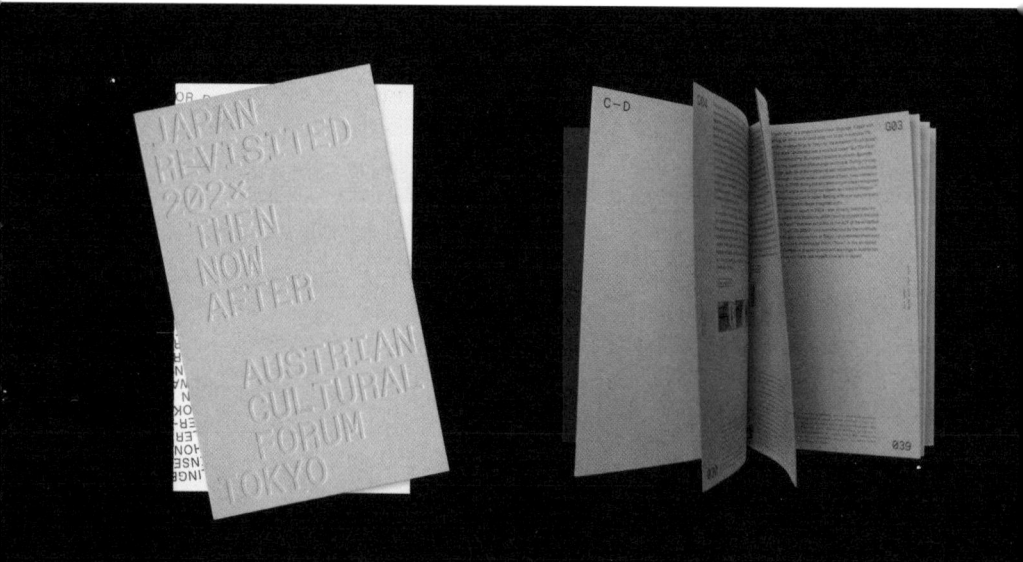

451 Book
TD. AD. Jan Vranovský
D (assistance). TS. Yara Abu Aataya
E. Mario Vielgrader
CU. Sybilla Patrizia
PCO. Chia-Wen Lin Vranovská, Daisuke Orio
PB. SunM Color
CL. Austrian Cultural Forum Tokyo
PT. ABC Favorit+Mono, Noto Sans CJK

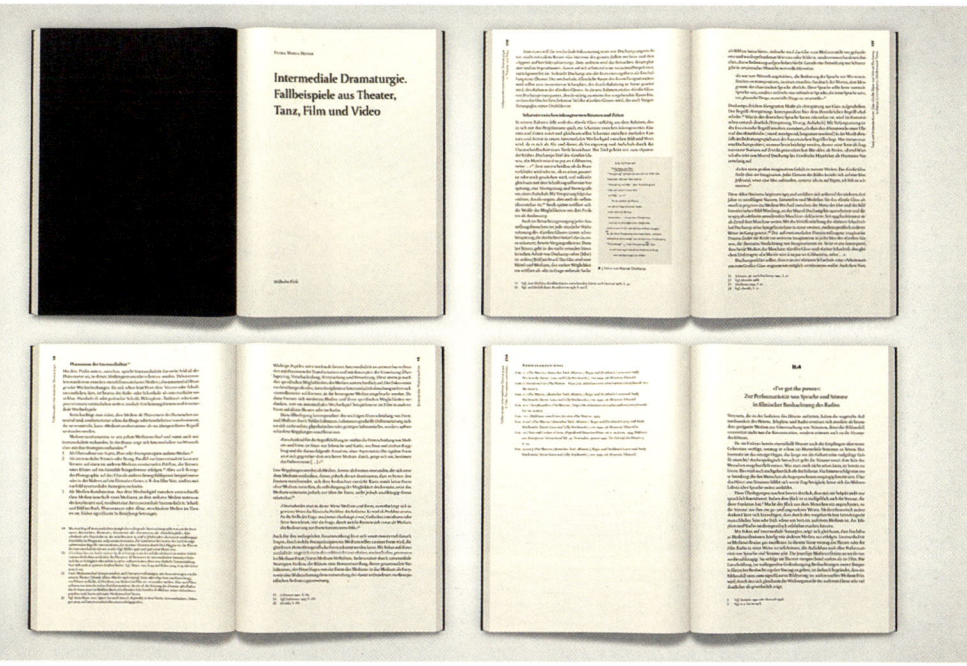

452 VI
TD. AD. D. P. Jan Vranovský
WDE. Tomáš Mrázek
PRO. Chia-Wen Lin Vranovská

CL. Austrian Cultural Forum Tokyo
PT. ABC Favorit+Mono, Noto Sans CJK

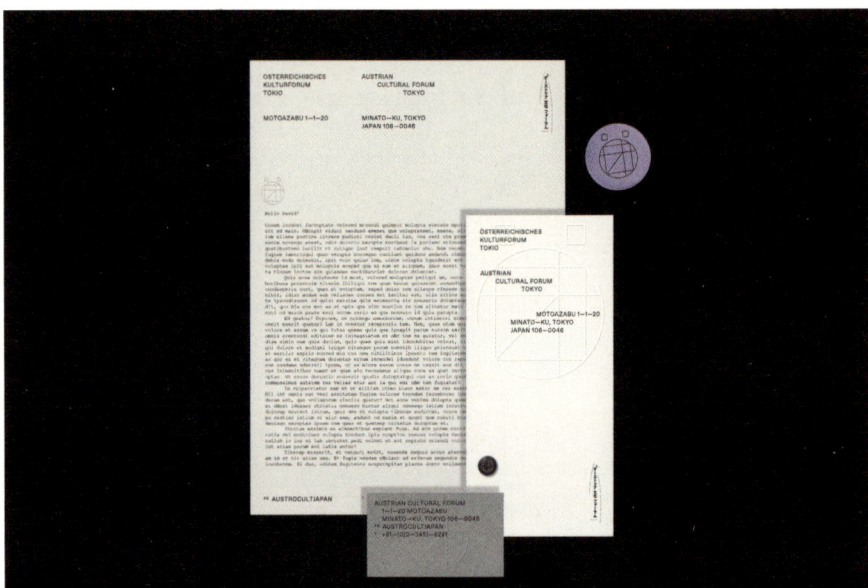
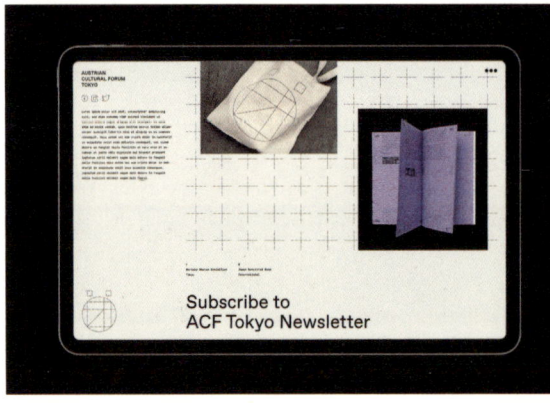
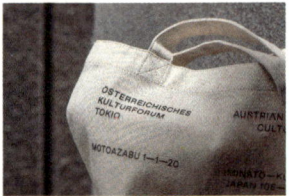
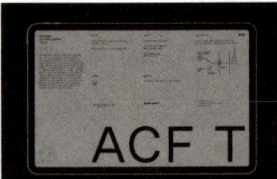
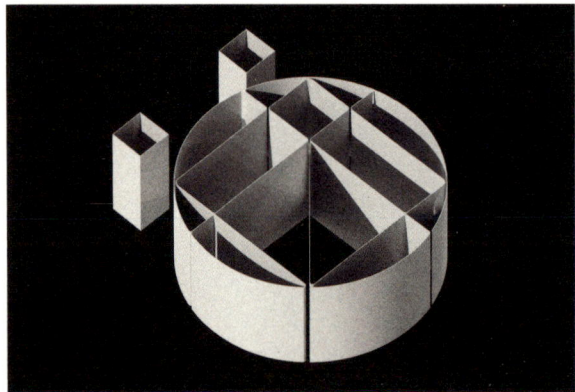
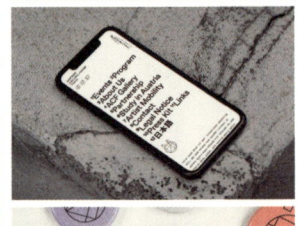
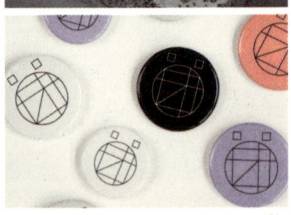

Prize Nominee Work

453 Poster
TD. Toan Vu-Huu
CL. DOC!
PT. Custom-made for the project, MT Grotesque

Alicia Zaton
09.01.–
22.01.21
jeu–sam
11–17h

Vernissage
09.01.
17–23h

Heure bleue

Eaux noires

DOC
26 rue
du
Docteur
Potain
75019
Paris

Prize Nominee Work

454 Branding
TD. Wang Pu
CL. Random Noise Rock Festival

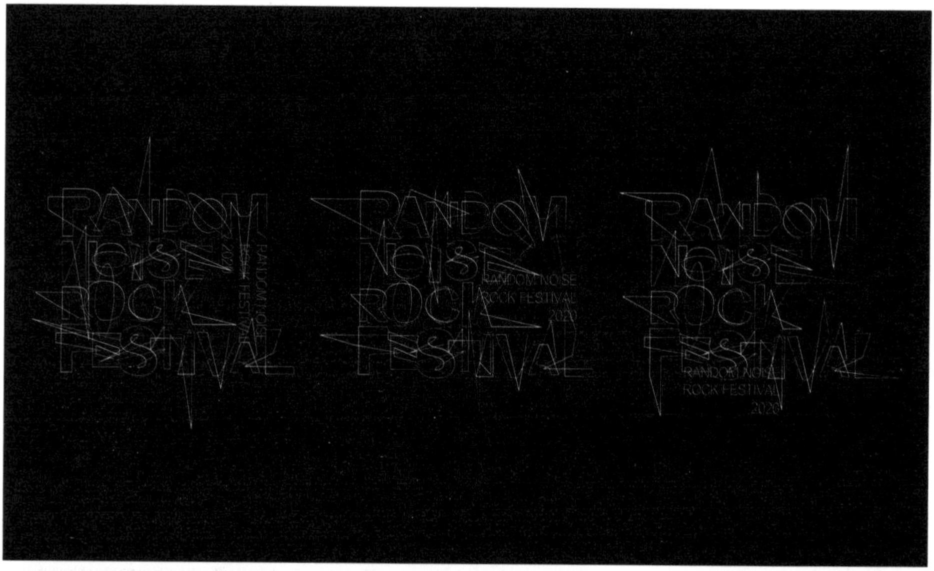

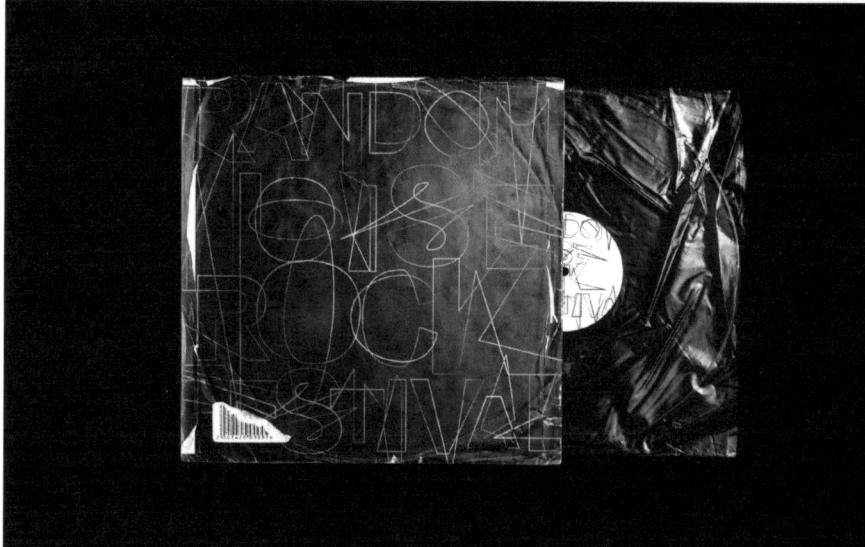

455 Book
TD. AD. Wang Zhihong
AD. Yuwen Hsu
CL. The Reserach and Preservation Society
for Dahong Wang's Architecture
PT. GT Super Display Trial

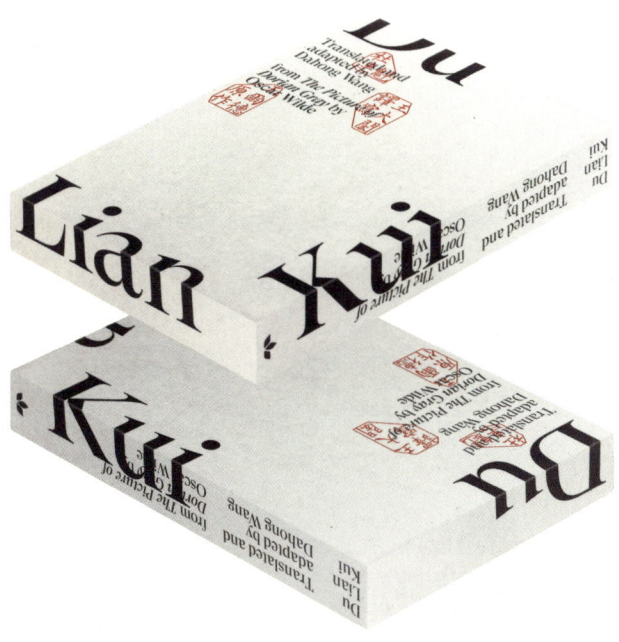

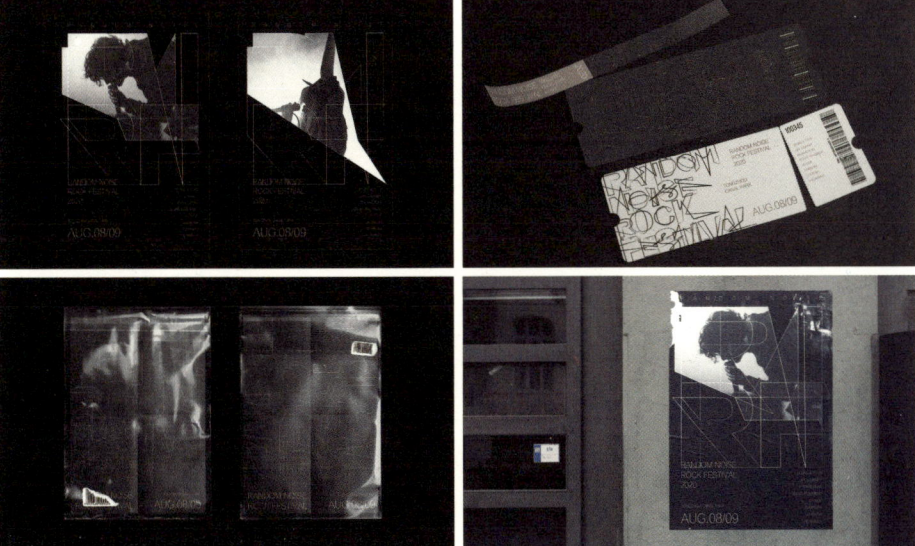

456 Art book
TD. AD. D. P. Mulan Wang
CL. Non-commercial work
PT. Neutro Bold

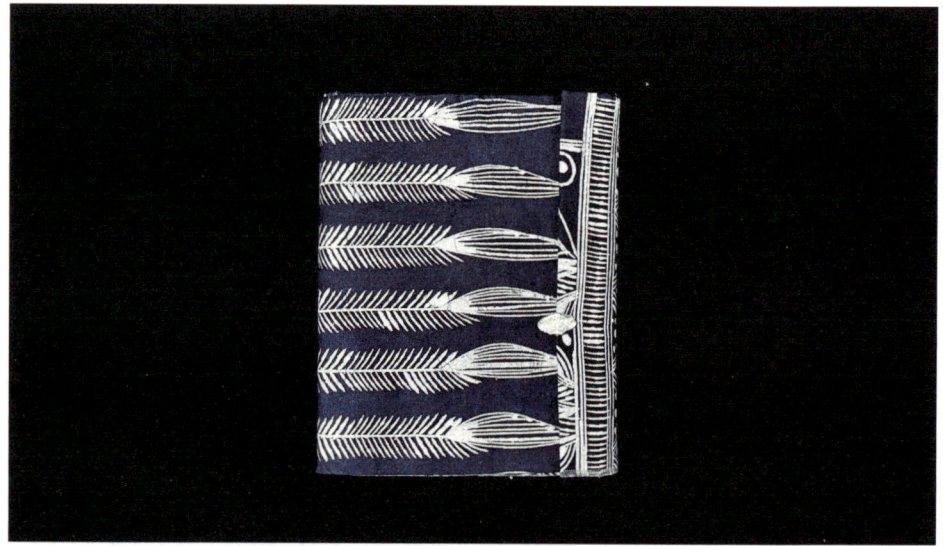

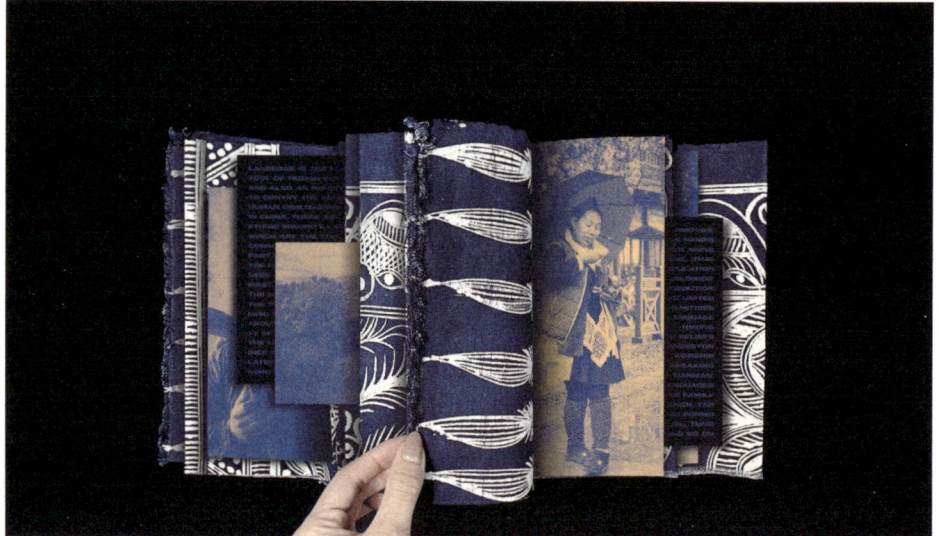

457 Cassette tape jacket
TD. AD. D. 王睿宇 Ruiyu Wang
CL. Allright Music, Only In Dreams

458 Flyer
TD. AD. D. 王睿宇 Ruiyu Wang
CL.（株）シブヤテレビジョン Shibuya Television

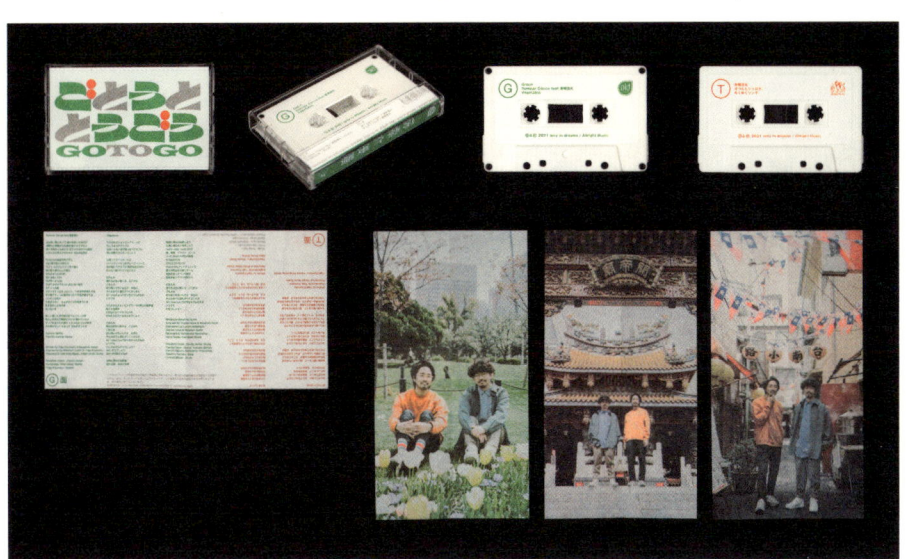

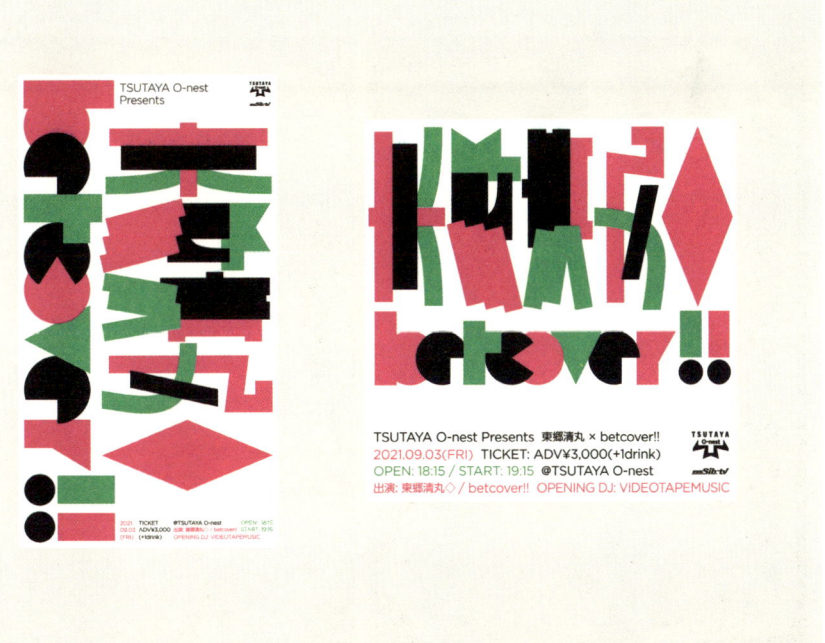

459 Experimental work
TD. Qin Wang
CL. Non-commercial work
PT. Custom-made for the project

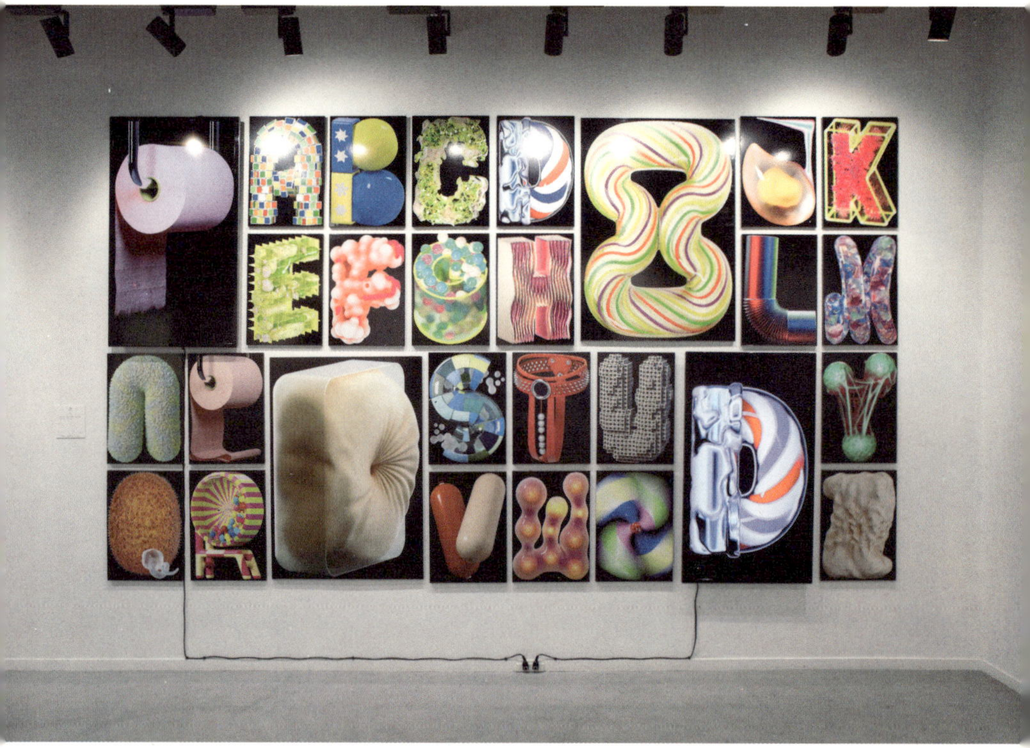

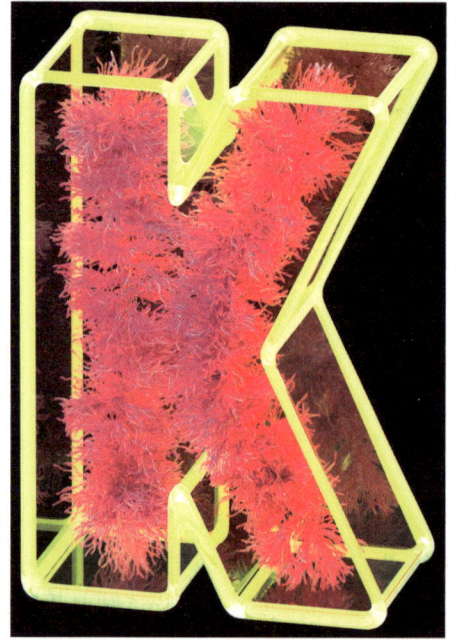
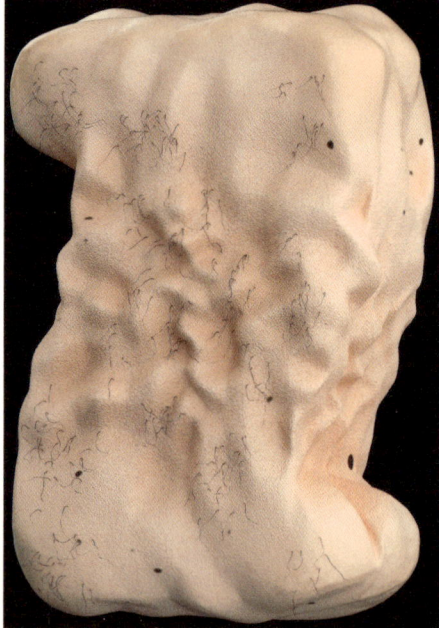

460 Catalogue
TD. AD. 渡辺和音 Kazune Watanabe
D. 宮垣朱音 Ayane Miyagaki, 手塚朋子 Tomoko Tezuka
CL. 専門学校 桑沢デザイン研究所 Kuwasawa Design School
PT. イワタゴシック, Akzidenz Grotesk

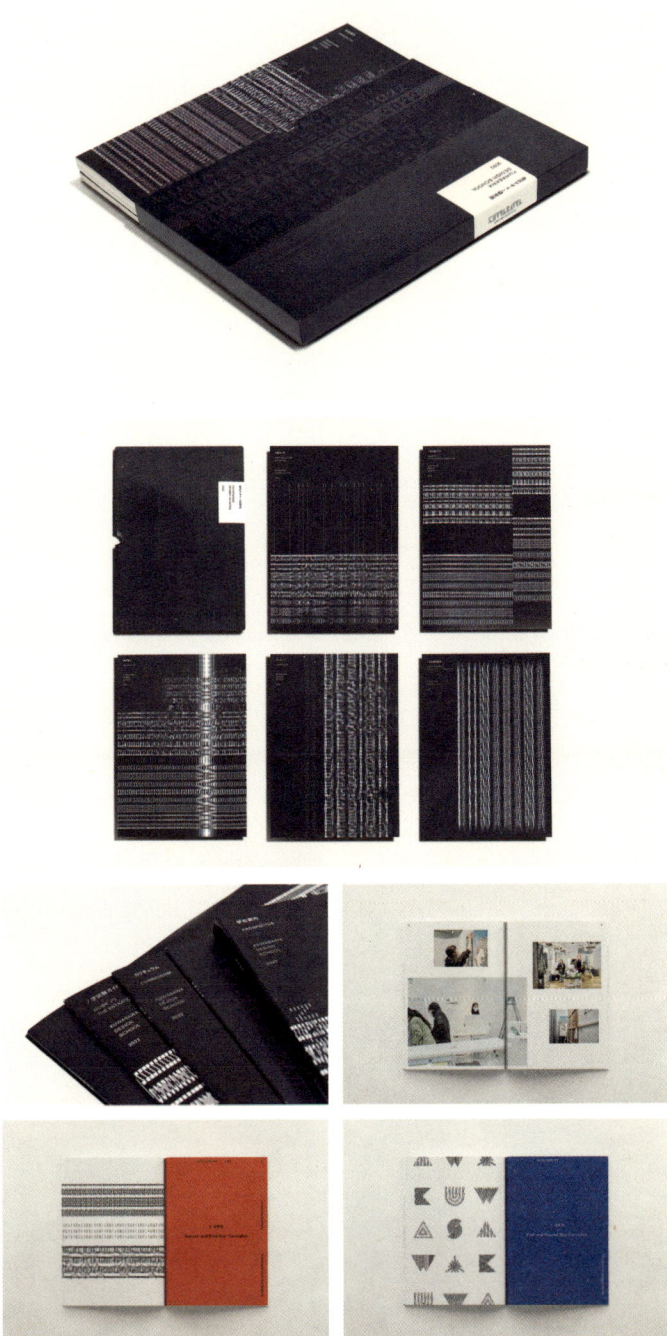

461 Packaging
TD. AD. D. I. 渡邊良重 Yoshie Watanabe
D. 森本麻友 Mayu Morimoto
CL.（株）プレジール Plaisir Co., Ltd.
PT. Custom-made for the project

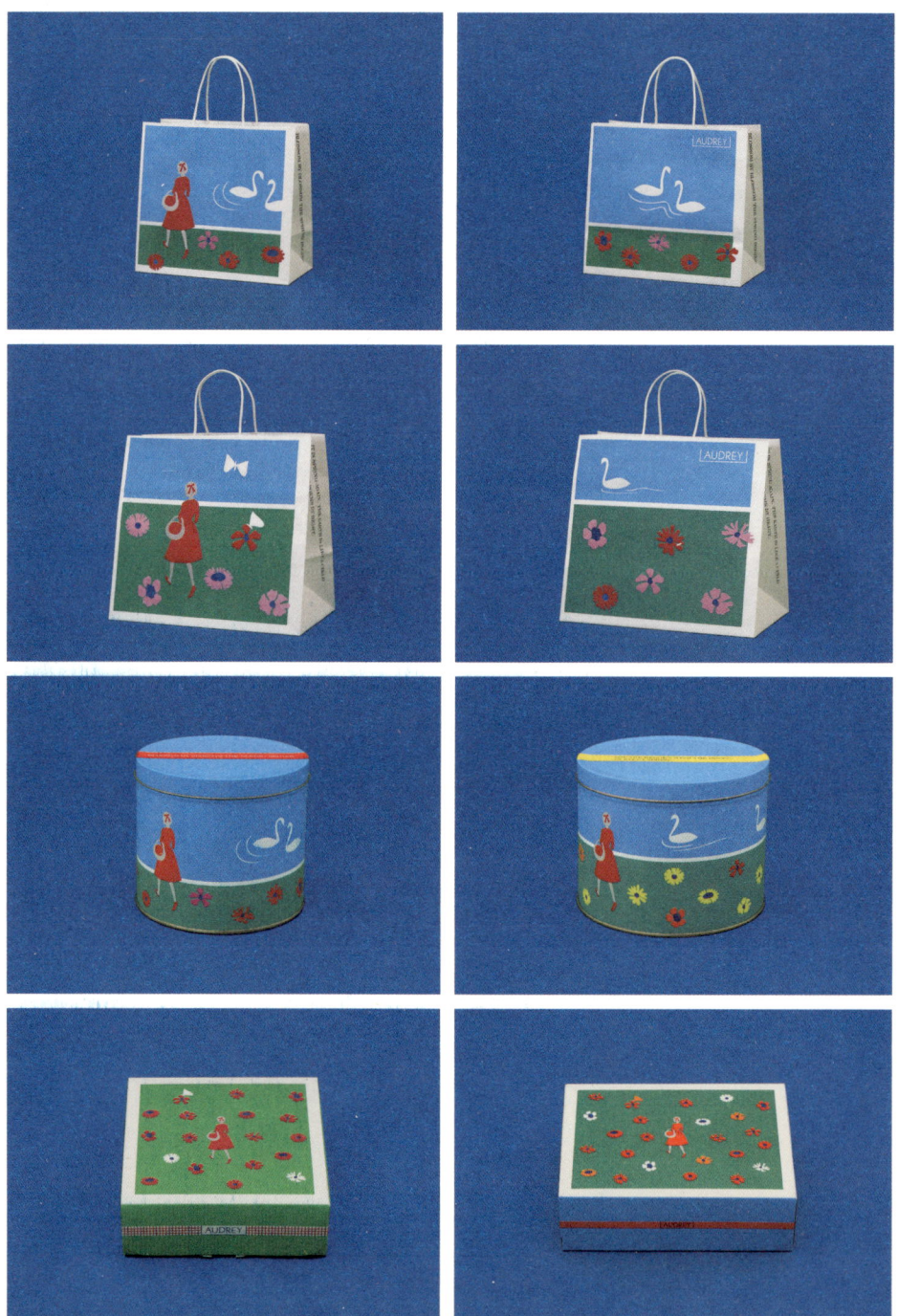

462 Poster
TD. AD. D. I. 渡邊良重 Yoshie Watanabe
CL. Our Favorite Shop
PT. Custom-made for the project

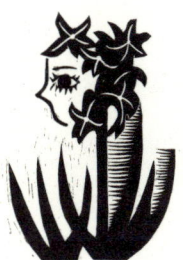
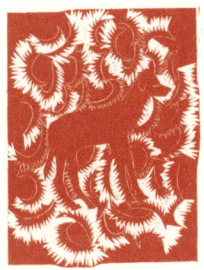
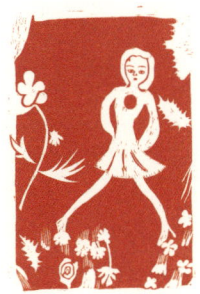
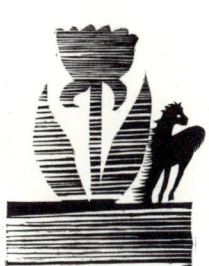
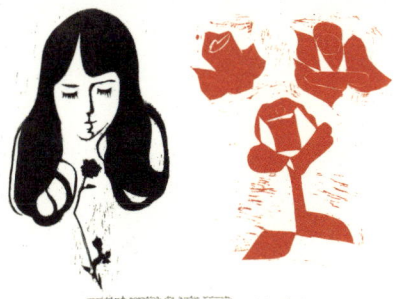
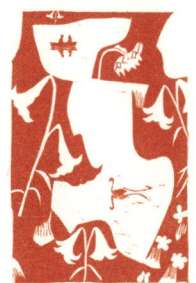
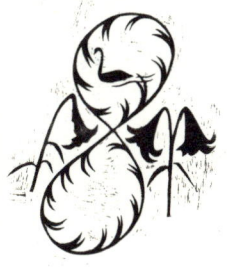
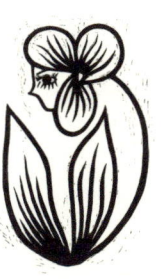
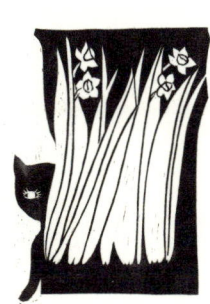
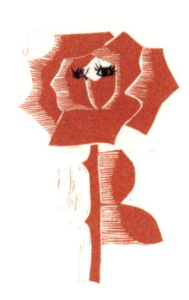
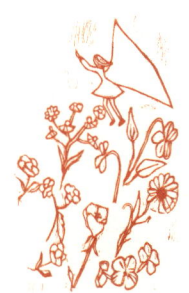
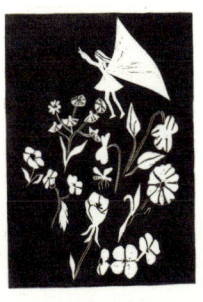
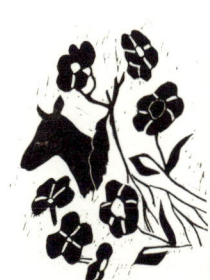
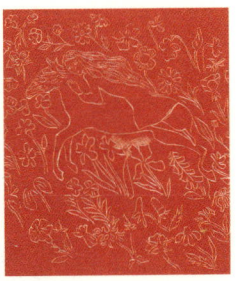

463 Poster
TD. AD. 渡邊裕文 Hirofumi Watanabe
AD. 小柳祐介 Yusuke Koyanagi
D. 土細工雅也 Masaya Dozaiku, 唐鎌大也 Daiya Karakama
P. 西部裕介 Yusuke Nishibe
C. 小川祐人 Yuto Ogawa
PR. 祥見知生 Tomoo Shoken
CL. Shoken inc.
PT. Axis Std, Custom-made for the project

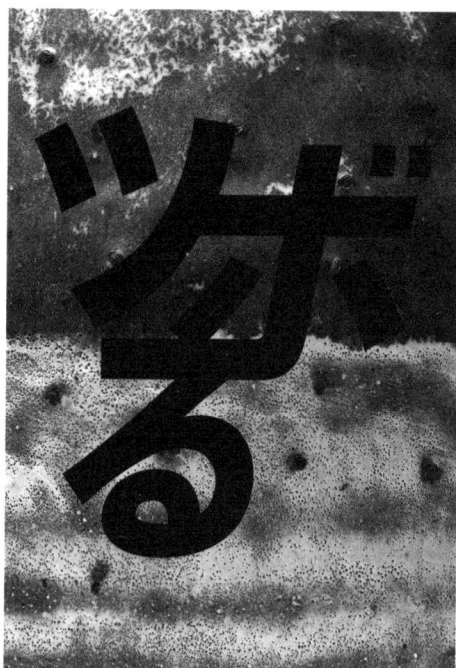
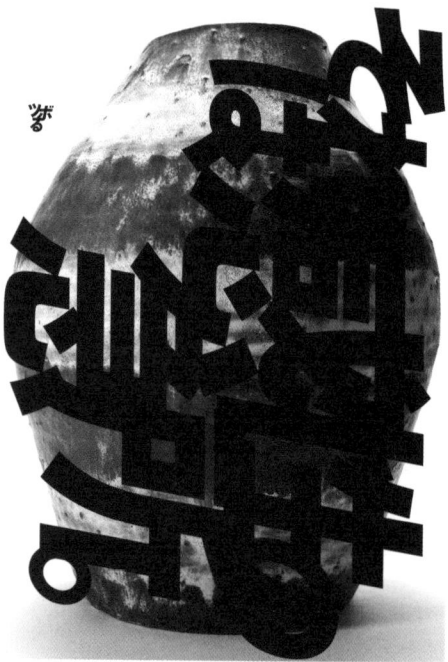

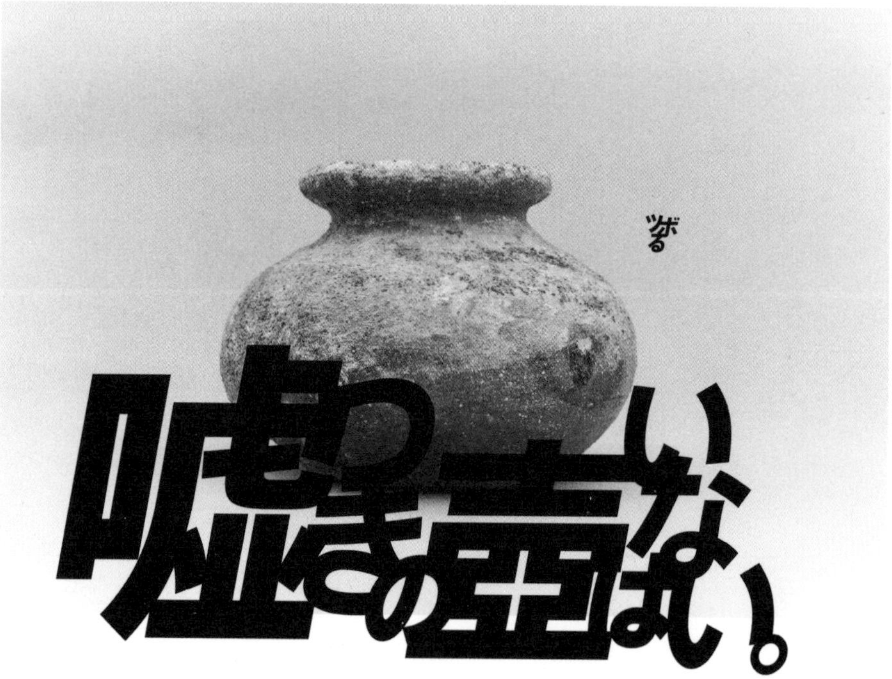

464 Book
TD. AD. D. Liao Wei
P. Chang Shao Ting
CL. Faces Publications
PT. Custom-made for the project

465 BI
TD. what
AD. D. Caspar Ip, Anissa Fung
CL. Project In Progress Studio
PT. Custom-made for project, Euclid Circular A

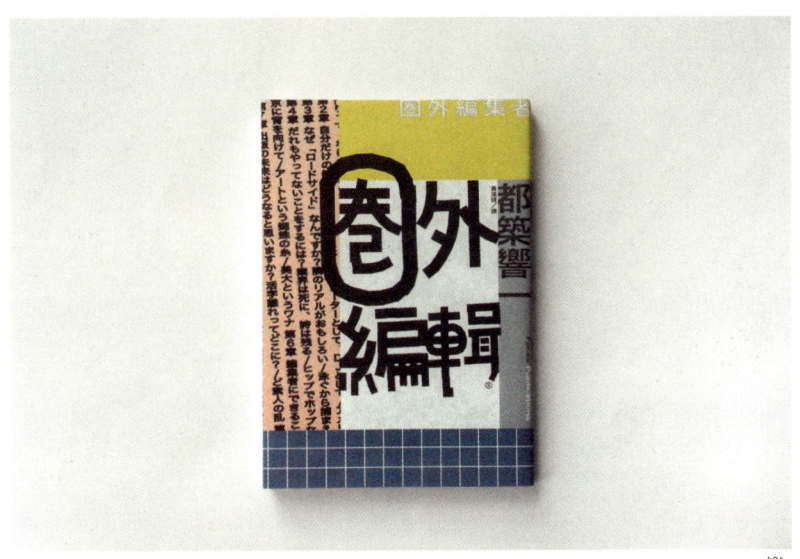

464

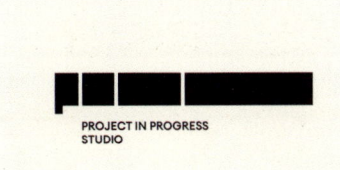
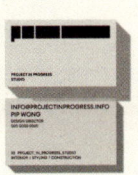

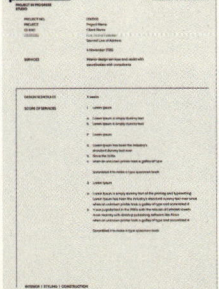
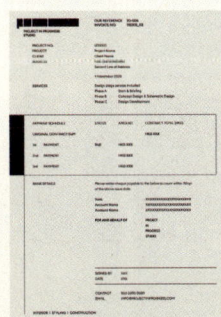
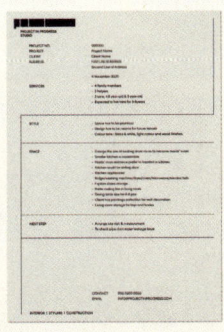

465

Prize Nominee Work

466 Book
TD. D. Daniel Wiesmann
D. Jule Erner, Robert Radziejewski
P. Georgios Michaloudis
CL. Stiftung Buchkunst
PT. Oracle & Oracle Triple

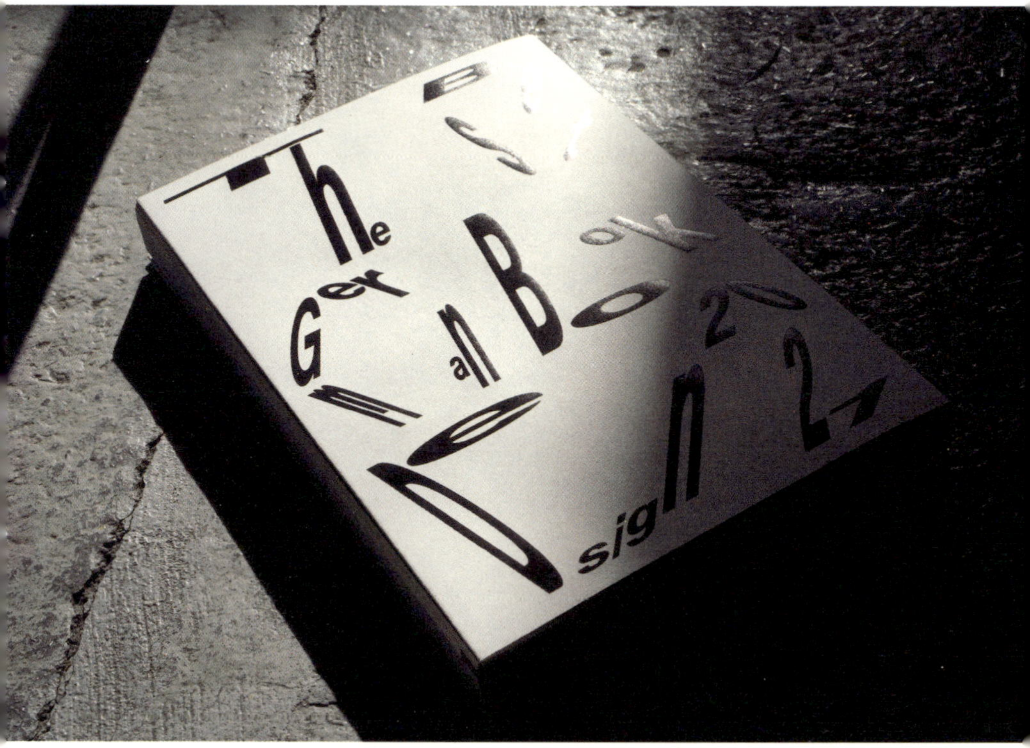

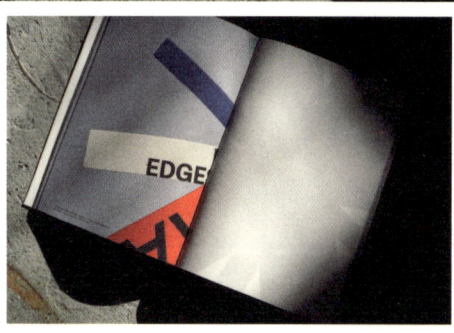
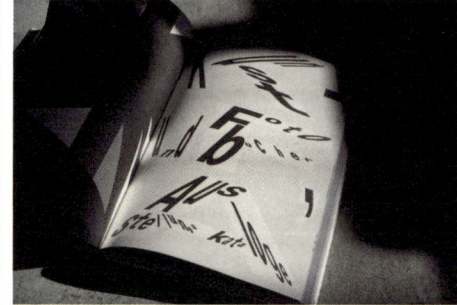
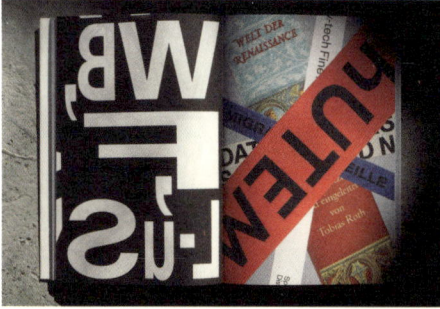
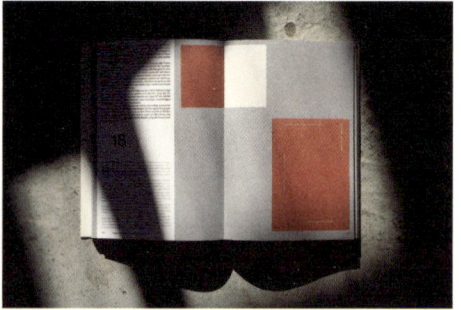

467 Book
TD. Benjamin Wurster
CL. PU. Slanted Publishers
PT. Acumin Pro Wide, Acumin Pro

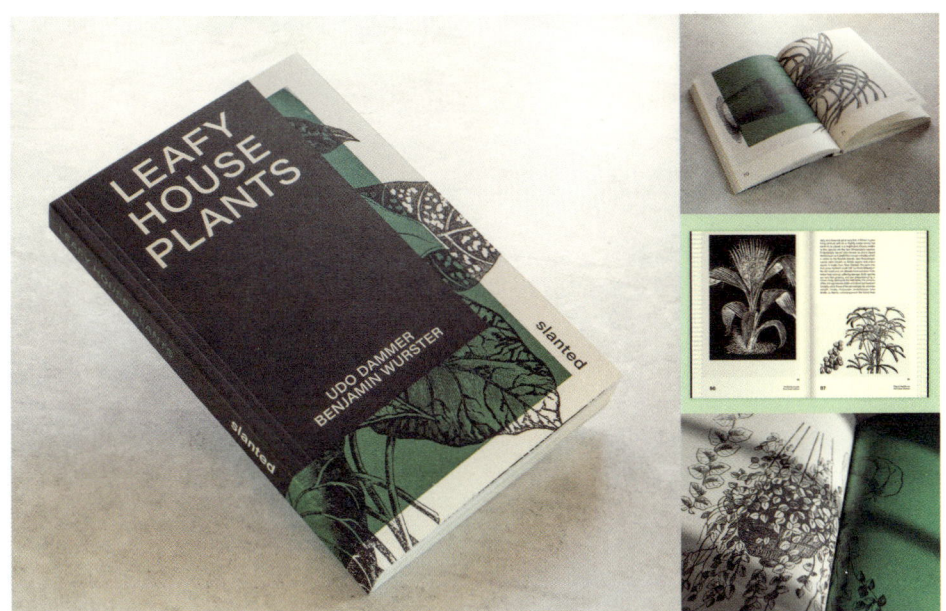

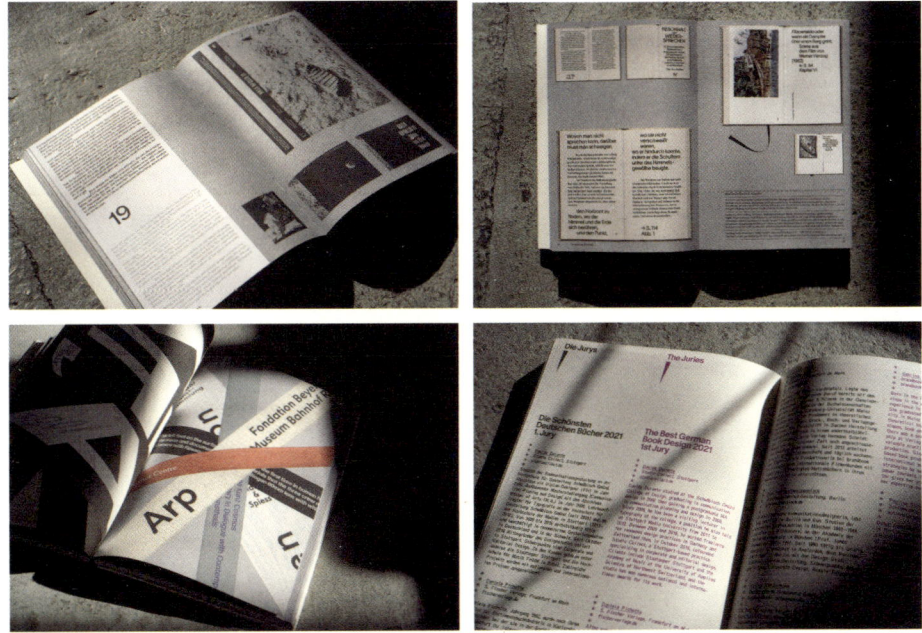

468 Pamphlet
TD. Wolfe Hall : Jason Wolfe, Luke Hall
CL. Hollybush Gardens
PT. Moreau, WH Zagreus

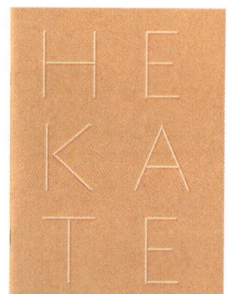
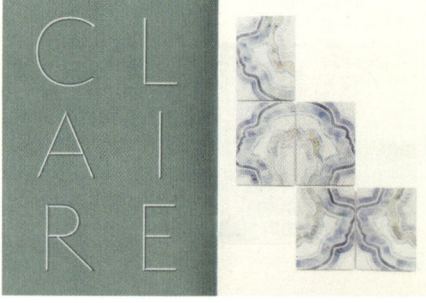
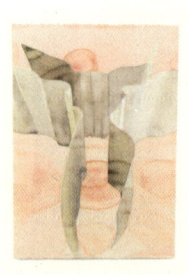
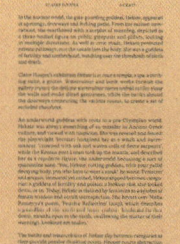
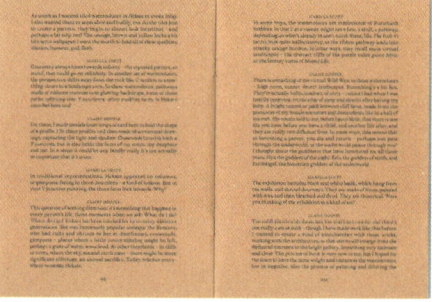
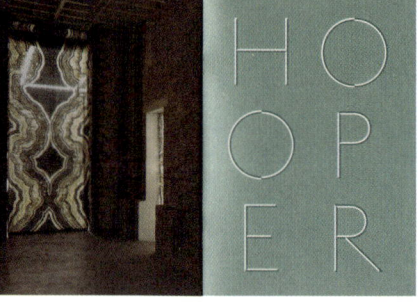
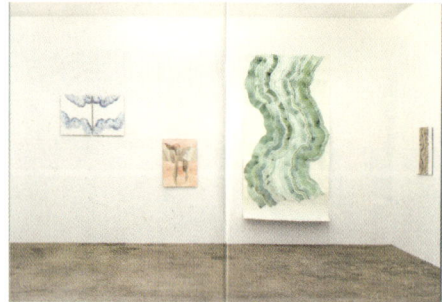

405 **Prize Nominee Work**

469 Poster
TD. AD. D. Siguang Wu
CL. Non-commercial work
PT. Custom-made for the project

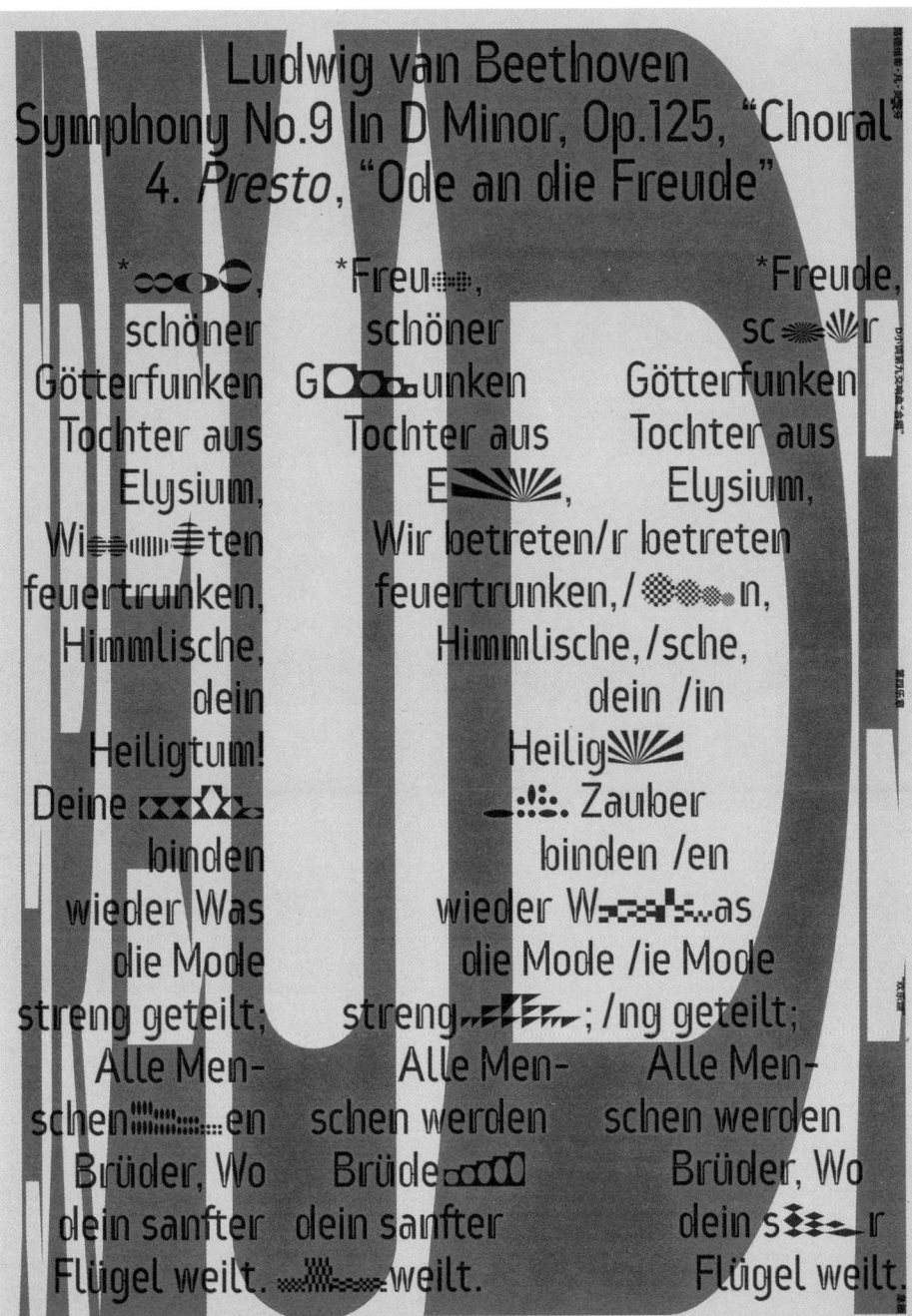

Prize Nominee Work

470 Mark & Logo, Corporate stationery
TD. AD. Nan Xiao
D. Chang Kai
MD. Qian Huang
P. Zi Wang
C. Ruiyan Wang
CL. 山地土壤 Mountain Soil
PT. Custom-made for the project

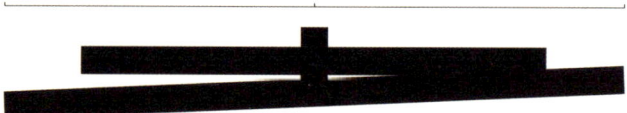

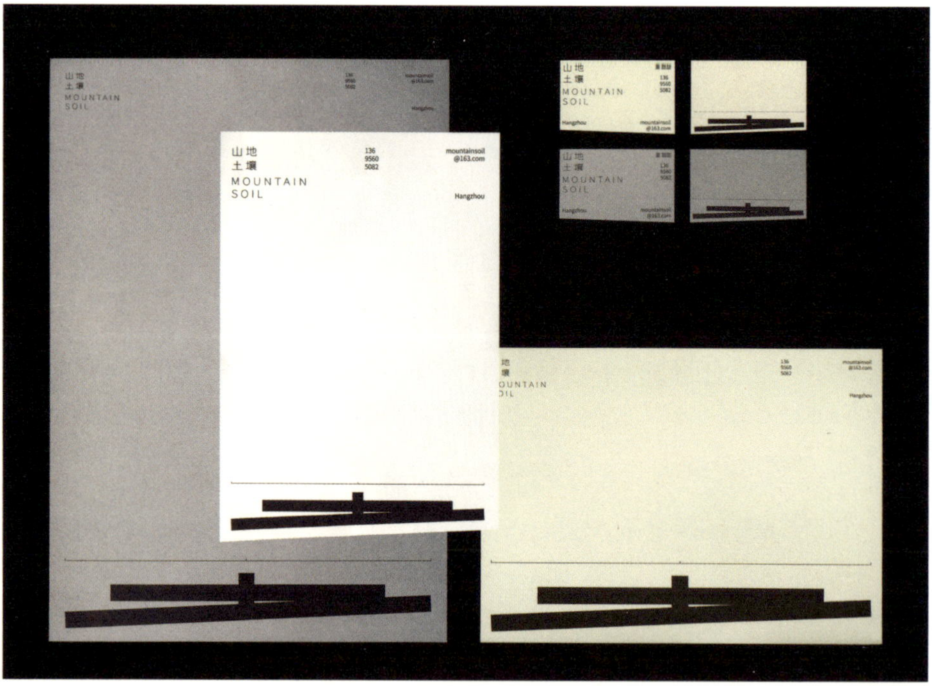

471 Exhibition VI
TD. Chun Sing Wong
AD. Zachary Chan, Allan Chan
CL. School of Art, Design and Media, NTU Singapore
PT. Custom-made for the project, Dazzed

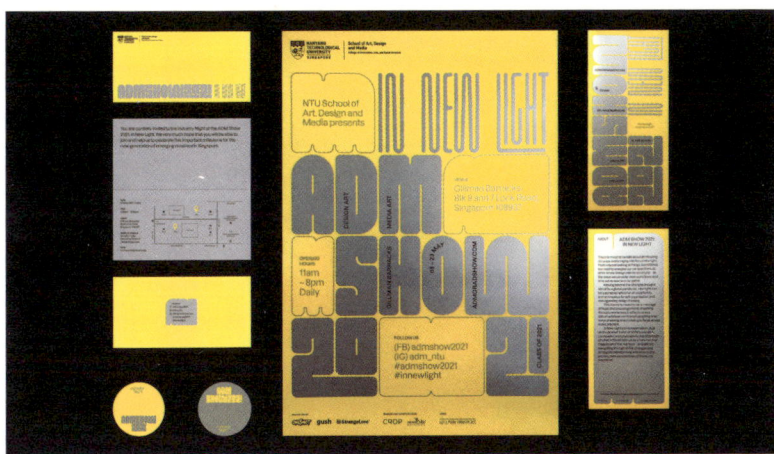

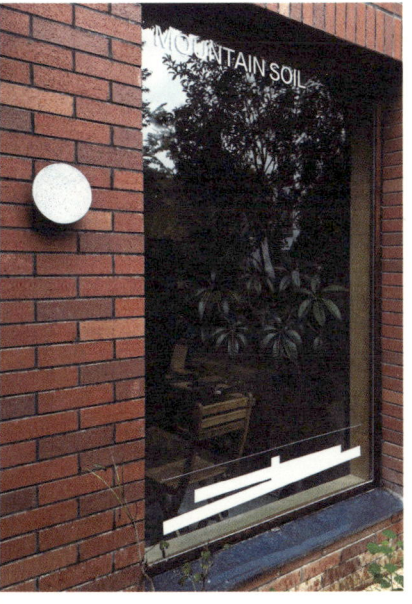

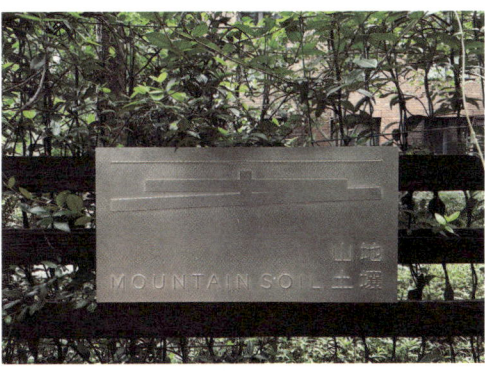

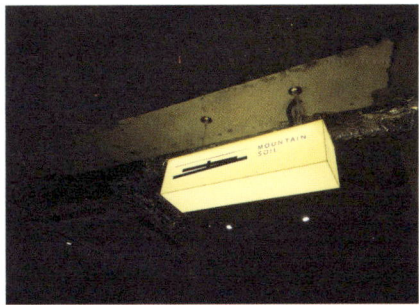

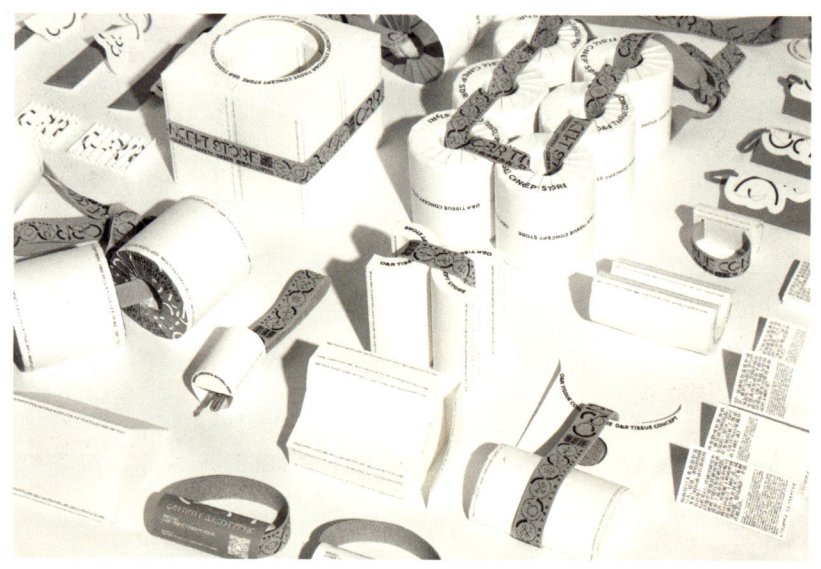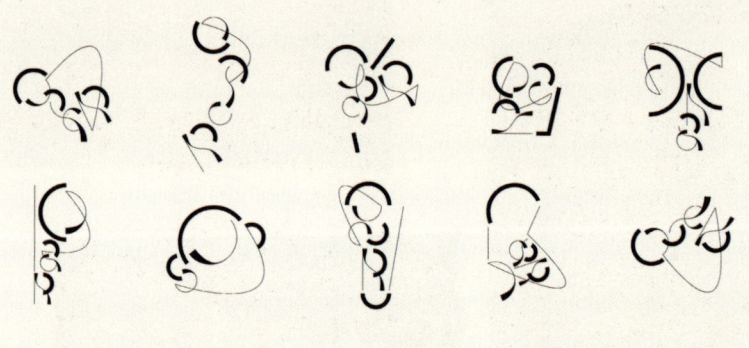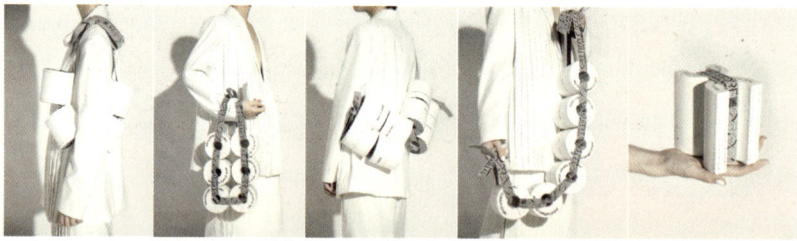

473 Branding
TD. AD. Chen Xing
TD. Xiang Li
D. Shuyao Bian, Yinan Wang, Qinglu Guo
P. Di Wang
CL. delicates
PT. Custom-made for the project

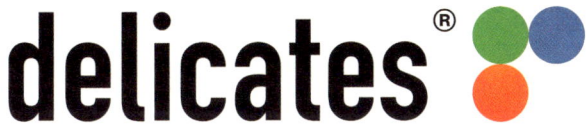

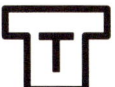 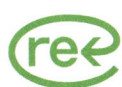 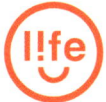 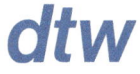

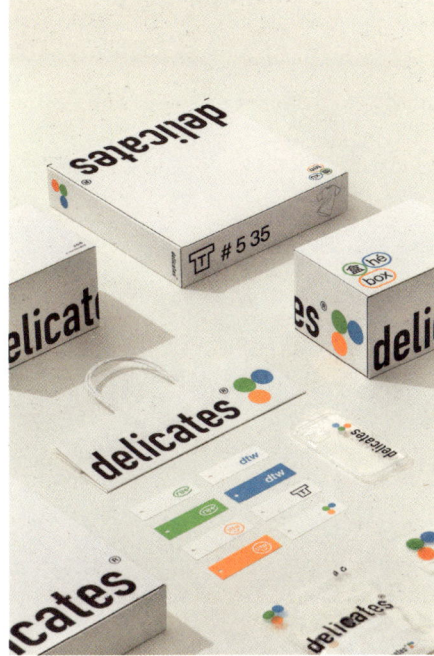
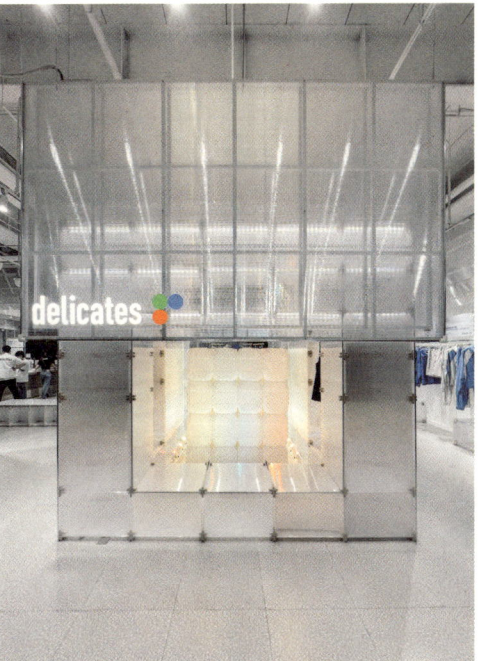

474 Branding
TD. AD. D. Hunk Xing
CL. Beijing Creative Minds Technology Co., Ltd.
PT. MingLan_Orz, HK Grotesk

475 Packaging
TD. Chen Xing
TD. AD. Xiang Li
D. Qinglu Guo
P. Di Wang
CL. Maison Margiela
PT. Helvetica, Graphik

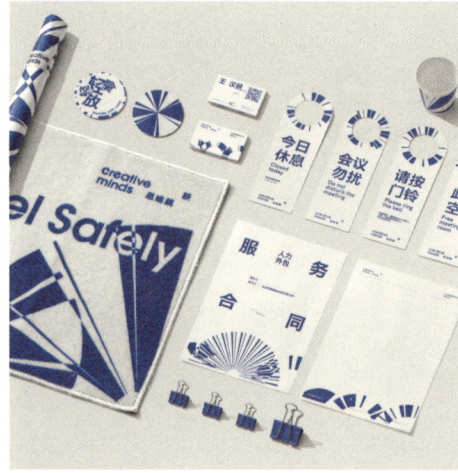
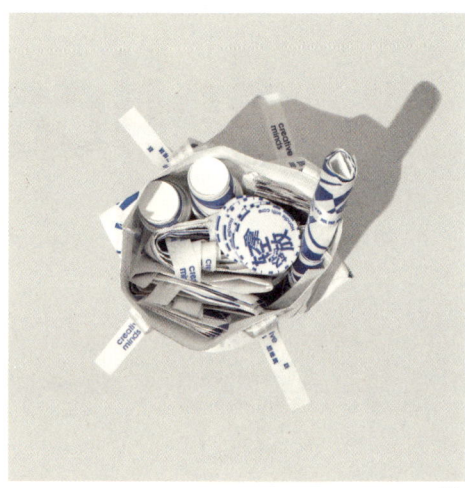

474

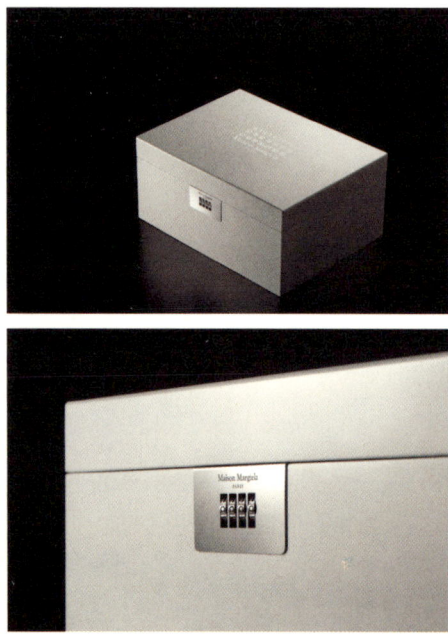
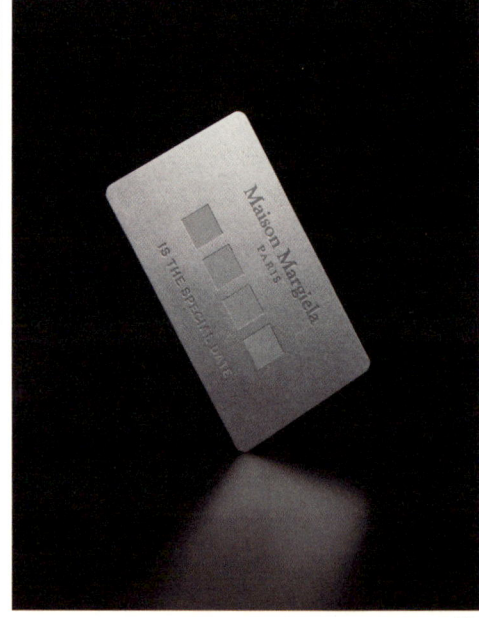

475

476 Poster
TD. Xu Weixin
CL. Reserve Land Design Library

477 Exhibition graphics
TD. Xu Weixin
CL. Reserve Land Design Library

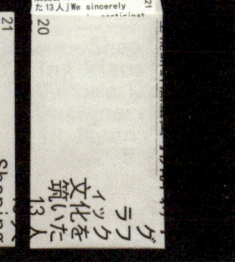
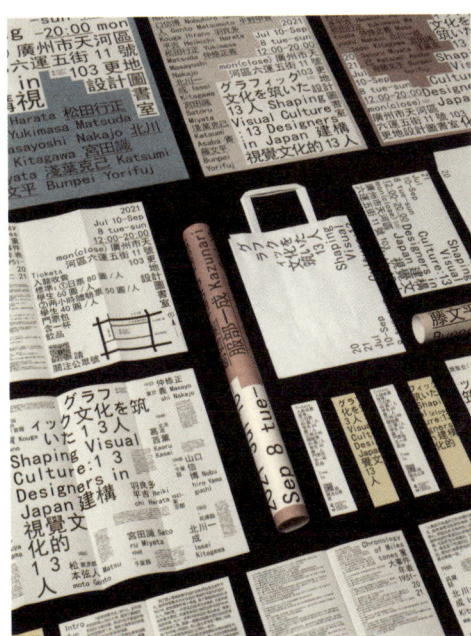
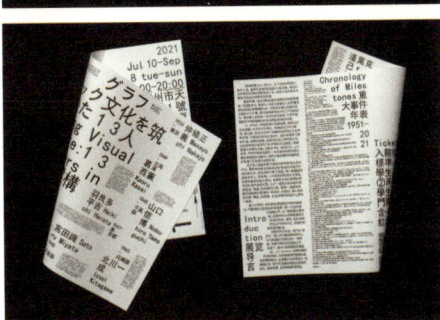

Prize Nominee Work

478 Poster
TD. AD. D. 矢後直規 Naonori Yago
CL. (株)サクラムラボ Sakuramurabo Ltd.
PT. AG Old Face

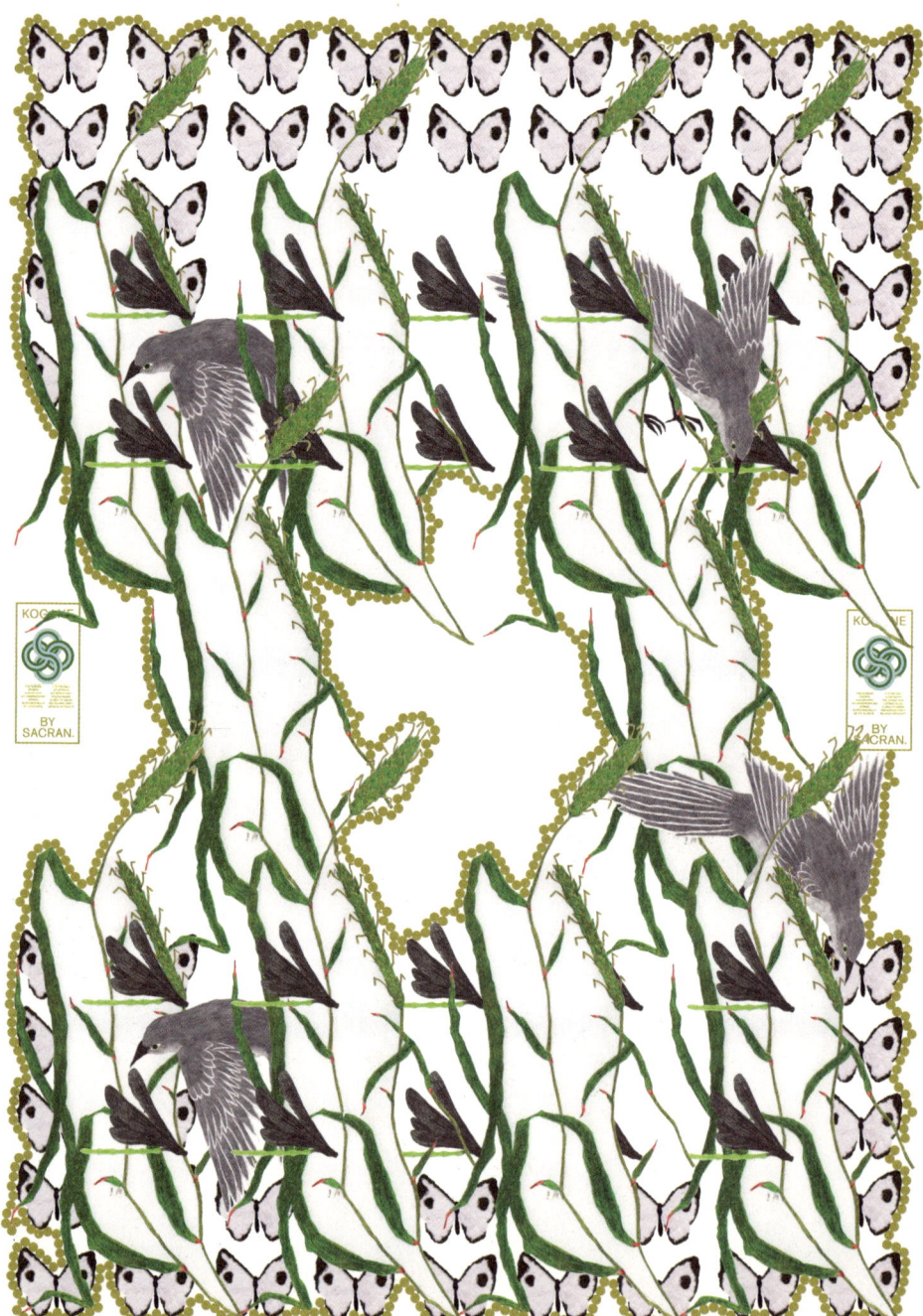

479 Letter
TD. AD. D. 矢後直規 Naonori Yago
CL.（株）サクラムラボ Sakuramurabo Ltd.
PT. AG Old Face

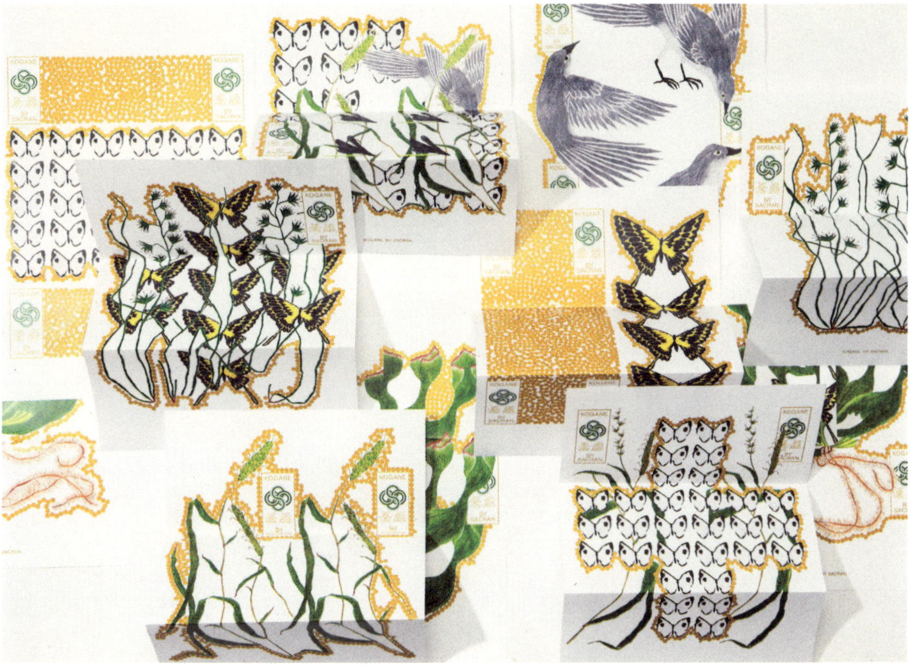

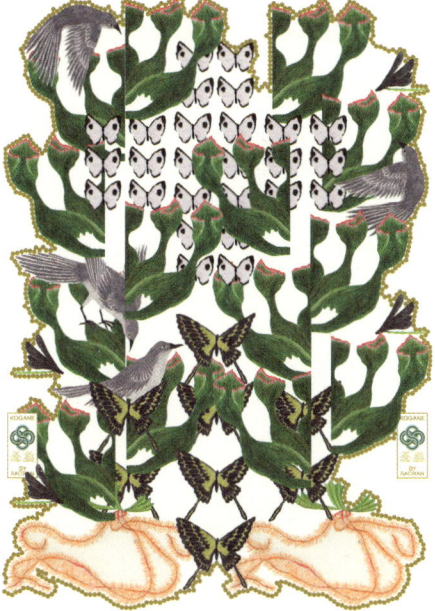
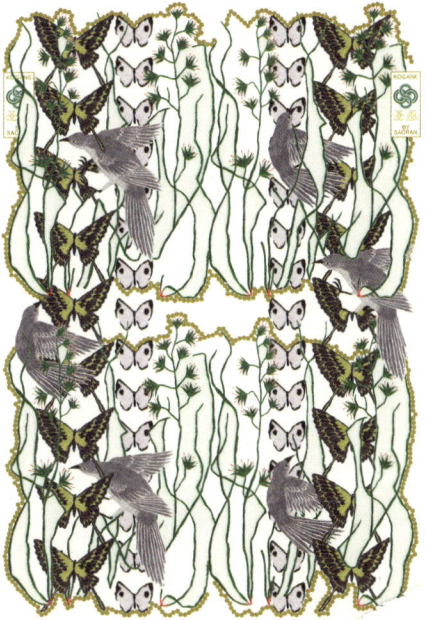

480 Book
TD. AD. D. 矢後直規 Naonori Yago
CL. Nick White
PT. 秀英明朝, AG Old Face

481 Poster
TD. AD. D. 山本ヒロキ Hiroki Yamamoto
CL. 渋谷美術学院 Shibuya Bijutu Gakuin
PT. Custom-made for the project

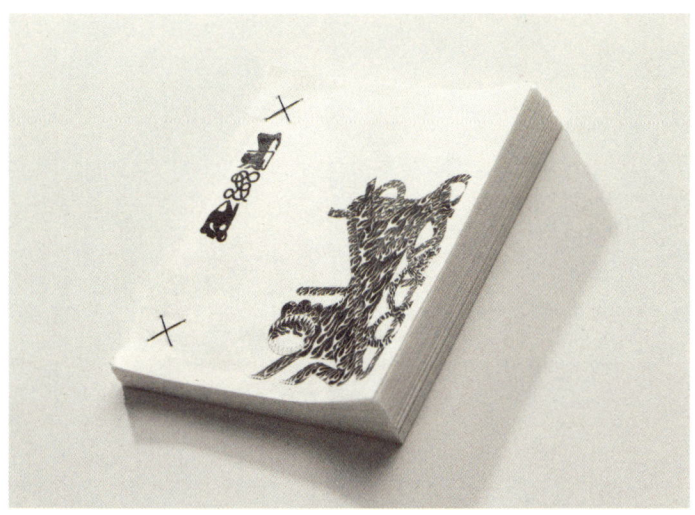

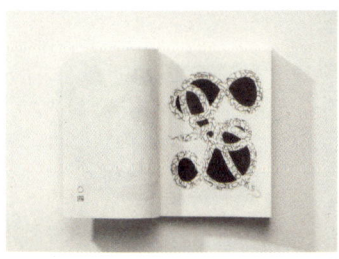

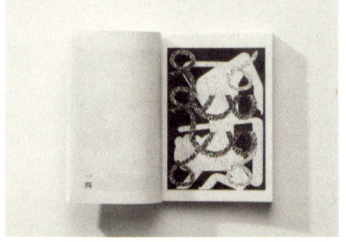

480

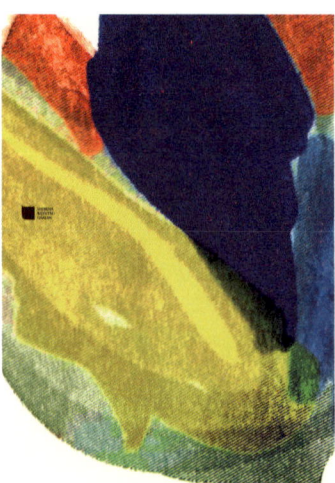

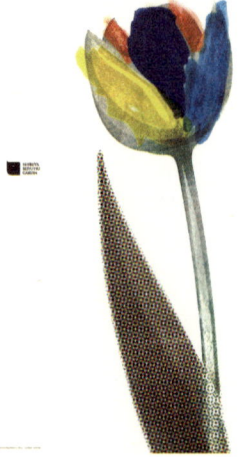

481

482 Seal
TD. AD. D. 山中桃子 Momoko Yamanaka
P. 玉村敬太 Keta Tamamura
COO. 東京ミッドタウン Tokyo Midtown
CL. カモ井加工紙（株）Kamoi Kakoshi Co., Ltd.
PT. A-OTF 見出ゴMB31 Pro MB31, A-OTF UD新丸ゴ Pro

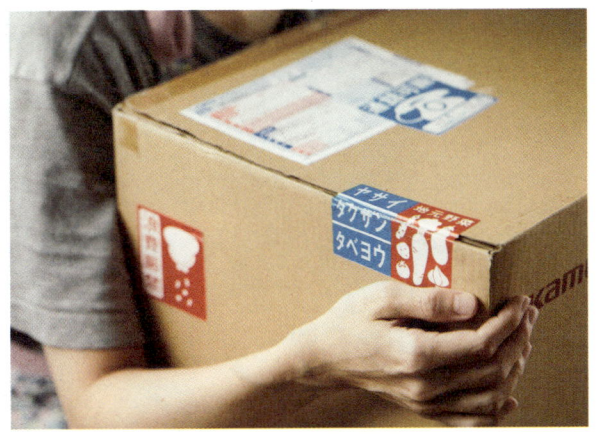

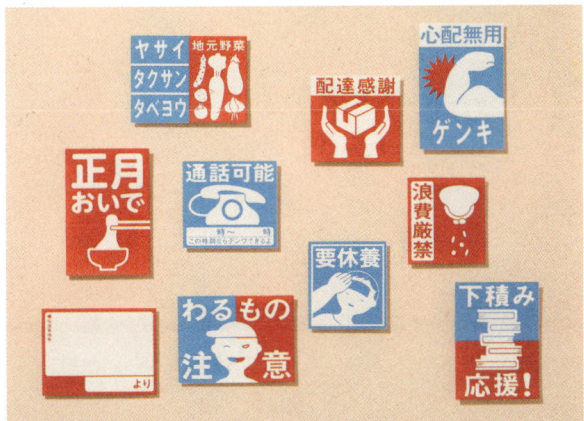

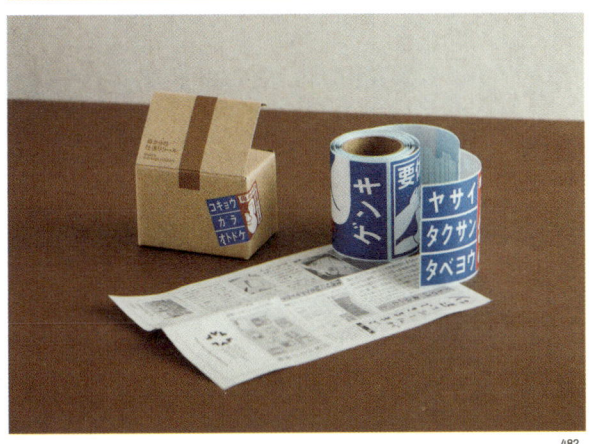

Prize Nominee Work

483 Record jacket
TD. AD. I. 矢入幸一 Koichi Yairi
CL. Non-commercial work
PT. Century Gothic, Custom-made for the project

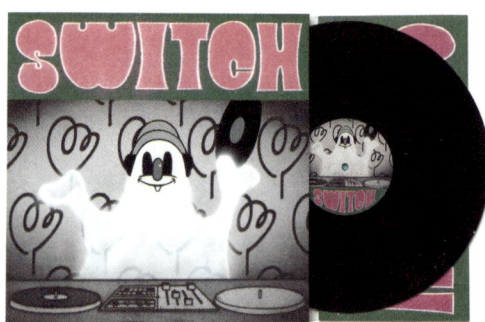
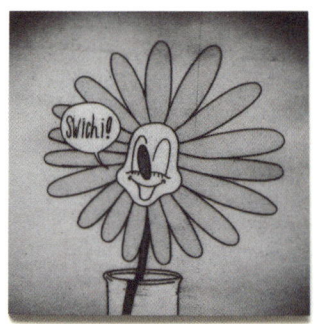
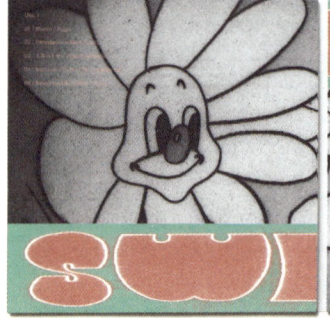
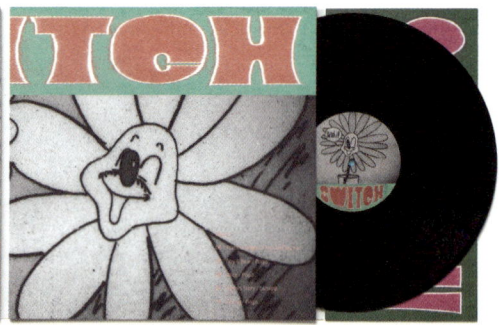
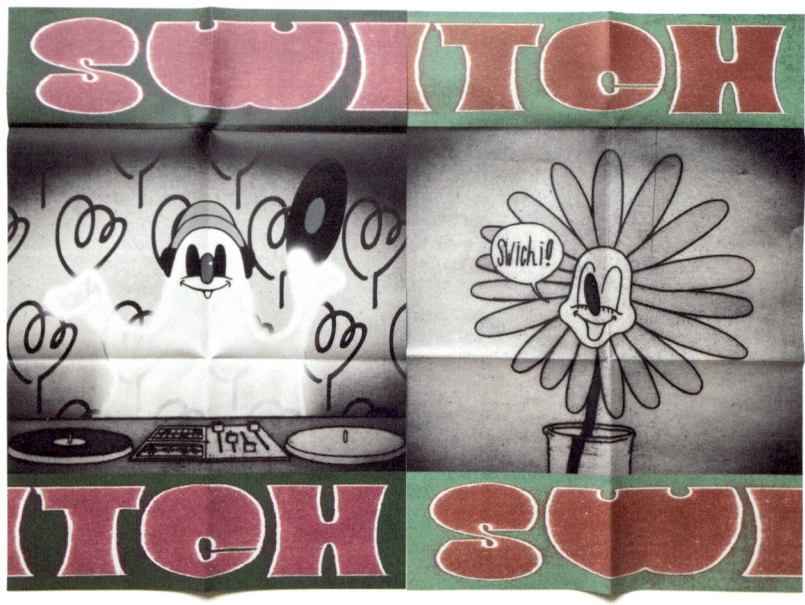

484 Calendar
TD. AD. I. 矢入幸一 Koichi Yairi
CL.（株）サン・アド Sun Ad Co., Ltd.
PT. Garamond, Custom-made for the project

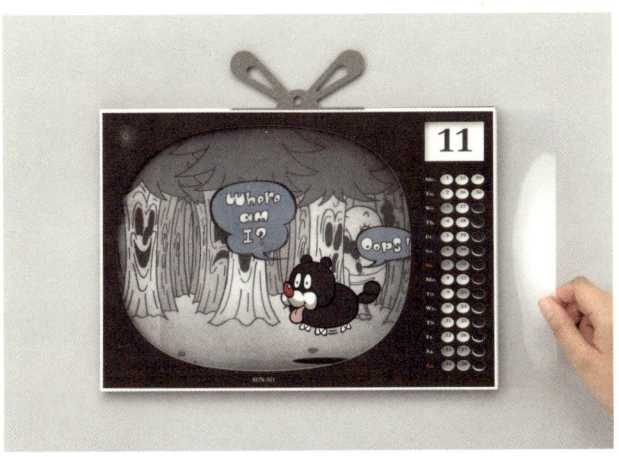

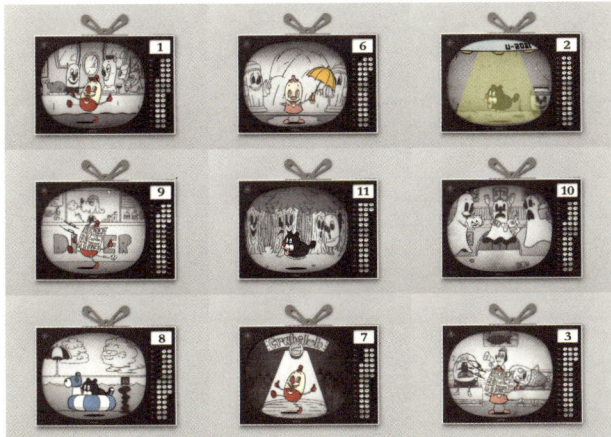

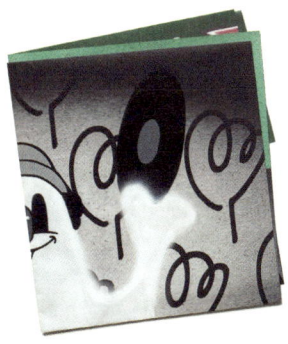
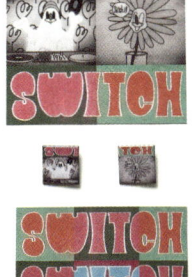
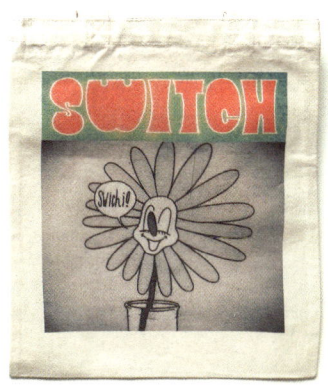

485 Book
TD. 山本浩貴 Hiroki Yamamoto
CL. (株)思潮社 Shichosha Co., Ltd.
PT. 貂明朝, FOT-筑紫Aオールド明朝 Pr6,
FOT-筑紫ゴシック Pro

486 Book
TD. AD. D. 山下ともこ Tomoko Yamashita
CL. モンターニュ Montagne
PT. Century Gothic Regular

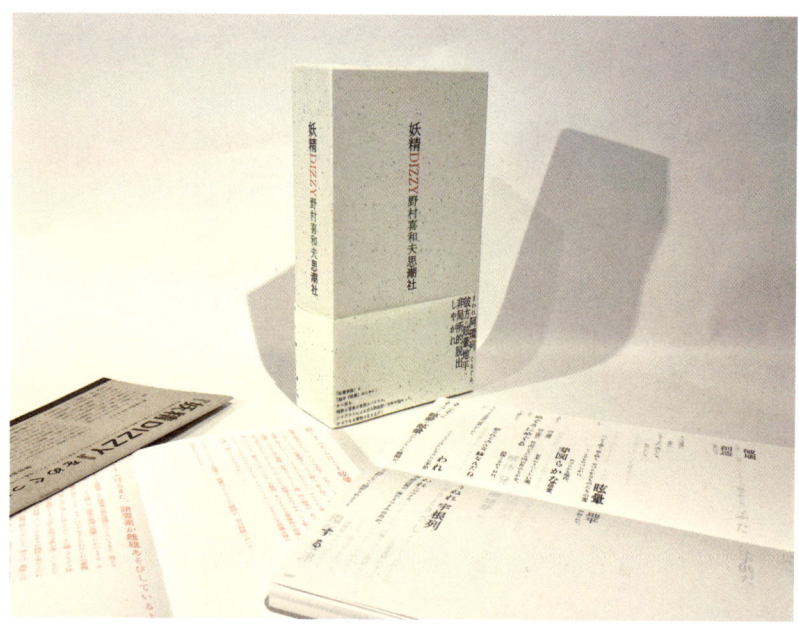

485

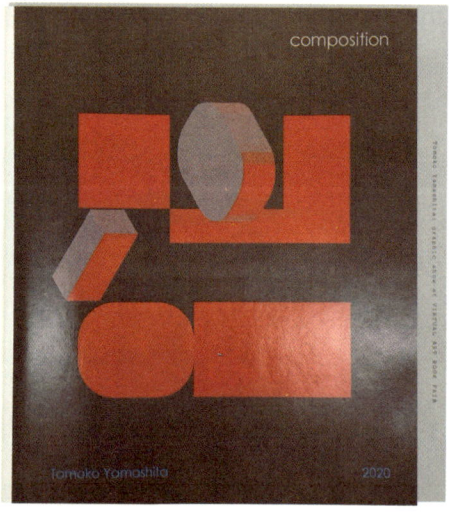

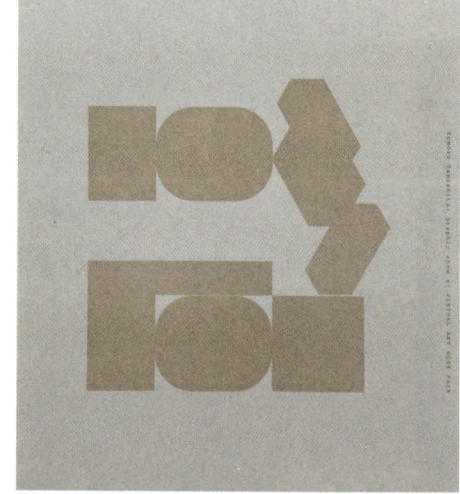

486

487 VI
TD. Yaoming Yan, Mijia Liu
CL. South South

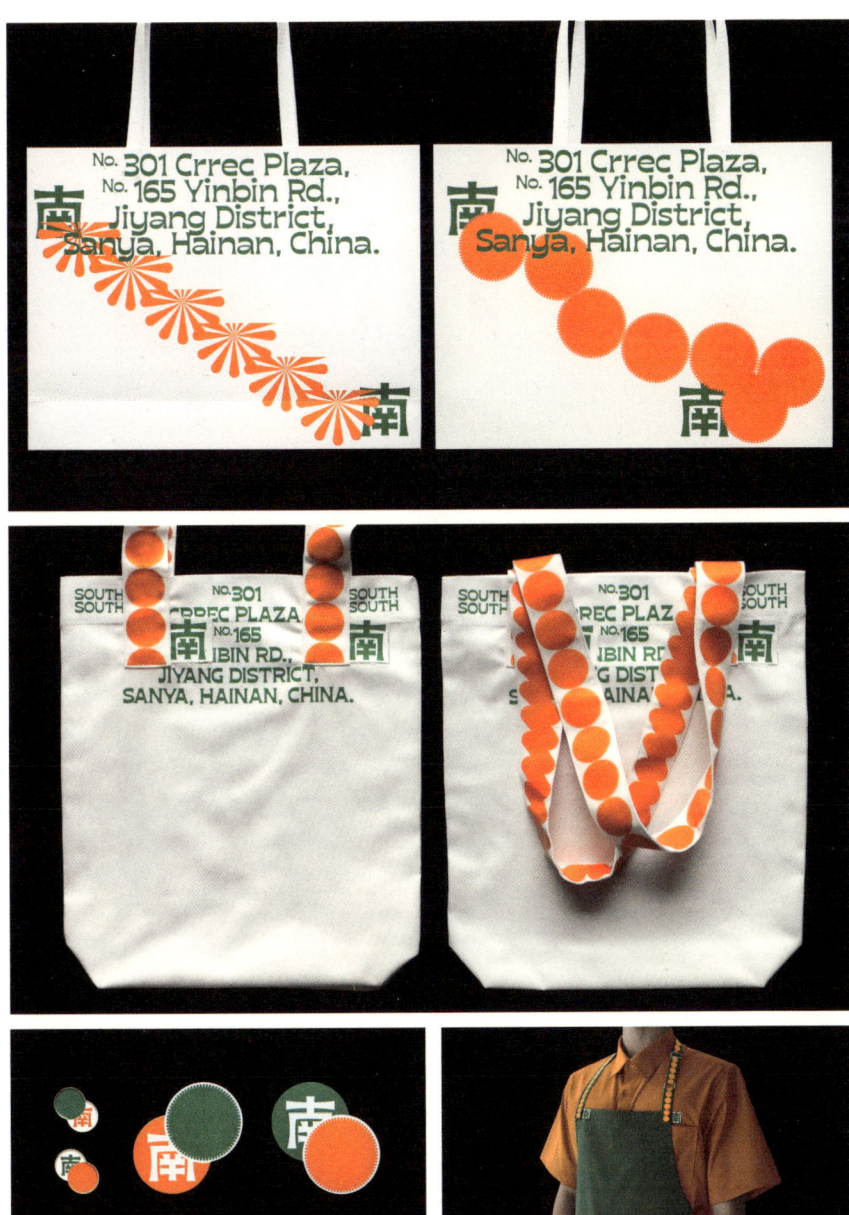

488 VI
TD. Yaoming Yan, Mijia Liu
CL. cheeer Studio

489 Exhibition
TD. AD. D. Senyu Yang
D. Kaizheng Hao, Ruiping Lai
CL. Tencent
PT. Custom-made for the project

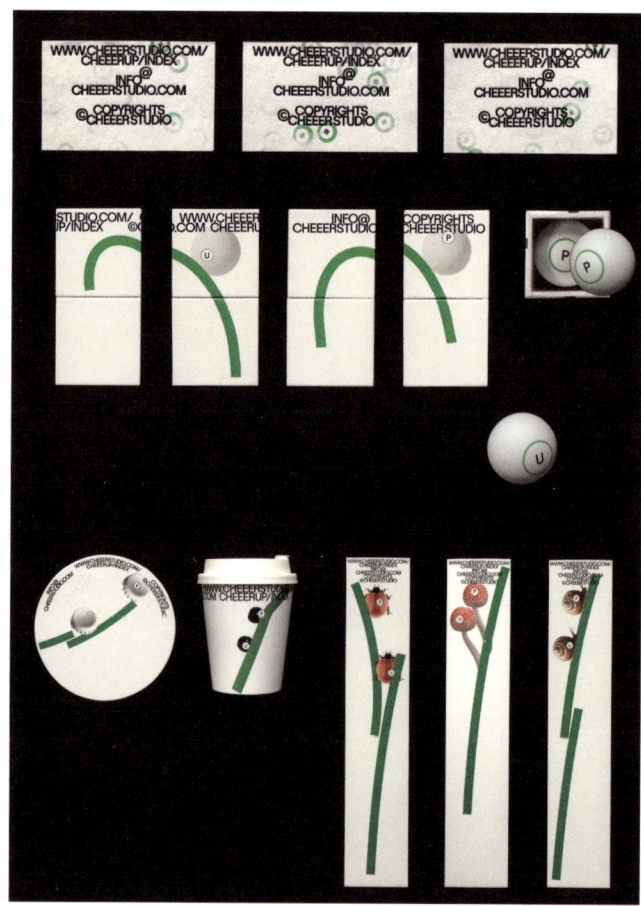

488

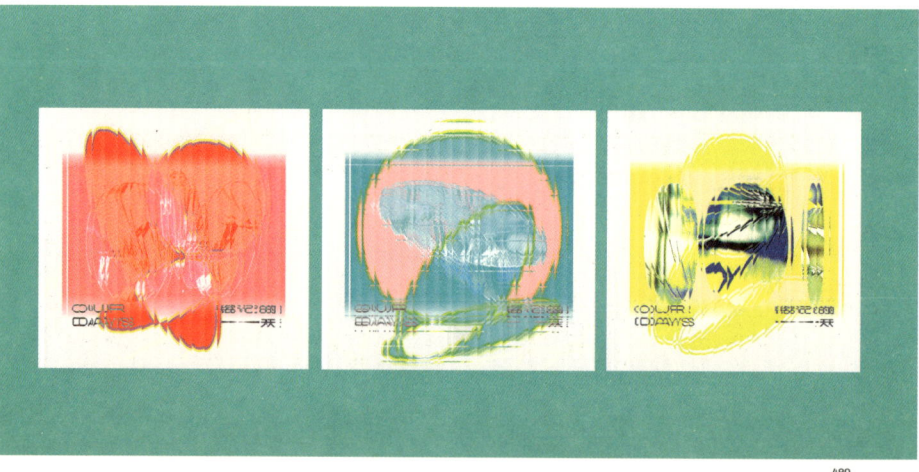

489

490 Packaging
TD. Yaoming Yan, Mijia Liu
CL. 十点一刻 22:15

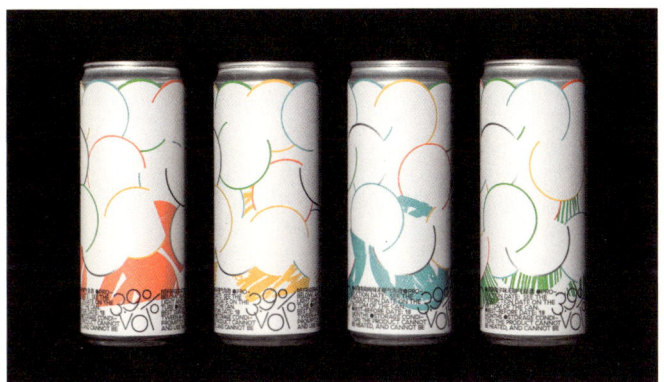

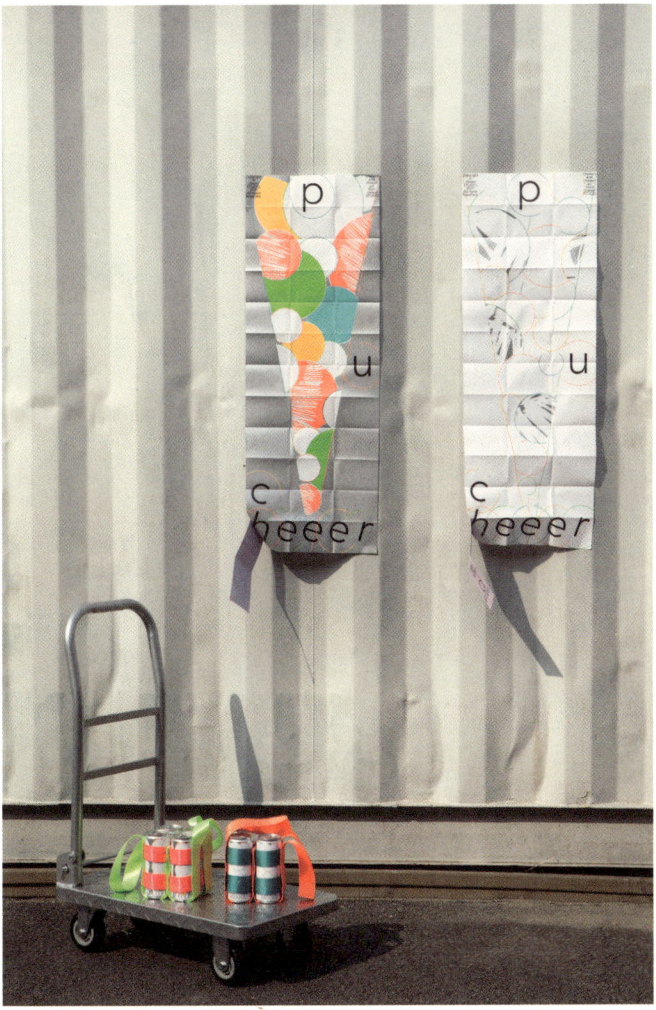

491 Book
TD. AD. D. P. Sun Yao
CL. Hongik University Visual Design Studio
PT. Caslon

492 BI
TD. Randy Yeo
CL. National Arts Council
PT. Founders Grotesk

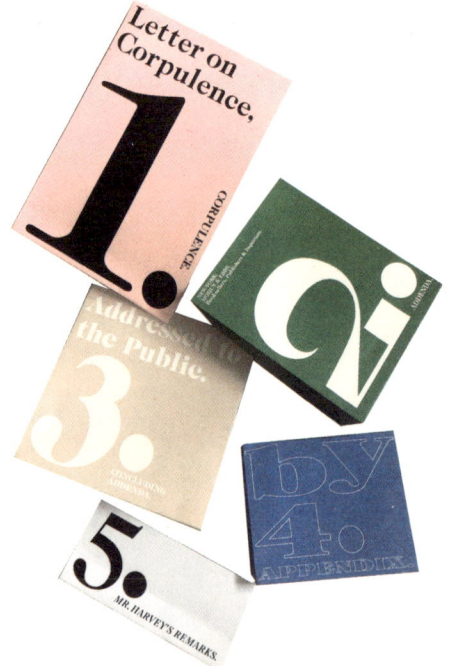

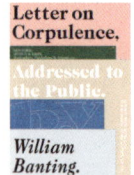
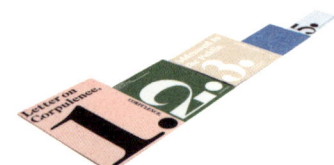
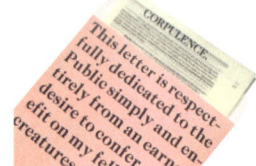

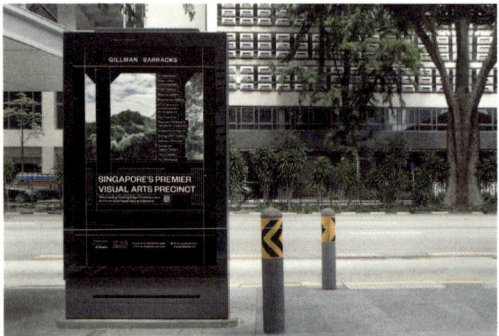
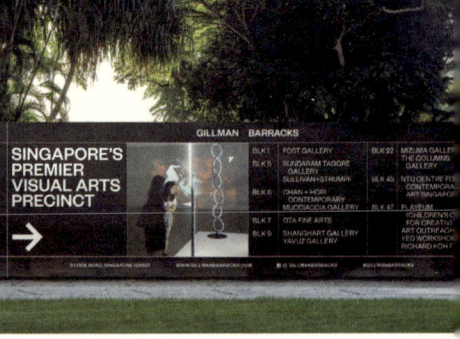

493 Book
TD. Yaping Guang
CL. Jiangxi Normal University

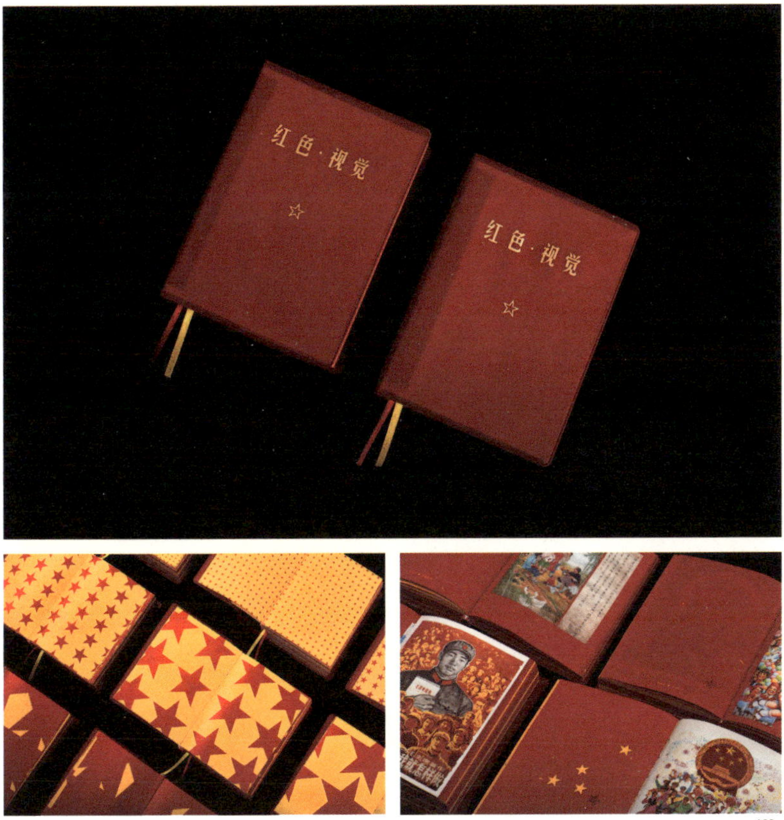

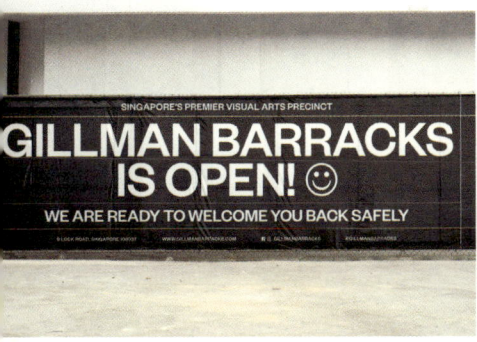
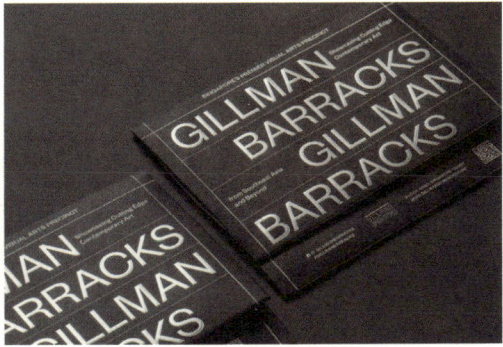

494 Book
TD. Randy Yeo
D. Martin Chen
P. Don Wong
CL. In Plain Words
PT. Visuelle by Mark de Winne

495 Branding
TD. Randy Yeo
D. Grace Duong
CL. SUNN
PT. Custom made for the project, Akzidenz Grotesk

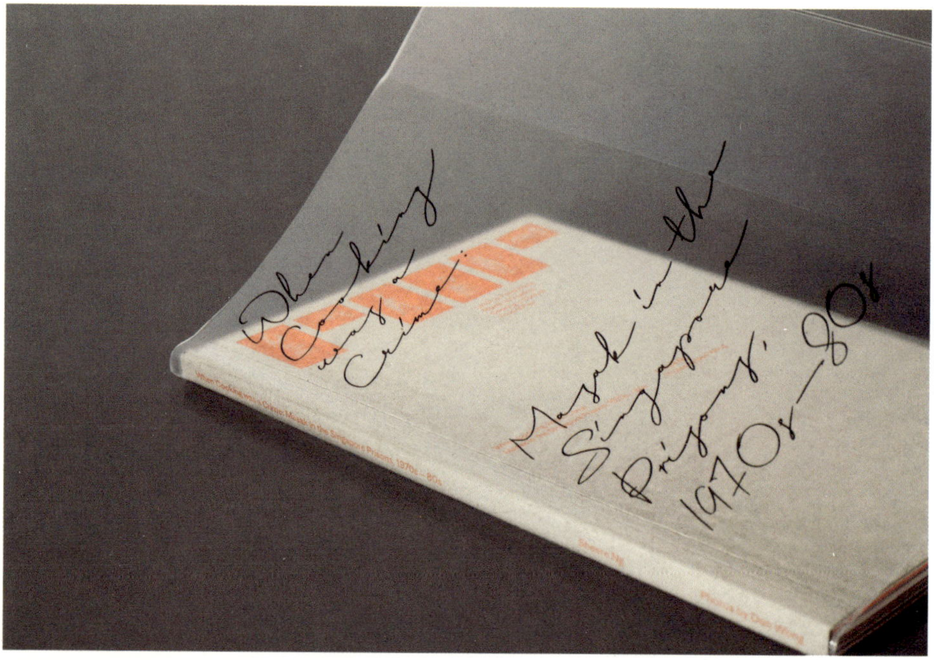

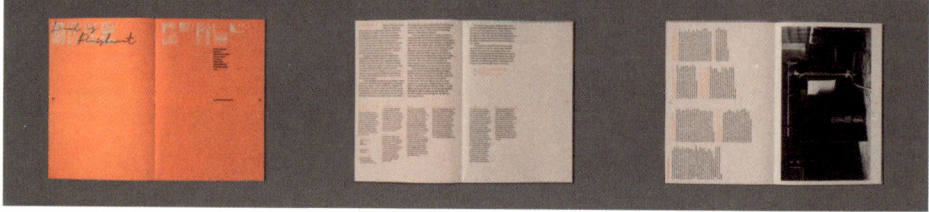

494

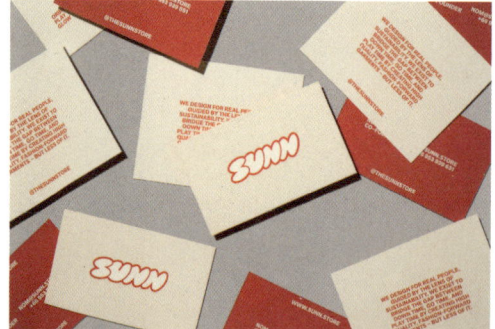
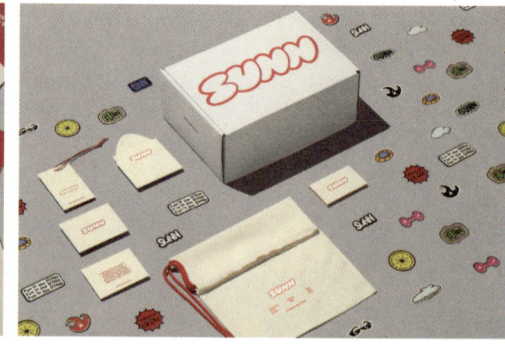

496 Label
TD. Tsan Yu Yin
CL. Ugly Half Beer
PT. Suisse Int'l Mono

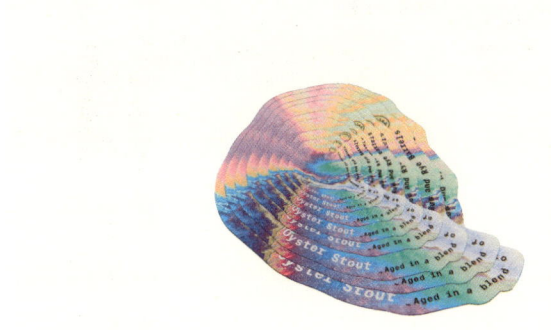

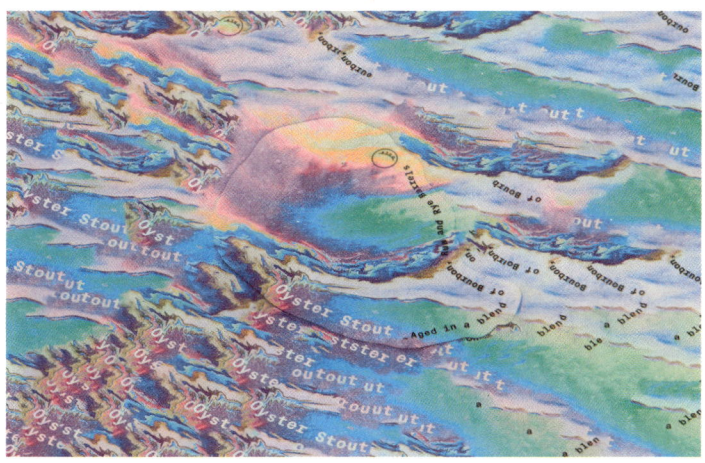

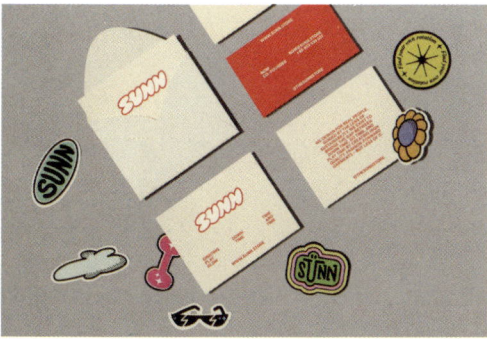

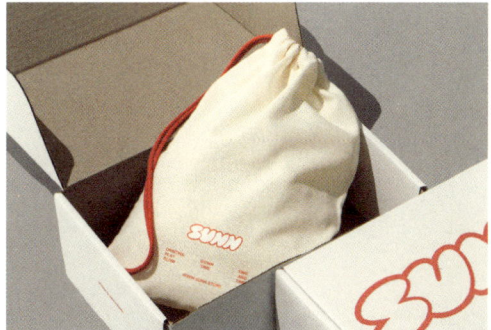

497 Poster
TD. AD. D. Zhongjun Yin
CL. The 4th Shenzhen International Poster Festival
PT. Source Han Sans

498 Book
TD. CD. AD. Yah-Leng Yu
D. Tess Sweeney, Sharon Choy
E. Lucy Lou
CL. Alwyn Chong
PT. Ogg Roman, Prestige Elite, Typewriter Elite, MinionPro, Universe

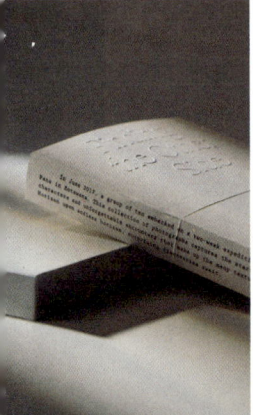
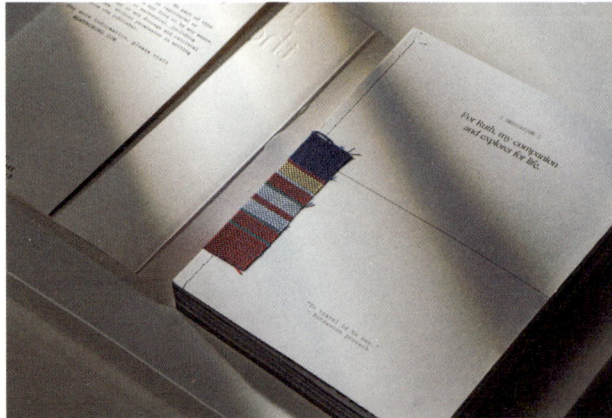
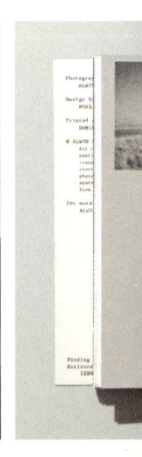

499 Book
TD. Mira Ying
D. Yang Hengbin, Chen Yan
T. Eonway Ying
P. Colleague Dong, Shen Jianwen, Shi Jiayu
CL. The Type
PT. Custom-made for the project, Plantin, SinoType Songti

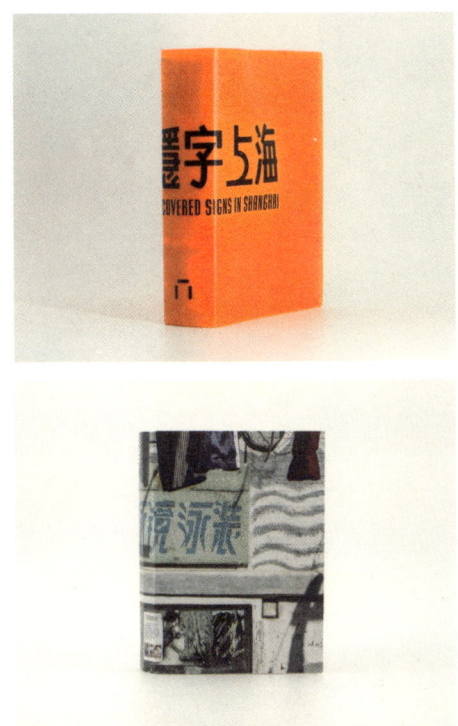

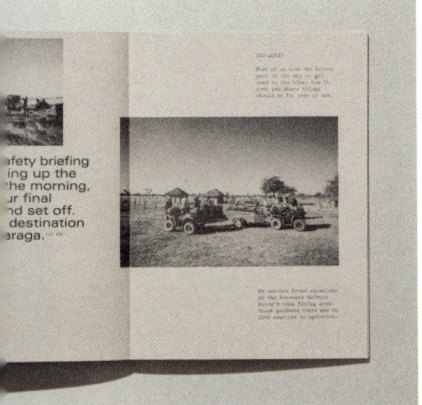

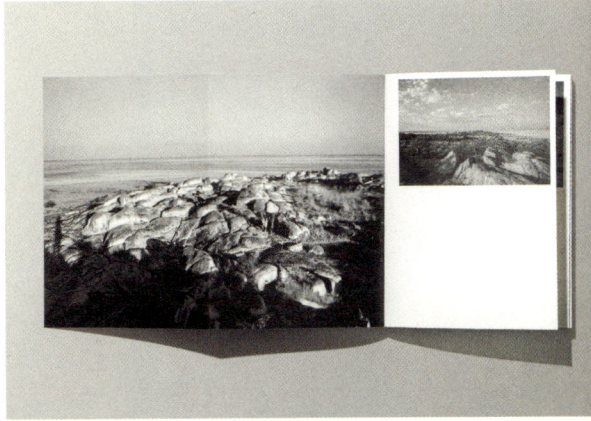

500 Branding
TD. CD. AD. Yah-Leng Yu
D. Dandy Hartono, Jiani Lu, Celsy Sabilla
CL. Figment
PT. Custom-made for Logo, Mazius, Sharp Grotesk

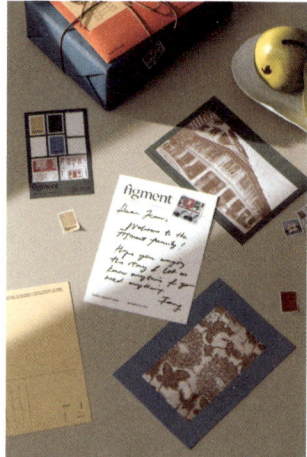
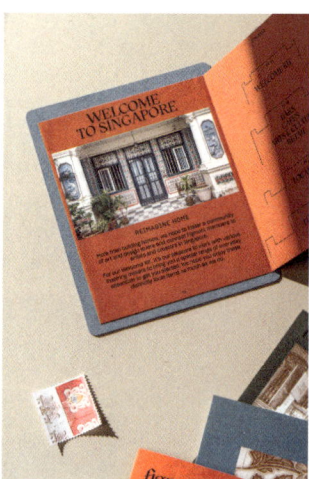
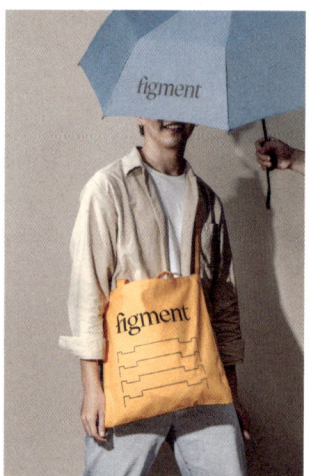
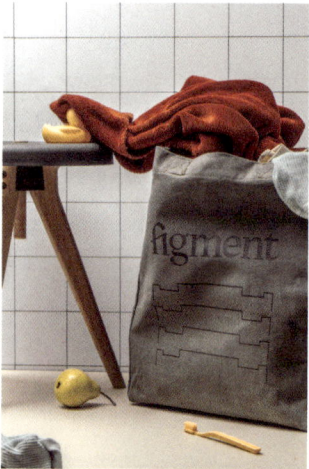
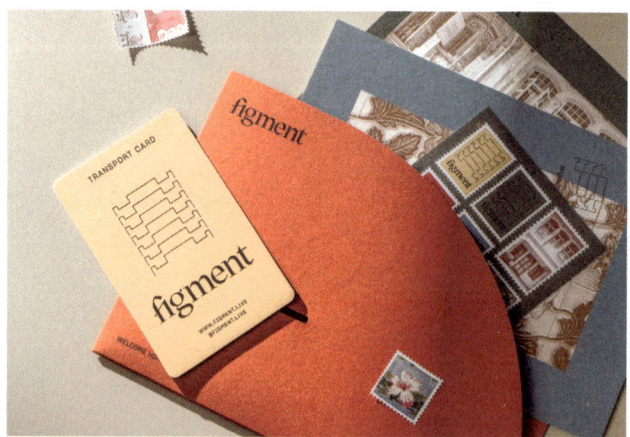
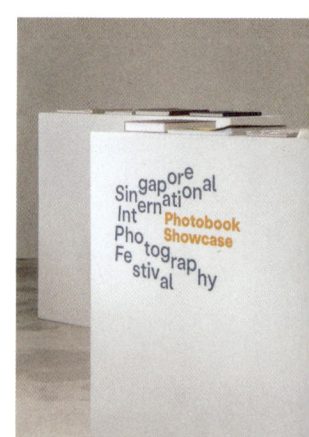

501 BI
TD. CD. AD. Yah-Leng Yu
D. Dandy Hartono
CL. Singapore International Photography Festival
PT. Stabil Grotesk

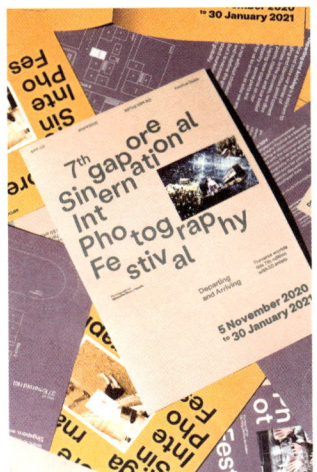
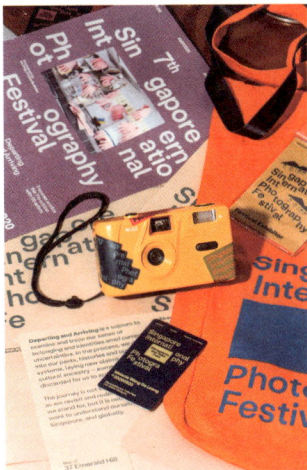
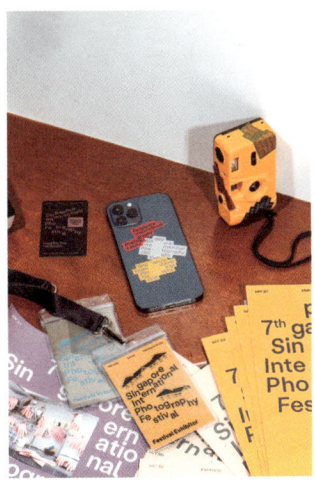
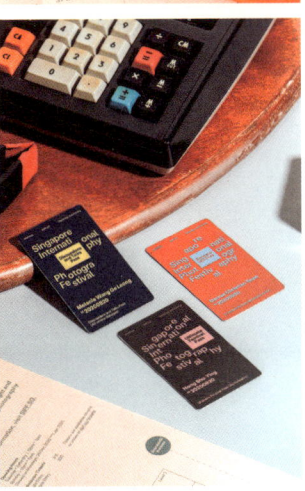
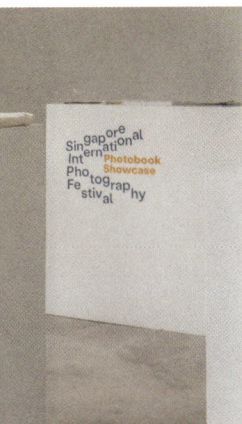
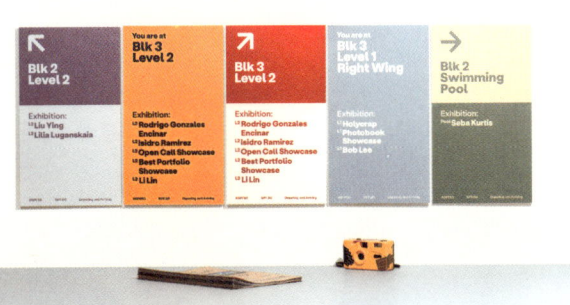

502 Type design
TD. 余秋子 Qiuzi Yu
CL. FounderType design Competition
PT. Custom-made for the project

503 Type design
TD. Junyi Yu
CL. Non-commercial work
PT. Costom-made for the project

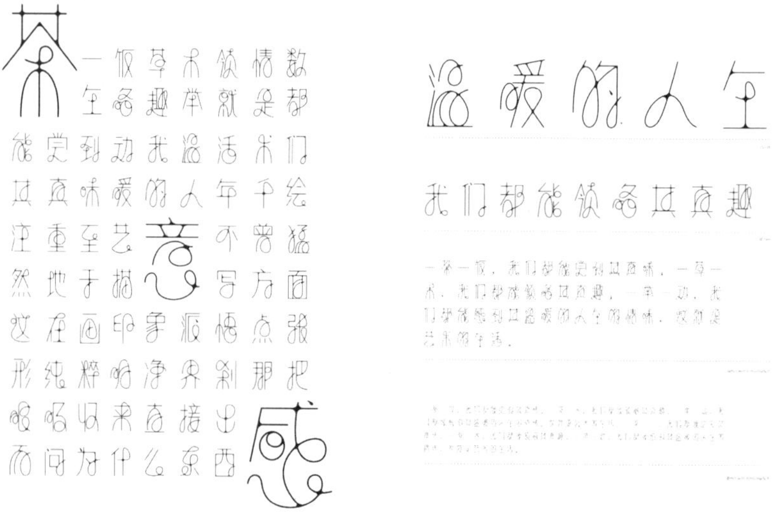

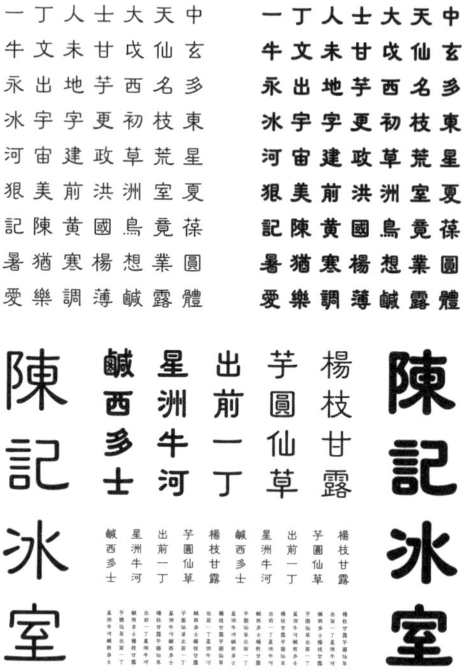

504 Book
TD. Zak Group
CL. Nike, Off-White c/o Virgil Abloh ™, Taschen
PT. Diatype, Monument Grotesk Mono

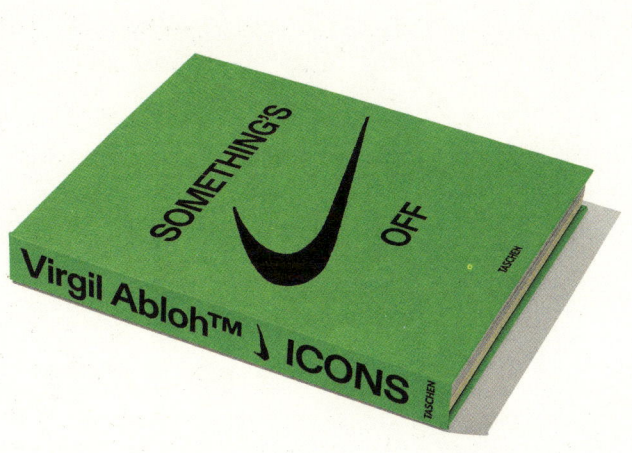

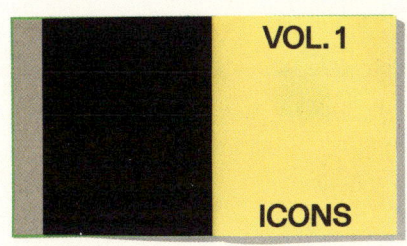

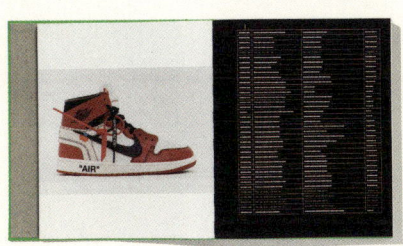

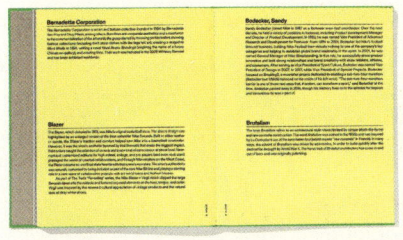

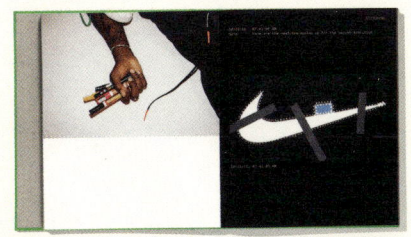

505 Exhibition design
TD. AD. D. Haocheng Zhang
D. Jua Klein Nina
P. Andrew Meredith
CL. University of the Arts London
PT. Body Experimental Type design by Haocheng Zhang

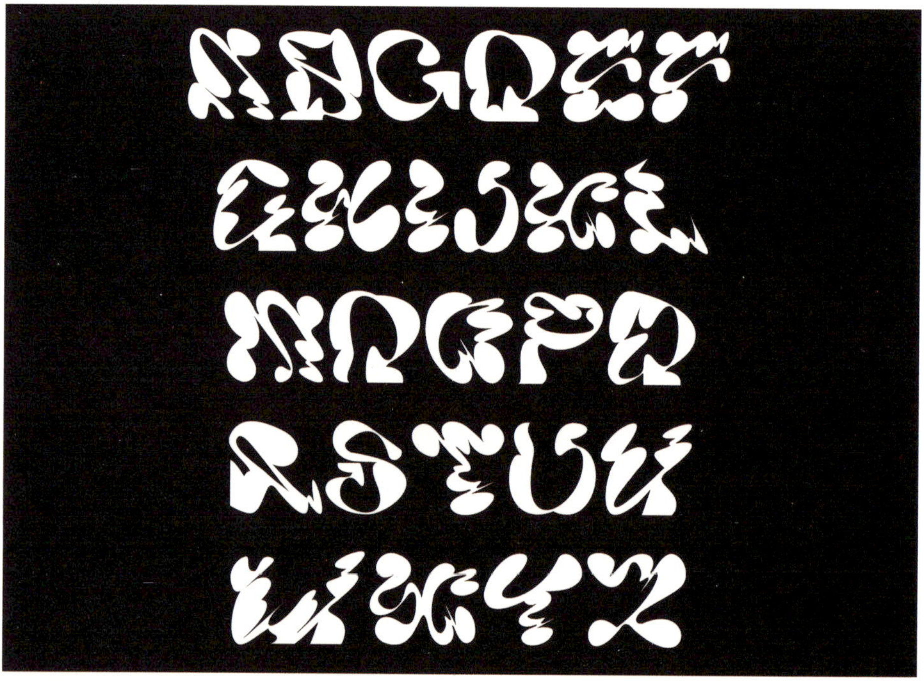

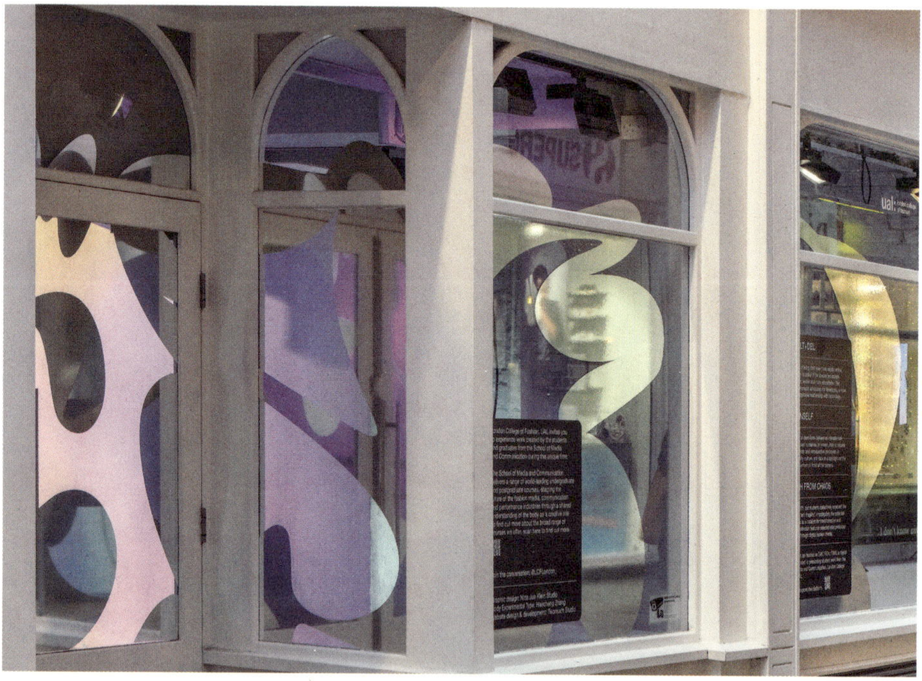

506 Book
TD. AD. D. P. Eager Zhang
CL. Non-commercial work
PT. Custom-made for the project, Neue Haas Unica

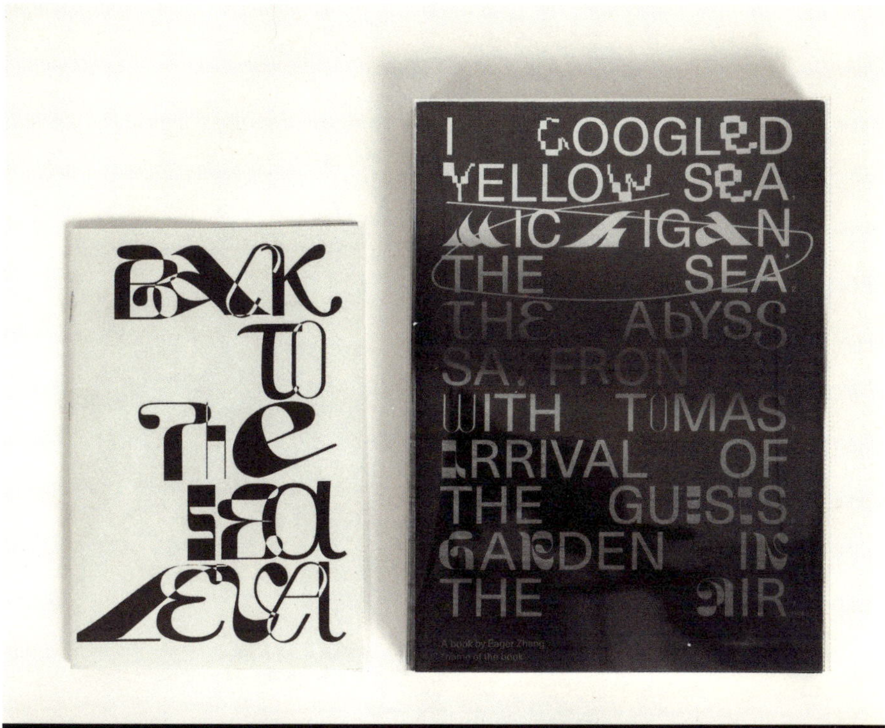

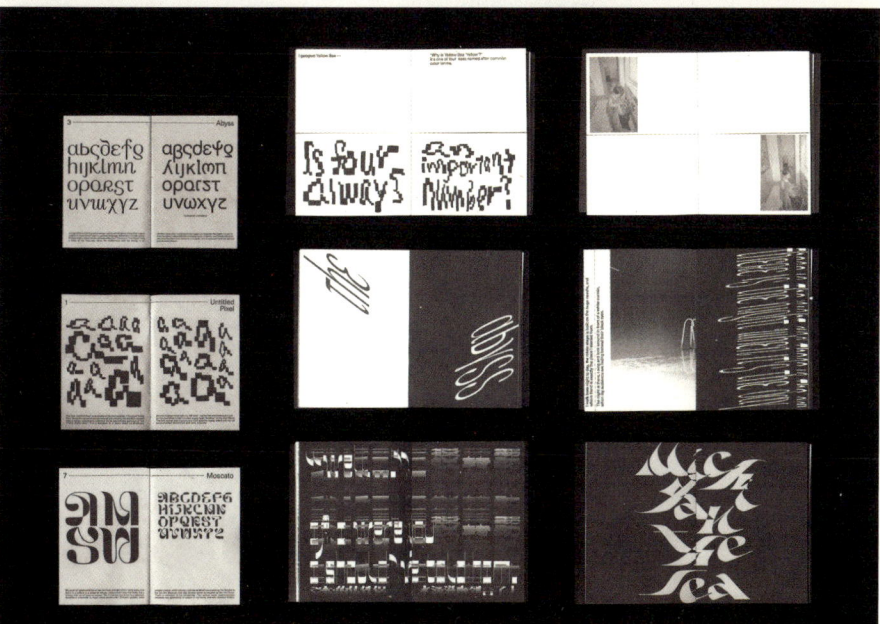

507 Poster
TD. Zexuan Zeng
CL. Club Space Ganzhou
PT. Custom-made for the project

508 Poster
TD. Zexuan Zeng
CL. The Exodus Project
PT. Custom-made for the project

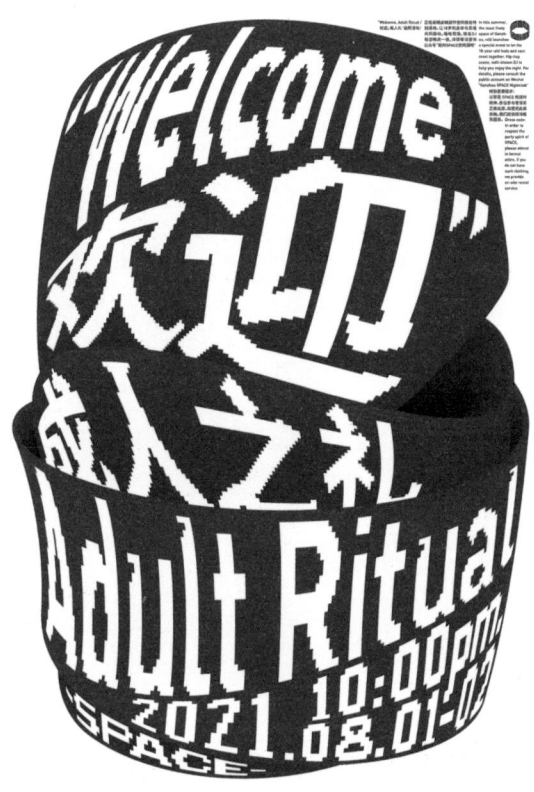

507

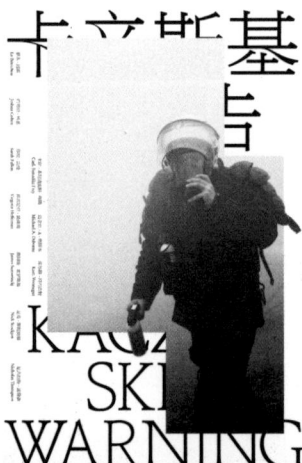

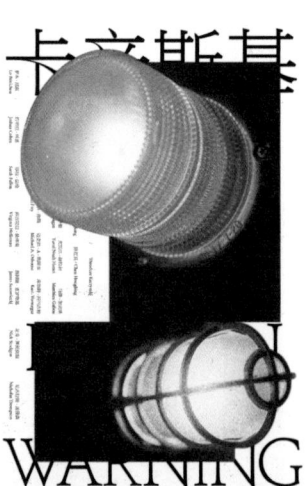

508

509 Poster
TD. AD. D. P. Eager Zhang
CL. Non-commercial work
PT. Custom-made for the project

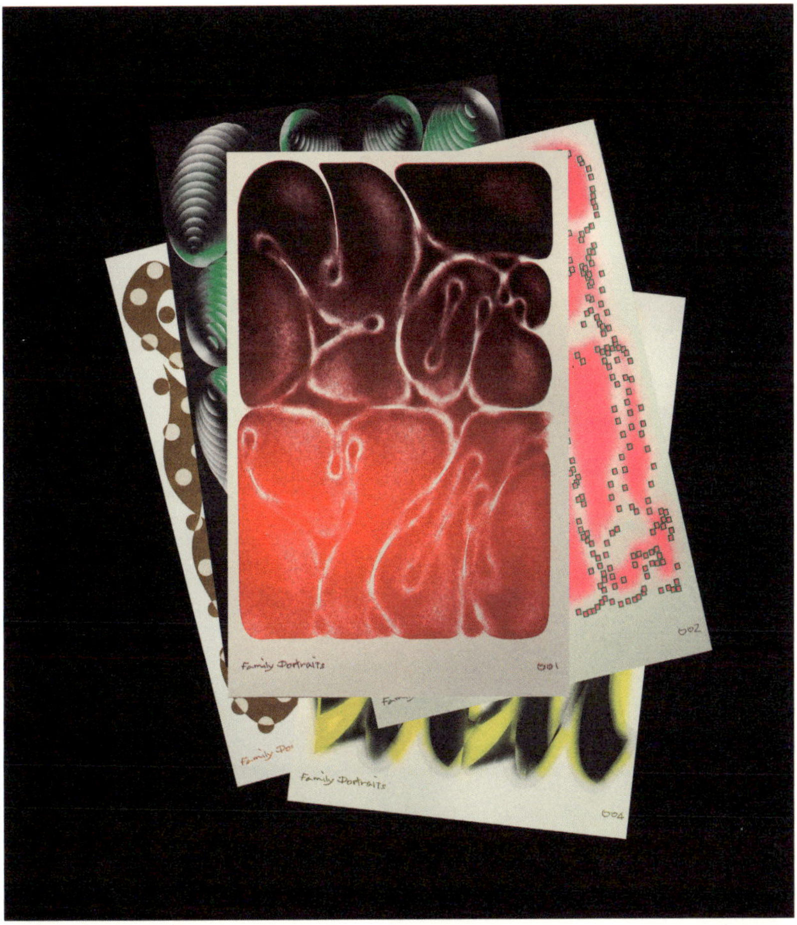

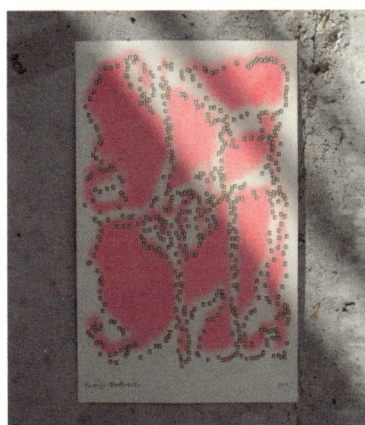
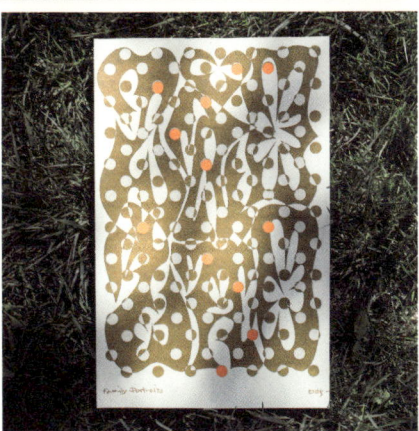

510 Branding
TD. AD. Wentian Zhang
D. Mengtong Li, Fan Zhou
PRO. Seethe Design
CL. Shin
PT. Ao Grotesque

511 Book
TD. AD. D. P. Zhao Yifeng
AD. Sun Hua, Feng Yu
AD. D. P. Huang Shu
AD. P. Zhang Yazhou
CL. Xu Bing
PT. FZFWZhuZiMincho, PTximing, Adobe Garamond

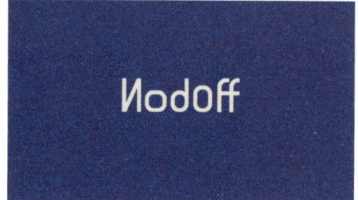
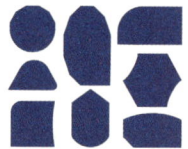
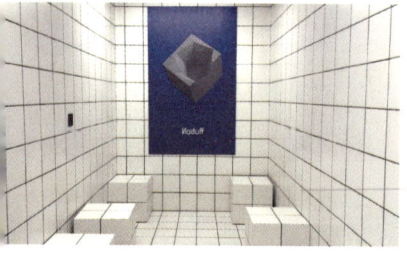
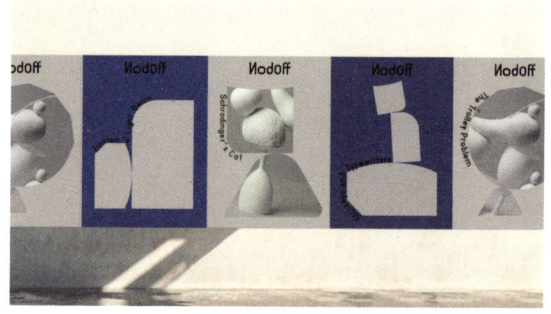
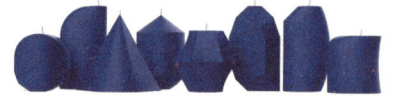
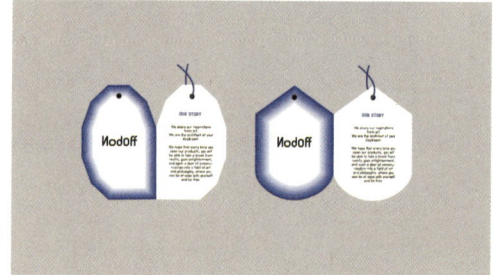

510

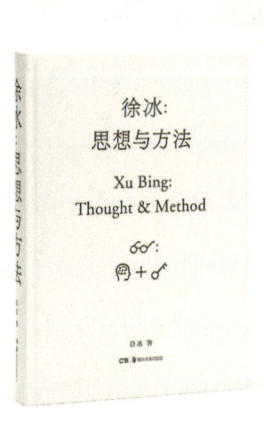
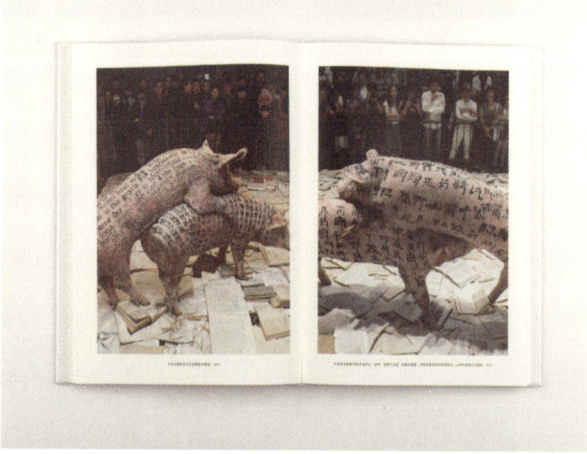

511

512 Poster
TD. AD. Zen Zheng
DS. CC Chen, Karo Hong
D. Kawing Feng
CL. Leaping Creative
PT. Custom-made for the project, HK Grotesk

re-defining >
brand experience design

leaping creative

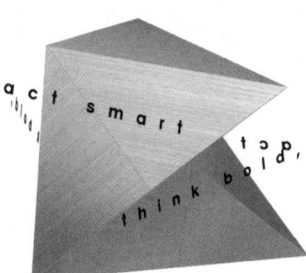

leaping creative

re-defining >
brand experience design

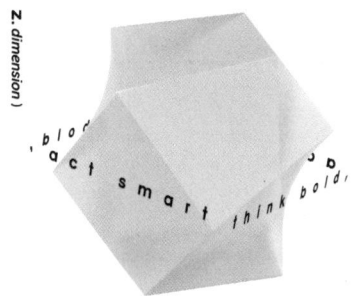

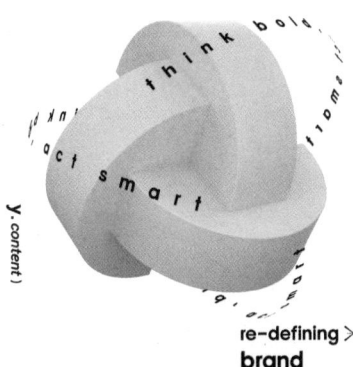

re-defining >
brand experience design

513 Experimental work
TD. Rozi Zhu
ADV. Richard The, Kyle Li, Anezka Sebek, Anna Harsanyi
CL. Non-commercial work
PT. Bubble Type

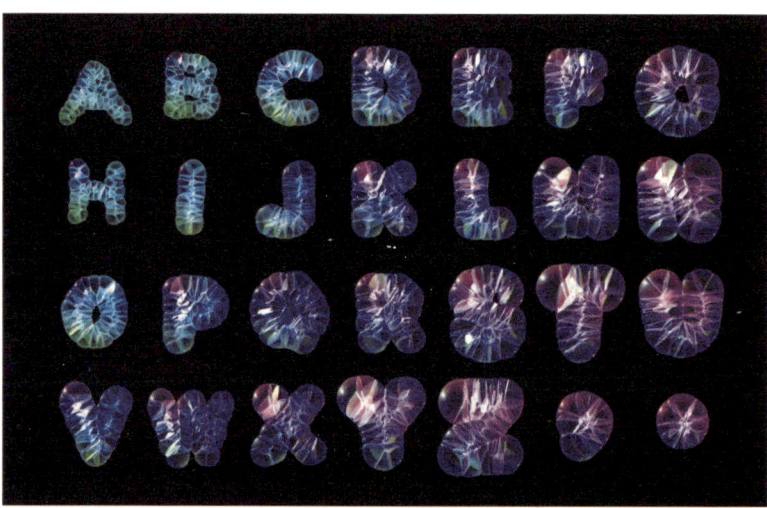

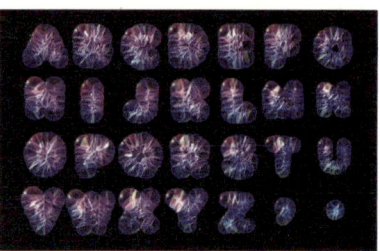
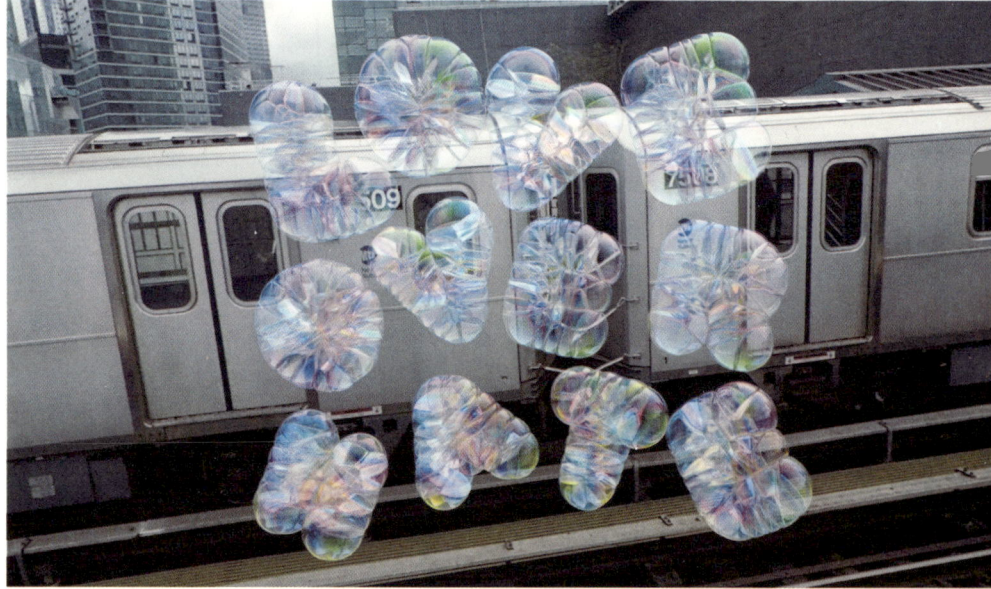

514 Book
TD. PU. Zolo Press
E. D. Arno Baudin
E. Julia Rommel
E (Interviewer). Rebecca Bengal
E (Assistant). Angela Baudin García
CE. PRR. Robert Morris Levine,
Romy Dolgin, Rachel Valinsky
P. Barb Choit, Brian Forrest, Vegard Kleven,
Dario Lasagni, Gunter Lepkowski,
Jason Mandella, Adam Reich, Paul Salveson
CS. Olivier Dengis
PT. Bradford LL

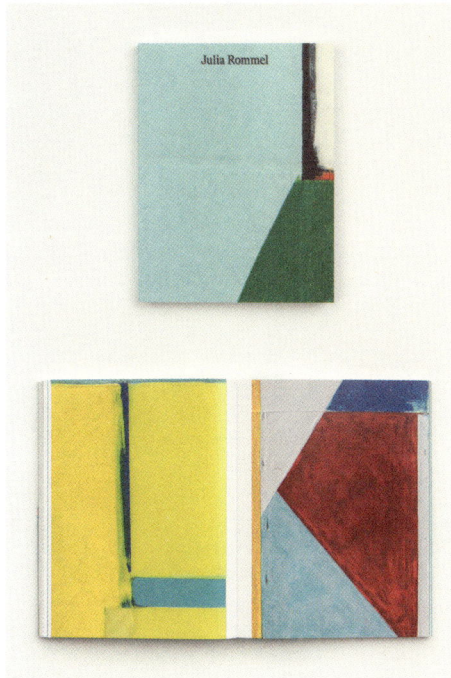
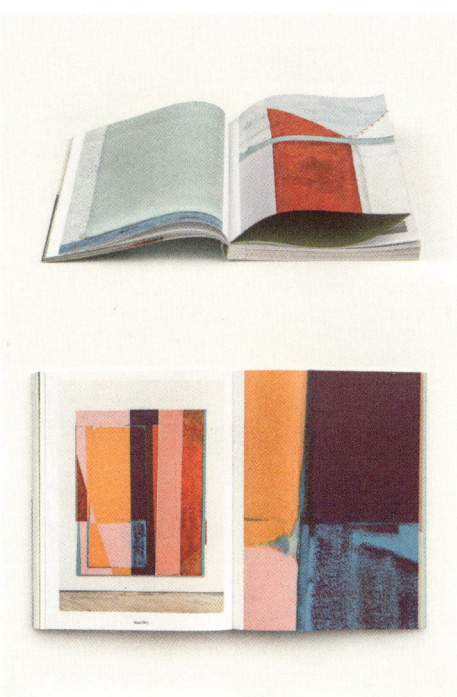

514

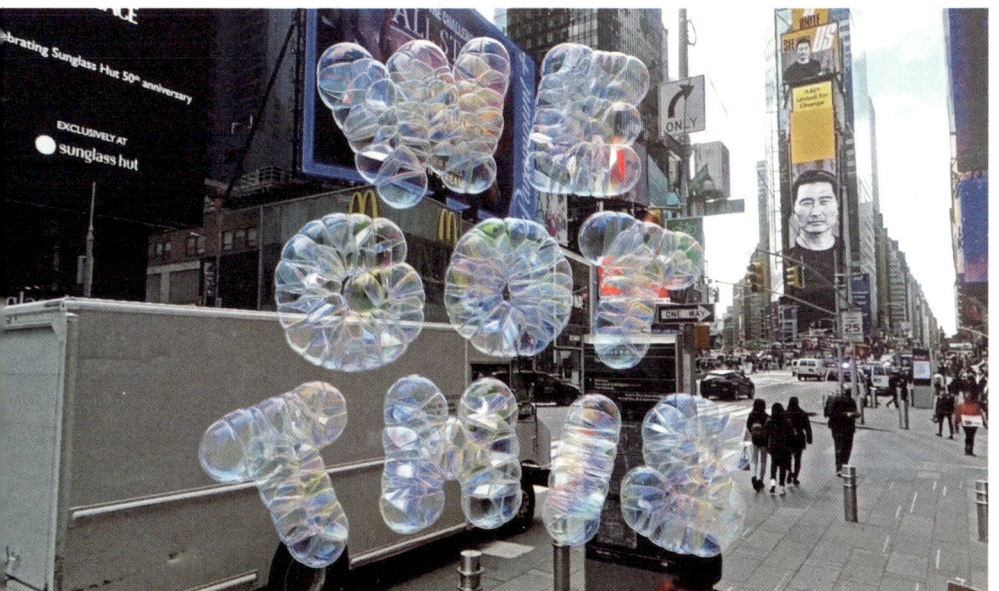

凡例
Usage Guide

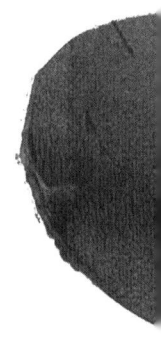

TD.	Type Director	ECO.	Editorial Coordinator
AD.	Art Director	EE.	English Editing
C.	Copy Writer	EN.	Engineering
CD.	Creative Director	FD.	Film Director
CA.	Calligrapher	LD.	Lettering Designer
D.	Designer	LP.	Letterpress Printing
DI.	Director	MD.	Motion Designer
E.	Editor	MO.	Model
I.	Illustrator	MU.	Music
P.	Photographer	OR.	Organizer
T.	Type Designer	PB.	Printing and Binding
W.	Writer	PCO.	Production Coordinator
CL.	Client	PM.	Project Manager
PT.	Principal Typeface	PR.	Producer
		PRG.	Programmer
		PRI.	Print
A.	Artist	PRO.	Production
ADV.	Advisor	Prof.	Professor
AP.	Animation Programmer	PRR.	Proofreading
AU.	Author	PRM.	Product Manager
BA.	Book Author	PU.	Publisher
BD.	Branding Designer	PUM.	Publishing Manager
CA.	Creative Agency	RE.	Retoucher
CCO.	Creative Coordinator	SD.	Sound Designer
CE.	Copyediting	SPD.	Space Design
COMP.	Composer	ST.	Stylist
CON.	Concept	SV.	Supervisor
CS.	Color Separation	TDI.	Technical Director
DC.	Design Collaboration	TS.	Typesetting
DCO.	Design Coordinator	3DM.	3D Modelling
DEV.	Developer	V.	Videographer
DP.	Director of Photography / Cinematographer	W.	Writer (Text)
		WD.	Web Design
DS.	Design Strateg	WDE.	Website Development

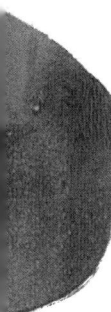

获奖者感言与简介
Winners' Comments and Outline of Their Careers

全场大奖
Grand Prize

名曲集+《安魂曲》曼努埃尔·卡多索
(Manuel Cardoso) 作曲
Meikyoku Album +「Manuel Cardoso: Requiem」

大西景太
Keita Onishi

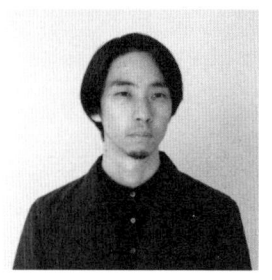

这是为《NHK名曲集+》创作的影像作品。《NHK名曲集+》是通过音乐可视化表现各种古典音乐杰作的NHK特别节目。我以16至17世纪的音乐家曼努埃尔·卡多索创作的无伴奏合唱曲《安魂曲》为对象进行了音乐的可视化表现。

《安魂曲》是由多个独立旋律，包含不同音高以及节奏构成的复调音乐。我使用笔记体字体书写的歌词动态地表现不同的音高、音长，从而展现6位歌者合唱中各自的旋律，以求让听众从视觉上理解现已经很难听到的复调音乐。而画面中的每一根线条均代表歌者的一次发声。

我完全没有想到这样的作品能获得评委的高度评价，在大感惊讶的同时，还强烈感受到将评价标准置于经济效益之外的东京TDC所具备的深刻的社会意义。我认为，《安魂曲》的获奖将给各种创意人以希望。深表感谢。

—

影像艺术家，常驻日本东京和神奈川。毕业于东京艺术大学研究生院美术研究系(设计学)。使用动画手法表现音乐的构造以及声音的质感，以制作影像装置作品以及音乐视频。此外，还从事电视广告、概念电影、动态CI等广告以及电视媒体的制作活动。

This video was made for the NHK program, "Meikyoku Album + (plus)," showcasing works that visualize masterpieces of classical music, made by various visual creators. For my own visualization, I chose Requiem, a piece for an unaccompanied chorus by 16th century composer Manuel Cardoso.

It is a "polyphonic" composition of multiple melodies that consist of notes of varying pitch and length. The voices of the six vocalists, who each sing a different melody, are expressed through an animation of the lyrics written in longhand style, according to the pitch and length of each note. The idea was to help the viewer/listener understand by way of visual perception the structure of the polyphony—a style that has become rare these days. Each line represents at once the respective singer's breath.

While being highly surprised at the high evaluation given to this kind of work, it also made me feel very strongly the significance of the TDC's evaluation of design beyond economic aspects. I think the fact that I received this reward will be encouraging for various types of creators. Thank you very much.

—

A video artist based in Tokyo and Kanagawa, Japan. Graduated the master's program (Design) at Tokyo University of the Arts, graduate school of Fine Arts. Onishi produces video installation works and music videos using animation methods to express the structure of music and the texture of sound. He is also involved in advertising, such as commercials, concept movies and motion CIs.

书籍设计奖
Book Design Prize

20th Century Women Screenplay Book

Actual Source, Davis Ngarupe & JP Haynie

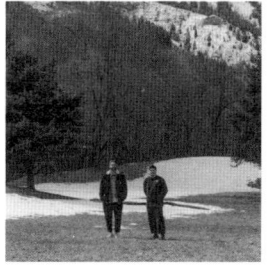

本书是A24 Screenplay Collection的第5本。收录了Mike Mills撰写的完整的剧本、Greta Gerwig的序言、纪录片导演Matt Wolf的随笔、Mike Mills与Maggie Nelson的对谈、以及Mike Mills在电影拍摄过程中手写的笔记。

-

Actual Source是Davis Ngarupe（库克群岛，美国）与JP Haynie（美国）共同经营的设计事务所。他们为各种不同领域的客户提供各种规模的出版设计、VI设计、网页设计、包装设计、时装设计以及空间设计等领域的服务。最近的主要设计项目包括：Nike Design Exploration的品牌识别系统、HBO / A24's Euphoria的8册书籍套装、Shoplifters Issue 10等。

Book 005 in the A24 Screenplay Collection features the complete screenplay by Mike Mills, a foreword by Greta Gerwig, an essay by documentary filmmaker Matt Wolf, a conversation between Mike Mills and Maggie Nelson, and an annotated selection of Mike Mills' handwritten notecards from the making of the film.

—

Actual Source is the collaborative design practice of Davis Ngarupe (Cook Islands / USA) and JP Haynie (USA). Together, and with their community of collaborators, they design and produce publications, visual identities, websites, packaging, apparel, and physical spaces for clients in many diverse fields at large and small scale. Recent projects include an identity system for Nike Design Exploration (NDE), an 8 book boxed set for *HBO / A24's Euphoria* and *Shoplifters Issue 10*.

字体设计奖
Type Design Prize

Altesse

Jean François Porchez

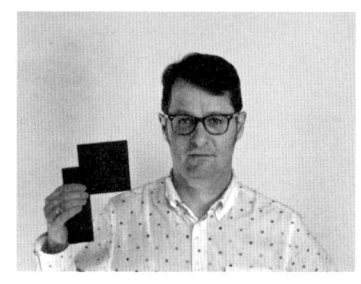

Altesse 是以 19 至 20 世纪的法国铜版雕刻师的文字为蓝本设计的字体。

其风格受到数世纪以来广泛使用的法国铜版雕刻文字的直接影响。我们的构想并非是要再现某个时代的著名人物书写的文字，而是以日常书写的文字为蓝本确立设计样式。19 世纪初以来，正式的笔记体成为法国贵族公告用铜版雕刻文字的标准，为此，活字铸造所也曾尝试将手工铜版雕刻文字铸造为金属活字。但在金属活字技术之中必须分别铸造每一个字母，还必须巧妙、精确地连接各个字母以表现其连续性，其操作异常复杂。究其原因是正式的笔记体具有自然的倾斜，其极具装饰性的终笔部的形状以及连接处无法安放于垂直的金属活字的字身之中。为此，正式的笔记体字体开发不得不等待到预示数字字体的照相排版技术普及，字体设计得以从金属活字的物理限制获得解放之时。然而，照相排版技术也并未能提供笔画更多的丰富变化以及相应的技术。我们致力于尽可能地为使用者提供自动的、圆滑的Altesse字体的丰富变化。

—

Typofonderie的创立者、ZeCraft的字体指导、数字字体的先驱者之一。作为信息传播者和人才挖掘者，团队合作是他关注的核心。正因如此，他在2015年创办TypeParis。他曾作为平面设计师接受严格的训练，在此期间开始专注于字体设计，其后在Dragon Rouge担任字体指导，90年代初任职于Le Monde报社。2004年至2007年间任ATypI（国际文字设计协会）主席。2011年至2019年间任ECV Master design & Typography创办人兼代表。他还是Club des Directeurs Artistiques in Paris的理事、NY TDC会员。1998 年他获得Prix Charles Peignot奖，并凭借其字体设计获得了无数奖项。2009年入选法国名人录。2014年，Perrousseaux出版了他的专著。2015 年获得艺术与文学骑士勋章。2017年开始，法国总统埃马纽埃尔·马克龙开始使用他设计的字体。

Altesse is a typographic adaptation of the scripts engraved by the French copperplate masters from the 19th and 20th centuries.

The drawings are directly influenced by French copperplate engravings in use over the centuries. The idea was to identify a style based on daily practices and not the search for the work of a writing master from a given period. Since the beginning of the 19th century, the use of formal script became the standard for the announcements copperplate of the French aristocracy. Foundries tried to adapt typographically copperplate scripts: each letter must be engraved separately but linked to the next. A complex operation, because the formal script is naturally slanted while the punches and metal type shot are perpendicular, which leaves no room to draw the shapes and their connections as well as the flourished endings. It was necessary to wait for photocomposition, which foreshadows the transition to digital typography, to be completely freed from the metal type. Photocomposition does not yet provide the many necessary variants and the technology for contextualizing letters. This is where we put our efforts, to make the use of the Altesse variations as smooth as possible by automating as much as possible.

—

Founder of Typofonderie, type director of ZeCraft, Jean François Porchez is one of the pioneers of digital typography. Transmitter of knowledge and discoverer of talents, teamwork is at the heart of his concerns. It is also for these reasons that he launched TypeParis in 2015. After training as a graphic designer, during which he focused on type design, Jean François Porchez (1964) worked as a type director at Dragon Rouge, then at Le Monde newspaper in early 90s. He was President of the Association Typographique Internationale in 2004–2007. Founder and head of ECV Master design & Typography between 2011–2019. He is board member of the Club des Directeurs Artistiques in Paris and member of the Type Directors Club in New York. He was awarded the Prix Charles Peignot in 1998 and numerous prizes for his typefaces. Introduced to French Who's Who in 2009. In 2014, Perrousseaux publishes his monograph. Knight in the order of Arts and Letters in 2015. The President of France, Emmanuel Macron use his typefaces for his communication since 2017.

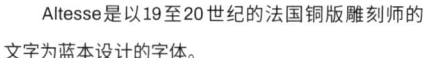

RGB 奖
RGB Prize

3&bC Website

北川一成 Issay Kitagawa + Semitransparent Design

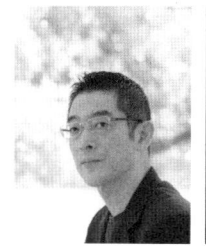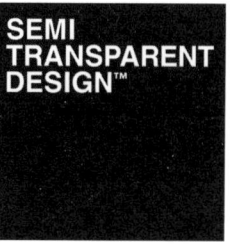

这是将"3&bC 不受约束"的品牌概念巧妙地利用网络的响应性（其构图与尺寸随终端设备可变）进行崭新表现的网站设计。

无论对于何种终端设备都能"不受约束"地鲜明地展现出商品的色彩且能依据各种终端设备的尺寸最大限度地表现商品的尺寸。该网站的设计中体现出网络特有的技术和独具匠心的表现方式的共存。

-

北川一成
GRAPH公司执行董事/首席设计师
1965年生于日本兵库县加西市。1987年毕业于筑波大学。1989年入职GRAPH公司（旧称：北川纸器印刷株式会社）。将创造能引人共鸣的设计视为目标，贯彻于品牌、设计、知识产权管理、角色设计、造物等各类活动之中。他立足于经营者以及设计师双方的视角而提出的"作为经营资源的设计方法"的理念，获得了从本地中小企业至海外知名奢侈品品牌等众多客户的广泛支持。

Semitransparent Design
创立于2003年。业务范围包括网站策划和制作、平面设计、国内外的美术馆和画廊的作品展览等。曾经策展、执行的主要活动有，在山口信息艺术中心"YCAM"举办的创意团体"Semitra"的"tFont/fTime"展、在CREATION GALLERY G8举办的"Illuminating Graphics 0、1、2"展、在ginza graphic gallery举办的"Semitransparent Design Tikutu"展，此外还曾参加 ICC（NTT InterCommunication Center）举办的open space 2008、2015等展览。

This website communicates the brand concept of "3&bC wa, torawarenai" ("3&bC is independent") with a tongue-in-cheek reference to the aspect ratio for the responsiveness of device browsers connecting to the internet (i.e., in the variability of layouts and sizes to fit any device size).

Products are displayed as large as possible in response to the size of the user's device, in order to make colors appear vividly "independent of" device sizes. This site was constructed as a website that boldly combines distinctive web technologies and expressions.

—

Issay Kitagawa
CEO and head designer of GRAPH
Born 1965 in Kasai, Hyogo Prefecture, Japan. Graduated from the University of Tsukuba in 1987. Joined GRAPH in 1989 (when the company was still called "Kitagawa Shiki Printing Co."). Aiming to create a form of communication design that resonates with people, Kitagawa has been involved in branding, design, intellectual property management, character development, and manufacturing activities. By proposing "design as a management resource" that represents the viewpoints of businessmen and designers alike, Kitagawa has gained the support of a broad clientele, from local SMEs to famous international luxury brands.

Semitransparent Design
Established in 2003. The company engages in projects ranging from website planning and production to graphic design and the exhibition of works at art museums and galleries in Japan and abroad. Past activities include hosting the Semitra exhibition "tFont/fTime" (Yamaguchi Center for Arts and Media [YCAM]) and the "Illuminating Graphics 0," "Illuminating Graphics 1," and "Illuminating Graphics 2" exhibitions (Creation Gallery G8), and participating in the "Semitransparent Design: Boring/Bored" exhibition (ginza graphic gallery) and in the "Open Space 2008" and "2015" exhibitions (NTT InterCommunication Center [ICC]).

TDC 奖
TDC Prize

GT Maru Minisite

Grilli Type, Thierry Blancpain & Noël Leu

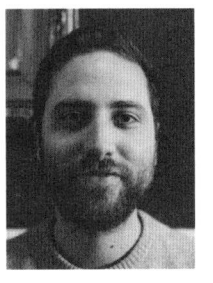 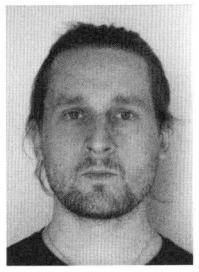

　　GT Maru Minisite是为纪念和介绍"GT Maru"字体的问世而设计的网站，内容包括了我们去日本旅游时遇到的趣闻轶事。Thierry对拉丁字母的文字设计如何用于日本的公共标识抱有强烈的兴趣。不懂日语的我们通过日本的标识以及文字设计，让我们对我们自身的瑞士设计的背景也有了更多的认识。在网站中，我们尝试说明了这种对视觉传达设计的探索究竟如何催生了GT Maru字体。对于个人而言，这个项目不仅是一封献给日本的情书，也让我们认识到日本的视觉文化给我们的设计带来的影响。
—
Grilli Type是Thierry Blancpain和Noël Leu于2009年创立的瑞士的字体公司兼设计工作室，这个国际化设计团队的7名成员分别活跃于瑞士和美国。团队秉承瑞士现代平面设计的传统——极简主义、概念驱动的细致性，但在如何实施这一理念方面并不拘泥于任何教条。Grilli Type始终探求基于概念性方法的崭新的视觉表现形式，其设计不但具备独特的视角同时还具备丰富的表现力和个性。不同于那些受过专业训练的字体设计师创作的字体，Grilli Type基于平面设计师的视角、立足于使用者的需求进行字体设计。正如GT Maru Minisite所介绍的，他们认为，字体并非仅仅是一种工具，还具有独特的个性。

This website celebrates the introduction of our typeface GT Maru. It tells the story of our visits to Japan, where Thierry became interested in the ways Latin typography is used in public wayfinding. The experience of interacting with signage and typography as a non-Japanese speaker led us to many observations about our own background in Swiss design. The minisite explains how these explorations of visual communication led to the creation of GT Maru. On a more personal level, this project is a love letter to Japan, and an acknowledgement of the impact Japanese visual culture has on our own appreciation of design.
—
Grilli Type is a Swiss type foundry and design studio, founded in 2009 by Thierry Blancpain and Noël Leu. Our international team of seven is based in both Switzerland and the US. We lead with the traditions of Swiss modernist graphic design—minimalist, concept-driven precision—but we're not stuck with any dogmas on how we implement this philosophy. We constantly search for new visual expressions of this conceptual approach. Our designs have a point of view, an expressive personality. Most typefaces are designed by trained type designers. Our method is different: We are graphic designers, and approach typeface design from the user's perspective. Typefaces are not only a tool, but have an individual personality that we showcase in our minisites.

TDC 奖
TDC Prize

The Curtain Rises & Falls

LOW sek-vai

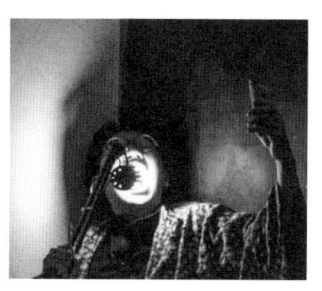

能获得东京TDC奖，我感到不胜荣幸。特别要感谢设计师吕旻，如果没有吕旻，我不可能完成这个平面作品。在这张海报中，设计师吕旻要表现的是"对比之美"。吕旻不仅喜欢中国传统的民族文化、古典音乐和法国的装帧设计，他还对视频游戏、手作玩具、先锋文化抱有强烈的兴趣。"幕间休息"（after intermission）项目是他的主要的成果之一，其间，他将出版设计视为"舞台上的表演"，而将自费出版项目视为"舞台下的娱乐"。他独特的个性构成整体展览的核心，而我则尝试从平面设计的视角出发表达这种喜悦。幸运的是，我没有毁掉这个作品。祈祷世界和平。

-

平面设计师、手工艺人。与Web艺术家xoesan共同创办TTTLAX。北京的YAN BOOKS的驻场设计师。致力于为受主要出版商限制的出版提供替代方案。

Before showing grateful to be awarded the Tokyo TDC prize, I would like to express my appreciation to designer Lu Min since I would not be able to create this graphic work without the illumination from him. As the main body of this poster, Designer Lu represents "the beauty of contrasts". He likes traditional Chinese folk culture, classical music and French binding, and also interested in video games, handmade toys and pioneering culture...... His main achievement involves with the "after intermission" project, which considers publication design as an "on-stage performance" and self-publishing projects as "backstage entertainment". His unique personality is the core of this exhibition and what I did was to express this ritualistic joy from a graphic perspective. Lucky that I didn't ruin it. May the world be at peace.

—

Graphic designer. Craftsman. Co-founder of TTTLAX with web artist xoesan. Residence designer of YAN BOOKS in Beijing. Dedicated to provide an alternative to publishing restricted by the constraints of major publishers.

TDC 奖
TDC Prize

无用之盒
Useless boxes

佐藤 丰
Yutaka Sato

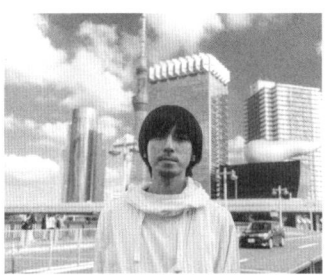

我在火柴盒大小的白色盒子上用中性笔描绘自作的平面图形。最初仅仅是为了打发时间，但是在这些盒子上的创作逐渐成为我一天之中唯一的目的，往往在不经意之间，我就已经画完了手边的白盒子。

虽然一字排开的画好的盒子令人赏心悦目，但与此同时更重要的是，这些盒子的"无意义性"也逐渐浮现而出。我猜想，其中可能还隐藏了一些无法用语言表达的"某种事物"。我意识到，迄今为止我始终为能够触及到"某种事物"才投入到不断的创作之中，但是时至今日我仍然无法了解，那些事物究竟是否是我所能触及的。

一方面，文字和平面图形似乎在表达"某种事物"，但是另一方面也经常会掩盖它们。

—

1990年出生于福岛县。2013年毕业于桑泽设计研究所设计学科。在仙台的设计事务所任职后，2014年入职服部一成设计事务所。2020年开始成为自由设计师。

I used a gel ink ballpoint pen to draw my own graphics onto white, matchbox-sized containers. It was just for killing time at first, but creating these boxes gradually developed into my sole "purpose of the day," and before I knew it, I had used up all the boxes that I had.

Looking at the painted boxes all lined up in one place was exhilarating in its own way, but what began to stand out first and foremost was the utter meaninglessness of these boxes.

However at the same time, I also felt that there was something in them that I couldn't put into words. It appears to me that my entire work to date has been inspired by the desire to connect to that "something," but I still don't know whether it is something that is within my reach.

Letters and graphics are supposed to express things, but sometimes they also obscure things.

—

Born 1990 in Fukushima Prefecture, Japan. Graduated from Kuwasawa Design School in 2013. After working for a design office in Sendai, joined Kazunari Hattori Co., Ltd. in 2014. Has been working as a freelance designer since 2020.

TDC 奖
TDC Prize

女子美术大学
Joshibi University of Art and Design

林 规章
Noriaki Hayashi

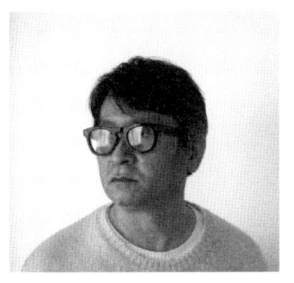

这是面向全国的高中生以及美术预科学校学生的意象海报。以"JOSHIBI"中的"J"为基本元素，尝试表现自由、灵活以及个性、创意的视觉化。想要表现奋不顾身的勇气和无形的冲动是此海报的主题所在。
JOSHIBI UNIVERSITY OF ART AND DESIGN
利用字母"J"的曲线部分作为要素，在各种不同组合方式的变化中与支撑物联系在一起。在不改变视觉印象的前提下，创造能联想起多种艺术创作的设计构造。只需改变组合方式就能形成各种造型的图标。有限的要素仅仅是伴装为有限的无限。首先描绘有气势的弧线。起笔处的"点"是重心所在，"线"则表示距离，换而言之，产生形状的行为正是"运动"本身。图形是变化的、浮游的，在其被描绘的瞬间就已经成为过去。如同禅宗公案一般反复的概念，打破了先入为主的"规则"。所谓表现这一行为是冲动，而其原点是思考。无论什么颜色都可以，拿出勇气尝试描绘自己独特的"点"，画出自己独特的"线条"。而这就是新的"形状"产生的瞬间、也是艺术的开始。

-

艺术指导、平面设计师。女子美术大学大学院教授。东京ADC会员、东京TDC会员、JAGDA会员。1964年生于日本岐阜县。1987年毕业于名古屋艺术大学美术学部设计系（毕业设计作品被学校购买收藏）。1987年4月开始作为平面设计师崭露头角。主要作品包括："MUNARI I LIBRI 1929—1999" "Wim Crouwel: A Graphic Odyssey" "Wabi-Sabi for Artists, Designers, Poets & Philosophers" "Design Ah! A Book for Seeing" "The Bonin Islanders Shinichiro Nagasawa"等书籍设计；以及"女子美术大学""MTV JAPAN VMAJ""东京TDC2019"等项目的全部平面设计。主要获奖包括：NY ADC特别奖、JAGDA新人奖、ONE SHOW DESIGN Gold Pencil、东京ADC奖等。

These are image posters made for national high schools and preparatory art schools. The "J" in "Joshibi" was used as a basic element to visualize aspects of liberty, flexibility, individuality, and ingenuity, themed around the invisible impulse and courage that is required for taking the first step whenever one feels the desire to express something.
JOSHIBI UNIVERSITY OF ART AND DESIGN
The idea was to take the curved part of the letter "J" and put it together in various combinations for each support, yet without changing the visual image, to create a design language that evokes all kinds of artistic creations. Playing around with the combinations resulted in variously shaped icons. Limited factors only feign limitedness, but possibilities are unlimited. Start by drawing a dynamic arc. The point where you start is the "center of gravity," while the line from there expresses "distance." In other words, it is this very "motion" that defines the act of creating a shape. The image floats around and becomes a matter of the past the moment it is drawn. It's a concept that is repeated over and over like a Zen riddle, and that breaks down rules of preconception. Expression is impulse, and intention is the starting point. Take any color you like, don't be shy, set your own points, and start drawing lines. That's where a new shape emerges and where art begins.

—

Art director, Graphic designer. Professor of Joshibi University of Art and Design.Member of Japan Graphic Designers Association Inc,Tokyo Type Directors Club,Tokyo Art Directors Club.1964 Born in Gifu Prefecture Japan.1987 Graduate Department of Design at the Nagoya University of Arts, B.A.Received the honor of his graduation work be purchased by his school.1987 Work as a freelance graphic designer. Major works includeed; Book Design =*"Munari's Books"*, *"Wim Crouwel:A Graphic Odyssey"*, *"Wabi-Sabi for Artists, Designers, Poets & Philosophers"*, *"Design Ah!-A Book for Seeing"*, *"The Bonin Islanders Shinichiro Nagasawa"*. Graphic Design="Joshibi University of Art and Dsign", "MTV JAPAN Video Music Awards Japan", "Tokyo Type Directors Club 2019". Major Awards included; The Art Directors Club of New York. Distinctive Merit, Japan Graphic Designers Association Inc. New Designer Award, The One Show Design. Gold Pencil, and Tokyo Art Directors Club ADC Prize.

TDC 奖
TDC Prize

San Francisco Symphony Rebrand

COLLINS + Louis Mikolay + Erik Berger Vaage

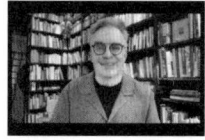
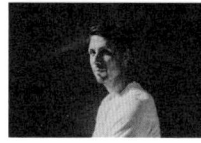
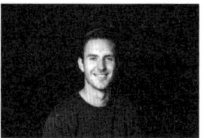

旧金山交响乐团是一个拥有108年历史的文化传奇,享誉国际,在改写规则方面有着深厚的传承,并且正处于重新构想其未来的关键时刻。

COLLINS受邀明确定义设计构想和表现旧金山交响乐团的新蓝图。其目标是帮助他们将古典音乐作为至关重要的全球当代艺术形式重新认知,同时保持扎根于社区并强化使他们成功超过一个世纪的纽带。

宛如交响乐团尝试新的技术、先进的数字技术、声音和文字设计的实验构成COLLINS的设计的核心。那不断响应、不断发展的视觉系统,生动地表现出古典音乐富有活力的特质。以传统的文字设计为基础,我们积极利用响应式网页设计、可变字体等技术,无论是版式还是文字,都能即刻反映不同的声音、音乐的变化,从而营造出其不意的、现代性的表现。以白色和黑色为基调,融入湾区当代独特色彩和景观的设计进一步增加了艺术表现力。在不断发展和变化的媒体以及数字技术环境中,为唤起交响乐丰富的感情世界,追求更好、更新的设计。

—

COLLINS是一家以企业战略、设计、信息传播为业务的独立设计公司。通过创意、手工艺和技术的结合,为人们提供改善生活的创意和独特体验。将敏锐的洞察力和丰富的想象力视为所有活动的核心,创造富于魅力的品牌,促进社会发展、实现更好的未来。

The San Francisco Symphony is a 108-year old cultural legend with international acclaim and a deep legacy of rewriting the rules, and was at a crucial moment to reimagine its future.

COLLINS was invited to help clarify, define and express this new vision for the Symphony, and help them re-assert classical music as a crucial, global contemporary art form — all while staying rooted in our community and strengthening the bonds that have made them so successful for over a century.

As the Symphony experiments with emerging technologies, our work's heart lies in new digital, sonic, and typographic experimentation. An ever-responsive, evolving visual system brings to life the dynamic qualities of classical music itself. Starting with traditional typography that speaks to the art form's heritage — we used responsive and variable font technology to add an unexpected contemporary behavior — giving each typographic character the ability to immediately change form in reaction to sound and music. We also crafted a more expressive voice that juxtaposes the timeless formality of black and white with a contemporary palette inspired by the unique colors and landscape of the Bay Area. All now better designed to evoke the rich emotional range of symphonic music across an always-changing media and digital landscape.

—

We are COLLINS.
We are an independent strategy, design and communications company.
We combine creativity, craft and technology into ideas and experiences that improve people's lives.
We put insight and imagination at the center of everything we do.
To make brands that can't be ignored.
To accelerate growth.
To build better futures at scale.

特别奖
Special Prize

仲条 NAKAJO

服部一成
Kazunari Hattori

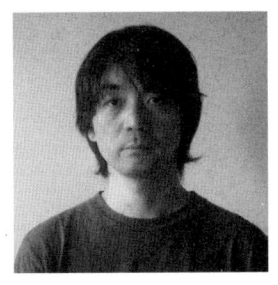

　　仲条先生并不愿意出版他的作品回顾集。虽然他举出的理由是不想给出版商添麻烦，但事实上可能是他并不愿意被过去所束缚。ADP出版社的久保田启子女士成功地说服仲条先生，本书才得以开始编辑，葛西薫先生和我任编辑委员，具体的设计工作由我负责。然而我并不知道如何推进这一重任，在我的无所作为中时间不断流逝。正如仲条先生最初的声明"等书出版的时候我会看"，他并未在设计过程中有过任何过问，仅仅是偶尔打电话给我："尽快做完就好""做成70来页的小册子就可以""按照你的想法来，让他成为你的作品""不要做成一本看起来很了不起的书""作品按顺序摆放就可以""不要总选择那些奇怪的作品"等等。他也曾说："我感觉这本书出版的时候一切都会结，慢慢做吧"。

　　书中的作品并未刻意安排，而是以年代顺序构成。封面上使用了仲条先生各个时代的作品。书函则选择了仲条先生1973年个展中的心形图案。

-
1964年生于东京。1988年毕业于东京艺术大学美术学部设计系后，入职Light Publicity公司。2001年开始成为自由设计师。主要作品包括："kewpie half"的广告；杂志《流行通信》"here and there"《真夜中》的艺术指导；Hermes的"petit h"的会场设计以及"梦想的形状Hermès Bespoke Objects"的平面设计；"三菱一号馆美术馆""新潟市美术馆""弘前红砖仓库美术馆"的VI设计；"隈研吾展为创造新的公共性的猫的五原则""声之间: 全身诗人、吉増刚造展"等展览会的招贴、物料和图录；书籍设计有Petit Royal French-Japanese Dictionary等。曾获得的奖项包括：每日设计奖、龟仓雄策奖、东京ADC奖、东京TDC全场大奖等。

Mr. Nakajo was reluctant to publish a book compiling his work to date. He explained that in terms of the inconvenience that he thought he might cause the publisher, but maybe he just doesn't like to get caught up in things past. Ms. Keiko Kubota at Art Design Publishing eventually managed to persuade him, and work on the book started with Mr. Kaoru Kasai and myself taking over editorial duties. I was also in charge of design. I didn't really know how to go about this rather frightening task, and I ended up neglecting my job several times along the way. Mr. Nakajo kept his initial promise to "look at the book when it's done" and did not see the progress of the work. He would just call a couple of times to tell us to "Get it done quickly!" "A 70-page booklet will do!" "Feel free to chop my work into pieces and make it all your own!" "Don't make it look pretentious!" "It'll be fine if you just line it all up in order!" "Don't choose only the weird stuff!" etc. But then again, he also said things like, "I have a feeling that it might be the end once the book is out, so take your time."

Rather than making grand arrangements, we simply lined the works up chronologically by decade and wrapped it all in a cover that features Nakajo's creations from several different eras. For the front cover of the box, we took a heart motif from his exhibition back in 1973.

—

Born in Tokyo in 1964. Graduated from the Department of Design, Faculty of Fine Arts, Tokyo National University of Fine Arts and Music (the present-day Tokyo University of the Arts) and joined Light Publicity Co., Ltd. in 1988. Have been working as a freelance designer since 2001. Main works include advertisement for "Kewpie Half"; art direction for magazines (*Ryuko Tsushin*, *here and there*, and *Mayonaka*); venue design for Hermès event "petit h"; graphic design for "Hermès Bespoke Objects"; VI plans for "Mitsubishi Ichigokan Museum, Tokyo," "Niigata City Museum" and "Hirosaki Museum of Contemporary Art"; exhibition posters, announcement materials and catalogues for "Kuma Kengo: Five Purr-fect Points for a New Public Space" and "The Voice Between: The Art and Poetry of Yoshimasu Gozo", and book design for "*Petit Royal French-Japanese Dictionary*." Has won awards including the Mainichi Design Award, the Yusaku Kamekura Design Award, the Tokyo ADC Award, and the Tokyo TDC Grand Prix.

特别奖
Special Prize

佐藤 卓展 "MILK"
Taku Satoh Exhibition "MILK"

佐藤 卓
Taku Stash

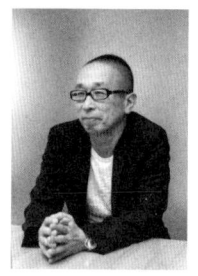

这些是我在位于东京银座的巷房画廊举办的个展的展场照片。在此展示的立体作品是将我设计的在日本销售的牛奶包装的一部分进行放大，以纤维增强复合材料制作的。此前我曾以此牛奶为主题，举办过基于设计视角的，从包装设计的表面追溯至牛饲料、牛粪便的"设计的解剖展"，而在本次展览中，我以相同的牛奶包装为主题，尝试将其作为艺术进行剖析。究其原因，是我认为，即便是日常商品，在部分地切取、展示后，也可以进入当代艺术的殿堂。在本次展览中，我还展示了将牛奶的包装盒切割成细小的废弃物状态，再将其重新构成圆形的作品。不言而喻，这是尝试唤醒对大规模生产的日用品带来的垃圾问题，以及环境问题的关注。我尝试从设计的形成开始剖析并将其发展为艺术。对我而言，这些事物并非各自独立存在而是处于同一谱系之中。作品能获得东京TDC奖的高度评价，我感到不胜荣幸。非常感谢。

—

平面设计师
1979年毕业于东京艺术大学设计系，1981年毕业于东京艺术大学研究生院。经过在电通公司的任职后，1984年创办佐藤卓设计事务所（现TSDO公司）。曾负责"Nikka Whiskey Pure Malt"的商品开发、LOTTE XYLITOL Gum、明治牛奶的包装设计、PLEATS PLEASE ISSEY MIYAKE的平面设计、金泽21世纪美术馆、国立科学博物馆的LOGO设计，以品牌策划和企业CI设计为中心活跃于多个领域。此外，还担任NHK教育频道"Nihongo de Asobo"的艺术指导、"Design Ah!"的综合指导、"21_21 DESIGN SIGHT"的馆长，策划和实施了众多的展览。主要著作有"Sosuru Shiko"（新潮社）等。

These are photos of my solo exhibition at Gallery Kobo in Tokyo's Ginza district. The objects unveiled here I made from FRP using enlarged parts of my design for a milk package. I had done the "Design Anatomy Exhibition" before, and that was also themed around milk, where I went from the package all the way back to cow feed and dung, from a design point of view. The idea for this exhibition was to try and focus on the same subject as art, because it had appeared to me that I could probably do something that is almost contemporary art, if I focused on certain parts of familiar products. In the exhibition, I dismantled the package into small parts, and put those together again to create items including a circular panel. Needless to mention, it is a nod to the garbage problem of mass-produced articles—and to environmental problems at large. From the establishment of design to its dissection, and further, to art—I consider these not as separate things, but they are all part of the same flow. I am very thankful for the high evaluation that my work received on this occasion. Thank you very much.

—

Graphic Designer
Graduated from Tokyo University of the Arts, Department of Design, in 1979, then from its Graduate School in 1981. Worked for Dentsu Inc., before establishing Taku Satoh Design Office (TSDO Inc.) in 1984. Satoh's work includes product development (Nikka Whiskey Pure Malt), packaging design (LOTTE XYLITOL Gum, Meiji Oishii gyunyu), graphic design (PLEATS PLEASE ISSEY MIYAKE), logo design (21st Century Museum of Contemporary Art, Kanazawa; National Museum of Nature and Science, Tokyo), as well as on branding and corporate identity (CI) programs. He provides art direction on the educational channel of NHK Television, Nihongo de Asobo, overall direction for Design Ah! on the same channel, and overall direction of 21_21 DESIGN SIGHT. He has planned and held many exhibitions. His publications include *Sosuru Shiko* (Shinchosha, 2017).

设计论坛
TDCDAY 2022

东京TDC奖2022的11组获奖者的获奖作品解说以及嘉宾的感言影像,于2022年4月8日在YouTube上公开。
https://youtu.be/FOf_41nTKzE

Design Forum TDCDAY 2022
The creators of the twelve prize-winning works will engage in a rich discussion focused on their work and a message from the guests are archived at the 8 April 2022 on YouTube.
https://youtu.be/pONg3c3o1vg

开场
Balmer Hählen, Balmer Priscilla + Yvo Hählen

分享会 01
大西景太 Keita Onishi
点评人: 松本弦人 Gento Matsumoto,
平面设计师

分享会 02
服部一成 Kazunari Hattori
点评人: 久保田启子 Keiko Kubota,
ADP 出版社

分享会 03
Jean François Porchez
点评人: Cyrus Highsmith,
字体设计师

分享会 04
LOW sek-vai
点评人: 室贺清德 Kiyonori Muroga,
编辑

分享会 05
Actual Source, Davis Ngarupe & JP Haynie
点评人: Balmer Hählen,
Balmer Priscilla + Yvo Hählen,
平面设计师

分享会 06
林 规章 Noriaki Hayashi
点评人: Mei Shuzhi,
艺术指导

分享会 07
Grilli Type, Thierry Blancpain & Noël Leu
点评人: 伊藤Gabin Gabin Ito,
编辑

分享会 08
佐藤 卓 Taku Satoh
点评人: John Warwicker, tomato

分享会 09
COLLINS
点评人: 田中义久 Yoshihisa Tanaka,
平面设计师

分享会 10
北川一成+田中良治+有本诚司
Issay Kitagawa + Ryoji Tanaka + Seiji Arimoto
点评人: 菊地敦己 Atsuki Kikuchi,
平面设计师

分享会 11
佐藤 丰 Yutaka Sato
点评人: 中村至男 Norio Nakamura,
平面设计师

主办: 东京字体指导俱乐部
共同主办: DNP文化振兴财团
Organize =
Tokyo Type Directors Club (Tokyo TDC)
Co-Organizer =
DNP Foundation for Cultural Promotion

東京TDC会員名簿
Tokyo TDC Members List

2022年8月末日現在
TDCのWebサイトで会員の代表作およびプロフィールをご覧いただけます。
The list dates from August 2022
You can refer to the TDC website for the major works and profiles of the members:
https://tokyotypedirectorsclub.org/

法人会員
Corporate Members

（公財）DNP文化振興財団
DNP Foundation for Cultural Promotion
〒104-0061 東京都中央区
銀座7-7-2 DNP銀座ビル
Tel. 03-5568-8224
Fax. 03-5568-8225
https://www.dnpfcp.jp/foundation/

（株）竹尾
Takeo Co., Ltd.
〒101-0054 東京都千代田区
神田錦町3-12-6
Tel. 03-3292-3611
Fax. 03-3292-9202
http://www.takeo.co.jp/

（株）ピラミッドフィルム
Pyramid Film Inc.
〒108-0023 東京都港区
芝浦2-12-16
Tel. 03-5576-4743
Fax. 03-5576-4746
http://www.pyramidfilm.co.jp/

（株）モリサワ
Morisawa Inc.
〒556-0012 大阪市浪速区
敷津東2-6-25
Tel. 06-6649-2151（main）
Fax. 06-6649-2153
http://www.morisawa.co.jp

個人会員
Members

青木克憲　Katsunori Aoki
バタフライ・ストローク・株式會社
butterfly・stroke inc.
〒104-0054 東京都中央区
勝どき2-8-19
近富ビル倉庫3F・3A
Tel. 03-5144-0330
info@btf.co.jp
https://www.butterfly-stroke.com/
https://www.shopbtf.com/

赤迫 仁　Hitoshi Akasako
THE END
〒151-0051 東京都渋谷区
千駄ヶ谷2-10-7
Tel. 03-5413-3591
Fax. 03-5413-3286
theend@end-tokyo.com
http://www.end-tokyo.com/

秋元克士　Yoshio Akimoto
秋元克士制作室
Yoshio Akimoto Office
〒174-0043 東京都板橋区
坂下3-20-1-213
Tel. Fax. 03-5918-9128
yazyo3@u04.itscom.net

秋山カズオ　Kazuo Akiyama
（株）Deluxe
Deluxe Co., Ltd.
〒108-0074 東京都港区
高輪2-14-18
グレイス高輪408
Tel. 03-6432-9766
Fax. 03-6432-9767
a@dx-d.jp
http://dx-d.jp/

秋山具義　Gugi Akiyama
デイリーフレッシュ（株）
Dairy Fresh
〒153-0042 東京都目黒区
青葉台1-25-7
ブルーウッド青葉台1F
Tel. 03-6303-4976
Fax. 03-6303-4973
info@d-fresh.com
http://www.d-fresh.com

浅葉克己　Katsumi Asaba
（株）浅葉克己デザイン室
Asaba Design Co., Ltd.
〒107-0062 東京都港区
南青山3-9-2
Tel. 03-3479-0471
Fax. 03-3402-0694
asaba@asaba-d.co.jp

味岡伸太郎　Shintaro Ajioka
（有）スタッフ
Design Studio STAFF
〒441-8011 愛知県豊橋市菰口町1-43
Tel. 0532-32-4871
Fax. 0532-32-7134
shintaro@ajioka3.com
http://www.ajioka3.com

有山達也　Tatsuya Ariyama
ariyama design store
〒103-0001 東京都中央区
日本橋小伝馬町20-4
東洋ハットビル2F
Tel. 03-3808-1414
Fax. 03-3808-1313
info@ariyamadesignstore.com

池越顕尋　Akihiro Ikegoshi
(有) GW
GWG Inc.
〒152-0012 東京都渋谷区
恵比寿4-5-23
ルイシャトレ恵比寿203
〒540-0004 大阪府大阪市中央区
玉造2-16-25-3F
info@gwg.ne.jp
http://www.gwg.ne.jp/

石橋政美　Masami Ishibashi
いしばしデザイン
Ishibashi Design
midesign@fuga.ocn.ne.jp
tokyotypedirectorsclub.org/member/
masami_ishibashi/

板倉敬子　Keiko Itakura
FRMA (株)
FRMA Co., Ltd.
info@keikoitakura.com

糸井重里　Shigesato Itoi
(株) ほぼ日
Hobonichi Co., Ltd.
https://www.1101.com/

井上嗣也　Tsuguya Inoue
ビーンズ
BEANS
〒106-0041 東京都港区
麻布台1-6-10 パークハビオ麻布台201
Tel. 03-3586-8005
Fax. 03-3588-1003
beans@poppy.ocn.ne.jp

後 智仁　Tomohito Ushiro
WHITE DESIGN inc.
〒107-0062 東京都港区
南青山6-3-14-204
Tel. 03-6805-1320
Fax. 03-6805-1321
info@whitedesign.jp
http://whitedesign.jp/

ゑ藤隆弘　Takahiro Eto
STUDY LLC.
eto.t.study@gmail.com
https://studyllc.tokyo

大杉 学　Gaku Ohsugi
(株) ナナマルニ・ワークス
702 Design Works Co., Ltd.
〒151-0064 東京都渋谷区
上原3-6-6 オークハウス1-A
Tel. 03-3468-9702
Fax. 03-3468-9797
gaku@702design.co.jp
http://www.702design.co.jp/

大橋清一　Seiichi Ohashi
クリエイティブコミュニケイションズ
(株) レマン
C.C. LES MAINS, Inc.
〒150-0002 東京都渋谷区
渋谷1-19-2 nalu ビル 3階
Tel. 03-3407-1013
Fax. 03-3407-1598
info@cc-lesmains.co.jp
http://www.cc-lesmains.co.jp/

大原健一郎　Kenichiro Ohara
NIGN ((株) ナイン)
NIGN Co., Ltd.
info@nign.co.jp
http://www.nign.co.jp/

大森 剛　Tsuyoshi Omori
(有) トリプレットデザイン
TRIPLET DESIGN INC.
〒156-0042 東京都世田谷区
羽根木1-21-23 羽根木の森 06
Tel. 03-6265-7273
https://tsuyoshiomori.com/

岡室 健　Ken Okamuro
(株) 博報堂
HAKUHODO Inc.
〒107-6322 東京都港区
赤坂5-3-1 赤坂Bizタワー
Tel. 03-6441-8153

奥野正次郎　Shojiro Okuno
ポロロッカ
POROROCA
〒150-0001 東京都渋谷区
神宮前3-18-42 ル・シヤージュ
神宮前109
Tel. 03-5770-0700
okuno@prrc.jp
https://www.prrc.jp/

奥村靫正　Yukimasa Okumura
TSTJ inc.
〒141-0031 東京都品川区
西五反田1-32-8
ぐれいぷハウス3F
Tel. 03-5434-8031
Fax. 03-5434-6212
oua@tstj-inc.co.jp
http://www.tstj-inc.co.jp/

尾崎伸行　Nobuyuki Ozaki
(株) 百舌／モズデザイン
MOZU Co., Ltd.
〒150-0013 東京都渋谷区
恵比寿2-17-5
Tel. 03-5449-7716
Fax. 03-5449-0024
nozaki@mozu.co.jp

押見健太郎　Kentaro Oshimi
Beatness inc.
oshimix@beatness.jp
https://beatness.jp/

葛西 薫　Kaoru Kasai
(株) サン・アド
SUN-AD Co., Ltd.
〒107-0061 東京都港区
北青山2-11-3 A-Place青山
Tel. 03-5785-6800
Fax. 03-3796-3850
https://sun-ad.co.jp/

梶山かつみ　Katsumi Kajiyama
(有) インテグラルプラス
Integral-Plus Inc.
〒162-0855 東京都新宿区
二十騎町2-12-V-32
Tel. 03-5206-3320
kajiyama@integral-plus.jp
http://integral-plus.jp/

葛本京子　Kyoko Katsumoto
(株) 視覚デザイン研究所
Visual Design Laboratory, Inc.
〒559-0034 大阪府大阪市住之江区
南港北2-1-10
アジア太平洋トレードセンタービル
ITM 棟 10F
Tel. 06-6615-0800
Fax. 06-6615-0801
https://www.vdl.co.jp/

加納佳之　Yoshiyuki Kano
contact@moji-to-design.com

川畑明日佳　Asuka Kawabata
専門学校 桑沢デザイン研究所
Kuwasawa Design School
〒150-0041 東京都渋谷区
神南1-4-17
Tel. 03-3463-2431
Fax. 3-3463-2435
kawabata@kds.ac.jp
https://www.kds.ac.jp/

菊地敦己　Atsuki Kikuchi
(株)菊地敦己事務所
Atsuki Kikuchi Ltd.
studio@akltd.jp
http://atsukikikuchi.com/

木口章人　Akito Kiguchi
(有)イノセンスグラフィック
INNOCENCE GRAPHIC
〒150-0021 東京都渋谷区
恵比寿西1-16-1 #401
Te. 03-6455-0027
Fax. 03-6455-0028
kiguchi@igraphic.jp
http://www.igraphic.jp/

木住野彰悟　Shogo Kishino
6D
〒107-0062 東京都港区
南青山5-10-12
青山EDGEビル3F
Tel. 03-6427-3752
Fax. 03-6427-3753
info@6d-k.com
http://www.6d-k.com/

北川一成　Issay Kitagawa
グラフ(株)
GRAPH Co. Ltd.
〒150-0033 東京都渋谷区
猿楽町29-9 D25
Tel. 03-5489-6931
Fax. 03-5489-6933
info@moshi-moshi.jp
http://www.moshi-moshi.jp

金田一 剛　Kou Kindaichi
(株)金田一デザイン
Kindaichi Design
〒112-0012 東京都文京区
大塚3-8-1 #901
Tel. 03-6902-9922
Fax. 03-6902-9923
design@kindaichi.jp

草谷隆文　Takafumi Kusagaya
(有)草谷デザイン
Kusagaya Design Inc.
〒168-0082 東京都杉並区
久我山4-9-3
Tel. 03-5938-9493
Fax. 03-6761-9493
kusagaya@kt.rim.or.jp
http://www.kusagayadesign.com/

工藤青石　Aoshi Kudo
コミュニケーションデザイン研究所
Communication Design Laboratory
〒107-0051 東京都港区
元赤坂1-3-9
Tel. 03-3478-9777
Fax. 03-3478-4777
info@cdlab.jp
http://www.cdlab.jp/

工藤規雄　Norio Kudo
(有)グリフ
Griffe Inc.
〒136-0073 東京都江東区
北砂3-4-2,1503
Tel. 03-6666-8653
Fax. 03-6666-8654
n-kudo@japan.email.ne.jp

國定勝利　Katsutoshi Kunisada
花王(株)作成センター
コミュニケーション作成部
Creative Department, Kao Corporation
〒103-8210 東京都中央区
日本橋茅場町1-14-10
kunisada.katsutoshi@kao.com
http://www.kao.com/

栗林和夫　Kazuo Kuribayashi
クリとグラフィック
Kuri + Graphic
Tel. Fax. 03-5930-0660
kurivo.1@jcom.home.ne.jp
http://kuri-graphic.com/

小島潤一　Junichi Kojima
(株)サン・アド
SUN-AD Co., Ltd.
〒107-0061 東京都港区
北青山2-11-3 A-Place青山
Tel. 03-5785-6800
Fax. 03-3796-3852
j-kojima@sun-ad.co.jp

小島利之　Toshiyuki Kojima
小島デザイン事務所
Kojima Design Office Inc.

小林一毅　Ikki Kobayashi
graphic.ikki.kobayashi@gmail.com
https://www.instagram.com/kobayashi.ikki/

後藤 宏　Hiroshi Goto
〒819-1314 福岡県糸島市
志摩師吉355-11

近藤一弥　Kazuya Kondo
(株)カズヤコンド
Kazuya Kondo Inc.
〒604-8076 京都市中京区
海老野町323-3-603
Tel. 075-251-6562
info@kazuyakondo.com
http://www.kazuyakondo.com/

七種泰史　Yasushi Saikusa
(株)デザインシグナル
Design Signal Inc.
〒216-0007 神奈川県川崎市宮前区
小台2-6-6-802
Tel. 044-854-9822
yes-c@design-signal.co.jp
http://design-signal.co.jp/

斉藤正明　Masaaki Saito
(株)ライトパブリシティ
Light Publicity Co., Ltd.

坂元 純　Jun Sakamoto
〒180-0002 武蔵野市吉祥寺東町
1-4-23 FOCO 204
Tel. 0422-27-5322
sakamoto@gekkodo.co.jp

佐藤可士和　Kashiwa Sato
SAMURAI
〒150-0011 東京都渋谷区
東2-14-11 1F
info@samurai.sh
http://kashiwasato.com/

佐藤 卓　Taku Satoh
(株)TSDO
TSDO Inc.
〒104-0061 東京都中央区
銀座3-2-10 並木ビル6F
Tel. 03-3538-2051
Fax. 03-3538-2054
tsdo@tsdo.co.jp
http://www.tsdo.jp

沢田耕一　Koichi Sawada
(株)電通
Dentsu Inc.
Kosawada06@gmail.com

澤田泰廣　Yasuhiro Sawada
澤田泰廣デザイン室
Yasuhiro Sawada Design Studio
〒150-0034 東京都渋谷区
代官山町4-1 代官山マンション710
Tel. 03-5459-3383
Fax. 03-3463-4822
sy28@apricot.ocn.ne.jp

三近 淳　Atsushi Sanchika
(株)電通
Dentsu Inc.
〒105-7001 東京都港区
東新橋1-8-1
Tel. 080-8030-9408
atsushi.sanchika@dentsu.co.jp

澁谷克彦　Katsuhiko Shibuya
〒150-0001 東京都渋谷区
神宮前5-53-67 コスモス青山
EAST-B1F FOTON
shibuya@k.email.ne.jp

シマダタモツ　Tamotsu Shimada
(有)シマダデザイン
Shimada Design Inc.
http://www.shimada-d.com/

清水正己　Masami Shimizu
(有)清水正己デザイン事務所
Shimizu Masami Design Office
〒150-0002 東京都渋谷区
渋谷1-15-15 テラス渋谷美竹1203
Tel. 03-5467-0581
Fax. 03-5467-0584
info@shimizu-design.co.jp
http://www.shimizu-design.co.jp/

末廣峰治　Mineji Suehiro
パワーデザイン
Power Design
東京都新宿区四谷4-6
mineji.suehiro@gmail.com

杉崎真之助　Shinnoske Sugisaki
(株)真之助デザイン
SHINNOSKE Design
〒540-0035 大阪市中央区
釣鐘町2-1-8 都住創釣鐘町6階
Tel. 06-6943-9077
Fax. 06-6943-9078
shinn@shinn.co.jp
http://www.shinn.co.jp/

関根慎一　Shinichi Sekine
関根慎一デザイン室
Shinichi Sekine Design Room

関本明子　Akiko Sekimoto
(株)ヒダマリ
HIDAMARI Ltd.
Tel. 03-6805-1085
contact@hltd.jp
https://www.akikosekimoto.com/

祖父江 慎　Shin Sobue
(有)コズフィッシュ
cozfish
〒153-0061 東京都目黒区
中目黒3-11-13 1F
Tel. 03-3793-2225
Fax. 03-3793-2226
tamao@cozfish.jp

大日本タイポ組合
Dainippon Type Organization
〒150-0011 東京都渋谷区
東2-20-16 エストマニヴィア2F
dainippon@type.org
https://dainippon.type.org/

髙橋正実　Masami Takahashi
(有)マサミデザイン
MASAMI DESIGN Co., Ltd.
〒131-0033 東京都墨田区
向島3-3-1 ミリアレジデンス押上
1101号室
Tel. 03-5619-1550
http://www.masamidesign.co.jp/

高橋善丸　Yoshimaru Takahashi
(株)広告丸
Kokokumaru Co., Ltd.
〒530-0052 大阪府大阪市北区
南扇町7-2 ユニ東梅田502
Tel. 06-6314-0881
yoshimaru@kokokumaru.com
http://www.kokokumaru.com/

高原 宏　Hiroshi Takahara
(有)高原宏デザイン事務所
Hiroshi Takahara Design Office
〒151-0053 東京都渋谷区
代々木2-23-1
ニューステイトメナー 1106
Tel. 03-6265-0735
Fax. 03-6265-0736
YRL03026@nifty.ne.jp
http://takahara.fri.macserver.jp/

竹内一峰　Ippo Takeuchi
(株)博報堂プロダクツ
Hakuhodo Product's Inc.
〒135-8619 東京都江東区
豊洲5-6-15 NBF豊洲ガーデンフロント
Tel. 03-5144-7280
Fax. 03-5144-7277
ippo.takeuchi@hakuhodo.co.jp

竹村真太郎　Shintaro Takemura
(株)グライド
GRIDE Inc.
〒141-0031 東京都品川区
西五反田4-27-10
s_takemura@gride.co.jp

立花ハジメ　Hajime Tachibana
(株)立花ハジメデザイン
Tachibana Hajime Design

立花文穂　Fumio Tachibana
立花文穂プロ.
TACHIBANA FUMIO PRO.
kyutai@230pro.jp

田中良治　Ryoji Tanaka
(株)セミトランスペアレント・デザイン
Semitransparent Design
〒154-0004 東京都世田谷区
太子堂4-26-9 コロニス三軒茶屋2F
Tel. Fax. 03-6903-7637
info@semitransparentdesign.com
http://www.semitransparentdesign.com/

玉置太一　Taichi Tamaki
(株)電通
クリエーティブ・ディレクション・センター
クリエーティブ・ディレクション5部
Dentsu Inc.
Tel. 03-6216-8654
Fax. 03-6217-5800
taichi.tamaki@dentsu.co.jp

塚田男女雄　Minao Tsukada
ツカダデザイン
Minao Tsukada Design
〒123-0843 東京都足立区
西新井栄町3-1-1-811
Tel. Fax. 03-3848-0831
minao.t@tokyo.email.ne.jp
http://www.ne.jp/asahi/minaotsukada/design/

塚本 陽　Kiyoshi Tsukamoto
eraplatonico@gmail.com
http://eraplatonico.tumblr.com/

豊島 晶　Aki Toyoshima
(株)AKIPON DESIGN HOUSE
aki@akipon.com
http://www.akipon.com/

トウサワ　Dong Ze
日中未来デザイン交流センター
Communication Center of China
And Japan Future Design Conception
〒176-0012 東京都練馬区
豊玉北6-15-13-401
Tel. 070-4293-6896
Fax. 03-6781-0708
japanartstudio@yahoo.com
https://www.fdcj-design.com

永井裕明　Hiroaki Nagai
(株)エヌ・ジー
N.G. inc.
〒107-0062 東京都港区
南青山5-4-19
The Upper Residences at南青山403
Tel. 03-3486-0800
Fax. 03-3486-3509
ng@nginc.jp
http://www.nginc.jp/

中島祥文　Shobun Nakashima
ウエーブクリエーション
Wave Creation Inc.
〒107-0062 東京都港区
南青山6-15-13-503
Tel. 03-5778-9711
Fax. 03-5778-9712
jdw06140@nifty.ne.jp

中村至男　Norio Nakamura
中村至男制作室
Norio Nakamura Studio
https://norionakamura.com/

中村勇吾　Yugo Nakamura
tha ltd.
info@tha.jp
http://tha.jp/

南部俊安　Toshiyasu Nanbu
(有)テイスト
Taste Inc.
〒572-0825 大阪府寝屋川市
萱島南町18-10
Tel. 072-824-5538
Fax. 072-824-5583
tasteinc@osk.3web.ne.jp
http://www.tasteinc.net/

西村 武　Takeshi Nishimura
(株)コンプレイトデザイン
Completo Design Inc.
〒107-0062 東京都港区
南青山2-15-6 ループ青山ビルB1F
Tel. 03-6427-0435
Fax. 03-6427-0436
info@completo.co.jp
http://www.completo.co.jp/

野村勝久　Katsuhisa Nomura
(株)野村デザイン制作室
NOMURA DESIGN FACTORY INC.
〒753-0087 山口県山口市
米屋町2-26-3F
Tel. Fax. 083-924-8625
info@nomura-design.com
http://www.nomura-design.com/

橋本明花　Haruka Hashimoto
I&CO Tokyo
〒150-0033 東京都渋谷区
猿楽町17-10 Art Village TOKO 3F
hashimoto103172@gmail.com
https://www.harukahashimoto.com

長谷川踏太　Tota Hasegawa
totahasegawa@gmail.com

畑野憲一　Kenichi Hatano
(株)電通 第1CRプランニング局
Dentsu Inc.
〒105-7001 東京都港区
東新橋1-8-1
Tel. 080-6501-1686
kenichi.hatano@dentsu.co.jp

服部一成　Kazunari Hattori
(有)服部一成
Kazunari Hattori Inc.
〒106-0031 東京都港区
西麻布3-20-13 木村ビル5F
Tel. 03-3478-2591
Fax. 03-3478-2592
hattori@flyingcake.com

浜田武士　Takeshi Hamada
h@hamada-takeshi.com
http://www.hamada-takeshi.com/

林 規章　Noriaki Hayashi
HAYASHI DESIGN
〒107-0062 東京都港区
南青山3-6-10
Tel. Fax. 03-6804-6570
hayashid@me.com
http://hayashinoriaki.com

原 健三　Kenzo Hara
(株)ハイフン
HYPHEN Inc.
Tel. 03-6455-3680
Fax. 03-6455-3681
hara@hy-phen.jp
http://www.hy-phen.jp/

針谷建二郎　Kenjiro Harigai
THINKR inc.
〒153-0042 東京都目黒区
青葉台3-6-16 HF青葉台ビル2F
Tel. 03-6455-2862
Fax. 03-6455-2863
info@thinkr.jp
http://thinkr.jp/
http://www.kenjiroharigai.com/

日比野克彦　Katsuhiko Hibino
(株)ヒビノスペシャル
HIBINO SPECIAL Co., Ltd.
〒101-0021 東京都千代田区
外神田6-11-14 千代田アーツ3331
308号室 日々の明々後日
https://www.hibinospecial.com

平野篤史　Atsushi Hirano
AFFORDANCE inc.
〒253-0021 神奈川県茅ヶ崎市
浜竹2-2-51 山友5ビル4階
Tel. 0467-81-3785
Fax. 0467-81-4655
hirano@affordance.tokyo
https://www.affordance.tokyo

平野湟太郎　Kotaro Hirano
(有)平野湟太郎デザイン研究所
Kotaro Hirano Design Laboratory
〒639-3432 奈良県吉野郡吉野町
大字窪垣内515
Tel. 0746-39-9176
yoshino@hiranodesign.jp
http://www.hiranodesign.jp/

平林奈緒美　Naomi Hirabayashi
PLUG-IN GRAPHIC
info@plug-in.co.uk
http://www.plug-in.co.uk/

廣村正彰　Masaaki Hiromura
(株)廣村デザイン事務所
Hiromura Design Office
http://www.hiromuradesign.com/

福島 治　Osamu Fukushima
福島デザイン
Fukushima Design
〒135-0045 東京都江東区
古石場3-11-17
Tel. Fax. 03-5621-3036
fukushima-design@gol.com
http://www.fukushima-design.jp/

福田秀之　Hideyuki Fukuda
(有)スタジオ福デ
studio Fuku-De
〒154-0002 東京都世田谷区
下馬3-32-3
Tel. 090-8791-0215
fukude@fsinet.or.jp
http://www.fuku-de.com/

古川智基　Tomoki Furukawa
SAFARI inc.
post@safari-design.com
http://www.safari-design.com/

細島雄一　Yuichi Hosojima
(株)Tottemo Designing
〒107-0052 東京都港区
赤坂9-6-28 アルベルゴ乃木坂406
Tel. 03-6721-1366
Fax. 03-6721-1367
hoso@tottemoinc.com
http://www.tottemoinc.com/

奔保彰良　Akira Hombo
(株)マイリアルビジョン
MY REAL VISION INC.
〒153-0051 東京都目黒区
上目黒3-13-10
Tel. 03-3715-5411
Fax. 03-3715-5412
hombo@mrv.co.jp
http://mrv.co.jp/

間嶋龍臣　Tatsuomi Majima
間嶋デザイン事務所
MAJIMA TATSUOMI DESIGN Inc.
〒771-0144 徳島県徳島市
川内町榎瀬846-6
Tel. Fax. 088-665-1243
majix@peach.ocn.ne.jp
https://t-majima.jimdo.com/

松下 計　Kei Matsushita
(有)松下計デザイン室
Kei Matsushita Design Room Inc.

松本弦人　Gento Matsumoto
SB
saru@sarubrunei.com
http://sarubrunei.com/

松山智一　Norikazu Matsuyama
(有)松山デザイン
Matsuyama Design Inc.
Tel. 090-9685-8895
design@matsuyamadesign.co.jp

三浦 遊　Yu Miura
Shiseido Americas Corporation

三木 健　Ken Miki
三木健デザイン事務所
Ken Miki & Associates
http://www.ken-miki.net/

水垣 淳　Jun Mizugaki
(株)マッシーン
Machine Inc.
Tel. 03-6300-6212
Fax. 03-6300-6218
jun@machine.ne.jp
https://www.machine.ne.jp/

水野 学　Manabu Mizuno
(株)グッドデザインカンパニー
good design company
contact@gooddesigncompany.com

三宅 孝　Takashi Miyake

村松丈彦　Takehiko Muramatsu
むDESIGN室
MU DESIGN ROOM
〒112-0002 東京都文京区
小石川2-15-5
muramatsu.takehiko@gmail.com
https://mu-design-room.com

杢谷吉也　Yoshinari Mokutani
モクタニデザイン
Mokutani Design
mokutani_d@h05.itscom.net

森本千絵　Chie Morimoto
(株) goen°
〒150-0033 東京都渋谷区
猿楽町4-6 代官山宝ビル4F
goen@goen-goen.co.jp
http://www.goen-goen.co.jp/

安原和夫　Kazuo Yasuhara
YASUHARA DESIGN
〒150-0001 東京都渋谷区
神宮前4-14-13 ハイシティ表参道213
Tel. 03-3401-1564
yasuharadesign@yahoo.co.jp

柳 圭一郎　Keiichiro Yanagi
(株) 原宿デザイン
Harajuku DESIGN Inc.
〒150-0001 東京都渋谷区
神宮前3-25-18 THE SHARE 217-a
info@harajuku-design.co.jp
http://www.harajuku-design.co.jp/

山口 馨　Kaoru Yamaguchi
(有) バウ広告事務所
Bau Advertising Office
〒106-0032 東京都港区
六本木3-16-35 イースト六本木ビル4F
Tel. 03-3568-6711
Fax. 03-3568-6712
yamaguchi@bau-ad.co.jp
http://www.bau-ad.co.jp/

山本哲次　Tetsuji Yamamoto
(株) 山本哲次デザイン室
Tetsuji Yamamoto Design Office
Co., Ltd.
〒135-0034 東京都江東区
永代2-31-5 内田ビル4F
Tel. 03-3643-9807
Fax. 03-3643-9808
tetsu@kc4.so-net.ne.jp

山本ヒロキ　Hiroki Yamamoto
マーヴィン (同)
MARVIN LLC
〒150-0031 東京都渋谷区
桜丘16-6-2F-A
Tel. 03-6452-5930
Fax. 03-6452-5940
info@marvin-ltd.com
https://marvin-ltd.com/

山本洋司　Yoji Yamamoto
(株) ビジュアルメッセージ研究所
Visual Message Inc.
〒261-0003 千葉県千葉市美浜区
高浜4-5 稲毛マリンハイツ6-205
Tel. 043-301-5750
Fax. 043-301-5780
yamamoto@visual2004.com
http://www.visual2004.com/

吉田直樹　Naoki Yoshida

渡辺卓也　Takuya Watanabe
渡辺卓也デザイン室
Takuya Watanabe Design Room
〒156-0043 東京都世田谷区
松原3-23-19 松原フラット B104号
Tel. Fax. 03-3324-6495
d.room01@m5.dion.ne.jp

和田由里子　Yuriko Wada
(株) ペーパーパレード
Paper Parade Inc.
〒151-0051 東京都渋谷区
千駄ヶ谷3-59-8-208
info@paperparade.tokyo
http://paperparade.tokyo

Benny Au [Hong Kong, China]
Amazing Angle Design Co., Ltd.
http://www.amazingangle.com/

Alexander Gelman [USA / Japan]
http://studioglmn.com/

Jianping He [Germany / China]
http://www.hesign.com/

John Maeda [USA]
Maeda Studio
http://www.maedastudio.com/

Non-Format [USA / Norway]
Jon Forss, Kjell Ekhorn
http://non-format.com/

Guang Yu [China]
A Black Cover Design
http://www.ablackcover.com

John Warwicker [UK / Australia]
http://www.johnwarwicker.com/

Xu Wang [China]
Wang Xu & Associates Ltd.
http://www.wangxu.com.cn/

NPO法人
東京タイプディレクターズクラブ
〒111-0032 東京都台東区
浅草2-1-14 2F
Tel. 03-6276-5210
Fax. 03-6276-5211

Tokyo Type Directors Club Office
2F, 2-1-14 Asakusa, Taito-ku,
Tokyo 111-0032 Japan
Tel. +81-3-6276-5210
Fax. +81-3-6276-5211
contact@tokyotypedirectorsclub.org
https://tokyotypedirectorsclub.org/